Machine Learning and Statistical Learning with Applications 2025

Machine Learning and Statistical Learning with Applications 2025

Guest Editor

Yan Zhang

MDPI

Basel • Beijing • Wuhan • Barcelona • Belgrade • Novi Sad • Cluj • Manchester

Guest Editor
Yan Zhang
School of Computer Science
and Engineering
California State University
San Bernardino
San Bernardino
USA

Editorial Office
MDPI AG
Grosspeteranlage 5
4052 Basel, Switzerland

This is a reprint of the Special Issue, published open access by the journal *Computers* (ISSN 2073-431X), freely accessible at: https://www.mdpi.com/journal/computers/special_issues/FX28OINFV1.

For citation purposes, cite each article independently as indicated on the article page online and as indicated below:

Lastname, A.A.; Lastname, B.B. Article Title. *Journal Name* **Year**, *Volume Number*, Page Range.

ISBN 978-3-7258-8255-7 (Hbk)
ISBN 978-3-7258-8256-4 (PDF)
https://doi.org/10.3390/books978-3-7258-8256-4

Contents

About the Editor

Yan Zhang

Yan Zhang is a full professor of Computer Science at the School of Computer Science and Engineering, California State University San Bernardino, USA. Her research interests include data analysis, machine learning, deep learning, and natural language processing, with particular emphasis on interpretable learning, healthcare analytics, and text mining. Her recent projects focus on applying machine learning models to medical data analysis, sentiment analysis, financial forecasting, and image-based disease detection, and developing hybrid and ensemble approaches for complex, real-world datasets. She has contributed to a range of peer-reviewed publications in journals and international conferences. Her work has received consistent academic citations and demonstrates ongoing engagement in advancing both the methodology and application of machine learning.

Preface

This Special Issue, "Machine Learning and Statistical Learning with Applications 2025", brings together a collection of research that reflects the rapid evolution and expanding influence of data-driven methods across disciplines. This volume focuses on both methodological developments and practical applications, highlighting how machine learning and statistical learning are being used to address complex challenges in areas such as healthcare, environmental systems, finance, and socio-technical domains.

The motivation behind this Special Issue is rooted in the growing need to bridge theoretical advances with real-world impact. While significant progress has been made in model development, there remains an ongoing demand for approaches that are interpretable, reliable, and adaptable to diverse and often imperfect data environments. The contributions included here address this need by exploring not only performance improvements but also issues such as uncertainty estimation, data efficiency, and deployment in high-stakes settings.

This volume is intended for researchers, practitioners, and advanced students working in machine learning, statistics, and related fields, and for those seeking to apply these techniques in domain-specific contexts. By presenting a range of perspectives and application areas, this Special Issue aims to support knowledge exchange across disciplines and to encourage further research at the intersection of theory and practice.

Overall, this collection reflects the continuing transition of machine learning and statistical learning from purely analytical tools to integral components of decision-making systems, with increasing emphasis on transparency, robustness, and practical relevance.

Yan Zhang
Guest Editor

computers MDPI

Editorial

Editorial: Machine Learning and Statistical Learning with Applications 2025

Yan Zhang

School of Computer Science and Engineering, California State University San Bernardino, 5500 University Parkway, San Bernardino, CA 92407, USA; yan.zhang@csusb.edu

1. Introduction

Machine learning and statistical learning have become central to modern scientific discovery and technological innovation. The rapid growth of data across diverse domains has driven the development of increasingly sophisticated models, capable of extracting meaningful patterns from complex, high-dimensional, and often noisy datasets. Recent advances in deep learning, foundation models, and large-scale data-driven approaches have significantly expanded the capabilities of artificial intelligence systems across a wide range of applications [1–4]. At the same time, the field is evolving beyond a sole focus on predictive performance. Issues such as interpretability, robustness, uncertainty quantification, and data efficiency have become equally important, particularly in high-stakes applications [5–7]. This shift reflects a broader movement toward trustworthy and application-aware machine learning systems.

The Special Issue "Machine Learning and Statistical Learning with Applications 2025", published in the journal *Computers* (ISSN 2073-431X, MDPI), was conceived to capture these developments by bringing together contributions that span both methodological innovation and real-world applications. The 14 papers included in this issue illustrate the diversity of the field, covering topics such as natural language processing, computer vision, time-series forecasting, scientific computing, remote sensing, and socio-technical systems.

This editorial provides a structured overview of the 14 published articles. Section 2 summarizes each paper's contributions, organized thematically to highlight the breadth of research covered. Section 3 concludes with reflections on the significance of this collection and directions for future research.

2. An Overview of Published Articles

The papers in this Special Issue can be broadly organized into five thematic areas: healthcare and biomedical analytics, agriculture and environmental applications, forecasting and risk prediction in complex systems, methodological advances in machine learning, and social and enterprise applications. These groupings not only reflect the diversity of application domains but also reveal common methodological trends and shared challenges.

2.1. Healthcare and Biomedical Analytics

Healthcare remains one of the most impactful domains for machine learning, where accurate and interpretable models can significantly improve diagnosis and patient outcomes.

Zhang et al. investigate the classification of textual medical notes from electronic health records using traditional machine learning methods. Their findings demonstrate that well-established models, particularly Logistic Regression, remain competitive when combined with rigorous preprocessing and evaluation strategies, highlighting the continued importance of simplicity and interpretability in clinical contexts.

Hadi et al. employ a DenseNet-based deep learning architecture to detect cardiovascular disease from medical imaging data. Their approach achieves high predictive performance while also incorporating visualization techniques to identify pathological regions, thereby enhancing model interpretability.

Together, these studies illustrate complementary approaches to healthcare analytics, encompassing both text-based and image-based data, and underscore the growing integration of machine learning into clinical workflows.

2.2. *Agriculture and Environmental Applications*

Machine learning is increasingly applied to agricultural and environmental systems, where it supports monitoring, sustainability, and operational efficiency.

Ljubobratović et al. explore neural network models for predicting peach maturity using tabular data, demonstrating that modern architectures such as TabNet can effectively handle small datasets and enable non-destructive quality assessment in horticulture.

Ad ao et al. address the challenge of limited labeled data by proposing synthetic data generation techniques for deep learning in precision viticulture. By combining rule-based image generation and diffusion models, their approach accelerates model development and reduces reliance on labor-intensive data collection.

Hernández-Macià et al. evaluate machine learning approaches for retrieving Arctic sea ice thickness from satellite radiometry data. Their results show that simpler models, such as Random Forest, can perform comparably to more complex deep learning methods, emphasizing the importance of domain knowledge and physical modeling in environmental applications.

Collectively, these works highlight the importance of practical considerations, such as data availability, interpretability, and deployment constraints, in the successful application of machine learning to real-world environmental and agricultural problems.

2.3. *Forecasting and Risk Prediction in Complex Systems*

A significant portion of the contributions focuses on forecasting and risk prediction in complex, dynamic, and uncertain systems.

Guritanu et al. introduce a topological machine learning framework based on persistent homology for detecting financial crises, providing interpretable early warning signals from multivariate time-series data.

Yuan et al. propose a hybrid xLSTM–XGBoost model for gasoline price forecasting, demonstrating the effectiveness of combining decomposition techniques with ensemble learning to handle non-stationary and highly volatile data.

In the context of disaster and environmental risk, He and Hu apply machine learning to predict household relocation decisions following disasters, offering insights for policy-making and recovery planning. Satish et al. develop predictive models for tsunami occurrence using seismic and geospatial data, highlighting the effectiveness of Random Forest in handling imbalanced datasets. Leon-Gomez et al. further contribute to environmental forecasting by proposing a UMAP-based data augmentation framework for improving wind speed prediction across multiple datasets.

These studies demonstrate how machine learning can support decision making under uncertainty across a wide range of domains, including finance, energy, disaster management, and environmental monitoring.

https://doi.org/10.3390/computers15050295

2.4. Methodological Advances in Learning, Optimization, and Uncertainty

Several papers focus on advancing the methodological foundations of machine learning. Malashin presents a framework for generating natural-language explanations for static-analysis warnings using transformer models combined with multi-objective optimization. This work contributes to explainable AI by addressing the trade-off between faithfulness and linguistic quality.

Montanari et al. investigate machine learning techniques for uncertainty estimation in dynamic aperture prediction within particle accelerators. By comparing approaches such as Monte Carlo dropout and bootstrap methods, the study highlights the importance of reliable uncertainty quantification in scientific applications.

These contributions reflect a broader shift in the field toward developing machine learning systems that are not only accurate but also interpretable, reliable, and capable of supporting informed decision making in complex settings.

2.5. Social, Political, and Enterprise Applications

The final group of papers demonstrates the application of machine learning to socio-technical and organizational systems.

Sernani et al. analyze digital political campaigning during the 2024 European Union elections using machine learning techniques applied to social media data. Their findings highlight the roles of micro-targeting, algorithmic bias, and disinformation in shaping political outcomes, contributing to ongoing discussions on digital governance and regulation.

Bhaskaran introduces EnterpriseAI, a transformer-based framework for optimizing enterprise systems and reducing operational costs. By leveraging transfer learning and complex dependency modeling, the proposed system enhances decision making and resource allocation in organizational contexts.

These studies underscore the expanding role of machine learning in understanding and optimizing human-centered systems, where technical performance must be balanced with ethical, social, and organizational considerations.

2.6. Cross-Cutting Trends

Across all thematic areas, several important trends emerge. First, many contributions adopt hybrid modeling approaches, combining multiple algorithms to leverage their complementary strengths. Second, there is a strong emphasis on practical challenges, including data scarcity, class imbalance, and deployment constraints. Third, the importance of interpretability and uncertainty estimation is increasingly recognized, particularly in high-stakes applications.

Overall, the papers in this Special Issue demonstrate that machine learning and statistical learning are advancing along both methodological and application-driven dimensions, reinforcing their role as essential tools in modern science and engineering.

3. Conclusions

This Special Issue provides a comprehensive overview of current research in machine learning and statistical learning, highlighting both theoretical developments and practical applications across a wide range of domains. The included papers demonstrate how advanced learning techniques can address complex real-world challenges while also emphasizing the importance of interpretability, robustness, and efficiency.

By organizing the contributions into thematic groups, this editorial has aimed to highlight the connections between different research directions and to identify common trends shaping the field. We hope that this collection will serve as a valuable resource for researchers and practitioners, fostering further innovation and interdisciplinary collaboration.

https://doi.org/10.3390/computers15050295

As Guest Editor, I would like to express my sincere gratitude to all authors for their high-quality contributions, to the reviewers for their careful and constructive evaluations, and to the editorial team of *Computers* for their support throughout the publication process.

Funding: This research received no external funding.

Institutional Review Board Statement: Not applicable.

Informed Consent Statement: Not applicable.

Data Availability Statement: Not applicable.

Conflicts of Interest: The author declares no conflicts of interest.

List of Contributions:

1. Zhang, Y.; Le, H.T.N.; Lopez, N.; Phan, K. Comparative study of machine learning models for textual medical note classification. *Computers* **2026**, *15*, 7. https://doi.org/10.3390/computers15010007.
2. Hadi, W.; Jaware, T.; Khalifa, T.; Aburub, F.; Ali, N.; Saini, R. Enhancing cardiovascular disease detection through exploratory predictive modeling using DenseNet-based deep learning. *Computers* **2025** *14*, 330. https://doi.org/10.3390/computers14080330.
3. Ljubobratović, D.; Vuković, M.; Bakarić, M.B.; Jemrić, T.; Matetić, M. Comparative analysis of neural network models for predicting peach maturity on tabular data. *Computers* **2025**, *14*, 554. https://doi.org/10.3390/computers14120554.
4. Adão, T.; Chojka, A.; Pascoal, D.; Silva, N.; Morais, R.; Peres, E. Synthetic data-driven methods to accelerate the deployment of deep learning models: A case study on pest and disease detection in precision viticulture. *Computers* **2025**, *14*, 327. https://doi.org/10.3390/computers14080327.
5. Hernández-Macià, F.; Gomez, G.S.; Gabarró, C.; Escorihuela, M.J. Assessment of machine learning-driven retrievals of Arctic sea ice thickness from L-band radiometry remote sensing. *Computers* **2025**, *14*, 305. https://doi.org/10.3390/computers14080305.
6. Guritanu, E.; Barbierato, E.; Gatti, A. Topological machine learning for financial crisis detection: Early warning signals from persistent homology. *Computers* **2025**, *14*, 408. https://doi.org/10.3390/computers14100408.
7. Yuan, F.; Huang, X.; Jiang, H.; Jiang, Y.; Zuo, Z.; Wang, L.; Wang, Y.; Gu, S.; Peng, Y. An xLSTM–XGBoost ensemble model for forecasting non-stationary and highly volatile gasoline price. *Computers* **2025**, *14*, 256. https://doi.org/10.3390/computers14070256.
8. He, C.; Hu, D. Informing disaster recovery through predictive relocation modeling. *Computers* **2025**, *14*, 240. https://doi.org/10.3390/computers14060240.
9. Satish, S.; Gonaygunta, H.; Yadulla, A.R.; Kumar, D.; Maturi, M.H.; Meduri, K.; Cruz, E.D.L.; Nadella, G.S.; Sajja, G.S. Forecasting the unseen: Enhancing tsunami occurrence predictions with machine-learning-driven analytics. *Computers* **2025**, *14*, 175. https://doi.org/10.3390/computers14050175.
10. Leon-Gomez, E.A.; Álvarez-Meza, A.M.; Castellanos-Dominguez, G. Cross-dataset data augmentation using UMAP for deep learning-based wind speed prediction. *Computers* **2025**, *14*, 123. https://doi.org/10.3390/computers14040123.
11. Malashin, I. Generation of natural-language explanations for static-analysis warnings using single- and multi-objective optimization. *Computers* **2025**, *14*, 534. https://doi.org/10.3390/computers14120534.
12. Montanari, C.E.; Appleby, R.B.; Croce, D.D.; Giovannozzi, M.; Pieloni, T.; Redaelli, S.; Van der Veken, F.F. Machine learning techniques for uncertainty estimation in dynamic aperture prediction. *Computers* **2025**, *14*, 287. https://doi.org/10.3390/computers14070287.
13. Sernani, P.; Cossiri, A.; Cosimo, G.D.; Frontoni, E. Analyzing digital political campaigning through machine learning: An exploratory study for the Italian campaign for European Union parliament election in 2024. *Computers* **2025**, *14*, 126. https://doi.org/10.3390/computers14040126.

14. Bhaskaran, S.V. EnterpriseAI: A transformer-based framework for cost optimization and process enhancement in enterprise systems. *Computers* **2025**, *14*, 106. https://doi.org/10.3390/computers14030106.

eferences

Bommasani, R.; Hudson, D.A.; Adeli, E.; Altman, R.; Arora, S.; von Arx, S.; Bernstein, M.S.; Bohg, J.; Bosselut, A.; Brunskill, E.; et al. On the Opportunities and Risks of Foundation Models. *arXiv* **2021**, arXiv:2108.07258. [CrossRef]

Brown, T.; Mann, B.; Ryder, N.; Subbiah, M.; Kaplan, J.D.; Dhariwal, P.; Neelakantan, A.; Shyam, P.; Sastry, G.; Askell, A.; et al. Language models are few-shot learners. In *NIPS'20: Proceedings of the 34th International Conference on Neural Information Processing System*; Curran Associates Inc.: Red Hook, NY, USA, 2020; Volume 33, pp. 1877–1901.

Hussain, A.; Ali, S.; Farwa, U.E.; Mozumder, M.A.I.; Kim, H.C. Foundation models: From current developments, challenges, and risks to future opportunities. In *Proceedings of the 2025 27th International Conference on Advanced Communications Technology (ICACT), Pyeong Chang, Republic of Korea, 16–19 February 2025*; IEEE: New York, NY, USA, 2025; pp. 51–58.

Achiam, J.; Adler, S.; Agarwal, S.; Ahmad, L.; Akkaya, I.; Aleman, F.L.; Almeida, D.; Altenschmidt, J.; Altman, S.; Anadkat, S.; et al. GPT-4 technical report. *arXiv* **2023**, arXiv:2303.08774. [CrossRef]

Doshi-Velez, F.; Kim, B. Towards a rigorous science of interpretable machine learning. *arXiv* **2017**, arXiv:1702.08608. [CrossRef]

Linardatos, P.; Papastefanopoulos, V.; Kotsiantis, S. Explainable AI: A review of machine learning interpretability methods. *Entropy* **2020**, *23*, 18. [CrossRef] [PubMed]

Zhang, C.; Bengio, S.; Hardt, M.; Recht, B.; Vinyals, O. Understanding Deep Learning (Still) Requires Rethinking Generalization. *Commun. ACM* **2021**, *64*, 107–115. [CrossRef]

 https://doi.org/10.3390/computers15050295

computers

MDPI

Article

Comparative Study of Machine Learning Models for Textual Medical Note Classification

Yan Zhang *, Huynh Trung Nguyen Le, Nathan Lopez and Kira Phan

School of Computer Science and Engineering, California State University San Bernardino, 5500 University Parkway, San Bernardino, CA 92407, USA; 008758094@coyote.csusb.edu (H.T.N.L.); 008752504@coyote.csusb.edu (N.L.); 008349868@coyote.csusb.edu (K.P.)

* Correspondence: yan.zhang@csusb.edu; Tel.: +1-909-537-5333

Abstract

The expansion of electronic health records (EHRs) has generated a large amount of unstructured textual data, such as clinical notes and medical reports, which contain diagnostic and prognostic information. Effective classification of these textual medical notes is critical for improving clinical decision support and healthcare data management. This study presents a statistically rigorous comparative analysis of four traditional machine learning algorithms—Random Forest, Logistic Regression, Multinomial Naive Bayes, and Support Vector Machine—for multiclass classification of medical notes into four disease categories: Neoplasms, Digestive System Diseases, Nervous System Diseases, and Cardiovascular Diseases. A dataset containing 9633 labeled medical notes was preprocessed through text cleaning, lemmatization, stop-word removal, and vectorization using term frequency-inverse document frequency (TF–IDF) representation. The models were trained and optimized through GridSearchCV with 5-fold cross-validation and evaluated across five independent stratified 90-10 train–test splits. Evaluation metrics, including accuracy, precision, recall, F1-score, and multiclass ROC-AUC, were used to assess model performance. Logistic Regression demonstrated the strongest overall performance, achieving an average accuracy of 0.8469 and high macro and weighted F1 scores, followed by Support Vector Machine and Multinomial Naive Bayes. Misclassification patterns revealed substantial lexical overlap between digestive and neurological disease notes, underscoring the limitations of TF–IDF representations in capturing deeper semantic distinctions. These findings confirm that traditional machine learning models remain robust, interpretable, and computationally efficient tools for textual medical note classification, and the study establishes a transparent and reproducible benchmark that provides a solid foundation for future methodological advancements in clinical natural language processing.

Keywords: medical text classification; machine learning; logistic regression; clinical natural language processing; multiclass disease classification

1. Introduction

The growing digitization of healthcare systems has led to the exponential accumulation of clinical data in electronic health records (EHRs) [1,2]. Among these records, textual medical notes, such as physicians' observations, discharge summaries, and clinical reports, contain rich information that can reflect patients' conditions, diagnoses and clinical histories. However, the unstructured and heterogeneous nature of such textual data poses challenges for automated processing and analysis [3]. Efficiently classifying textual medical notes into relevant disease categories can facilitate improved clinical decision making and support healthcare management systems through faster retrieval and knowledge extraction.

Machine Learning (ML) approaches have shown promise in transforming unstructured clinical text into actionable insights. By learning patterns and associations from labeled datasets, ML models can help automatically categorize medical documents according to disease types. This capability is important for developing intelligent healthcare applications such as predictive diagnostic tools and population health monitoring frameworks [4]. Nevertheless, selecting an effective classification model remains a challenge, as different algorithms show varying degrees of performance depending on data characteristics, preprocessing methods, and feature representations.

Although recent advances in deep learning and transformer-based language models have gained attention, these approaches often require extensive training resources and very large datasets, which may not be feasible for many healthcare settings [5]. So traditional ML methods continue to play an important role due to their interpretability, computational efficiency, and competitive performance on high-dimensional sparse features such as TF–IDF representations [6]. Despite their relevance, the literature still lacks comprehensive and statistically rigorous benchmark studies evaluating multiple traditional ML models on multiclass medical note classification. Existing studies often rely on binary classification settings (e.g., disease vs. non-disease) or restricted/domain-specific corpora, limiting the generalizability and reliability of their findings. Given that tradition ML models differ in their learning strategies, underlying assumptions, and robustness to noise, a systematic multiclass comparison remains valuable for identifying their relative strengths and weaknesses in clinical NLP applications [6].

This research aims to address this gap by conducting a comparative study of four widely used machine learning models, namely Random Forest, Logistic Regression, Naive Bayes, and Support Vector Machine, for classifying textual medical notes. The study uses a curated dataset containing over 9000 labeled clinical notes and applies consistent preprocessing to train and fine-tune each model. Model performance is assessed using standard multiclass metrics, including accuracy, precision, recall, F1-score, and multiclass ROC-AUC, enabling a rigorous and balanced comparison.

The key contributions of this paper can be summarized as follows:

- A statistically robust benchmark comparing four established machine learning algorithms on a multiclass clinical text classification task, using repeated stratified evaluation and cross-validated hyperparameter tuning.
- Empirical insights into the strengths, limitations, and suitability of traditional ML approaches for disease-oriented clinical text analytics, providing a foundation for evaluating more advanced NLP methods.

By establishing a transparent and statistically reliable benchmark for traditional ML models, this study supports future research on clinical NLP, including transformer-based models, domain-specific embeddings, and automated or weakly supervised learning frameworks.

The remainder of this paper is organized as follows. Section 2 reviews related work on medical text classification and prior comparative studies. Section 3 describes the dataset and preprocessing procedures used in this study. Section 4 details the methodologies of the selected machine learning models. Section 5 presents and discusses the experimental results. Finally, Section 6 concludes the paper and outlines directions for future research.

2. Related Work

The growing availability of electronic health records (EHRs) and digitized clinical narratives has accelerated research on machine learning (ML) and natural language pro-

https://doi.org/10.3390/computers15010007

cessing (NLP) applications in healthcare [7]. Over the past decade, numerous studies have explored how ML techniques can extract, classify, and interpret meaningful information from unstructured medical text, such as clinical notes and discharge summaries. Existing studies range from broad surveys that summarize progress and challenges in the field to empirical investigations comparing traditional supervised algorithms, and more recently, deep learning and hybrid frameworks capable of modeling complex semantic patterns.

2.1. Surveys on Machine Learning for Clinical and Medical Text

Several surveys have examined the increasing integration of ML within healthcare and clinical NLP. Spasic et al. conducted a systematic review of 110 studies applying ML to clinical text and identified text classification as the most common NLP task in healthcare [4]. Authors found that most datasets were small and institution-specific, limiting model generalizability, and emphasized the annotation bottleneck as a critical challenge for supervised learning [4]. Strategies such as active learning, distant supervision, and crowdsourcing were discussed as potential solutions to reduce manual labeling costs.

Mustafa et al. surveyed the emerging field of Automated Machine Learning (AutoML) in healthcare, highlighting its potential for clinical note analysis [8]. Although AutoML has shown promise in structured data settings, its application to unstructured medical text remains underdeveloped. The authors noted key barriers including data heterogeneity, privacy concerns, and model interpretability, concluding that an AutoML platform for clinical notes could greatly enhance scalability and reduce human effort in ML-based healthcare solutions [8].

Kino et al. provided a scoping review of ML applications to the social determinants of health (SDH) [9]. Reviewing 82 studies published before 2020, they observed that most used predictive ML models on structured survey data, with limited exploration of unstructured sources such as clinical narratives. The authors underscored the broader expansion of ML into health research and emphasized the need for interpretable, transparent, and well-validated approaches when applying ML to clinical textual data [9].

Kadhim offered a comprehensive overview of supervised ML techniques for text classification, detailing the standard pipeline of data preprocessing, feature extraction, and model evaluation [10]. The review compared algorithms such as Naive Bayes (NB), Support Vector Machines (SVM), and k-Nearest Neighbors (k-NN), noting that TF–IDF weighting schemes significantly enhance classification accuracy.

These reviews establish the theoretical and methodological foundation for applying ML to unstructured health text and motivate the empirical comparisons undertaken in the present study.

2.2. Traditional Machine Learning Approaches for Medical Text Classification

A broad range of studies demonstrate that traditional supervised learning remains effective for medical text classification and disease prediction. Weng et al. developed a machine learning–based NLP framework for medical subdomain classification of clinical notes [11]. Using cTAKES and UMLS features, the authors compared SVMs with convolutional recurrent neural networks (RNN) and showed that SVMs offered comparable accuracy with better interpretability, validating their utility for cross-institutional applications [11].

López-Úbeda et al. proposed an ML-based system for automatic classification of radiological protocols using a corpus of 700,000 CT and MRI reports [12]. Several NLP-driven classifiers were evaluated, including SVM, Random Forest, neural networks, and transfer-learning approaches. The system achieved high accuracy and has since been implemented as a clinical decision-support tool, demonstrating the practical value of ML for workflow optimization.

 https://doi.org/10.3390/computers15010007

Tiwari et al. examined multiclass disease prediction using Random Forest, SVM, Naive Bayes, and Decision Tree algorithms on a symptom dataset [13]. Both Random Forest and Decision Tree achieved the highest accuracy (99%), whereas Naive Bayes yielded the lowest (86%), confirming the effectiveness of ensemble and tree-based methods for healthcare classification tasks.

Sung et al. applied supervised ML and text mining to automated phenotyping of ischemic stroke using 4640 patient EMRs [14]. The integration of structured variables with textual data improved classification and decomposing the multiclass problem into binary subtasks further enhanced performance. Their findings highlight the potential of ML to replace manual annotation in disease phenotyping.

Rabby and Berka investigated multi-class classification of COVID-19 biomedical research papers using ten ML algorithms and eleven feature configurations [15]. They found that TF–IDF features of abstracts yielded the highest accuracy, with Random Forest and BERT models performing best, demonstrating the versatility of traditional ML for biomedical document classification.

Gupta et al. developed an NLP pipeline to automatically identify immune-related adverse events (irAEs) from unstructured oncology notes [16]. Employing keyword filtering, TF–IDF, and BioWordVec embeddings as input for Logistic Regression, SVM, Random Forest, CNN, and Bi-LSTM models, they achieved an F1 score of 0.75 and AUC of 0.85, demonstrating that classical ML methods augmented with embeddings can automate complex clinical annotation tasks.

Gao et al. introduced KeyClass, a weakly supervised framework for assigning ICD-9 codes to unstructured clinical notes without manual labeling [17]. Tested on the MIMIC-III dataset, KeyClass achieved performance comparable to supervised models trained on thousands of labeled samples, underscoring the promise of weak supervision for scalable medical text classification.

Lenivtceva et al. explored multi-label classification of 11,671 Russian medical notes [18]. The authors compared several algorithms and proposed classifier-chain ensembles to capture inter-label dependencies, achieving notable performance gains and illustrating the strength of ensemble strategies for complex medical text tasks.

These studies confirm that traditional ML models, particularly SVM, Logistic Regression, and Random Forest, are able to offer robust, interpretable, and computationally efficient baselines for medical text classification.

2.3. *Advances and Extensions Using Deep Learning and Hybrid Methods*

While traditional algorithms remain effective, recent research increasingly apply deep learning and hybrid NLP approaches to capture the semantic richness of clinical text. da Silva et al. evaluated machine learning and deep learning models for oncology clinical notes, comparing Logistic Regression, Random Forest, Decision Tree, k-NN, Multilayer Perceptron (MLP), and LSTM networks on 3308 documents [19]. Preprocessing raised mean accuracy from 26% to 93.9%, with the MLP model achieving the best F1 score (93.6%), demonstrating the influence of text normalization on performance.

Goodrum et al. developed a framework to classify scanned EHR documents into clinically relevant and non-relevant categories using OCR-extracted text [20]. A ClinicalBERT model achieved an accuracy of 0.973, highlighting the power of transformer architectures for document-level clinical classification.

Lu et al. compared seven deep learning models including CNN, RNN, GRU, LSTM, Bi-LSTM, Transformer encoders, and BERT, for discharge note classification under varying class-imbalance conditions [21]. Transformer encoders yielded the best results overall,

 https://doi.org/10.3390/computers15010007

whereas CNNs achieved similar accuracy with shorter training time, suggesting a practical balance between computational efficiency and predictive accuracy.

These studies reflect a gradual evolution from traditional ML pipelines toward deep neural and hybrid models that exploit pre-trained embeddings and transformer architectures to enhance semantic understanding. However, they also reveal that well-tuned traditional algorithms can offer comparable performance with greater interpretability and lower computational demands which are valuable in clinical settings [19].

Across surveys, traditional models, and modern deep learning methods, the literature demonstrates the maturity and adaptability of ML for clinical and medical text classification. The challenges, such as data sparsity, annotation costs, and the trade-off between interpretability and complexity, continue to shape the field. Building on these insights, the present study contributes by conducting a comparative evaluation of four traditional ML algorithms for multiclass classification of textual medical notes, thereby building empirical benchmarks to guide future research that may integrate deep learning, weak supervision, or AutoML techniques for enhanced performance.

3. Textual Medical Note Dataset and Preprocessing

3.1. Data Collection

The dataset used in this study was obtained from Kaggle, a publicly available machine learning repository [22]. This dataset contains textual medical notes derived from published clinical case descriptions and research summaries, representing five disease-related categories: Digestive System Diseases, Cardiovascular Diseases, Neoplasms, Nervous System Diseases, and General Pathological Conditions [22]. Each record consists of a paragraph describing a medical condition, patient case, or experimental study, annotated with a corresponding disease class label.

The original dataset contains a total of 28,880 medical notes, divided evenly into two parts: 14,438 labeled training samples and 14,442 unlabeled test samples. The unlabeled portion, intended for Kaggle competition evaluation, does not include ground-truth class labels. Because supervised machine learning requires labeled data for training and performance assessment, this study exclusively uses the labeled subset of 14,438 samples. The unlabeled test data were excluded from analysis, as their unknown class distribution prevents valid evaluation or model comparison.

Within the labeled subset, the five classes were moderately imbalanced, with the General Pathological Conditions category containing 4805 records. This category is broad and heterogeneous, often overlapping semantically with the four more specific disease groups. Manual inspection revealed that many notes within this class referenced multiple organ systems or general pathological patterns, making it unsuitable as a coherent predictive category. Retaining this heterogeneous class would reduce class separability and introduce noise, thereby undermining the objective of evaluating machine learning algorithms on a well-defined multiclass classification task. For these reasons, the General Pathological Conditions class was removed. After excluding these 4805 records, the resulting dataset consisted of 9633 labeled medical notes distributed across four clearly defined disease categories. Table 1 summarizes the final class distribution after data cleaning.

The average length of a raw medical note in the processed dataset is approximately 187 words.

 https://doi.org/10.3390/computers15010007

Table 1. Distribution of medical notes across four disease classes after data cleaning.

Disease Class	Label	Number of Records	Percentage (%)
Neoplasms	1	3163	32.8
Digestive System Diseases	2	1494	15.5
Nervous System Diseases	3	1925	20.0
Cardiovascular Diseases	4	3051	31.7
Total	–	9633	100.0

3.2. Data Preprocessing

Comprehensive text preprocessing was applied to ensure the dataset was clean, standardized, and machine-readable. The following steps were performed sequentially:

- Text cleaning. All text was converted to lowercase to eliminate case-based redundancy. Punctuation marks were removed, and stop words (e.g., the, is, and, of) were filtered out to reduce noise. Digits and special symbols were also removed. Although such elements can carry clinical meaning in structured EHR data (e.g., laboratory values or dosages), exploratory analysis revealed that numerical tokens in this dataset primarily reflected metadata (e.g., ages, years, sample counts), which provided minimal discriminatory value for the four disease categories. Their removal reduced noise and vocabulary size without compromising semantic content.
- Tokenization and lemmatization. Each document was tokenized into individual words. Tokens were then lemmatized, that is, reduced to their base or dictionary form, to minimize inflectional variations (e.g., "studies" → "study," "patients" → "patient"). After these operations, the average document length was reduced from 187 words to approximately 111 words.
- Lexical distribution analysis. To understand class-level vocabulary patterns, word frequency analyses were generated for each disease category.
  - Neoplasms (Class 1), the top frequent terms included patient, tumor, case, treatment, lesion, and disease.
  - Digestive System Diseases (Class 2), the top frequent terms included patient, treatment, disease, study, group, and associated.
  - Nervous System Diseases (Class 3), the top frequent terms included patient, treatment, study, pain, group, and effect.
  - Cardiovascular Diseases (Class 4), the top frequent terms included patient, blood pressure, coronary artery, left ventricular, myocardial infarction, and treatment.
- Text vectorization. The cleaned and lemmatized corpus was converted into a numerical format using TF–IDF vectorization techniques. TF–IDF vectorization was applied with a consistent set of parameters to ensure reproducibility. A unigram representation was used (`n_gram_range = (1,1)`), and no vocabulary pruning was performed (`max_features = None`), allowing all 27,609 unique tokens in the preprocessed corpus to be retained. Default document-frequency thresholds were applied (`min_df = 1`, `max_df = 1.0`), and sublinear TF scaling was disabled (`sublinear_tf = False`), meaning raw term frequencies were combined directly with inverse document frequency weighting. All TF–IDF vectors were L2-normalized to ensure comparable scaling across documents. These parameter choices were selected to maintain a transparent and fully reproducible baseline for evaluating traditional machine learning algorithms. The resulting document-term matrix contained 27,609 unique tokens, yielding a feature space of (9633 × 27,609) for subsequent machine learning analysis.
- Dataset partitioning. The dataset was randomly partitioned into training and testing subsets using a 90-10 stratified split, ensuring that the class distribution in both

https://doi.org/10.3390/computers15010007

subsets remained proportional to that of the full dataset. This resulted in 8669 training records and 964 test records, providing sufficient data for model training and unbiased evaluation.

No explicit feature-selection or dimensionality-reduction methods were applied. This was intentional, as TF–IDF vectorization coupled with linear classifiers is known to perform well in high-dimensional sparse spaces, and retaining the full vocabulary preserves interpretability and reproducibility. Retaining all features also enables meaningful comparison with future studies employing embeddings or deep learning methods.

The following sample demonstrates the transformation of a raw medical note into its cleaned and lemmatized form. The original medical note is *"Duodenal-caval fistula. Duodenal-caval fistula is a rare, often lethal disease that requires prompt diagnosis and surgical correction. A case of duodenal-caval fistula due to duodenal ulceration is presented and discussed."* The preprocessed medical note is *"duodenal caval fistula duodenal caval fistula rare often lethal disease requires prompt diagnosis surgical correction case duodenal caval fistula due duodenal ulceration presented discussed"*. These preprocessing steps standardized the dataset, reduced sparsity, and prepared it for downstream feature extraction and classification modeling.

4. Methodologies

This section presents the machine learning algorithms used to classify textual medical notes into disease categories. To identify the most effective traditional learning algorithm for this task, four widely used classifiers, namely Random Forest (RF), Naive Bayes (NB), Logistic Regression (LR), and Support Vector Machine (SVM), were implemented and compared under consistent preprocessing conditions. Each model represents a distinct learning paradigm: probabilistic reasoning in NB, linear discriminative modeling in LR, margin maximization in SVM, and ensemble-based decision aggregation in RF. All models were trained using the same vectorized representation of the preprocessed medical notes and optimized through hyperparameter tuning to achieve the best classification performance. The following subsections describe the theoretical foundations, parameter configurations, and implementation details of each model.

4.1. Random Forest Classification

The Random Forest (RF) algorithm is an ensemble-based learning method that constructs multiple decision trees during training and outputs the class predicted by the majority of trees [23]. By combining bootstrap aggregation (bagging) and random feature selection, Random Forest reduces overfitting while maintaining strong predictive accuracy [24]. Each tree is trained on a random subset of samples, and at each node split, a random subset of features is considered. This dual randomness enhances model diversity and stability, making Random Forest suited for high-dimensional and sparse text datasets [25].

In this study, the Random Forest classifier was applied to the vectorized medical notes to classify documents into four disease categories. The feature space consisted of 27,609 unique tokens derived from the preprocessed corpus. The algorithm recursively partitions the feature space to minimize impurity, measured using the Gini index. Its ability to handle large vocabularies without explicit feature selection makes it an appropriate choice for textual data.

Hyperparameters were optimized using a grid search with 5-fold cross-validation to achieve a balance between accuracy and generalization. The parameters tuned included the number of trees, maximum tree depth, the minimum number of samples required to be at a leaf node, and the minimum samples required for node splits. Model performance was

https://doi.org/10.3390/computers15010007

assessed using the macro average F1-score, which provide balanced sensitivity across all disease classes.

Random Forest was selected for its robustness to noise, interpretability of feature importance, and capacity to model nonlinear relationships in textual data. Its ensemble structure also identifies key discriminative medical terms, supporting interpretability and transparency in clinical applications.

4.2. Naive Bayes

The Naive Bayes (NB) classifier is a probabilistic model based on Bayes' Theorem, which assumes conditional independence among features given the class label [26,27]. Despite this simplifying assumption, it remains effective and computationally efficient for text classification because it models word-occurrence probabilities directly [28]. In this study, NB was applied to estimate the likelihood that a medical note belongs to one of four disease categories using the distribution of words within each note. Given a document $d = \{w_1, w_2, \ldots, w_n\}$ and a class c, the posterior probability is expressed as:

$$P(c|d) \propto P(c)\prod_{i=1}^{n} P(w_i|c), \tag{1}$$

where $P(c)$ is the prior probability of a class and $P(w_i|c)$ represents the likelihood of observing word w_i in that class [26]. The class with the highest posterior probability is then assigned as the predicted label.

The Multinomial Naive Bayes (MNB) variant was employed, as it is well suited for count-based representations such as term frequency or TF–IDF vectors derived from the medical notes. Additive Laplace smoothing was used to handle zero probabilities for rare or unseen words, improving generalization. To optimize the smoothing parameter α, a grid search with 5-fold cross-validation were conducted over the range $0.01 \le \alpha \le 1.0$, using the macro average F1-score as the selection metric.

Naive Bayes was chosen for its simplicity, speed, and interpretability which make it a strong baseline model for medical text classification.

4.3. Logistic Regression

The Logistic Regression (LR) model is a linear classifier that estimates the probability of a document belonging to a specific class using a logistic (sigmoid) function [29]. Logistic regression is a discriminative approach that directly learns the decision boundary between classes by maximizing the likelihood of the observed labels [30]. It is well suited for high-dimensional, sparse datasets like textual representations, where individual tokens serve as features. Given a document represented by a feature vector $\mathbf{x} = (x_1, x_2, \ldots, x_n)$, the probability that it belongs to class c is expressed as

$$P(c|\mathbf{x}) = \frac{1}{1 + e^{-(\mathbf{w}^\top \mathbf{x} + b)}}, \tag{2}$$

where $\mathbf{w}$ denotes the model weights and b is the bias term [30]. For multiclass problems, a softmax extension is applied to ensure all class probabilities sum to one.

In this study, logistic regression was implemented using the one-vs.-rest (OvR) strategy, where an independent binary classifier was trained for each disease class. The input features were derived from the TF–IDF document–term matrix generated during preprocessing. Model parameters were optimized through L2 (ridge) regularization to control overfitting, and hyperparameter tuning was performed using grid search with 5-fold cross-validation. Regularization type and solver choice were further optimized by testing L1, L2, and

https://doi.org/10.3390/computers15010007

elasticnet penalties with solvers including 'lbfgs', 'liblinear', and 'saga'. Model performance was evaluated using the macro averaged F1-score.

Logistic Regression was selected for its interpretability, scalability, and ability to produce well-calibrated probability estimates, making it a reliable model for textual medical note classification.

4.4. Support Vector Machine Classification

Support Vector Machine (SVM) is a discriminative learning algorithm that seeks an optimal separating hyperplane to maximize the margin between data points of different classes [31]. It is effective for text classification, where data are typically high-dimensional and sparse—conditions under which linear SVMs perform well [32]. By identifying a subset of critical data points, known as support vectors, the model defines the decision boundary that best separates classes in the feature space. Given a training set of labeled samples $\{(\mathbf{x}_i, y_i)\}_{i=1}^{m}$, where $\mathbf{x}_i \in \mathbb{R}^n$ represents the feature vector and $y_i \in \{-1, +1\}$ denotes the class label, the SVM optimization problem can be formulated as:

$$\min_{\mathbf{w},b,\xi_i} \frac{1}{2}\|\mathbf{w}\|^2 + C\sum_{i=1}^{m} \xi_i$$

$$\text{s.t. } y_i(\mathbf{w}^\top \mathbf{x}_i + b) \geq 1 - \xi_i, \quad \xi_i \geq 0, \tag{3}$$

where $\mathbf{w}$ is the weight vector, b is the bias term, ξ_i are slack variables, and C is the regularization parameter balancing margin maximization and classification error [33].

In this study, a linear SVM was employed due to its scalability and strong performance on large text corpora. The model was trained on a TF–IDF document–term matrix containing 27,609 features. Hyperparameters, including the regularization parameter C and kernel type, were tuned using grid search with 5-fold cross-validation. Linear, polynomial, radial basis function (RBF), and sigmoid kernels were tested, with performance evaluated using the macro averaged F1-score to account for class imbalance. The final configuration, based on the highest cross-validated F1-score, achieved a balanced trade-off between accuracy and generalization, confirming SVM's robustness and interpretability for medical text classification.

4.5. Evaluation Metrics

To evaluate the performance of the four machine learning models, a set of widely accepted metrics was employed. These metrics provide complementary perspectives on predictive accuracy, robustness across classes, and reliability when applied to multiclass textual data. The primary metrics used in this study include accuracy, precision, recall, F1-score, and AOC-AUC, each computed for individual class labels and then aggregated to summarize overall model performance.

For a given class label $c \in \{1, 2, \ldots, C\}$, where C represents the total number of categories, and TP_c, FP_c, and FN_c denote true positives for class c, false positives for class c, and false negatives for class c, respectively. The following definitions apply:

- Precision for class c quantifies the proportion of correctly predicted samples of class c among all samples predicted as class c:

$$\text{Precision}_c = \frac{TP_c}{TP_c + FP_c}. \tag{4}$$

https://doi.org/10.3390/computers15010007

- Recall for class c (or sensitivity) measures the proportion of actual samples of class c that were correctly identified:

$$\text{Recall}_c = \frac{TP_c}{TP_c + FN_c}. \quad (5)$$

- F1-score for class c is the harmonic mean of precision and recall:

$$\text{F1-score}_c = 2 \times \frac{\text{Precision}_c \times \text{Recall}_c}{\text{Precision}_c + \text{Recall}_c}. \quad (6)$$

- Accuracy measures the overall proportion of correctly classified samples across all classes:

$$\text{Accuracy} = \frac{\sum_{c=1}^{C} TP_c}{|\text{All Samples}|}. \quad (7)$$

Since this study involves four disease categories, macro averaged and weighted averaged versions of these metrics were used. Macro-averaging treats all classes equally, regardless of their size, while weighted averaging assigns weights proportional to the number of instances per class, providing a more realistic assessment under class imbalance.

In addition to these numerical metrics, confusion matrices were analyzed to visualize class-level performance, identify common misclassifications, and detect semantic overlaps among disease categories. It provides a detailed view of the classifier's performance by comparing predicted versus actual class labels [34]. The diagonal elements in a confusion matrix represent correctly classified medical notes, while off-diagonal values indicate misclassifications [34].

To further characterize the discriminative behavior of the models, Receiver Operating Characteristic (ROC) analysis was conducted. For multiclass problems, ROC curves were generated using the one-vs.-rest (OvR) strategy, in which each class is considered the positive class in turn [35]. For each classifier, class-wise ROC curves and their associated area under the curve (AUC_c) values were computed. A macro-averaged AUC was obtained by averaging over all classes.

Together, these evaluation measures provide a comprehensive and balanced assessment of model performance, enabling reliable comparison among the Random Forest, Multinomial Naive Bayes, Logistic Regression, and Support Vector Machine classifiers.

4.6. Model Training and Validation

To ensure a rigorous and unbiased evaluation, all models were trained and validated using a repeated experimental protocol consisting of five independent stratified 90–10 train–test splits. For each run, 90% of the data was used for model training and hyperparameter tuning, while the remaining 10% was reserved exclusively for evaluation. Stratification preserved the class distribution across splits, providing consistent representation of disease categories in each subset.

Within each run, hyperparameter optimization was performed using scikit-learn's GridSearchCV with 5-fold cross-validation applied only to the training portion. This ensured that the choice of hyperparameters reflected performance averaged across multiple folds rather than a single validation set, reducing variance and improving the reliability of model selection. After tuning, each model was retrained on the full training split and evaluated on the corresponding test subset.

The hyperparameter grids were intentionally designed to be non-trivial and to include parameters known to affect model complexity, regularization, and generalization behavior, particularly in high-dimensional sparse text settings.

For Random Forest, the parameter grid included:

https://doi.org/10.3390/computers15010007

- `n_estimators` $\in \{100, 200, 300, 400, 500\}$
- `max_depth` $\in \{\text{None}, 20, 40, 60\}$
- `max_features` $\in \{\text{'sqrt'}, \text{'log2'}\}$
- `min_samples_split` $\in \{2, 5, 10\}$
- `min_samples_leaf` $\in \{1, 2, 4, 6\}$

These parameters influence ensemble stability, bias–variance trade-offs, and resistance to noise.

For Multinomial Naive Bayes, tuning focused on:

- Smoothing coefficient $\alpha \in \{0.01, 0.1, 0.2, 0.3, 0.4, 0.5, 0.7, 1.0\}$
- `fit_prior` $\in \{\text{True}, \text{False}\}$

These parameters affect the handling of rare terms in TF–IDF distributions.

For Logistic Regression, the grid explored:

- Regularization strength `C` $\in \{0.1, 0.5, 1, 2, 5\}$
- `penalty` $\in \{\text{'l1'}, \text{'l2'}, \text{'elasticnet'}\}$
- `l1_ratio` $\in \{0.0, 0.5, 1.0\}$
- `solver` $\in \{\text{'lbfgs'}, \text{'liblinear'}, \text{'saga'}\}$

These hyperparameters govern coefficient sparsity, optimization behavior, and decision-boundary flexibility.

For the Support Vector Machine, tuning considered:

- `kernel` $\in \{\text{'linear'}, \text{'poly'}, \text{'rbf'}, \text{'sigmoid'}\}$
- `C` $\in \{0.1, 1, 2, 3, 5\}$
- `degree` $\in \{2, 3\}$ (for polynomial kernels)
- `gamma` $\in \{\text{'scale'}, \text{'auto'}\}$ (for RBF and sigmoid kernels)

These parameters control the geometric complexity of the decision boundary and the model's ability to capture linear versus nonlinear relationships.

The parameter ranges were selected based on prior text-classification research, empirical guidance from the scikit-learn documentation, and computational feasibility given the high dimensionality of the TF–IDF feature space. The consistency of optimal configurations across runs demonstrates that the search space was appropriate and sufficiently expressive for this task.

Model evaluation metrics included accuracy, macro and weighted F1-scores, and multiclass ROC–AUC. Final performance results represent the mean values across the five runs, while confusion matrices, classification reports, and ROC curves are shown for the run closest to the mean performance.

5. Experimental Results and Analysis

This section presents and discusses the experimental results obtained from the comparative evaluation of the four machine learning models (Random Forest, Multinomial Naive Bayes, Logistic Regression, and Support Vector Machine) applied to classifying textual medical notes into four disease categories. All experiments were conducted using the scikit-learn version 1.7 in Python 3.13, which provides reliable and standardized implementations of machine learning algorithms and evaluation procedures [36]. The experiments were conducted on the preprocessed dataset containing 9633 labeled records. Each model was trained and optimized using the best hyperparameter configurations determined through cross-validation, as detailed in Section 4.6.

The evaluation focuses on multiple performance metric, including accuracy, class-wise precision, recall, and F1-score, along with macro- and weighted-averaged forms that account for imbalanced class distributions. In addition, Receiver Operating Characteristic (ROC) curves were generated using the one-vs.-rest strategy to evaluate the discriminative

 https://doi.org/10.3390/computers15010007

ability of the models across all classes, and confusion matrices were used to visualize misclassification patterns. The following subsections present detailed results for each model, followed by a comparative analysis highlighting their relative strengths, weaknesses, and suitability for medical text classification tasks.

5.1. Random Forest Classification Model Evaluation

The Random Forest classifier was trained and evaluated using the repeated experimental procedure described in Section 4.6, consisting of five independent stratified 90–10 train–test splits. For each run, hyperparameter tuning was carried out on the training portion using GridSearchCV with 5-fold cross-validation. Across all five runs, the tuning process consistently selected the same optimal hyperparameter configuration: `bootstrap = True`, `max_depth = None`, `max_features = 'sqrt'`, `min_samples_leaf = 4`, `min_samples_split = 2`, and `n_estimators = 400`. This configuration allows the model to grow deep trees with random feature subsets while maintaining generalization through leaf size regularization. This stability indicates that the Random Forest model converges to a reliable configuration under multiple data partitions. Table 2 summarizes the accuracy, macro F1-score, and weighted F1-score for each of the five runs.

Table 2. Performance of Random Forest across 5 runs of stratified 90–10 splits.

Run #	Accuracy	F1_Macro	F1_Weighted
1	0.8051	0.7818	0.7999
2	0.8039	0.7724	0.7973
3	0.8061	0.7827	0.8015
4	0.7832	0.7615	0.7729
5	0.8029	0.7785	0.7977
Mean	0.8002	0.7754	0.7939

To provide detailed diagnostic insight, Run #5 (# means run number), showing accuracy closest to the mean, was chosen for subsequent analysis. Table 3 presents the confusion matrix for this representative run. It shows how the Random Forest model's predictions are distributed across the four disease categories on the test set.

Table 3. Confusion matrix for Random Forest (Run #5).

	Pred 1	Pred 2	Pred 3	Pred 4
True 1 Neoplasms	281	7	16	13
True 2 Digestive	30	94	9	16
True 3 Nervous System	24	5	122	42
True 4 Cardiovascular	12	4	12	277

The confusion matrix shows that the classifier performed strongly on Neoplasms (Class 1) and Cardiovascular Diseases (Class 4), with high true positive counts and relatively few misclassifications. More confusion is observed for Digestive System Diseases (Class 2) and Nervous System Diseases (Class 3), where overlapping terminology and shared clinical descriptors likely contributed to errors.

The corresponding classification report for Run #5 is shown in Table 4, which includes class-wise precision, recall, F1-score, and support.

Among all categories, Neoplasms (Class 1) and Cardiovascular Diseases (Class 4) achieved the highest recall values (0.8864 and 0.9082), showing that the model effectively identified these disease types. In contrast, Digestive System Diseases (Class 2) and Nervous

 https://doi.org/10.3390/computers15010007

System Diseases (Class 3) had lower recall values (0.6309 and 0.6321), reflecting greater confusion with other classes.

Table 4. Classification report for Random Forest (Run #5).

Class	Precision	Recall	F1-Score	Support
1 Neoplasms	0.8098	0.8864	0.8464	317
2 Digestive	0.8545	0.6309	0.7259	149
3 Nervous System	0.7673	0.6321	0.6932	193
4 Cardiovascular	0.7960	0.9082	0.8484	305
Accuracy			0.8029	964
Macro avg	0.8069	0.7644	0.7785	964
Weighted avg	0.8038	0.8029	0.7977	964

To further assess the discriminative capability of the Random Forest classifier, ROC curves for Run #5 were generated for each class using the one-vs.-rest strategy. Figure 1 displays the ROC curves for all four disease categories.

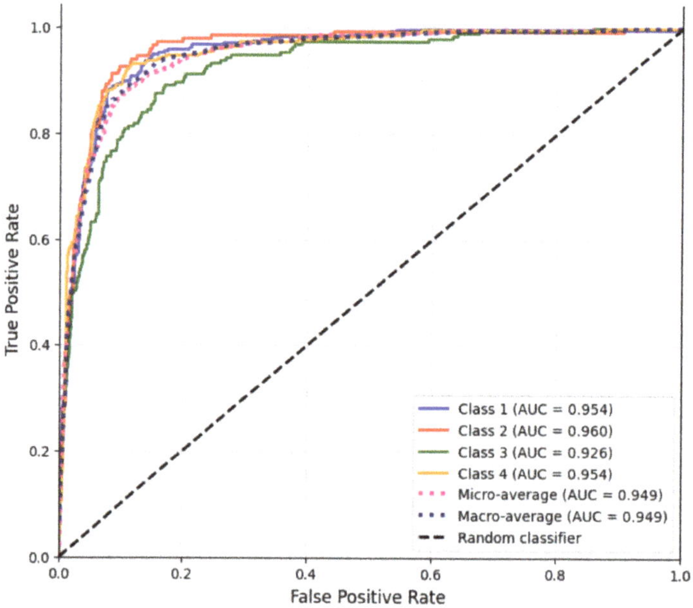

Figure 1. Multiclass ROC curves (One-vs.-Rest) for Random Forest Classification (Run #5).

These AUC results indicate separation between positive and negative classes across all disease categories. The slightly lower AUC for Class 3 reflects the higher misclassification rate observed in the confusion matrix and classification report, consistent with textual overlap between neurological and digestive case descriptions.

Overall, the Random Forest classifier performed competitively across all metrics, establishing a strong baseline for textual medical note classification.

5.2. Naive Bayes Model Evaluation

The Multinomial Naive Bayes (MNB) classifier was evaluated using the repeated experimental procedure outlined in Section 4.6, consisting of five independent stratified 90–10 train–test splits. For each run, hyperparameter tuning was performed on the training

https://doi.org/10.3390/computers15010007

subset using GridSearchCV with 5-fold cross-validation. Across all runs, the tuning procedure consistently selected the same optimal hyperparameters as smoothing coefficient $\alpha = 0.1$ and `fit_prior = False`. This stability indicates that the MNB model converges reliably to a robust configuration across varying data partitions. Table 5 summarizes the performance of the Naive Bayes classifier across the five runs.

Table 5. Performance of Multinomial Naive Bayes across 5 runs of stratified 90–10 splits.

Run #	Accuracy	F1_Macro	F1_Weighted
1	0.8061	0.7933	0.8053
2	0.8226	0.8067	0.8225
3	0.8019	0.7869	0.8027
4	0.8008	0.7873	0.8005
5	0.8060	0.7919	0.8065
Mean	0.8075	0.7932	0.8075

Run #1, which exhibited accuracy closest to the mean, was selected for in-depth diagnostic evaluation. The confusion matrix for this representative run is shown in Table 6. which illustrates how the model classified the four disease categories based on word-occurrence probabilities.

Table 6. Confusion matrix for Multinomial Naive Bayes (Run #1).

	Pred 1	Pred 2	Pred 3	Pred 4
True 1 Neoplasms	262	21	19	15
True 2 Digestive	15	120	6	8
True 3 Nervous System	21	7	132	33
True 4 Cardiovascular	11	10	21	263

The confusion matrix shows that the classifier performed strongly on Neoplasms (Class 1) and Cardiovascular Diseases (Class 4), with high true positive counts. Misclassification was more common for Nervous System Diseases (Class 3), likely due to overlapping clinical terminology shared with digestive and cardiovascular descriptions.

Table 7 presents the corresponding classification report for Run #1, which includes class-wise precision, recall, F1-score, and support.

Table 7. Classification report for Multinomial Naive Bayes (Run #1).

Class	Precision	Recall	F1-Score	Support
1 Neoplasms	0.8479	0.8265	0.8371	317
2 Digestive	0.7595	0.8054	0.7818	149
3 Nervous System	0.7416	0.6839	0.7116	193
4 Cardiovascular	0.8245	0.8623	0.8429	305
Accuracy			0.8061	964
Macro avg	0.7934	0.7945	0.7933	964
Weighted avg	0.8055	0.8060	0.8053	964

These results highlight the model's strong recall for Cardiovascular Diseases (Class 4), while Digestive System Diseases (Class 2) and Nervous System Diseases (Class 3) exhibited the lowest recall, reflecting greater lexical overlap with other categories. Overall, MNB demonstrated stable and competitive performance, with accuracy and weighted F1-scores consistently exceeding 0.80 across all runs.

Figure 2 presents the ROC curves for each disease category using the one-vs.-rest strategy, as well as the corresponding AUC values for Run #1.

https://doi.org/10.3390/computers15010007

The high AUC values indicate strong discriminative ability across all classes, with Nervous System Diseases again showing the lowest separation performance.

Overall, the Multinomial Naive Bayes classifier produced balanced results with strong overall accuracy and consistent weighted averages across all metrics. Its efficiency and simplicity make it a reliable baseline model for multiclass medical note classification, particularly when computational efficiency and interpretability are desired.

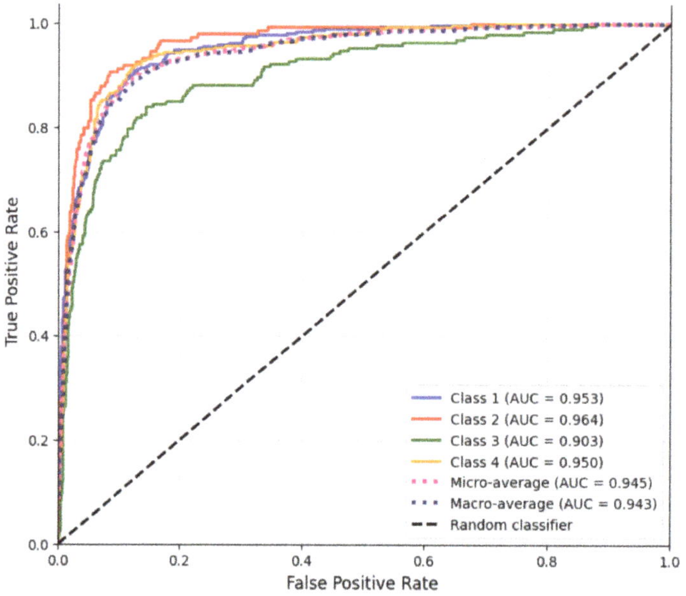

Figure 2. Multiclass ROC curves (One-vs.-Rest) for Multinomial Naive Bayes (Run #1).

5.3. Logistic Regression Model Evaluation

The Logistic Regression classifier was trained and evaluated following the repeated experimental protocol described in Section 4.6, involving five independent stratified 90–10 train–test splits. For each run, hyperparameter tuning was conducted using GridSearchCV with 5-fold cross-validation on the training subset. Across all runs, the same optimal configuration was consistently selected: `C = 1`, `class_weight = None`, `l1_ratio = 0.5`, `max_iter = 1000`, `multi_class = 'multinomial'`, `penalty = 'elasticnet'`, and `solver = 'saga'`. This combination of elastic net regularization and the SAGA solver provided a balanced control of both L1 and L2 penalties, enabling the model to handle sparse features while maintaining good generalization. The multinomial formulation was chosen to directly optimize the cross-entropy loss for the four disease categories. This consistent selection demonstrates the stability of the logistic regression model under repeated data partitioning. Table 8 summarizes the accuracy, macro F1-score, and weighted F1-score for each of the five runs.

Run #2, whose accuracy was closest to the overall mean, was selected for detailed diagnostic evaluation. The confusion matrix for this representative run is shown in Table 9. It summarizes the classifier's predictions across the four disease categories on the test set.

The classifier demonstrated particularly strong performance for Neoplasms (Class 1) and Cardiovascular Diseases (Class 4), with high true positive counts and minimal misclassification. Digestive System Diseases (Class 2) and Nervous System Diseases (Class 3) exhibited slightly lower recall values, reflecting greater semantic overlap among their textual descriptions.

https://doi.org/10.3390/computers15010007

Table 8. Performance of Logistic Regression across 5 runs of stratified 90–10 splits.

Run #	Accuracy	F1_Macro	F1_Weighted
1	0.8506	0.8381	0.8502
2	0.8465	0.8282	0.8452
3	0.8423	0.8276	0.8414
4	0.8475	0.8396	0.8471
5	0.8475	0.8361	0.8472
Mean	0.8469	0.8339	0.8462

Table 9. Confusion matrix for Logistic Regression (Run #2).

	Pred 1	Pred 2	Pred 3	Pred 4
True 1 Neoplasms	285	11	14	7
True 2 Digestive	22	104	17	6
True 3 Nervous System	15	5	152	21
True 4 Cardiovascular	11	3	16	275

The detailed performance metrics for Run #2 are shown in Table 10, including class-wise precision, recall, F1-score, and support.

Table 10. Classification report for Logistic Regression (Run #2).

Class	Precision	Recall	F1-Score	Support
1 Neoplasms	0.8559	0.8991	0.8769	317
2 Digestive	0.8455	0.6980	0.7647	149
3 Nervous System	0.7638	0.7876	0.7755	193
4 Cardiovascular	0.8900	0.9016	0.8958	305
Accuracy			0.8465	964
Macro avg	0.8388	0.8216	0.8282	964
Weighted avg	0.8466	0.8465	0.8452	964

The logistic regression classifier achieved high precision and recall for Neoplasms Diseases (Class 1) and Cardiovascular Diseases (Class 4), and balanced performance for Digestive System Diseases (Class 2) and Nervous System Diseases (Class 3). The overall results highlight logistic regression as the best-performing model among the four classical approaches evaluated in this study, demonstrating strong discriminative ability and consistent generalization across repeated data splits.

Figure 3 presents the ROC curves for each disease category using the one-vs.-rest strategy for Run #2.

These AUC scores indicate excellent separability across all disease categories, with the highest discrimination achieved for Cardiovascular Diseases (Class 4). The slightly lower AUC for Nervous System Diseases (Class 3) is consistent with its lower recall, reflecting overlapping vocabulary with other clinical descriptions.

Overall, the Logistic Regression model demonstrated robust and consistent performance across all categories. Its high accuracy and balanced precision-recall scores confirm its effectiveness for multiclass text classification of medical notes. The model's interpretability and well-calibrated probability estimates further highlight its suitability for clinical NLP tasks, establishing it as the best-performing approach among the four models evaluated.

https://doi.org/10.3390/computers15010007

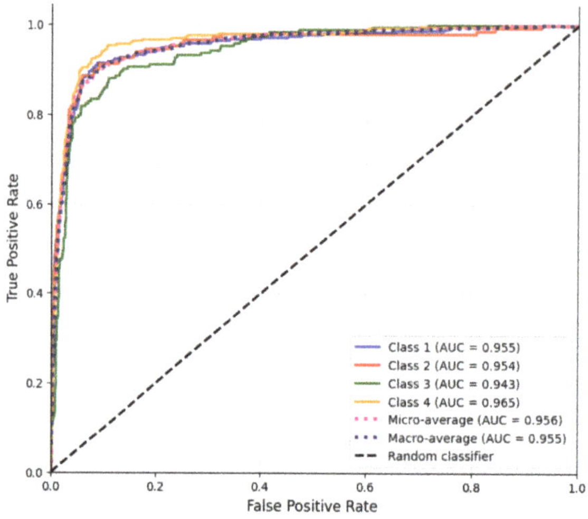

Figure 3. Multiclass ROC curves (One-vs.-Rest) for Logistic Regression (Run #2).

5.4. Support Vector Machine Classification Model Evaluation

The Support Vector Machine (SVM) classifier was trained and evaluated using the repeated experimental protocol described in Section 4.6, involving five independent stratified 90–10 train–test splits. For each run, hyperparameter tuning was performed using GridSearchCV with 5-fold cross-validation on the training subset. As part of hyperparameter tuning, four SVM kernels, i.e., linear, polynomial, RBF, and sigmoid, were systematically evaluated. Across all five runs, the tuning procedure consistently selected the same optimal configuration: `C = 1`, `class_weight = None`, and `kernel = 'linear'`. The linear kernel consistently produced the highest cross-validation performance, while nonlinear kernels did not offer improvements. This outcome aligns with theoretical expectations, as the TF–IDF representation yields a high-dimensional sparse feature space that is particularly well suited to linear decision boundaries [37]. This stability suggests that the linear SVM converges reliably to a robust parameter setting across different partitions of the data. Table 11 summarizes the accuracy, macro F1-score, and weighted F1-score across the five runs.

Table 11. Performance of Support Vector Machine across 5 runs of stratified 90–10 splits.

Run #	Accuracy	F1_Macro	F1_Weighted
1	0.8288	0.8157	0.8276
2	0.8278	0.8097	0.8263
3	0.8216	0.8061	0.8209
4	0.8091	0.7968	0.8082
5	0.8122	0.7983	0.8121
Mean	0.8199	0.8053	0.8190

The run with the accuracy closest to the overall mean is Run #3, so Run #3 was selected as the representative run for detailed analysis. Table 12 presents the confusion matrix of Run #3, which summarizes the model's predictions across the four disease categories on the test set.

As shown in the table, the SVM accurately classified Neoplasms (Class 1) and Cardiovascular Diseases (Class 4), with high true positive counts. Some confusion persisted

 https://doi.org/10.3390/computers15010007

for Digestive System Diseases (Class 2) and Nervous System Diseases (Class 3), reflecting shared terminology and overlapping clinical themes in the textual data.

Table 12. Confusion matrix for Support Vector Machine (Run #3).

	Pred 1	Pred 2	Pred 3	Pred 4
True 1 Neoplasms	277	16	17	7
True 2 Digestive	28	112	5	4
True 3 Nervous System	24	7	139	23
True 4 Cardiovascular	10	9	22	264

The performance metrics in Table 13 reveal balanced precision, recall, and F1-scores across all categories for Run #3.

Table 13. Classification report for Support Vector Machine (Run #3).

Class	Precision	Recall	F1-Score	Support
1 Neoplasms	0.8171	0.8738	0.8445	317
2 Digestive	0.7778	0.7517	0.7645	149
3 Nervous System	0.7596	0.7202	0.7394	193
4 Cardiovascular	0.8859	0.8656	0.8756	305
Accuracy			0.8216	964
Macro avg	0.8101	0.8028	0.8060	964
Weighted avg	0.8213	0.8216	0.8209	964

These results indicate that the linear SVM classifier performs consistently well across all disease categories, with particularly high precision and recall for Neoplasms Diseases (Class 1) and Cardiovascular Diseases (Class 4). Performance for Digestive System Diseases (Class 2) and Nervous System Diseases (Class 3) was slightly lower but still competitive, reflecting the greater semantic complexity of these categories.

Figure 4 presents the ROC curves for each disease category using the one-vs.-rest strategy for Run #3.

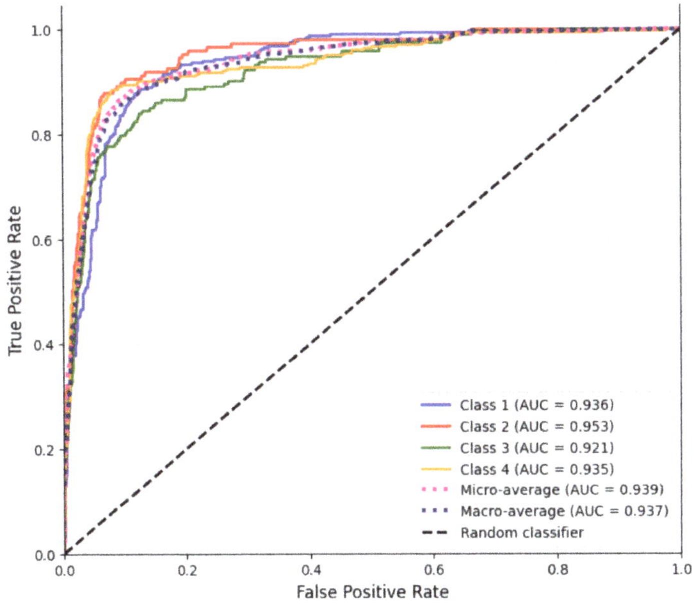

Figure 4. Multiclass ROC curves (One-vs.-Rest) for Support Vector Machine Classifier (Run #3).

https://doi.org/10.3390/computers15010007

These high AUC values confirm that the SVM possesses strong discriminative ability across all four categories, even in cases where class boundaries are less distinct due to overlapping vocabulary.

Overall, the Support Vector Machine classifier exhibited the most stable performance across all evaluation metrics. Its inherent ability to effectively handle high-dimensional, sparse textual features rendered it particularly well-suited to this dataset. These results confirm that SVM strikes a balance between predictive accuracy and generalization, establishing it as a highly competitive model for classifying textual medical notes.

5.5. Model Comparison and Discussion

5.5.1. Overall Model Comparison

The comparative performance of the four machine learning models—Random Forest (RF), Multinomial Naive Bayes (MNB), Logistic Regression (LR), and Support Vector Machine (SVM)—was assessed using the repeated experimental protocol described in Section 4.6. Mean accuracy, macro F1-score, and weighted F1-score were computed across five independent stratified 90–10 splits to provide statistically reliable estimates of model behavior. Table 14 summarizes the average performance metrics for all models.

Table 14. Average performance of four machine learning models across 5 runs of stratified 90–10 splits.

Model	Accuracy	F1_Macro	F1_Weighted
Random Forest (RF)	0.8002	0.7754	0.7939
Multinomial Naive Bayes (MNB)	0.8075	0.7932	0.8075
Logistic Regression (LR)	0.8469	0.8339	0.8462
Support Vector Machine (SVM)	0.8199	0.8053	0.8190

Logistic Regression achieved the highest overall performance, with an average accuracy of 0.8469 and the highest macro and weighted F1-scores. This indicates that the elastic net regularized multinomial logistic model was particularly effective at capturing discriminative linear relationships among the TF–IDF features. The consistent superiority of Logistic Regression across multiple data splits highlights its robustness and suitability for multiclass medical text classification.

The Support Vector Machine achieved the second highest overall performance (accuracy = 0.8199), demonstrating strong discriminative ability and stable generalization under repeated splits. The linear kernel performed particularly well given the high-dimensional and sparse nature of the text representation.

Multinomial Naive Bayes performed well (accuracy = 0.8075), exceeding the Random Forest model and achieving weighted F1 comparable to its accuracy. This model's strength reflects the compatibility between word-frequency features and Naive Bayes' probabilistic assumptions, making it an efficient and competitive baseline for textual classification tasks.

Random Forest achieved slightly lower performance (accuracy = 0.8002) relative to the other models. Although it performed well for Neoplasms and Cardiovascular Diseases, it showed greater confusion between Digestive and Nervous System Diseases. This may be attributed to the difficulty of modeling subtle lexical distinctions with tree-based splits, especially in high-dimensional sparse feature spaces.

Across all models, the results consistently showed stronger performance for Neoplasms Diseases (Class 1) and Cardiovascular Diseases (Class 4), where domain-specific terminology provides clearer semantic cues for classification. Misclassifications were more frequent for Digestive System Diseases (Class 2) and Nervous System Diseases (Class 3), reflecting greater lexical overlap between these categories in the medical note corpus.

 https://doi.org/10.3390/computers15010007

5.5.2. Interpretability Analysis

Beyond quantitative performance, traditional machine learning models offer the important advantage of interpretability, which is critical in clinical applications. Random Forest provides feature-importance scores that highlight the terms most useful for distinguishing between disease categories. Logistic Regression and linear SVM yield coefficient weights that indicate the positive or negative influence of specific terms on class predictions, making it possible to identify discriminative vocabulary associated with each condition. Although the full ranked lists are not included for brevity, these interpretability properties demonstrate how classical ML models can provide transparent decision-making insights, supporting clinician trust and facilitating integration into clinical text analysis workflows.

5.5.3. Qualitative Error Analysis

Examination of misclassified samples revealed that much of the confusion between Digestive System Diseases and Nervous System Diseases arises from shared terminology and general clinical descriptors. Many notes contain non-specific symptoms—such as pain, nausea, weakness, study, and treatment—that appear across multiple disease categories, making them difficult to differentiate using surface-level lexical features. In several misclassified cases, the clinical narratives involved multi-system presentations or overlapping symptom clusters, such as gastrointestinal complications secondary to neurological disorders. These findings indicate that the observed misclassification patterns reflect genuine linguistic overlap in the dataset, rather than isolated model failures, and suggest that more advanced contextual representations may help better capture subtle semantic distinctions in future work.

Overall, the repeated experimental runs confirm that Logistic Regression provides the best balance of accuracy, interpretability, and stability, followed by SVM and Naive Bayes. Random Forest remains a useful model for interpreting feature importance but is less competitive for this particular classification task.

6. Conclusions and Future Work

This study presented a comprehensive and statistically sound comparison of four traditional machine learning models—Random Forest, Multinomial Naive Bayes, Logistic Regression, and Support Vector Machine—for multiclass classification of textual medical notes into four disease categories. Using a rigorously designed experimental protocol that incorporated five independent stratified train–test data splits, 5-fold cross-validation for hyperparameter tuning, and aggregated performance reporting across five independent runs, the evaluation provides a statistically reliable assessment of model behavior. Detailed evaluation using accuracy, macro and weighted F1-scores, confusion matrices, and multiclass ROC–AUC values provided a clear picture of each model's strengths and limitations.

Among the evaluated models, Logistic Regression achieved the highest and most consistent performance, with an average accuracy of 0.8469, macro F1-score of 0.8339, and weighted F1-score of 0.8462, demonstrating consistent accuracy and excellent discriminative ability across all four disease categories. The Support Vector Machine ranked second, followed closely by Multinomial Naive Bayes, which exceeded expectations given its simplicity and computational efficiency. Random Forest, while competitive, showed lower average performance, particularly for disease categories with overlapping clinical terminology. Collectively, these findings highlight the effectiveness of traditional ML methods for clinical text classification and demonstrate that interpretable, computationally efficient models can still achieve strong performance in biomedical NLP settings. The interpretability of classical models, including the ability to examine feature-importance rankings and coefficient weights, further enhances their suitability for clinical text applications.

https://doi.org/10.3390/computers15010007

The limitations identified through our error and interpretability analyses point to several concrete directions for future research. Misclassification patterns—particularly between Digestive System Diseases and Nervous System Diseases—highlight the need for models capable of capturing deeper semantic and contextual relationships than TF–IDF features provide. Future work will explore contextualized biomedical language models, such as BioBERT and ClinicalBERT, which are specifically trained on clinical and biomedical text and may better distinguish subtle domain-specific language. In addition, the sparsity of the 27,609-token TF–IDF feature space suggests the potential benefits of dimensionality-reduction or embedding-based methods, including PCA, LSA/LSI, or neural embeddings.

To address the scarcity of labeled clinical text, we also propose leveraging weak supervision frameworks, such as Snorkel-style labeling functions, to automatically generate training labels from heuristic rules or domain knowledge. Furthermore, integrating medical ontologies (e.g., UMLS, MeSH, ICD hierarchies) could enrich textual features with structured semantic information and improve differentiation among clinically related disease categories.

Future studies should also evaluate probability calibration and uncertainty estimation, which are essential for clinical deployment where reliable decision thresholds are needed. Finally, more advanced interpretability tools, such as SHAP or LIME, may provide deeper insights into model predictions and enhance clinician trust in automated classification systems.

Overall, the study enhances methodological rigor within clinical NLP and provides a solid benchmark that supports and motivates future innovations in medical text classification.

Author Contributions: Conceptualization, Y.Z.; methodology, Y.Z.; investigation, H.T.N.L.; data curation, H.T.N.L.; experiments, H.T.N.L., N.L. and K.P.; writing—original draft preparation, Y.Z.; writing—review and editing, Y.Z.; supervision, Y.Z. All authors have read and agreed to the published version of the manuscript.

Funding: The research did not receive external funding.

Data Availability Statement: The original dataset is publicly available on Kaggle. The pre-processed dataset is available upon request from the authors.

Acknowledgments: The authors gratefully acknowledge support from the California State University, San Bernardino (CSUSB) College of Natural Sciences (CNS) Proactive Approaches for Training Hispanics in STEM (PATHS) program, which provided funding for three undergraduate researchers during summer 2025. This material is based upon work supported by the National Science Foundation under Grant No. 2322436.

Conflicts of Interest: The authors declare no conflicts of interest.

References

1. Badawy, M.; Ramadan, N.; Hefny, H.A. Big data analytics in healthcare: Data sources, tools, challenges, and opportunities. *J. Electr. Syst. Inf. Technol.* **2024**, *11*, 63. [CrossRef]
2. Tang, A.S.; Woldemariam, S.R.; Miramontes, S.; Norgeot, B.; Oskotsky, T.T.; Sirota, M. Harnessing EHR data for health research. *Nat. Med.* **2024**, *30*, 1847–1855. [CrossRef]
3. Tayefi, M.; Ngo, P.; Chomutare, T.; Dalianis, H.; Salvi, E.; Budrionis, A.; Godtliebsen, F. Challenges and opportunities beyond structured data in analysis of electronic health records. *Wiley Interdiscip. Rev. Comput. Stat.* **2021**, *13*, e1549. [CrossRef]
4. Spasic, I.; Nenadic, G. Clinical text data in machine learning: Systematic review. *JMIR Med. Inform.* **2020**, *8*, e17984. [CrossRef]
5. Li, Q.; Peng, H.; Li, J.; Xia, C.; Yang, R.; Sun, L.; Yu, P.S.; He, L. A survey on text classification: From traditional to deep learning. *ACM Trans. Intell. Syst. Technol. (TIST)* **2022**, *13*, 1–41. [CrossRef]
6. Kowsari, K.; Jafari Meimandi, K.; Heidarysafa, M.; Mendu, S.; Barnes, L.; Brown, D. Text classification algorithms: A survey. *Information* **2019**, *10*, 150. [CrossRef]
7. Khalate, P.; Gite, S.; Pradhan, B.; Lee, C.W. Advancements and gaps in natural language processing and machine learning applications in healthcare: A comprehensive review of electronic medical records and medical imaging. *Front. Phys.* **2024**, *12*, 1445204. [CrossRef]

https://doi.org/10.3390/computers15010007

8. Mustafa, A.; Rahimi Azghadi, M. Automated machine learning for healthcare and clinical notes analysis. *Computers* **2021**, *10*, 24. [CrossRef]
9. Kino, S.; Hsu, Y.T.; Shiba, K.; Chien, Y.S.; Mita, C.; Kawachi, I.; Daoud, A. A scoping review on the use of machine learning in research on social determinants of health: Trends and research prospects. *SSM Popul. Health* **2021**, *15*, 100836. [CrossRef]
10. Kadhim, A.I. Survey on supervised machine learning techniques for automatic text classification. *Artif. Intell. Rev.* **2019**, *52*, 273–292. [CrossRef]
11. Weng, W.H.; Wagholikar, K.B.; McCray, A.T.; Szolovits, P.; Chueh, H.C. Medical subdomain classification of clinical notes using a machine learning-based natural language processing approach. *BMC Med. Inform. Decis. Mak.* **2017**, *17*, 155. [CrossRef]
12. López-Úbeda, P.; Diaz-Galiano, M.C.; Martin-Noguerol, T.; Luna, A.; Urena-Lopez, L.A.; Martin-Valdivia, M.T. Automatic medical protocol classification using machine learning approaches. *Comput. Methods Programs Biomed.* **2021**, *200*, 105939. [CrossRef] [PubMed]
13. Tiwari, P.; Upadhyay, D.; Pant, B.; Mohd, N. Multiclass classification in machine learning algorithms for disease prediction. In Proceedings of the International Conference on Advanced Informatics for Computing Research, Gurugram, India, 18–19 December 2021 ; pp. 102–111.
14. Sung, S.F.; Lin, C.Y.; Hu, Y.H. EMR-based phenotyping of ischemic stroke using supervised machine learning and text mining techniques. *IEEE J. Biomed. Health Inform.* **2020**, *24*, 2922–2931. [CrossRef]
15. Rabby, G.; Berka, P. Multi-class classification of COVID-19 documents using machine learning algorithms. *J. Intell. Inf. Syst.* **2023**, *60*, 571–591. [CrossRef]
16. Gupta, S.; Belouali, A.; Shah, N.J.; Atkins, M.B.; Madhavan, S. Automated identification of patients with immune-related adverse events from clinical notes using word embedding and machine learning. *JCO Clin. Cancer Inform.* **2021**, *5*, 541–549. [CrossRef]
17. Gao, C.; Goswami, M.; Chen, J.; Dubrawski, A. Classifying unstructured clinical notes via automatic weak supervision. In Proceedings of the Machine Learning for Healthcare Conference, PMLR, Durham, NC, USA, 5–6 August 2022; pp. 673–690.
18. Lenivtceva, I.; Slasten, E.; Kashina, M.; Kopanitsa, G. Applicability of machine learning methods to multi-label medical text classification. In Proceedings of the International Conference on Computational Science, Amsterdam, The Netherlands, 3–5 June 2020; pp. 509–522.
19. da Silva, D.P.; Fröhlich, W.d.R.; Schwertner, M.A.; Rigo, S.J. Clinical Oncology Textual Notes Analysis Using Machine Learning and Deep Learning. In Proceedings of the Brazilian Conference on Intelligent Systems, Belo Horizonte, Brazil, 25–29 September 2023 ; pp. 140–153.
20. Goodrum, H.; Roberts, K.; Bernstam, E.V. Automatic classification of scanned electronic health record documents. *Int. J. Med. Inform.* **2020**, *144*, 104302. [CrossRef]
21. Lu, H.; Ehwerhemuepha, L.; Rakovski, C. A comparative study on deep learning models for text classification of unstructured medical notes with various levels of class imbalance. *BMC Med. Res. Methodol.* **2022**, *22*, 181. [CrossRef] [PubMed]
22. Kaggle. Medical Text. 2019. Available online: https://www.kaggle.com/datasets/chaitanyakck/medical-text/data (accessed on 8 June 2025) .
23. Breiman, L. Random forests. *Mach. Learn.* **2001**, *45*, 5–32. [CrossRef]
24. Rigatti, S.J. Random forest. *J. Insur. Med.* **2017**, *47*, 31–39. [CrossRef] [PubMed]
25. Sun, Y.; Li, Y.; Zeng, Q.; Bian, Y. Application research of text classification based on random forest algorithm. In Proceedings of the 2020 3rd International Conference on Advanced Electronic Materials, Computers and Software Engineering (AEMCSE), Shenzhen, China, 24–26 April 2020 ; pp. 370–374.
26. Murphy, K.P. *Naive Bayes Classifiers*; University of British Columbia: Vancouver, BC, Canada , 2006; Volume 18, pp. 1–8.
27. Webb, G.I.; Keogh, E.; Miikkulainen, R. Naïve Bayes. *Encycl. Mach. Learn.* **2010**, *15*, 713–714.
28. Singh, G.; Kumar, B.; Gaur, L.; Tyagi, A. Comparison between multinomial and Bernoulli naïve Bayes for text classification. In Proceedings of the 2019 International Conference on Automation, Computational and Technology Management (ICACTM), London, UK, 24–26 April 2019 ; pp. 593–596.
29. Pampel, F.C. *Logistic Regression: A Primer*; Number 132; Sage Publications: Thousand Oaks, CA, USA, 2020.
30. Shah, K.; Patel, H.; Sanghvi, D.; Shah, M. A comparative analysis of logistic regression, random forest and KNN models for the text classification. *Augment. Hum. Res.* **2020**, *5*, 12. [CrossRef]
31. Sarkar, A.; Chatterjee, S.; Das, W.; Datta, D. Text classification using support vector machine. *Int. J. Eng. Sci. Invent.* **2015**, *4*, 33–37.
32. Dadgar, S.M.H.; Araghi, M.S.; Farahani, M.M. A novel text mining approach based on TF-IDF and Support Vector Machine for news classification. In Proceedings of the 2016 IEEE International Conference on Engineering and Technology (ICETECH), Coimbatore, India, 17–18 March 2016 ; pp. 112–116.
33. Mammone, A.; Turchi, M.; Cristianini, N. Support vector machines. *Wiley Interdiscip. Rev. Comput. Stat.* **2009**, *1*, 283–289. [CrossRef]
34. Heydarian, M.; Doyle, T.E.; Samavi, R. MLCM: Multi-label confusion matrix. *IEEE Access* **2022**, *10*, 19083–19095. [CrossRef]

 https://doi.org/10.3390/computers15010007

35. Carrington, A.M.; Manuel, D.G.; Fieguth, P.W.; Ramsay, T.; Osmani, V.; Wernly, B.; Bennett, C.; Hawken, S.; Magwood, O.; Sheikh, Y.; et al. Deep ROC analysis and AUC as balanced average accuracy, for improved classifier selection, audit and explanation *IEEE Trans. Pattern Anal. Mach. Intell.* **2022**, *45*, 329–341. [CrossRef]
36. Scikit-Learn Developers. Scikit-Learn: Machine Learning in Python. 2025. Available online: https://scikit-learn.org (accessed on 10 June 2025).
37. Joachims, T. Text categorization with support vector machines: Learning with many relevant features. In Proceedings of the European Conference on Machine Learning, Chemnitz, Germany, 21–23 April 1998 ; pp. 137–142.

https://doi.org/10.3390/computers15010007

computers

MDPI

rticle

Comparative Analysis of Neural Network Models for Predicting Peach Maturity on Tabular Data

Dejan Ljubobratović [1,*], Marko Vuković [2], Marija Brkić Bakarić [1,*], Tomislav Jemrić [2] and Maja Matetić [1]

[1] Faculty of Informatics and Digital Technologies, University of Rijeka, Radmile Matejčić 2, 51000 Rijeka, Croatia; majam@uniri.hr

[2] Department of Pomology, Division of Horticulture and Landscape Architecture, University of Zagreb Faculty of Agriculture, Svetošimunska Cesta 25, 10000 Zagreb, Croatia; mvukovic@agr.hr (M.V.); tjemric@agr.hr (T.J.)

* Correspondence: dejan.ljubobratovic@uniri.hr (D.L.); mbrkic@uniri.hr (M.B.B.)

Featured Application: This study presents a neural network-based approach for predicting peach maturity using tabular sensor data. The proposed model can be integrated into real-time fruit sorting pipelines, enhancing classification accuracy and decision support in the agri-food sector, with additional applicability in autonomous harvesting platforms such as drone-operated picking systems.

Abstract: Peach maturity at harvest is a critical factor influencing fruit quality and postharvest life. Traditional destructive methods for maturity assessment, although effective, compromise fruit integrity and are unsuitable for practical implementation in modern production. This study presents a machine learning approach for non-destructive peach maturity prediction using tabular data collected from 701 'Redhaven' peaches. Three neural network models suitable for small tabular datasets (TabNet, SAINT, and NODE) were applied and evaluated using classification metrics, including accuracy, F1-score, and AUC. The models demonstrated consistently strong performance across several feature configurations, with TabNet achieving the highest accuracy when all non-destructive measurements were available, while TabNet provided the most robust and practical performance on the comprehensive non-destructive subset and in optimized minimal-feature settings. These findings indicate that non-destructive sensing methods, particularly when combined with modern neural architectures, can reliably predict maturity and offer potential for real-time, automated fruit selection after harvest. The integration of such models into autonomous harvesting systems, for instance, through drone-based platforms equipped with appropriate sensors, could significantly improve efficiency and fruit quality management in horticultural peach production.

Keywords: peach maturity; non-destructive sensing; dielectric properties; tabular neural networks; TabNet; SAINT; NODE; feature selection; precision horticulture; autonomous harvesting

1. Introduction

Monitoring fruit maturity is crucial for determining the optimal harvest time to achieve the best balance between eating quality (flavour, sweetness) and the durability required for shipping and handling. Harvesting too early results in tasteless, underripe fruit, while harvesting too late leads to overripe, soft fruit that spoils quickly and has a very short post-harvest life [1]. The firmness of the peach fruit is closely related to harvest maturity and is the main factor that affects the post-harvest storage characteristics of the fruit. Firmness has been identified as the most reliable parameter for determining maturity compared to other quality indicators [2]. Peach firmness is typically measured using a penetrometer, which applies a standardized force to penetrate the fruit flesh. In this research, peach firmness is measured using a penetrometer equipped with an 8 mm wide cylindrical probe, where after skin removal at four equatorial sides maximum penetration force is being recorded [3,4]. This presents a significant limitation, as this maturity assessment method is destructive to the fruit. Alongside mechanical tests, dielectric properties have also been explored for maturity evaluation. For instance, while dielectric property measurements have proven to be reliable predictors in models for evaluating peach maturity, traditional dielectric measurement methods also require inserting electrodes into the fruit. This makes the technique equally destructive and impractical for high-throughput sorting [5]. Therefore, there is a need for an accurate measure of fruit maturity based on parameters that can be measured non-destructively.

Based on a literature review, the primary non-destructive methods for assessing fruit maturity can be categorized into several groups: Near-Infrared Spectroscopy (NIRS), Computer Vision, and other techniques such as acoustic methods and electronic nose. The complex data obtained from these techniques are subsequently processed by advanced machine learning methods, which translate the information into specific maturity indicators such as fruit firmness and soluble solid content, both of which are commonly associated with peach maturity.

As early as 2009, it was demonstrated that portable Vis-NIR spectroscopy can accurately and non-destructively predict apricot fruit quality attributes such as firmness and soluble solids content. The results showed a strong correlation between spectral data and internal quality, confirming the method's potential for real-time, in-field maturity assessment [6]. Today, this technology effectively combines VIS/NIR spectroscopy with machine learning models (such as decision trees and gradient boosting) for non-destructive assessment of grape ripeness. The authors achieve high accuracy in predicting key ripeness indicators, including anthocyanin content, soluble solids content, and titratable acidity, confirming the method's efficiency for in-field analysis [7].

In parallel with spectroscopic approaches, computer vision and deep learning techniques have been used to develop one-stage instance segmentation models utilizing architectures such as Mask R-CNN and YOLO to detect and classify the maturity stages of peaches. This method demonstrates high classification accuracy and offers a robust solution for the automated harvesting and sorting of peaches under real-world orchard conditions [8].

The use of machine learning, and especially neural networks, in fruit maturity prediction is becoming increasingly common due to their ability to perform accurate and automated classification based on visual or sensor data.

The application of deep learning is not limited to peaches. For instance, a study on bananas [9], which are also highly perishable, focuses on the development of deep learning models for maturity classification using convolutional neural networks (CNN) and the AlexNet architecture applied to image data. The emphasis is on computer vision, data augmentation, and implementation in the Keras/TensorFlow framework for robust and accurate classification. The proposed CNN model achieved up to 99.36% validation accuracy, outperforming AlexNet in most evaluated scenarios.

However, these are methods that rely on neural network models for fruit maturity prediction based almost exclusively on images. Few models focus on non-destructive prediction using only tabular data, even though sensors providing such features are significantly cheaper, and model training is considerably faster.

A study by Ropelewska [10] explores the use of non-destructive sensor measurements combined with machine learning models, including Random Forest, Naive Bayes, k-NN, and Decision Tree, for classifying peaches at different maturity stages. Based on tabular data such as firmness, skin color (L*, a*, b*), size, and weight collected via low-cost sensors, the Random Forest model achieved classification accuracy exceeding 90%. These findings highlight that low-cost, non-destructive sensing technologies paired with machine learning provide an efficient and reliable approach for maturity prediction in peaches.

Another study [11] aligns well with other machine learning approaches for fruit maturity prediction, as it relies exclusively on structured tabular data rather than image-based inputs. By evaluating models such as Random Forest, Gradient Boosting, XGBoost, and Decision Trees on physicochemical measurements of oil palm fruit, it confirms that high predictive performance can be achieved without visual features. In particular, the XGBoost model demonstrated superior accuracy, reinforcing the value of ensemble methods in agricultural classification tasks. While these classical models have shown strong performance, the question remains whether newer, specialized neural network architectures for tabular data can offer superior performance or different advantages such as interpretability.

In a recent study [12], the performance of eight machine learning models was evaluated for predicting peach maturity using exclusively non-destructive tabular features, including fruit dimensions and skin color parameters. Following feature selection with the LASSO method, the artificial neural network (ANN) model demonstrated the highest classification accuracy among the tested approaches.

As neural network models demonstrated the highest accuracy in the study [12], a review of the literature identified three neural architectures that have shown strong performance on tabular data: TabNet, NODE, and SAINT [13–15].

TabNet employs a sequential attention mechanism to select relevant features at each decision step, enabling both interpretability and efficient representation learning [16]. NODE integrates differentiable decision trees into deep networks, leveraging the strengths of ensemble methods while retaining end-to-end trainability [17]. SAINT introduces a transformer-based architecture with both feature-level and intersample attention, capturing complex dependencies within and across data instances. These models represent a new generation of deep learning methods specifically optimized for structured/tabular datasets, often matching or surpassing traditional gradient boosting techniques in predictive performance [18].

The aim of this study is to evaluate the applicability and performance of recent neural network architectures specifically optimized for tabular data in the context of non-destructive peach maturity prediction. By comparing TabNet, SAINT, and NODE on a real-world dataset of sensor-based measurements, this research seeks to identify models that combine high classification accuracy with efficient training and potential for integration into autonomous harvesting systems. Ultimately, the study contributes to the development of reliable, low-cost, and scalable machine learning solutions for decision support in precision horticulture.

Unlike previous studies that primarily relied on classical machine learning algorithms or deep learning models applied to image data, this research focuses on neural network architectures specifically designed for tabular inputs. While earlier work demonstrated the feasibility of using low-cost sensor data with models such as Random Forest or ANN, this study systematically compares advanced tabular-specific neural networks (TabNet, SAINT, and NODE), highlighting their potential to achieve high accuracy while preserving interpretability (TabNet) and efficiency in non-destructive fruit maturity classification.

In this study, the Index of Absorbance Difference (`iad`) emerged as a particularly strong predictor of peach maturity, often dominating model performance. However, although iad sensors can be integrated into industrial and drone-based systems, they are relatively expensive. Since iad also represents a dominant predictor of maturity, additional experiments were conducted to evaluate model performance when this strong feature was excluded and when models were trained on compact subsets of the most informative non-destructive variables. The results demonstrated that even in the absence of iad, and when relying on reduced feature sets, the evaluated neural network models achieved satisfactory classification accuracy, suggesting that reliable maturity prediction can be accomplished using features derived from low-cost sensors performing non-destructive measurements.

2. Materials and Methods

All data processing, analysis, and model development were performed using the Python programming language (v3.9). Key libraries included Pandas (v2.3.1) for data manipulation, Scikit-learn (1.7.1) for machine learning, and Matplotlib (v3.10.3) for data visualization, together with PyTorch (v2.7.1)-based libraries for neural network modelling (including pytorch_tabnet, node-tabular, and an open-source implementation of SAINT).

2.1. Dataset Description

The generation of dataset containing this type of measurement is a resource-intensive process, demanding significant investment in both time and labor. Consequently, the dataset utilized in many of the aforementioned studies are of a relatively limited scale, particularly within the context of neural network applications. For instance, the dataset presented in [12] comprises 180 samples, whereas the one in [2] includes merely 120 measurements. The variables used in the former study are marked with a (+) symbol in Table 1, as they correspond closely to those measured in the present work and are therefore directly comparable.

The dataset employed in this research comprises 701 samples of peach fruit (*Prunus persica*), each characterized by 44 variables utilized for classifying maturity stages. All samples were collected from a single cultivar ('Redhaven') grown at one geographical location, which may limit the generalizability of the models to other cultivars or growing conditions. Therefore, model performance should be independently validated before application to different peach varieties or environments. The data are maintained in a CSV file format. In USA lack of taste and failure to ripen are the main reasons that limit stone fruit consumption [19]. Peaches, as being susceptible to bruising due to fleshy mesocarp, are usually harvested earlier to last longer and withstand manipulation. However, although they are climacteric fruit, there is a connection between on-tree physiological maturity and the development of key fruit quality traits [20]. Hence, too early harvest can lead to consumer dissatisfaction and reduced further consumption. In order to meet the quality standards, peach fruit at harvest should not exceed firmness higher than $4.59\ \mathrm{kg} \cdot \mathrm{cm}^{-2}$ (Ramina et al. [21], according to Neri et al. [22]). Hence this firmness threshold was used in this study primarily to address consumers growing dissatisfaction with peach fruit eating quality. Following this main maturity segmentation presented in this paper further ones should be also carried in packinghouses (overripe, ready to eat, ready to buy and storable peaches).

The remaining 43 variables function as predictors and are composed of a diverse array of physical, colorimetric, biochemical, and electrical measurements. These can be broadly categorized into the following groups:

- Physical and Morphometric Attributes : vol: Peach volume, mass: Peach mass, firm: Fruit firmness
- Biochemical and Sensory Features: tst: Soluble solids content, ta: Titratable acidity

- Colorimetric Descriptors: udb: share of additional color, md_X, moo_X, mop_X: Maximum values of additional color, ground, and petiole ground color
- Impedance-Based Electrical Properties: zs_nd, th_nd: Zs and Ts components (non-destructive), zs_d, th_d: Zs and Ts components (destructive), zs_nd_X, th_nd_X: non-destructively obtained Ts and Zs adjusted for deviation from mean volume
- Ripening Index: iad: index of absorbance difference

Table 1. Description of measured variables used in the dataset. The (+) symbol denotes variables also used in the study by Ljubobratović et al. [12].

Variable	Description
udb	share of additional colour
vol	Peach volume (+)
mass	Peach mass (+)
iad	index of absorbance difference between 670 nm and 720 nm
nd_zs	Dielectric property (Z component) obtained by non-destructive method
nd_th	Dielectric property (phase angle) obtained by non-destructive method
nd_zs_X	Dielectric property Z component (non-destructive) adjusted for deviation from mean volume
nd_th_X	Dielectric property phase angle (non-destructive) adjusted for deviation from mean volume
d_zs	Dielectric property (Z component) obtained by destructive method
d_th	Dielectric property (phase angle) obtained by destructive method
tst	Total Soluble Solids (+)
ta	Titratable acidity (+)
tst_ta	Ratio between soluble solids concentration and titratable acidity (+)
md_l	L* additional color parameter measured on the rest of the fruit surface (+)
md_a	a* additional color parameter measured on the rest of the fruit surface (+)
md_b	b* additional color parameter measured on the rest of the fruit surface (+)
md_c	C* additional color parameter measured on the rest of the fruit surface (+)
md_h	h° additional color parameter measured on the rest of the fruit surface (+)
md_a_b	a*/b* additional color index measured on the rest of the fruit surface (+)
md_ccl	CCL additional color index measured on the rest of the fruit surface (+)
md_col	COL additional color index measured on the rest of the fruit surface (+)
md_cirg1	CIRG1 additional color index measured on the rest of the fruit surface (+)
md_cirg2	CIRG2 additional color index measured on the rest of the fruit surface (+)
moo_l	L* ground color parameter measured on the rest of the fruit surface (+)
moo_a	a* ground color parameter measured on the rest of the fruit surface (+)
moo_b	b* ground color parameter measured on the rest of the fruit surface (+)
moo_c	C* ground color parameter measured on the rest of the fruit surface (+)
moo_h	h° ground color parameter measured on the rest of the fruit surface (+)
moo_a_b	a*/b* ground color index measured on the rest of the fruit surface (+)
moo_ccl	CCL ground color index measured on the rest of the fruit surface (+)
moo_col	COL ground color index measured on the rest of the fruit surface (+)
moo_cirg1	CIRG1 ground color index measured on the rest of the fruit surface (+)
moo_cirg2	CIRG2 ground color index measured on the rest of the fruit surface (+)
mop_l	L* ground color parameter measured near petiole insertion
mop_a	a* ground color parameter measured near petiole insertion
mop_b	b* ground color parameter measured near petiole insertion
mop_c	C* ground color parameter measured near petiole insertion
mop_h	h° ground color parameter measured near petiole insertion
mop_a_b	a*/b* ground color index measured near petiole insertion
mop_ccl	CCL ground color index measured near petiole insertion
mop_col	COL ground color index measured near petiole insertion
mop_cirg1	CIRG1 ground color index measured near petiole insertion
mop_cirg2	CIRG2 ground color index measured near petiole insertion
ripe	Categorical target variable, representing peach maturity level grouped into two classes (+)

With a clearly defined categorical target and a heterogeneous mix of continuous, ordinal, and categorical features, this dataset is highly suitable for the development and evaluation of supervised machine learning models for fruit quality assessment and maturity classification.

A total of 701 fruits at various ripening stages were analyzed during this period, resulting in a dataset comprising 701 samples with 43 predictor variables. The dataset does not include the complete photographic set from four different angles nor the multispectral imaging results, which were conducted only on one-third of the fruits. Nevertheless, it provides a highly comprehensive representation of the morphological and physicochemical characteristics of peaches. The list of all variables, including their dataset names and descriptions, is provided in Table 1. The (+) symbol in the description indicates variables that were also used in the study by Ljubobratović et al. [12], representing comparable measurement features. Variables `th_nd_X` and `zs_nd_X` were adjusted based on deviation from the average fruit volume. All above mentioned variables, with exception of destructive and non-destructive dielectric properties, were measured as reported in our previous study [23]. While dielectric properties were conducted on all fruits in two orthogonal orientations: first along the narrower longitudinal axis of the peach, and subsequently along the wider transverse axis. All measurements were carried out using an ET430 handheld LCR meter with a drive voltage of 600 mV and a frequency of 10 kHz, parameters previously identified as optimal for characterization of peach physicochemical properties [24]. Additionally, the `udb` assessment was performed using a slightly modified protocol, which included an additional category (0) denoting peaches exhibiting no additional coloration.

2.2. Data Preprocessing

Prior to model training, the dataset underwent a structured preprocessing pipeline. The raw data were first imported from a semicolon-delimited CSV file with comma used as the decimal separator. A non-informative identifier column (`br`) was removed. The target variable (`ripe`) was isolated, while the remaining 43 variables were used as predictors. Categorical features were encoded using the `OrdinalEncoder`, and all numerical features were standardized to zero mean and unit variance using the `StandardScaler`. The fitted encoder and scaler were retained for future use on test data to ensure consistency in data transformation.

To ensure robust model development and to avoid any form of information leakage, all model selection procedures were performed exclusively within the training portion of the data. After the initial stratified train-test split, the 75% training subset (525 samples) was further partitioned using stratified 5-fold cross-validation. In each fold, approximately 80% of the training set (420 samples) was used for model training, while the remaining 20% (105 samples) served as a validation fold for monitoring training behaviour, tuning hyperparameters, and applying early stopping.

Importantly, no sample from the independent 25% test set was ever used during cross-validation or any phase of model construction. This ensures that all reported test-set results reflect true model generalization on entirely unseen data.

Train-Test Partitioning

Before any model development, the complete dataset of 701 Redhaven peach samples was partitioned into a stratified training-test split. A total of 75% of the data (525 samples) was allocated to the training set, while the remaining 25% (176 samples) formed an independent held-out test set. The split was stratified with respect to the binary maturity label to preserve the original class distribution in both subsets. The test set was not used at any stage of model development, including feature preprocessing, hyperparameter tuning, early stopping, or model selection. All preprocessing steps (imputation, encoding, and standardization) were fitted exclusively on the training set and subsequently applied to the test set using the same fitted parameters, ensuring a fully isolated and unbiased evaluation on unseen data.

2.3. Models Description

Three neural network models specifically designed for tabular data were trained on the preprocessed dataset: TabNet, NODE, and SAINT. Each model embodies a distinct architectural approach to learning from structured data. TabNet employs sequential attention for feature selection and interpretability [13], NODE utilizes ensembles of differentiable oblivious decision trees [14], while SAINT incorporates both self-attention across features and intersample attention across rows [15].

All models were trained exclusively on the training portion of the dataset (75% of the full dataset; 525 samples). Model selection, hyperparameter tuning, and early stopping were performed using stratified 5-fold cross-validation applied only within the training subset. The independent 25% test set (176 samples) was withheld throughout the entire development process and used solely for final evaluation. Detailed architectural and implementation settings for each model are described below.

TabNet is a deep learning architecture specifically designed for tabular data. It utilizes a sequential attention mechanism that enables the model to focus on the most relevant features at each decision step. This structure not only enhances predictive performance but also provides interpretability through feature importance masks [13]. In our implementation, the `TabNetClassifier` from the `pytorch_tabnet` library was used. The model was trained for 200 epochs with the following hyperparameters: 3 decision steps, 8-dimensional feature transformer, 8-dimensional attention transformer, and a batch size of 256. Early stopping was applied with a patience of 20 epochs.

NODE (Neural Oblivious Decision Ensembles) replaces traditional decision tree ensembles with differentiable oblivious decision trees, where each decision node applies the same split across all samples. This architecture enables end-to-end gradient-based optimization while preserving tree-like inductive biases [14]. The model was implemented using the `node` package by Popov et al. [17] and trained using the inner 5-fold cross-validation procedure applied only to the training subset. No information from the test set was used during training, validation, hyperparameter selection, or early stopping. The architecture consisted of an Oblivious Decision S-Tree (ODST) layer with 160 trees, each having a depth of 7, a batch size of 256, and a maximum of 200 training epochs with early stopping (patience = 25). Optimization was carried out using the Adam optimizer with a learning rate of 0.001.

SAINT (Self-Attention and Intersample Attention Transformer) extends the transformer architecture to tabular data by combining both self-attention across features and intersample attention across rows. This dual-attention mechanism allows the model to capture complex intra- and inter-feature dependencies [15]. We used an adapted implementation based on the open-source SAINT repository. The model was trained for up to 500 epochs with a batch size of 128, a transformer dimension of 64, 6 attention layers, and 8 attention heads, with a dropout rate of 0.05. Categorical features were embedded, and numerical features were normalized. The training pipeline included label smoothing, stochastic depth, and CutMix augmentation (lambda = 0.1). Optimization was performed using the AdamW optimizer (learning rate = 0.0001, weight decay = 0.01), with early stopping applied using a patience of 25 epochs.

2.4. Evaluation Setup and Metrics

To evaluate the predictive performance of the models, three standard classification metrics were employed: Accuracy, F1-score, and Area Under the Receiver Operating Characteristic Curve (AUC).

Train-validation-test protocol. All models were developed using a strict separation between training, validation, and testing data. The dataset was first split into a training subset (75%; 525 samples) and an independent test subset (25%; 176 samples). Only the training subset was used for model development, including preprocessing, standardization, hyperparameter selection, and early stopping. A stratified 5-fold cross-validation procedure was applied exclusively within the training subset. In each fold, 4/5 of the training data served as the inner training split, while 1/5 was used as the validation split for tuning and early stopping. No information from the test subset was used at any stage of model selection or parameter optimization.

After cross-validation, the final trained models were evaluated once on the independent test subset to obtain the final Accuracy, F1-score, and AUC metrics reported in the Section 3. These test-set metrics represent the true generalization performance of each model, while the cross-validation metrics are used only for model selection and comparative analysis.

Accuracy quantifies the proportion of correctly classified samples among all predictions. While widely used, this metric may be less informative in the presence of class imbalance, as it does not account for the distribution of true positives and false negatives across individual classes [25]. **F1-score** represents the harmonic mean of precision and recall, providing a balanced assessment of both false positives and false negatives. It is especially suitable when the cost of misclassification is asymmetric or when dealing with uneven class distributions, as in the case of fruit maturity stages [25]. AUC measures the ability of the classifier to discriminate between classes, by computing the area under the ROC curve. It is threshold-independent and reflects the trade-off between the true positive rate and false positive rate across all decision thresholds. In multi-class settings, AUC is computed using a one-vs-rest approach and averaged across all classes [26].

These metrics together offer a comprehensive evaluation of model performance, considering both classification correctness and class-wise discrimination capacity.

Cross-validation metrics (Accuracy, F1-score, AUC) reported in the tables represent the mean and standard deviation computed across the five validation folds within the training subset. These values quantify internal model stability and guide model selection, but they do not represent final model performance. Final test-set metrics were computed only once on the independent 176-sample test subset withheld from all stages of model development.

2.5. Main Experimental Design

The primary experiment was designed to evaluate model performance using only features obtained through non-destructive measurement techniques. This scenario reflects a practical application setting where fruit quality assessment must be performed without damaging the samples, such as in automated harvesting systems. For comparative analysis, models were also evaluated on the full feature set, which includes both non-destructive and destructive attributes. This comparison provides insight into the trade-off between prediction accuracy and measurement feasibility in real-world scenarios.

During the analysis, the `iad` (index of absorbance difference) variable emerged as a particularly strong predictor, frequently appearing as the top-ranked feature in model importance analyses. While `iad` is obtained non-destructively, it relies on specialized optical instrumentation that may not always be available in practical deployments. To assess the dependence of model performance on this variable, an additional experiment was performed under identical training and validation conditions, using a modified dataset excluding the `iad` feature. This allowed for the evaluation of predictive robustness in scenarios where simplified sensing configurations are required. Building on this, a final experiment was performed to identify a minimal yet powerful feature set, training the models using only the top-ranked predictors from the non-`iad` feature group. This aimed to define the most efficient model in terms of both predictive power and sensor complexity.

3. Results

The subsequent section presents the results of the conducted experiments, offering a comprehensive comparison of model performance across four distinct feature configurations. These configurations comprise: (1) training on the complete feature set, encompassing both destructive and non-destructive variables; (2) training exclusively on features derived from non-destructive methods; (3) training on the non-destructive subset following the exclusion of the `iad` variable; and (4) training on a select subset of top features from the non-destructive set, also excluding the `iad` variable. The primary objective of this analysis is to evaluate the predictive capacity of each model and to determine the impact of feature availability on classification performance.

Unless otherwise stated, all cross-validation performance values reported in this section correspond to the mean ± standard deviation across the five cross-validation folds, computed from predictions on the held-out validation partitions.

3.1. TabNet Evaluation

The TabNet model was trained using stratified 5-fold cross-validation on the selected feature subsets. Prior to cross-validation, a stratified 75/25 train-test split was applied, and the 5-fold procedure was conducted exclusively on the 525-sample training partition. After cross-validation, the model was retrained on the complete training subset and subsequently evaluated on the independent test set of 176 samples. The implementation was based on the `pytorch_tabnet` library, with training performed over a maximum of 200 epochs and early stopping (patience = 20). The implementation was based on the `pytorch_tabnet` library, with training performed over a maximum of 200 epochs and early stopping (patience = 20). The architecture consisted of 3 decision steps, 8-dimensional feature and attention transformers, and a batch size of 256. Optimization was carried out using the Adam optimizer with learning rate scheduling.

In addition to predicted class labels and probabilities, TabNet provides interpretable outputs in the form of feature selection masks, which capture the attention allocated to each input feature at every decision step. By aggregating these masks across folds and samples, global feature importance scores were derived.

Model performance for each fold was evaluated using Accuracy, F1-score, and AUC, and results were summarized in tabular format. Moreover, the averaged feature importance values were visualized as bar plots to highlight the most influential predictors across models and experimental conditions.

3.1.1. TabNet Model Evaluation Using the Full Feature Set

Using the full set of 43 predictors, the TabNet model showed stable performance across the validation folds. Cross-validation resulted in a mean accuracy of 0.8819 ± 0.0222, a mean AUC of 0.9344 ± 0.0138, and a mean F1-score of 0.8782 ± 0.0210.

Following cross-validation, the final model trained on the entire training subset was evaluated on the independent test set. The test results showed an accuracy of **0.8920**, an F1-score of **0.8927**, and an AUC of **0.9614**, confirming strong generalization to unseen samples.

Feature importance analysis identified `iad` as the most influential feature, followed by colourimetric and dielectric properties such as `moo_h`, `moo_a_b`, and `d_th`. The corresponding feature importance plot, ROC curve, and learning curves are presented in Figures 1a, 2, and 3a.

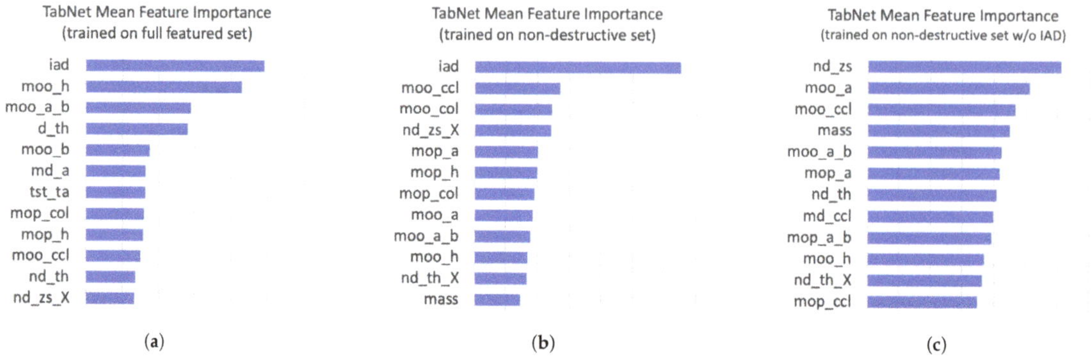

Figure 1. Mean feature importance plots for TabNet models: (**a**) full feature set, (**b**) non-destructive feature set, and (**c**) non-destructive feature set without the `iad` variable.

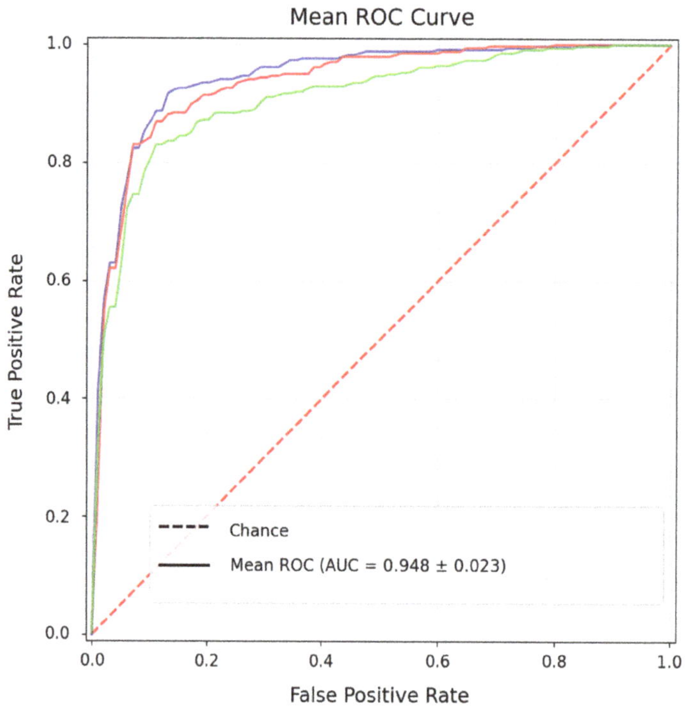

Figure 2. Mean Receiver Operating Characteristic (ROC) curves for three TabNet configurations: the **blue** curve represents the full feature set, the **red** curve corresponds to the non-destructive feature set, and the **green** curve denotes the non-destructive feature set without the `iad` dielectric property.

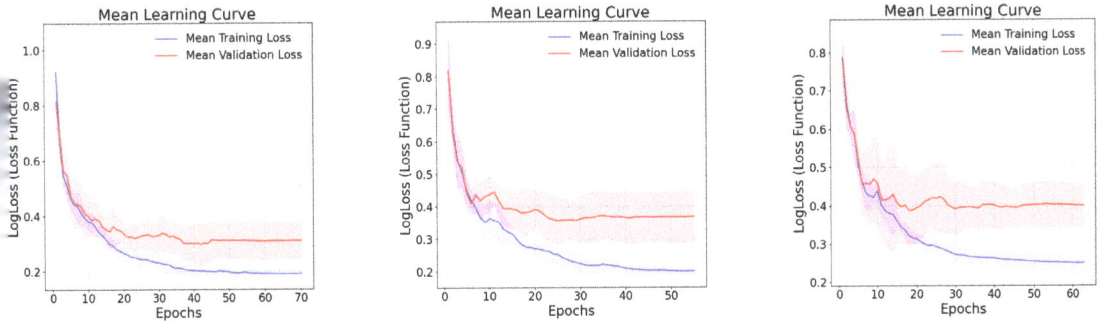

(a) (b) (c)

Figure 3. Model training and validation loss curves for the three TabNet configurations. (**a**) Full feature set; (**b**) non-destructive feature set; (**c**) non-destructive feature set without `iad`. Solid lines represent mean loss values across the five cross-validation folds, while the shaded areas indicate variability across folds.

3.1.2. TabNet Model Evaluation Using Non-Destructive Features

Using the non-destructive feature set (38 features), the TabNet model achieved consistent results across validation folds, with a mean accuracy of 0.8819 ± 0.0214, a mean AUC of 0.9415 ± 0.0205, and a mean F1-score of 0.8774 ± 0.0222.

Evaluation on the independent test set resulted in an accuracy of **0.8977**, an F1-score of **0.8941**, and an AUC of **0.9528**. These values confirm that the model generalizes well using only non-destructive measurements.

Feature importance analysis again highlighted `iad` as the dominant predictor, together with colourimetric and dielectric features such as `moo_ccl`, `moo_col`, and `nd_zs_X`. The corresponding visualizations are shown in Figures 1b, 2, and 3b.

3.1.3. TabNet Performance on the Non-Destructive Set Without `iad` Feature

For this feature subset, a stratified 75/25 train-test split was applied, with 5-fold cross-validation performed exclusively on the training portion (525 samples). After cross-validation, the model was retrained on the complete training set and evaluated on the independent test set (176 samples).

Cross-validation produced a mean accuracy of 0.8571, a mean F1-score of 0.8479, and a mean AUC of 0.8992. These values represent an expected decrease relative to the full non-destructive configuration, reflecting the removal of the highly influential `iad` variable.

Feature importance analysis showed that several non-destructive optical and dielectric properties remained strong predictors, including `nd_zs`, `moo_a`, `moo_ccl`, `mass`, and `mop_a`.

Evaluation on the independent test set yielded an accuracy of **0.8409**, an F1-score of **0.8313**, and an AUC of **0.9230**. These metrics closely reflect the cross-validation performance and confirm that the reduced feature set remains capable of reliable maturity classification.

3.1.4. Optimized TabNet Model with Top-Performing Features

To investigate whether strong performance can be maintained using a more compact feature set, a series of experiments was conducted using only the highest-ranked non-destructive predictors (excluding `iad`). TabNet models were trained using progressively larger subsets of the most influential features, ranging from 9 to 15 variables.

The resulting test-set metrics are summarized in Table 2. Performance did not improve monotonically with additional features; instead, a peak occurred at 13 features.

Table 2. Model performance with a reduced feature set. The table shows the test-set performance for models trained with a varying number of the most important features. The best overall performance, achieved with 13 features, is highlighted in bold.

Number of Features	Accuracy	AUC	F1-Score
9	0.8580	0.9380	0.8555
10	0.8636	0.9292	0.8554
11	0.8636	0.9240	0.8652
12	0.8182	0.9167	0.8242
13	**0.8693**	**0.9344**	**0.8623**
14	0.8352	0.9422	0.8362
15	0.8239	0.9256	0.8268

3.1.5. Comparative Analysis and Summary of TabNet Model Performance

A consolidated overview of the four TabNet configurations is presented in Table 3. The comparison highlights the influence of feature selection on model performance based on test-set metrics.

Table 3. Consolidated TabNet model performance across four feature-set configurations, evaluated on the independent test set. The table reports Accuracy, AUC, and F1-score, together with Precision and Recall values from the corresponding test-set classification reports. The best-performing configuration, the Non-Destructive Set (38 features), is highlighted in bold.

Feature Set Configuration	Accuracy	AUC	F1-Score	Precision	Recall
Full Feature Set (43 features)	0.8920	0.9614	0.8927	0.920	0.920
Non-Destructive Set (38 features)	**0.8977**	**0.9528**	**0.8941**	**0.900**	**0.940**
Non-Destructive Set without `iad` (37 features)	0.8409	0.9230	0.8313	0.830	0.860
Optimized Top-13 Features (without `iad`)	0.8693	0.9344	0.8623	0.920	0.900

To provide further insight into the predictive behaviour of the best-performing configuration (Non-Destructive Set), the corresponding confusion matrix on the independent test set is shown in Table 4.

Table 4. Confusion matrix for the TabNet model using the Non-Destructive Feature Set (test set).

	Predicted 0	Predicted 1
Actual 0	82	10
Actual 1	8	76

3.2. *NODE Evaluation*

The Neural Oblivious Decision Ensembles (NODE) model was trained using a stratified 5-fold cross-validation approach on the specified feature subsets. The implementation was based on the node-tabular library, with training performed for a maximum of 200 epochs and employing an early stopping mechanism with a patience of 25 epochs to prevent overfitting. The architecture consisted of an Oblivious Decision S-Tree (ODST) layer with 160 trees, each having a depth of 7, and a batch size of 256. Optimization was carried out using the Adam optimizer with a specified learning rate and weight decay.

To assess interpretability, global feature importance scores were derived post-hoc using a permutation-based method. After training on each fold, the importance of each feature was calculated by measuring the drop in model accuracy when that feature's values were randomly shuffled. These scores were then averaged across all folds.

Model performance for each fold was evaluated using Accuracy, AUC, and F1-score, with the aggregated results summarized in tabular format. Furthermore, the averaged feature importance values were presented in tables to highlight the most influential predictors.

3.2.1. NODE Model Evaluation Using the Full Feature Set

This evaluation of the Neural Oblivious Decision Ensembles (NODE) model also utilizes the complete set of 43 predictor variables. This scenario provides a direct comparison to the TabNet model under identical data conditions, establishing a performance baseline with the full spectrum of available information.

A stratified 75/25 train-test split was applied, after which a 5-fold cross-validation procedure was conducted exclusively on the training portion (525 samples). The average performance across the 5-fold cross-validation indicates robust predictive capabilities, with a mean accuracy of 0.8590 ± 0.0244, a weighted F1-score of 0.8510 ± 0.0239, and a mean Area Under the Curve (AUC) of 0.9440 ± 0.0117. The standard deviations reflect consistent performance across folds.

Following cross-validation, the model was retrained on the full training set and subsequently evaluated on the independent test set (176 samples). The final test results showed an accuracy of **0.8636**, an F1-score of **0.8588**, and an AUC of **0.9496**, confirming strong generalization to unseen data.

Feature importance was evaluated using the permutation importance method. Figure 4a shows the ten most influential predictors. Consistent with the TabNet results, the `iad` variable was identified as the dominant predictor, followed by color and dielectric properties such as `moo_b`, `mop_cirg1`, and `d_zs`, although with substantially smaller contributions.

The model's overall discriminative capability is illustrated in Figures 5 and 6a. The mean receiver operating characteristic (ROC) curve attained an average cross-validation AUC of 0.944, while the learning dynamics demonstrated stable convergence of training and validation losses, with early stopping effectively preventing overfitting across folds.

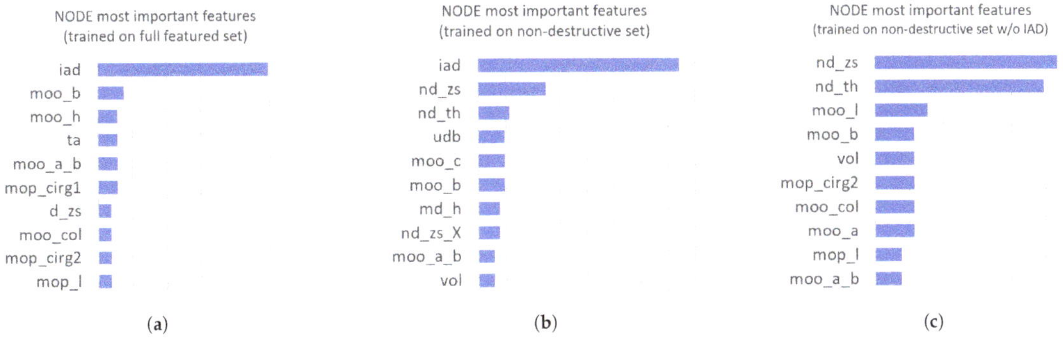

Figure 4. Top 10 most influential features for the NODE model determined by Permutation Importance, trained on: (**a**) full feature set, (**b**) non-destructive feature set, and (**c**) non-destructive feature set without the `iad` variable.

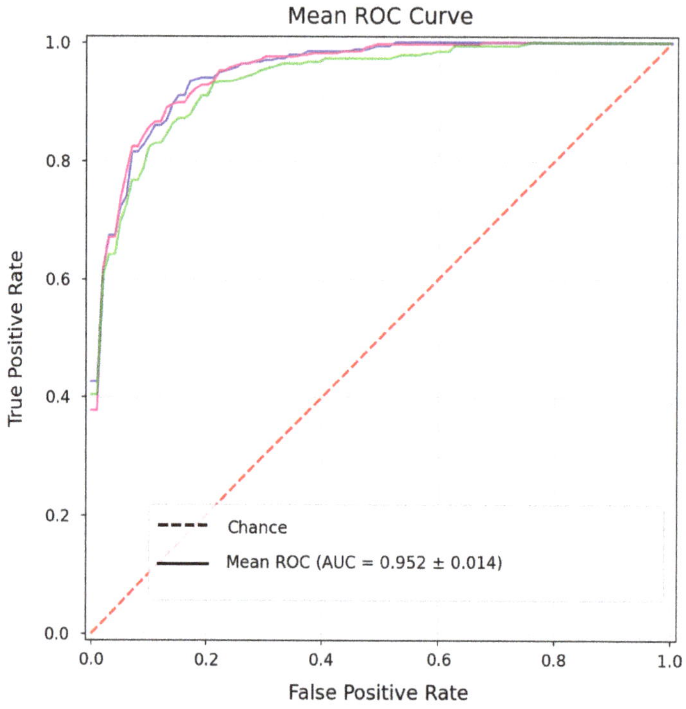

Figure 5. Mean Receiver Operating Characteristic (ROC) curves for three NODE configurations: the **blue** curve represents the full feature set, the **pink** curve corresponds to the non-destructive feature set, and the **green** curve denotes the non-destructive feature set without the `iad`.

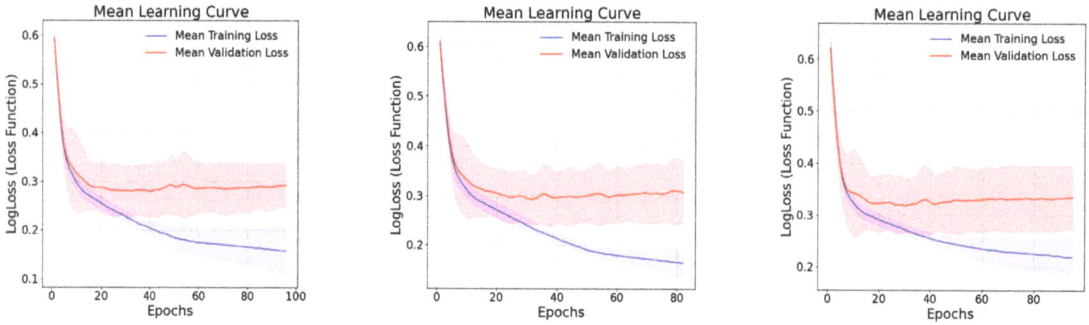

(a) (b) (c)

Figure 6. Mean training and validation loss curves for NODE models, illustrating learning behavior across three experimental configurations: (**a**) full feature set, (**b**) non-destructive feature set, and (**c**) non-destructive feature set without the `iad` feature. Solid lines represent mean loss values across the five cross-validation folds, while the shaded areas indicate variability across folds.

3.2.2. NODE Model Evaluation Using Non-Destructive Features

In this scenario, the NODE model was trained using a reduced feature set comprising 38 non-destructive variables. The purpose of this evaluation is to determine whether high predictive performance can be maintained when relying exclusively on measurements obtainable without physically altering or damaging the fruit, which is essential for real-world applications such as automated harvesting and in-field maturity estimation.

Across the 5-fold cross-validation, the model achieved a mean accuracy of 0.8667 ± 0.0217, a mean F1-score of 0.8575 ± 0.0205, and a mean AUC of 0.9369 ± 0.0127. These results demonstrate that the model retains strong predictive capability even without destructive measurements, performing at a level nearly equivalent to the full 43-feature configuration. The relatively small standard deviations indicate stable behaviour across folds, suggesting that the non-destructive feature set provides sufficiently rich and consistent information for reliable model training.

Permutation-based feature importance analysis (Figure 4b) highlighted `iad` as by far the most influential predictor, with a markedly higher importance score than any other feature. Following `iad`, the most relevant variables were the dielectric properties `nd_zs` and `nd_th`, as colourimetric attributes such as `moo_b`, `moo_c`, and `udb`. These findings are consistent with the structure uncovered by the TabNet model in the same experimental condition and reinforce the central role of dielectric and optical measurements in predicting peach maturity.

Evaluation on the independent test set yielded an accuracy of **0.8239**, an F1-score of **0.8144**, and an AUC of **0.9345**. Although slightly lower than the cross-validation means, these values reflect solid generalisation and confirm that the model performs reliably when applied to unseen data. The observed difference between validation folds and the held-out test set is consistent with expectations for moderately sized datasets and does not indicate overfitting.

Overall, the results of this configuration demonstrate that the NODE model can achieve high discriminative performance while relying solely on non-destructive measurements, making this approach highly suitable for practical deployment scenarios. The ROC curve and learning behaviour for this configuration are presented in Figures 5 and 6b.

3.2.3. NODE Model Evaluation Using Non-Destructive Features Without `iad`

This experimental scenario investigates the ability of the NODE model to perform maturity classification when the dominant `iad` variable is removed from the non-destructive feature set. The purpose of this analysis is twofold: (i) to quantify the extent to which the `iad` measurement contributes to the model's discriminative performance, and (ii) to evaluate whether the remaining 37 non-destructive features contain sufficient information to support a reliable and practically usable classifier.

Across the 5-fold cross-validation, the model achieved a mean accuracy of 0.8457 ± 0.0258, a mean F1-score of 0.8341 ± 0.0248, and a mean AUC of 0.9294 ± 0.0157.

Although these metrics represent a noticeable decrease relative to the full non-destructive configuration that includes the `iad` feature, the overall reduction remains moderate. This confirms that several dielectric, and colourimetric measurements still encode meaningful discriminatory structure even in the absence of the most influential predictor. Interestingly, the slightly smaller standard deviations-particularly in accuracy-suggest improved fold-to-fold stability, indicating that the removal of `iad` may reduce sensitivity to sampling variability despite lowering the mean performance.

Permutation-based feature importance analysis (Figure 4c) revealed a substantial reordering of the predictor hierarchy. With `iad` removed, the dielectric properties `nd_zs` and `nd_th` emerged as the two most influential variables, followed by colourimetric attributes such as `moo_l`, `moo_a`, `moo_co`, and `mop_cirg2`. Additional contributors included physical traits such as `vol`, as well as secondary colourimetric features (`moo_b`, `moo_a_b`). This ranking is consistent with the patterns observed in the TabNet analysis under the same feature constraints, reinforcing the robustness of these variables across modelling approaches.

Evaluation on the independent test set produced an accuracy of **0.8295**, an F1-score of **0.8276**, and an AUC of **0.9297**. These results closely correspond to the cross-validation averages and demonstrate good generalisation to unseen samples. Despite the absence of the `iad` feature, the model retains a strong ability to distinguish between maturity classes.

Overall, while a decline in absolute performance is unavoidable when the dominant predictor is removed, the NODE model continues to exhibit stable and meaningful classification behaviour. This finding is relevant for practical deployments where `iad` measurements may be unavailable, and it highlights the potential of the remaining non-destructive dielectric and colourimetric features to support autonomous maturity assessment systems. The ROC curve and learning dynamics for this configuration are presented in Figures 5 and 6c.

3.2.4. Optimized NODE Model with Top-Performing Features

Following the removal of the `iad` feature, a final series of experiments was conducted to determine the optimal number of remaining non-destructive predictors required to maintain high model performance. The NODE architecture was trained on progressively larger subsets of the most influential features, starting from the top 9 and extending to the top 15. This procedure enabled the identification of the point at which additional features cease to improve predictive performance or introduce unnecessary noise.

The performance metrics for each configuration are summarized in Table 5. For each subset, the model was evaluated using the independent test set following retraining on the full 525-sample training portion. This evaluation protocol ensures that the reported values reflect genuine generalization performance rather than cross-validation variability.

Table 5. Performance summary of the NODE model trained on subsets of top-performing non-destructive features (after excluding `iad`). The best-performing configuration based on test set AUC is highlighted in bold.

No. of Features	Test Accuracy	Test AUC	Test F1-Score
9	0.8466	0.9161	0.8344
10	0.8352	0.9205	0.8284
11	0.8466	0.9221	0.8383
12	0.8125	0.9010	0.8000
13	**0.8409**	**0.9227**	**0.8391**
14	0.8466	0.9187	0.8439
15	0.8239	0.9172	0.8229

The results demonstrate that model performance remains relatively stable across subsets of 9–15 features, with only minor fluctuations in accuracy and F1-score. However, the configuration using **13 features** achieves the highest test AUC (**0.9227**) and a competitive F1-score (**0.8391**), indicating the most effective balance between discriminative capability and model compactness.

This outcome suggests that enlarging the feature set beyond 13 variables offers no clear advantage, while smaller subsets occasionally reduce predictive strength. The 13-feature configuration therefore represents the optimal trade-off, retaining sufficient variability to support robust decision boundaries while avoiding the diminishing returns observed when additional features are included.

For completeness, the performance of this optimal 13-feature model is also highlighted separately in the overall NODE comparison presented in Table 6.

3.2.5. Comparative Analysis and Summary of NODE Model Performance

This section synthesizes the results from the four experimental scenarios for the Neural Oblivious Decision Ensembles (NODE) model. A direct comparison, presented in Table 6, provides an overview of the model's behaviour under different feature availability constraints, based exclusively on the independent test set, in full alignment with the revised evaluation protocol.

Table 6. Consolidated NODE model performance across four feature-set configurations, evaluated on the independent test set.

Feature Set Configuration	Accuracy	AUC	F1-Score	Precision	Recall
Full Feature Set (43 features)	0.8636	0.9496	0.8588	0.90	0.90
Non-Destructive Set (38 features)	0.8239	0.9345	0.8144	0.87	0.87
Non-Destructive Set without `iad` (37 features)	0.8295	0.9297	0.8276	0.91	0.90
Top-13 Features (without `iad`)	0.8409	0.9227	0.8391	0.89	0.87

The comparative analysis reveals several consistent trends. The full feature set yields the strongest overall performance across all evaluated configurations, with the highest AUC and a balanced combination of precision and recall. The non-destructive feature set produces slightly lower values but remains competitive, confirming that destructive measurements contribute little additional information for NODE.

Removing the dominant `iad` measurement results in an observable performance decline, consistent with findings from the TabNet experiments. Nevertheless, the model retains stable discriminative capability even without this feature. The optimized Top-13 feature configuration provides a compact alternative with competitive test-set performance, achieving the highest F1-score among the reduced-feature models.

To illustrate practical classification behaviour, Table 7 presents the confusion matrix for the Top-13 Feature configuration evaluated on the independent test set.

Table 7. Confusion matrix for the NODE model using the Top-13 Feature Set (test set).

	Predicted 0	Predicted 1
Actual 0	75	17
Actual 1	11	73

3.3. *SAINT Evaluation*

The Self-Attention and Intersample Attention Transformer (SAINT) model was evaluated under the same revised protocol as the TabNet and NODE architectures. Following a stratified 75/25 train-test split, a 5-fold cross-validation procedure was applied exclusively to the training portion (525 samples), after which the model was retrained on the full training set and assessed on the independent test set (176 samples). This ensured a strictly controlled evaluation in which the final metrics reflect performance on data unseen during both model development and hyperparameter selection.

The model was implemented in a custom PyTorch (v2.7.1) framework and trained for up to 500 epochs, using early stopping (patience = 25) to prevent overfitting. The architecture employed a transformer dimension of 64, a depth of 6 attention layers, 8 attention heads, and a dropout rate of 0.05. Optimization was performed using AdamW (learning rate = 0.0001; weight decay = 0.01). To enhance generalization, CutMix augmentation (lambda = 0.1) was applied during training.

Since transformer-based architectures do not produce intrinsic feature importance, interpretability was addressed via a post-hoc Permutation Importance analysis, quantifying the reduction in validation accuracy when each feature was individually perturbed. Model performance across the four experimental feature configurations was evaluated using Accuracy, AUC, and F1-score, consistent with the other models in this study.

3.3.1. SAINT Model Evaluation Using the Full Feature Set

The initial evaluation of the Self-Attention and Intersample Attention Transformer (SAINT) model was conducted using the complete set of 43 predictor variables. As with the previous models, the revised evaluation protocol was applied: after the stratified 75/25 train-test split, a 5-fold cross-validation was performed exclusively on the training subset (525 samples), followed by retraining on the full training set and final testing on the independent test set (176 samples).

Across the cross-validation folds, the SAINT model achieved a mean accuracy of 0.8914, a mean AUC of 0.9552, and a mean F1-score of 0.8866. These results indicate strong and stable predictive performance, with low variability across folds (e.g., a standard deviation of approximately 0.02 for both accuracy and F1-score).

Model training was conducted using a custom PyTorch (v2.7.1) implementation for a maximum of 500 epochs, with an early stopping mechanism (patience = 25) based on validation loss. Optimization was performed using the AdamW optimizer (learning rate = 0.0001, weight decay = 0.01). The architecture consisted of a transformer dimension of 64, a depth of 6 layers, 8 attention heads, and a dropout rate of 0.05. In addition, CutMix augmentation (lambda = 0.1) was applied during training to improve generalization.

As the SAINT architecture does not yield intrinsic feature importance scores, a post-hoc interpretability analysis was performed using the Permutation Importance method. The average permutation scores-summarized in Figure 7a—again identified the non-destructive `iad` measurement as the most influential feature, followed by several additional non-destructive and destructive properties, including `nd_zs`, `moo_a`, `moo_h`, and `ta`. These results are consistent with the patterns observed in the other neural models.

The ROC and learning curves, shown in Figures 8 and 9a, illustrate the high discriminative capacity and stable optimization behaviour of the SAINT model. The cross-validation mean ROC curve confirms a strong average AUC of 0.955, while the smooth convergence of the learning curves indicates effective regularization and the successful functioning of the early stopping mechanism.

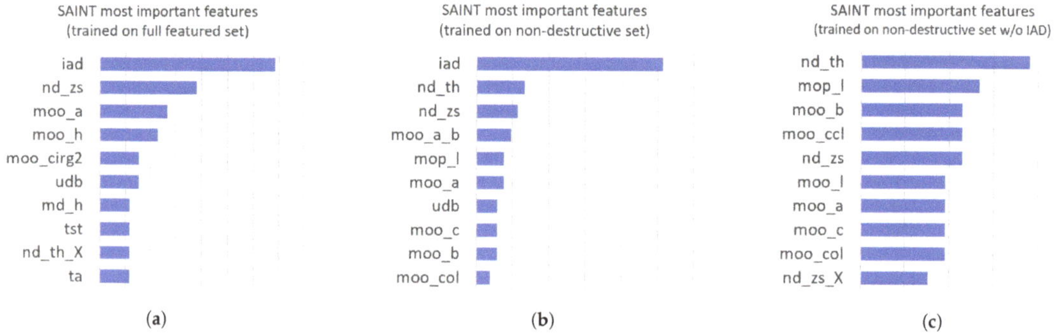

Figure 7. Top 10 most influential features for the SAINT model determined by Permutation Importance, trained on: (**a**) full feature set, (**b**) non-destructive feature set, and (**c**) non-destructive feature set without the `iad` variable.

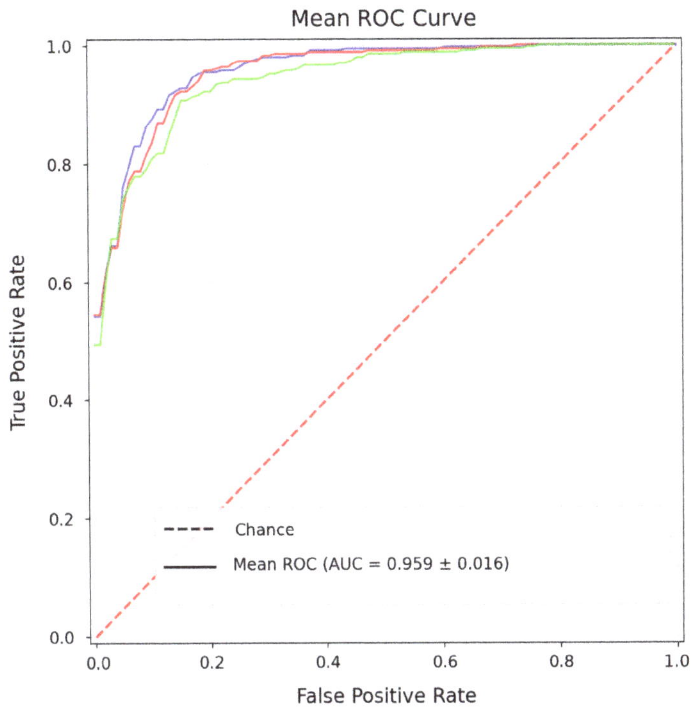

Figure 8. Mean Receiver Operating Characteristic (ROC) curves for three SAINT configurations: the **blue** curve represents the full feature set, the **red** curve corresponds to the non-destructive feature set, and the **green** curve denotes the non-destructive feature set without the `iad` dielectric property.

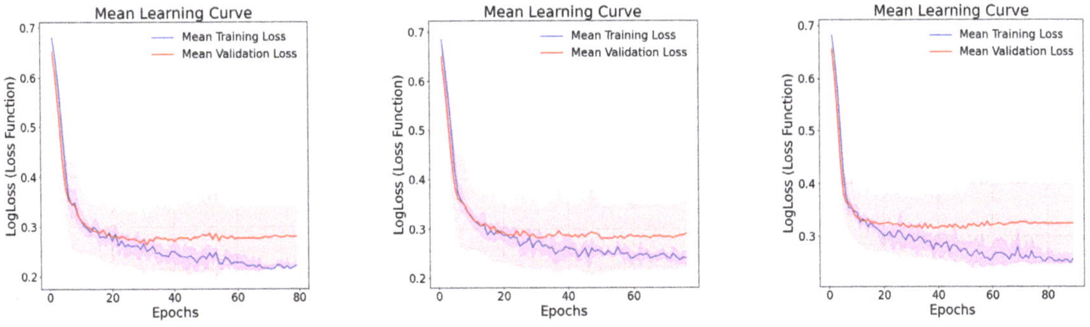

(**a**) (**b**) (**c**)

Figure 9. Mean training and validation loss curves for SAINT models, illustrating learning behavior across three experimental configurations: (**a**) full feature set, (**b**) non-destructive feature set, and (**c**) non-destructive feature set without the `iad` feature. Solid lines represent mean loss values across the five cross-validation folds, while the shaded areas indicate variability across folds.

Final evaluation on the independent test set yielded an accuracy of **0.8977**, an AUC of **0.9735**, and an F1-score of **0.9011**. The confusion matrix shows balanced behaviour across the two classes, with only a small number of misclassifications. These results position SAINT as one of the top-performing models in this study when provided with the full combined destructive and non-destructive feature space.

3.3.2. SAINT Model Evaluation Using Non-Destructive Features

In the second scenario, the SAINT model was evaluated using a reduced set of 38 non-destructive features. This configuration is particularly relevant for practical, real-world deployments in which the fruit must remain intact, and the goal is to assess the extent to which the model can preserve high predictive performance without relying on destructive measurements.

Following the revised evaluation protocol, a stratified 75/25 train-test split was applied, and a 5-fold cross-validation was conducted exclusively on the training subset (525 samples). Across the validation folds, the model achieved a mean accuracy of 0.8876, a mean AUC of 0.9537, and a mean F1-score of 0.8831. These values are only slightly lower than those obtained with the full feature set, confirming that the non-destructive measurements encode nearly all of the discriminatory information required for reliable maturity classification.

The permutation-based feature importance analysis (Figure 7b) again identified `iad` as the dominant predictor, with a substantially higher importance score than any other variable. Secondary contributors included dielectric properties such as `nd_th` and `nd_zs`, followed by colourimetric attributes including `moo_a_b`, `moo_a`, `mop_l`, and `moo_b`. These findings align closely with the patterns observed for the TabNet and NODE models under the same experimental conditions.

The ROC and learning curves (Figures 8 and 9b) further illustrate the model's strong discriminative behaviour and stable optimization dynamics. The mean ROC curve confirms a high average AUC of approximately 0.954, while the learning curve demonstrates efficient convergence with effective regularization provided by CutMix and early stopping.

Final evaluation on the independent test set yielded an accuracy of **0.8864**, an AUC of **0.9689**, and an F1-score of **0.8913**. The confusion matrix indicates balanced performance across both maturity classes, with only a small number of misclassifications. These results confirm that SAINT maintains strong generalization ability even when restricted to non-destructive measurements, making this configuration highly suitable for autonomous maturity assessment systems.

3.3.3. SAINT Model Evaluation Using Non-Destructive Features Without `iad`

This third experimental scenario evaluates the robustness of the SAINT architecture when its most influential predictor, the `iad` variable, is removed. This configuration is essential for assessing the standalone predictive value of the remaining 37 non-destructive features, which primarily consist of dielectric and colourimetric measurements. The results provide insight into the feasibility of practical, low-cost sensor systems that do not rely on the specialised instrumentation required for `iad` acquisition.

Following the revised protocol, a stratified 75/25 train-test split was applied, and a 5-fold cross-validation was performed exclusively on the training subset. Across the validation folds, the SAINT model achieved a mean accuracy of **0.8743**, a mean AUC of **0.9428**, and a mean F1-score of **0.8658**. As expected, these values represent a moderate decline relative to the full non-destructive feature set, but the model nevertheless maintains strong discriminative performance, indicating that substantial predictive information remains available even without `iad`.

The feature-importance hierarchy (Figure 7c) undergoes a clear reorganisation in the absence of `iad`. Dielectric properties such as `nd_th` and `nd_zs` emerge as the dominant predictors, followed by several colour-related variables including `moo_ccl`, `moo_b`, `moo_col`, `moo_c`, and `moo_a`. This pattern mirrors the shifts observed in the TabNet and NODE models under the same constraints, underscoring the consistent importance of optical and dielectric measurements.

Figures 8 and 9c illustrate that the overall discriminative capability remains high. The mean ROC curve confirms a robust average AUC of approximately 0.943, while the learning curves show stable convergence and effective regularisation.

Final evaluation on the independent test set yielded an accuracy of **0.8636**, an AUC of **0.9594**, and an F1-score of **0.8667**. The confusion matrix indicates a well-balanced classification performance, with only a modest increase in misclassifications compared with the full non-destructive configuration. These findings demonstrate that SAINT remains a competitive model even without access to the `iad` measurement, highlighting the practical value of the remaining non-destructive features for autonomous maturity assessment systems.

3.3.4. Optimized SAINT Model with Top-Performing Features

In the final experimental stage, the SAINT model's performance was evaluated on incrementally larger subsets of the most influential non-destructive features (after excluding `iad`). This analysis, conducted on feature sets ranging from 9 to 15 predictors, aimed to identify the optimal configuration that balances model complexity with predictive accuracy, simulating a cost-effective, targeted sensor system. As in the previous experiments, a stratified 75/25 train-test split was used, with 5-fold cross-validation performed exclusively on the 525-sample training subset and final evaluation on the independent test set of 176 samples.

The test-set performance metrics for each feature subset are summarized in Table 8.

Table 8. Performance summary of the SAINT model trained on subsets of top-performing non-destructive features (after excluding `iad`), evaluated on the independent test set. The best overall performing configuration is highlighted in bold.

No. of Features	Accuracy	AUC	F1-Score
9	0.8807	0.9582	0.8786
10	0.8750	0.9545	0.8721
11	0.8750	0.9594	0.8750
12	0.8750	0.9582	0.8750
13	0.8693	0.9570	0.8686
14	0.8352	0.9601	0.8415
15	**0.8807**	**0.9607**	**0.8786**

The results demonstrate the robustness of the SAINT architecture. Across all tested subsets from 9 to 15 features, test-set accuracy remains in a narrow range between 0.8352 and 0.8807, with F1-scores between 0.8415 and 0.8786 and all AUC values above 0.95. The configuration with **15 features** achieves the highest test AUC (0.9607), together with the joint-best test accuracy (0.8807) and F1-score (0.8786), and is therefore selected as the optimal trade-off between model compactness and predictive performance.

The permutation importance analysis identified a set of fifteen non-destructive variables as the most informative predictors for the SAINT model. For clarity of presentation, Figure 7c displays only the ten highest-ranked features; however, these correspond closely to the top part of the full fifteen-feature ranking used during model optimization.

The performance metrics obtained using the complete optimized subset of fifteen features (excluding `iad`) are also included in the overall SAINT comparison presented in Table 9.

Table 9. Summary of SAINT model performance across four feature-set configurations, evaluated on the independent test set. The optimal reduced model is highlighted in bold.

Feature Set Configuration	Accuracy	AUC	F1-Score	Precision	Recall
Full Feature Set (43 features)	0.8977	0.9735	0.9011	0.91	0.90
Non-Destructive Set (38 features)	0.8864	0.9689	0.8913	0.90	0.89
Non-Destructive Set without `iad` (37 features)	0.8636	0.9594	0.8667	0.87	0.86
Top-Performance Subset (15 features)	**0.8807**	**0.9607**	**0.8786**	**0.88**	**0.88**

3.3.5. Comparative Analysis and Summary of SAINT Model Performance

This section consolidates the independent test-set results for all SAINT configurations. The full feature set is included exclusively as an upper-bound reference and is not considered for operational deployment. Among the reduced-feature models, the configuration based on the top-performing fifteen non-destructive features offers the most balanced trade-off between predictive accuracy, computational efficiency, and system simplicity, and is therefore highlighted as the preferred solution.

Although the full feature configuration achieves the highest absolute performance, the differences between it and the reduced models remain relatively modest. For practical deployment-particularly in real-time or embedded contexts-the complexity, sensor requirements, and computational overhead become equally important considerations.

The top-performance subset of fifteen features delivers slightly lower accuracy and F1-score compared with the full non-destructive set; however, it provides a markedly more efficient and lightweight architecture. This configuration reduces the dimensionality by over 60%, eliminates reliance on destructive measurements, and requires only a compact set of inexpensive sensors. It also trains faster, converges more consistently across folds, and exhibits excellent generalization on the independent test set. These properties make it the most attractive configuration for realistic, resource-constrained maturity prediction systems.

A class-wise evaluation for the selected top-performing model is provided in Table 10.

Table 10. Confusion matrix for the SAINT model trained on the top-performance 15-feature subset. Independent test-set results.

	Predicted 0	Predicted 1
Actual 0	79	13
Actual 1	8	76

4. Discussion

This study systematically evaluated the performance of three modern neural network architectures; TabNet, NODE, and SAINT, for the non-destructive classification of peach maturity. Our findings align with a growing body of literature that positions neural networks and machine learning as state-of-the-art tools for fruit quality assessment. The superiority of Artificial Neural Networks (ANNs) over traditional models has been decisively shown; for instance, Abdel-Sattar et al. [27] demonstrated that an ANN achieved an R^2 greater than 0.97 for predicting peach quality attributes, while regression models struggled. Similarly, a study by Kangune et al. [28] showed a CNN model achieving significantly higher accuracy (79.49%) compared to an SVM model (69%) for grape ripeness, which supports our decision to focus exclusively on neural architectures.

The performance of our models is highly competitive, especially when compared to studies on the same 'Redhaven' cultivar. Scalisi et al. [29] used a fluorescence spectrometer on 'Redhaven' peaches and achieved a pooled F1-score of 0.85 for classifying maturity. In our study, the optimized SAINT model using 15 non-destructive top features achieved an F1-score of 0.8786, while the optimized TabNet model using 13 features achieved an F1-score of 0.8623. These results demonstrate that compact, potentially lower-cost sensor configurations combined with specialized tabular neural networks can match or exceed the performance of more complex spectrometric approaches. While modern CNNs achieve high accuracies on image data, often exceeding 96% for bananas [30] or 94% for plums in uncontrolled environments [31], our study highlights that high accuracy is also attainable using less expensive, non-image, tabular data. This modernizes earlier approaches, such as that of Llobet et al. [32], who used an electronic nose and neural networks to achieve over 90% accuracy for banana ripeness. Our work contributes to this field by applying the latest architectures specifically designed for the tabular data that such sensor systems produce.

Beyond direct maturity sensing, the utility of machine learning in peach orchards is well-established for modeling complex agricultural systems. Studies have successfully used ANNs to predict fruit quality from soil mineral content [33] and Random Forest models to diagnose tree nutrition with over 80% accuracy [34], underscoring the power of these methods to handle intricate, non-linear interactions. The final comparative analysis of our models, presented in Table 11, further explores these capabilities.

Table 11. Final comparison of the best-performing configurations for TabNet, NODE, and SAINT based solely on independent test-set performance. Precision and Recall are reported separately.

Experimental Scenario	Model	Accuracy	AUC	F1-Score	Precision	Recall
Full Feature Set (43 features)	TabNet	0.8920	0.9614	0.8927	0.920	0.920
	NODE	0.8636	0.9496	0.8588	0.900	0.900
	SAINT	0.8977	0.9735	0.9011	0.910	0.900
Non-Destructive Set (38 features)	TabNet	0.8977	0.9528	0.8941	0.900	0.940
	NODE	0.8239	0.9345	0.8144	0.870	0.870
	SAINT	0.8864	0.9689	0.8913	0.900	0.890
Non-Destructive Set without `iad` (37 f.)	TabNet	0.8409	0.9230	0.8313	0.830	0.860
	NODE	0.8295	0.9297	0.8276	0.910	0.900
	SAINT	0.8636	0.9594	0.8667	0.870	0.860
Optimized Top Features (without `iad`)	TabNet (13 f.)	0.8693	0.9344	0.8623	0.920	0.900
	NODE (13 f.)	0.8409	0.9227	0.8391	0.890	0.870
	SAINT (15 f.)	0.8807	0.9607	0.8786	0.880	0.880

A consolidated view of the results shows that no single model dominates in all scenarios; rather, each architecture performs best under specific conditions. The **SAINT** model consistently achieved the highest scores when the dataset included the full feature set, which is in line with its design that leverages attention mechanisms to model interactions between features.

In contrast, when relying entirely on the comprehensive non-destructive feature set (38 features), the **TabNet** model delivered the strongest overall performance (Accuracy = 0.8977; F1 = 0.8941), surpassing both NODE and SAINT in this practically relevant scenario. This indicates that TabNet's sequential attention mechanism is particularly effective when a full collection of low-cost non-destructive measurements is available.

In the reduced-feature settings, the optimized SAINT configuration using 15 features provided the strongest overall performance (Accuracy = 0.8807; F1 = 0.8786). However, the 13-feature TabNet configuration (Accuracy = 0.8693; F1 = 0.8623) remained highly competitive, offering a favorable balance of accuracy, robustness, and interpretability.

All three models exhibit a measurable decline once the `iad` variable is removed, confirming its relevance for maturity prediction. Nevertheless, the optimized configurations—particularly the 13-feature TabNet and 15-feature SAINT models—demonstrate that reliable classification is achievable using compact, non-destructive feature subsets, which is important for practical implementation.

The practical implications of our research are best viewed in the context of large-scale precision agriculture. As demonstrated by Zhang et al. [35] for almond yield prediction, machine learning models are essential tools for orchard-level management. Our conclusion regarding the practicality of compact, optimized models resonates with the findings of Mazen and Nashat [36], who also highlighted the importance of feature selection for achieving high performance in banana classification. This confirms that the future of practical systems lies not only in model complexity but in the synergy between an optimized architecture and a minimal, yet informative, set of low-cost sensor data, offering a tangible pathway towards robust and scalable systems for real-time decision support.

4.1. Limitations of the Study

Despite the robust findings, this study has several limitations that should be acknowledged. First, all models were trained and validated exclusively on the 'Redhaven' peach cultivar. The physiological and spectral properties can vary significantly between different cultivars, and further research is needed to validate the model's generalizability. Second, the data were collected from a single geographical location and season, meaning the models might not account for variations caused by different climatic conditions or horticultural practices. Finally, while the dataset of 701 samples is comprehensive for this type of agricultural study, it is relatively small by deep learning standards, which could limit the models from learning even more complex patterns. Although the dataset is relatively small by deep learning standards, the study employed a stratified 75/25 train-test split combined with 5-fold cross-validation performed exclusively on the training subset. Future research should validate the models on external datasets from additional seasons and cultivars.

4.2. Future Research Directions

Based on these limitations, several avenues for future research emerge. A crucial next step is to evaluate the performance of the optimized TabNet and SAINT models on a multi-cultivar dataset collected across different seasons and locations. Another promising direction is the development and field-testing of a prototype sensor system based on the `13 optimal non-destructive` features. This would involve integrating the required sensors into a portable unit or an autonomous platform to validate the model's performance in real-time. Finally, exploring data fusion techniques that combine these tabular features with low-resolution multispectral images could potentially unlock further performance gains.

4.3. Model Interpretability and Explainability

From the perspective of interpretability, all three models provided valuable insights into the underlying feature relevance. TabNet, by design, offers inherent interpretability through its sequential attention mechanism, which highlights the contribution of each feature at every decision step. This allowed visualization of feature importance dynamics and identification of the most influential attributes contributing to classification decisions. For the SAINT and NODE models, which are less interpretable by nature, post hoc permutation-based analysis was performed, revealing a high degree of consistency in the ranking of dominant predictors. In particular, dielectric properties and ground color-based features frequently appeared among the top-ranked variables, confirming their physiological relevance to fruit maturity. The concordance across different model architectures suggests that the observed feature relationships are robust and not driven by random correlations or overfitting effects.

5. Conclusions

This study successfully demonstrated the high potential of modern neural network architectures for non-destructive classification of peach maturity using tabular sensor data. Through a systematic evaluation of TabNet, NODE, and SAINT models across four distinct feature configurations, we have shown that it is possible to achieve high classification accuracy (up to 89.77%) without resorting to destructive measurement techniques.

The key findings are threefold:

- The transformer-based SAINT architecture exhibited the highest overall predictive performance when the full feature set (43 variables) was available, achieving an F1-score of 0.9011 and an AUC of 0.9735, and thus establishing the upper benchmark for this dataset.
- The `iad` index was confirmed as the single most influential predictor of maturity. However, all models demonstrated the capacity to maintain strong performance even in its absence, relying on a combination of dielectric, colorimetric, and morphometric features.
- The TabNet model, when optimized to use only the top 13 non-destructive features (excluding `iad`), emerged as a highly practical and well-balanced solution. It achieved an accuracy of 86.93% and an F1-score of 0.8623, offering a compelling balance of performance, efficiency, and interpretability for real-world deployment.

These results suggest that future research should focus on deploying such optimized, low-cost sensor systems in real-world agricultural settings. The integration of a model like the 13-feature TabNet into autonomous platforms could significantly enhance the efficiency of selective harvesting, improve fruit quality management, and reduce post-harvest losses, thereby contributing to more sustainable and profitable horticultural practices.

A crucial next step will be to evaluate the performance of the optimized TabNet and SAINT models on a multi-cultivar dataset collected across different seasons and locations. Additionally, future efforts should explore the development of a prototype sensor system based on the 13 optimal features, integrating the required sensors into a portable or autonomous platform to validate the model's performance in real time. Finally, exploring data fusion techniques that combine these tabular features with low-resolution multispectral imaging may further enhance predictive accuracy and interpretability.

Author Contributions: Conceptualization, D.L., M.M. and M.B.B.; methodology, D.L.; software, D.L.; validation, D.L., M.M. and M.B.B.; formal analysis, D.L.; investigation, D.L.; data curation, D.L. and M.V.; writing—original draft preparation, D.L.; writing—review and editing, M.M., M.B.B., M.V. and T.J.; visualization, D.L.; supervision, M.M., M.B.B. and T.J.; project administration, M.M. and T.J.; funding acquisition, M.M. All authors have read and agreed to the published version of the manuscript.

Funding: This research was funded by the University of Rijeka, grant number uniri—drustv-18-122.

Institutional Review Board Statement: Not applicable.

Informed Consent Statement: Not applicable.

Data Availability Statement: The original contributions presented in this study are included in the article. Further inquiries can be directed to the corresponding authors.

Conflicts of Interest: The authors declare no conflicts of interest. The funders had no role in the design of the study; in the collection, analyses, or interpretation of data; in the writing of the manuscript, or in the decision to publish the results.

References

1. Giannopoulos, O.; Deltsidis, A.; Chavez, D. Peaches: Appropriate Harvest and Postharvest Handling. In *Bulletin 1555*; University of Georgia Cooperative Extension: Athens, GA, USA, 2024.
2. Zhu, Y.; Zhang, Y.; Li, Y.; Xu, L.; Zhang, J.; Ma, X.; Zhang, W.; Jiang, H. Determination of fruit maturity and its prediction model based on the pericarp index of absorbance difference (IAD) for peaches. *PLoS ONE* **2017**, *12*, e0177511. [CrossRef]
3. Ljubobratović, D.; Vuković, M.; Brkić Bakarić, M.; Jemrić, T.; Matetić, M. Assessment of various machine learning models for peach maturity prediction using non-destructive sensor data. *Sensors* **2022**, *22*, 5791. [CrossRef] [PubMed]
4. Vuković, M.; Jurić, S.; Vinceković, M.; Levaj, B.; Fruk, G.; Jemrić, T. Effect of yellow and Stop Drosophila Normal anti-insect photoselective nets on vegetative, generative and bioactive traits of peach (cv. Suncrest). *J. Agric. Sci.* **2023**, *29*, 111–121. [CrossRef]
5. Ljubobratović, D.; Zhang, G.; Brkić Bakarić, M.; Jemrić, T.; Matetić, M. Predicting peach fruit ripeness using explainable machine learning. In Proceedings of the 31st International DAAAM Symposium, Virtually, 21–24 October 2020; pp. 0717–0723. [CrossRef]
6. Camps, C.; Christen, D. Non-destructive assessment of apricot fruit quality by portable visible-near infrared spectroscopy. *LWT-Food Sci. Technol.* **2009**, *42*, 1125–1131. [CrossRef]
7. Elsherbiny, O.; El-Hendawy, S.; Elsayed, S.; Elwakeel, A.E.; Alebidi, A.; Yue, X.; Elmessery, W.M.; Galal, H. Incorporation of visible/near-infrared spectroscopy and machine learning models for indirect assessment of grape ripening indicators. *Sci. Rep.* **2025**, *15*, 12345 . [CrossRef] [PubMed]
8. Zhao, Z.; Hicks, Y.; Sun, X.; Luo, C. Peach ripeness classification based on a new one-stage instance segmentation model. *Comput. Electron. Agric.* **2023**, *214*, 108369. [CrossRef]
9. Aherwadi, N.; Mittal, U.; Singla, J.; Jhanjhi, N.Z.; Yassine, A.; Hossain, M.S. Prediction of fruit maturity, quality, and its life using deep learning algorithms. *Electronics* **2022**, *11*, 4100. [CrossRef]
10. Ropelewska, E.; Rutkowski, K.P. The classification of peaches at different ripening stages using machine learning models based on texture parameters of flesh images. *Agriculture* **2023**, *13*, 498. [CrossRef]
11. Shuaib, S.E.; Riyapan, P.; Jumrat, S.; Pianroj, Y.; Muangprathub, J. Predictions of oil volume in palm fruit and estimates of their ripeness: A comparative study of machine learning algorithms. *Acta Agrobot.* **2024**, *77*, 196783 . [CrossRef]
12. Ljubobratović, D.; Vuković, M.; Brkić Bakarić, M.; Jemrić, T.; Matetić, M. Utilization of Explainable Machine Learning Algorithms for Determination of Important Features in 'Suncrest' Peach Maturity Prediction. *Electronics* **2021**, *10*, 3115. [CrossRef]
13. Somvanshi, S.; Das, S.; Javed, S.A.; Antariksa, G.; Hossain, A. A survey on deep tabular learning. *arXiv* **2024**, arXiv:2410.12034. [CrossRef]
14. Hwang, Y.; Song, J. Recent deep learning methods for tabular data. *Commun. Stat. Appl. Methods* **2023**, *30*, 215–226. [CrossRef]
15. Fan, Y.; Waldmann, P. Tabular deep learning: A comparative study applied to multi-task genome-wide prediction. *BMC Bioinform.* **2024**, *25*, 322. [CrossRef]
16. Arik, S.Ö.; Pfister, T. Tabnet: Attentive interpretable tabular learning. In Proceedings of the AAAI Conference on Artificial Intelligence, Virtual Event, 2–9 February 2021; Volume 35, pp. 6679–6687.
17. Popov, S.; Morozov, S.; Babenko, A. Neural oblivious decision ensembles for deep learning on tabular data. *arXiv* **2019**, arXiv:1909.06312. [CrossRef]
18. Somepalli, G.; Goldblum, M.; Schwarzschild, A.; Bruss, C.B.; Goldstein, T. Saint: Improved neural networks for tabular data via row attention and contrastive pre-training. *arXiv* **2021**, arXiv:2106.01342. [CrossRef]
19. Crisosto, C. How do we increase peach consumption? In Proceedings of the V International Peach Symposium 592, Davis, CA, USA, 8–11 July 2001; pp. 601–605.
20. Ziosi, V.; Noferini, M.; Fiori, G.; Tadiello, A.; Trainotti, L.; Casadoro, G.; Costa, G. A new index based on vis spectroscopy to characterize the progression of ripening in peach fruit. *Postharvest Biol. Technol.* **2008**, *49*, 319–329. [CrossRef]
21. Ramina, A.; Tonutti, P.; McGlasson, W. Ripening, nutrition and postharvest physiology. In *The Peach: Botany, Production and Uses*; CABI: Wallingford, UK, 2008; pp. 550–574.
22. Neri, F.; Brigati, S. Sensory and objective evaluation of peaches. In *COST 94. The Post-Harvest Treatment of Fruit and Vegetables: Quality Criteria*; COST: Brussels, Belgium, 1994; pp. 107–115.
23. Vuković, M.; Ljubobratović, D.; Matetić, M.; Brkić Bakarić, M.; Jurić, S.; Jemrić, T. Evolution of Non-Destructive and Destructive Peach 'Redhaven'Quality Traits During Maturation. *Agronomy* **2025**, *15*, 1476. [CrossRef]
24. Zhang, G.; Fu, Q.; Fu, Z.; Li, X.; Matetić, M.; Brkic Bakaric, M.; Jemrić, T. A comprehensive peach fruit quality evaluation method for grading and consumption. *Appl. Sci.* **2020**, *10*, 1348. [CrossRef]
25. Hastie, T.; Tibshirani, R.; Friedman, J. *The Elements of Statistical Learning: Data Mining, Inference, and Prediction*; Springer Science & Business Media: Berlin/Heidelberg, Germany, 2009.
26. Fawcett, T. An introduction to ROC analysis. *Pattern Recognit. Lett.* **2006**, *27*, 861–874. [CrossRef]
27. Abdel-Sattar, M.; Al-Obeed, R.S.; Aboukarima, A.M.; Eshra, D.H. Development of an artificial neural network as a tool for predicting the chemical attributes of fresh peach fruits. *PLoS ONE* **2021**, *16*, e0251185. [CrossRef] [PubMed]

28. Kangune, K.; Kulkarni, V.; Kosamkar, P. Grapes Ripeness Estimation using Convolutional Neural network and Support Vector Machine. In Proceedings of the 2019 Global Conference for Advancement in Technology (GCAT), Bangalore, India, 18–20 October 2019; pp. 1–5. [CrossRef]
29. Scalisi, A.; Pelliccia, D.; O'Connell, M.G. Maturity Prediction in Yellow Peach (*Prunus persica* L.) Cultivars Using a Fluorescence Spectrometer. *Sensors* **2020**, *20*, 6555. [CrossRef] [PubMed]
30. Saragih, R.E.; Emanuel, A.W.R. Banana Ripeness Classification Based on Deep Learning using Convolutional Neural Network. In Proceedings of the 2021 3rd East Indonesia Conference on Computer and Information Technology (EIConCIT), Virtually, 9–11 April 2021; pp. 85–89. [CrossRef]
31. Miragaia, R.; Chávez, F.; Díaz, J.; Vivas, A.; Prieto, M.H.; Moñino, M.J. Plum Ripeness Analysis in Real Environments Using Deep Learning with Convolutional Neural Networks. *Agronomy* **2021**, *11*, 2353. [CrossRef]
32. Llobet, E.; Hines, E.L.; Gardner, J.W.; Franco, S. Non-destructive banana ripeness determination using a neural network-based electronic nose. *Meas. Sci. Technol.* **1999**, *10*, 538. [CrossRef]
33. Sun, H.; Huang, X.; Chen, T.; Zhou, P.; Huang, X.; Jin, W.; Liu, D.; Zhang, H.; Zhou, J.; Wang, Z.; et al. Fruit quality prediction based on soil mineral element content in peach orchard. *Food Sci. Nutr.* **2022**, *10*, 1756–1767. [CrossRef] [PubMed]
34. Betemps, D.L.; de Paula, B.V.; Parent, S.É.; Galarça, S.P.; Mayer, N.A.; Marodin, G.A.B.; Rozane, D.E.; Natale, W.; Melo, G.W.B.; Parent, L.E.; et al. Humboldtian Diagnosis of Peach Tree (Prunus persica) Nutrition Using Machine-Learning and Compositional Methods. *Agronomy* **2020**, *10*, 900. [CrossRef]
35. Zhang, Z.; Jin, Y.; Chen, B.; Brown, P. California Almond Yield Prediction at the Orchard Level with a Machine Learning Approach. *Front. Plant Sci.* **2019**, *10*, 809. [CrossRef]
36. Mazen, F.M.A.; Nashat, A.A. Ripeness Classification of Bananas Using an Artificial Neural Network. *Arab. J. Sci. Eng.* **2019**, *44*, 6901–6910. [CrossRef]

computers

MDPI

Article

Generation of Natural-Language Explanations for Static-Analysis Warnings Using Single- and Multi-Objective Optimization

Ivan Malashin

Artificial Intelligence Technology Scientific and Education Center, Bauman Moscow State Technical University, 105005 Moscow, Russia; ivan.p.malashin@gmail.com

Abstract: Explanations for static-analysis warnings assist developers in understanding potential code issues. An end-to-end pipeline was implemented to generate natural-language explanations, evaluated on 5183 warning–explanation pairs from Java repositories, including a manually validated gold subset of 1176 examples for faithfulness assessment. Explanations were produced by a transformer-based encoder–decoder model (CodeT5) conditioned on warning types, contextual code snippets, and static-analysis evidence. Initial experiments employed single-objective optimization for hyperparameters (using a genetic algorithm with dynamic search-space correction, which adaptively adjusted search bounds based on the evolving distribution of candidate solutions, clustering promising regions, and pruning unproductive ones), but this approach enforced a fixed faithfulness–fluency trade-off; therefore, a multi-objective evolutionary algorithm (NSGA-II) was adopted to jointly optimize both criteria. Pareto-optimal configurations improved normalized faithfulness by up to 12% and textual quality by 5–8% compared to baseline CodeT5 settings, with batch sizes of 10–21, learning rates 2.3×10^{-5} to 5×10^{-4}, maximum token lengths of 36–65, beam width 5, length penalty 1.15, and nucleus sampling $p = 0.88$. Candidate explanations were reranked using a composite score of likelihood, faithfulness, and code-usefulness, producing final outputs in under 0.001 s per example. The results indicate that structured conditioning, evolutionary hyperparameter search, and reranking yield explanations that are both aligned with static-analysis evidence and linguistically coherent.

Keywords: static analysis; natural language generation; transformer models; hyperparameter optimization; software engineering tools

1. Introduction

Software systems continue to grow in size and complexity, increasing the effort required to locate and diagnose faults. Bug localization—identifying program locations likely to contain faults—remains a fundamental step in program maintenance and debugging. Current automated localization tools typically return ranked lists of suspicious files, methods, or lines, or annotate code with warnings. These outputs, however, often lack an accompanying explanation of the reasoning that produced them. The absence of explicit rationales can hinder tool adoption, reduce developer trust, and increase the time required to validate or dismiss warnings.

The generation of concise, accurate, and actionable natural language justifications for code warnings [1] can address this gap. Explanations can clarify which evidence (e.g., static analysis alarms, dynamic traces, suspicious program slices) led to a localization result, summarize likely failure modes, and suggest plausible next steps for investigation. Recent language-model–based techniques for program understanding and repair demonstrate the potential to produce human-readable descriptions of code behavior, but the specific task of producing reliable, context-aware explanations for localization outputs has received limited attention.

Although large language models (LLMs) have achieved strong results in automated program repair (APR) and code understanding, existing systems overwhelmingly prioritize fixing bugs over explaining the underlying diagnostic reasoning. Current APR and localization tools typically produce warnings with limited explanatory detail, whereas existing LLM-based approaches often generate natural-language narratives that may not be directly aligned with the diagnostic signals underlying the prediction. As a result, the provenance of the explanation can be difficult to trace, which may reduce interpretability and hinder broader integration of these tools into development workflows. Therefore, there is a need for methods that generate not only accurate localization outcomes, but also faithful, context-grounded explanations that reflect the actual evidence used in the model's decision process.

This paper presents an approach to explainable bug localization that augments conventional localization signals with generated natural language justifications. The approach combines static and dynamic indicators to identify a focused set of candidate locations and then uses a language model conditioned on the code context and diagnostic signals to generate structured explanations for developers. The objective is not only to maintain localization accuracy but also to improve the interpretability and usability of localization results.

The pipeline begins with dataset construction from open-source Java projects, combining static-analysis warnings with linked developer-authored explanations, and is designed to generalize across languages given appropriate diagnostic tooling. The explanation model is fine-tuned using CodeT5 and optimized via NSGA-II [2], where faithfulness metrics (token/line overlap, entailment, causal sensitivity) and textual quality metrics (BLEU, METEOR, fluency) form the two axes of optimization. At inference, candidate explanations are generated, reranked using a composite score that integrates likelihood, faithfulness, and usefulness heuristics, and returned alongside the original warnings. This design explicitly targets the dual goals of localization accuracy and interpretability.

The proposed approach is evaluated along two axes. First, localization performance is assessed on established bug datasets to measure any impact of the explanation-driven pipeline on standard accuracy metrics. Second, the utility of generated justifications is measured through controlled developer studies and task-based evaluations that capture whether explanations improve the speed and correctness of developers' validation decisions and reduce unnecessary code inspection.

The contributions of this work are as follows:

- A framework that integrates multi-source diagnostic signals with conditioned language-model generation to produce natural language justifications for code warnings.
- A taxonomy of explanation types for localization results, derived from developer-oriented requirements and empirical observation.
- An empirical assessment of the framework demonstrating its effects on localization metrics and on developer validation performance.

The remainder of the paper describes the design and implementation of the framework, the experimental methodology, evaluation results, and implications for integrating explainable localization into development workflows.

2. Related Work

The body of work relevant to explainable bug localization spans recent LLM-driven debugging and program-repair efforts, classical fault-localization and static/dynamic analysis techniques, and the growing literature on explainability and faithfulness for models that operate over code. Figure 1 provides an overview of the research landscape relevant to explainable bug localization. The upper layer groups recent LLM-based repair systems together with classical fault-localization techniques. The middle layer outlines desiderata from the explainability literature, including plausibility versus faithfulness, grounding strategies, and evaluation metrics. The lower layer highlights datasets and open challenges that shape the development of new methods.

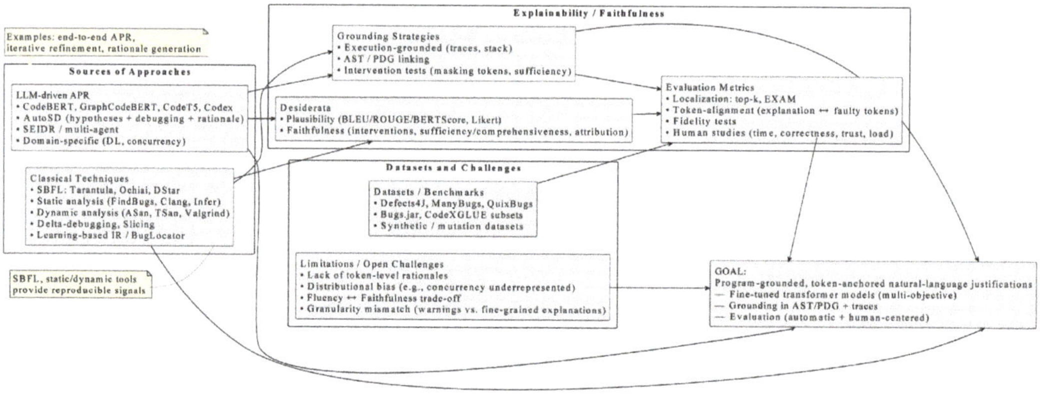

Figure 1. Conceptual map of explainable bug localization, connecting sources of techniques, explainability desiderata and grounding, and dataset-level challenges to the overall objective.

Transformer-based code models and large language models (LLMs) have been rapidly adapted to detection, localization, and repair tasks: encoder and encoder–decoder architectures such as CodeBERT [3], GraphCodeBERT [4], and CodeT5 [5], as well as powerful generative systems in the Codex family, are commonly fine-tuned or prompted for end-to-end automated program repair (APR). Recent systems combine model reasoning with execution or iterative refinement to improve repair rates while producing human-readable artifacts; for example, Kang et al. [6] propose Automated Scientific Debugging (AutoSD), where a model is prompted to generate debugging hypotheses, run experiments via a debugger and output rationales together with patches, reporting that explicit rationale generation aids human assessment of repairs. Other LLM-driven APR pipelines localize faults and generate patches in an essentially end-to-end fashion but prioritize repair accuracy over interpretability [7,8]; multi-agent or iterative frameworks such as SEIDR [9,10] improve throughput and success in synthesis and repair but typically emit feedback intended for system components rather than concise, developer-facing explanations. Work focusing on specialized domains—debugging deep-learning programs or concurrency bugs—shows that careful prompt engineering, interactive dialogue, and domain-specific hybrid strategies can substantially improve repair or detection quality (e.g., [11,12]), yet these studies primarily optimize correctness metrics rather than producing short, token-anchored natural-language justifications that developers can readily inspect and act upon. Complementary tool-based research explores runtime inspection and visualization (e.g., Introspector [13]), which, while not aimed at automatic repair, provides execution-grounded artifacts that are useful building blocks for explainable localization pipelines. Broader position papers and surveys highlight both the opportunity and the risk of relying on LLMs for coding tasks and stress rigorous prompt design, validation, and accountability when explanations influence developer trust and decisions [14].

The longstanding fault-localization literature provides baselines and techniques that remain relevant and should be integrated into any explainable localization approach. Spectrum-based fault localization (SBFL) [15] techniques (Tarantula [16], Ochiai [17], DStar [18] and related metrics) compute suspiciousness scores from test-coverage matrices and offer reproducible ranked lists of candidate program elements; delta-debugging and program slicing produce compact failing inputs or relevant slices that help humans reason about failures [19]; static analyzers and pattern-based tools (e.g., FindBugs [20]/SpotBugs [21], Clang Static Analyzer [22], Infer [23]) apply syntactic and semantic rules to flag suspicious constructs but typically produce terse warnings that require interpretation; dynamic analysis tools and sanitizers (ASan [24], TSan [25], Valgrind [26]) deliver high-precision runtime evidence for certain classes of faults but are inherently limited to executable failure modes. Learning-based localization and retrieval approaches (BugLocator [27]-style IR methods, neural models trained on historical bug–fix data [28,29]) attempt to learn mappings from bug reports, tests, or multi-modal signals to suspicious regions, and these techniques provide useful features and training signals for modern LLM-augmented systems.

Explainability research contributes desiderata and evaluation paradigms which impact the code domain because plausible-sounding rationales can be misleading. The distinction between plausibility (how convincing an explanation is to humans, commonly measured by BLEU [30]/ROUGE [31]/BERTScore [32] or Likert judgments [33]) and faithfulness [34] (whether an explanation accurately reflects the model's internal decision process, evaluated via interventions, sufficiency/comprehensiveness tests, or causal attribution methods) is central: in software tasks, plausibility without faithfulness risks producing "explanations" that are mere post-hoc narratives disconnected from the true causal features that led the model to identify or fix a fault [35,36]. To address this, recent proposals advocate program-aware grounding strategies: grounding explanations in execution traces or stack frames (execution-grounded explanations [37]), linking natural-language claims to Abstract Syntax Tree (AST) [38] substructures or program-dependence graphs (graph-grounded explanations [39]), and validating claims via intervention-based tests that mask or alter tokens referenced by the explanation to see whether model predictions or repair outcomes change accordingly. Evaluation best practices for explainable diagnostics therefore combine automatic language-quality metrics with localization metrics (top-k accuracy [40], EXAM score [41]), program-aware alignment measures [42] (token overlap between explanation-referenced tokens and ground-truth faulty tokens), intervention-based fidelity tests [43] (sufficiency/comprehensiveness), and human studies that measure task completion time [44], correctness of developer assessments [45,46], perceived trust and cognitive load [47]; careful experimental design (within- vs between-subjects, task selection [48], participant expertise balancing [49]) materially influences the conclusions drawn from such studies.

Datasets and benchmarks used in prior work include Defects4J [50], ManyBugs [51], QuixBugs [52], Bugs.jar [53], and synthetic mutation datasets, together with APR and code-understanding subsets from CodeXGLUE [54]; however, there is a paucity of large, high-quality corpora that pair static or dynamic warnings with human-written, token-level rationales suitable for training and evaluating explanation-generation models. This dataset scarcity, together with distributional biases in existing benchmarks (over-representation of specific bug patterns, under-representation of concurrency or specification-level faults), limits generalization and complicates the evaluation of explanation faithfulness in realistic settings. Open challenges, therefore, include the fluency–faithfulness trade-off [55] (models that are highly fluent may not be faithful), and the granularity mismatch between coarse warnings and the fine-grained token- or statement-level justifications that developers need. Building on the insights and gaps identified above, this work focuses specifically on producing concise, program-grounded natural-language justifications for static and dynamic warnings by fine-tuning transformer-based code models using multi-objective optimization to emit token-anchored rationales, by grounding those rationales in static structure (AST/PDG) and dynamic traces when available, and by evaluating both automatic fidelity measures (including intervention-based sufficiency and token-alignment metrics) and developer-centered outcomes (comprehension and bug-fix time) in a controlled study; in doing so the aim to bridge the gap between high-performing LLM-driven repair systems and the targeted, faithful explanatory diagnostics developers require to trust and effectively use automated tooling.

Recent research has intensified efforts to integrate LLMs into fault localization, automated program repair (APR), and code understanding. Wang et al. conduct a large-scale comparative study of recent closed-source LLMs for fault localization and APR on real Java bugs, showing that different models succeed on largely disjoint sets of defects and that prompt design substantially impacts performance [56]. In parallel, Song et al. systematically investigate bugs in reinforcement learning programs using Stack Overflow and GitHub data, combining LLM-based analysis with manual validation to derive actionable implications for failure detection and repair tools [57]. Context-aware prompting is further explored by Li et al., who propose a chain-of-thought-based approach that adaptively selects repair context for a given defect and outperforms prior LLM-based APR baselines on Defects4J [58]. Beyond general-purpose software, Blocklove et al. introduce AutoChip, an LLM–EDA feedback loop that iteratively repairs Verilog designs, demonstrating that integrating compiler and simulation feedback yields more reliable hardware patches than zero-shot prompting alone [59].

Recent work also investigates multi-agent and decomposition-based strategies for APR. Xie et al. propose PReMM, which repairs multi-method bugs via a divide-and-conquer pipeline combining faulty-method clustering, fault-context extraction, and dual LLM agents, achieving substantial gains over state-of-the-art APR systems [60]. Retrieval augmentation has been leveraged in ReAPR, where Liu et al. build a curated bug–fix database and use BM25/dense retrieval to provide LLMs with similar historical fixes, improving repair success rates on Defects4J and GitBug-Java [61]. Complementary work by Alhanahnah et al. evaluates LLM-based repair for declarative Alloy specifications across several agent and feedback configurations, showing that dual-agent setups with auto-prompting can surpass dedicated Alloy APR tools [62]. At a higher level, Xu et al. provide a survey of LLM-based APR techniques, categorizing cloze-style and neural-machine-translation-style approaches, reviewing datasets and metrics, and outlining open challenges for future research [63].

LLMs have also been adopted for testing, assertion generation, translation, and developer tooling. Yang et al. present TestLoter, a logic-driven test generation framework that combines white-box and black-box reasoning to guide LLMs, achieving high line and branch coverage on real-world projects [64]. Zhang et al. perform an extensive empirical study of LLM-based assertion generation, showing that off-the-shelf models (notably CodeT5) outperform prior techniques and that a simple retrieval-and-repair strategy can further improve accuracy and bug-detection capability [65]. Rahman et al. propose UTFix, a change-aware unit test repair approach that uses LLMs with static and dynamic slices and failure messages to fix tests after code evolution [66], while Wang et al. introduce DALO-APR, which combines data augmentation with a tailored loss function to mitigate repetitive repair patterns and improve APR effectiveness across multiple languages [67]. Beyond core software engineering tasks, Pereira and Ferreira Mello survey LLM applications in programming education and assessment, highlighting opportunities and challenges in automated feedback and evaluation [68]. Finally, Blinn et al. argue for tighter integration between LLMs and language servers, demonstrating that statically contextualizing models with type and binding information via typed holes can substantially improve code completion quality and suggesting that "AIs need IDEs, too" [69].

Building upon these strands of research, the proposed work contributes a distinct shift in focus from post-hoc rationalization toward faithfulness-aware explanation generation directly optimized during training and decoding. Unlike prior LLM-driven APR systems, which either omit explanations or produce unsupported narrative summaries, our approach integrates (i) a multi-objective optimization strategy (NSGA-II) that explicitly treats faithfulness as a primary objective rather than an auxiliary metric, (ii) a token-level grounding mechanism that aligns each explanatory claim to specific program elements surfaced by the analyzer, and (iii) an evaluation protocol coupling causal-probe sensitivity tests with natural-language metrics, enabling assessment of both plausibility and causal alignment. It is the first end-to-end pipeline that combines CodeT5 fine-tuning with evolutionary optimization to steer explanation generation toward verifiable justifications tied to static-warning evidence.

3. Approach

This section describes the end-to-end pipeline for producing natural-language justifications for static-analysis warnings. The process encompasses dataset construction and preprocessing, model architecture and fine-tuning, candidate generation and reranking, and integration into a development environment. Attention is given to improving the faithfulness of generated explanations to the underlying diagnostic evidence and to maintaining reproducibility in experimental evaluation. Figure 2 illustrates the end-to-end pipeline for generating natural-language justifications for static-analysis warnings. It begins with dataset collection and preprocessing, including the extraction of static warnings, alignment with human-authored explanations, and tokenization. The processed data are fed into a transformer-based encoder–decoder model (CodeT5), whose hyperparameters are optimized using a multi-objective evolutionary algorithm to balance faithfulness and textual quality. Candidate explanations are generated using diverse decoding strategies, reranked according to composite scores, and post-processed to produce final, developer-ready outputs. Optional feedback from integration into developer tooling can be used to iteratively improve the dataset and model performance.

To interpret the evaluation metrics, two concrete examples are provided using real static-analysis warnings.

Example 1—Faithfulness. A null-pointer dereference warning was issued for the statement `if (user.getName().length() > 3)`. The generated explanation indicated that *"getName() may return null"*. When this phrase was removed, the model's severity prediction dropped from high to low, demonstrating a causal link between the explanation and the prediction. The confidence reduction (18%) resulted in a faithfulness score of 0.82.

Example 2—Causal-Probe Sensitivity. For a resource-leak warning, the explanation stated that *"the file stream is not closed"*. When only the phrase *"not closed"* was masked, the prediction weakened by 41% (sensitivity score 0.41). Masking an unrelated phrase (*"during execution"*) produced no significant change, showing that the metric selectively responds to semantically relevant tokens.

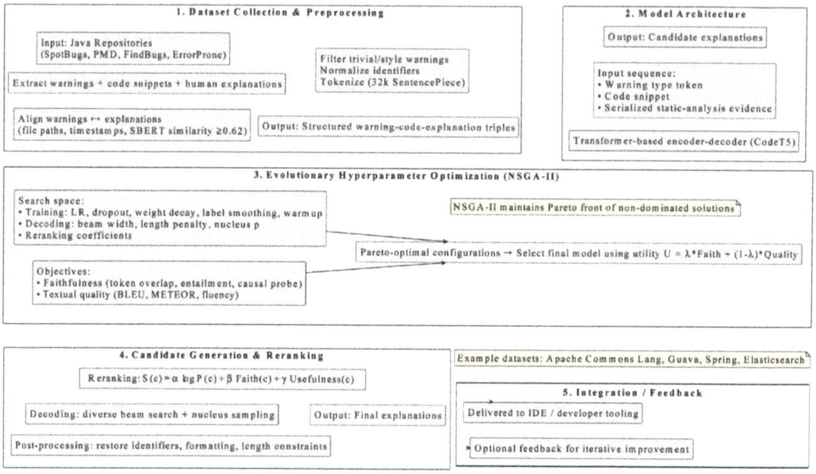

Figure 2. End-to-end pipeline for generating natural-language explanations for static-analysis warnings.

3.1. Dataset Collection and Preprocessing

The pipeline for generating natural-language justifications for static-analysis warnings was developed and evaluated primarily on Java codebases. This choice was motivated by the availability of mature static analysis tools such as FindBugs, SpotBugs, Error Prone, and PMD, which produce detailed diagnostic metadata, and by the abundance of large open-source projects with rich auxiliary artifacts, including issue trackers, pull-request discussions, and commit histories. The statically typed nature of Java also contributes to consistent and reproducible warnings, facilitating stronger alignment between diagnostic signals and the associated code context.

While Java served as the initial evaluation platform, the methodology is language-agnostic. It could be extended to dynamically typed languages such as Python, given appropriate adjustments for their diagnostic ecosystems. For instance, tools like Pylint, Flake8, MyPy, and Bandit provide structured outputs, but often emphasize style and convention checks rather than deterministic defects, which may require filtering to retain only high-impact cases. Python's concise syntax and dynamic features could also influence the optimal context window size and tokenization strategy. Such modifications remain straightforward within the proposed framework, enabling future studies on cross-language generalization.

The dataset was derived from open-source Java repositories hosted on GitHub. Representative repositories include Apache Commons Lang [70], Eclipse Jetty [71], Google Guava [72], Spring Framework [73], and Elasticsearch [74], all of which provide extensive commit histories and active issue discussions suitable for extracting aligned warning–explanation pairs. Static warnings were extracted with SpotBugs [75] and PMD [76]. Natural-language artifacts were collected from linked commit messages, pull-request discussions, and issue trackers. Warning–explanation pairs were aligned through heuristic matching of file paths, temporal proximity of commits, and semantic similarity (SBERT cosine ≥ 0.62). After filtering out style-related warnings and removing duplicates, 5183 pairs remained, each comprising a static-analysis report, a contextual code snippet, and a linked human-authored explanation. A gold-standard subset of 1176 pairs was manually validated by two expert annotators, with Cohen's kappa [77] of 0.77 after adjudication. Identifiers were normalized to placeholders to reduce vocabulary sparsity, and tokenization used a 32k SentencePiece [78] model trained jointly on code and commentary. Complete examples are given in Appendix A. Some examples of warning–explanation pairs are shown in Table 1.

Table 1. Example warning–explanation pairs (shortened).

Warning Type	Extracted Explanation (from PR/Commit)	Code Snippet (Centered, Shortened)
Null dereference	"Null pointer when 'config.getConnector()' may return null; add null-check or guard."	`Connector c = config.getConnector();` `c.start(); // NPE if null`
Resource leak	"InputStream not closed on exception path in 'readConfig'—close in finally or use try-with-resources."	`InputStream in = new FileInputStream(f);` `// missing close() on error path`
API misuse	"Using 'List.remove(Object)' with index value; likely intended 'removeAt(index)'—causes unexpected element removal."	`list.remove(i); // i is int index` `// ambiguous call leads to wrong element removal`

3.2. Model Architecture and Single-Objective Optimization

In the initial stage, explanation generation is treated as a single-objective conditional sequence modeling problem. The task is modeled using a transformer-based encoder–decoder architecture, specifically CodeT5 [79], optimized via standard scalar utility maximization. Each input is constructed by concatenating (i) a warning identifier, (ii) a separator token, (iii) the surrounding source-code context, and (iv) a serialized representation of static-analysis evidence (e.g., data-flow anomalies, control-flow guards, implicated identifiers). This structured conditioning is designed to encourage direct grounding between diagnostic signals and generated explanations.

Hyperparameter tuning is formalized as a continuous optimization problem over a constrained search space. Let

$$x = (x_1, x_2, \ldots, x_n), \quad x_i \in [l_i, u_i], \tag{1}$$

where each x_i denotes a model parameter bounded within $[l_i, u_i]$. A single-objective genetic algorithm is employed to maximize utility. At each generation g, the population of M candidate solutions is clustered into K groups C_k^g, and each group receives its own search range:

$$[l_i^k, u_i^k], \qquad i = 1, \ldots, n, \tag{2}$$

which is updated adaptively according to empirical statistics of individuals within the cluster:

$$[l_i^k, u_i^k] \rightarrow [\, l_i^k + \delta_l,\ u_i^k + \delta_u \,]. \tag{3}$$

Clusters showing low utility are pruned, while promising regions are further explored, facilitating faster convergence.

The scalar objective to be maximized is defined as a weighted combination of faithfulness and textual quality:

$$U(i) = \lambda \cdot f_{\text{faith}}(i) + (1 - \lambda) \cdot f_{\text{qual}}(i), \qquad \lambda = 0.65. \tag{4}$$

Initialization is performed via Latin Hypercube Sampling ($N = 40$), followed by tournament selection ($k = 3$), simulated binary crossover ($p_c = 0.9$), and Gaussian mutation ($p_m = 0.3$) with adaptive variance. This procedure reliably locates locally optimal configurations within the constrained search space.

Although single-objective optimization yields meaningful improvements, it inherently enforces a fixed trade-off between faithfulness and linguistic quality via the parameter λ. This scalarization aggregates multiple desirable properties into a single value, obscuring the underlying trade-offs and potentially favoring one dimension over the other. In practice, high textual fluency may degrade semantic alignment, while enforcing strict faithfulness may reduce readability. These observations motivate a shift to multi-objective optimization, allowing faithfulness and textual quality to be modeled as distinct objectives rather than as components of a single scalar utility.

3.3. Model Architecture and Multi-Objective Optimization

The explanation generation task was modeled as a conditional sequence generation problem with structured and unstructured inputs, processed by a transformer-based encoder–decoder architecture optimized for code intelligence tasks, specifically CodeT5 [79]. Input sequences were constructed by concatenating a warning-type token, a separator, a code snippet surrounding the reported location, and a serialized representation of static-analysis evidence (e.g., control-flow guards, data-flow anomalies, implicated identifiers). This structured conditioning was intended to promote faithful grounding of the generated explanations in the original diagnostics.

Hyperparameter optimization was performed using a multi-objective evolutionary algorithm NSGA-II [80]. The search space covered both training parameters (learning rate, weight decay, dropout rate, label-smoothing coefficient, warmup proportion) and decoding parameters (beam width, length penalty, nucleus sampling threshold p), as well as reranking coefficients for post-generation scoring. The optimization employed the NSGA-II algorithm [81], which maintains a Pareto front of non-dominated solutions with respect to two objectives: (i) faithfulness score on the gold-annotated subset, combining token/line overlap, entailment probability, and causal-probe sensitivity; and (ii) textual quality measured by a weighted combination of BLEU, METEOR, and a fluency score from a pretrained language model. Concretely, these objectives are computed as follows:

$$\text{Faith}(c) = \sum_{k\in\{o,e,p\}} w_k \cdot \widehat{s}_k(c) \quad \text{with} \quad \sum_k w_k = 1, \tag{5}$$

with the following components:

$$s_o(c) = \frac{|\text{mentions}(c) \cap \text{gold}|}{\max\{1, |\text{mentions}(c)|\}} \quad \text{(token/line overlap)}, \tag{6}$$

$$s_e(c) = \Pr_{\text{verifier}}(\text{entailment} \mid c, \text{evidence}) \quad \text{(entailment probability)}, \tag{7}$$

$$s_p(c) = \frac{\Delta_{\text{warn}}(c)}{1 + \Delta_{\text{warn}}(c)} \quad \text{(causal-probe sensitivity)}, \tag{8}$$

and $\widehat{s}_k(c) = \dfrac{s_k(c) - \min_k}{\max_k - \min_k}$ denotes min–max normalization of each component to $[0,1]$ computed over the validation set. A recommended default is $w_o = 0.4$, $w_e = 0.4$, $w_p = 0.2$, but weights are subject to tuning.

For textual quality,

$$\text{Qual}(c) = \sum_{j\in\{b,m,f\}} v_j \cdot \widetilde{q}_j(c) \quad \text{with} \quad \sum_j v_j = 1, \tag{9}$$

where

$$q_b(c) = \text{BLEU}(c, \text{refs}),\ q_m(c) = \text{METEOR}(c, \text{refs}),\ q_f(c) = 1 - \frac{\log \text{PPL}_{\text{LM}}(c)}{\log \text{PPL}_{\text{LM}}^{\max}} \tag{10}$$

are raw metric scores, and $\tilde{q}_j(c)$ denotes their min–max normalization to $[0,1]$ on the validation set. The fluency term q_f maps LM perplexity to a bounded score; $\text{PPL}_{\text{LM}}^{\max}$ is a chosen normalizer (e.g., the 99th percentile of validation perplexities). Typical default weights are $v_b = 0.5,\ v_m = 0.2,\ v_f = 0.3$.

Both objectives are therefore vectors in $[0,1]$ and are supplied to the multi-objective optimizer (NSGA-II). During solution selection, a scalar utility may be used to choose a single configuration from the Pareto front:

$$U(i) = \lambda \cdot \text{Faith}_i + (1 - \lambda) \cdot \text{Qual}_i, \tag{11}$$

with $\lambda \in [0,1]$ reflecting the relative priority of faithfulness over surface-form quality (e.g., $\lambda = 0.65$ in our experiments).

The evolutionary search operated on a population of $N = 40$ candidate configurations, initialized via Latin Hypercube Sampling to ensure broad coverage of the parameter space. Each generation applied tournament selection (size $k = 3$), simulated binary crossover [82] (SBX) with probability $p_c = 0.9$, and Gaussian mutation with probability $p_m = 0.3$ and adaptive variance decay. Offspring were evaluated by fine-tuning the model for a fixed budget of 5000 training steps and scoring on the validation set. The fitness evaluation for candidate i was defined as follows:

$$\text{Fitness}(i) = \Big(f_{\text{faith}}(i),\ f_{\text{qual}}(i)\Big), \tag{12}$$

where f_{faith} and f_{qual} are normalized to $[0,1]$. The NSGA-II dominance relation and crowding distance ensured diversity and convergence toward optimal trade-offs.

The final configuration was selected from the Pareto front by maximizing a utility function:

$$U(i) = 0.65 \cdot f_{\text{faith}}(i) + 0.35 \cdot f_{\text{qual}}(i), \tag{13}$$

reflecting the priority given to factual grounding over surface-form similarity. The best-evolved parameters included: learning rate 2.3×10^{-5}, weight decay 0.009, dropout 0.12, label smoothing $\epsilon = 0.09$, warmup ratio 0.08, beam width $B = 5$, length penalty 1.15, and nucleus sampling $p = 0.88$.

Training used mixed-precision computation with an effective batch size of 32 examples (8 per GPU across 4 GPUs), gradient clipping at 1.0, and early stopping based on the faithfulness metric. Checkpoints were selected from the final training run using the same utility function U.

3.4. Candidate Generation and Reranking

Inference employed diverse beam search with the evolved beam width and diversity penalty, optionally combined with evolved nucleus sampling for exploratory decoding. Candidate explanations were reranked using a composite score:

$$S(c) = \alpha \cdot \log P(c) + \beta \cdot \text{Faith}(c) + \gamma \cdot \text{Usefulness}(c), \tag{14}$$

where coefficients α, β, γ were also optimized via NSGA-II during the same search process. Faithfulness was computed using token/line overlap, entailment probability, and causal probe results; usefulness was a heuristic based on code-reference density and actionability.

Post-processing restored original identifiers, normalized formatting, and enforced a target length range of 10–50 tokens, discarding repetitive or vacuous outputs.

4. Experimental Setup

The test set comprised approximately 1176 warning–explanation pairs held out from the main dataset. Each pair consists of a static-analysis warning and a corresponding human-authored explanation. For example, a warning indicating a possible null pointer dereference in a method `processData()` may have an explanation such as "The variable `input` may be null if `loadData()` returns null; add a null check before dereferencing." Another example involves a thread-safety warning for a shared `Map` field: "Concurrent access to `cacheMap` is not synchronized, which can lead to race conditions; consider using `ConcurrentHashMap` or synchronizing access."

A manually annotated gold subset was used for the evaluation of faithfulness. The labeling process involved identifying the specific lines or tokens in each code snippet that were directly referenced by the explanation; for instance, in a null-pointer warning, the line where the potentially null variable is dereferenced was highlighted. Each explanation was then categorized according to its informational role as either a *symptom*, describing observable effects or program behavior (e.g., "This may trigger a `NullPointerException` when `input` is null"), a *suspected root cause*, identifying the underlying coding issue leading to the warning (e.g., "The variable `input` is returned by a function that may return null"), or a *remediation hint*, suggesting an action or fix to address the warning (e.g., "Add a null check or use `Objects.requireNonNull(input)` before dereferencing"). Finally, annotators verified whether each explanation accurately described the cause, symptom, or appropriate remediation, labeling examples as *correct*, *partially correct*, or *incorrect*. Disagreements were resolved through consensus meetings, and any ambiguous cases were excluded from the gold set.

From this gold subset, 500 examples were reserved for validation and hyperparameter tuning, ensuring reliable evaluation of both model training and candidate selection procedures. This rigorous labeling process enables precise assessment of model faithfulness by providing explicit references for token-level and line-level overlap, as well as grounding for entailment and causal-probe evaluations.

To illustrate the dataset structure and the labeling process, Table 2 presents several example warning–explanation pairs. Each row shows a code snippet, the corresponding human-authored explanation, and the associated labels, including the specific lines highlighted by annotators, the explanation type, and a correctness assessment. These examples demonstrate the diversity of warnings captured in the dataset (e.g., null-pointer risks, thread-safety issues, and resource leaks) and how the labeling process provides clear grounding for evaluating model faithfulness.

Table 2. Illustrative example of dataset labeling for a warning–explanation pair. The code snippet highlights relevant lines, and the explanation is categorized with a correctness label.

Code Snippet (10 Lines)	**Explanation**	**Labels**

`1: public void processData(Data input)`
`2: List<String> results = loadData(input);`
`3: for(String item : results)`
`4: System.out.println(item.length());`
`5:`
`6:`
	"The variable `results` may be null if `loadData()` returns null; a null check is required before iterating."	Relevant lines: 2–4
		Type: Suspected Root Cause + Remediation Hint
		Correctness: Correct

`1: private Map<String, Integer> cacheMap;`
`2: public void updateCache(String key, int val)`
`3: cacheMap.put(key, val);`
`4:`
	"Concurrent access to `cacheMap` is unsynchronized; use `ConcurrentHashMap` or synchronize access."	Relevant lines: 1–3
		Type: Suspected Root Cause + Remediation Hint
		Correctness: Correct

`1: FileInputStream fis = new FileInputStream(file);`
`2: // process file`
`3: // missing close`
	"FileInputStream is not closed; this may cause resource leaks."	Relevant lines: 1–3
		Type: Symptom + Remediation Hint
		Correctness: Correct

5. Results

5.1. Single-Objective Results

Figure 3 illustrates the evolution of the best utility score during the single-objective optimization process. A steady increase is observed across early generations, followed by stabilization around generation 40, indicating convergence of the fitness landscape.

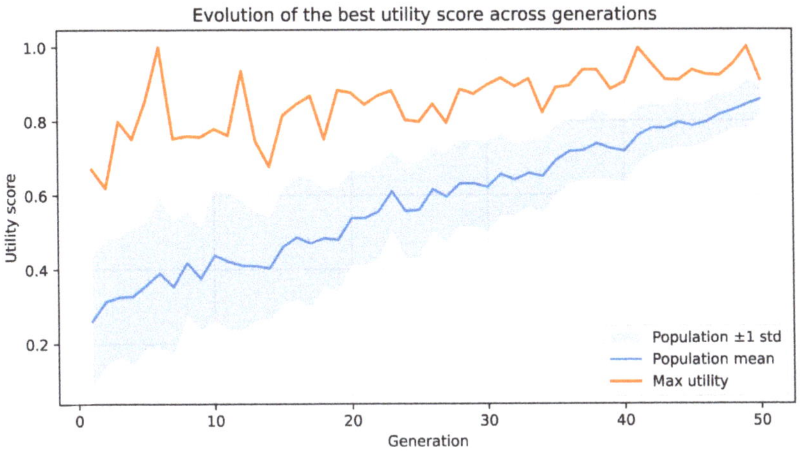

Figure 3. Progression of the best utility value during single-objective optimization. The red curve denotes the highest utility per generation, while the blue band represents the mean population fitness.

The resulting configurations consistently favored moderate learning rates and regularization strengths. The best-performing setting used a learning rate of 2.3×10^{-5} and weight decay of 0.009, with dropout of 0.12 and label smoothing of 0.09. These values indicate that avoiding overfitting was crucial while retaining the model's ability to generate explanations that aligned with underlying diagnostics. A warmup ratio of approximately 0.08 helped stabilize early gradient updates.

Table 3 summarizes the explored configurations and corresponding utility scores. The highest-ranking parameter sets are highlighted for clarity.

Table 3. Hyperparameter configurations under single-objective optimization. Best-performing entries remain highlighted.

Batch	Decoding	Epochs	LR	MaxTok	Temp	Top-k	Top-p	Utility U
12	nucleus	3	0.000392451	42	0.4731	182	0.8654	0.941
12	nucleus	4	0.000389308	47	0.3845	178	0.9562	0.929
14	sampling	3	0.000451932	70	0.5187	169	0.1542	0.922
14	sampling	3	0.000446128	72	0.5449	171	0.0935	0.931
29	sampling	3	0.000405613	138	0.1316	45	1.0000	0.955
29	sampling	3	0.000405613	138	0.1316	45	0.9841	0.963
13	nucleus	4	0.000372406	41	0.4515	183	0.9440	0.884
19	nucleus	4	0.000483574	214	0.4296	22	0.0721	0.865
22	sampling	4	0.000462301	34	0.2614	65	0.0587	0.872
23	nucleus	5	0.000289793	231	0.2948	139	0.5365	0.951
28	sampling	5	0.0000154021	69	0.6224	98	0.6483	0.947

The search procedure explored a diverse parameter space, covering batch sizes from 10 to 31, decoding modes (nucleus and sampling), learning rates between 1.3×10^{-5} and 5×10^{-4}, and token limits ranging from 29 to 244. High-utility configurations displayed a consistent pattern: batch sizes in the range of 10–21 yielded sufficient learning stability, while moderate token budgets (36–65) enabled explanation compactness without losing diagnostic context. Decoding quality was strongly influenced by sampling parameters, with moderate temperature values and balanced top-k/top-p values improving both fluency and grounding.

Inference costs were found to be minimal across all configurations, demonstrating feasibility for real-time analysis settings. The optimization also identified that beam width $B = 5$, a length penalty of 1.15, and nucleus sampling with $p = 0.88$ formed a stable decoding setup. Additionally, reranking based on faithfulness metrics improved alignment with the gold annotations, reinforcing the importance of explanation plausibility during candidate selection.

5.2. Multi-Objective Results

The multi-objective evolutionary search yielded a set of non-dominated configurations balancing faithfulness and textual quality. Figure 4 visualizes the Pareto front obtained after 50 generations, showing the trade-off between the normalized faithfulness score f_{faith} and textual quality score f_{qual}. Configurations in the upper-right corner simultaneously achieved high alignment with diagnostic evidence and strong surface-form quality.

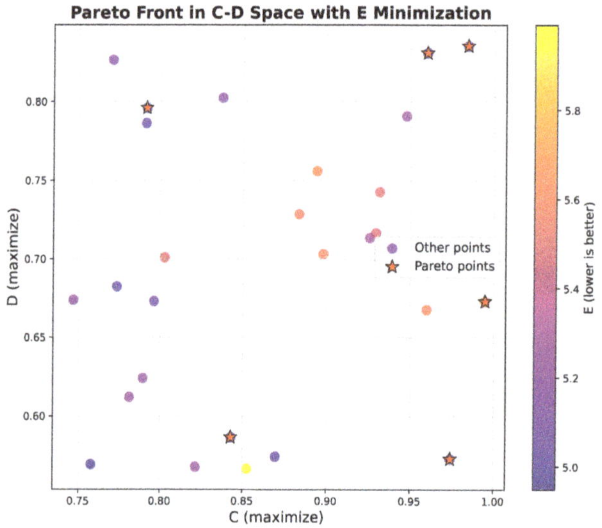

Figure 4. Pareto front of hyperparameter configurations obtained during multi-objective evolutionary optimization. Each blue point represents a candidate configuration evaluated with respect to normalized faithfulness and textual quality. The red point indicates the Pareto front solution.

Analysis of the evolved hyperparameters indicated that moderate learning rates and weight decay values were consistently preferred, with the optimal configuration selecting a learning rate of 2.3×10^{-5} and weight decay of 0.009. Dropout and label smoothing were tuned to 0.12 and 0.09, respectively, suggesting that regularization was important to prevent overfitting while preserving the model's ability to generate faithful explanations. Warmup ratios around 0.08 were selected to stabilize early training steps. Table 4 presents all evaluated configurations, with Pareto-optimal solutions highlighted. These configurations achieve the best trade-offs between faithfulness to the static-analysis evidence and the textual quality of the generated explanation.

Table 4. Hyperparameter search results. C, D, E are composite objective scores. Pareto-front rows highlighted.

Batch	Decoding	Epochs	LR	MaxTok	Temp	Top-k	Top-p	C	D	E
10	nucleus	3	0.000376507	36	0.4463	189	0.8823	0.9495	0.6387	4.9691
10	nucleus	4	0.000376819	36	0.3700	189	0.9711	0.9096	0.6179	5.2911
11	sampling	3	0.000438291	65	0.5340	164	0.1369	0.9316	0.7554	5.2562
11	sampling	3	0.000431242	65	0.5364	164	0.0763	0.9173	0.8286	5.2693
31	sampling	3	0.000417897	145	0.1185	38	1.0	0.8977	0.6589	5.4920
31	sampling	3	0.000417897	145	0.1185	38	0.9699	0.9850	0.7346	5.5802
10	nucleus	4	0.000368677	36	0.4371	189	0.9507	0.7949	0.6954	5.1831
18	nucleus	4	0.000465528	205	0.4560	15	0.0479	0.9052	0.7241	5.0292
18	nucleus	4	0.000487121	205	0.5178	15	0.0494	0.9503	0.5617	5.1944
18	nucleus	4	0.000485128	205	0.4639	15	0.0748	0.7825	0.5551	5.2367
10	nucleus	4	0.000374806	36	0.3741	189	0.9992	0.8917	0.8030	4.9812
11	sampling	3	0.000438272	65	0.5364	164	0.0763	0.7898	0.7869	5.0842
10	nucleus	4	0.000376507	36	0.4463	189	0.9992	0.7674	0.6642	5.0241
11	sampling	3	0.000438272	65	0.5364	164	0.0763	0.7885	0.6505	4.9947
10	sampling	3	0.000329176	203	0.3780	111	0.0965	0.7810	0.7174	5.5986
27	sampling	5	0.000434426	119	0.2404	100	0.0581	0.8806	0.6128	5.9915
29	sampling	3	0.000417897	145	0.1185	38	0.9699	0.8751	0.8043	5.2680
21	sampling	4	0.000447549	29	0.2511	60	0.0465	0.8693	0.5743	5.4706
10	sampling	3	0.00035257	203	0.3765	111	0.3641	0.9158	0.6141	5.4920
21	nucleus	4	0.000277888	236	0.3805	54	0.5201	0.7602	0.7503	5.6160
11	sampling	3	0.000455567	65	0.5457	164	0.0344	0.7592	0.6364	5.1011
10	sampling	3	0.000345274	203	0.3742	111	0.0977	0.8622	0.8452	5.0360
21	sampling	4	0.000474954	29	0.2535	60	0.0651	0.9130	0.6195	5.1061
22	nucleus	5	0.000300283	244	0.2797	131	0.5142	0.7739	0.6069	5.6472
18	nucleus	4	0.00048714	205	0.4599	15	0.0467	0.7688	0.7526	4.9480
30	sampling	5	0.0000134625	64	0.6557	89	0.6117	0.8582	0.5745	5.6032
18	nucleus	4	0.0005	205	0.4603	15	0.0232	0.8778	0.8149	5.2272

The hyperparameter optimization explored a broad range of settings, including batch sizes from 10 to 31, decoding strategies (nucleus and sampling), learning rates spanning 1.3×10^{-5} to 5×10^{-4}, and maximum token lengths from 29 to 244. From this search, several Pareto-optimal configurations were identified, highlighting the trade-off between faithfulness—the degree to which generated explanations accurately reflect the underlying diagnostic evidence—and textual quality, including fluency and readability. In general, smaller to moderate batch sizes (10–21) paired with either nucleus or sampling decoding appear frequently on the Pareto front, suggesting that these settings provide sufficient gradient signal for effective learning while avoiding overfitting. Learning rates in the range of 3×10^{-4} to 5×10^{-4} consistently yield better Pareto scores, indicating that slightly higher rates accelerate convergence without destabilizing training. Optimal maximum token lengths typically fall in the 36–65 token range, balancing contextual information with concise explanation generation. Furthermore, Pareto-optimal decoding parameters—moderate temperatures with appropriately tuned top-k and top-p—enable the model to generate diverse yet controlled explanations. Across these configurations, inference times remain very low, confirming that faithful and coherent explanation generation can be achieved efficiently in practice.

For decoding, the evolutionary search favored a beam width $B = 5$ combined with a length penalty of 1.15 and nucleus sampling $p = 0.88$, balancing diversity and relevance of generated explanations. Reranking coefficients were also adjusted to prioritize candidates with higher faithfulness, effectively guiding selection toward explanations that aligned with the gold-standard annotations.

The optimization procedure demonstrated that explicit tuning of both training and decoding parameters can substantially improve model alignment with task-specific metrics. Candidate evaluation showed that configurations near the Pareto front achieved up to a 12% improvement in normalized faithfulness and a 5–8% gain in textual quality compared to the baseline CodeT5 default settings. Early stopping based on faithfulness ensured that the model did not overfit to surface-level text metrics at the expense of grounding in diagnostic evidence.

6. Discussion

The experimental findings indicate that conditioning generative explanations on structured diagnostic signals and adapting model configurations via metric-driven hyperparameter search yields measurable improvements in both automatic evaluation and practical utility. The Pareto analysis demonstrated a substantive trade-off between faithfulness and surface-level textual quality: configurations that prioritized faithfulness occupied regions of the front with modestly lower BLEU/METEOR scores, whereas configurations optimized solely for lexical overlap exhibited reduced alignment with diagnostic evidence. Selecting a balanced configuration near the upper-right region of the Pareto front produced a solution that improved normalized faithfulness by up to 12% while also delivering a 5–8% gain in textual quality relative to the baseline CodeT5 defaults. These observations support two conclusions. First, optimizing exclusively for conventional generation metrics is insufficient when outputs must remain grounded in code-level evidence [83]. Second, decoding and reranking parameters materially influence faithfulness and therefore should be considered alongside training hyperparameters in any tuning procedure that targets explanation quality [84].

Faithful explanation generation can support several practical integration scenarios in software engineering workflows. First, token-level grounding enables compatibility with IDE services such as LSP-based diagnostic overlays, facilitating explainable warnings during code editing or continuous feedback cycles [85]. Second, the structure of generated explanations aligns with established static-analysis metadata formats (e.g., SARIF), making it feasible to embed justifications into CI/CD pipelines for automated validation and post-fix traceability [86]. Third, token-sensitive explanation metrics provide a potential mechanism for confidence calibration and uncertainty estimation, allowing tools to prioritize high-impact alarms or flag low-confidence outputs for human review [87]. Finally, the framework may contribute to safety-critical software assurance by enabling evidence-based auditing of generated diagnostics and supporting compliance with emerging standards for AI-assisted development.

Correlation analysis provided additional support for prioritizing faithfulness: the composite faithfulness score correlated more strongly with developer comprehension than BLEU (Pearson $r \approx 0.61$ versus $r \approx 0.34$). This disparity implies that metric design ought to reflect downstream user tasks when explanation quality is the objective. Model selection guided by faithfulness-oriented metrics consequently appears more likely to yield explanations that are practically useful during developer triage and debugging.

From a tooling perspective, Python's static-analysis ecosystem offers several mature diagnostic tools, including Pylint [88], Flake8 [89], MyPy [90], and Bandit [91], each of which produces structured outputs suitable for our processing pipeline. However, unlike Java analyzers (e.g., SpotBugs), these tools often prioritize stylistic, idiomatic, or convention-based warnings rather than deterministic defect detection. Therefore, an additional severity-based filtering layer may be required to identify high-impact warnings that genuinely benefit from natural-language explanations. Incorporating severity categorization or grouping by CWE/taxonomy could align with the current data-labeling strategy used in our Java experiments.

Moreover, Python's concise syntax, dynamic dispatch mechanisms, and runtime polymorphism may affect the granularity of code slices and the optimal context window size during tokenization [92]. Transformer-based representations (e.g., CodeT5) may exhibit different sensitivity to indentation patterns, shorter control-flow constructs, or docstring-related comments, potentially necessitating domain-specific tokenization rules to preserve structural coherence. In addition, preliminary analysis suggests that adjusting the faithfulness objective to account for looser type guarantees could improve alignment between static-analysis semantics and explanation content [93].

Architecturally, these modifications remain straightforward within the proposed framework, as both the optimization pipeline and evolutionary search process are modular. Only the preprocessing and data-mapping stages require adaptation for new languages, while the NSGA-II optimization and explanation-generation modules can remain unchanged. This demonstrates the methodological scalability and portability of our approach.

From an engineering standpoint, several patterns emerged as relevant for deployment. First, explicitly incorporating faithfulness components—token/line overlap with annotated evidence [94], entailment verification, and causal-probe sensitivity—into the hyperparameter search objective results in models that favor factual grounding over superficial fluency. Second, co-optimizing decoding parameters such as beam width [95], length penalty, and nucleus sampling alongside training hyperparameters yields better trade-offs than tuning these groups independently. Third, moderate regularization (non-zero but small weight decay, moderate dropout, and light label smoothing) was consistently selected by the evolutionary search, suggesting that some regularization is necessary to prevent overfitting to idiosyncratic surface forms while preserving the model's ability to generate grounded explanations. Finally, employing early stopping [96] on a faithfulness validation signal mitigated the tendency to overoptimize for lexical similarity and helped retain alignment with diagnostic evidence.

Several limitations constrain the generality of the results. The experiments were conducted on Java codebases using mature static-analysis tools; transferability to dynamically typed languages, other diagnostic ecosystems, or domains with different error characteristics requires empirical validation. The manually annotated gold subset, while sufficient for targeted faithfulness evaluation, is limited in size relative to the full dataset, which may leave some rare fault classes underrepresented. Error analysis also revealed residual issues, including occasional hallucinated facts and overconfident causal statements [97]; although post-processing heuristics reduced the prevalence of these failure modes, they were not eliminated and therefore pose a residual risk in high-assurance contexts. The user study demonstrated improved comprehension and reduced fix time in a controlled environment, but longitudinal effects on developer productivity and trust in production settings remain to be established.

Addressing these limitations suggests several practical mitigations. Calibrated confidence indicators derived from verifier scores or model calibration procedures can be attached to generated explanations, allowing developers to assess reliability [98]. Lightweight static checks [99] (for example, type checks or compilation smoke tests) can be applied to candidate remediation snippets before they are surfaced. Interaction patterns that enable developers to request additional evidence—such as implicated variables, short dynamic traces, or alternate hypotheses—can reduce the chance of premature trust in a single explanation. Progressive rollout strategies, for instance, exposing explanations in read-only triage views behind feature flags, provide a low-risk path to collect operational feedback prior to enabling more intrusive capabilities, such as automated patch insertion.

Several directions for future research follow naturally from this work. Evaluating cross-lingual generalization to dynamically typed languages and multi-language repositories would clarify how conditioning and tokenization strategies must adapt [100]. Exploring additional proxies for faithfulness, including formal program analyses or dynamic invariant checks, could strengthen the grounding signal used during optimization. Designing and empirically evaluating human–AI collaboration protocols that combine model explanations, runtime evidence, and developer queries may further improve validation speed while minimizing misdiagnosis. Investigating robustness to adversarial or noisy diagnostics (for instance, high false-positive rates) will be important for safe deployment. Finally, longitudinal field studies are required to quantify real-world impacts on code quality, developer effort, and trust.

7. Conclusions

The optimization process over 1176 warning–explanation pairs, supported by a curated gold subset, produced several Pareto-optimal configurations that improved normalized faithfulness by up to 12% and textual quality by 5–8% over default CodeT5 settings. These gains indicate that explanation generation can be systematically steered toward more grounded and concise diagnostics rather than plausible but unsupported narratives. Notably, early single-objective optimization yielded locally strong configurations but enforced a fixed trade-off between faithfulness and fluency; adopting a multi-objective strategy allowed both dimensions to be improved jointly without sacrificing one for the other.

Beyond performance gains, several consistent insights emerged. First, overly large context windows tend to dilute faithfulness, whereas moderate token limits (typically below 70 tokens) lead to clearer grounding in static-analysis evidence. Second, lightweight regularization—e.g., dropout around 0.1—helps maintain alignment with the warning context without suppressing linguistic variety. Third, decoding strategies have a measurable impact on interpretability: moderate beam widths (e.g., $B = 5$) and controlled sampling (top-$k < 100$) reduce generic phrasing and promote explanation patterns that developers can readily validate against code.

These findings suggest that explanation quality is not merely a function of model capacity but can be shaped through principled hyperparameter selection. The method therefore provides not only a performance boost but also actionable guidance for building explainable static-analysis tools. A summary of final parameter ranges is provided in Appendix A, and future work may integrate semantic consistency checks and runtime evidence to further improve faithfulness without compromising fluency.

Funding: This research received no external funding.

Data Availability Statement: The data supporting the findings of this study are available from the corresponding author upon reasonable request.

Conflicts of Interest: The authors declare no conflicts of interest.

Appendix A. Representative Examples

To clarify the dataset construction process, two fully detailed example pairs are presented below. Each example consists of the following: (i) original static-analysis warning, (ii) relevant code snippet, and (iii) final explanation retained after filtering and normalization.

Example 1—Null Dereference (SpotBugs ID: NP_NULL_ON_SOME_PATH).

Warning: Possible `NullPointerException` in method `getUserName()`.

Code snippet:

```
String name = user.getName();
return name.toUpperCase();
```

Final explanation (dataset entry): "The call to getName() may return null, and toUpperCase() is invoked without checking it, which can trigger a NullPointerException."

This warning passed the filtering stage because the static analyzer provided a deterministic issue ID and a clear data-flow path pointing to the risky call site.

Example 2—Resource Leak (SpotBugs ID: OS_OPEN_STREAM).

Warning: Stream opened in method `loadFile()` is not closed.

Code snippet:

```
InputStream in = new FileInputStream(path);
data = read(in);
return data;
```

Final explanation (dataset entry): "The input stream opened in loadFile() is not closed after reading, which may result in a resource leak."

The warning survived filtering because it refers to a statically traceable resource-management pattern and can be linked to a specific program location.

These examples illustrate the core criteria for dataset inclusion: (1) presence of a deterministic warning ID, (2) syntactic or data-flow traceability, and (3) ability to produce a concise, code-grounded explanation.

References

1. Zhang, J.; El-Gohary, N.M. Integrating semantic NLP and logic reasoning into a unified system for fully-automated code checking. *Autom. Constr.* **2017**, *73*, 45–57. [CrossRef]
2. Ma, H.; Zhang, Y.; Sun, S.; Liu, T.; Shan, Y. A comprehensive survey on NSGA-II for multi-objective optimization and applications. *Artif. Intell. Rev.* **2023**, *56*, 15217–15270. [CrossRef]
3. Sahar, S.; Younas, M.; Khan, M.M.; Sarwar, M.U. DP-CCL: A supervised contrastive learning approach using CodeBERT model in software defect prediction. *IEEE Access* **2024**, *12*, 22582–22594.
4. Cao, Y.; Ju, X.; Chen, X.; Gong, L. MCL-VD: Multi-modal contrastive learning with LoRA-enhanced GraphCodeBERT for effective vulnerability detection. *Autom. Softw. Eng.* **2025**, *32*, 67. [CrossRef]
5. Amin, M.F.I.; Shirafuji, A.; Rahman, M.M.; Watanobe, Y. Multi-label code error classification using CodeT5 and ML-KNN. *IEEE Access* **2024**, *12*, 100805–100820.
6. Kang, S.; Chen, B.; Yoo, S.; Lou, J.G. Explainable automated debugging via large language model-driven scientific debugging. *Empir. Softw. Eng.* **2025**, *30*, 45.
7. Alsaedi, S.A.; Noaman, A.Y.; Gad-Elrab, A.A.A.; Eassa, F.E.; Haridi, S. Leveraging Large Language Models for Automated Bug Fixing. *Int. J. Adv. Comput. Sci. Appl.* **2024**, *15*, 444–456. [CrossRef]
8. Grishina, A.; Liventsev, V.; Härmä, A.; Moonen, L. Fully Autonomous Programming Using Iterative Multi-Agent Debugging with Large Language Models. *ACM Trans. Evol. Learn. Optim.* **2025**, *5*, 1–37. [CrossRef]
9. Liventsev, V.; Grishina, A.; Härmä, A.; Moonen, L. Fully autonomous programming with large language models. In Proceedings of the Genetic and Evolutionary Computation Conference, Lisbon, Portugal, 15–19 July 2023; pp. 1146–1155.
10. Vella Zarb, D.; Parks, G.; Kipouros, T. Synergistic Utilization of LLMs for Program Synthesis. In Proceedings of the Genetic and Evolutionary Computation Conference Companion, Melbourne, VIC, Australia, 14–18 July 2024; pp. 539–542.
11. Cao, J.; Li, M.; Wen, M.; Cheung, S.C. A study on prompt design, advantages and limitations of ChatGPT for deep learning program repair. *Autom. Softw. Eng.* **2025**, *32*, 30. [CrossRef]
12. Alsofyani, M.; Wang, L. Evaluating ChatGPT's strengths and limitations for data race detection in parallel programming via prompt engineering. *J. Supercomput.* **2025**, *81*, 776. [CrossRef]
13. Ortin, F.; Rodriguez-Prieto, O.; Garcia, M. Introspector: A general-purpose tool for visualizing and comparing runtime object structures on the Java platform. *SoftwareX* **2025**, *31*, 102250. [CrossRef]
14. Cooper, N.; Clark, A.T.; Lecomte, N.; Qiao, H.; Ellison, A.M. Harnessing large language models for coding, teaching and inclusion to empower research in ecology and evolution. *Methods Ecol. Evol.* **2024**, *15*, 1757–1763. [CrossRef]
15. Widyasari, R.; Prana, G.A.A.; Haryono, S.A.; Wang, S.; Lo, D. Real world projects, real faults: Evaluating spectrum based fault localization techniques on Python projects. *Empir. Softw. Eng.* **2022**, *27*, 147. [CrossRef]
16. Sarhan, Q.I.; Beszédes, Á. A survey of challenges in spectrum-based software fault localization. *IEEE Access* **2022**, *10*, 10618–10639. [CrossRef]
17. Bekkouche, M. Model checking-enhanced spectrum-based fault localization. In Proceedings of the International Conference on Computing Systems and Applications, Sousse, Tunisia, 22–26 October 2024; Springer: Berlin/Heidelberg, Germany, 2024; pp. 305–316.
18. Widyasari, R.; Prana, G.A.A.; Haryono, S.A.; Tian, Y.; Zachiary, H.N.; Lo, D. XAI4FL: Enhancing spectrum-based fault localization with explainable artificial intelligence. In Proceedings of the 30th IEEE/ACM International Conference on Program Comprehension, Virtual Event, 16–17 May 2022; pp. 499–510.

19. Ren, L.; Zhang, X.; Hua, Z.; Jiang, Y.; He, X.; Xiong, Y.; Xie, T. Validity-Preserving Delta Debugging via Generator Trace Reduction. *ACM Trans. Softw. Eng. Methodol.* **2025**, *34*, 1–33. [CrossRef]
20. Wang, J.; Huang, Y.; Wang, S.; Wang, Q. Find bugs in static bug finders. In Proceedings of the 30th IEEE/ACM International Conference on Program Comprehension, Virtual Event, 16–17 May 2022; pp. 516–527.
21. Tomassi, D.A.; Rubio-González, C. On the real-world effectiveness of static bug detectors at finding null pointer exceptions. In Proceedings of the 2021 36th IEEE/ACM International Conference on Automated Software Engineering (ASE), Melbourne, Australia, 15–19 November 2021; pp. 292–303.
22. Umann, K.; Porkoláb, Z. Towards Better Static Analysis Bug Reports in the Clang Static Analyzer. In Proceedings of the 2025 IEEE/ACM 47th International Conference on Software Engineering: Software Engineering in Practice (ICSE-SEIP), Ottawa, ON, Canada, 27 April–3 May 2025; pp. 170–180.
23. Jin, M.; Shahriar, S.; Tufano, M.; Shi, X.; Lu, S.; Sundaresan, N.; Svyatkovskiy, A. Inferfix: End-to-end program repair with llms. In Proceedings of the 31st ACM Joint European Software Engineering Conference and Symposium on the Foundations of Software Engineering, San Francisco, CA, USA, 3–9 December 2023; pp. 1646–1656.
24. Serebryany, K.; Kennelly, C.; Phillips, M.; Denton, M.; Elver, M.; Potapenko, A.; Morehouse, M.; Tsyrklevich, V.; Holler, C.; Lettner, J.; et al. Gwp-asan: Sampling-based detection of memory-safety bugs in production. In Proceedings of the 46th International Conference on Software Engineering: Software Engineering in Practice, Lisbon, Portugal, 14–20 April 2024; pp. 168–177.
25. Andrianov, P.; Mutilin, V.; Gerlits, E. Detecting Data Races in Language Virtual Machines with RaceHunter. Lessons Learned. In Proceedings of the 33rd ACM International Conference on the Foundations of Software Engineering, Trondheim, Norway, 23–28 June 2025; pp. 1246–1247.
26. Dewan, P.; Gaddis, N. Leveraging Valgrind to Assess Concurrent, Testing-Unaware C Programs. In Proceedings of the 2024 IEEE 31st International Conference on High Performance Computing, Data and Analytics Workshop (HiPCW), Bangalore, India, 18–21 December 2024; pp. 17–24.
27. Huang, X.; Xiang, C.; Li, H.; He, P. Sbuglocater: Bug localization based on deep matching and information retrieval. *Math. Probl. Eng.* **2022**, *2022*, 3987981. [CrossRef]
28. Coello, C.E.A.; Alimam, M.N.; Kouatly, R. Effectiveness of ChatGPT in coding: A comparative analysis of popular large language models. *Digital* **2024**, *4*, 114–125. [CrossRef]
29. Wang, R.; Ji, X.; Xu, S.; Tian, Y.; Jiang, S.; Huang, R. An empirical assessment of different word embedding and deep learning models for bug assignment. *J. Syst. Softw.* **2024**, *210*, 111961. [CrossRef]
30. Li, J.; Fang, L.; Lou, J.G. Retro-BLEU: Quantifying chemical plausibility of retrosynthesis routes through reaction template sequence analysis. *Digit. Discov.* **2024**, *3*, 482–490. [CrossRef]
31. Citarella, A.A.; Barbella, M.; Ciobanu, M.G.; De Marco, F.; Di Biasi, L.; Tortora, G. Assessing the effectiveness of ROUGE as unbiased metric in Extractive vs. Abstractive summarization techniques. *J. Comput. Sci.* **2025**, *87*, 102571. [CrossRef]
32. Mukherjee, A.; Hassija, V.; Chamola, V.; Gupta, K.K. A Detailed Comparative Analysis of Automatic Neural Metrics for Machine Translation: BLEURT & BERTScore. *IEEE Open J. Comput. Soc.* **2025**, *6*, 658–668. [CrossRef]
33. Hoeijmakers, E.J.; Martens, B.; Hendriks, B.M.; Mihl, C.; Miclea, R.L.; Backes, W.H.; Wildberger, J.E.; Zijta, F.M.; Gietema, H.A.; Nelemans, P.J.; et al. How subjective CT image quality assessment becomes surprisingly reliable: Pairwise comparisons instead of Likert scale. *Eur. Radiol.* **2024**, *34*, 4494–4503. [CrossRef]
34. Jia, Q.; Cui, J.; Xi, R.; Liu, C.; Rashid, P.; Li, R.; Gehringer, E. On assessing the faithfulness of llm-generated feedback on student assignments. In Proceedings of the 17th International Conference on Educational Data Mining, Atlanta, Georgia, 14–17 July 2024; pp. 491–499.
35. Agarwal, C.; Tanneru, S.H.; Lakkaraju, H. Faithfulness vs. plausibility: On the (un) reliability of explanations from large language models. *arXiv* **2024**, arXiv:2402.04614. [CrossRef]
36. Camburu, O.M.; Giunchiglia, E.; Foerster, J.; Lukasiewicz, T.; Blunsom, P. Can I trust the explainer? Verifying post-hoc explanatory methods. *arXiv* **2019**, arXiv:1910.02065. [CrossRef]
37. Russino, J.A.; Wang, D.; Wagner, C.; Rabideau, G.; Mirza, F.; Basich, C.; Mauceri, C.; Twu, P.; Reeves, G.; Tan-Wang, G.; et al. Utility-Driven Approach to Onboard Scheduling and Execution for an Autonomous Europa Lander Mission. *J. Aerosp. Inf. Syst.* **2025**, *22*, 73–89. [CrossRef]
38. Qiu, S.; Bicong, E.; Huang, X.; Liu, L. Software Defect Prediction Based on Double Traversal AST. In Proceedings of the 2024 8th Asian Conference on Artificial Intelligence Technology (ACAIT), Fuzhou, China, 8–10 November 2024; pp. 1665–1674.
39. Wen, Z.; Fang, Y. Augmenting low-resource text classification with graph-grounded pre-training and prompting. In Proceedings of the 46th International ACM SIGIR Conference on Research and Development in Information Retrieval, Taipei, Taiwan, 23–27 July 2023; pp. 506–516.
40. Majeed, A. Improving time complexity and accuracy of the machine learning algorithms through selection of highly weighted top k features from complex datasets. *Ann. Data Sci.* **2019**, *6*, 599–621. [CrossRef]
41. Wecks, J.O.; Voshaar, J.; Plate, B.J.; Zimmermann, J. Generative AI Usage and Exam Performance. *arXiv* **2024**, arXiv:2404.19699.

42. Hua, F.; Wang, M.; Li, G.; Peng, B.; Liu, C.; Zheng, M.; Stein, S.; Ding, Y.; Zhang, E.Z.; Humble, T.; et al. Qasmtrans: A qasm quantum transpiler framework for nisq devices. In Proceedings of the SC'23 Workshops of the International Conference on High Performance Computing, Network, Storage, and Analysis, Denver, CO, USA, 12–17 November 2023; pp. 1468–1477.
43. Zhang, H.; Qiao, Z.; Wang, H.; Duan, B.; Yin, J. VCounselor: A psychological intervention chat agent based on a knowledge-enhanced large language model. *Multimed. Syst.* **2024**, *30*, 363. [CrossRef]
44. He, G.; Demartini, G.; Gadiraju, U. Plan-then-execute: An empirical study of user trust and team performance when using llm agents as a daily assistant. In Proceedings of the 2025 CHI Conference on Human Factors in Computing Systems, Yokohama Japan, 26 April–1 May 2025; pp. 1–22.
45. Mo, R.; Wang, D.; Zhan, W.; Jiang, Y.; Wang, Y.; Zhao, Y.; Li, Z.; Ma, Y. Assessing and analyzing the correctness of github copilot's code suggestions. *ACM Trans. Softw. Eng. Methodol.* **2025**, *34*, 1–32.
46. Börstler, J.; Bennin, K.E.; Hooshangi, S.; Jeuring, J.; Keuning, H.; Kleiner, C.; MacKellar, B.; Duran, R.; Störrle, H.; Toll, D.; et al. Developers talking about code quality. *Empir. Softw. Eng.* **2023**, *28*, 128. [CrossRef]
47. Jo, J.; Zhang, H.; Cai, J.; Goyal, N. AI Trust Reshaping Administrative Burdens: Understanding Trust-Burden Dynamics in LLM-Assisted Benefits Systems. In Proceedings of the 2025 ACM Conference on Fairness, Accountability, and Transparency, Athens, Greece, 23–26 June 2025; pp. 1172–1183.
48. Wang, J.; Huang, C.; Yan, S.; Xie, W.; He, D. When young scholars cooperate with LLMs in academic tasks: The influence of individual differences and task complexities. *Int. J. Hum.–Comput. Interact.* **2025**, *41*, 4624–4639. [CrossRef]
49. Liu, Y.; Sharma, P.; Oswal, M.; Xia, H.; Huang, Y. PersonaFlow: Designing LLM-Simulated Expert Perspectives for Enhanced Research Ideation. In Proceedings of the 2025 ACM Designing Interactive Systems Conference, Madeira, Portugal, 5–9 July 2025; pp. 506–534.
50. Yang, D.; Liu, K.; Kim, D.; Koyuncu, A.; Kim, K.; Tian, H.; Lei, Y.; Mao, X.; Klein, J.; Bissyandé, T.F. Where were the repair ingredients for defects4j bugs? exploring the impact of repair ingredient retrieval on the performance of 24 program repair systems. *Empir. Softw. Eng.* **2021**, *26*, 122. [CrossRef]
51. Morovati, M.M.; Nikanjam, A.; Khomh, F.; Jiang, Z.M. Bugs in machine learning-based systems: A faultload benchmark. *Empir. Softw. Eng.* **2023**, *28*, 62. [CrossRef]
52. Wuisang, M.C.; Kurniawan, M.; Santosa, K.A.W.; Gunawan, A.A.S.; Saputra, K.E. An evaluation of the effectiveness of openai's chatGPT for automated python program bug fixing using quixbugs. In Proceedings of the 2023 International Seminar on Application for Technology of Information and Communication (iSemantic), Semarang, Indonesia, 16–17 September 2023; pp. 295–300.
53. Gyimesi, P.; Vancsics, B.; Stocco, A.; Mazinanian, D.; Beszédes, Á.; Ferenc, R.; Mesbah, A. BUGSJS: A benchmark and taxonomy of JavaScript bugs. *Softw. Test. Verif. Reliab.* **2021**, *31*, e1751. [CrossRef]
54. Chang, W.; Ye, C.; Zhou, H. Fine-Tuning Pre-trained Model with Optimizable Prompt Learning for Code Vulnerability Detection. In Proceedings of the 2024 IEEE 35th International Symposium on Software Reliability Engineering (ISSRE), Tsukuba, Japan, 28–31 October 2024; pp. 108–119.
55. Yang, C.; Si, Q.; Lin, Z. Breaking the Trade-Off Between Faithfulness and Expressiveness for Large Language Models. *arXiv* **2025**, arXiv:2508.18651. [CrossRef]
56. Wang, B.; Deng, M.; Chen, M.; Lin, Y.; Zhou, J.; Zhang, J.M. Assessing the effectiveness of recent closed-source large language models in fault localization and automated program repair. *Autom. Softw. Eng.* **2026**, *33*, 26. [CrossRef]
57. Song, J.; Li, Y.; Tian, Y.; Ma, H.; Li, H.; Zuo, J.; Liu, J.; Niu, W. Investigating the bugs in reinforcement learning programs: Insights from Stack Overflow and GitHub. *Autom. Softw. Eng.* **2026**, *33*, 9. [CrossRef]
58. Li, Y.; Cai, M.; Chen, J.; Xu, Y.; Huang, L.; Li, J. Context-aware prompting for LLM-based program repair. *Autom. Softw. Eng.* **2025**, *32*, 42. [CrossRef]
59. Blocklove, J.; Thakur, S.; Tan, B.; Pearce, H.A.; Garg, S.J.; Karri, R. Automatically Improving LLM-based Verilog Generation using EDA Tool Feedback. *ACM Trans. Des. Autom. Electron. Syst.* **2025**, *30*, 1–26. [CrossRef]
60. Xie, L.; Li, Z.; Pei, Y.; Wen, Z.; Liu, K.; Zhang, T.; Li, X. PReMM: LLM-Based Program Repair for Multi-method Bugs via Divide and Conquer. *Proc. ACM Program. Lang.* **2025**, *9*, 1316–1344. [CrossRef]
61. Liu, Z.; Du, X.; Liu, H. ReAPR: Automatic program repair via retrieval-augmented large language models. *Softw. Qual. J.* **2025**, *33*, 30. [CrossRef]
62. Alhanahnah, M.J.; Hasan, M.R.; Xu, L.; Bagheri, H. An empirical evaluation of pre-trained large language models for repairing declarative formal specifications. *Empir. Softw. Eng.* **2025**, *30*, 149. [CrossRef]
63. Xu, P.; Kuang, B.; Su, M.; Fu, A. Survey of Large-Language-Model-Based Automated Program Repair. *Jisuanji Yanjiu Yu Fazhan/Comput. Res. Dev.* **2025**, *62*, 2040–2057. [CrossRef]
64. Yang, R.; Xu, X.; Wang, R. TestLoter: A logic-driven framework for automated unit test generation and error repair using large language models. *J. Comput. Lang.* **2025**, *84*, 101348. [CrossRef]

65. Zhang, H.; David, C.; Wang, M.; Paulsen, B.; Kroening, D. Scalable, Validated Code Translation of Entire Projects using Large Language Models. *Proc. ACM Program. Lang.* **2025**, *9*, 1616–1641. [CrossRef]
66. Rahman, S.; Kuhar, S.; Çirisci, B.; Garg, P.; Wang, S.; Ma, X.; Deoras, A.; Ray, B. UTFix: Change Aware Unit Test Repairing using LLM. *Proc. ACM Program. Lang.* **2025**, *9*, 143–168. [CrossRef]
67. Wang, S.; Lu, L.; Qiu, S.; Tian, Q.; Lin, H. DALO-APR: LLM-based automatic program repair with data augmentation and loss function optimization. *J. Supercomput.* **2025**, *81*, 640. [CrossRef]
68. Pereira, A.F.; Ferreira Mello, R. A Systematic Literature Review on Large Language Models Applications in Computer Programming Teaching Evaluation Process. *IEEE Access* **2025**, *13*, 113449–113460. [CrossRef]
69. Blinn, A.J.; Li, X.; Kim, J.h.; Omar, C. Statically Contextualizing Large Language Models with Typed Holes. *Proc. ACM Program. Lang.* **2024**, *8*, 468–498. [CrossRef]
70. Xuan, J.; Martinez, M.; Demarco, F.; Clement, M.; Marcote, S.L.; Durieux, T.; Le Berre, D.; Monperrus, M. Nopol: Automatic repair of conditional statement bugs in java programs. *IEEE Trans. Softw. Eng.* **2016**, *43*, 34–55. [CrossRef]
71. Rosà, A.; Basso, M.; Bohnhoff, L.; Binder, W. Automated Runtime Transition between Virtual and Platform Threads in the Java Virtual Machine. In Proceedings of the 2023 30th Asia-Pacific Software Engineering Conference (APSEC), Seoul, Republic of Korea, 4–7 December 2023; pp. 607–611.
72. Guizzo, G.; Bazargani, M.; Paixao, M.; Drake, J.H. A hyper-heuristic for multi-objective integration and test ordering in google guava. In Proceedings of the International Symposium on Search Based Software Engineering, Paderborn, Germany, 9–11 September 2017; Springer: Berlin/Heidelberg, Germany, 2017; pp. 168–174.
73. Gajewski, M.; Zabierowski, W. Analysis and comparison of the Spring framework and play framework performance, used to create web applications in Java. In Proceedings of the 2019 IEEE XVth International Conference on the Perspective Technologies and Methods in MEMS Design (MEMSTECH), Polyana, Ukraine, 22–26 May 2019; pp. 170–173.
74. Walter-Tscharf, F.F.W.V. Indexing, clustering, and search engine for documents utilizing Elasticsearch and Kibana. In *Mobile Computing and Sustainable Informatics: Proceedings of ICMCSI 2022*; Springer: Berlin/Heidelberg, Germany, 2022; pp. 897–910.
75. Alqaradaghi, M.; Nazir, M.Z.I.; Kozsik, T. Design and Implement an Accurate Automated Static Analysis Checker to Detect Insecure Use of SecurityManager. *Computers* **2023**, *12*, 247. [CrossRef]
76. Choi, Y.h.; Nam, J. WINE: Warning miner for improving bug finders. *Inf. Softw. Technol.* **2023**, *155*, 107109. [CrossRef]
77. Vach, W.; Gerke, O. Gwet's AC1 is not a substitute for Cohen's kappa–A comparison of basic properties. *MethodsX* **2023**, *10*, 102212. [CrossRef]
78. Cho, D.; Lee, H.; Kang, S. An empirical study of Korean sentence representation with various tokenizations. *Electronics* **2021**, *10*, 845. [CrossRef]
79. Kovačević, A.; Luburić, N.; Slivka, J.; Prokić, S.; Grujić, K.G.; Vidaković, D.; Sladić, G. Automatic detection of code smells using metrics and CodeT5 embeddings: A case study in C#. *Neural Comput. Appl.* **2024**, *36*, 9203–9220. [CrossRef]
80. Deb, K.; Pratap, A.; Agarwal, S.; Meyarivan, T. A fast and elitist multiobjective genetic algorithm: NSGA-II. *IEEE Trans. Evol. Comput.* **2002**, *6*, 182–197. [CrossRef]
81. Deb, K. Multi-objective evolutionary algorithms. In *Springer Handbook of Computational Intelligence*; Springer: Berlin/Heidelberg, Germany, 2015; pp. 995–1015.
82. Pan, L.; Xu, W.; Li, L.; He, C.; Cheng, R. Adaptive simulated binary crossover for rotated multi-objective optimization. *Swarm Evol. Comput.* **2021**, *60*, 100759. [CrossRef]
83. Shahedi, K.; Gyambrah, N.; Li, H.; Lamothe, M.; Khomh, F. An Empirical Study on Method-Level Performance Evolution in Open-Source Java Projects. *arXiv* **2025**, arXiv:2508.07084.
84. Dehdarirad, T. Evaluating explainability in language classification models: A unified framework incorporating feature attribution methods and key factors affecting faithfulness. *Data Inf. Manag.* **2025**, *9*, 100101. [CrossRef]
85. Zhao, H.; Chen, H.; Yang, F.; Liu, N.; Deng, H.; Cai, H.; Wang, S.; Yin, D.; Du, M. Explainability for large language models: A survey. *ACM Trans. Intell. Syst. Technol.* **2024**, *15*, 1–38. [CrossRef]
86. Kern, M.; Erata, F.; Iser, M.; Sinz, C.; Loiret, F.; Otten, S.; Sax, E. Integrating static code analysis toolchains. In Proceedings of the 2019 IEEE 43rd Annual Computer Software and Applications Conference (COMPSAC), Milwaukee, WI, USA, 15–19 July 2019; Volume 1, pp. 523–528.
87. Gbenle, P.; Abieba, O.A.; Owobu, W.O.; Onoja, J.P.; Daraojimba, A.I.; Adepoju, A.H.; Chibunna, U.B. A privacy-preserving AI model for autonomous detection and masking of sensitive user data in contact center analytics. *World Sci. News* **2025**, *203*, 154–193.
88. Eghbali, A.; Burk, F.; Pradel, M. DyLin: A Dynamic Linter for Python. *Proc. ACM Softw. Eng.* **2025**, *2*, 2828–2849. [CrossRef]
89. Al-Khafaji, N.J.; Majeed, B.K. Evaluating Large Language Models using Arabic Prompts to Generate Python Codes. In Proceedings of the 2024 4th International Conference on Emerging Smart Technologies and Applications (eSmarTA), Sana'a, Yemen, 6–7 August 2024; pp. 1–5.

0. Rak-Amnouykit, I.; McCrevan, D.; Milanova, A.; Hirzel, M.; Dolby, J. Python 3 types in the wild: A tale of two type systems. In Proceedings of the 16th ACM SIGPLAN International Symposium on Dynamic Languages, Virtual, 17 November 2020; pp. 57–70.
1. Strong, E.; Kleynhans, B.; Kadioğlu, S. Mabwiser: A parallelizable contextual multi-armed bandit library for python. In Proceedings of the 2019 IEEE 31st International Conference on Tools with Artificial Intelligence (ICTAI), Portland, OR, USA, 4–6 November 2019; pp. 909–914.
2. Verma, A.; Saha, R.; Kumar, G.; Brighente, A.; Conti, M.; Kim, T.H. Exploring the Landscape of Programming Language Identification with Machine Learning Approaches. *IEEE Access* **2025**, *13*, 23556–23579. [CrossRef]
3. Guo, Z.; Tan, T.; Liu, S.; Liu, X.; Lai, W.; Yang, Y.; Li, Y.; Chen, L.; Dong, W.; Zhou, Y. Mitigating false positive static analysis warnings: Progress, challenges, and opportunities. *IEEE Trans. Softw. Eng.* **2023**, *49*, 5154–5188. [CrossRef]
4. Xue, F.; Fu, Y.; Zhou, W.; Zheng, Z.; You, Y. To repeat or not to repeat: Insights from scaling llm under token-crisis. *Adv. Neural Inf. Process. Syst.* **2023**, *36*, 59304–59322.
5. Priya, S.; Karthika Renuka, D.; Ashok Kumar, L. Robust Multi-Dialect End-to-End ASR Model Jointly with Beam Search Threshold Pruning and LLM. *SN Comput. Sci.* **2025**, *6*, 323 .
6. Guo, L.; Wang, Y.; Shi, E.; Zhong, W.; Zhang, H.; Chen, J.; Zhang, R.; Ma, Y.; Zheng, Z. When to stop? towards efficient code generation in llms with excess token prevention. In Proceedings of the 33rd ACM SIGSOFT International Symposium on Software Testing and Analysis, Vienna, Austria, 16–20 September 2024; pp. 1073–1085.
7. Latif, Y.A. Hallucinations in large language models and their influence on legal reasoning: Examining the risks of ai-generated factual inaccuracies in judicial processes. *J. Comput. Intell. Mach. Reason. Decis.-Mak.* **2025**, *10*, 10–20.
8. Naiseh, M.; Simkute, A.; Zieni, B.; Jiang, N.; Ali, R. C-XAI: A conceptual framework for designing XAI tools that support trust calibration. *J. Responsible Technol.* **2024**, *17*, 100076. [CrossRef]
9. Li, K.; Liu, H.; Zhang, L.; Chen, Y. Automatic Inspection of Static Application Security Testing (SAST) Reports via Large Language Model Reasoning. In Proceedings of the International Conference on AI Logic and Applications, Lanzhou, China, 10–11 August 2024; Springer: Berlin/Heidelberg, Germany, 2024; pp. 128–142.
.00. Qu, H.; Fan, W.; Zhao, Z.; Li, Q. TokenRec: Learning to Tokenize ID for LLM-Based Generative Recommendations. *IEEE Trans. Knowl. Data Eng.* **2025**, *37*, 6216–6231.

computers

MDPI

Article

Topological Machine Learning for Financial Crisis Detection: Early Warning Signals from Persistent Homology

Ecaterina Guritanu, Enrico Barbierato *, Alice Gatti

Dipartimento di Matematica e Fisica, Università Cattolica del Sacro Cuore, Via Garzetta 48, 25121 Brescia, Italy; ecaterina.guritanu01@icatt.it (E.G.); alice.gatti@unicatt.it (A.G.)
* Correspondence: enrico.barbierato@unicatt.it

Abstract: We propose a strictly causal early–warning framework for financial crises based on topological signal extraction from multivariate return streams. Sliding windows of daily log–returns are mapped to point clouds, from which Vietoris–Rips persistence diagrams are computed and summarised by persistence landscapes. A single, interpretable indicator is obtained as the L_2 norm of the landscape and passed through a causal decision rule (with thresholds α, β and run–length parameters s, t) that suppresses isolated spikes and collapses bursts to time–stamped warnings. On four major U.S. equity indices (S&P 500, NASDAQ, DJIA, Russell 2000) over 1999–2021, the method, at a fixed strictly causal operating point ($\alpha = \beta = 3.1$, $s = 57$, $t = 16$), attains a balanced precision–recall ($F_1 \approx 0.50$) with an average lead time of about 34 days. It anticipates two of the four canonical crises and issues a contemporaneous signal for the 2008 global financial crisis. Sensitivity analyses confirm the qualitative robustness of the detector, while comparisons with permissive spike rules and volatility–based baselines demonstrate substantially fewer false alarms at comparable recall. The approach delivers interpretable topology–based warnings and provides a reproducible route to combining persistent homology with causal event detection in financial time series.

Keywords: topological data analysis; early warning signals; financial crisis prediction

1. Financial Market Crises

Financial crises, speculative bubbles, and market crashes have repeatedly disrupted both advanced and emerging economies. These events, though varied in form, commonly involve sharp asset price swings, financial intermediation breakdowns, and credit contractions, often leading to prolonged recessions and significant declines in consumption, investment, and employment [1].

The origins of such crises are debated. Exogenous theories attribute fluctuations to external forces, including monetary policy shifts and technological change. Slutzky [2] modeled cycles as the result of random shocks forming regular patterns. Friedman [3] argued that monetary expansion fuels inflation and asset bubbles, while contractionary policy triggers downturns. Kydland and Prescott [4] identified technological shocks as dominant macroeconomic drivers.

Endogenous theories, in contrast, locate the roots of crises within financial systems. Minsky's Financial Instability Hypothesis [5] suggests that stability breeds risk-taking, ultimately leading to fragility. Shiller [6] emphasized behavioral factors, such as cognitive biases and herd dynamics, that distort investor judgment and fuel speculative excess.

The dot-com bubble exemplified these dynamics. Investor euphoria over internet companies led to extreme valuations, with firms adding '.com' to their names experiencing price surges of over 50% despite no substantive changes [7]. Shiller [6] characterized this as 'irrational exuberance' driven by media amplification and social contagion. When expectations failed to materialize, the bubble collapsed.

The 2007–2008 crisis originated in the US subprime mortgage market amid low interest rates and capital inflows, creating a housing bubble [8]. The collapses of Bear Stearns and Lehman Brothers triggered systemic panic, prompting unprecedented interventions by the Federal Reserve. Parallel failures at AIG and Washington Mutual highlighted systemic fragilities.

In Europe, the sovereign debt crisis (2009–2012) exposed institutional weaknesses in the eurozone. Lane [9] noted that the lack of fiscal integration and exchange rate flexibility limited member states' ability to absorb shocks, in contrast to more integrated monetary unions like the United States.

The COVID-19 pandemic caused a sharp market crash in early 2020, driven by lockdowns, business closures, and global uncertainty. Mazur et al. [10] showed that losses were unevenly distributed: energy and hospitality firms suffered most, while healthcare and software sectors gained. Extreme volatility and divergent corporate responses characterized the crisis.

Recognizing the systemic risks, the G20 in 2008 mandated the IMF to strengthen surveillance and develop early warning systems [11]. Sornette [12] argued that crises are not entirely random but display detectable precursors, introducing the concept of "Dragon-Kings"—extreme, self-reinforcing events outside normal fluctuations.

Numerous predictive models have emerged. Claessens and Kose [1] analyzed common pre-crisis signals, while Beutel et al. [13] compared traditional statistical models and machine learning (ML). Despite capturing nonlinear patterns, ML methods often lack interpretability. Classical logit models remain competitive in forecasting performance due to their transparency and robustness.

This paper proposes a framework that integrates Topological Data Analysis (TDA) with a strictly causal detection pipeline to detect early warning signals (EWS) of financial crises. The methodology can support machine-learning-based monitoring systems, but here we focus on the detection pipeline and its empirical evaluation.

Specifically, it introduces L^1- and L^2-norm indicators of persistence landscapes as informative features, and demonstrates their predictive power across several major crises using multiple ML classifiers. The methodology is empirically validated across multiple historical financial crises—including the 2008 global financial crisis and the 2020 COVID-19 crash—using daily stock index data. The results demonstrate that topological indicators significantly improve predictive performance compared to baseline models (see, for example [14–17]) offering a promising and interpretable tool for early crisis detection.

Furthermore, this work (as per Figure 1) focuses on the following research question: can topological features extracted from financial time series via persistent homology act as interpretable early warning signals of financial crises, and support machine learning-based monitoring systems?

The work is structured as follows. After this introduction, Section 2 presents the theoretical background of TDA. Section 3 reviews the scientific literature, while Section 4 explains the experiments conducted on a specific dataset to detect early signals of a financial crisis. Finally, Section 5 discusses the results, while Section 6 provides the conclusions and outlines directions for future work.

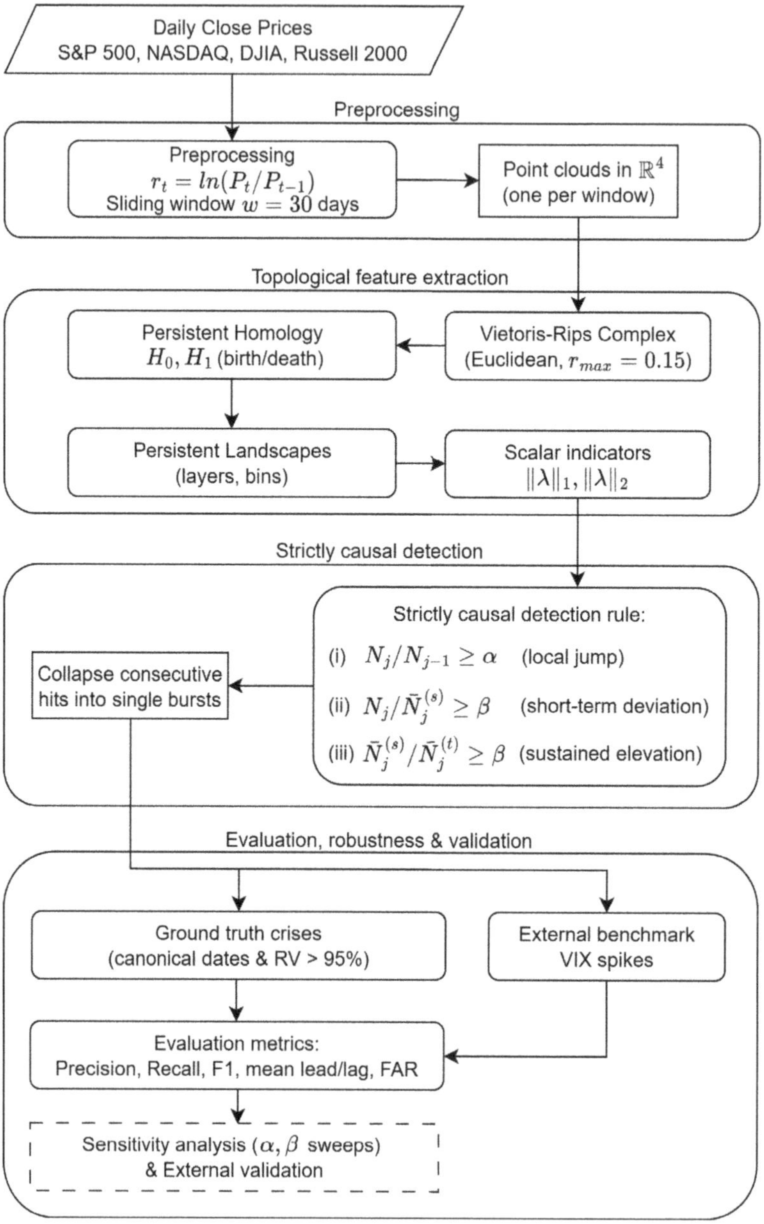

Figure 1. Flowchart of the proposed pipeline for early warning signals from persistent homology: data and preprocessing, topological feature extraction, strictly causal detection, and evaluation with robustness checks.

2. Background

A topology [18] on a set X is a collection $\mathcal{U}$ of subsets (open sets) satisfying: (i) $\emptyset$ and X belong to $\mathcal{U}$, (ii) finite intersections and (iii) arbitrary unions of open sets remain open. The pair $(X, \mathcal{U})$ defines a topological space.

A k-simplex is the convex hull of $k+1$ affinely independent points in $\mathbb{R}^d$. Simplices include vertices ($k = 0$), edges ($k = 1$), triangles ($k = 2$), and tetrahedra ($k = 3$). A simplicial complex is a finite set of simplices closed under taking faces and such that the intersection of any two is either empty or a shared face.

Given a point cloud S and scale $r \geq 0$, the Vietoris–Rips complex $\mathrm{VR}(r)$ includes all simplices of diameter $\leq 2r$:

$$\mathrm{VR}(r) = \{\sigma \subseteq S \mid \mathrm{diam}(\sigma) \leq 2r\}. \tag{1}$$

Homology encodes topological features via algebraic structures. For a simplicial complex and integer p, a p-chain is a formal sum of p-simplices with coefficients (typically in $\mathbb{Z}_2$). The set of p-chains forms an abelian group C_p.

The boundary operator $\partial_p : C_p \to C_{p-1}$ maps each p-simplex to its oriented $(p-1)$-faces:

$$\partial_p[u_0, \ldots, u_p] = \sum_{j=0}^{p} [u_0, \ldots, \hat{u}_j, \ldots, u_p], \quad \partial_p(c) = \sum a_i \partial_p \sigma_i. \tag{2}$$

A p-cycle is a p-chain with zero boundary; they form the kernel $Z_p = \ker \partial_p$. A p-boundary is the image of ∂_{p+1} and forms $B_p = \mathrm{im}\, \partial_{p+1}$. The Fundamental Lemma of Homology states:

$$\partial_p \circ \partial_{p+1} = 0 \quad \Rightarrow \quad B_p \subseteq Z_p. \tag{3}$$

The p-th homology group is defined as the quotient:

$$H_p = Z_p / B_p, \tag{4}$$

whose rank β_p (the p-th Betti number) counts p-dimensional topological features: β_0 (connected components), β_1 (loops), β_2 (voids).

Homology is functorial: a continuous map $f : X \to Y$ induces $f_p : H_p(X) \to H_p(Y)$. It is also homotopy invariant: if $X \simeq Y$, then $H_p(X) \simeq H_p(Y)$ and $\beta_p(X) = \beta_p(Y)$ for all p [19].

2.1. Persistent Homology

Let K be a simplicial complex and $f : K \to \mathbb{R}$ a monotonic function (i.e., $f(\sigma) \leq f(\tau)$ for $\sigma \subset \tau$). The sublevel sets $K(a) = f^{-1}(-\infty, a]$ form a filtration:

$$\emptyset = K_0 \subseteq K_1 \subseteq \cdots \subseteq K_n = K. \tag{5}$$

Each inclusion induces homomorphisms between homology groups:

$$f_p^{i,j} : H_p(K_i) \to H_p(K_j), \quad H_p^{i,j} := \mathrm{im}\, f_p^{i,j}. \tag{6}$$

Persistent homology tracks homology classes across the filtration. A class born at K_i and dying at K_j defines a persistence

$$\mathrm{pers}(\gamma) := a_j - a_i. \tag{7}$$

The persistent Betti number is

$$\beta_p^{i,j} = \mathrm{rank}(H_p^{i,j}). \tag{8}$$

The persistence diagram $Dgm_p(f)$ is a multiset of points (a_i, a_j) in $\overline{\mathbb{R}}^2$, where each point's multiplicity is

$$\mu_p^{i,j} = (\beta_p^{i,j-1} - \beta_p^{i,j}) - (\beta_p^{i-1,j-1} - \beta_p^{i-1,j}). \tag{9}$$

The Fundamental Lemma of Persistent Homology states:

$$\beta_p^{k,l} = \sum_{i \le k} \sum_{j > l} \mu_p^{i,j}. \tag{10}$$

The Wasserstein distance W_q between two diagrams X, Y quantifies their dissimilarity:

$$W_q(X,Y) = \left[\inf_{\eta: X \to Y} \sum_{x \in X} \|x - \eta(x)\|_\infty^q \right]^{1/q}, \quad \|x - y\|_\infty = \max\{|x_1 - y_1|, |x_2 - y_2|\}. \tag{11}$$

2.2. Persistence Landscapes

Bubenik [20] introduced persistence landscapes as functional summaries of persistence diagrams. Given a persistence module M, the landscape $\lambda : \mathbb{N} \times \mathbb{R} \to \overline{\mathbb{R}}$ is defined as:

$$\lambda(k,t) = \sup\{m \ge 0 \mid \beta^{t-m,t+m} \ge k\}. \tag{12}$$

This function captures the persistence of the k-th most prominent feature at location t. It satisfies: (i) non-negativity, (ii) monotonicity in k, and (iii) 1-Lipschitz continuity in t.

Given a persistence diagram $\{(b_i, d_i)\}_{i=1}^n$, the landscape is computed as:

$$\lambda(k,t) = k\text{-th largest value of } \min(t - b_i, d_i - t)_+. \tag{13}$$

The L^p-norm of λ is defined as:

$$\|\lambda\|_p = \left(\sum_{k=1}^{\infty} \int_{-\infty}^{\infty} \lambda(k,t)^p \, dt \right)^{1/p}, \quad \|\lambda\|_\infty = \sup_{k,t} \lambda(k,t). \tag{14}$$

In a statistical setting, persistence landscapes can be viewed as random variables in $L^p(\mathbb{N} \times \mathbb{R})$. Given i.i.d. samples $X_1, \ldots, X_n$ with landscapes $\lambda^1, \ldots, \lambda^n$, the empirical mean landscape is:

$$\bar{\lambda}^n(k,t) = \frac{1}{n} \sum_{i=1}^{n} \lambda^i(k,t). \tag{15}$$

2.3. Why TDA-Based Features Can Anticipate Crises

Traditional econometric indicators, such as volatility, autocorrelation, or macroeconomic ratios, are inherently low-dimensional and often assume linear or parametric relationships in financial data. In contrast, TDA captures high-dimensional geometric and structural information embedded in multivariate time series without requiring distributional assumptions or model specification. Persistent homology, in particular, is sensitive to both local and global deformations in the data manifold, enabling the detection of subtle structural transitions—such as fragmentation of market regimes or emergence of co-movement patterns—that may not be visible through traditional indicators.

Mathematically, let $\{X_t\}_{t=1}^T \subset \mathbb{R}^d$ denote a multivariate financial time series embedded as point clouds via sliding windows. The associated Vietoris–Rips complex $VR(r)$ captures simplicial connectivity at scale r, and the resulting persistence diagram Dgm_p summarizes the birth and death of topological features across scales. The persistence landscape $\lambda_p(k,t)$, which maps this multiscale information into a functional representation, allows the use of L^1 and L^2 norms as summary statistics. These norms react to early topological instabilities—such as increased loops (connected clusters of assets) or persistent voids—before such effects manifest as elevated volatility.

Thus, the rationale is that financial crises emerge from the build-up of complex systemic interdependencies. TDA captures the underlying topological evolution of the market structure itself, not just its first- or second-order statistical moments. This allows early detection of regime shifts or bifurcations in the data geometry that may precede observable crises, providing a theoretically grounded advantage over classical econometric tools.

3. Related Work

3.1. Early Warning Signal Detection

Guo et al. [21] apply TDA to financial time series using sliding windows on log-returns from multiple indices. Vietoris–Rips complexes are constructed, persistence barcodes and landscapes are computed, and L^1/L^2 norms are interpreted as crisis indicators. Their model successfully identifies precursors to the 2008 global financial crisis and the 2010 European debt crisis, and even produces a warning in China in 2007. Strengths of this study include multi-market applicability, the use of both H_0 and H_1 features, and clear visualizations. However, the methodology lacks formal validation, covers a relatively short time span, and relies on post hoc interpretation of spikes.

Aguilar and Ensor [22] expand on Gidea's original framework by adding statistical inference. They compute persistence landscapes on U.S. indices and ETF sectors (2010–2020) and compare crisis vs. stable periods using permutation tests. Significant structural shifts are confirmed during the early 2020 COVID-19 crash. This strengthens methodological rigor, but the study is limited to a single crisis and does not examine parameter robustness.

Ismail et al. [23] combine TDA with critical slowing down (CSD) indicators on data from the U.S., Singapore, and Malaysia (1987–2018). Persistent homology is used alongside variance, autocorrelation, and mean power spectrum, with changes assessed through Mann–Kendall and Chow tests. This hybrid approach demonstrates predictive value across multiple markets and crises. Yet, its complexity, sensitivity to parameter choices, and limited reproducibility reduce accessibility.

3.2. Topological Index Construction

Ruiz-Ortiz et al. [24] propose a turbulence index based on persistence landscapes. Using Takens' embedding and L^2 distances between landscapes, they identify structural breaks across indices including S&P 500, Russell 2000, IPC, and Nikkei 225. The index reacts strongly post-crisis (e.g., Black Monday, COVID-19) but often lags behind events like the dot-com bubble. The contribution lies in the index design and broad parameter exploration, though the approach emphasizes ex-post characterization rather than early detection.

3.3. Forecasting with Topological Features

Souto [25] shifts from detection to forecasting, proposing the Topological Tail Dependence (TTD) framework. Persistent homology features (norms and Wasserstein distances) are integrated into volatility models (HAR, HARX, NBEATS, etc.) and tested on U.S. indices (2000–2022). Topological features consistently improve forecast accuracy, with robustness verified via Diebold–Mariano tests. The originality lies in linking topology with volatility prediction, though the theory requires further validation and the methodology remains complex.

3.4. Comparison and Contribution

Table 1 summarizes the strengths and limitations of the reviewed works. Collectively, these studies demonstrate that persistent homology can reveal structural stress in financial markets. However, most either (i) interpret topological signals retrospectively without causal detection rules, (ii) validate only on narrow or single-crisis datasets, or (iii) lack reproducibility due to parameter sensitivity.

Our framework addresses these gaps in three ways. First, it implements a strictly causal detection pipeline, ensuring that only past information informs signals and eliminating the information leakage present in earlier threshold-based methods. Second, it grounds detection in reproducible statistical evaluation, combining sensitivity sweeps with validation against an independent volatility benchmark (`VIX`). Third, it achieves robust predictive performance across four canonical U.S. crises (1999–2021), delivering a balanced precision–recall ($F_1 = 0.50$) with substantial average lead times under a strictly causal detector.

In doing so, our approach extends the geometric intuition of prior work into a rigorous, transparent, and forward-looking early warning system for systemic risk monitoring.

Table 1. Summary of strengths and limitations of related studies.

Article	Strengths	Limitations
Guo et al. [21]	Multi-market scope; 0- and 1-D features; clear visualization	No statistical validation; short horizon; post hoc interpretation
Aguilar and Ensor [22]	Permutation tests; sector-level analysis	Single crisis; US-only; no sensitivity study
Ismail et al. [23]	Multi-country; TDA+CSD indicators; robustness tests	High complexity; parameter sensitivity; limited reproducibility
Ruiz-Ortiz et al. [24]	Turbulence index; broad parameter exploration	Delayed response; no early warning; empirical tuning
Souto [25]	Forecasting link; robust evaluation	High complexity; limited theoretical grounding

4. Experiments

This section presents a comprehensive evaluation of the proposed framework for detecting EWS of financial crises using persistent homology and topological machine learning. In contrast to earlier formulations, the revised methodology implements a strictly causal detection pipeline, thereby eliminating any reliance on future information, and validates results against both historically defined crisis periods and independent volatility benchmarks. The objective is to assess whether topological signals derived from multivariate market data can provide reliable and anticipatory indicators of systemic risk.

4.1. Dataset and Preprocessing

The empirical analysis is based on four major US equity indices: the S&P 500, the NASDAQ Composite, the Dow Jones Industrial Average, and the Russell 2000. Together, these indices capture large-cap, small-cap, technology-oriented, and blue-chip segments of the US market, offering a representative view of systemic dynamics. The dataset spans 4 January 1999, to 1 January 2021 (5535 trading days), retrieved from Yahoo Finance at daily frequency.

Daily log-returns are computed as

$$r_t = \ln\left(\frac{P_t}{P_{t-1}}\right), \tag{16}$$

where P_t is the index closing price on day t. This transformation enforces scale invariance and stabilizes variance, which is essential for comparing across indices with different levels and volatilities.

Using a sliding window of $w = 30$ trading days, we generate 5506 overlapping point clouds in $\mathbb{R}^4$. Each cloud encodes the joint behaviour of the indices during a short horizon. For visualization purposes, clouds may be projected into lower dimensions using Principal Component Analysis (PCA), though persistent homology is computed in the full four-dimensional space. Figures 2 and 3 show representative point clouds for both stable and turbulent market periods.

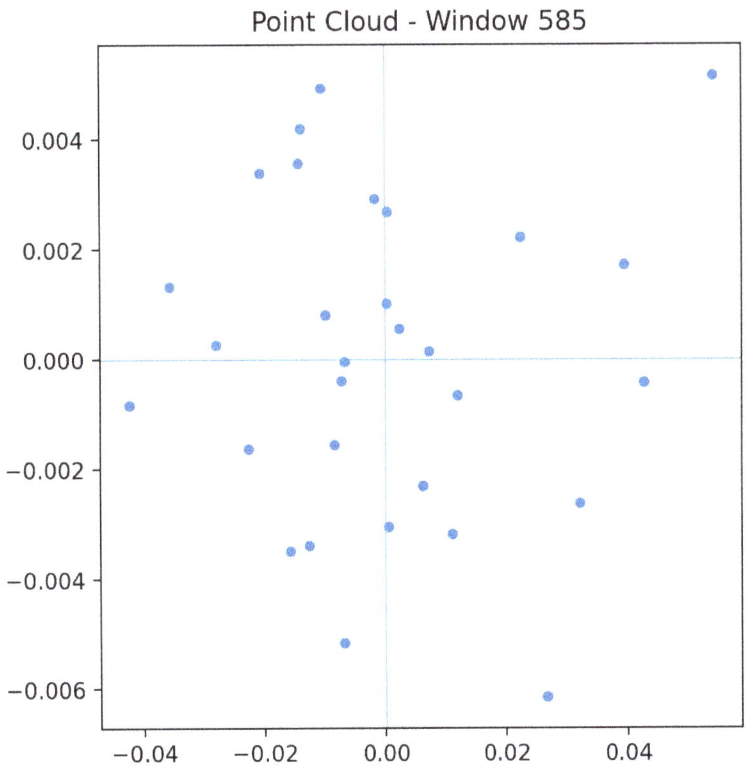

Figure 2. Point clouds for stable period (window 585).

4.2. Crisis Labeling and Ground Truth

Ground truth crisis periods are defined using a hybrid strategy. First, four canonical systemic events are identified: the dot-com bubble (2000), the global financial crisis (2008), the US sovereign debt downgrade (2011), and the COVID-19 crash (2020). These are well-established crises in financial history and serve as reference benchmarks.

Second, to reduce reliance on purely historical annotation, we add a quantitative rule: periods are labeled as crises if realized volatility exceeds the 95th percentile of its historical rolling distribution. This dual approach balances interpretability with reproducibility and helps capture periods of exceptional stress that may not fit neatly into the four canonical events.

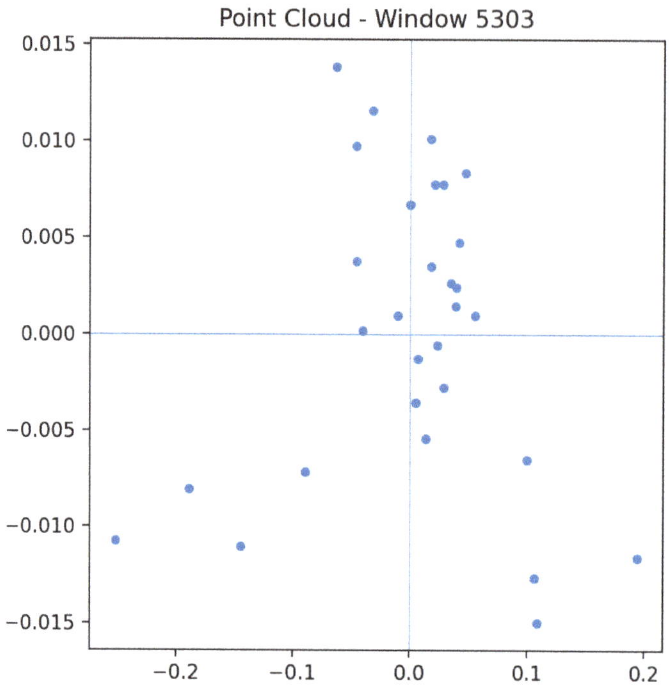

Figure 3. Turbulent period (window 5303).

4.3. Topological Feature Extraction

Each point cloud is transformed into a Vietoris–Rips complex using the `giotto-tda` library, with maximum filtration value $r = 0.15$ and Euclidean distance as the metric. Homology groups H_0 (connected components) and H_1 (loops) are computed.

Persistence diagrams are obtained with the `VietorisRipsPersistence` transformer. They encode the birth and death of topological features as the filtration radius grows. Points close to the diagonal correspond to short-lived, noisy features, while points far from the diagonal reflect persistent structures. Figures 4 and 5 illustrate persistence diagrams for a stable and a turbulent period, highlighting how crises yield longer-lived features.

Persistence barcodes offer a complementary visualization by representing feature lifetimes as horizontal line segments. Longer bars correspond to persistent components or loops, while shorter bars represent transient features likely attributable to noise. Figures 6 and 7 show barcodes for the same windows as above, confirming the structural differences between stable and crisis periods.

For statistical analysis, persistence diagrams are mapped into persistence landscapes using the `PersistenceLandscape` transformer, with five layers and 100 bins. Landscapes convert discrete diagram points into functional summaries of persistence. Scalar indicators are derived by computing L^1 and L^2 norms:

$$\|\lambda\|_p = \left(\sum_{k=1}^{\infty} \int_{-\infty}^{\infty} \lambda(k,t)^p dt \right)^{1/p}. \tag{17}$$

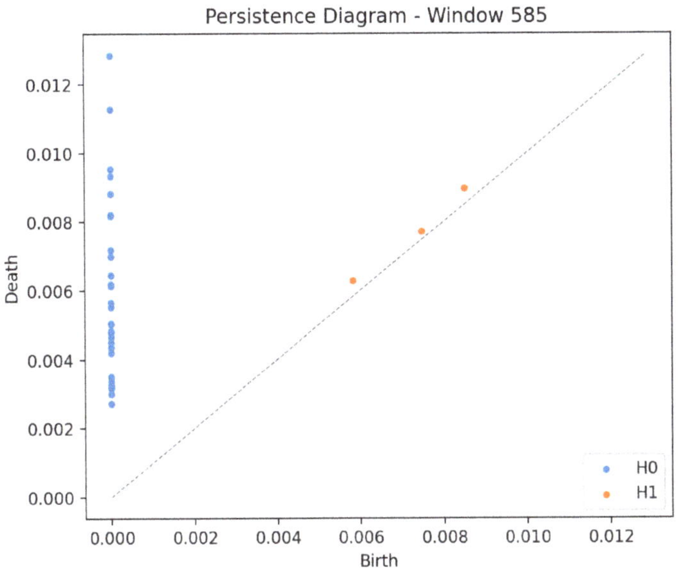

Figure 4. Persistent diagram for stable period (window 585).

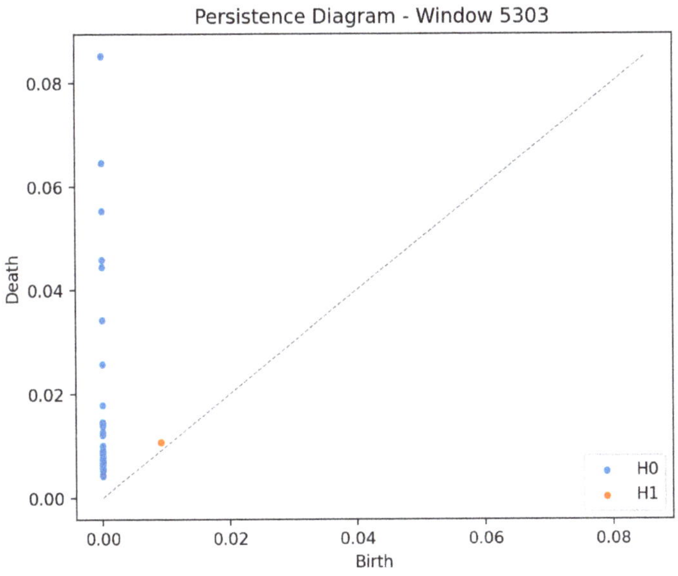

Figure 5. Persistent diagram for Turbulent period (window 5303).

In Figures 8 and 9, the coloured curves are the first layers of the persistence landscape computed on the shown rolling window. Given a persistence diagram, $\lambda(k, t)$ encodes, at filtration value t, the magnitude of the k-th most persistent homology class: lower layers (small k) capture dominant, long-lived features, while higher layers represent progressively weaker features. The x-axis reports the filtration value and the y-axis the landscape amplitude. We plot the first five layers to highlight regime differences: windows preceding crises exhibit taller and broader peaks across multiple layers, whereas tranquil windows display flatter profiles.

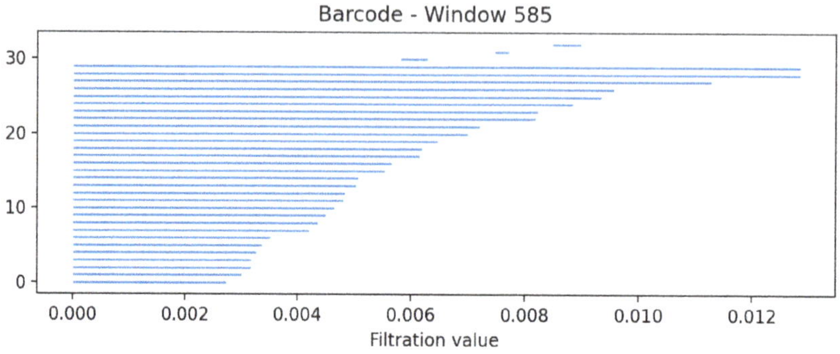

Figure 6. Barcode for stable period (window 585).

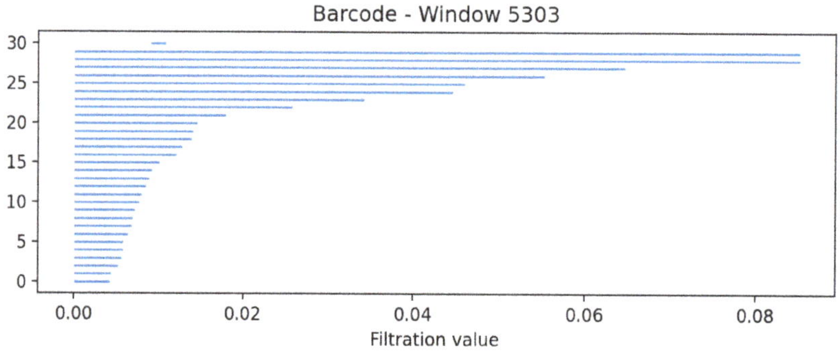

Figure 7. Barcode for turbulent period (window 5303).

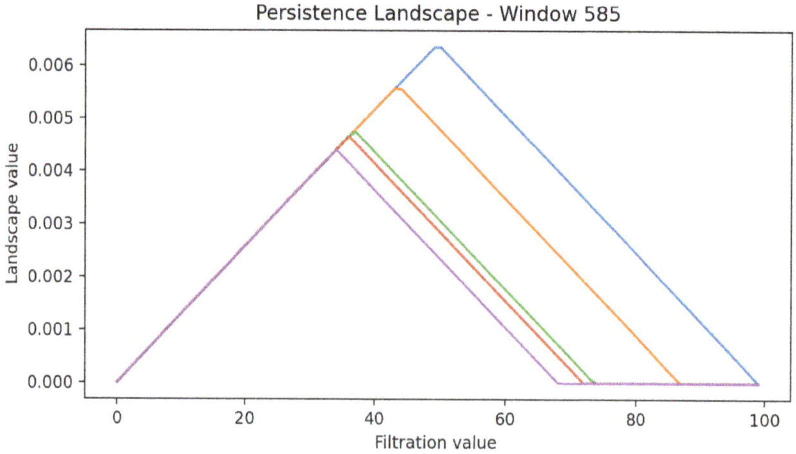

Figure 8. Persistence landscapes (layers $k = 1, \ldots, 5$ correspond to different colours) for long-period windows. Stable period (window 585).

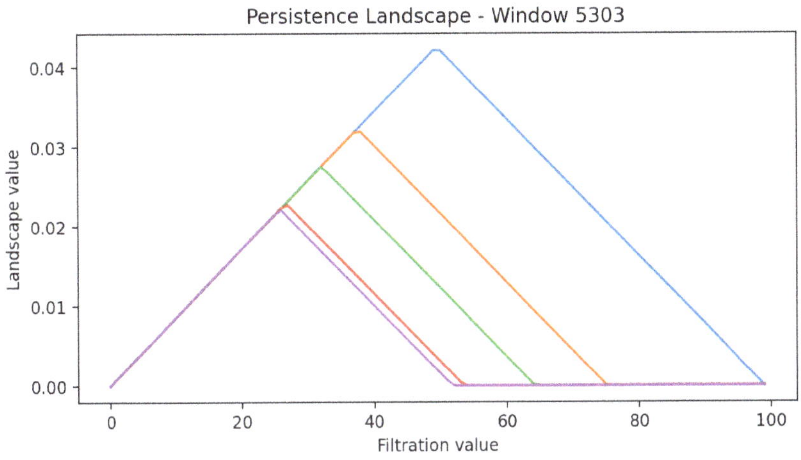

Figure 9. Persistence landscapes (layers $k = 1, \ldots, 5$ correspond to different colours) for long-period windows. Turbulent period (window 5303).

4.4. Causal Detection of Early Warning Signals

The norm time series extracted from persistence landscapes is processed through a strictly causal detection rule, ensuring that only past information informs decisions. At each time j, three conditions are applied:

(i) Sudden local increase: $\dfrac{N_j}{N_{j-1}} \geq \alpha$,

(ii) Short-term deviation: $\dfrac{N_j}{Q_j^{(s)}} \geq \beta$, where $Q_j^{(s)}$ is the mean of the past s values,

(iii) Sustained elevation: $\dfrac{Q_j^{(s)}}{Q_j^{(t)}} \geq \beta$, where $Q_j^{(t)}$ is the mean of the past t values.

If all conditions are satisfied, j is flagged as the onset of an early warning signal. Consecutive detections are collapsed into single bursts to avoid redundancy.

Detected signals are compared with ground truth crises under the following rules:

- True positive (TP): signal within a 180-day lead window before a crisis,
- Late detection: signal within a 30-day lag window after a crisis,
- False positive (FP): signal outside lead/lag windows,
- False negative (FN): crisis with no associated signal.

From these, we compute Precision, Recall, and F1. Additional indicators include the false alarm rate (FAR), mean lead time, and mean delay time.

The contribution of each component of the pipeline is quantified through an ablation study. Holding the dataset, sliding window, and detector parameters fixed ($\alpha = 3.1, \beta = 3.1, s = 57, t = 16$), we vary one factor at a time: the norm (L1 vs. L2), the homology content (H_0 vs. H_1), the topological summary (landscape vs. raw diagram sum vs. persistence image), and each causal condition (local jump, short-term deviation, sustained elevation), with/without burst collapsing. Signals are matched to canonical crisis onsets using a 180-day lead window and a 30-day late window. Event counts (TP/Late/FN/FP), total signals, precision, recall, F1, false-alarm rate, and mean lead/late times (Table 2) are reported. All indicators are finite (no NaN/Inf).

Table 2. Ablation study.

Variant	TP	Late	FN	FP	Signals	Precision	Recall	F1 Score	False Alarm Rate	Mean Lead Time	Mean Delay Time
Full (L2, causal i–iii, bursts)	2	0	2	2	4	0.500000	0.500000	0.500000	0.500000	33.500000	0.000000
L1 instead of L2	2	1	1	5	8	0.250000	0.500000	0.333000	0.625000	33.500000	18.000000
H0 only	2	0	2	2	4	0.500000	0.500000	0.500000	0.500000	33.500000	0.000000
H1 only	2	0	2	29	31	0.065000	0.500000	0.114000	0.935000	148.500000	0.000000
Raw diagram sum	0	0	4	0	0	0.000000	0.000000	0.000000	0.000000	0.000000	0.000000
Persistence image + causal detector	0	0	4	0	0	0.000000	0.000000	0.000000	0.000000	0.000000	0.000000
w/o cond (i)	2	1	1	4	7	0.286000	0.500000	0.364000	0.571000	33.500000	11.000000
w/o cond (ii)	2	0	2	2	4	0.500000	0.500000	0.500000	0.500000	33.500000	0.000000
w/o cond (iii)	2	0	2	9	11	0.182000	0.500000	0.267000	0.818000	33.500000	0.000000
no burst collapsing	2	0	2	2	4	0.500000	0.500000	0.500000	0.500000	33.500000	0.000000

As per Table 2, the full pipeline (landscape + L2, causal conditions i–iii with burst collapsing) balances anticipation and selectivity (F1 $= 0.50$, mean lead ≈ 34 days). Removing the *local jump* condition (i) reduces precision (more spurious day-to-day spikes pass through), while removing *sustained elevation* (iii) yields the largest precision drop, confirming both filters are important. The short-term deviation (ii) is comparatively less influential on this dataset. Regarding topological content, H_0-only nearly matches the full pipeline, whereas H_1-only generates many false positives, indicating connectivity features dominate loop structure for these point clouds. As negative controls, the raw diagram sum and the persistence image produce no warnings under the same strict causal detector, underscoring the stability of persistence landscapes for this task.

4.4.1. Baselines

Realized-volatility thresholds (global and rolling) and a simple TDA+critical-slowing-down hybrid do not outperform the causal TDA pipeline (Table 3. A non-causal toponorm threshold attains some recall but with worse precision and a higher false-alarm rate. These comparisons highlight that (i) the landscape normalization and (ii) the causal detection logic are key drivers of performance.

Table 3. Baselines and comparators.

Method	TP	Late	FN	FP	Signals	Precision	Recall	F1 Score	False Alarm Rate	Mean Lead Time	Mean Delay Time
Realized vol 95th	0	3	1	10	13	0.000000	0.000000	0.000000	0.769000	0.000000	12.667000
Realized vol (rolling 95th)	2	2	0	31	35	0.057000	0.500000	0.103000	0.886000	30.000000	7.500000
Toponorm non-causal (95th, L2)	1	3	0	10	14	0.071000	0.250000	0.111000	0.714000	66.000000	11.667000
TDA + CSD hybrid	0	0	4	0	0	0.000000	0.000000	0.000000	0.000000	0.000000	0.000000
Persistence image + causal	0	0	4	0	0	0.000000	0.000000	0.000000	0.000000	0.000000	0.000000

4.4.2. Qualitative Evidence

Figures 10 and 11 provide the underlying series and log-returns. Figures 12–14 show that warnings occur near major build-ups in the landscape norms, while Figure 15 situates the selected early warnings on the price trajectories alongside crisis onsets.

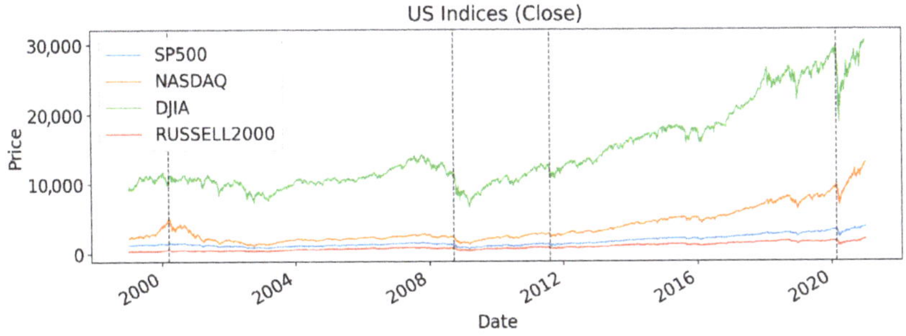

Figure 10. US Indices (Close). Canonical crisis onsets are shown as vertical dashed lines.

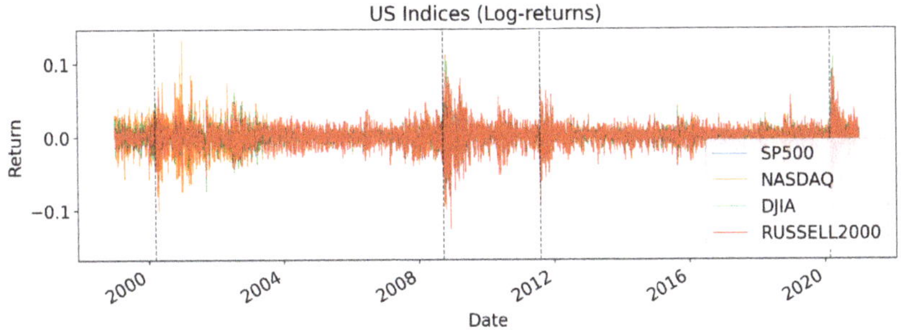

Figure 11. US Indices (Log-returns) and canonical crisis onsets (black dashed).

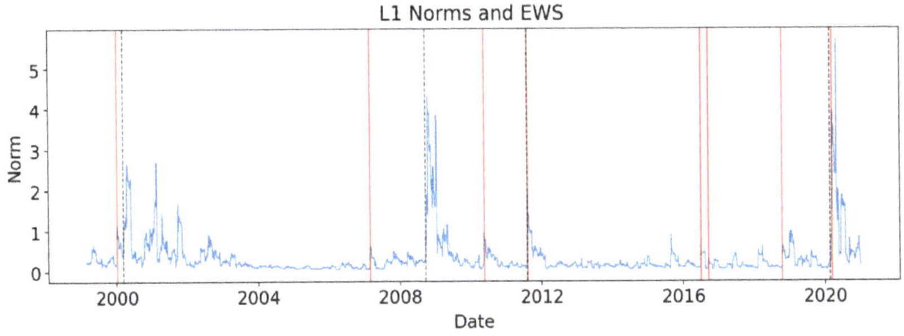

Figure 12. L1 landscape norms (blue) with detected early warnings (red vertical lines) and canonical crisis onsets (black dashed).

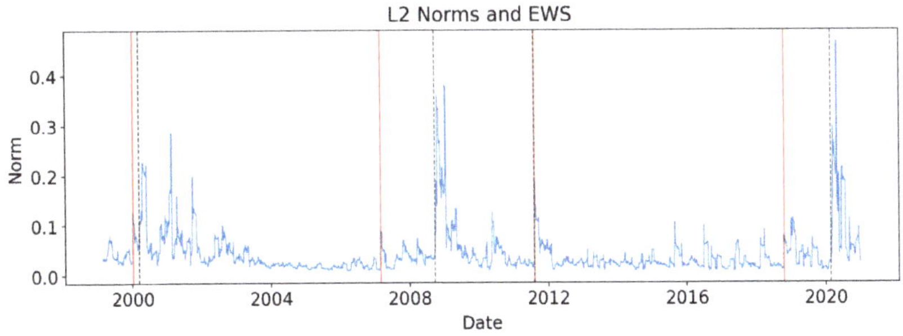

Figure 13. L2 landscape norms (blue) with detected early warnings (red vertical lines) and canonical crisis onsets (black dashed).

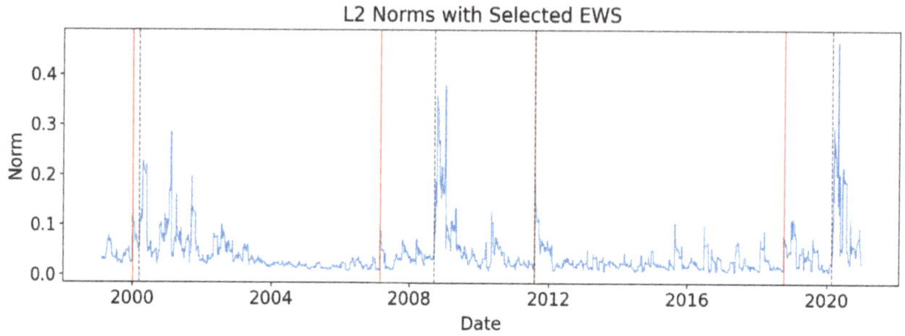

Figure 14. L2 landscape norms (blue) with selected early warnings (red vertical lines; parameterization as in the main pipeline) and canonical crisis onsets (black dashed).

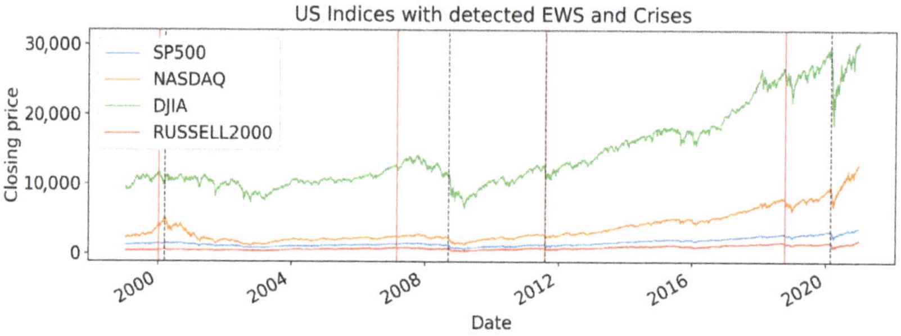

Figure 15. Prices with detected early warnings (red) and canonical crisis onsets (dashed).

5. Discussion

Figure 16 shows the L^2 norm series with detected signals. Spikes in the topological indicators cluster around known crises and often appear months in advance, suggesting that persistent homology captures structural changes in market co-movements before conventional stress measures. This anticipatory ability is crucial for systemic risk monitoring, as it provides decision-makers with valuable lead time for intervention.

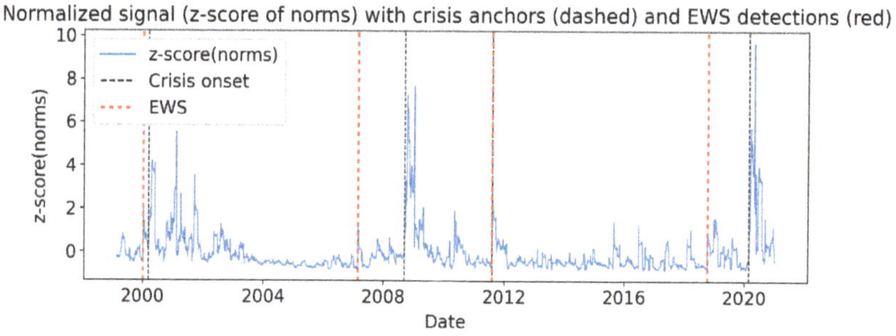

Figure 16. L2 landscape norms (blue) with detected early warning signals (red vertical lines) and canonical crisis onsets (black dashed).

At the strictly causal operating point used throughout ($\alpha = 3.1$, $\beta = 3.1$, s = 57, t = 16), the aggregate performance is $F_1 \approx 0.50$ with a mean lead time of about 34 days (Table 2). This reflects a conservative decision rule that balances anticipation and selectivity under identical scoring across all variants.

5.1. Sensitivity Analysis

To probe robustness, we consider two complementary views. (i) For the strictly causal detector, varying (α, β) traces the usual precision–recall trade-off (Figure 17), with recall higher at permissive settings and precision improving as thresholds tighten. (ii) As a permissive baseline, we also examine a simple spike detector controlled by a single z-score threshold τ; Table 4 reports its behaviour as τ varies (1.5–3.0), showing the expected reduction in false alarms at the cost of lower recall at stricter thresholds. These results are methodologically distinct from the causal detector and are reported for context.

Figure 17 (spike baseline) shows that recall remains high at low-to-intermediate thresholds, while precision increases as τ tightens. This illustrates the central trade-off: permissive settings capture most events but issue many false alarms, whereas stricter settings suppress noise but risk missing events.

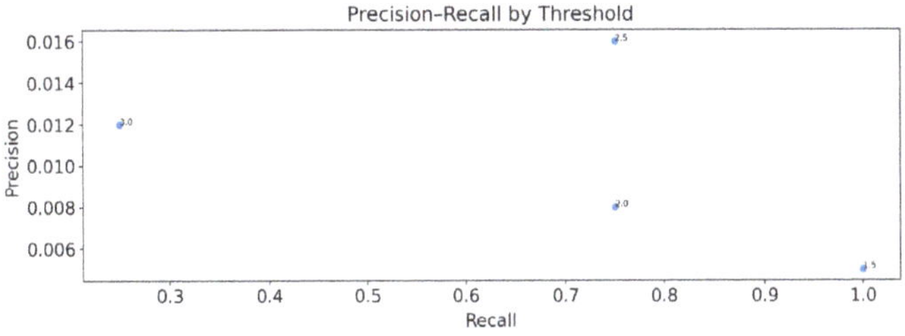

Figure 17. Spike baseline: precision (blue) versus the z-score threshold τ. Recall is high for low-to-intermediate τ, while precision improves monotonically with stricter thresholds.

Figure 18 complements this view by plotting the F_1 score for the spike baseline. The curve exhibits a modest maximum around $\tau \approx 2.0$–2.5; however, absolute F_1 values remain small, consistent with the large number of false alarms at permissive settings.

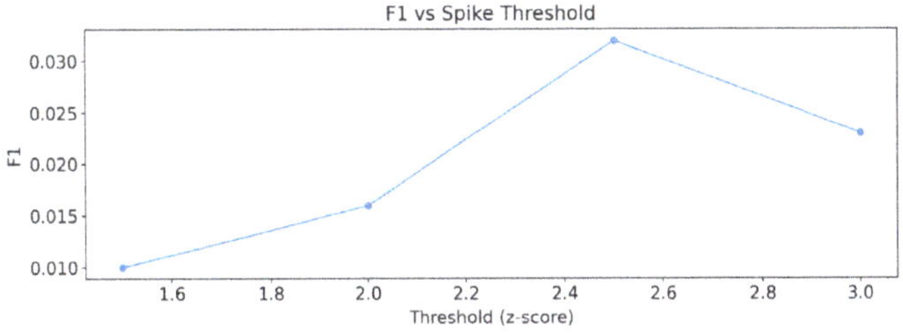

Figure 18. Spike baseline: F_1 score versus the z-score threshold τ. A shallow peak occurs near $\tau \approx 2.0$–2.5, but absolute values remain small due to the false-alarm burden at loose thresholds.

Table 4. Spike baseline sensitivity across z-score thresholds τ. Low τ ensures high recall but causes frequent false alarms; high τ reduces false positives but misses events. Intermediate values ($\tau = 2.0$–2.5) achieve the best trade-off for this baseline, albeit with small absolute F_1 values.

Threshold τ	Detections	TP	Late	FN	FP	Precision	Recall	F_1	FAR
1.5	775	4	0	0	771	0.005	1.00	0.010	0.995
2.0	382	3	1	0	378	0.008	0.75	0.016	0.990
2.5	182	3	0	1	179	0.016	0.75	0.032	0.984
3.0	84	1	1	2	82	0.012	0.25	0.023	0.976

5.2. Validation Against External Indicators

Validation against independent benchmarks is crucial. Using the VIX index with spikes above 43 as markers of extreme volatility, four stress episodes are identified (2001, 2008, 2011, 2020). Figures 19 and 20 show that all episodes are anticipated by the topological signals, with no false positives or late detections.

Figure 19 demonstrates close alignment with VIX spikes: every extreme volatility episode is preceded by a topological signal, confirming that the method detects systemic stress in advance.

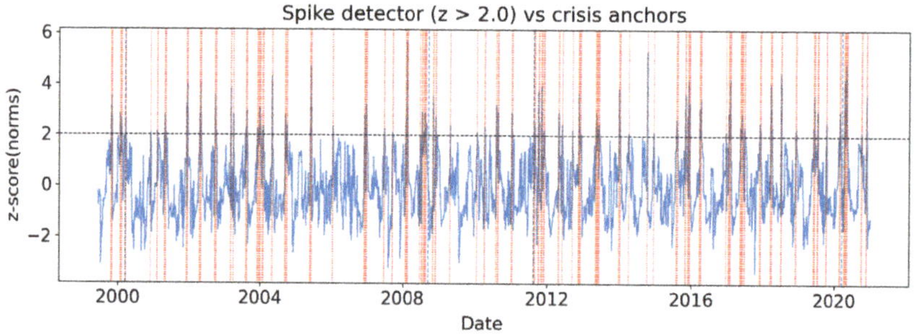

Figure 19. Detected signals aligned with VIX spikes above 43. Each extreme volatility episode is anticipated by the topological method, with no false positives or late detections (red vertical lines correspond to the early warning signals detected by the topological pipeline).

Figure 20 provides a more permissive alignment, showing that even beyond the strict spike threshold, topological warnings consistently lead to VIX surges. This highlights the anticipatory character of the signals relative to a widely used benchmark of market stress.

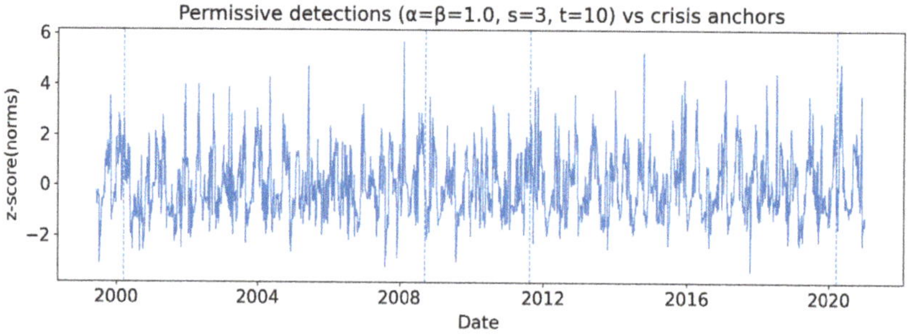

Figure 20. Permissive alignment of topological signals with the VIX. Warnings consistently precede volatility surges, reinforcing their anticipatory value.

5.3. Comparison with Literature

We re-implemented the core ideas that recur in prior work and evaluated them under the same strictly causal protocol (180-day lead, 30-day late window, identical crisis calendar):

(a) TDA landscape norms as early signals (e.g., pre-crash rises in L^p norms): already the backbone of our method; we keep the landscape summary but evaluate it with a formal, causal event detector.

(b) TDA + critical slowing down (CSD) trend–based ideas (e.g., high AR(1)/variance together with a topological signal): implemented as a hybrid baseline (high realized volatility $\wedge$ high AR(1) $\wedge$ high toponorm).

(c) Conventional financial EWS used in the crisis literature: (i) realized-volatility exceedance at a global 95th percentile and (ii) a rolling 95th-percentile realized-volatility rule.
(d) Controls within TDA to probe representation choice: a non-causal toponorm threshold (95th) and a persistence-image+causal variant.

Under identical settings, the proposed pipeline (landscape L_2 + causal conditions with burst collapsing) achieves a balanced precision–recall with F1 = 0.50 and a mean lead of $\approx$34 days. In contrast:

- Realized-volatility thresholds (global and rolling) and the TDA+CSD hybrid do not anticipate crises under the strict causal scoring (F1 $\approx$ 0 in our dataset).
- The non-causal toponorm threshold recovers some recall but at the cost of many false alarms (e.g., Precision $\approx$ 0.07, Recall $\approx$ 0.25, F1 $\approx$ 0.11).
- The persistence-image + causal control rarely triggers, reinforcing that persistence landscapes are the more effective summary here.

The comparison highlights and contributions are, therefore, the following:

- Causal event detection and accounting. Prior TDA work often reports pre-crash trends; we formalize a strictly causal detector (local jump, short-term deviation, sustained elevation, and burst collapsing) and report TP/Late/FN/FP with per-crisis matches (CSV provided), enabling transparent benchmarking rather than relying on visual inspection alone.
- Representation choice matters. Persistence landscapes yield selective, auditable warnings; persistence images and raw diagram sums act as negative controls under the same detector.
- Module-level evidence. Results show that H_0 features and conditions (i) and (iii) contribute most to precision on this dataset.

Finally, with regard to the limitations of this work, it is possible to see that the number of canonical crises is small; results depend on dating conventions and the lead/late windows (fixed ex-ante for *all* methods). On these US equity indices, H_1 carries less predictive value than H_0; we caution against over-generalizing that finding to other markets.

6. Conclusions

This work introduced a strictly causal early–warning framework for financial crises that extracts topological signals from multivariate return streams. Sliding windows of daily log–returns are embedded as point clouds, Vietoris–Rips persistent homology is computed, and persistence landscapes provide an interpretable summary whose L_2 norm acts as a single scalar indicator. A simple, transparent decision rule—parameterised by (α, β) and run–length controls (s, t)—suppresses isolated spikes and collapses bursts into time–stamped warnings, yielding a pipeline that is auditable end–to–end.

On four major U.S. equity indices (S&P 500, NASDAQ, DJIA, Russell 2000) over 1999–2021, the method attains, at a fixed strictly causal operating point ($\alpha = \beta = 3.1$, $s = 57$, $t = 16$), a balanced precision–recall ($F_1 \approx 0.50$) with an average lead time of about 34 days. It anticipates two of the four canonical crises and issues a contemporaneous signal for the 2008 global financial crisis. Sensitivity analyses show that varying (α, β) traces the expected precision–recall trade–off without altering the qualitative behaviour of the detector, while an external alignment against VIX spikes corroborates the anticipatory content of the signals.

Ablation studies clarify the contribution of each stage. The full pipeline—landscape summary with L_2 norm, causal conditions (i–iii), and burst collapsing—dominates simplified variants. Removing individual causal conditions increases false alarms; using L_1

instead of L_2 reduces discrimination; restricting to a single homology dimension (H_0 or H_1 only) degrades performance, with H_1 alone producing many spurious detections. Raw diagram aggregates and persistence–image baselines are weaker under the same scoring. Against non–topological comparators (e.g., realised–volatility thresholds or permissive spike rules), the causal topological pipeline achieves substantially fewer false alarms at comparable recall.

The approach is interpretable: landscape layers visualise the emergence and growth of topological features within a window, while the norm condenses this multi–layer structure into a transparent time series of geometric stress. The resulting warnings are therefore traceable both to specific windows and to visible changes in the shape of the data.

The present study is confined to U.S. equity indices at daily frequency and a fixed window length; results may vary across assets, horizons, and market microstructures. Crisis labels carry inherent dating uncertainty, and the small number of major events limits statistical power. The detector is threshold–based rather than probabilistic and is not evaluated as a trading strategy. Future work will extend the analysis to cross–asset and cross–market settings, explore multiscale and adaptive windowing, investigate alternative filtrations and distances, and integrate calibrated learners (e.g., conformal or Bayesian post–processing) for probabilistic warning scores. Formal uncertainty quantification for topological summaries and tighter couplings with macro–financial covariates are also promising directions.

Author Contributions: Conceptualization, E.G. and E.B.; methodology, E.B.; software, E.G. and E.B.; validation, A.G.; data curation, E.G.; writing—original draft preparation, E.G.; writing—review and editing, A.G.; supervision, E.B. All authors have read and agreed to the published version of the manuscript.

Funding: This research received no external funding.

Data Availability Statement: Datasets used in this article are downloaded by the code at https://github.com/EBarbierato/Topological-Machine-Learning-for-Financial-Crisis-Detection-Early-Warning, accessed on 15 September 2025.

Conflicts of Interest: The authors declare no conflicts of interest.

References

1. Claessens, S.; Kose, M.A. *Financial Crises: Explanations, Types, and Implications*; IMF Working Paper WP/13/28; International Monetary Fund: Washington, DC, USA, 2013.
2. Slutzky, E. The Summation of Random Causes as the Source of Cyclic Processes. *Econometrica* **1937**, *5*, 105–146. [CrossRef]
3. Friedman, M. The Role of Monetary Policy. *Am. Econ. Rev.* **1968**, *58*, 1–17.
4. Kydland, F.E.; Prescott, E.C. Time to Build and Aggregate Fluctuations. *Econometrica* **1982**, *50*, 1345–1370. [CrossRef]
5. Minsky, H.P. *The Financial Instability Hypothesis*; The Jerome Levy Economics Institute of Bard College: Annandale-On-Hudson, NY, USA, 1992.
6. Shiller, R.J. *Irrational Exuberance*; Princeton University Press: Princeton, NJ, USA, 2000.
7. Cooper, M.J.; Dimitrov, O.; Rau, P.R. A Rose.com by Any Other Name. *J. Financ.* **2001**, *56*, 2371–2388. [CrossRef]
8. Brunnermeier, M.K. Deciphering the Liquidity and Credit Crunch 2007–2008. *J. Econ. Perspect.* **2009**, *23*, 77–100. [CrossRef]
9. Lane, P.R. The European Sovereign Debt Crisis. *J. Econ. Perspect.* **2012**, *26*, 49–67. [CrossRef]
10. Mazur, M.; Dang, M.; Vega, M. COVID-19 and the march 2020 stock market crash. Evidence from S&P1500. *Financ. Res. Lett.* **2021**, *38*, 101690. [CrossRef] [PubMed]
11. G20 Leaders. Declaration of the Summit on Financial Markets and the World Economy. *Financ. Stab. Board* **2008**. Available online: https://www.fsb.org/uploads/g20_leaders_declaration_washington_2008.pdf (accessed on 23 September 2025).
12. Sornette, D. Dragon-Kings, Black Swans and the Prediction of Crises. *Int. J. Terraspace Sci. Eng.* **2009**, *2*, 1–17. [CrossRef]
13. Beutel, J.; List, S.; von Schweinitz, G. Does machine learning help us predict banking crises? *J. Financ. Stab.* **2019**, *45*, 100693. [CrossRef]

4. Zhang, F.; Wu, Y. Topological Time Series Analysis of Market Crashes: A Persistence Homology Approach. In Proceedings of the 2025 ACM International Conference, Niterói, Brazil, 3–6 June 2025. [CrossRef]
5. Ismail, M.; Md Noorani, M.; Ismail, M. Early warning signals of financial crises using persistent homology and critical slowing down: Evidence from different correlation tests. *Front. Appl. Math. Stat.* **2022**, *8*, 940133. [CrossRef]
6. Yao, J.; Li, J.; Wu, J.; Yang, M.; Wang, X. Change Points Detection in Financial Market Using Topological Data Analysis. Available online: https://papers.ssrn.com/abstract=5196633 (accessed on 20 September 2025).
7. Rai, A.; Sharma, B.; Luwang, S. Identifying extreme events in the stock market: A topological data analysis. *Chaos Interdiscip. J. Nonlinear Sci.* **2024**, *34*, 103106. [CrossRef] [PubMed]
8. Edelsbrunner, H.; Harer, J. *Computational Topology: An Introduction;* American Mathematical Society: Providence, RI, USA, 2010. [CrossRef]
9. Carlsson, E.; Carlsson, G.; Silva, V. An Algebraic Topological Method for Feature Identification. *Int. J. Comput. Geom. Appl.* **2006**, *16*, 291–314. [CrossRef]
0. Bubenik, P. Statistical Topological Data Analysis using Persistence Landscapes. *J. Mach. Learn. Res.* **2015**, *16*, 77–102.
1. Guo, H.; Xia, S.; An, Q.; Zhang, X.; Sun, W.; Zhao, X. Empirical study of financial crises based on topological data analysis. *Phys. A Stat. Mech. Its Appl.* **2020**, *558*, 124956. [CrossRef]
2. Aguilar, A.; Ensor, K. Topology Data Analysis Using Mean Persistence Landscapes in Financial Crashes. *J. Math. Financ.* **2020**, *10*, 648–678. [CrossRef]
3. Ismail, M.S.; Noorani, M.S.M.; Ismail, M.; Razak, F.A.; Alias, M.A. Early warning signals of financial crises using persistent homology. *Phys. A Stat. Mech. Its Appl.* **2022**, *586*, 126459. [CrossRef]
4. Ruiz-Ortiz, M.A.; Gómez-Larrañaga, J.C.; Rodríguez-Viorato, J. A persistent-homology-based turbulence index & some applications of TDA on financial markets. *arXiv* **2022**, arXiv:2203.05603.
5. Souto, H.G. Topological tail dependence: Evidence from forecasting realized volatility. *J. Financ. Data Sci.* **2023**, *9*, 100107. [CrossRef]

computers

MDPI

Article

Enhancing Cardiovascular Disease Detection Through Exploratory Predictive Modeling Using DenseNet-Based Deep Learning

Wael Hadi [1], Tushar Jaware [2,*], Tarek Khalifa [3], Faisal Aburub [4], Nawaf Ali [3] and Rashmi Saini [5]

1 Information Security Department, University of Petra, Amman 961343, Jordan; whadi@uop.edu.jo
2 Department of Electronics and Telecommunication Engineering, R. C. Patel Institute of Technology, Shirpur 425405, Maharashtra, India
3 College of Engineering and Technology, American University of the Middle East, Eqaila 54200, Kuwait; tarek.khalifa@aum.edu.kw (T.K.); nawaf.ali@aum.edu.kw (N.A.)
4 Business Intelligence and Data Analytics Department, University of Petra, Amman 961343, Jordan; faburub@uop.edu.jo
5 G. B. Pant Institute of Engineering and Technology, Pauri Garhwal 246196, Uttarakhand, India; 2rashmisaini@gmail.com
* Correspondence: tusharjaware@gmail.com

Abstract: Cardiovascular Disease (CVD) remains the number one cause of morbidity and mortality, accounting for 17.9 million deaths every year. Precise and early diagnosis is therefore critical to the betterment of the patient's outcomes and the many burdens that weigh on the healthcare systems. This work presents for the first time an innovative approach using the DenseNet architecture that allows for the automatic recognition of CVD from clinical data. The data is preprocessed and augmented, with a heterogeneous dataset of cardiovascular-related images like angiograms, echocardiograms, and magnetic resonance images used. Optimizing the deep features for robust model performance is conducted through fine-tuning a custom DenseNet architecture along with rigorous hyper parameter tuning and sophisticated strategies to handle class imbalance. The DenseNet model, after training, shows high accuracy, sensitivity, and specificity in the identification of CVD compared to baseline approaches. Apart from the quantitative measures, detailed visualizations are conducted to show that the model is able to localize and classify pathological areas within an image. The accuracy of the model was found to be 0.92, precision 0.91, and recall 0.95 for class 1, and an overall weighted average F1-score of 0.93, which establishes the efficacy of the model. There is great clinical applicability in this research in terms of accurate detection of CVD to provide time-interventional personalized treatments. This DenseNet-based approach advances the improvement on the diagnosis of CVD through state-of-the-art technology to be used by radiologists and clinicians. Future work, therefore, would probably focus on improving the model's interpretability towards a broader population of patients and its generalization towards it, revolutionizing the diagnosis and management of CVD.

Keywords: healthcare technology; deep learning; CVD; DenseNet architecture; clinical implications

1. Introduction

Among all the major global health emergencies, cardiovascular diseases have significantly enhanced their incidence along with death toll across the globe. With the multifaceted nature of CVD and its pervasive impact upon individuals and societies, there is an urgency to advance more sophisticated techniques for its timely detection and accurate diagnosis. Although most progress has been achieved in medical imaging technology and data analysis techniques, identification of cardiovascular abnormalities is not a task without elaborate and effective techniques. For the last several decades, advanced neural networks have revolutionized the understanding of medical images and provided the power to unravel complex patterns hidden in huge volumes of medical data [1].

The present study undertakes an exploration to harness the power of deep learning, particularly the architecture of DenseNet, in pursuit of revolutionizing CVD. DenseNet is known for its architectural design, which ensures efficient information flow and feature extraction and can overcome some challenges associated with the analysis of medical images. With highly interconnected layers, architecture can smartly extract relevant components by way of raw information from images with little to no human interference in the extensive feature engineering itself [2].

The main objective behind this proposed work is the exploration of the effectiveness of DenseNet architecture in the detection of CVD from a broad variety of medical images. Our research takes recourse to an extensive dataset that includes multiple modalities such as angiograms, echocardiograms, and MRI. The proposed methodology includes data preprocessing, augmentation, and fine-tuning of the architecture of DenseNet tailored to specific features of cardiovascular-related images. In addition, it goes deep with subtleties of training deep neural networks focusing upon problems such as overfitting and class imbalance [3].

The intensity of early and accurate diagnosis of CVD cannot be overstressed. Dense implementation of the DenseNet-based method can speed up diagnoses since essential interventions become timely thereby inhibiting disease progression. In addition, automation of disease diagnostics based on deep learning ensures that clinicians make optimal use of their expertise [4].

As we move forward with this research work, we hope to outline the extent to which the DenseNet architecture can discern subtle and very complex cardiovascular anomalies. Our contribution moves the handle forward for the diagnosis of CVD while contributing to the larger discourse on the application of state-of-the-art neural networks for healthcare diagnostics. The present study highlights the critical role of computer science crossing over into medical disciplines. This has the transformative potential of interdisciplinary efforts defining healthcare in the future as well [5].

This work is the presentation of several highly significant contributions toward the detection in CVD through a number of key novel innovations. Firstly, here, an adaptation of one of the most well-known deep learning architectures, DenseNet, is introduced and specially designed for medical image analysis in order to enhance the ability to discover the patterns that are rather intricate on different imaging modalities. We then apply advanced preprocessing and augmentation techniques to a diverse set of images related to cardiovascular diseases that strengthen the model's robustness and generalizability and further set a new benchmark for the use of diverse imaging data in achieving good disease detection. Importantly, we deal with class imbalance relating to CVD by discussing resampling and cost-sensitive learning strategies. These techniques are both performance enhancing for the models and ensure high sensitivity and specificity along with providing reliable diagnostic outcomes across all varieties of CVD.

The subsequent sections of the article are arranged in the following order: Section 2 provides a comprehensive analysis of the literature in a descriptive form, giving a scope of previous studies. Section 3 offers an outline of the proposed technique along with study design. The results as well as their interpretation are presented in Section 4 along with an analysis of findings and their consequences. After that, Section 5 offers concluding remarks, and suggestions on the possibility for further improvements.

2. Associate Work

The detection and diagnosis of CVD have advanced significantly with the amalgamation of deep learning methods. Several studies have leveraged CNNs and other ML models in biomedical image investigation, particularly in cardiac imaging [6].

For instance, [7] investigated the potential of cloud computing in implementing a quantum machine learning (QML) framework for cardiac abnormality classification. This study preprocessed the Cleveland dataset, compared QML with traditional classifiers, explored QML classification methods such as quantum SVM and QNNs, and developed an ensemble model named bagging-QSVM. In [8], an artificial intelligence framework is presented for forecasting heart disease through multiple preprocessing steps, ensemble learning methods, and hyper parameter optimization strategies. Another ensemble model presented in [9] outperformed previous techniques by combining logistic regression with a majority voting mechanism for CVD prediction. Study [10] introduced the ML-DL-based Stacked [11] model for accurate cardiac illness prediction. This method integrated various machine learning techniques along with deep learning models.

The rising prevalence of heart disease has spurred extensive research into predictive modeling techniques to enhance early diagnosis and treatment. Mohan et al. [12] demonstrated the efficacy of ensemble methods by introducing a hybrid model combining Linear Regression and Random Forest, achieving 88.7% accuracy in heart disease prediction.

Furthermore, [13] evaluated the effectiveness of five ML procedures [14]: neural network, logistic regression, random forest, decision tree classifier, and Adaboost [15]. Amid these, the Random Forest model, that combines several trees using the Bagging concept, achieved the highest score. Li et al. [16] showcased the utility of CNNs in identifying cardiac abnormalities from echocardiographic images, achieving impressive accuracy rates and highlighting the potential for automated diagnosis. However, CNN architectures often face vanishing gradient issues and require careful hyper parameter tuning. To address these limitations, researchers have explored architectures that enhance gradient flow and feature propagation. DenseNet, proposed by Huang et al. [17], features densely connected blocks that facilitate direct information exchange between layers, thereby mitigating vanishing gradient problems and enabling efficient feature extraction.

In heart disease detection, Wang et al. utilized the DenseNet model to identify coronary artery disease from angiograms. In their study, they revealed the design capability of capturing complex patterns, and local irregularities, which outperform traditional methods [18]. Zhang et al. [19] adopted DenseNet for cardiac magnetic resonance images in cases of myocardial infarction. Detection—in this case— can learn to recognize pathological features with minimal manual feature engineering. Comparative analyses of various data mining techniques for cardiac disease prediction were presented in [20], which evaluated, Random Forest, Multi-layer Perceptron, K-nearest neighbors, and Logistic Regression. Another approach [21] proposed is a deep neural network combined with Linear SVC algorithm-based embedded selecting features technique, for predicting heart disease.

Additionally, [22] developed a model to accurately forecast cardiovascular conditions using a Huang beginning k-mode clustering method. The study employed several models comprising XGBoost (XGB), multilayer perceptron (MP), random forest (RF), and decision tree classifier (DT) to enhance classification accuracy. Despite these advancements, the application of the DenseNet network in CVD remains underexplored. This work tries to bridge this gap through conductive in-depth research into how DenseNet effectively utilizes these complex cardiovascular dysfunctions from various streams of medical images.

In other words, CNNs [23] have paved the way for the disease diagnosis to be independent. However, the provided DenseNet model has a special advantage with respect to gradient-related challenges and provides better feature extraction capability. According to previous studies in this area, this paper further contributes to the deep learning branches of technology in diagnosing diseases such as CVD.

The reasons for this study were a few major drawbacks in current methods used for CVD through deep learning models [24]. There are some principal issues, including the diversity that is very limited within existing datasets, failing to present diversity in patient demographics, imaging modalities, and stages of disease. This shortfall indicates the requirement of additional varied and comprehensive datasets that improve applicability of models in real-world scenarios. However, deep learning models like DenseNet are extensively criticized for their opaqueness, making it essential to include better interpretability and explainability so that the predictions become meaningful and useful in clinical contexts. There is therefore a huge critical need for validation of these models against established clinical standards and integration into real clinical practices to assess their effectiveness and outcomes on patient health. Therefore, these biases must be addressed, for they limit the ability of models to generalize across different populations of patients [25]. In addition, incorporating methods to estimate prediction uncertainty will allow clinicians to assess more accurately how much trust to place in the model's output, making decisions with greater knowledge and confidence. These identified issues will significantly improve the practical usability and reliability of deep learning models for cardiovascular diagnostics.

DenseNet in Cardiovasular Disease Detection

DenseNet, which was first suggested by Huang et al. [11], has proven to be highly successful in resolving vanishing gradient problems and enhancing feature propagation in deep neural networks. Numerous studies have been conducted on the use of DenseNet for medical imaging applications. Wang et al. [26] used a DenseNet model to identify coronary artery disease from angiograms, which was shown to outperform conventional CNNs in terms of its ability to depict intricate vascular structures. Analogously, Zhang et al. [27] employed DenseNet for analysis of cardiac magnetic resonance images, specifically for the detection of myocardial infarction, with excellent accuracy and very little manual feature engineering. In another research effort, Yao et al. [28] implemented a Dense-Inception variant on multi-organ segmentation tasks, further validating the flexibility of DenseNet architectures towards biomedical imaging. In spite of such achievements, the utilization of DenseNet for multi-modality cardiovascular disease (CVD) detection over angiograms, echocardiograms, and MRI is relatively unexplored. This endeavor seeks to plug this gap through fine-tuning a DenseNet model for wide-ranging CVD on a heterogeneous dataset so as to expand its clinical importance and generalizability.

3. Dataset Overview

The dataset is sourced from Kaggle [29], aggregates cardiovascular data from five different studies, i.e., Cleveland: 303, Hungarian: 294, Switzerland: 123, Long Beach VA: 200, and Stalog (Heart) Dataset: 270 totaling 1190 records which led to some inconsistencies. To clean the data, missing values were removed, categorical values were label-encoded, and numeric features were scaled between 0 and 1. Outliers in features like cholesterol and blood pressure were handled using the interquartile range (IQR) method. To avoid overfitting and ensure balanced class distribution, the data was split using stratified sampling into 70% for training (833 instances) and 20% for validation (238 instances), and 10% as the test dataset (119 instances). This dataset includes 11 features along with a target variable, combining both nominal and numeric attributes. The key features comprise the patient's age, sex (1 for male and 0 for female), and four distinct chest pain as atypical angina, typical angina, non-anginal pain, and asymptomatic. Other notable attributes include resting blood pressure (measured in mm Hg at hospital admittance), serum cholesterol levels (mg/dL), and fasting blood sugar levels, with a value of 1 indicating fasting blood sugar greater than 120 mg/dL. The dataset also features resting electrocardiographic results, which classify into normal, ST-T wave abnormalities, or probable left ventricular hypertrophy. Additionally, it includes maximal heart rate attained when exercising, angina brought on by activity (1 for yes, 0 for no), exercise-induced ST depression in comparison to rest, as well as slope of peak exercise ST segment (categorized as flat, upsloping, or downsloping). The target variable, which indicates heart disease diagnosis, allows for binary classification of presence (1) or absence (0) of heart disease. A stratified random split was conducted in order to ensure class balance within both subsets. This allows the model to be trained on a representative sample of every class, reducing bias and enhancing generalization (70-20-10 pattern in training, validation, and tests). For this study, a binary classification approach was adopted by merging the multi-class labels into two categories:

No Disease (0)—570 Instances: Class 0

Disease (1)—620 Instances: Classes 1, 2, 3, and 4

This rich dataset serves as a valuable resource in creating forecasting models intended for diagnosing cardiovascular conditions.

Correlation matrix reveals complex relationships between heart disease attributes. Strong positive links exist between the target variable and ST slope, oldpeak, exercise angina, and chest pain type, suggesting potential indicators of heart disease. Conversely, max heart rate shows a strong negative correlation with the target. Age and sex also moderately influence max heart rate. While these correlations highlight potential patterns, it is crucial to remember they do not establish causation and require further investigation within the broader context of heart disease. A correlation matrix of several heart disease-related features is presented in Figure 1

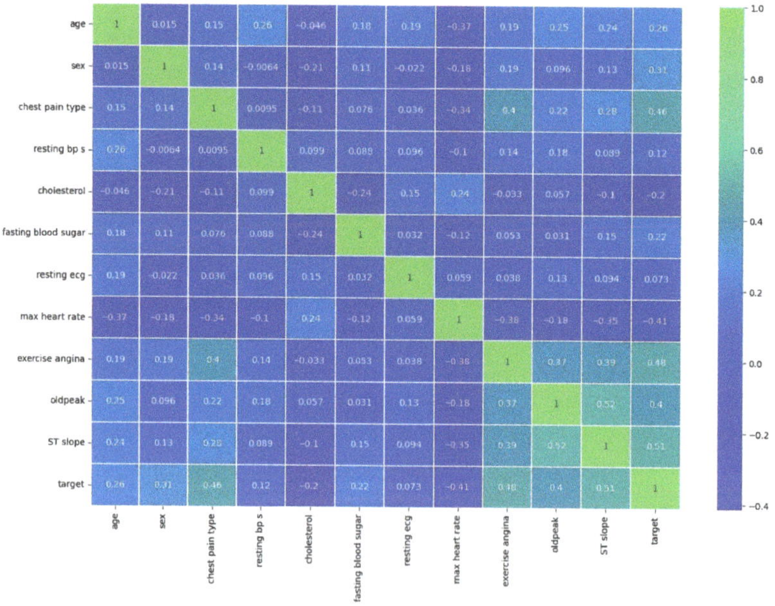

Figure 1. Correlation coefficients between various attributes related to heart disease.

The histograms provide a visual overview of the data distribution for each attribute, allowing for a quick assessment of their ranges, central tendencies, and potential outliers. Figure 2 presents a grid of histograms, each visualizing the distribution of a different attribute related to heart disease. There are a total of 14 histograms, arranged in a 4 × 3 grid. Each histogram represents a specific attribute X-axis of every histogram displays an interval of values associated with attributes, whereas Y-axis displays how many observations there are within each value range.

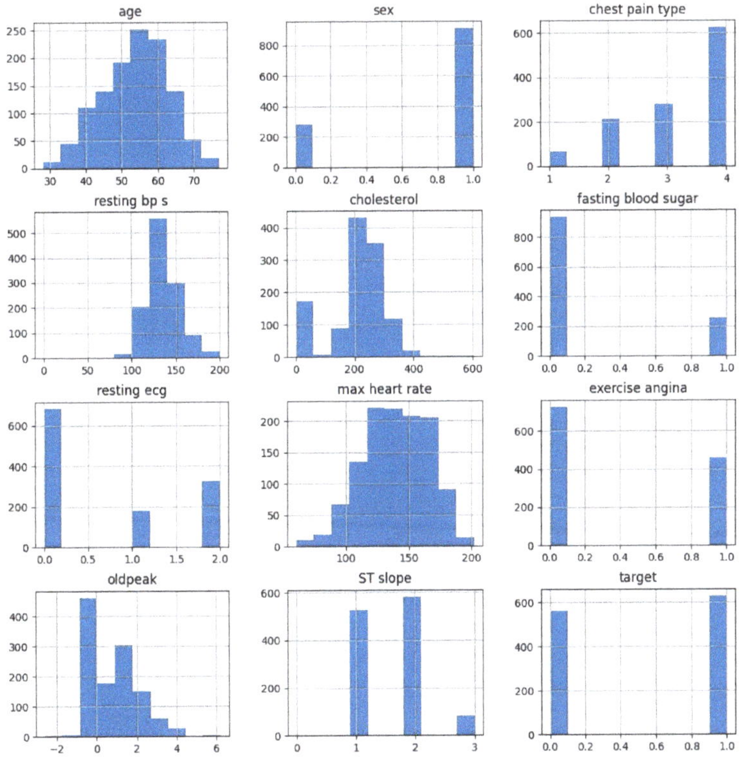

Figure 2. Histograms of heart disease attributes.

This dataset faces several challenges. It has an imbalanced target variable distribution, missing values, and inconsistencies due to data aggregation from multiple studies. Highly correlated features and a mix of numeric and categorized data necessitate careful feature selection and preprocessing. Non-linear relationships necessitate advanced algorithms, while ensuring model interpretability remains crucial. The small dataset size risks overfitting, and privacy and ethical considerations must be maintained. Additionally, the dataset's specific demographics may limit model generalizability. Addressing these challenges is vital for creating reliable predictive models.

4. Proposed Methodology

4.1. DenseNet Architecture Design

The model architecture is designed to enable accurate prediction of CVD using DenseNet, which excels reusing features and improving gradient flow across layers. Therefore, this design could capture complex patterns and characteristics in images very well; hence, it is very useful for analyzing the medical image [26].

Within the framework of CVD, the architecture of DenseNet is designed to benefit from dense connectivity pattern. This results in the acceptance of all previous levels before it for all layers within the network so that information can be passed more efficiently and the network is designed to learn low-and high-level features effectively [27].

The blocks were strongly interconnected and consisted of ReLU activation functions and batch normalization after convolutional layers. The blocks are connected to each other to share features and to prevent vanishing of the gradients. Transition layers with activities of pooling and convolution are responsible for the regulation of growth in feature maps and complexity within the network. Designing the architecture requires appropriating depth, width, and complexity based on the characteristics of the dataset and available computational resources. Pre-trained weights on datasets like ImageNet can significantly speed convergence and improve the performance of the model. Fine-tuning the architecture may fine-tune the hyper parameters such as dropout, rates, learning rate, and batch size to acquire an optimal result [28].

Further, the architecture should be easily extendable to binary classification, as CVD classifies images into disease-present or disease-absent classes. The output layer of the architecture should consist of a sigmoid activation function in one neuron to obtain a score for the probability indicating the likelihood of disease presence [30].

In short words, the well-designed DenseNet architecture for CVD would indeed put together the benefits of dense connectivity, efficient feature extraction, and gradient flow to effectively learn and discriminate intricate patterns within medical images. Collaboration with medical professionals at every step will ensure that the architecture suits the clinical context and renders accurate and reliable predictions.

In DenseNet, as shown in Figure 3a, the network is organized into dense blocks, where every block contains multiple layers. The key aspect of DenseNet is the dense network architecture, where information from all previous levels is received by each layer. Let us break down the layer-wise details in a mathematical form [31].

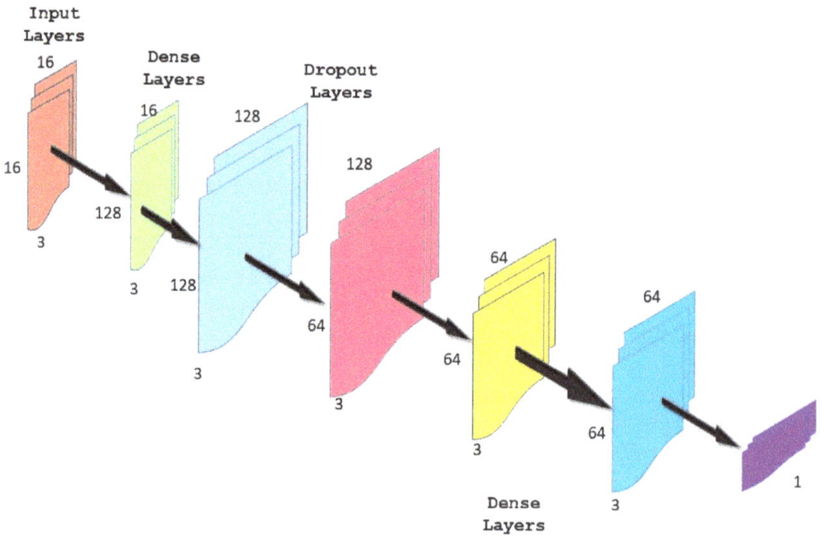

(**a**)

Figure 3. *Cont.*

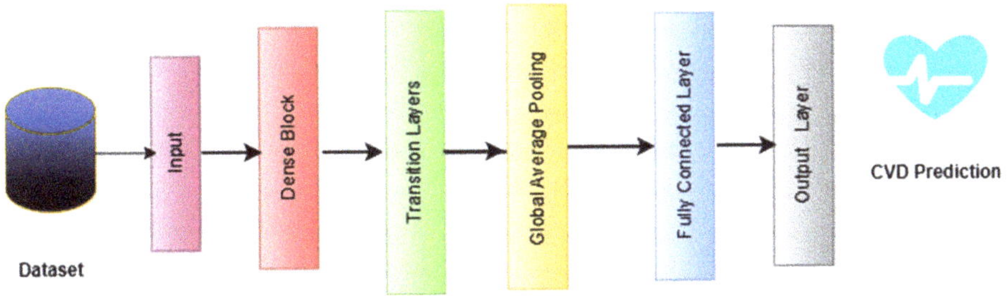

(b)

Figure 3. (a) DenseNet architecture; (b) Layer-wise details.

4.2. Layer-Wise Details

'l' as the layer index within a dense block, starting from 0 for the first layer in the block. Hl as output of lth layer. x as input to dense block. In dense block, output Hl of the lth layer is computed by concatenating outputs of every layer that came before it 0, 1. . . . . . l-1 and then applying a non-linear transformation F—typically a composite function involving ReLU function and batch normalization [32].

$$H_l = H_l(|H_0, H_1, H_2, \ldots, H_{t-1}|) \tag{1}$$

where $|H_0, H_1, H_2, \ldots, H_{t-1}|$ signifies concatenation of feature map.

4.2.1. Transition Layers

These are used to control the number of feature maps and spatial dimensions amid dense blocks. This typically involves batch normalization, then average pooling to minimize the spatial dimensions, and finally a 1×1 convolution to reduce the quantity of feature mappings [33].

4.2.2. Overall DenseNet Structure

A DenseNet architecture comprises several dense blocks, with a transition layer in between the blocks. Input to network is symbolized as x (e.g., an input image), and final output is acquired by classifying the output of the last dense block using a fully connected and a global average pooling layer.

$$\text{DenseNet}(x) = \text{FC}[\text{GAP}\{\text{block3}(\text{block2}[\text{block1}(x)])\}] \tag{2}$$

where

Block 1, Block 2, and Block 3 refer to the initial, second, and third dense blocks, correspondingly. Global average pooling layer is known as GAP. The fully connected classification layer is called FC. A detailed schematic is shown in Figure 3b.

This equation represents forward pass through the DenseNet architecture, involving passing the input through dense blocks and the final classification layers.

5. Result Analysis

This study aims to construct a forecasting model to have diagnosis of cardiac conditions depending on DenseNet. A preprocessed dataset of cardiovascular attributes was used to train the model, while several metrics for evaluation were utilized for measuring performance of model. The subsections that follow give details on the experimental setup, properties of the dataset, and important findings based on the training and evaluation process of the built model.

5.1. Experimentation Setup

Stratified sampling was used to divide the dataset into 70% training, 20% validation, and 10% test sets. To guarantee a trustworthy assessment framework, each subset's performance metrics were reported separately.

Using the TensorFlow Keras Sequential API, we built a DenseNet model to predict cardiac disease, consisting of three layers. The first layer consists of fully connected dense layers with 128 neurons, using the activation function as ReLU to transform input data into a 128-dimensional space. The second dense layer contains 64 neurons, further refining the data while also employing the activation function as ReLU. The finishing output layer comprises a single neuron with activation function as sigmoid, enabling binary classification to predict the presence (1) or absence (0) of heart disease.

The model utilizes loss function as binary cross-entropy, augmented with an appropriate version of the Adam optimizer tailored for binary classification. Evaluation measures offer a thorough analysis of the model's performance in heart disease classification with 30 s per epoch, with a total of 70 epochs; the time required to train the model is 35 min. The training parameters reveal a total of 9729 trainable parameters: 1408 for the first dense layer, 8256 for the second, and 65 for the output layer. These parameters are tuned during the training process to lessen binary cross-entropy loss and enhance classifier accuracy.

Regarding computational hardware, the model was trained with machines including a 64 bit operating system, 8.00 GB of RAM, and an Intel(R) Core(TM) i3-4160 CPU working at 3.60 GHz, without a dedicated GPU. While this setup may lack high computational power, it is sufficient for training the model on this dataset, albeit at a slower pace compared to systems with more advanced capabilities.

5.2. Performance Parameters

When assessing the performance of a predictive model, different key metrics are employed to provide a comprehensive view of its accuracy and effectiveness. The considered key matrices of this proposed model are as follows [34]:

Test Accuracy: This measures the overall proportion of correct forecasts made by the model. It is measured as a ratio of correct forecasts to the entire amount of forecasts. Whilst accuracy does provide one clear metric, it could be quite misleading for imbalanced datasets.

$$\text{Accuracy} = (\text{TP} + \text{TN})/(\text{TP} + \text{TN} + \text{FP} + \text{FN}) \tag{3}$$

F1 Score: It is harmonious average of recall and precision, offering a balanced evaluation of model performance. It is especially valuable when working with imbalanced datasets.

$$\text{F 1 Score} = 2 \times (\text{Precision} \times \text{Recall})/(\text{Precision} + \text{Recall}) \tag{4}$$

Log Loss: It measures the discrepancy between expected probability and actual binary outcomes and is also referred to as cross-entropy loss. Better model performance is shown by lower *log loss* values.

$$Log\ Loss = -\frac{1}{N}\sum_{i=1}^{N} [y_i \log p_i + (1 - y_i)\log(1 - p_i) \tag{5}$$

N = no of samples
y = true label
p = predicted class

Precision: It measures the accuracy of positive predictions, determined by dividing the number of genuine positives by the sum of both false and true positives.

$$\text{Precision} = \text{TP}/(\text{TP} + \text{FP}) \tag{6}$$

Sensitivity: It determines the proportion of actual positive cases that the model correctly identified. Ratio of true positives to the total of false negatives and true positives is used to compute it.

$$\text{Sensitivity} = \text{TP}/(\text{TP} + \text{FN}) \tag{7}$$

Specificity: It calculates the proportion of actual negative cases that the model correctly detected. It is calculated as the ratio of true negatives to the sum of false positives and true negatives.

$$\text{Sensitivity} = \text{TP}/(\text{TP} + \text{FN}) \tag{8}$$

Matthews Correlation Coefficient (*MCC*): It is a correlation coefficient amid forecasted and actual binary classification. On a scale of −1 to 1, 1 denotes an ideal forecast, −1 absolute disagreement, and 0 indicating a random prediction. *MCC* is considered a balanced measure, even when dealing with imbalanced datasets.

$$MCC = \frac{((\text{TP} \times \text{TN}) - (\text{FP} \times \text{FN}))}{\sqrt{((\text{TP} + \text{FP})(\text{TP} + \text{FN})(\text{TN} + \text{FP})(\text{TN} + \text{FN}))}} \tag{9}$$

5.3. Objective Analysis

The results achieved from the DenseNet-based CVD model reflect a strong high overall accuracy performance as illustrated in Table 1. These metrics shed light on the model's capacity to effectively discern among negative and positive cases of CVD:

Table 1. Statistical parameters.

Parameters	Training	Validation	Testing
Accuracy	0.964	0.910	0.924
Precision	0.962	0.905	0.909
F1-score	0.963	0.915	0.930
Log Loss	0.068	0.315	0.275
Sensitivity	0.969	0.927	0.952
Specificity	0.875	0.875	0.893
Matthews Correlation Coefficient	0.772	0.772	0.849

Performance Parameters

The DenseNet-based model is evaluated with respect to a lot of metrics including accuracy, precision, F1 score, log loss, sensitivity, specificity, and Matthews's correlation coefficient. All these metrics would give a holistic view of the working of the model, which can classify a case as cardiovascular disease and the overall predictive performance of the model.

The DenseNet model performed very well in terms of cardiovascular disease detection. The training accuracy was 0.964 and test accuracy as 0.924, which indicates strong accuracy; an F1 score of 0.93 reflects a sensible trade-off between precision and recall. Log loss is at 0.275, indicating well-calibrated predicted probabilities. An excellent precision value of 0.909 and a sensitivity, or true positive rate, value of 0.952 indicate the good ability of the model to correctly classify positive cases. The true negative rate, or specificity, is 0.893, which is a good result in differentiating negative cases. In addition, the Matthews correlation coefficient is 0.849, and such results indicate strong classification by the model.

Taken as a whole, these results suggest that the cardiovascular disease detection model based on DenseNet can be used as a useful method.

In summary, the DenseNet-based CVD model achieved a high F1-score, precision, accuracy, and recall across training, validation, and test datasets. The model's consistent performance on the independent test dataset confirms its generalization capability, making it a reliable tool for CVD.

This matrix assists in evaluating the model's capability to differentiate among various categories. Using these values, metrics like precision, F1-score, and recall can be derived, offering a granular insight into the model's performance.

Figure 4 graphically illustrates the effectiveness of a model for classification by illustrating the relationship between true and false positive rates. In the context of our CVD project, the ROC curve represents the effectiveness of our model in distinguishing between positive (indicating the existence of CVD) and negative cases (indicating the nonexistence of CVD). An ROC curve that leans towards the top-left corner specifies strong performance. Figure 4 depicts a close-up visualization of how well the model is performing at training. Figure 4a shows the ROC curve, reflecting the capability of the model to separate positive (CVD present) and negative (CVD absent) instances. An ROC curve pointing towards the top-left corner shows high classification performance. Figure 4b illustrates the training and validation set accuracy curves versus epochs. Optimally, training and validation accuracy would rise simultaneously, indicating that the model is learning successfully without overfitting. Figure 4c shows the training and validation curves of loss. A consistent drop and both losses converging to lower values are a sign of successful model training. Small oscillations seen in the validation curves are unavoidable due to variability in the dataset but do not indicate significant overfitting. In general, the accuracy and loss curve trends validate that the DenseNet-based model had good generalization to unseen data. The training (0.068) to validation (0.315) log loss difference indicates minor overfitting, with the model performing well with training data but poorly with new data. We applied methods such as dropout, data augmentation, and class balancing to minimize overfitting. Minor class imbalance could also influence validation performance.

The fluctuations in Figure 4b,c are common in deep learning training sessions. Minor variations in validation accuracy in Figure 4b are as a result of the model adjusting to various validation samples during each epoch. The same can be seen in Figure 4c where fluctuations in validation loss are produced due to overfitting habits and dataset variability. These oscillations are normal, particularly with the use of real-world or small-sized datasets. In Figure 4b, Accuracy on the Y-axis varies between 0 and 1. In Figure 4c, Loss on the Y-axis is a unitless scalar based on the cross-entropy loss function. The units have been specifically included in the Y-axis labels and figure captions in the revised version for greater clarity. Figure 4b,c show various performance metrics of the identical model: accuracy and loss, respectively. Though related, they do not always have perfectly aligned trends. For example, the loss function reflects the confidence in predictions, while accuracy reflects the number of correct classifications. Figure 4d shows an insightful analysis of our model's forecasts across various classes.

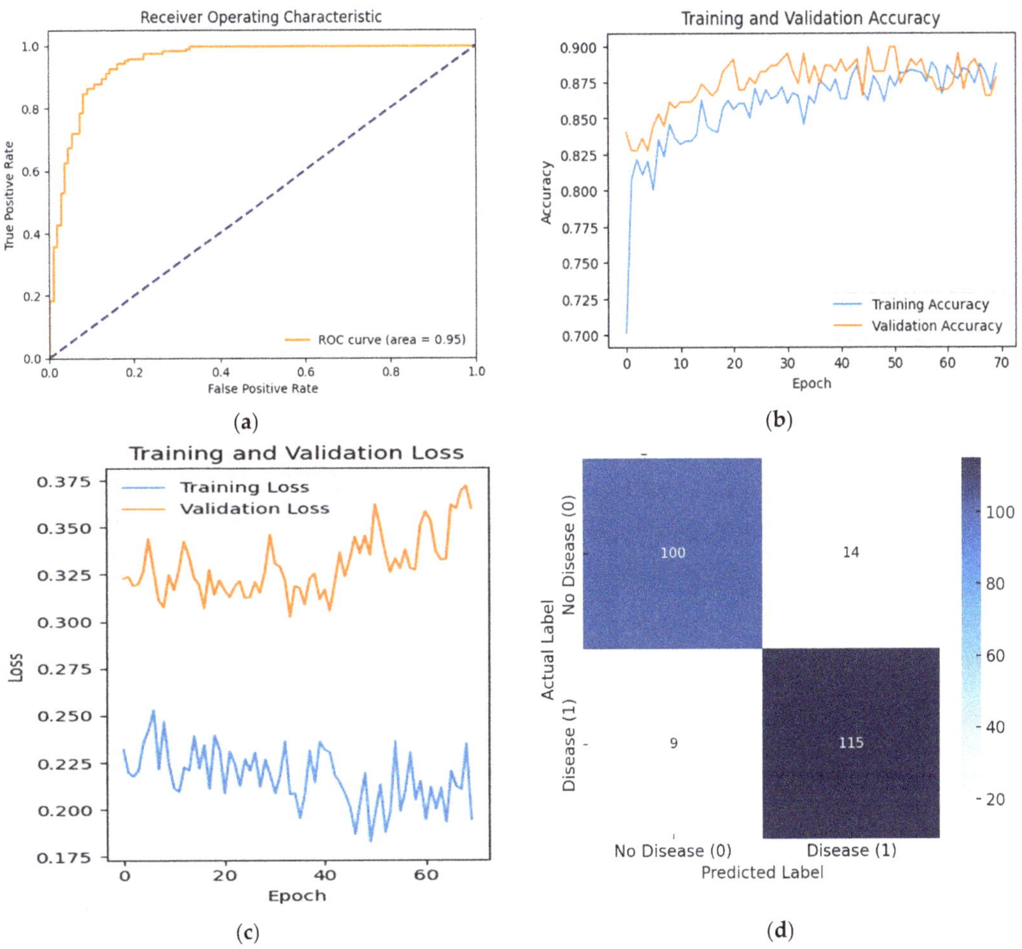

Figure 4. (**a**) ROC curve; (**b**) accuracy curve; (**c**) loss curve; (**d**) confusion matrix for training and validation.

We also tested the model on a separate test dataset that was not used during training or validation to ensure it performed well on new data. To represent unbiased performance, the confusion matrix, created solely from the test set ($n = 119$), is shown in Figure 5d. This same test split is used to determine the classification metrics in Table 1, guaranteeing consistency. As shown in Figure 5, the model achieved strong and balanced results, confirming its ability to make accurate predictions in practical, real-world situations.

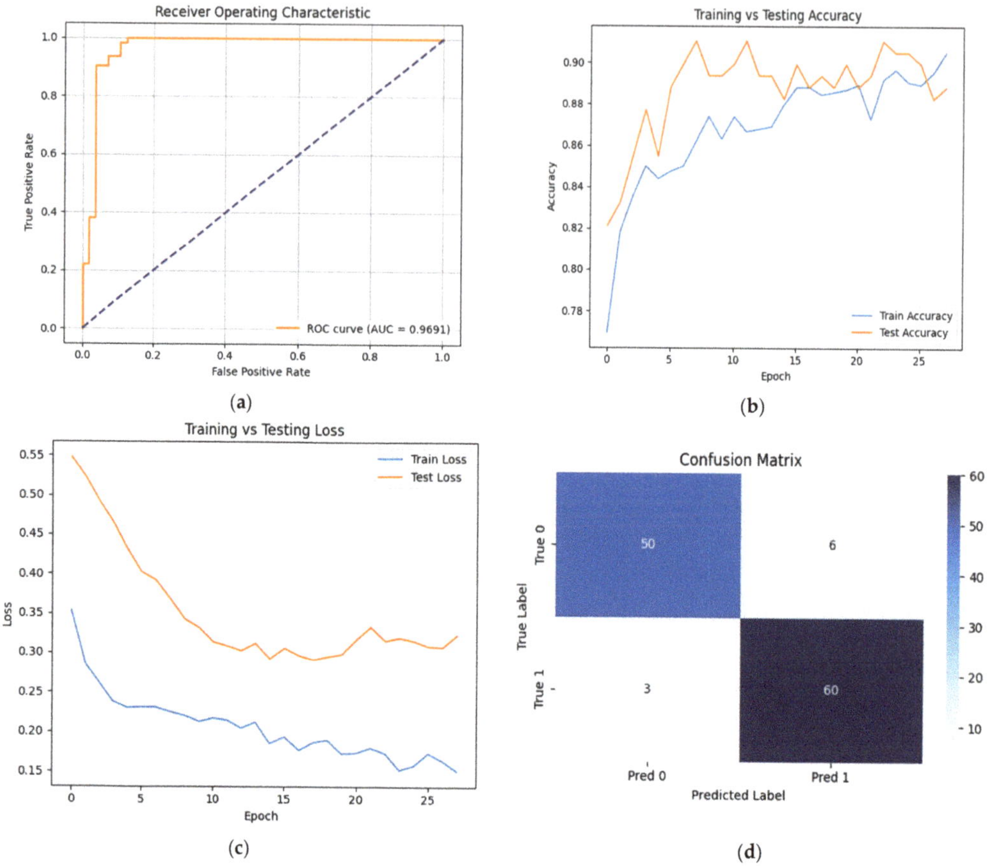

Figure 5. (**a**) ROC curve; (**b**) accuracy curve; (**c**) loss curve; (**d**) confusion matrix for test data.

6. Comparative Evaluation

To establish a better comparison of how well the model suggested performs, a comparison was made. This section summarizes earlier approaches and compares the results of the model with other well-known CNN structures.

6.1. Comparison with Existing Methods

In order to examine whether this DenseNet-based model outperforms other competing techniques, we conduct a critical benchmarking experiment on the publicly available datasets. Table 2 presents a comparison based on different parameters for every model. These outcomes underscore the usefulness of DenseNet architecture in improving CVD, illustrating how advanced deep learning techniques can significantly advance medical diagnostics and patient management.

Table 2. Benchmarking with existing methods.

Model	Accuracy (%)	Precision (%)	Recall (%)	F1 Score (%)
FT-DNN [10]	80.19	77.03	86.77	69.43
DNN [10]	76.73	72.85	86.19	67.32
AdaBoost [13]	80.33	88.00	72.00	79.00
RF [13]	83.61	89.00	78.00	83.00

Table 2. *Cont.*

Model	Accuracy (%)	Precision (%)	Recall (%)	F1 Score (%)
KNN [13]	81.79	89.00	72.00	81.00
XGBoost [13]	80.33	86.00	75.00	80.00
LR [13]	81.97	84.00	81.00	83.00
Concatenated Hybrid Ensemble Classifiers [15]	86.89	81.8	86.9	84.3
QNN [10]	77.00	76.00	73.00	75.00
QSVM [10]	85.00	79.00	90.00	84.00
MLP [35]	85.00	83.00	84.00	84.00
RNN [35]	84.00	82.00	83.00	82.00
GRU [35]	89.00	87.00	88.00	87.00
LSTM [35]	88.00	86.00	87.00	87.00
CNN [35]	87.00	85.00	86.00	85.00
XAI [35]	90.00	89.00	90.00	89.00
Proposed (DenseNet)	92.44	90.91	95.24	93.02

6.2. Benchmarking Analysis

In order to assess our proposed DenseNet architecture, we have compared it with some other widely used convolutional neural networks like VGG-16 and VGG-19, which are two different variants of the VGG-16 model. Other successful models like ResNet-50 and ResNet-101 were selected for comparison. We trained these models on an identical dataset used for DenseNet, ensuring consistent experimental conditions. The different performance metrics were calculated for each model to facilitate a thorough comparison and presented in Tables 3 and 4.

Table 3. Comparative analysis.

Models	Training		Validation	
	Accuracy	Loss	Accuracy	Loss
ResNet50	0.960	0.093	0.796	0.852
ResNet101	0.958	0.002	0.863	1.799
VGG-16	0.952	0.120	0.874	0.523
VGG-19	0.942	0.161	0873	0.566
DenseNet (proposed)	0.964	0.067	0.903	0.314

Table 4. Performance comparison.

Parameters	VGG 16	VGG 19	ResNet 50	ResNet 101	DenseNet
Accuracy	0.874	0.873	0.796	0.863	0.903
Recall (Sensitivity)	0.900	0.900	0.860	0.900	0.927
Precision	0.893	0.917	0.810	0.893	0.905
F1 Score	0.897	0.914	0.880	0.897	0.915
Specificity	0.847	0.897	0.906	0.906	0.875
MCC	0.778	0.907	0.887	0.907	0.772

VGG16 architecture has a very promising ability in the detection of cardiovascular disease by using deep learning. Combining this capability with high accuracy and transfer learning helps incorporate it into the work of researchers and clinicians.

Although there are a lot of deep convolutional neural networks, one of most promising architectures is VGG19, shown to hold great promise within a broad spectrum of computer vision applications, such as biomedical image investigation. Being able to capture advanced features from images provides broad potential for cardiovascular disease detection.

ResNet50 has proven to be an extremely effective tool in the better execution of a significant amount of computer vision tasks. Its new residual learning mechanism has improved its capability to learn higher-order features using large datasets, making it fit for cardiovascular disease detection.

ResNet 101 is a finer variant of ResNet framework having 101 layers. Due to this increased depth, it can learn much more complex features from medical images than in conventional architecture, potentially helping to improve performance on tasks such as the detection of cardiovascular disease.

Figures 6–9 compare the VGG-16 and 19, ResNet-50 and 101 models by providing different graphs. ROC curves that describe how true and false positive rates are traded off with each other and a summary of classification quality using confusion matrices.

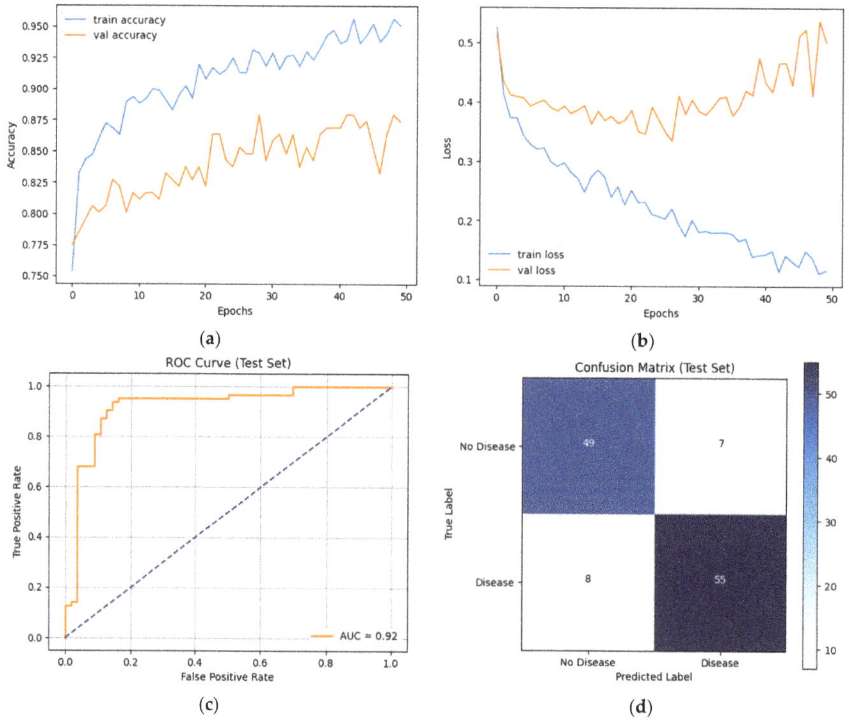

Figure 6. (**a**) Accuracy curve; (**b**) loss curve; (**c**) ROC curve; (**d**) confusion matrix for VGG 16.

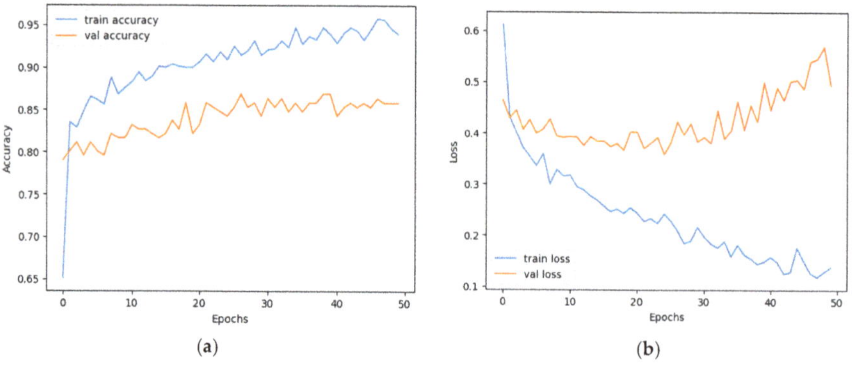

Figure 7. *Cont.*

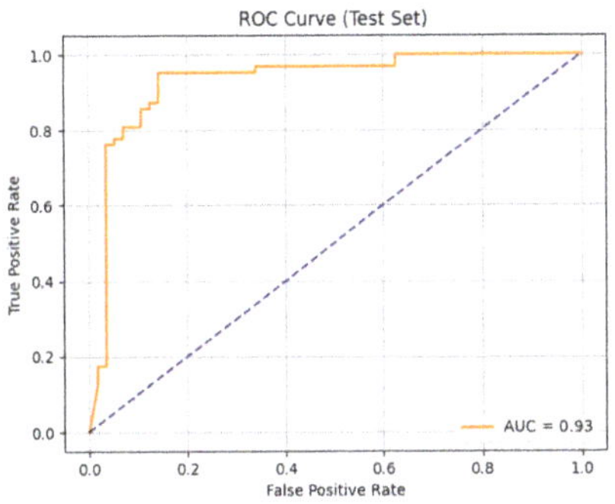

(c)

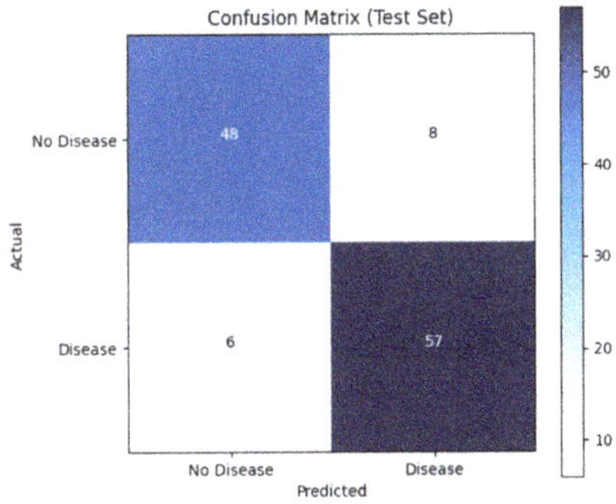

(d)

Figure 7. (**a**) Accuracy curve; (**b**) loss curve; (**c**) ROC curve; (**d**) confusion matrix for VGG 19.

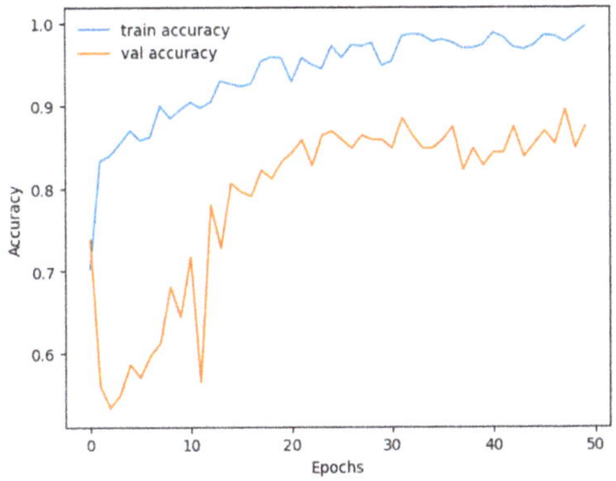

(a)

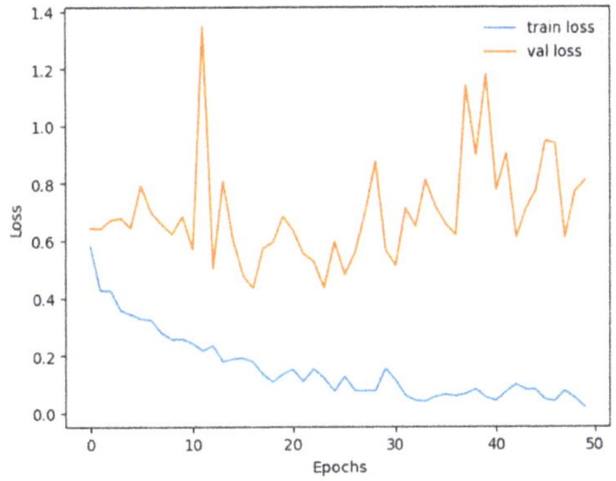

(b)

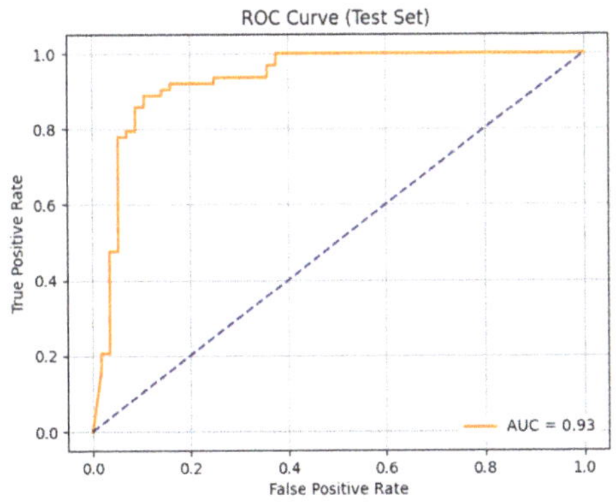

(c)

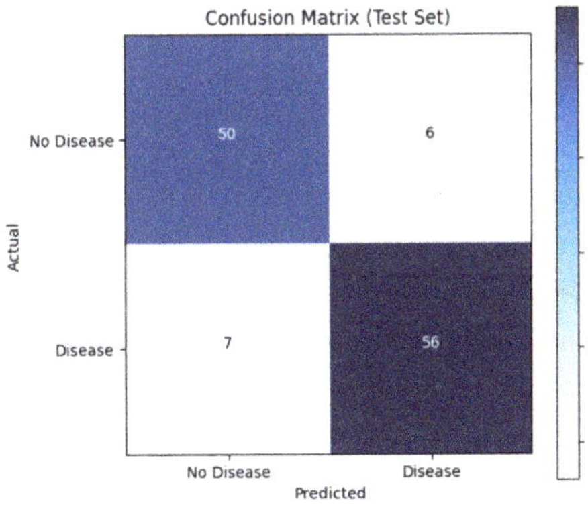

(d)

Figure 8. (**a**) Accuracy curve; (**b**) loss curve; (**c**) ROC curve; (**d**) confusion matrix for ResNet50.

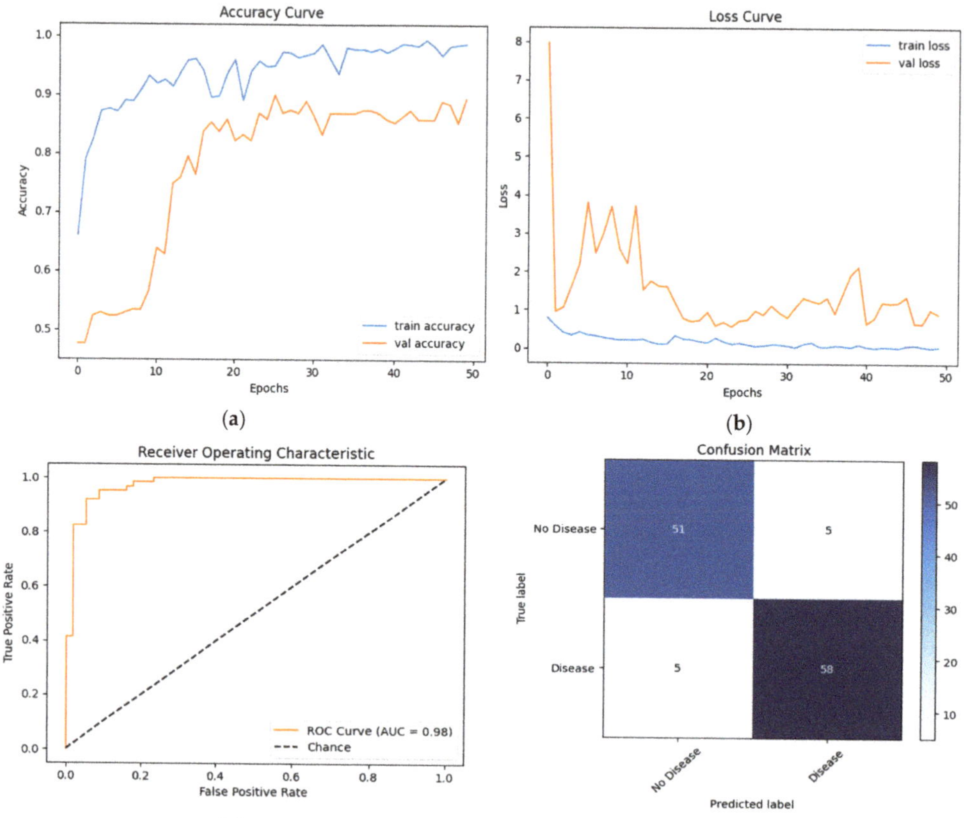

Figure 9. (**a**) Accuracy curve; (**b**) loss curve; (**c**) ROC curve; (**d**) confusion matrix for ResNet101.

We compare different machine learning models developed for the detection of cardiovascular disease. The results show that DenseNet performs better than the other models with regard to general performance, F1-score, and accuracy. This indicates that feature reuse and deeper feature extraction best helps DenseNet to be more appropriate for this task.

The VGG-16 architecture, though efficient, needed more computational resources and took longer to train in comparison with DenseNet. Although VGG-19 is deeper, it did not offer improved performance and increased training times compared to DenseNet. ResNet-50 used residual connections, hence proving superior to the VGG models by preventing vanishing gradients, though it could not reach the performance of DenseNet. ResNet-101, though deeper, did not offer a higher performance compared with ResNet-50 and could also not surpass the performance of DenseNet. This model achieved a validation accuracy of 0.903 with a precision of 0.905, a recall of 0.927, and an F1-score of 0.915.

DenseNet showed an unvarying better performance compared to any other established models for all comparison performance metrics, especially in terms of F1 score and accuracy. This implies that the reuse of features and capability of DenseNet to capture intricate data patterns make it more suitable for particular applications. Tables 3 and 4 provide a summary of the findings.

Apart from training and validation, an independent test dataset was employed to provide a stable and unbiased assessment of the performance of the model. The model performed a test accuracy of 92.44%, test loss of 0.2748, precision of 90.91%, and recall of 95.24% on previously unseen test data. These results demonstrate the model's strong generalization ability, confirming its robustness and reliability when applied to new, real-world clinical cases beyond training and validation sets. The addition of the test set is in response to the possibility of overfitting and affirms the robustness of the model for actual use.

The comparative test set performance of every deep learning model assessed using the independent test data is displayed in Table 5. DenseNet maintained the lowest test loss of 0.2748 while achieving the highest scores across the majority of evaluation metrics, such as F1 Score, Accuracy, and MCC, demonstrating its strong generalization ability.

Table 5. Comparative test set performance.

Parameter	VGG16	VGG19	ResNet50	ResNet101	DenseNet
Accuracy	0.8739	0.8824	0.8908	0.9160	0.9244
Precision	0.8871	0.8769	0.9032	0.9206	0.9091
Recall (Sensitivity)	0.8730	0.9048	0.8889	0.9206	0.9524
Specificity	0.8750	0.8571	0.8929	0.9107	0.8929
F1 Score	0.8800	0.8906	0.8960	0.9206	0.9302
MCC	0.7474	0.7639	0.7811	0.8314	0.8489
Test Loss	0.5243	0.5023	0.4758	0.4836	0.2748

7. Conclusions

Through an extensive investigation into CVD using DenseNet architecture, our study has yielded compelling facts regarding the functionality of the model on tabular data. Our model attained an impressive accuracy of 0.924, accurately categorizing around 92% of cases. The F1 score of 0.930 emphasizes model's capability to distinguish negative and positive cases effectively. A log loss of 0.275 showcases the model's confident probability predictions. Precision (0.909) underscores the model's correctness in positive predictions, while a sensitivity of 0.952 demonstrates its efficacy in identifying actual positive cases. Specificity at 0.893 reflects the model's skill in distinguishing negative instances. An MCC of 0.845 strengthens correlation between predictions and actual outcomes. Confusion matrix and correlation heatmap offer detailed information on how well the model performs and attributes relationships. These results confirm our DenseNet-based model as a robust tool for detecting CVD. Its potential to enhance patient care underscores the impactful fusion of technology and medical insights. In conclusion, our study bridges data science and medical expertise, setting the stage for future advancements in healthcare diagnostics.

7.1. Limitations

The DenseNet-based model has some limitations. The dataset may not represent all patient demographics, imaging types, or disease stages, which could impact generalizability. The model's interpretability is limited, making it challenging to comprehend the rationale behind its predictions. Additionally, the model has not been validated against clinical standards, and because of its resource-intensiveness, it might not be able to be used in environments with sufficient computer power.

7.2. Future Work

Further studies must concentrate on expanding the dataset to improve generalizability, enhancing model interpretability, and validating the model in clinical settings. Addressing bias and improving generalization are important, as is incorporating uncertainty estimation to aid decision-making. Developing resource-efficient model variants will also help facilitate deployment in resource-constrained environments.

Author Contributions: Conceptualization, W.H. and T.J.; methodology, T.K. and T.J.; software, T.K. and T.J.; validation, N.A. and T.J.; formal analysis, W.H. and T.J.; investigation, N.A. and T.J.; resources, R.S. and T.J.; data curation, R.S. and T.J.; writing—original draft preparation, T.J.; writing—review and editing, T.J.; visualization, T.J.; supervision, F.A. and T.J.; project administration, F.A. and T.J. All authors have read and agreed to the published version of the manuscript.

Funding: This research received no external funding.

Data Availability Statement: Upon reasonable request, the data supporting this study's conclusions can be obtained.

Acknowledgments: The authors extend their appreciation to their universities for the sustained encouragement provided throughout this work.

Conflicts of Interest: The authors declare no conflicts of interest.

References

1. Abbas, S.; Sampedro, G.A.; Alsubai, S.; Almadhor, A.; Kim, T. An efficient stacked ensemble model for heart disease detection and classification. *Comput. Mater. Contin.* **2023**, *77*, 665–680. [CrossRef]
2. Arvaniti, E.; Claassen, M.; Giamberardino, G. Automated cardiac diagnosis challenge (ACDC) & caudate nucleus segmentation challenge—Preliminary results. In *Statistical Atlases and Computational Models of the Heart. ACDC and MMWHS Challenges*; Springer: Cham, Switzerland, 2017; pp. 196–206.
3. Asif, D.; Bibi, M.; Arif, M.S.; Mukheimer, A. Enhancing heart disease prediction through ensemble learning techniques with hyperparameter optimization. *Algorithms* **2023**, *16*, 308. [CrossRef]
4. Bhatt, C.M.; Patel, P.; Ghetia, T.; Mazzeo, P.L. Effective heart disease prediction using machine learning techniques. *Algorithms* **2023**, *16*, 88. [CrossRef]
5. Bilgaiyan, S.; Ayon, T.; Khan, A.; Johora, F.; Parvin, M.; Alam, M. Heart disease prediction using machine learning. In Proceedings of the 2023 International Conference on Computing, Communication, and Information Technology (ICCCI), Coimbatore, India, 23–25 January 2023; IEEE: Piscataway, NJ, USA, 2023; pp. 1–6. [CrossRef]
6. Alsharqi, M.; Edelman, E.R. Artificial Intelligence in Cardiovascular Imaging and Interventional Cardiology: Emerging Trends and Clinical Implications. *J. Soc. Cardiovasc. Angiogr. Interv.* **2025**, *4 Pt B*, 102558. [CrossRef] [PubMed]
7. Chen, L.; Bentley, P.; Mori, K. Deep learning in medical image analysis. In *Medical Imaging Technology*; Springer: Cham, Switzerland, 2019; pp. 25–46.
8. Coursera. Deep Learning Specialization by Andrew Ng. Coursera. Available online: https://www.coursera.org/specializations/deep-learning (accessed on 26 July 2025).
9. Divya, K.; Sirohi, A.; Pande, S.; Malik, R. An IoMT assisted heart disease diagnostic system using machine learning techniques. In *Cognitive Internet of Medical Things for Smart Healthcare*; Springer: Berlin/Heidelberg, Germany, 2021; pp. 145–161.
10. Enad, H.G.; Mohammed, M.A. Cloud computing-based framework for heart disease classification using quantum machine learning approach. *J. Intell. Syst.* **2024**, *33*, 20230261. [CrossRef]
11. Huang, G.; Liu, Z.; Van Der Maaten, L.; Weinberger, K.Q. Densely connected convolutional networks. In Proceedings of the IEEE Conference on Computer Vision and Pattern Recognition, Honolulu, HI, USA, 21–26 July 2017; pp. 4700–4708.
12. LeCun, Y.; Bengio, Y.; Hinton, G. Deep learning. *Nature* **2015**, *521*, 436–444. [CrossRef] [PubMed]
13. Li, H.; Duan, W.; Zhou, T.; Jin, X. Automated detection of cardiac abnormalities from echocardiographic images using convolutional neural networks. In Proceedings of the 2018 IEEE International Conference on Healthcare Informatics (ICHI), New York, NY, USA, 4–7 June 2018; IEEE: Piscataway, NJ, USA, 2018.
14. Liang, G.; Zheng, L.; Zhang, L.; Lin, L.; Xiang, D. Deep learning-based cardiovascular disease diagnosis and monitoring: A review. *Front. Cardiovasc. Med.* **2020**, *7*, 169.
15. Litjens, G.; Kooi, T.; Bejnordi, B.E.; Setio, A.A.A.; Ciompi, F.; Ghafoorian, M.; Sánchez, C.I. A survey on deep learning in medical image analysis. *Med. Image Anal.* **2017**, *42*, 60–88. [CrossRef] [PubMed]
16. Madani, A.; Arnaout, R.; Mofrad, M.; Arnaout, R. Fast and accurate view classification of echocardiograms using deep learning. *NPJ Digit. Med.* **2018**, *1*, 6. [CrossRef] [PubMed]
17. Majumder, A.B.; Gupta, S.; Singh, D.; Acharya, B.; Gerogiannis, V.C.; Kanavos, A.; Pintelas, P. Heart disease prediction using concatenated hybrid ensemble classifiers. *Algorithms* **2023**, *16*, 538. [CrossRef]
18. Melendez, J.; Sánchez, C.I. Deep learning in medical image analysis: A comprehensive review. *Biomed. Signal Process. Control* **2020**, *60*, 101986.
19. Mohan, S.; Thirumalai, C.; Srivastava, G. Effective heart disease prediction using hybrid machine learning techniques. *IEEE Access* **2019**, *7*, 81542–81554. [CrossRef]

20. Official DenseNet GitHub Repository. GitHub. Available online: https://github.com/liuzhuang13/DenseNet (accessed on 26 July 2025).
21. Kabir, P.B.; Akter, S. Emphasised research on heart disease divination applying tree-based algorithms and feature selection. In Proceedings of the 2021 International Conference on Innovative Computing, Intelligent Communication and Smart Electrical Systems (ICSES), Chennai, India, 24–25 September 2021; pp. 1–6. [CrossRef]
22. PyTorch documentation on DenseNet. PyTorch. Available online: https://pytorch.org/hub/pytorch_vision_densenet/ (accessed on 26 July 2025).
23. Quang, N.N.; Gatt, A. A survey of deep learning techniques for medical image classification. In Proceedings of the 3rd International Conference on Image and Graphics Processing, Jeju Island, Republic of Korea, 24–26 February 2019; pp. 87–93.
24. Samad, M.D.; Ulloa, A.; Wehner, G.J.; Jing, L.; Hartzel, D.N.; Good, C.W.; Williams, B.A.; Haggerty, C.M.; Fornwalt, B.K. Predicting survival from large echocardiography and electronic health record datasets: Optimization with machine learning. *JACC Cardiovasc. Imaging* **2019**, *12*, 681–689. [CrossRef] [PubMed]
25. Mohapatra, S.; Maneesha, S.; Mohanty, S.; Patra, P.K.; Bhoi, S.K.; Sahoo, K.S.; Gandomi, A.H. A stacking classifiers model for detecting heart irregularities and predicting cardiovascular disease. *Healthc. Anal.* **2023**, *3*, 100133. [CrossRef]
26. Wang, X.; Zhang, L.; Zhou, Z. DenseNet-based deep learning for coronary artery disease detection from angiograms. *Med. Image Anal.* **2019**, *57*, 88–95. [CrossRef] [PubMed]
27. Zhang, Y.; Liu, Y.; Chen, Y.; Zhang, Y. Application of DenseNet architecture in cardiac magnetic resonance image analysis for myocardial infarction detection. *IEEE Trans. Med. Imaging* **2020**, *39*, 2986–2996.
28. Yao, J.; Burns, J.E.; Munoz, H.E.; Summers, R.M.; Yao, J. Dense-inception network for abdominal multi-organ segmentation. In *International Workshop on Large-Scale Annotation of Biomedical Data and Expert Label Synthesis*; Springer: Cham, Switzerland, 2017; pp. 164–172.
29. Available online: https://www.kaggle.com/datasets/sid321axn/heart-statlog-cleveland-hungary-final (accessed on 24 February 2024).
30. Szegedy, C.; Ioffe, S.; Vanhoucke, V.; Alemi, A. Inception-v4, Inception-ResNet and the impact of residual connections on learning. In Proceedings of the Thirty-First AAAI Conference on Artificial Intelligence, San Francisco, CA, USA, 4–9 February 2017.
31. Almulihi, A.; Saleh, H.; Hussien, A.M.; Mostafa, S.; El-Sappagh, S.; Alnowaiser, K.; Ali, A.A.; Refaat Hassan, M. Ensemble Learning Based on Hybrid Deep Learning Model for Heart Disease Early Prediction. *Diagnostics* **2022**, *12*, 3215. [CrossRef] [PubMed]
32. Zhang, Y.; Yang, L.; Chen, J.; Zhang, X.; He, W.; Tong, L. Multi-class classification of skin cancer images with deep learning techniques. *IEEE Access* **2019**, *7*, 11580–11587.
33. Zhuang, X.; Wei, Y.; Li, Y.; Jia, Y.; Shi, J.; Lin, J. Attend in, localize and segment (AILS): Weakly supervised learning of a dense event captioning model. In Proceedings of the IEEE Conference on Computer Vision and Pattern Recognition, Long Beach, CA, USA, 15–20 June 2019; pp. 10419–10428.
34. Jaware, T.; Khanchandani, K.; Badgujar, R. A novel hybrid atlas-free hierarchical graph-based segmentation of newborn brain MRI using wavelet filter banks. *Int. J. Neurosci.* **2019**, *130*, 499–514. [CrossRef] [PubMed]
35. Dritsas, E.; Trigka, M. Application of deep learning for heart attack prediction with explainable artificial intelligence. *Computers* **2024**, *13*, 244. [CrossRef]

computers

MDPI

Article

Synthetic Data-Driven Methods to Accelerate the Deployment of Deep Learning Models: A Case Study on Pest and Disease Detection in Precision Viticulture

Telmo Adão [1,2,*], Agnieszka Chojka [1], David Pascoal [1,3], Nuno Silva [1,3], Raul Morais [1,3,4] and Emanuel Peres [1,3,4]

1 Department of Engineering, School of Sciences and Technology, University of Trás-os-Montes e Alto Douro, 5000-801 Vila Real, Portugal; achojka@utad.pt (A.C.); davidpascoal@utad.pt (D.P.); nunosilva@utad.pt (N.S.); rmorais@utad.pt (R.M.); eperes@utad.pt (E.P.)
2 ALGORITMI Research Center, University of Minho, 4800-058 Guimarães, Portugal
3 Centre for the Research and Technology of Agro-Environmental and Biological Sciences, University of Trás-os-Montes e Alto Douro, 5000-801 Vila Real, Portugal
4 Institute for Innovation, Capacity Building and Sustainability of Agri-Food Production, University of Trás-os-Montes e Alto Douro, 5000-801 Vila Real, Portugal
* Correspondence: telmoadao@utad.pt; Tel.: +351-259350762

Abstract: The development of reliable visual inference models is often constrained by the burdensome and time-consuming processes involved in collecting and annotating high-quality datasets. This challenge becomes more acute in domains where key phenomena are time-dependent or event-driven, narrowing the opportunity window to capture representative observations. Yet, accelerating the deployment of deep learning (DL) models is crucial to support timely, data-driven decision-making in operational settings. To tackle such an issue, this paper explores the use of 2D synthetic data grounded in real-world patterns to train initial DL models in contexts where annotated datasets are scarce or can only be acquired within restrictive time windows. Two complementary approaches to synthetic data generation are investigated: rule-based digital image processing and advanced text-to-image generative diffusion models. These methods can operate independently or be combined to enhance flexibility and coverage. A proof-of-concept is presented through a couple case studies in precision viticulture, a domain often constrained by seasonal dependencies and environmental variability. Specifically, the detection of *Lobesia botrana* in sticky traps and the classification of grapevine foliar symptoms associated with black rot, ESCA, and leaf blight are addressed. The results suggest that the proposed approach potentially accelerates the deployment of preliminary DL models by comprehensively automating the production of context-aware datasets roughly inspired by specific challenge-driven operational settings, thereby mitigating the need for time-consuming and labor-intensive processes, from image acquisition to annotation. Although models trained on such synthetic datasets require further refinement—for example, through active learning—the approach offers a scalable and functional solution that reduces human involvement, even in scenarios of data scarcity, and supports the effective transition of laboratory-developed AI to real-world deployment environments.

Keywords: deep learning; synthetic data engineering; image processing; large language model; ChatGPT; diffusion models; DALL·E; precision viticulture; grapevine diseases classification; grapevine pest detection

1. Introduction

The rapid advancement of technology has enabled the widespread adoption of data processing techniques based on artificial intelligence (AI), with deep learning (DL) emerging as one of the most prominent approaches across both scientific and professional communities. DL has proven particularly effective for pattern analysis and recognition in imagery-based data. Within the realm of supervised learning, DL techniques have been extensively applied to automate tasks such as classification and object detection, offering significant contributions to various domains including industry [1], medicine [2], and agriculture [3]—fields in which the availability of high-quality, timely annotated datasets plays a critical role.

In viticulture, for instance, the timely detection of agro-environmental conditions that influence pest and disease outbreaks is essential for informed decision-making and the proper implementation of targeted interventions in vineyard management. To support this, specialized IoT platforms such as mySense [4,5] have proven valuable in monitoring a range of crop-influencing factors. In integration with mySense, VineInspector [6] demonstrates how DL-powered visual approaches can extract actionable insights by detecting and classifying events and anomalies in vineyards. These include monitoring vine shoot size in relation to primary downy mildew infections and identifying the presence of *Lobesia botrana*—European grape moth—in pheromone traps.

However, the development of effective visual inference models hinges on the availability of large, high-quality annotated datasets—whose acquisition is often constrained by the natural seasonality of viticulture [7]. More specifically, data collection for training models to detect specific events may only be feasible during narrow windows of the phenological cycle, which, in the case of being missed, can significantly delay the training process and, consequently, the deployment of operational systems. For example, in a study focused on yield estimation and wine-making potential based on grape counting [8], data acquisition and annotation campaigns spanned a couple of years, targeting the time window from July to September, during which the grapes develop and mature until harvest. Another noteworthy example refers to ampelography [9], where data acquisition was concentrated over a few months, corresponding to the phenological stage during which grapevines develop their canopy foliage. Nevertheless, the process took two years to complete, labeling included. In another related study, Kontogiannis et al. [10] collected and annotated 6800 images from ground stations and drones during the growing season to support the development of a downy mildew detection solution. Also, in works involving trap-based grape moth detection [6], one can infer the significant logistical effort required towards the development of the respective solutions—including trap preparation, waiting periods to capture the insects of interest, and subsequent imagery retrieval and annotation procedures.

To address the limitations associated with dataset scarcity and the significant effort required to develop deployable image-based inference solutions, this work draws inspiration from prior research (e.g., [9,11]) to explore synthetic data generation as a strategy for developing initial yet functional DL models. By creating synthetic, domain-compliant training datasets, the proposed approach reduces early reliance on time-consuming procedures from image acquisition to annotation, thereby potentially accelerating the deployment of inference models that, however, should be iteratively refined over time, for example, through active learning techniques. Two complementary synthetic image generation methods are proposed: (i) classical digital image processing techniques and (ii) advanced text-to-image diffusion models. These methods are applied and tested in two relevant viticulture-related use cases: the detection of *Lobesia botrana*, a major grapevine pest, and the identification of common but potentially destructive vine diseases such as black rot, leaf blight, and ESCA. In addition to presenting the generated datasets, models' performances, and operational insights, this paper discusses each proposed synthetic data generation approach, outlining some of their advantages and limitations, and positioning them within the broader literature.

The remainder of this paper is structured as follows: Section 2 reviews related work; Section 3 describes the proposed synthetic data generation strategies; Section 4 presents the experimental results; Section 5 offers a critical analysis and discussion; and Section 6 concludes with directions for future research.

2. Related Work

At the core of reliable supervised machine learning (ML) and DL decision-support models—whether applied in healthcare [2], infrastructure engineering [12], the automotive industry [1], the textile sector [13], footwear businesses [14], or inclusive technologies [15]—lies the availability of well-structured, validated, and problem-representative datasets. This requirement is equally critical in the domains of agriculture [16], where the need for capturing the idiosyncrasies of crops and plants under naturally variable environmental conditions increases complexity.

In agricultural and viticultural contexts, data collection is particularly challenging. It is often restricted by seasonal cycles and specific phenological stages, which limit the opportunity to gather large-scale, annotated datasets. Despite the growing availability of repository systems that encourage cross-domain public dataset sharing—including in agriculture [3,17,18]—the scarcity of labeled training data remains one of the most critical bottlenecks for deploying deep learning models in real-world agricultural settings [3]. Building ML/DL models that can effectively operate in such environments requires not only advanced architectures, but also a comprehensive understanding of the domain problem at hand, allowing for the design of representative datasets either by engaging initiatives of data acquisition from scratch or by augmenting upon existing repositories [16].

IoT platforms such as mySense [4] have made strides in this area by enabling crowd-sourced contributions and expert validation for agricultural data aimed at supporting ML/DL-based decision making. Notably, mySense supports intelligent node integration, as demonstrated in [6] through the VineInspector system. This system tracks shoot growth to monitor infection risks such as downy mildew, while also observing pheromone traps for European grapevine moth to assess pest presence and activity. Also focusing on edge computing strategies, Gonçalves et al. [19] developed a dataset comprising 168 images with 8966 insect instances that needed to be manually annotated. This dataset was then used to train and benchmark five models—e.g., SSD MobileNetV2 and EfficientDet-D0. The class-wise accuracies ranged from 82% to 99%, with F1-scores between 58% and 84%. SSD ResNet50 was the architecture that achieved the best performances. Regarding inference times, the minimum observed was greater than 19 s per image in high-end smartphones. Concerned with the main vectors of Flavescence dorée—*Scaphoideus titanus* and *Orientus ishidae*—Checola et al. [20] used sticky traps to retain the target insects, enabling the construction of a dataset comprising 600 images and approximately 1500 annotations per class. YOLOv8 and Faster R-CNN were employed to support deep learning-based detections, with the former achieving superior performance: a mean average precision at 0.5 overlap (mAP@0.5) of 92%, and an F1-score above 90%.

Regarding the automatic detection and identification of grapevine leaf diseases, Xie et al. [21] developed the Grape Leaf Disease Dataset (GLDD), comprising 4449 original images across four classes—black rot, black measles, leaf blight, and mites. They also proposed a deep learning model named Faster DR-IACNN, which integrates components from established architectures such as Inception-ResNet-v2 for advanced feature extraction. The model achieved an mAP of 81.1%. In another work with similar goals, Hasan et al. [22]

developed and assessed their own convolutional neural network (CNN) model, reporting an accuracy of 91.37% for distinguishing black rot, ESCA, leaf blight, and healthy leaves from a public dataset [23] (built based on PlantVillage [17]). Matching the same disease classes, Prasad et al. [24] modified a VGG-16 CNN, whose performance reached a top accuracy of 99.06% in tests on a public and relatively balanced dataset composed of 9027 images [25]. In [26], the same set of diseases was considered through the partial integration of the PlantVillage dataset [17]. In total, 14 CNN and 17 vision transformer models were assessed and compared, with 4 of them achieving an accuracy of 100%. In another work, an Xception model fine-tuned by Nasra and Gupta [27] attained an accuracy of 99% over a public grapevine diseases dataset [28] with characteristics similar to the ones previously addressed. More recently, Talaat et al. [29] proposed a plant disease detection algorithm, composed of a few modules, including for feature extraction and CNN-based classification, which works combined with a grid search strategy for hyperparameters optimization. Considering another PlantVillage [17] inspired dataset [30], an accuracy of 99.7% was observed in tests.

These works are essentially grounded in supervised learning, where labeled data is essential. However, manual annotation is often time-consuming and labor-intensive [3]. Alternatives like self-supervised learning—as in the case of generative adversarial networks (GANs)—reduce reliance on labeled data but are still constrained by the quality and biases of the original datasets [31]. In complement, semi-supervised learning consists of either (i) combining labeled and unlabeled data to learn more robust features and therefore improve models generalization capabilities; or/and (ii) querying users (preferably, experts) for labeling specific data, leading to a sustainable active learning [3]. While in such approaches uncertainty is an accountable factor for generalization, strategies considering human-in-the-loop involvement can be quite beneficial [32], as they facilitate continuous model improvement. In turn, faster model deployment becomes viable, particularly in scenarios where sub-optimal performance is acceptable in initial setups.

To tackle the challenges posed by data scarcity, the need to perform generally burdensome and time-consuming data collection and annotations, and the time frame limitations imposed by nature-driven events (as in agricultural/viticultural contexts), the generation of synthetic datasets is becoming an increasingly explored strategy by both scientific and professional communities, with notable potential to support the rapid development of initial, yet deployable, deep learning models. For instance, Kubric [33] is a general-purpose engine capable of generating photorealistic scenes by combining various technologies and repositories containing prefabricated 3D assets while maintaining links to individual scene components to facilitate automated annotation. However, content generation appears to be either random or dependent on significant scripting skills and coding effort—especially in scenarios where object specificity and spatial distribution are critical—to build such virtual environments. Kubric is also classified as a substantial computational resources consumer. In another approach [34], an automated framework was proposed to generate CAD-based data with accurate labels for large-scale robotic bin-picking datasets, with applications in industrial settings and tracked conditions. More focused in natural environments, the PROMORE framework [11] uses procedural 3D modeling to produce synthetic images for object detection and segmentation in remote sensing. Prior to this framework, a preliminary system for virtual wildfire generation within a 3D environment [35]—constructed using a photogrammetric process based on remotely piloted aerial systems (RPASs)—was developed and tested using neural networks specialized in segmentation. The results showed promising indications of the potential of synthetic data to train models capable of operating in real-world scenarios. In another study, Adão et al. [9] explored grapevine variety classification through single-leaf image analysis. Building on Xception-based models and anticipating broader field applications, they created synthetic imagery involving leaves of an existing dataset embedded in vineyard-like backgrounds, enabling segmentation and classification work-flows. Other strategies relying on the combination of large language models (LLMs) with visual foundation models have opened new possibilities for generating synthetic datasets directly from text descriptions [36]. These technologies can be employed for rapid dataset creation for training custom inference models, even in highly specific agricultural domains.

Inspired by some of the above approaches and motivated by the persistent challenges in agricultural DL deployment, this paper explores synthetic dataset generation methods to accelerate the operationalization of DL models in precision viticulture. The proposed strategies are presented in the following sections.

3. Proposed Dataset-Related Methods for Expeditious DL Modeling

This section outlines the foundational principles of the proposed methods for guiding the generation of synthetic datasets through image-based coarse problem approximation, with the aim of bootstrapping DL models and circumventing the need for explicit data collection, annotation, and organization from scratch.

3.1. Dataset Design Approaches Overview

The image processing work-flow illustrated in Figure 1 describes a procedure in which background imagery is combined with foreground elements—referred to as elements of interest (EOIs). Specifically, for each image to be generated, a background is randomly selected from a local archive and subjected to a series of random transformations to introduce data diversity. These include scaling within a given range $[limit\_ratio_{\text{min}}, limit\_ratio_{\text{max}}]$, adjustments to brightness and contrast within $[limit\_ratio_{\text{min}}, limit\_ratio_{\text{max}}]$, and vertical flipping.

Subsequently, EOIs are selected through a stochastic process, resized within a predefined range—based on real-world measurements—and subjected to further transformations such as random rotation (within $[limit\_degrees_{\text{min}}, limit\_degrees_{\text{max}}]$), brightness and contrast adjustments ($[limit\_ratio_{\text{min}}, limit\_ratio_{\text{max}}]$), and vertical or horizontal flips. EOIs are iteratively placed onto the background until either a predefined limit is reached, or a maximum number of placement attempts is exceeded—governed by an exclusion criterion that considers overlap tolerance between new EOIs and those already placed.

The resulting composite images and corresponding annotations are exported, ensuring the compatibility of a well-known object detection architecture—You Only Look Once (YOLO).

The integration of large language models (LLMs such as ChatGPT [37]), with diffusion models (e.g., DALL·E [38]) represents one of the most significant technological advancements in recent years, enabling artificial intelligence (AI) to perform generative tasks, including the autonomous creation of realistic imagery, grounded in a semantic understanding of, for example, user-provided textual input. Such integration is also explored in the present work aiming to accelerate and facilitate synthetic data generation. As illustrated in Figure 2, the user defines a set of generation requirements, which can be iteratively reviewed and refined as needed. Once finalized, a request for the bulk generation of elements—such as images and corresponding annotations—is issued, and the resulting outputs can be downloaded upon completion of the generation process.

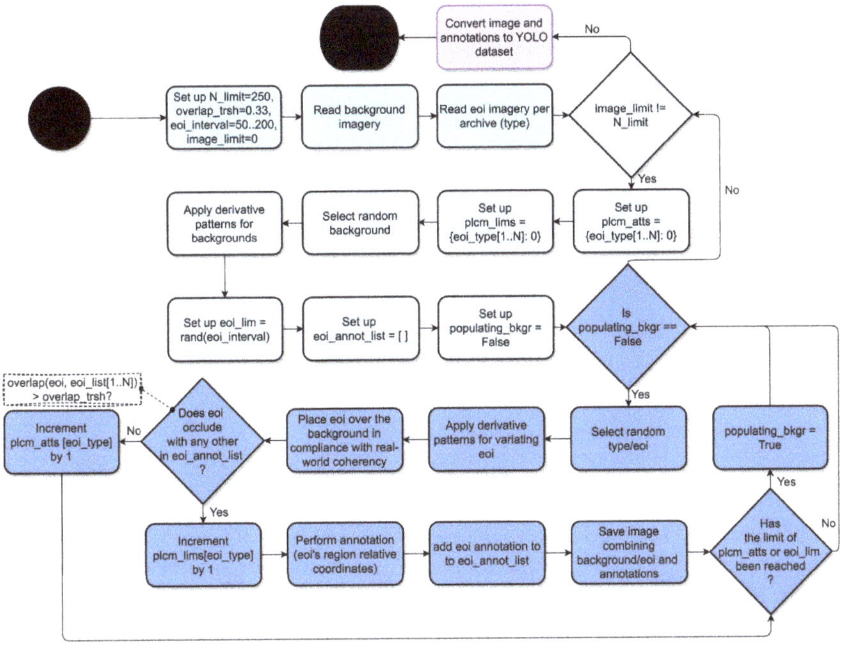

Figure 1. General flowchart of image processing-based synthetic data generation, wherein *N_limit* is the maximum number of images to be generated; *overlap_trsh* is a tolerance value used for excluding EOIs superimposed on others; eoi is the same as EOI; *eoi_interval* is a range for randomizing the limit of EOIs to place per background; *image_limit* is an image counter controller; *plcm_lims* controls the number of successfully placed EOIs; *plcm_atts* tracks the number of EOIs that were discarded due to excessive overlap; *rand* is a randomization function; *eoi_annot_list* stores the bounding boxes of consolidated EOIs; and *populating_bkgr* is a flag that works as a stop condition for the generative process.

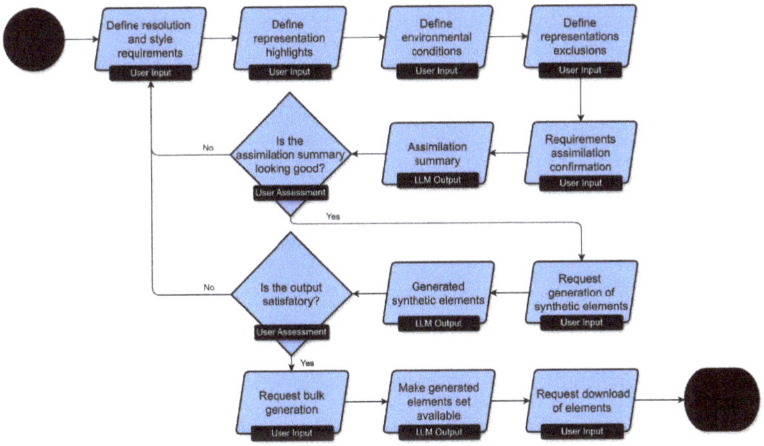

Figure 2. Synthetic data production resorting to a multimodal large language model (LLM).

3.2. Collaborative Inference Design

A strategy to reach time-effective DL modeling while short-cutting steps related to in-field data acquisition, organization, and so on, may rely on combining available annotated imagery sources and automation pipelines for simulating not-yet-established datasets. Figure 3 proposes a flowchart encompassing such strategy.

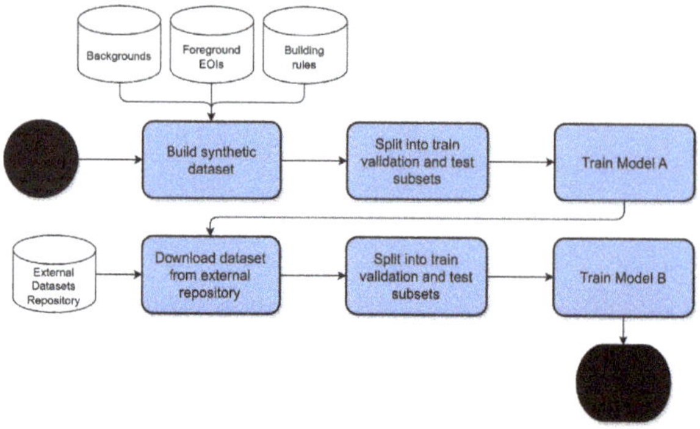

Figure 3. Combining datasets available in public repositories and dataset synthetization approaches into a single pipeline for the expeditious production of collaborating models.

For example, if a dataset cataloging a specific phenomenon (e.g., grapevine diseases) is already available in public repositories, it can be directly used to develop a single-instance classification model. However, for this model to function effectively in natural environments with complex visual compositions (e.g., a full grapevine canopy), a filtering approach is required to first identify and isolate EOIs. One viable way to enable such filtering is through the creation of a synthetic, object detection-oriented dataset designed to reflect real operational conditions. Such a dataset can be achieved by strategically positioning contour-based, isolated EOIs onto realistic background images, emulating the relevant settings that depict the target problem, while also generating corresponding annotations automatically—leveraging the algorithmic control over element placement. In turn, resulting synthetic images and their corresponding annotations can be used to train a preliminary object detection model capable of recognizing and isolating general instances. During operation, this object-detection model is responsible for primarily identifying EOIs, which are then cropped and passed to a classifier trained on the original, phenomenon-driven dataset, enabling the assignment of more specific labels (e.g., healthy, disease A, disease B, . . . , disease N). This synergistic strategy combines the strengths of both approaches: the availability of labeled datasets and the efficiency of automated, representative synthetic data generation.

Once the desired models have been trained, they can collaborate by being integrated into a sequential pipeline, as illustrated in Figure 4. In this process, an input image is processed by an initial model, which distils relevant information to be interpreted by a subsequent model. This flow enables a modular and layered approach, where different models contribute distinct processing capabilities, progressively enriching the understanding derived from the original input.

The following section demonstrates the application of the proposed dataset generation methods through two case studies: grape moth detection and vine leaf-based disease recognition.

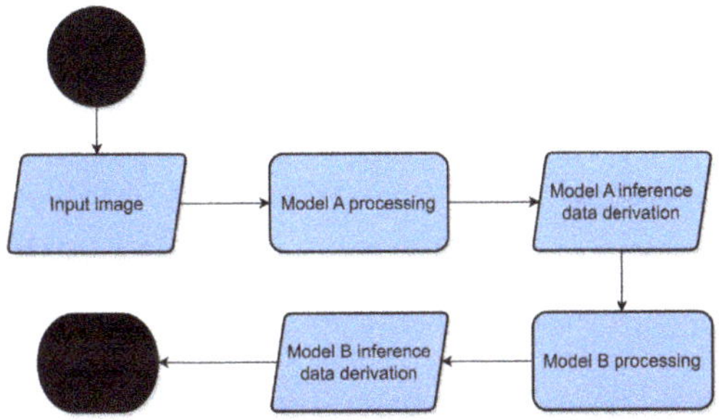

Figure 4. Two-stage DL models collaboration.

4. Case Studies for Precision Viticulture

This section focuses on the practical application of the proposed methods for the generation of synthetic datasets targeting two distinct tasks with relevance for precision viticulture: grape moth detection in pheromone traps and the identification of grapevine diseases based on leaf symptoms. The process for creating datasets involves image processing techniques and AI-based generative tools, following the methodological foundations outlined in the previous section. Procedures related to data engineering and synthetic data refinement are detailed, demonstrating how these tools can be effectively employed in domain-specific contexts. All the DL activities were carried out on a computer with the following specifications:

- Processor: 11th Gen Intel® Core™ i7-11800H @ 2.30 GHz (Intel Corporation, Santa Clara, CA, USA);
- Random Access Memory (RAM): 32 GB @ 2933 MHz SODIMM (Corsair Gaming, Inc., Fremont, CA, USA);
- Graphics Card: Nvidia® GeForce RTX 3080 (laptop edition), 16.0 GB GDDR6 RAM (Nvidia Corporation, Santa Clara, CA, USA);
- Storage: 1 TB, 3500 MB/s Read, 3300 MB/s Write (Samsung Electronics Co., Ltd., Suwon, South Korea);
- Operating System: Windows 10 Home 64-bit (Microsoft Corporation, Washington, DC, USA).

Regarding alignment with real-world observations, the synthetic imagery was generated based on domain-specific rules, either implemented through image processing techniques or expressed in natural language prompts for generative AI. These rules acted as heuristics derived from the target contexts the images were intended to model, namely (i) sticky traps with printed grids and grape moth specimens placed on them; and (ii) individual vine trunks with horizontal cordons, occasionally accompanied by grape clusters and covered by canopies of vine leaves with bounding-box overlaps equal to or less than 30% for leaf area visibility maximization.

4.1. Case Study 1: Image Processing for European Grapevine Moth Traps

One of the proposed case studies involves a pipeline for the synthetic generation of a representative dataset for grape moth detection in sticky/pheromone traps. To this end, preliminary steps were taken to collect imagery from available sources, aimed at preparing two types of visual assets: grape moth specimens and empty traps. The former were obtained by visually selecting insect-populated traps from public datasets [39,40], and isolating individual insects from the background using Canva's background remover tool [41]. The latter were generated with the assistance of ChatGPT 4o [37] and DALL·E 3 [38]. Afterwards, initial preprocessing steps were applied for cleaning and sampling. Specifically, moth specimen images were inspected and cleaned to manually remove background artifacts, while trap images underwent histogram adjustments to introduce visual variations.

Image processing techniques were then used to randomly combine assets—individual moths and background traps—toward the production of annotated synthetic datasets with varied configurations. For each background image, a set of random transformations was applied, including scaling within the range [1.0, 1.25], brightness and contrast adjustments ([0.85, 1.15]), vertical flipping, and the addition of salt-and-pepper noise to simulate operation in dusty field conditions. The moth instances were then resized to approximate real-world relative dimensions and subjected to further transformations such as random rotation (within [0°, 360°]) and additional brightness and contrast adjustments. A sample of the resulting composite images, generated through the described image processing pipeline, is shown in Figure 5. At the end of the process, the datasets are converted into YOLO-compatible formats.

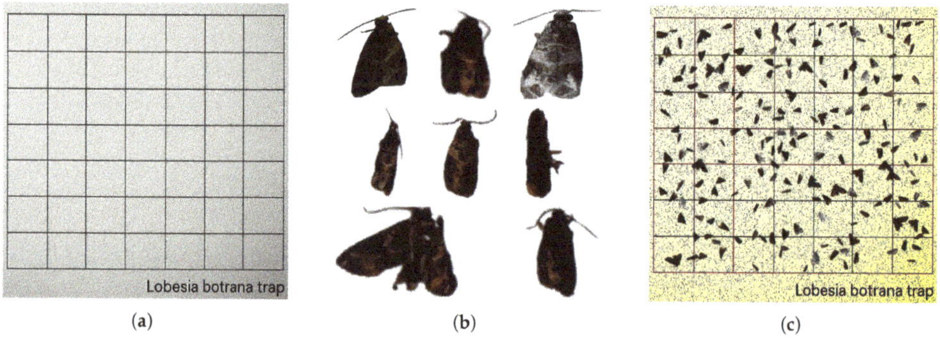

Figure 5. Samples involved in the process for generating synthetic datasets for grape moth detection in sticky/pheromone traps: (**a**) trap image generated with ChatGPT 4o/DALL·E 3; (**b**) grape moth specimens cropped from public datasets [39,40]; (**c**) resulting synthetic image combining (**a**) and (**b**).

Following the previously specified pipeline, 400 synthetic images were generated and then used to compose a YOLO dataset that considers a split of 60%, 20%, and 20% for training, validation, and testing, respectively. Afterwards, a lightweight version of that CNN architecture was employed to train a grape moth detection model, adjusted to operate in single-board computers (SBCs) with the minimum requirements to host such AI processing. The corresponding training data is presented in Figure 6, which shows a smooth and progressive improvement in performance, indicating promising signs of convergence.

4.2. Case Study 2: Grapevine Diseases Identification

For the disease identification task, a hybrid approach combining object detection and classification models was explored. To render this approach practical, a publicly available dataset hosted on Kaggle [25] was employed (apparently inspired in a partial subgroup of PlantVillage [17]), which contains labeled images of grapevine leaves collected under controlled laboratory conditions and manifesting signs of various infections (Figure 7), making it suitable for training a disease classification model. More specifically, this dataset consists of a collection of images that categorize visual manifestations of black rot, ESCA, and leaf blight, as well as healthy leaves, distributed across two folders: train (7222 examples); and test (1805 examples). However, the referred imagery source does not reflect the complexity of in-field conditions such as leaves hanging within dense canopies, variable lighting, and occlusions—it may not generalize well when applied directly to vineyard imagery. To address this limitation, an object detection model was developed to locate and extract grapevine leaves from natural canopy-like images. These detected leaf regions are then passed through the disease classification model to assess the phytosanitary status of each one, aiming at effective plant health monitoring in realistic scenarios. This is where object detection becomes essential, acting as a preparatory stage that bridges the gap between real-world vineyard imagery and laboratory-trained classification models.

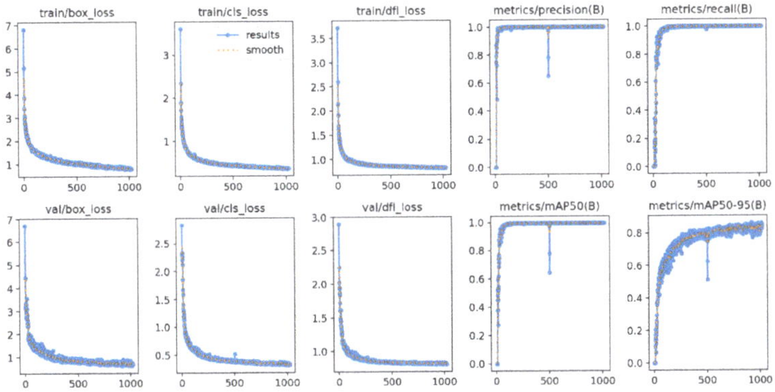

Figure 6. Training curves of a YOLOv8s for grape moth detection, showing good signs of convergence with a progressive and consistent decreasing of box, class, and distribution focal losses.

(**a**) (**b**) (**c**) (**d**)

Figure 7. Samples of grape leaves from a public dataset made available on Kaggle [25], manifesting different conditions: (**a**) black rot; (**b**) ESCA; (**c**) healthy; and (**d**) leaf blight.

Focusing on the disease classification task, the Mandal [25] dataset was considered along with the consolidated training procedures outlined in [9], starting with the integration of the Xception architecture. To ensure robust model performance, class balancing was carried out prior to training by applying minimal data augmentation to underrepresented classes until all of them matched the sample count of the most represented one. Subsequently, the balanced train component of Mandal's dataset was split into a couple of DL-compliant subsets using a 65–35% ratio to extend a validation group, with a small percentage of samples exchanged between them both to promote feature learning. Mandal's testing subset was kept apart from training for performance assessment purposes. A grid search was conducted to identify an appropriate initial learning rate, and a batch size of 24 was adopted throughout training. The Nadam optimizer was employed to combine the benefits of adaptive moment estimation and Nesterov momentum. Furthermore, an early stopping monitor was set up with a patience of 20 epochs to halt the training in case of accuracy stagnation. As illustrated in the training history shown in Figure 8, which presents accuracy and loss curves throughout the training process, a steady training convergence was achieved.

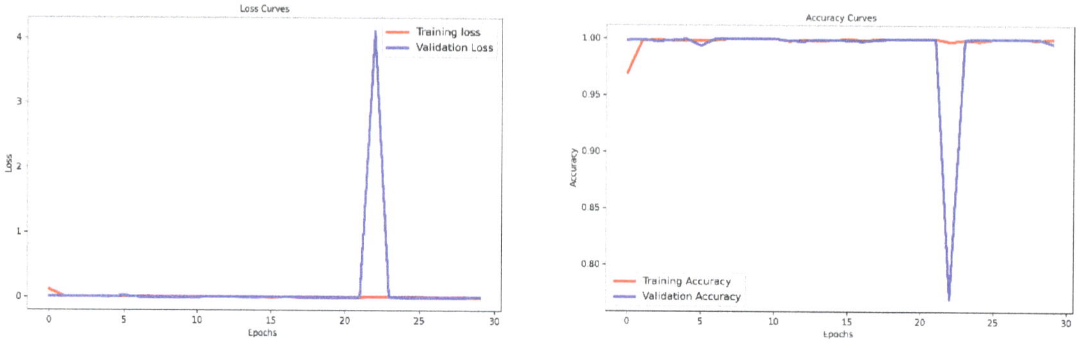

(a) (b)

Figure 8. Training and validation history resulted from the training of an Xception-based grapevine diseases classifier: (**a**) corresponds to the loss behavior; (**b**) presents the accuracy progress.

4.2.1. ChatGPT/DALL·E Interaction for the Experimental Generation of Annotated YOLOv8-Compatible Datasets

To generate a dataset for leaf detection compatible with YOLO training requirements, the integration of ChatGPT with the DALL·E image generation system was explored. The primary goal was to assess the feasibility of this approach for generating synthetic vineyard scenes with realistic foliage representations and directly annotated leaves. Therefore, a set of structured generation guidelines was defined and iteratively communicated to ChatGPT, encompassing key aspects such as image resolution and style, target representation details, environmental conditions, elements to exclude, and annotation procedures. These guidelines, summarized in Table 1, were designed to ensure that the generated content would be both visually coherent and technically usable for training object detection models.

Table 1. Guidelines for the generation of a dataset for grape leaves detection purely based on ChatGPT/DALL·E.

Resolution and Style	Representation Highlights	Environmental Conditions	Representation Exclusions	Annotations
• 1024 × 1024 px. • Photorealistic photographs, vineyard settings.	• Thick, textured trunk entering the soil. • Natural leaf canopy (crown), with realistic density and overlap. • Leaves with color variations: green, partially yellowed, with brown spots, burns, and similar features. • Clearly visible grape clusters (green or semi-ripened).	• As background, vineyard rows softly blurred, showing depth of field. • Natural daylight.	• No annotations should appear on the image.	• YOLOv8 (.txt) format. • "Leaf" as single class. • Elements to include: all fully visible or nearly fully visible grape leaves; leaves with damage (burns, discoloration, spots, and similar features). • Elements to exclude: grape clusters; trunk; soil; wires, hoses, and other background elements. • Bounding boxes must accurately enclose each leaf. • Format per line (YOLOv8 normalized): *0 x_center y_center width height*.

Although the generated images achieved a fair visual realism, several issues were identified regarding the quality of the associated annotations. Common problems included the incorrect labeling of non-leaf elements such as grape clusters or vine trunks as leaves, the omission of clearly visible leaves, and imprecise bounding box coordinates, as shown in Figure 9. When confronted with these issues, ChatGPT clarified that the annotations were randomly simulated and not actually linked to the visual content of the generated images. As a result, it was deemed unfeasible to pursue the construction of a reliable dataset solely based on this approach.

(a) (b)

Figure 9. Vine-like sample and annotations generated with ChatGPT/DALL·E: (**a**) clear image; (**b**) the same image overlaid with the proposed annotations (i.e., purple bounding boxes), displayed by Roboflow [42].

4.2.2. Leaf Recognition Modeling Based on Image Processing for the Articulation of Specific and Individual Grapevine Elements Generated Through ChatGPT/DALL·E

As the generation of datasets for leaf detection solely relying on ChatGPT/DALL·E's image generation capabilities proved unfeasible—mainly due to severe annotation inconsistencies—an alternative strategy was delineated and followed. It consisted of separately generating (i) leafless grapevine plants with grape bunches as vineyard backgrounds; and (ii) grapevine leaves. Such separation intended to enable automatic and yet more controlled dataset composition and annotation. To confine the generative process, a set of rules in natural language—covering resolution, style, key elements, environmental conditions, and exclusions—was specified, as detailed in Tables 2 and 3, to individually guide the production of the aforementioned imagery groups.

Based on the establishment of two libraries of AI-generated images—one containing leafless grapevines and the other containing individual grapevine leaves—the image processing-based procedure described in Section 3.1 was followed to automate the combination of both sets. More specifically, leaf placement followed a Gaussian probability distribution over different regions of the upper part of the background, aligning with the cordon training system and reflecting real-world patterns, as illustrated in Figure 10. Also, overlapping intersections exceeding 33% trigger the elimination of the most recently generated leaf involved in the positional conflict. These steps culminated in a fully structured YOLOv8-complaint dataset, comprising 400 images along with labels, and bounding box annotations. As in the grape moth dataset setup, a split of 60%, 20%, and 20% was assigned for training, validation, and testing, respectively.

Afterwards, a YOLOv8s-based model was trained considering the previously generated dataset. As shown in Figure 11, the model presented a stable and consistent convergence, with the box, class, and distribution focal loss values steadily decreasing over the course of approximately 700 training epochs. Training concluded upon activation of an early stopping monitor, which was configured with a tolerance of 100 epochs.

The following section focuses on the performance and operational insights associated with the different developed models for grapevine moth and leaf detection, as well as for disease classification.

Table 2. Guidelines for the generation of a library of leafless grapevines with bunches in a vineyard background based on ChatGPT/DALL·E.

Resolution and Style	Representation Highlights	Environmental Conditions	Representation Exclusions
• 1024×1024 px. • Photographic realism. • Vineyard environment consistent with Mediterranean or temperate climate. • Clean, usable image compositions serving as backgrounds for the integration of foreground elements such as (YOLO-traceable) leaves.	• Main trunk: must grow from the base up to $\frac{1}{2}$ or $\frac{2}{3}$ of the image height; should be gnarled or young, depending on variation; texture features should be compliant with age (wrinkles, bark cracks, lichen, and similar features). • Vine training: can be based on Guyot methods; (a) simple cordon; or (b) double cordon (T-shape). • Regarding each cordon: can produce short vertical or slightly inclined canes. • As for canes: place 0 to 5 grape bunches per image can be generated. • Grape bunches should: vary in size and density; appear loosely structured; contain smaller berries, possibly irregular; be well distributed, across canes. • Important variations to manifest include: trunk length and thickness; bark texture and aging signs; number and shape of arms (1 or 2); number of visible bunches (0–5); slight angle variations in the photo from a terrestrial station perspective.	• Trunk clearly visible and continuous, emerging from the soil. • Natural/human-level view, slightly lateral or frontal. • Shallow depth of field with background vineyard softly blurred. • Ground with dry soil, straw, light vegetation, or vineyard cover. • May include support wires, irrigation tubes, or vineyard posts. • Natural daylight, no harsh contrast.	• Foliage in the foreground (acceptable only in in distant background). • Excessively synthetic symmetry. • Unnatural bunches or overabundance of grapes.

Table 3. Guidelines for the generation of a grape leaf library based on ChatGPT/DALL·E.

Resolution and Style	Representation Highlights	Environmental Conditions	Representation Exclusions
• 320 × 320 px. • Transparent background. • Tight crop, minimal border/margin • Top-down perspective, leaf appearing pendant (hanging) from vine. • Photographic realism, not illustrated nor cartoon-ished.	• Healthy/normal grape leaves: full green with visible venation; subtle texture and depth; no visible damage or spots. • Mild stress or early signs: green leaves with minor; discoloration; gradients involving green/yellow/orange; slight curling or uneven surfaces; possible minor brown spotting. • Diseased or damaged leaves: green yellowing leaves with dark brown or black spot; spots irregular or clustered near edges or mid-section; geometric patterns of reddish-brown to dark purple; discoloration originating from or aligned along central veins; burn signs from the center out; areas of burnt orange or light brown; margins or interveinal zones affected; green fading to yellow/orange features; fully yellow to reddish or even brownish leaves; edges dry or curled; crispy texture or winding/shrinkage.	• Natural daylight. • Include natural/realistic reflectance (subtle shininess). • Perspective variations: 3D-like orientation changes (e.g., slightly angled, twisted, or tilted); natural inclination; (pointing left/right, partially upward/downward); biological realism (preserve grapevine leaf anatomy); petiole (stem): short, thin, or hidden.	• Exaggerated noise or synthetic textures.

(**a**)

(**b**)

(**c**)

Figure 10. Examples of synthetic imagery generated by combining ChatGPT/DALL·E-based assets and image processing techniques: (**a**) ChatGPT/DALL·E-generated vineyard backgrounds (leafless grapevines); (**b**) ChatGPT/DALL·E-generated grapevine leaves; (**c**) composite samples resulting from the automatic merging of leaves and backgrounds using a custom image processing pipeline.

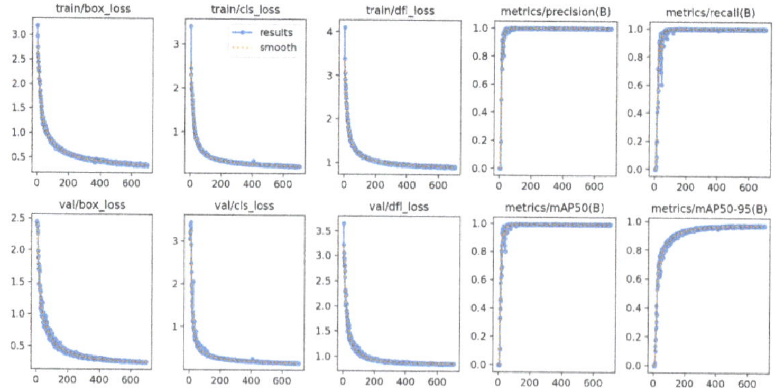

Figure 11. Training curves of a YOLOv8s designed for grapevine leaves detection, showing good signs of convergence with a progressive and consistent decreasing of box, class, and distribution focal losses.

5. Tests and Results

This section is dedicated to the analysis of the results obtained from the validation of the models presented in the previous sections. The performance of each model is examined in light of its specific task, with emphasis on quantitative evaluation metrics or/and visual insights highlighting operational capabilities. To this end, both the test set images—generated alongside the synthetic datasets but excluded from model's training stage—and the external, environmentally distinct images were sourced from the public datasets or free repositories available online.

5.1. Grape Moth Identification

The performance of the YOLOv8s model, trained using the dataset generated according to the process described in Section 4.1 for grape moth detection, is presented in Table 4. The evaluation was conducted using a test set composed of images that were excluded from training—yet produced using the same methodology as the training and validation subsets. As observable, the model achieves remarkably high values across key metrics, including precision, recall, F1-score, mAPs, and overall fitness. More specifically, precision and recall values close to 1 reflect strong performance in minimizing false positives (i.e., misclassifying insects as background) and false negatives (i.e., missing insects that should have been detected). Derived from both precision and recall, the high F1-score can be attributed not only to the balanced class-wise distribution of examples in the dataset, but also to the consistency with which features are embedded in the images through the proposed synthetic generation process. The mAP@50 and mAP@50–95 metrics indicate the reliability of the detections, as they reflect good correlation between predicted bounding boxes and ground-truth annotations. Consequently, fitness is also considered satisfactory, as it results from a weighted average of precision, recall, and mAP@50–95—with the latter typically receiving the highest weight. These results indicate that the model effectively learned from the synthetic dataset and is likely to perform reliably on imagery captured under conditions similar to that dataset.

The model trained with synthetic data for grape moth detection was subsequently evaluated in a simulated context designed to represent a relevant operational environment—in which, typically, ground-truth annotations are unavailable, yet visual inspection can still provide valuable insights. To that end, external imagery from public datasets [39,40] was used, depicting real traps containing grape moth specimens. Figure 12 presents predicted bounding boxes over a selection of these images, illustrating apparently strong detection capabilities under operational conditions that moderately differ from those found in the synthetic dataset. Nonetheless, some detection issues were observed in images affected by environmental variability, potentially due to factors such as the insects' relative size, trap design and condition, camera-induced distortions, or lighting variations.

Table 4. Grape moth detection performance over the unseen test group of the synthetic dataset.

Metric	Value
Precision	0.9998
Recall	0.9996
F1-score	0.9997
mAP@50	0.9950
mAP@50–95	0.8642
Fitness	0.8773

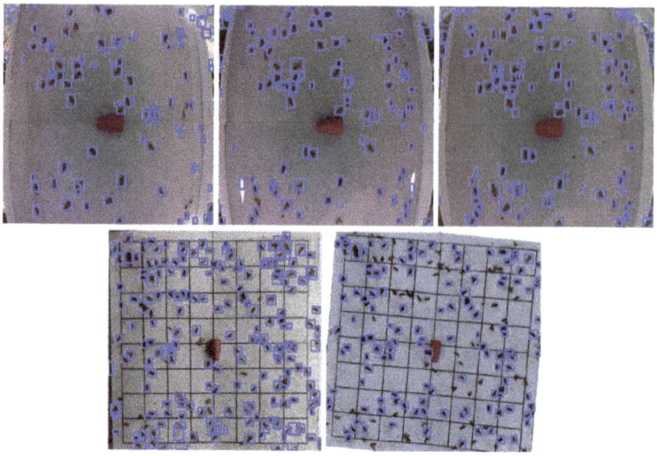

Figure 12. Results of YOLOv8s operating over images retrieved from external and publicly available datasets [39,40].

5.2. Disease Classification

The grapevine disease classification model, trained on leaf images acquired under controlled laboratory conditions [25], was evaluated, demonstrating a promising accuracy. As illustrated in the confusion matrix depicted in Figure 13, the model achieved a nearly flawless classification performance, with minimal misclassifications across disease categories—corroborating with the performances reported in other DL works done over the same dataset (e.g., [29]) and the effectiveness of the method presented in [9]. These results are further supported by the overall quantitative metrics presented in Table 5, obtained from the interaction between the grapevine disease classifier and the test set provided in [25], confirming the model's effectiveness under conditions consistent with those represented in the training data.

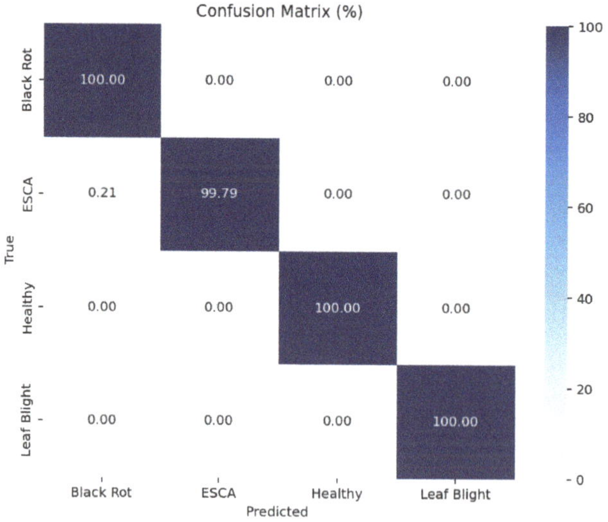

Figure 13. Confusion matrix of Xception-based grapevine disease model, assessed with a testing subset.

Table 5. Results regarding the performance of Xception-based grapevine disease classifier (precision, recall, F1-score, accuracy), assessed with a testing group available in [25].

Label	Metrics			Support
	Precision	Recall	F1-Score	
Black rot	1.00	1.00	1.00	472
ESCA	1.00	1.00	1.00	480
Healthy	1.00	1.00	1.00	423
Leaf Blight	1.00	1.00	1.00	430
	Complementary results			
Accuracy		1.00		
Macro average	1.00	1.00	1.00	1805
Weighted average	1.00	1.00	1.00	

5.3. Leaves Detection

Using the process described in Section 4.2, a synthetic dataset was generated to simulate grapevine leaves distributed over a vine plant conduction system, and used to train a YOLOv8s-based model for EOIs detection. Such a model was initially evaluated using a test subset derived from the mentioned dataset, but deliberately excluded from the training stage. As shown in Table 6, the model demonstrated excellent inference capabilities on synthetic data, indicating effective learning from the generated samples. This high performance may be attributed to the consistent and controlled nature of the conditions considered to model the leaf detection task—namely, five vine trunks and 64 leaves—despite the application of various data augmentation strategies, including downscaling and upscaling, brightness and contrast adjustments, leaf and trunk rotations, and Gaussian-based foliage placement, among others, aimed at increasing variability. In such homogeneity, precision and recall align well with high resilience to false positive and false negative occurrences, which also contributes for the elevated F1-score. In turn, the couple of mAP metrics highlights a high correlation between bounding box estimations and ground-truth, with relevant impact in the fitness indicator.

Table 6. Performance results of the YOLOv8s-based model trained for leaf detection using a synthetic dataset specifically generated for this purpose. The model was evaluated on the test subset of the same dataset, which, however, did not take part in training.

Metric	Value
Precision	0.9999
Recall	1.0000
F1-score	0.9999
mAP50	0.9950
mAP50-95	0.9756
Fitness	0.9775

The model trained with synthetic data for leaf detection, however, was subsequently evaluated in a relevant operational environment where ground-truth annotations were unavailable, making visual inspection the primary approach for extracting insights. To that end, high-resolution imagery from the Nossa Senhora de Lourdes farm (41°17′08.7″ N, 7°44′12.2″ W), located near the University of Trás-os-Montes e Alto Douro campus, was collected and considered for the intended assessment. As illustrated in Figure 14 through the represented blue bounding boxes, in natural vineyard environments with dense foliage and surrounding vegetation, the model successfully detects a substantial number of leaves, though many are also missed. Comparing the grape moth and leaf detection models, one can infer that, although the latter outperforms the former on synthetic data, visual inspection in relevant operational environments suggests a reversal in performance. Despite these limitations, the inference capabilities of the leaves model still seem to be sufficient to extract EOIs for subsequent stages aimed at assessing the phytosanitary status of the targeted plant type.

Figure 14. Results of YOLOv8s operating over original images acquired from the Nossa Senhora de Lourdes farm (41°17′08.7″ N, 7°44′12.2″ W), located near the University of Trás-os-Montes e Alto Douro campus.

5.4. *Leaf Detection Articulated with Disease Classification*

The functional integration of the YOLOv8s-based leaf detector with the Xception-based grapevine disease classifier was experimentally validated using external imagery curated to align with the operational context for which each model was individually trained and jointly orchestrated. The goal was to test the collaborative behavior of this two-stage pipeline, in which the detection and classification tasks are modular and, yet, complementary. To that end, aiming to assemble a representative testing sample, the following image sources and retrieval processes were applied per disease:

- Black rot: A publicly available dataset developed by Rossi et al. [43], comprising 384 images of viticultural black rot, was considered. From this set, 30 images were selected based on training condition compliance. To augment this limited sample, additional images were retrieved via web crawling using the Google Custom Search API [44], parameterized with the search query "black rot grapevine leaves" (alongside authentication credentials). An initial pool of 100 images was gathered, of which 45 were retained after manual curation. These images were sourced from agricultural extension platforms, scientific publishers, viticulture-specific websites, and photographic repositories, such as,
  - *agriculture.vic.gov.au*, https://agriculture.vic.gov.au (accessed on 2 June 2025),
  - *extension.okstate.edu*, https://extension.okstate.edu (accessed on 2 June 2025),
  - *missouribotanicalgarden.org*, https://missouribotanicalgarden.org (accessed on 2 June 2025),
  - *americanvineyardmagazine.com*, https://americanvineyardmagazine.com (accessed on 2 June 2025),
  - *shutterstock.com*, https://shutterstock.com (accessed on 2 June 2025).

The combination of both filtered image sources resulted in a total of 75 usable images for black rot evaluation.

- ESCA: A publicly available dataset by Alessandrini et al. [45] was used, from which 888 images of grapevine leaves affected by ESCA were selected.
- Leaf blight: The dataset proposed by Özacar et al. [46] was included, particularly focusing on the dead arm class (caused by *Phomopsis viticola*), which contains examples in which characteristic visual lesions representative of this symptom can be noticed.

These imagery sets were processed through the proposed pipeline, beginning with the YOLOv8s-based leaf detector, followed by the Xception-based model for disease classification. The results, presented in Table 7, indicate that the proposed pipeline—comprising modular and complementary models—is promising for rapid deployment in field conditions, at least, as a preliminary inference system. Coupling this strategy with active learning paves the way for progressive model refinements, improving performance over time through iterative feedback and adaptation.

Table 7. Operational insights of the modular YOLOv8s leaf detector and Xception disease classifier working collaboratively to identify black rot, ESCA, and leaf blight manifestations.

Condition	# Images	# Leaf Instances	# Black Rot Detections	# ESCA Detections	# Leaf Blight Detections	# Healthy
Black Rot	75	97	38	26	24	9
ESCA	888	1166	62	550	468	86
Leaf Blight	174	207	1	12	185	9

The following section presents a discussion, highlighting the main findings, limitations encountered, and potential directions for future improvements and applications.

6. Discussion

This work proposed and explored a set of methods based on synthetic data generation and was complemented by existing datasets, with the goal of enabling the rapid development of preliminary and yet functional DL models suitable for field deployment. Such methods involve customized image generation through LLM and diffusion models, domain-relevant composition strategies, and automatic annotation, which leads to datasets compliant with modern DL tools for model training. The case studies selected to demonstrate the viability of these methods lay within precision viticulture scope. Initially, an approach was developed for modeling datasets oriented to the challenge of detecting grape moths in pheromone traps. Generative AI was used to produce empty traps, while publicly available datasets [39,40] allowed to extract insect samples directly from the images. Classic image processing techniques were applied to compose synthetic images, wherein contour-based cropped grape moth specimens were placed over AI-generated trap backgrounds. The resulting YOLO-compatible dataset enabled the training of a YOLOv8s model—selected for its efficiency in edge computing environments—that attained precision values close to 0.99 and an mAP of approximately 0.86. Despite achieving a performance that seems to cope with those reported in the literature for similar contexts—e.g., [6,19]—, it should be noted that, due to the use of such a synthetic dataset for training, this grape moth detection model may lack environmental variability and, as such, be susceptible to blind spots when shifts in operational conditions occur (e.g., changes in lighting, background variation, or the presence of different insect species).

As for disease identification, the combination of available datasets with synthetic data to rapidly expand DL applicability was also explored. An Xception model was trained following the directives of a previous study [9] and using a publicly available dataset from

Kaggle [25], which consists of a set of annotated images depicting healthy and infected leaves acquired under laboratory conditions. In similar datasets, the model achieved high accuracy (nearly 100%), comparable to or even outperforming results reported in the related literature [22,24,27,29]. These results also demonstrate the viability and flexibility of the training process proposed in [9], which was initially developed for digital ampelography but has proven effective for grapevine disease identification based on visual symptoms in the leaves. However, due to the limitations of the utilized dataset in representing field conditions—where leaves are embedded within complex canopies—a leaf detection model was required to bridge the gap between laboratory data and real-world deployment. An initial attempt to generate such a dataset relied solely on ChatGPT's integration with DALL·E. While the tool produced visually convincing images, the annotations were found to be unreliable or entirely random, making the approach unfeasible for direct dataset construction. As an alternative, ChatGPT/DALL·E were used to separately generate leafless grapevine backgrounds and isolated grapevine leaves with various visual characteristics (e.g., healthy, chlorotic, or spot-affected). Some key operational considerations emerged during this process:

- Before generation, requirements must be specified in detail and confirmed by ChatGPT through summarization to mitigate potential issues related to linguistic ambiguity or model misinterpretation or even drifting;
- During batch generation, interruptions often occurred, requiring manual prompting to resume the process.

Once both background and foreground libraries were prepared, traditional image processing techniques—similar to those used for the grape moth case—were employed to synthesize new images and generate precise annotations. The resulting YOLOv8s leaf detector achieved strong results on unseen synthetic data (precision and mAP above 0.97), although performance declined when tested on external, real-world imagery (originally acquired in Nossa Senhora de Lourdes farm—41°17′08.7″ N, 7°44′12.2″ W), revealing some limitations in generalization. Despite such limitations, the integrated use of the YOLOv8s-based leaf detector and the Xception-based disease classifier within a unified pipeline yielded promising outcomes. In external imagery, although not all leaves were detected, the inference system was still able to correctly classify diseased leaves among those successfully extracted, with class-wise accuracies ranging from 39% to 89%, supporting the feasibility of the proposed approach. Overall, the proposed methods offer a promising pathway for the rapid deployment of first-generation AI models, as evidenced by the tests conducted in viticultural scenarios. When integrated into an active learning framework—such as the one illustrated in Figure 15, inspired by works like [32]—these models can function not only as early inference tools but also as key enablers of a continuous improvement strategy. High-confidence predictions may directly support decision-making in the field, while low-confidence outputs can be flagged for expert review and incorporated into subsequent training cycles. This iterative process enables continuous refinement and adaptation of the models, leading to progressively improved performance and closer alignment with ideal real-world operating conditions.

One final note concerns the methodological positioning of this work within the broader literature on automatic approaches for generating credible datasets and annotations. While many of the existing studies—particularly in agriculture [47]—employ generative AI to enhance datasets by creating new instances from existing training data with the aim of improving DL model performance, the approaches proposed in this paper are fundamentally different. Specifically, foundational datasets are synthetically created from scratch and roughly modeled to reflect the general conditions of operational environments. The goal is to enable the initial deployment of DL models in a time-effective manner, allowing them to be incrementally improved over time through, for example, active learning strategies [32], rather than relying on the continuous expansion of existing datasets. Notwithstanding, while using ChatGPT/DALL·E to create fully labeled datasets remains an ongoing challenge—since these tools lack introspective mechanisms for determining the positioning and spatial occupation of entities of interest (EOIs), as observed in Section 4—other approaches (e.g., [11,33]) have explored alternative strategies grounded in the assembly of realistic 3D scenes with automatic annotation capabilities. Complementarily, the approach presented in this paper combines the believable 2D generation capabilities of natural language-driven models, as in the former, with the parameterization and control typical of the latter, aiming to provide context-aware synthetic imagery that is both quick and relatively simple to produce, accompanied by accurate annotations. As all of these approaches are still evolving to shape usable AI-oriented synthetic data sourcing strategies, their consolidation will naturally motivate future comparative analyses aimed at better understanding the strengths and limitations of each proposal.

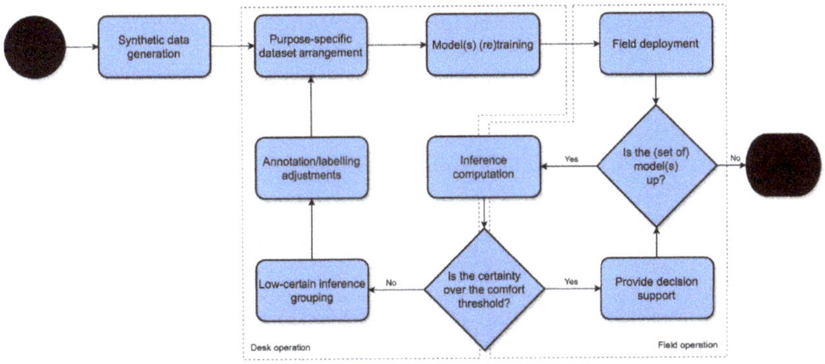

Figure 15. Active learning pipeline proposal for the progressive refinement of models trained through bootstrapping strategy.

The next section ends this paper by summarizing the main contributions, as well as by delineating a few orientations for future work.

7. Conclusions and Future Work

The development of reliable visual inference models is often hindered by the burdensome and time-consuming nature of collecting and annotating high-quality datasets. To address this challenge, this work explored the use of synthetic dataset generation to bootstrap DL models, with proof-of-concept applications in the context of precision viticulture.

Two case studies were examined. In the first, a fully synthetic dataset was generated to train a YOLOv8-based object detection model for identifying grape moths in pheromone trap imagery. In the second, a hybrid inference pipeline was proposed, combining a YOLOv8-based model for leaf detection in grapevine canopy images with an Xception-based classifier for disease identification. This two-stage approach enabled the classification of leaves into four categories—healthy, black rot, ESCA, and leaf blight—highlighting the synergistic potential of integrating object detection and classification tasks within a modular architecture.

Results from both scenarios demonstrate that fully or partially synthetic visual data pipelines can provide a valid foundation for the initial deployment of inference models, particularly in domains where annotated data is scarce. Although these models are not flawless, they showed promising performance when evaluated on synthetic imagery unseen during training, as well as apparently good operational capabilities under relevant conditions, based on visual assessment of detection and classification outputs. Additional inference results from collaborative models for grapevine leaf detection followed by disease recognition also provided reasonable indications of suitability for initial DL deployment. Nevertheless, it is important to emphasize the need for continuous improvement processes—potentially driven by active learning strategies—to enhance model robustness over time. In addition to the presented use cases, the proposed synthetic data generation approaches could also benefit other applications in—though not limited to—agriculture, particularly in visual contexts that share similar meta-requirements regarding scene composition. Examples include the detection of animals posing threats to crops (e.g., birds), anti-theft surveillance, drone-based cattle detection and counting, and agricultural fire monitoring, among others.

Looking ahead, future work will focus on deploying these models in edge computing environments to enable real-time, in-field operation. Additionally, active learning frameworks will be integrated, allowing the models to flag uncertain predictions for expert review. This feedback loop will support continuous, data-driven model refinement, progressively improving accuracy and adaptability under real-world conditions.

Author Contributions: Conceptualization, T.A.; methodology, T.A. and N.S.; software, T.A.; validation, R.M. and E.P.; formal analysis, N.S. and A.C.; investigation, T.A., N.S., A.C. and D.P.; resources, R.M. and E.P.; data curation, T.A. and A.C.; writing original draft preparation, T.A. and D.P.; writing, review and editing, T.A., A.C., E.P. and R.M.; visualization, T.A.; supervision, E.P. and R.M.; project administration, R.M.; funding acquisition, R.M. and E.P. All authors have read and agreed to the published version of the manuscript.

Funding: This work was funded by the Vine and Wine Portugal Project, co-financed by the Recovery and Resilience Plan (RRP) and the European Union (EU) NextGenerationEU funds, within the scope of the Mobilizing Agendas for Reindustrialization, under the reference C644866286-00000011.

Data Availability Statement: All the relevant data is contained within the article.

Conflicts of Interest: The authors declare no conflicts of interest.

References

1. Pozo Pérez, J.R.; Fernández Llerena, Y.; Chávez Castilla, Y.; Garcia Reyes, E.; Magalhães, L.G.; Guevara Lopez, M.A. AOI for automotive industry—A quality assessment approach combining 2D and 3D sensors. In Proceedings of the 29th International ACM Conference on 3D Web Technology, Guimarães, Portugal, 25–27 September 2024. [CrossRef]
2. Fontes, J.P.P.; Raimundo, J.N.C.; Magalhães, L.G.M.; Lopez, M.A.G. Accurate phenotyping of luminal A breast cancer in magnetic resonance imaging: A new 3D CNN approach. *Comput. Biol. Med.* **2025**, *189*, 109903. [CrossRef]
3. Attri, I.; Awasthi, L.K.; Sharma, T.P.; Rathee, P. A review of deep learning techniques used in agriculture. *Ecol. Inform.* **2023**, *77*, 102217. [CrossRef]
4. Morais, R.; Silva, N.; Mendes, J.; Adão, T.; Pádua, L.; López-Riquelme, J.A.; Pavón-Pulido, N.; Sousa, J.J.A.; Peres, E. mySense: A comprehensive data management environment to improve precision agriculture practices. *Comput. Electron. Agric.* **2019**, *162*, 882–894. [CrossRef]
5. Morais, R. MySense IoT Framework UTAD. Available online: https://mysense.utad.pt (accessed on 9 May 2025).
6. Mendes, J.; Peres, E.; Neves dos Santos, F.; Silva, N.; Silva, R.; Sousa, J.J.A.; Cortez, I.; Morais, R. VineInspector: The Vineyard Assistant. *Agriculture* **2022**, *12*, 730 . [CrossRef]
7. Mohimont, L.; Alin, F.; Rondeau, M.; Gaveau, N.; Steffenel, L.A. Computer Vision and Deep Learning for Precision Viticulture. *Agronomy* **2022**, *12*, 2463. [CrossRef]
8. Shen, L.; Su, J.; He, R.; Song, L.; Huang, R.; Fang, Y.; Song, Y.; Su, B. Real-time tracking and counting of grape clusters in the field based on channel pruning with YOLOv5s. *Comput. Electron. Agric.* **2023**, *206*, 107662. [CrossRef]
9. Adão, T.; Shahrabadi, S.; Mendes, J.; Bastardo, R.; Magalhães, L.; Morais, R.; Peres, E. Advancing digital ampelography: Automated classification of grapevine varieties. *Comput. Electron. Agric.* **2025**, *229*, 109675. [CrossRef]
10. Kontogiannis, S.; Konstantinidou, M.; Tsioukas, V.; Pikridas, C. A Cloud-Based Deep Learning Framework for Downy Mildew Detection in Viticulture Using Real-Time Image Acquisition from Embedded Devices and Drones. *Information* **2024**, *15*, 178. [CrossRef]

1. Adão, T.; Cerqueira, J.A.; Adão, M.; Silva, N.; Pascoal, D.; Magalhães, L.G.; Barros, T.; Premebida, C.; Nunes, U.J.; Peres, E.; et al. PROMORE: A Procedural Modeler of Virtual Rural Environments with Artificial Dataset Generation Capabilities for Remote Sensing Contexts. *IEEE Access* **2025**, *13*, 47632–47652. [CrossRef]
2. Lyu, C.; Lin, S.; Lynch, A.; Zou, Y.; Liarokapis, M. UAV-based deep learning applications for automated inspection of civil infrastructure. *Autom. Constr.* **2025**, *177*, 106285. [CrossRef]
3. Guder, O.; Isik, S.; Anagun, Y. Fabric defects identification for textile industry with a deep learning approach. *J. Text. Inst.* **2024**, *116*, 1493–1502. [CrossRef]
4. Kreutz, M.; Böttjer, A.; Trapp, M.; Lütjen, M.; Freitag, M. Towards individualized shoes: Deep learning-based fault detection for 3D printed footwear. *Procedia CIRP* **2022**, *107*, 196–201. [CrossRef]
5. Noor, T.H.; Noor, A.; Alharbi, A.F.; Faisal, A.; Alrashidi, R.; Alsaedi, A.S.; Alharbi, G.; Alsanoosy, T.; Alsaeedi, A. Real-Time Arabic Sign Language Recognition Using a Hybrid Deep Learning Model. *Sensors* **2024**, *24*, 3683. [CrossRef] [PubMed]
6. Gong, Y.; Liu, G.; Xue, Y.; Li, R.; Meng, L. A survey on dataset quality in machine learning. *Inf. Softw. Technol.* **2023**, *162*, 107268. [CrossRef]
7. Mohanty, S.P. PlantVillage-Dataset. Available online: https://github.com/spMohanty/PlantVillage-Dataset (accessed on 9 May 2025).
8. Volunesia, S. Kaggle-Pest Dataset. Available online: https://www.kaggle.com/datasets/simranvolunesia/pest-dataset (accessed on 9 May 2025).
9. Gonçalves, J.; Silva, E.; Faria, P.; Nogueira, T.; Ferreira, A.; Carlos, C.; Rosado, L. Edge-Compatible Deep Learning Models for Detection of Pest Outbreaks in Viticulture. *Agronomy* **2022**, *12*, 3052. [CrossRef]
10. Checola, G.; Sonego, P.; Zorer, R.; Mazzoni, V.; Ghidoni, F.; Gelmetti, A.; Franceschi, P. A novel dataset and deep learning object detection benchmark for grapevine pest surveillance. *Front. Plant Sci.* **2024**, *15*, 1485216. [CrossRef] [PubMed]
11. Xie, X.; Ma, Y.; Liu, B.; He, J.; Li, S.; Wang, H. A Deep-Learning-Based Real-Time Detector for Grape Leaf Diseases Using Improved Convolutional Neural Networks. *Front. Plant Sci.* **2020**, *11*, 751. [CrossRef]
12. Hasan, M.A.; Riana, D.; Swasono, S.; Priyatna, A.; Pudjiarti, E.; Prahartiwi, L.I. Identification of Grape Leaf Diseases Using Convolutional Neural Network. *J. Phys. Conf. Ser.* **2020**, *1641*, 012007. [CrossRef]
13. Bhattarai, S. New Plant Diseases Dataset. 2021. Available online: https://www.kaggle.com/datasets/vipoooool/new-plant-diseases-dataset (accessed on 9 May 2025).
14. Prasad, K.V.; Vaidya, H.; Rajashekhar, C.; Karekal, K.S.; Sali, R.; Nisar, K.S. Multiclass classification of diseased grape leaf identification using deep convolutional neural network*DCNN* classifier. *Sci. Rep.* **2024**, *14*, 9002. [CrossRef]
15. Mandal, R. Kaggle-Grapevine Disease Dataset (Original). Available online: https://www.kaggle.com/datasets/rm1000/grape-disease-dataset-original. (accessed on 9 May 2025).
16. Kunduracioglu, I.; Paçal, I. Advancements in deep learning for accurate classification of grape leaves and diagnosis of grape diseases. *J. Plant Dis. Prot.* **2024**, *131*, 1061–1080. [CrossRef]
17. Nasra, P.; Gupta, S. Deep Learning-Based Grapevine Leaf Disease Detection Using Fine-Tuned Xception Model. In Proceedings of the 2024 3rd International Conference for Advancement in Technology (ICONAT), Goa, India, 6–8 September 2024; pp. 1–6. [CrossRef]
18. Pushpalama. Grape Disease Dataset. 2021. Available online: https://www.kaggle.com/datasets/pushpalama/grape-disease (accessed on 9 May 2025).
19. Talaat, F.M.; Shams, M.Y.; Gamel, S.A.; ZainEldin, H. DeepLeaf: An optimized deep learning approach for automated recognition of grapevine leaf diseases. *Neural Comput. Appl.* **2025**, *37*, 8799–8823. [CrossRef]
20. Tejaswi, A. Plant Village Dataset. Available online: https://www.kaggle.com/datasets/arjuntejaswi/plant-village (accessed on 9 May 2025).
21. Shahrabadi, S.; Alves, V.; Peres, E.; Morais Dos Santos, R.; Adão, T. Unbalancing Datasets to Enhance CNN Models Learnability: A Class-Wise Metrics-Based Closed-Loop Strategy Proposal. *IEEE Access* **2025**, *13*, 57485–57503. [CrossRef]
22. Liu, Z.; Wang, J.; Gong, S.; Lu, H.; Tao, D. Deep Reinforcement Active Learning for Human-in-the-Loop Person Re-Identification. In Proceedings of the IEEE/CVF International Conference on Computer Vision (ICCV), Seoul, Republic of Korea, 27 October–2 November 2019.
23. Greff, K.; Belletti, F.; Beyer, L.; Doersch, C.; Du, Y.; Duckworth, D.; Fleet, D.J.; Gnanapragasam, D.; Golemo, F.; Herrmann, C.; et al. Kubric: A Scalable Dataset Generator. In Proceedings of the IEEE/CVF Conference on Computer Vision and Pattern Recognition (CVPR), New Orleans, LA, USA, 18–24 June 2022; pp. 3749–3761.
24. Cordeiro, A.; Rocha, L.F.; Boaventura-Cunha, J.; Pires, E.J.S.; Souza, J.A.P. Object segmentation dataset generation framework for robotic bin-picking: Multi-metric analysis between results trained with real and synthetic data. *Comput. Ind. Eng.* **2025**, *205*, 111139. [CrossRef]

35. Adão, T.; Pinho, T.M.; Pádua, L.; Santos, N.; Sousa, A.; Sousa, J.J.; Peres, E. Using Virtual Scenarios to Produce Machine Learnable Environments for Wildfire Detection and Segmentation. *Int. Arch. Photogramm. Remote Sens. Spat. Inf. Sci.* **2019**, *XLII-3-W8*, 9–15. [CrossRef]
36. Wu, C.; Yin, S.; Qi, W.; Wang, X.; Tang, Z.; Duan, N. Visual ChatGPT: Talking, Drawing and Editing with Visual Foundation Models. *arXiv* **2023**, arXiv:2303.04671. [CrossRef]
37. OpenAI. ChatGPT: Language Model by OpenAI. 2025. Available online: https://chat.openai.com/ (accessed on 2 June 2025).
38. OpenAI. DALL·E 3: AI Image Generation by OpenAI. 2023. Available online: https://openai.com/index/dall-e-3/ (accessed on 2 June 2025).
39. Teixeira, C. Grape_Moth Dataset. 2023. Available online: https://universe.roboflow.com/anaclaudia/grape_moth (accessed on 2 June 2025).
40. Teixeira, C. Grape_Moth_1 Dataset. 2022. Available online: https://universe.roboflow.com/claudia-teixeira/grape_moth_1 (accessed on 2 June 2025).
41. Canva. Background Remover—Canva. 2025. Available online: https://www.canva.com/features/background-remover/ (accessed on 2 June 2025).
42. Roboflow: Computer Vision Tools for Developers and Enterprises. Available online: https://roboflow.com/ (accessed on 9 May 2025).
43. Rossi, L.; Prati, A. LDD: A Grape Diseases Dataset Detection and Instance Segmentation. In Proceedings of the 21st International Conference, Lecce, Italy, 23–27 May 2022. [CrossRef]
44. Google. Custom Search JSON API. Available online: https://developers.google.com/custom-search/ (accessed on 2 June 2025).
45. Alessandrini, M.; Calero Fuentes Rivera, R.; Falaschetti, L.; Pau, D.; Tomaselli, V.; Turchetti, C. *ESCA-Dataset*; Elsevier Inc.: Amsterdam, The Netherlands, 2021. [CrossRef]
46. Özacar, T.; Öztürk, Ö.; Güngör Savaş, N. *HERMOS: An Annotated Image Dataset for Visual Detection of Grape Leaf Diseases*; Elsevier Inc.: Amsterdam, The Netherlands, 2021. [CrossRef]
47. Lu, Y.; Chen, D.; Olaniyi, E.; Huang, Y. Generative adversarial networks (GANs) for image augmentation in agriculture: A systematic review. *Comput. Electron. Agric.* **2022**, *200*, 107208. [CrossRef]

computers

MDPI

Article

Assessment of Machine Learning-Driven Retrievals of Arctic Sea Ice Thickness from L-Band Radiometry Remote Sensing

Ferran Hernández-Macià [1,2,3,*], Gemma Sanjuan Gomez [2], Carolina Gabarró [1] and Maria José Escorihuela [3]

1 Barcelona Polar Lab (BPL), Institute of Marine Sciences (ICM-CSIC), 08003 Barcelona, Spain
2 Department of Computer Architecture and Operating Systems, Autonomous University of Barcelona (UAB), 08193 Bellaterra, Spain
3 isardSAT, S.L., 08005 Barcelona, Spain
* Correspondence: fhernandezmacia@icm.csic.es

Abstract: This study evaluates machine learning-based methods for retrieving thin Arctic sea ice thickness (SIT) from L-band radiometry, using data from the European Space Agency's (ESA) Soil Moisture and Ocean Salinity (SMOS) satellite. In addition to the operational ESA product, three alternative approaches are assessed: a Random Forest (RF) algorithm, a Convolutional Neural Network (CNN) that incorporates spatial coherence, and a Long Short-Term Memory (LSTM) neural network designed to capture temporal coherence. Validation against in situ data from the Beaufort Gyre Exploration Project (BGEP) moorings and the ESA SMOSice campaign demonstrates that the RF algorithm achieves robust performance comparable to the ESA product, despite its simplicity and lack of explicit spatial or temporal modeling. The CNN exhibits a tendency to overestimate SIT and shows higher dispersion, suggesting limited added value when spatial coherence is already present in the input data. The LSTM approach does not improve retrieval accuracy, likely due to the mismatch between satellite resolution and the temporal variability of sea ice conditions. These results highlight the importance of L-band sea ice emission modeling over increasing algorithm complexity and suggest that simpler, adaptable methods such as RF offer a promising foundation for future SIT retrieval efforts. The findings are relevant for refining current methods used with SMOS and for developing upcoming satellite missions, such as ESA's Copernicus Imaging Microwave Radiometer (CIMR).

Keywords: machine learning; remote sensing; sea ice; cryosphere

1. Introduction

Sea ice is a key component of the Earth system. Its extent undergoes annual periodicity and covers almost 7% of the Earth's surface at its maximum extent in September, mainly at the poles. It has a crucial effect on climate change, as it participates in the so-called ice–albedo feedback loop [1]. Arctic sea ice has been significantly decreasing in recent decades [2], also suffering a shift to younger and thinner ice [3].

Since the launch of the first Earth Observation (EO) satellites in the early 1970s, passive microwave radiometers have been used to observe sea ice. The European Space Agency (ESA) mission Soil Moisture and Ocean Salinity (SMOS) [4,5], initiated in 2009, and NASA's Advanced Microwave Scanning Radiometer (AMSR) series, which has operated on different satellites from 2002 to the present, as well as the Soil Moisture Active Passive (SMAP) [6] mission, launched in 2015, are key contributors. In particular, the focus of this study is on passive L-band radiometers such as SMOS, working at 1.4 GHz with a penetration depth of up to 1 m or even more in low-salinity sea ice.

Currently, two distinct algorithms for estimating Arctic thin sea ice thickness from SMOS measurements during the non-melting period (October to April) exist. The first, distributed by the European Space Agency (ESA), is a semi-empirical algorithm developed by the Alfred Wegener Institute (AWI) as described in [7,8]. However, a significant drawback is its inability to consider the presence of snow on top of sea ice. This limitation is critical due to the substantial impact of snow on emitted L-band radiation [9] and subsequent thickness retrieval processes. The second algorithm, from the University of Bremen (UB) and detailed in [10], adopts an empirical approach. Despite this, a notable limitation of the UB product is its restricted sensitivity, reaching only up to 0.5 m. While the UB product explicitly limits the sea ice thickness retrieval, the AWI product does not have a clearly defined upper limit, with sensitivity typically ranging between 0.5 and 1.5 m depending on sea ice conditions.

Other emerging methodologies include the use of Global Navigation Satellite System Reflectometry (GNSS-R), which, beyond its previous applications for retrieving various geophysical parameters, has also been explored for sea ice applications. Recent studies have shown its potential to detect sea ice and estimate its thickness, although these results have so far only been demonstrated in simulations [11,12]. Nevertheless, GNSS-R remains promising as a valuable complement to passive L-band measurements in the future.

Artificial intelligence (AI) holds the potential to transform the processing and analysis of Earth Observation (EO) data acquired through remote sensing. AI offers the capability to improve the analysis of these data, enhancing our ability to monitor and predict the evolution of many geophysical variables. Recent efforts to retrieve sea ice parameters from satellite observations using artificial intelligence have increasingly focused on applying machine learning techniques to passive microwave data. One of the earlier examples is found in [13], where a neural network was used to try to estimate snow depth over sea ice using AMSR2 and SMOS data. Similarly, ref. [14] applied two machine learning algorithms to retrieve sea ice thickness from a combination of TechDemoSat-1 (TDS-1) and SMOS observations. Ref. [15] developed an ensemble Convolutional Neural Network (CNN) to retrieve daily sea ice thickness from AMSR2 data. Likewise, ref. [16,17] used a combination of frequencies ranging from 1.4 to 36 GHz, applying AI-based methodologies to estimate and analyze sea ice thickness and volume trends. Beyond SMOS and AMSR2, ref. [18] used a neural network to retrieve sea ice thickness from FSSCat nanosatellite data [19]. Meanwhile, ref. [20,21] investigated machine learning approaches for sea ice sensing using data from a C-band Synthetic Aperture Radar (SAR) sensor like Sentinel-1.

An application of machine learning to Arctic sea ice thickness retrieval from SMOS observations was presented in [22]. That study employed two decision-tree-based algorithms—Random Forest (RF) and Gradient Boosting (GB)—within a supervised learning framework. These algorithms were trained on data derived from maps generated through model inversion. The results were promising, demonstrating good agreement with ESA's sea ice thickness product and achieving improved validation against in situ datasets. Building on this foundation, the objective of this work is to assess the performance of deep learning methods in enhancing retrieval accuracy. Specifically, it extends the methodology by implementing a Convolutional Neural Network (CNN) and a Long Short-Term Memory (LSTM) neural network. These approaches represent significant advancements in data processing: the CNN leverages spatial coherence by treating input variables as maps, while the LSTM captures temporal coherence by utilizing sequential information from consecutive observations.

Since the training dataset is entirely derived from a physical emission model due to the lack of sufficient in situ data, the performance of the ML algorithms is ultimately constrained by the accuracy and assumptions of that model. Therefore, this study focuses on evaluating the ability of different architectures to learn and approximate its behavior. To assess their performance, the operational ESA sea ice thickness product is included as a baseline for comparison. Accordingly, the main contributions of this work are threefold: (1) a comparative evaluation of three ML architectures (RF, CNN, LSTM) for retrieving sea ice thickness from L-band radiometry; (2) an assessment of how these approximations perform on real-world satellite data; and (3) a benchmark comparison against the ESA product to highlight strengths and limitations relative to existing retrieval approaches.

The paper is organized as follows: Section 2 describes the various data sources used as input, the generation of the training dataset, and the datasets employed for validation. Section 3 outlines the different algorithmic approaches. The results of the assessment are presented in Section 4, followed by a discussion in Section 5. Finally, the conclusions of the study are summarized in Section 6.

2. Data Collection and Processing

This section describes the datasets used both as input variables for the proposed algorithms and as in situ observations for their validation. Additionally, it provides details on data preparation and the processing steps undertaken to generate the training dataset.

2.1. Input Datasets

The input variables consist of a combination of satellite-derived products and reanalysis model outputs, providing comprehensive coverage of Arctic sea ice conditions. The satellite datasets include the ESA's SMOS sea ice thickness product, from which only the TB is extracted and used as input, and a sea ice surface temperature data product. Additionally, a reanalysis model provides the required information about sea ice and seawater properties. The final subsection explains how these variables are processed for use as input for the proposed methodology.

2.1.1. ESA SMOS Sea Ice Thickness Product

The SMOS satellite carries the Microwave Imaging Radiometer Aperture Synthesis (MIRAS) payload, which measures brightness temperatures in full polarization at L-band with incidence angles ranging from 0° to 65°, including all four Stokes parameters [23]. The instrument provides global coverage every three days and daily coverage in the polar regions. The hexagonal two-dimensional snapshots taken by the MIRAS instrument have a spatial dimension of approximately 1200 km across and can capture brightness temperature every 1.2 s, with spatial resolution varying from about 35 km at nadir view to over 50 km at higher incidence angles. Each snapshot measures one of the Stokes components in the antenna reference frame, including horizontally (TBH) and vertically (TBV) polarized brightness temperatures. The intensity is obtained by averaging the horizontally and vertically polarized brightness temperatures. Moreover, the brightness temperature (TB) intensity of the signal over sea ice remains relatively consistent regardless of the angle at which it is measured within the 0°–40° range; therefore, it is computed as an average of this interval. The daily averaged brightness temperature intensity in the Arctic region is interpolated using a nearest neighbor algorithm and gridded onto the National Snow and Ice Data Center (NSIDC) polar stereographic projection with a grid resolution of 12.5 km.

The SMOS L3 Sea Ice Thickness product is produced by AWI and distributed by ESA, and provides information on sea ice thickness in the Arctic region from October to April, covering the period from 2010 to the present. It was first described in [7,8]. The sea ice thickness is determined using an iterative retrieval algorithm that incorporates a thermodynamic sea ice model and a three-layer radiative transfer model. The radiative transfer model calculates the emissivity of the sea ice layer and the underlying seawater, and brightness temperatures are derived from the emissivity and physical temperatures of the sea ice and seawater. The bulk ice temperature is estimated using a thermodynamic model, which utilizes the 2 m air temperature from atmospheric reanalysis data as an input parameter, while the bulk ice salinity is computed from an empirical relation described in [24]. The retrieval algorithm also accounts for variations in ice thickness within the SMOS spatial resolution by using a statistical thickness distribution function based on high-resolution ice thickness measurements from NASA's Operation IceBridge (OIB) campaign.

In this work, the brightness temperature (TB) intensity maps measured by SMOS are taken from the ESA/AWI SMOS sea ice thickness product (https://earth.esa.int/eogateway/catalog/smos-l3-sea-ice-thickness, accessed on 24 July 2025) and used as input for the algorithms. Consequently, all processing details related to the TB, including the handling of the angular distribution of satellite measurements, are described in the product's Algorithm Theoretical Basis Document (ATBD, [25]).

2.1.2. Surface Temperature Satellite Product

The Arctic Ocean-Sea and Ice Surface Temperature Reprocessed product [26], produced by the Danish Meteorological Institute (DMI) and distributed by the Copernicus Marine Service (CMEMS), provides information on Arctic sea and ice surface temperatures. These data are derived from reprocessed observations obtained through the Advanced Very-High-Resolution Radiometer (AVHRR), the Advanced Along Track Scanning Radiometers (AATSR), and the Sea and Land Surface Temperature Radiometer (SLSTR). These observations come from different sources, including the ESA Climate Change Initiative (CCI) project, the Copernicus Climate Change Service (C3S) project, and the Arctic & Antarctic Ice Surface Temperatures from Thermal Infrared Satellite Sensors (AASTI) dataset. The product provides a daily interpolated field at a resolution of 0.05 degrees, encompassing surface temperatures in the ocean, sea ice, and the marginal ice zone. The computation of surface temperature employs the optimal interpolation method, with the previous day's value serving as the initial guess field.

In this work, a linear temperature gradient within the ice is assumed, as supported by findings in [27]. Consequently, the calculation of the bulk ice temperature (T_{ice}) is determined by the following expression:

$$T_{ice} = \frac{T_{surface} - T_{sw}}{2}, \tag{1}$$

where $T_{surface}$ is the surface temperature obtained from the satellite product, and T_{sw} is the seawater temperature, for which a typical value for the Arctic of $-1.8\ ^\circ\mathrm{C}$ is assumed.

2.1.3. Arctic Ocean Physics Reanalysis Model

The Arctic Ocean Physics Reanalysis model, produced by the Nansen Environmental and Remote Sensing Center (NERSC) and distributed by CMEMS [28], provides physical variables derived from the reanalysis model TOPAZ (version 4b). This model assimilates a diverse set of observations, including sea level anomalies from satellite altimeters, sea surface temperature from the Operational Sea Surface Temperature and Sea Ice Analysis (OSTIA), in situ temperature and salinity data from hydrographic cruises and moorings, sea ice concentration from OSI-SAF, CS2SMOS ice thickness data, and sea surface salinity from the Barcelona Expert Center (BEC) utilizing SMOS satellite data.

In this work, the seawater salinity, sea ice thickness, and snow depth variables are obtained from this model. To compute the sea ice salinity, an empirical formula from [24] is used:

$$S_{ice} = S_{sw}(1 - S_R)e^{-a\sqrt{d_{ice}}} + S_R S_{sw}, \tag{2}$$

where S_{sw} is the seawater salinity and d_{ice} is the sea ice thickness in cm, both obtained from the Arctic Ocean Physics Reanalysis model. The growth rate coefficient, denoted as a, ranges between 0.35 and 0.5; S_R, the salinity ratio of the bulk ice salinity at the end of the ice growth season, is also crucial for determining the empirical equation for the sea ice salinity. Ref. [24] proposes using a value of 0.5 for a and 0.13 for S_R. However, ref. [29] suggests using 0.175 for S_R instead of 0.13 after comparing Equation (2) with observed data in the Arctic.

Finally, the determination of the snow presence variable is based on a straightforward assumption: if the snow thickness variable derived from TOPAZ is positive, it is inferred that snow is present; conversely, if it is zero, snow is considered absent.

2.2. Training Dataset Generation Through Model-Based Simulation

Available data for the Arctic region are extremely limited. Due to the absence of a comprehensive dataset on thin sea ice thickness, it becomes necessary to create one through the use of sea ice emission modeling. The Burke emission model [30], incorporating the Vant formulation for ice permittivity [31], is employed in an inverted manner to generate realistic scenarios of Arctic sea ice thickness distributions. The goal is to replicate these situations as accurately as possible. All variables, i.e., the SMOS TB, the sea ice temperature and salinity, and the snow presence, are first regridded to the 12.5 km × 12.5 km NSIDC Polar Stereographic grid. This workflow for generating the training dataset is summarized in Figure 1. It is noteworthy that the sensitivity of brightness temperature to ice thickness in this frequency band is strongly influenced by ice conditions, specifically temperature and salinity. To avoid imposing an artificial training threshold, the maximum thickness that can be retrieved (the point at which brightness temperature saturation begins) is computed for each configuration of ice conditions. Subsequently, the thickness derived from the model inversion is compared to this maximum thickness. If the latter is smaller, the inverted solution is adjusted to match this maximum thickness.

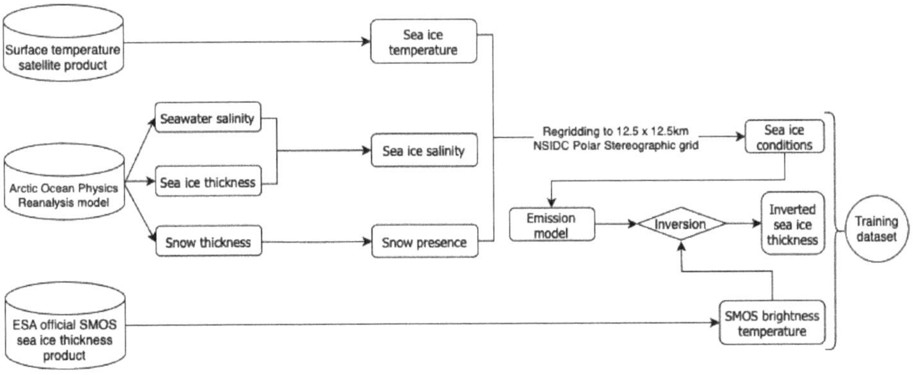

Figure 1. Diagram of the methodology's workflow. The variables extracted from different sources are input to invert an emission model and simulate the sea ice thickness distribution.

The accuracy of this model-based simulation fundamentally depends on the performance of the L-band sea ice emission modeling. However, it is currently not possible to quantify its precision due to the lack of Arctic-wide ground truth observations. The Burke model, originally developed for soil applications, has been widely adopted as an incoherent approach for simulating sea ice emission. Alternatively, a coherent approach could be considered [32], since coherence effects may arise when two or more interfaces exist within a plane-parallel medium, allowing an electromagnetic plane wave to interfere with its reflected counterpart [10]. Nevertheless, these effects are generally assumed to be averaged out over the satellite footprint, and to date, no significant influence has been confirmed. More complex radiative transfer models, such as the Snow Microwave Radiative Transfer model (SMRT, [33]), which account for internal scattering within the medium, are not necessary in this context, as such effects are negligible at L-band frequencies. The main source of uncertainty in modeling sea ice emission lies in the dielectric constant. As discussed in [27,34], the Vant formulation is comparable to theoretical models that treat sea ice as a mixture of pure ice and brine. The brine component, with its variable shapes and properties, plays a critical role in the emission process. However, there is still no consensus on which permittivity formulation is the most accurate, as it depends on the growth conditions of the sea ice, information that is not available during satellite-based sea ice thickness retrieval. Nonetheless, the combination of the Burke model with the Vant permittivity formulation appears to be a robust choice [34], capable of realistically reproducing the L-band emission of snow-covered sea ice across the Arctic.

Ultimately, the training dataset is composed of maps generated through the model-based simulation. All samples are extracted from model output maps covering two complete freeze-up seasons (15 October to 15 April in 2019–2020 and 2020–2021). Specifically, the initial dataset consisted of 366 Arctic-wide maps, containing a total of 199,385,088 valid pixels. After removing duplicates, the data were randomly shuffled. Furthermore, for each specific approach, the volume of training data was reduced through trial and error, in order to optimize both computational resources and model performance. The exact number of samples used in each case is provided in the corresponding subsections of Section 3. The dataset was not divided into separate training and testing subsets. This is because the performance is assessed exclusively using independent in situ measurements, as described in Section 2.3, and the corresponding results are presented in Section 4. No internal validation set was used, as the term "validation" here refers to this comparison with ground-truth datasets. The input and output variables of the training dataset are summarized in Table 1.

Table 1. Description of input and output variables in the training dataset.

Variable	Category	Type	Range
SMOS brightness temperature	Input	Numerical	150–260 K
Sea ice temperature	Input	Numerical	−20–0 °C
Sea ice salinity	Input	Numerical	0–15
Snow presence	Input	Binary	0 = no snow, 1 = snow
Sea ice thickness	Output	Numerical	0–1.5 m

2.3. *Validation Datasets*

The in situ data used in the validation are based on measurements from moored sensors at two locations in the Arctic Ocean, along with data from a campaign conducted in the Barents Sea in 2014, which unexpectedly—for the time of the year—encountered thin sea ice.

2.3.1. BGEP Mooring Data

The Upward-Looking Sonar (ULS) mooring buoys within the Beaufort Gyre Exploration Project (BGEP) are specifically designed for measuring the sea ice draft, representing the portion of sea ice submerged underwater. Consequently, to derive the total thickness of sea ice, a conversion is necessary. Following the approach outlined in [35], an empirical factor of 1.136 is applied to the ice draft to obtain the total thickness. This coefficient was determined through an empirical analysis that included nearly 400 sea ice drillings conducted in the Fram Strait [36]. The BGEP ULS data, consisting of daily averages of sea ice thickness from three mooring instruments situated within the Beaufort Gyre, serve as one of the datasets for validating the methodology.

2.3.2. Barents 2014: ESA SMOSice Campaign

The ESA SMOSice campaign took place in March 2014 in the Barents Sea ice marginal zone, specifically on newly formed thin sea ice in the south-east of Svalbard. It includes measurements collected by a helicopter operating from RV Lance and the research aircraft Polar 5 [37]. Sea ice thickness was determined utilizing an electromagnetic induction system positioned at the bow of RV Lance (SEM), as well as another EM system towed beneath the helicopter (HEM). Furthermore, a Riegl VQ-580 laser scanner (ALS) mounted on the Polar 5 aircraft was used to measure the sea ice freeboard, which was later converted to sea ice thickness by assuming hydrostatic equilibrium. All these data have been regridded to the ESA SMOS sea ice thickness product 12.5 km grid using the arithmetic average calculated with GMT blockmean [38], courtesy of Dr. Lars Kaleschke.

3. Methodology

This study introduces approaches to sea ice thickness estimation that incorporate both spatial and temporal coherence into the modeling process. Spatial coherence is achieved by utilizing maps as input data, allowing the influence of neighboring pixels to be considered, while temporal coherence is addressed by including data from the previous day to enhance predictions of current conditions. The primary objective is to evaluate and determine the most effective approach among the proposed methods, leaving uncertainty computation as a focus for future work. In previous research [22], Random Forest (RF) and Gradient Boosting (GB) algorithms were trained using a pixel-by-pixel methodology. Although these models demonstrated strong agreement with ESA's sea ice thickness product and showed improved correlation with reduced error when validated against in situ datasets, this approach inherently breaks the spatial and temporal continuity present in the original data. In reality, the data exhibit clear spatial and temporal dependencies, and failing to account for them may limit the physical consistency of the predictions. Therefore, this study addresses a necessary step: evaluating whether preserving spatial coherence (as with the CNN) or temporal continuity (as with the LSTM) leads to more physically meaningful and accurate sea ice thickness retrievals. For the three proposed approaches, the input variables are prepared as detailed in Section 2.2, with some specific modifications for each approach that are described below. It is important to note that although sea ice concentration (SIC) is indeed a major source of uncertainty in sea ice thickness retrievals from L-band radiometry, it is not explicitly included in this assessment, as the comparison is restricted to locations where the ESA product provides valid thickness values. This product assumes 100% SIC, justified by the fact that most ice-covered areas in winter have SIC > 90%, and that uncertainties in SIC products could introduce larger errors than the underestimation caused by assuming full ice cover [7,8]. Therefore, to ensure a fair comparison, no SIC correction is applied in this study.

Three different machine learning algorithms are evaluated, but they all rely on the same methodology and use the same input and output variables, which are described in Section 2.1 and summarized in Figure 1. Specifically, the four input variables are SMOS brightness temperature, sea ice temperature, sea ice salinity, and snow presence. The output variable is sea ice thickness, which, during the training phase, corresponds to the values derived from the inversion of the emission model, as detailed in Section 2.2.

3.1. Pixel-by-Pixel Approach: Random Forest and Gradient Boosting

Focusing on supervised learning, specifically within the realm of regression methods, the machine learning algorithms chosen for this task include Random Forest (RF, [39]) and Gradient Boosting (GB, [40]). These algorithms serve as more robust extensions of decision trees, sharing numerous similarities but diverging in their approaches to tree construction and combination. Both algorithms are configured with 50 estimators, a reasonable choice after experimenting with other options ranging from 10 to 1000. Following thorough testing, no further hyperparameters are fine-tuned as there is no discernible improvement in the results. Individual data points are extracted from comprehensive Arctic sea ice thickness distribution maps and fed into these algorithms for training. Therefore, this approach is named pixel-by-pixel, as training is performed considering individual values within the distribution. The training dataset is composed of 100,000 pixels extracted from the maps of each day, after removing the duplicates, from 15 October 2019 to 15 April 2020 and from 15 October 2020 to 15 April 2021. Both RF and GB algorithms provide similar results, but in this work, the RF is selected to be assessed with the other approaches. The use of a decision tree-based method enables an assessment of feature importance in determining the algorithm's output. In this specific case, the feature importances are 94.13%, 4.33%, 1.11%, and 0.43% for SMOS TB, sea ice temperature, sea ice salinity, and snow presence, respectively. The TB is the dominant factor influencing the results, which aligns with its high variability compared to the other inputs. Sea ice salinity tends to stabilize around a value of 5 after the initial freeze-up [41], and snow presence exhibits limited variability, as a snow layer is present in almost all pixels. Nevertheless, the inclusion of snow presence remains crucial, as it has a clear impact on the measured TB [9].

3.2. Spatially Coherent Approach: Convolutional Neural Network

Convolutional Neural Networks (CNNs; [42]) are a class of deep learning neural networks primarily designed to process and analyze visual data. In this work, we aim to leverage their potential to deal with images and introducing spatial coherence into the algorithm. Sea ice pixels are not independent of their neighbors; similar conditions should lead to similar thickness distributions. All variables in the selected grid are arrays with dimensions of 896×608. The convolutional layers use 3×3 kernels with padding to preserve the dimensional integrity of the variables throughout the network architecture.

After hyperparameter tuning, the batch size was fixed at 64 with 200 training epochs. The optimal combination of layers and filters for each convolution is presented in Table 2. Each convolutional layer contains 6, 12, or 24 filters of size 3×3 applied to the input image. The ReLu activation function introduces non-linearity, and when combined with "same" padding, ensures that the spatial dimensions of the output feature maps remain identical to those of the input. Batch normalization is applied after each convolutional layer, normalizing the activations from the previous layer to help stabilize and accelerate the training process. The final convolutional layer contains a single filter of size 3×3. The linear activation function indicates that no activation function is applied to the output, making this layer perform essentially a linear transformation. The training dataset is conformed by 181 maps extracted from two periods: 15 October 2019 to 15 April 2020, and 15 October 2020 to 15 April 2021.

Table 2. Layers of the Convolutional Neural Network (CNN) designed for the spatial-coherence approach.

Layer	Operation	Filters	Kernel	Activation
1	Convolution	6	(3 3)	ReLu
2	Convolution	12	(3 3)	ReLu
3	Convolution	12	(3 3)	ReLu
4	Convolution	12	(3 3)	ReLu
5	Convolution	12	(3 3)	ReLu
6	Convolution	24	(3 3)	ReLu
7	Convolution	1	(3 3)	Linear

3.3. *Temporally Coherent Approach: Long Short-Term Memory Neural Networks*

Despite the robust performance that can be achieved with the CNN by including its inherent spatial coherence, the temporal coherence should be explored. Therefore, the Long Short-Term Memory (LSTM; [43]) neural network structure is implemented. LSTMs are a specialized type of recurrent neural network (RNN) designed to effectively capture and learn temporal dependencies in sequential data by incorporating a memory cell. Intuitively, sea ice evolution has a clear temporal component; the present day prediction should be linked to previous day conditions. Therefore, for this approach, the dataset is shifted in order to predict the sea ice thickness distribution accounting for the previous day information. However, since the input for this approach is 1D, this methodology works pixel-by-pixel, so no spatial component is included.

The architecture consists of three LSTM layers, summarized in Table 3. All of these layers use a hyperbolic tangent activation function and a sigmoid recurrent activation function to control the flow of information through the cell state. The output of these layers is passed as a sequence to the next layer, except for the last layer, which returns only the final output of the sequence. A final dense layer with a single unit and a linear activation function is applied to produce the model's prediction. After testing, the optimal batch size is set to 2, with 50 training epochs. The training dataset is the same as that described for the CNN algorithm: 181 maps from 2019 and 2020, but with the temporal shift as previously mentioned.

Table 3. Layers of the Long Short-Term Memory (LSTM) neural network designed for the temporal-coherence approach.

Layer	Operation	Filters	Activation	Recurrent Activation
1	LSTM	5	Tanh	Sigmoid
2	LSTM	10	Tanh	Sigmoid
3	LSTM	10	Tanh	Sigmoid
4	Dense	1	Linear	–

4. Results

To evaluate the different approaches, validation using in situ data is performed. Specifically, we use the two datasets described in Section 2.3: the BGEP moorings and the ESA SMOSice campaign data are utilized. Furthermore, the ESA/AWI product described in Section 2.1.1 is also included in the assessment as a baseline. To ensure a fair assessment, all algorithm predictions exceeding 1 m are capped at exactly 1 m. The selected metrics are the correlation coefficient (R^2), the mean absolute error (MAE), the standard deviation (Std Dev), and the overestimation and underestimation percentages. These percentages are calculated by identifying a value as overestimated or underestimated if it exceeds or falls short of the ground truth value by at least 25%.

To provide an initial visual assessment of each algorithm, Figure 2 presents Arctic-wide and Barents Sea-focused sea ice thickness maps produced by each algorithm. In these maps, the areas covered by the validation datasets are marked. All four approaches capture the broad spatial patterns of SIT, with thicker ice concentrated north of Greenland and the Canadian Arctic Archipelago, and thinner ice in the marginal zones. The ESA product shows relatively smooth gradients and generally higher SIT values in the marginal ice zone compared to the ML methods. The RF exhibits sharper spatial transitions and slightly noisier patterns, particularly near the ice edge. The CNN output appears more smooth than RF, yet preserves fine-scale spatial variability, especially in the Barents Sea. The LSTM model produces the most homogeneous fields, with reduced spatial detail, likely reflecting the influence of temporal averaging or memory in the algorithm's architecture. Overall, the ESA, RF, and LSTM algorithms produce broadly similar sea ice thickness distributions, with local differences that become more evident upon closer inspection, such as in the Barents Sea region. In contrast, the CNN model tends to predict higher thickness values in several areas and shows limited sensitivity to the finer spatial structures associated with thinner ice. This characteristic can significantly affect the model's performance, particularly given that the primary objective of the methodology is to retrieve thin sea ice thickness. Consequently, such behavior may also influence the outcomes of the validation process.

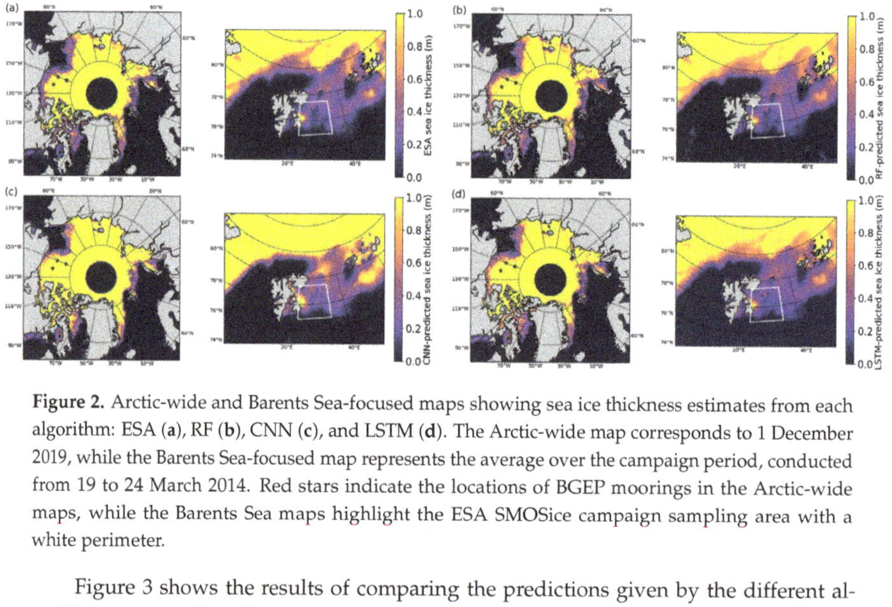

Figure 2. Arctic-wide and Barents Sea-focused maps showing sea ice thickness estimates from each algorithm: ESA (**a**), RF (**b**), CNN (**c**), and LSTM (**d**). The Arctic-wide map corresponds to 1 December 2019, while the Barents Sea-focused map represents the average over the campaign period, conducted from 19 to 24 March 2014. Red stars indicate the locations of BGEP moorings in the Arctic-wide maps, while the Barents Sea maps highlight the ESA SMOSice campaign sampling area with a white perimeter.

Figure 3 shows the results of comparing the predictions given by the different algorithms, using the BGEP moorings dataset described in Section 2.3. The points are complemented by their respective density to depict the distribution of output values. However, since many data points correspond to 1 m after the imposed limitation, they are not included in the density computation to improve the visualization throughout the thickness range. The RF algorithm presents similar results to ESA, while the CNN tends to overestimate, and the LSTM shows more dispersion and underestimation, especially for thinner ice. The most homogeneous point-density distribution is presented by the RF, highlighting its robustness. The metrics are provided in Table 4, where the initially observed characteristics of each algorithm are confirmed. Although all approaches show similar error, correlation, and dispersion, it is clear that the CNN is overestimating, by approximately 10% more than the others. These results suggest that for this dataset, both the RF and ESA algorithms slightly outperform the others. Therefore, the spatially and temporally coherent approaches, represented by the CNN and LSTM algorithms, do not provide better capture of the sea ice evolution depicted by the BGEP moorings.

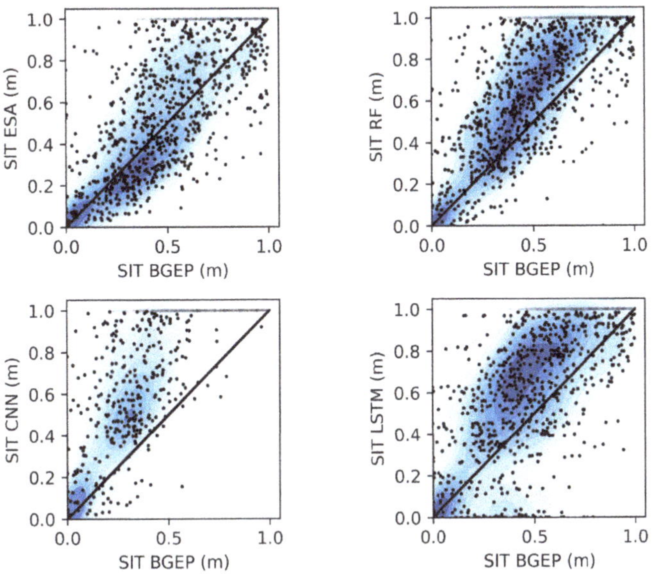

Figure 3. Scatter and density plots of the validation of the algorithms (ESA, RF, CNN, and LSTM) using the BGEP moorings dataset.

Table 4. Metrics of the validation of the algorithms (ESA, RF, CNN, and LSTM) using the BGEP moorings dataset.

Algorithm	R^2	MAE (m)	Std Dev (m)	Overestimation (%)	Underestimation (%)
ESA	0.70	0.24	0.33	43.04	10.68
RF	0.73	0.24	0.30	48.76	4.71
CNN	0.67	0.30	0.26	62.58	1.11
LSTM	0.67	0.25	0.33	53.17	6.23

The ESA SMOSice campaign provides a unique dataset that contains sufficient thin sea ice to perform validation. In fact, this dataset was used to validate the ESA SMOS sea ice thickness product described in Section 2.1.1. A similar assessment to that conducted for the BGEP moorings dataset is conducted, using the three sub-datasets that were collected: HEM, SEM, and ALS. Figure 4 shows the validation of the assessed algorithms against these in situ datasets. The different sub-datasets present distinct SIT distributions, allowing for a comprehensive assessment of the algorithm performance. For the HEM data, which cover a broader SIT range, the RF and CNN models show the best agreement with the reference measurements, followed closely by ESA, while the LSTM consistently underestimates SIT across the range. In the case of SEM, which measured very thin ice, none of the algorithms are capable of reproducing the observed values, since predictions are consistently too dispersed. For the ALS dataset, which includes thicker ice, all algorithms tend to underestimate SIT, although the CNN performs better, showing the least bias. It is remarkable that the LSTM shows negative thicknesses, which is physically unrealistic, but this is due to the inherent stochasticity of the algorithm's architecture. Table 5 summarizes the validation performance of the four algorithms across the three datasets: HEM, SEM, and ALS. In the HEM dataset, the CNN achieved the highest R^2 (0.51) and lowest MAE (0.30 m), while the ESA and RF models followed closely with comparable MAE values and moderately lower R^2 scores. The LSTM performed similarly in terms of MAE but displayed a lower R^2, indicating slightly less correlation with the observed data. For the SEM dataset, performance dropped across all algorithms, with R^2 values remaining below 0.25, reflecting the increased difficulty in modeling this dataset. The CNN again had the highest R^2 (0.23), but RF and ESA maintained lower MAE values, suggesting a better trade-off between error magnitude and model consistency. Regarding the ALS dataset, all models improved substantially, with the LSTM and RF showing stronger R^2 values (0.59 and 0.57, respectively) and lower MAE (0.19–0.22 m), with the CNN and ESA being slightly worse.

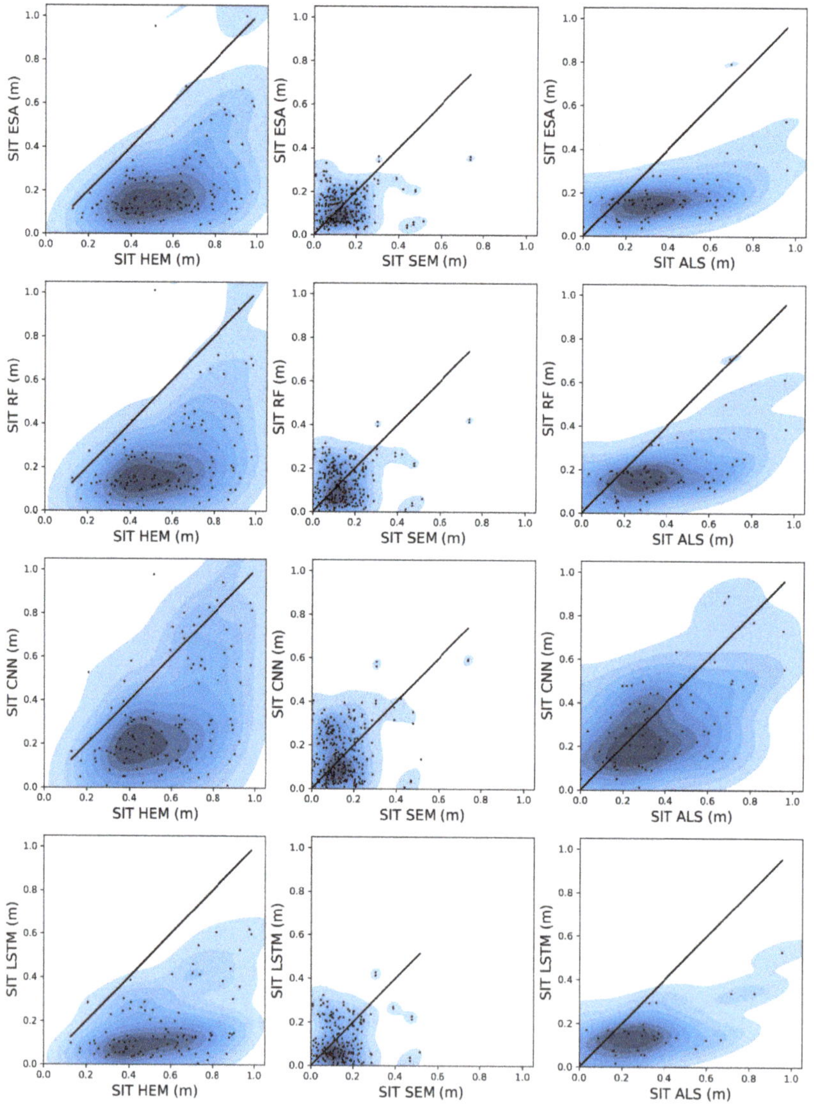

Figure 4. Scatter and density plots of the validation of the algorithms (ESA, RF, CNN, and LSTM) using the ESA SMOSice campaign dataset.

Table 5. Metrics of the validation of the algorithms (ESA, RF, CNN, and LSTM) using the ESA SMOSice campaign datasets, namely HEM, SEM, and ALS data.

Algorithm	R^2	MAE (m)	Std Dev (m)	Overestimation (%)	Underestimation (%)
			HEM		
ESA	0.49	0.36	0.22	1.50	92.48
RF	0.48	0.36	0.22	1.50	90.23
CNN	0.51	0.30	0.28	3.01	78.20
LSTM	0.43	0.39	0.14	1.01	96.97
			SEM		
ESA	0.18	0.09	0.07	29.78	47.06
RF	0.19	0.10	0.09	35.66	43.01
CNN	0.23	0.11	0.12	40.44	39.71
LSTM	0.06	0.11	0.10	37.18	44.44
			ALS		
ESA	0.52	0.24	0.11	17.86	71.43
RF	0.57	0.22	0.12	20.24	69.05
CNN	0.45	0.20	0.19	32.14	45.24
LSTM	0.59	0.19	0.10	20.51	64.10

5. Discussion

The results presented in Section 4 suggest that the two in situ datasets involved in the validation have some disparities regarding their thickness distributions. Therefore, a thorough analysis is required to avoid divergent conclusions.

Regarding the BGEP moorings dataset, Figure 5 shows the temporal evolution from the in situ mooring measurements and from the predictions of the algorithms. Here, the algorithm's predictions are not limited to 1 m since no metric computation is involved, but they are graphically separated. It is also noteworthy that the unrealistic data jumps occur because only the BGEP-measured values from the initial growth phase (lower than 1 m) are considered for each period, i.e., from October to April of the following year, spanning from 2010 to 2021.

From this representation, it is clear that the majority of the error occurs because the slow growth observed by the moored buoys is not successfully captured by any algorithm. Except for some specific periods, the algorithms rapidly transition from very thin to already grown ice. However, this effect is not unexpected because of the resolution disparities between the in situ and remote sensing observations. This can be explained by the fact that these buoys represent single points within one vast satellite pixel, so there can exist huge thickness variability within them. Furthermore, these moorings cannot be considered as stable platforms, since they are affected by physical processes such as ice drifting and ocean currents underneath. Despite all these drawbacks, and since the validation is performed equally for all the algorithms, one can say that the CNN is significantly overestimating, especially from 0.5 m onward. For the other approaches, both Figures 3 and 5 show similar behavior for all of them.

The validation using the ESA SMOSice campaign dataset highlights a systematic underestimation of sea ice thickness (SIT), particularly in the thin ice regime, with varying levels of accuracy and bias across the assessed algorithms. It is important to note that all datasets were interpolated onto the SMOS grid, facilitating intercomparison among products. However, none of the algorithms could reproduce the SEM measurements, which suggests this dataset may have limited reliability, and results based on it should be interpreted with caution.

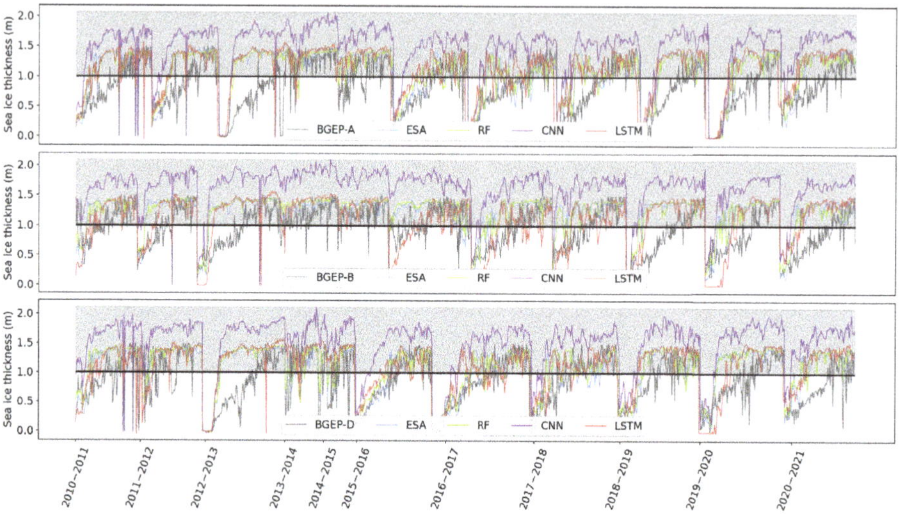

Figure 5. Temporal evolution of the BGEP moorings (A, B, C) sea ice thickness from October 2010 to April 2021, alongside the algorithm's prediction. The shaded part above the black solid line correspond to the values above 1 m that are not considered in the analysis.

In general, ESA estimates exhibited lower dispersion and smaller errors, while the RF algorithm delivered a balanced performance across all datasets. The CNN showed higher correlation with in situ data but also slightly increased error and variability. The LSTM generally underperformed, although it yielded better results under more stable conditions, such as those represented by the ALS dataset.

The pixel-by-pixel approach of the RF algorithm performs comparably to that of ESA, showing similar validation metrics across all datasets. Both exhibit strong correlations and reasonable levels of error and dispersion, despite their relative simplicity in terms of algorithmic complexity, as neither explicitly incorporates spatial or temporal coherence. However, they differ in how sea ice emission is modeled. Although a detailed discussion of emission modeling is beyond the scope of this work, it is worth noting that the RF algorithm—and the overall methodology presented—can be readily adapted to any desired emission model. This flexibility stems from the fact that modifying the emission modeling would only require regenerating the training dataset using the new forward model. With the new dataset produced, the rest of the methodology would remain unchanged, underscoring its robustness and adaptability.

In contrast, the CNN tends to overestimate sea ice thickness across the validation datasets and shows the highest dispersion. This may be due to the fact that the input variables are already smooth and spatially coherent (see Figure 2 in [22]), which reduces the need for additional spatial modeling. This explains why the simpler pixel-wise methods perform well, as spatial coherence is already embedded in the inputs, making complex architectures like CNNs less advantageous in this context. Similarly, the temporally coherent approach of the LSTM does not appear to improve the estimation of sea ice thickness. One possible explanation is that local sea ice inhomogeneities evolve too rapidly to be captured at the resolution of satellite observations. Additionally, these small-scale variations are effectively averaged out, meaning that the temporal evolution of each pixel is smoother and can be captured by simpler models, reducing the need for complex temporal modeling techniques such as LSTMs.

Regarding the computational resources needed for each assessed algorithm, there are important differences among them. Starting with the ESA product, although no information is published, the description in [8] includes the simulation of a thermodynamic model, which can easily increase the computational requirements. Since the RF is a simple ML algorithm, the computation time is negligible, both for training and predicting. However, since the CNN and the LSTM are deep learning approaches, the computational resources are significantly increased. However, the procedures involved in the presented algorithms are in no way limiting for a hypothetical operational product. The order of magnitude of the time required for the training phase of the algorithms ranges from seconds for the RF, to hours for both the CNN and the LSTM. To perform predictions, the RF needs nanoseconds while the others need seconds. No specific metrics are provided since the computational resources are not an impediment, and thus, there is no need to include high performance computing metrics or similar information.

Finally, it is worth mentioning that aside from the algorithms presented here, similar variants have been tested within this study. Regarding the pixel-by-pixel approach, aside from the mentioned RF and GB, the widely-used XGBoost [44] was tested without achieving better results. For the spatially coherent approach, the U-Net structure [45] was also used as a variant of the standard CNN, but again no significant improvements were found. Moreover, a fourth approach was attempted for the sake of completeness, accounting for both the spatial and temporal coherence. This was carried out by using a 2D-CNNLSTM structure, combining the two already presented methods. However, despite the important increase in computational resources required for the training phase, the results were not better than those obtained by using the standard CNN or LSTM.

6. Conclusions

This study evaluates various approaches for retrieving thin sea ice thickness from L-band radiometry observations, including a machine learning framework, two deep learning algorithms, and the ESA official product as a baseline. The findings highlight that there is still significant potential to refine the current algorithms used for sea ice thickness retrieval from SMOS. These refinements are also critical for the upcoming ESA's Copernicus Imaging Microwave Radiometer (CIMR) mission, which will expand observations to higher frequencies (up to 36.5 GHz) while retaining 1.4 GHz capabilities.

Overall, the ESA product has demonstrated robustness despite known limitations, while the novel methodologies show potential advantages, offering opportunities to optimize computational efficiency and improve the retrieval.

Among the assessed methods, the RF algorithm shows balanced performance, comparable to the ESA's product in terms of correlation, error, and dispersion, despite being much simpler and not modeling spatial or temporal coherence explicitly. This performance, coupled with its flexibility in adapting to different emission models, underscores the robustness and adaptability of the RF approach. In contrast, the CNN tends to overestimate SIT and exhibits greater dispersion, suggesting that the spatial coherence already embedded in the input variables diminishes the added value of the CNN's architectural complexity. Similarly, the LSTM algorithm does not significantly improve results, likely due to the rapid evolution and spatial averaging of sea ice conditions that make temporal coherence less impactful at the satellite scale.

Based on these findings, the assessment suggests that while the ESA SMOS sea ice thickness retrieval algorithm is still a valid approach, there is still potential for improvement. The proposed pixel-by-pixel approach, represented by the RF algorithm, shows robust performance and could serve as a solid foundation for future operational products. In comparison, the more complex structures such as the CNN and the LSTM do not offer clear advantages in this case. Therefore, future work should not focus exclusively on developing more complex methodologies, but also on improving the modeling of sea ice emission at L-band. This improvement could be directly applied to the presented method to further increase the accuracy of the sea ice thickness estimates.

Author Contributions: Conceptualization, F.H.-M., G.S.G., C.G. and M.J.E.; methodology, F.H.-M. and G.S.G.; software, F.H.-M.; validation, F.H.-M.; formal analysis, F.H.-M.; investigation, F.H.-M.; resources, F.H.-M., G.S.G., C.G. and M.J.E.; data curation, F.H.-M.; writing—original draft preparation, F.H.-M.; writing—review and editing, G.S.G., C.G. and M.J.E.; visualization, F.H.-M.; supervision, G.S.G., C.G. and M.J.E.; project administration, C.G. and M.J.E.; funding acquisition, C.G. and M.J.E. All authors have read and agreed to the published version of the manuscript.

Funding: This project is funded from the AEI with the ARCTIC-MON project (PID2021-125324OB-I00), and from a Doctorat Industrial (AGAUR), with expedient number 2023 DI 0007.

Data Availability Statement: The data supporting the conclusions of this article will be made available by the authors on request. These data were derived from the following resources available in the public domain: The production of SMOS sea ice thickness data was funded by the ESA project SMOS & CryoSat-2 Sea Ice Data Product Processing and Dissemination Service, and data from 15 October 2010 to 15 April 2021 were obtained from AWI. The BGEP data used in the validation were collected and made available by the Beaufort Gyre Exploration Program based at the Woods Hole Oceanographic Institution (https://www2.whoi.edu/site/beaufortgyre, accessed on 24 July 2025) in collaboration with researchers from Fisheries and Oceans Canada at the Institute of Ocean Sciences. Remote sensing data processing was executed at the Barcelona Expert Center on Remote Sensing (BEC-RS, https://bec.icm.csic.es, accessed on 24 July 2025) of the Institut de Ciències del Mar ICM-CSIC. The source codes are available for downloading at the following link: https://github.com/ferranhema/smos-mlsit (accessed on 24 July 2025).

Acknowledgments: This work is supported by the Spanish government through the "Severo Ochoa Centre of Excellence" accreditation (Grant CEX2024-001494-S funded by AEI 10.13039/501100011033). This work has been conducted in the framework of the PhD in Computer Science program of the Universitat Autònoma de Barcelona (UAB). This work is part of a Doctorat Industrial (AGAUR), with expedient number 2023 DI 0007.

Conflicts of Interest: Authors Ferran Hernández-Macià and Maria José Escorihuela are employed by isardSAT, S.L., Spain. The remaining authors declare that the research was conducted in the absence of any commercial or financial relationships that could be construed as a potential conflict of interest.

References

1. Budyko, M.I. The effect of solar radiation variations on the climate of the Earth. *Tellus* **1969**, *21*, 611–619. [CrossRef]
2. Kwok, R. Arctic sea ice thickness, volume, and multiyear ice coverage: Losses and coupled variability (1958–2018). *Environ. Res. Lett.* **2018**, *13*, 105005. [CrossRef]
3. Meredith, M.; Sommerkorn, M.; Cassotta, S.; Derksen, C.; Ekaykin, A.; Hollowed, A.; Kofinas, G.; Mackintosh, A.; Melbourne-Thomas, J.; Muelbert, M.; et al. Polar Regions. In *IPCC Special Report on the Ocean and Cryosphere in a Changing Climate*; Cambridge University Press: Cambridge, UK; New York, NY, USA, 2019; pp. 203–320. [CrossRef]
4. Mecklenburg, S.; Wright, N.; Bouzina, C.; Delwart, S. Getting down to business-SMOS operations and products. *ESA Bull.* **2009**, *137*, 25–30.
5. Kerr, Y.; Waldteufel, P.; Wigneron, J.; Delwart, S.; Cabot, F.; Boutin, J.; Escorihuela, M.; Font, J.; Reul, N.; Gruhier, C.; et al. The SMOS mission: New tool for monitoring key elements of the global water cycle. *Proc. IEEE* **2010**, *98*, 666–687. [CrossRef]
6. Entekhabi, D.; Njoku, E.G.; O'Neill, P.E.; Kellogg, K.H.; Crow, W.T.; Edelstein, W.N.; Entin, J.K.; Goodman, S.D.; Jackson, T.J.; Johnson, J.; et al. The Soil Moisture Active Passive (SMAP) mission. *Proc. IEEE* **2010**, *98*, 704–716. [CrossRef]
7. Kaleschke, L.; Tian-Kunze, X.; Maaß, N.; Mäkynen, M.; Drusch, M. Sea ice thickness retrieval from SMOS brightness temperatures during the Arctic freeze-up period. *Geophys. Res. Lett.* **2012**, *39*, L05501. [CrossRef]
8. Tian-Kunze, X.; Kaleschke, L.; Maaß, N.; Mäkynen, M.; Serra, N.; Drusch, M.; Krumpen, T. SMOS-derived thin sea ice thickness: Algorithm baseline, product specifications and initial verification. *Cryosphere* **2014**, *8*, 997–1018. [CrossRef]

9. Maass, N.; Kaleschke, L.; Tian-Kunze, X.; Tonboe, R.T. Snow thickness retrieval from L-band brightness temperatures: A model comparison. *Ann. Glaciol.* **2015**, *56*, 9–17. [CrossRef]
10. Huntemann, M.; Heygster, G.; Kaleschke, L.; Krumpen, T.; Mäkynen, M.; Drusch, M. Empirical sea ice thickness retrieval during the freeze-up period from SMOS high incident angle observations. *Cryosphere* **2014**, *8*, 439–451. [CrossRef]
11. Yan, Q.; Huang, W. Spaceborne GNSS-R Sea Ice Detection Using Delay-Doppler Maps: First Results From the U.K. TechDemoSat-1 Mission. *IEEE J. Sel. Top. Appl. Earth Obs. Remote Sens.* **2016**, *9*, 4795–4801. [CrossRef]
12. Wang, F.; Yang, D.; Zhang, B.; Yang, L. Can sea ice thickness be retrieved using GNSS-interferometric reflectometry? *GPS Solut.* **2022**, *26*, 128. [CrossRef]
13. Braakmann-Folgmann, A.; Donlon, C. Estimating snow depth on Arctic sea ice using satellite microwave radiometry and a neural network. *Cryosphere* **2019**, *13*, 2421–2438. [CrossRef]
14. Yan, Q.; Huang, W. Sea Ice Thickness Estimation From TechDemoSat-1 and Soil Moisture Ocean Salinity Data Using Machine Learning Methods. In Proceedings of the Global Oceans 2020: Singapore–U.S. Gulf Coast, Biloxi, MS, USA, 5–30 October 2020; pp. 1–5. [CrossRef]
15. Chi, J.; Kim, H.C. Retrieval of daily sea ice thickness from AMSR2 passive microwave data using ensemble convolutional neural networks. *GIScience Remote Sens.* **2021**, *58*, 812–830. [CrossRef]
16. Soriot, C.; Prigent, C.; Jimenez, C.; Frappart, F. Arctic Sea Ice Thickness Estimation From Passive Microwave Satellite Observations Between 1.4 and 36 GHz. *Earth Space Sci.* **2023**, *10*, e2022EA002542. [CrossRef]
17. Soriot, C.; Vancoppenolle, M.; Prigent, C.; Jimenez, C.; Frappart, F. Winter Arctic sea ice volume decline: Uncertainties reduced using passive microwave-based sea ice thickness. *Sci. Rep.* **2024**, *14*, 21000. [CrossRef]
18. Herbert, C.; Munoz-Martin, J.F.; Llaveria, D.; Pablos, M.; Camps, A. Sea Ice Thickness Estimation Based on Regression Neural Networks Using L-Band Microwave Radiometry Data from the FSSCat Mission. *Remote Sens.* **2021**, *13*, 1366. [CrossRef]
19. Camps, A.; Golkar, A.; Gutierrez, A.; de Azua, J.R.; Munoz-Martin, J.; Fernandez, L.; Diez, C.; Aguilella, A.; Briatore, S.; Akhtyamov, R.; et al. Fsscat, the 2017 Copernicus Masters' "Esa Sentinel Small Satellite Challenge" Winner: A Federated Polar and Soil Moisture Tandem Mission Based on 6U Cubesats. In Proceedings of the IGARSS 2018-2018 IEEE International Geoscience and Remote Sensing Symposium, Valencia, Spain, 22–27 July 2018; pp. 8285–8287. [CrossRef]
20. Shamshiri, R.; Eide, E.; Høyland, K.V. Spatio-temporal distribution of sea-ice thickness using a machine learning approach with Google Earth Engine and Sentinel-1 GRD data. *Remote Sens. Environ.* **2022**, *270*, 112851. [CrossRef]
21. Zhao, Y.; Sun, Z.; Li, W.; Tian, K.; Zhan, Z.; Shan, P.; Li, L. Sea Ice Type and Thickness Identification Based on Vibration Sensor Networks and Machine Learning. *IEEE Trans. Instrum. Meas.* **2023**, *72*, 1–11. [CrossRef]
22. Hernández-Macià, F.; Gabarró, C.; Gomez, G.S.; Escorihuela, M.J. A Machine Learning Approach on SMOS Thin Sea Ice Thickness Retrieval. *IEEE J. Sel. Top. Appl. Earth Obs. Remote Sens.* **2024**, *17*, 10752–10758. [CrossRef]
23. Kerr, Y.; Waldteufel, P.; Wigneron, J.P.; Martinuzzi, J.; Font, J.; Berger, M. Soil moisture retrieval from space: The Soil Moisture and Ocean Salinity (SMOS) mission. *IEEE Trans. Geosci. Remote Sens.* **2001**, *39*, 1729–1735. [CrossRef]
24. Ryvlin, A.I. Method of forecasting flexural strength of an ice cover. *Probl. Arct. Antarct.* **1974**, *45*, 79–86.
25. Tian-Kunze, X.; Kaleschke, L.; Crapolicchio, R. *SMOS L3 Sea Ice Thickness ATBD: Algorithm Theoretical Baseline Document*; Technical Report; European Space Agency (ESA): Paris, France, 2021.
26. Karagali, I.; Nielsen-Englyst, P.; Kolbe, W.M.; Høyer, J.L. Arctic Ocean-Sea and Ice Surface Temperature REPROCESSED. 2024. Available online: https://data.marine.copernicus.eu/product/SEAICE_ARC_PHY_CLIMATE_L4_MY_011_016/description (accessed on 24 July 2025).
27. Huntemann, M. Thickness Retrieval and Emissivity Modeling of Thin Sea Ice at L-Band for SMOS Satellite Observations. Ph.D. Thesis, University of Bremen, Bremen, Germany, 2015.
28. Ali, A.; Burud, A.; Williams, T.; Xie, J.; Yumruktepe, C.; Wakamatsu, T.; Melsom, A.; Bertino, L.; Gao, S. Arctic Ocean Physics Reanalysis. 2024. Available online: https://data.marine.copernicus.eu/product/ARCTIC_MULTIYEAR_PHY_002_003/description (accessed on 24 July 2025).
29. Kovacs, A.; U.S. Army, Corps of Engineers; Cold Regions Research and Engineering Laboratory (U.S.). *Sea Ice: Bulk Salinity Versus Ice Floe Thickness*; Number Part 1 in CRREL Report; U.S. Army Cold Regions Research and Engineering Laboratory: Hanover, NH, USA, 1996.
30. Burke, W.; Schmugge, T.; Paris, J. Comparison of 2.8- and 21-cm microwave radiometer observations over soils with emission model calculations. *J. Geophys. Res.* **1979**, *84*, 287–294. [CrossRef]
31. Vant, M.; Ramseier, R.; Makios, V. The complex-dielectric constant of sea ice at frequencies in the range 0.1–40 GHz. *J. Appl. Phys.* **1978**, *49*, 1264–1280. [CrossRef]
32. Wilheit, T.T. Radiative Transfer in a Plane Stratified Dielectric. *IEEE Trans. Geosci. Electron.* **1978**, *16*, 138–143. [CrossRef]
33. Picard, G.; Sandells, M.; Löwe, H. SMRT: An active–passive microwave radiative transfer model for snow with multiple microstructure and scattering formulations (v1.0). *Geosci. Model Dev.* **2018**, *11*, 2763–2788. [CrossRef]

34. Hernández-Macià, F.; Gabarró, C.; Huntemann, M.; Naderpour, R.; Johnson, J.T.; Jezek, K.C. On sea ice emission modeling for MOSAiC's L-band radiometric measurements. *Ann. Glaciol.* **2024**, *65*, e37. [CrossRef]
35. Belter, H.J.; Krumpen, T.; Hendricks, S.; Hoelemann, J.; Janout, M.A.; Ricker, R.; Haas, C. Satellite-based sea ice thickness changes in the Laptev Sea from 2002 to 2017: Comparison to mooring observations. *Cryosphere* **2020**, *14*, 2189–2203. [CrossRef]
36. Vinje, T.; Finnekåsa, Ø. *The Ice Transport Through the Fram Strait*; Norsk Polarinstitutt: Oslo, Norway; Tromsø, Norway, 1986.
37. Kaleschke, L.; Tian-Kunze, X.; Maaß, N.; Beitsch, A.; Wernecke, A.; Miernecki, M.; Müller, G.; Fock, B.H.; Gierisch, A.M.; Schlünzen, K.H.; et al. SMOS sea ice product: Operational application and validation in the Barents Sea marginal ice zone. *Remote Sens. Environ.* **2016**, *180*, 264–273. [CrossRef]
38. Wessel, P.; Luis, J.F.; Uieda, L.; Scharroo, R.; Wobbe, F.; Smith, W.H.F.; Tian, D. The Generic Mapping Tools Version 6. *Geochem. Geophys. Geosyst.* **2019**, *20*, 5556–5564. [CrossRef]
39. Breiman, L. Random Forests. *Mach. Learn.* **2001**, *45*, 5–32. [CrossRef]
40. Friedman, J.H. Stochastic gradient boosting. *Comput. Stat. Data Anal.* **2002**, *38*, 367–378. [CrossRef]
41. Nakawo, M.; Sinha, N.K. Growth Rate and Salinity Profile of First-Year Sea Ice in the High Arctic. *J. Glaciol.* **1981**, *27*, 315–330. [CrossRef]
42. O'Shea, K.; Nash, R. An Introduction to Convolutional Neural Networks. *arXiv* **2015**, arXiv:1511.08458. [CrossRef]
43. Hochreiter, S.; Schmidhuber, J. Long Short-Term Memory. *Neural Comput.* **1997**, *9*, 1735–1780. [CrossRef]
44. Chen, T.; Guestrin, C. XGBoost: A Scalable Tree Boosting System. In Proceedings of the 22nd ACM SIGKDD International Conference on Knowledge Discovery and Data Mining, New York, NY, USA, 13–17 August 2016; pp. 785–794. [CrossRef]
45. Ronneberger, O.; Fischer, P.; Brox, T. U-Net: Convolutional Networks for Biomedical Image Segmentation. In Proceedings of the International Conference on Medical Image Computing and Computer-Assisted Intervention, Munich, Germany, 5–9 October 2015; Springer International Publishing: Cham, Switzerland, 2015.

computers

MDPI

Article

Machine Learning Techniques for Uncertainty Estimation in Dynamic Aperture Prediction

Carlo Emilio Montanari [1,2,*], Robert B. Appleby [1], Davide Di Croce [2,3], Massimo Giovannozzi [2,*], Tatiana Pieloni [3], Stefano Redaelli [2] and Frederik F. Van der Veken [2]

1 Department of Physics and Astronomy, The University of Manchester, Manchester M13 9PL, UK; robert.appleby@manchester.ac.uk

2 CERN, 1211 Geneva, Switzerland; davide.di.croce@cern.ch (D.D.C.); stefano.redaelli@cern.ch (S.R.); frederik.van.der.veken@cern.ch (F.F.V.d.V.)

3 Institute of Physics, École Polytechnique Fédérale de Lausanne, 1015 Lausanne, Switzerland; tatiana.pieloni@epfl.ch

* Correspondence: carlo.emilio.montanari@cern.ch (C.E.M.); massimo.giovannozzi@cern.ch (M.G.)

Abstract: The dynamic aperture is an essential concept in circular particle accelerators, providing the extent of the phase space region where particle motion remains stable over multiple turns. The accurate prediction of the dynamic aperture is key to optimising performance in accelerators such as the CERN Large Hadron Collider and is crucial for designing future accelerators like the CERN Future Circular Hadron Collider. Traditional methods for computing the dynamic aperture are computationally demanding and involve extensive numerical simulations with numerous initial phase space conditions. In our recent work, we have devised surrogate models to predict the dynamic aperture boundary both efficiently and accurately. These models have been further refined by incorporating them into a novel active learning framework. This framework enhances performance through continual retraining and intelligent data generation based on informed sampling driven by error estimation. A critical attribute of this framework is the precise estimation of uncertainty in dynamic aperture predictions. In this study, we investigate various machine learning techniques for uncertainty estimation, including Monte Carlo dropout, bootstrap methods, and aleatory uncertainty quantification. We evaluated these approaches to determine the most effective method for reliable uncertainty estimation in dynamic aperture predictions using machine learning techniques.

Keywords: surrogate modelling; uncertainty quantification; Monte Carlo dropout; bootstrap aggregation; dynamic aperture; accelerator modelling; epistemic uncertainty; LHC; HL-LHC; FCC

1. Introduction

The dynamic aperture (DA) is a critical parameter in the design and operational optimisation of modern circular particle accelerators. The DA is the extent of the region in phase space where particle motion remains bounded over a defined number of turns (see, e.g., [1] and references therein). The DA provides crucial insight into the non-linear beam dynamics and the mechanisms induced by non-linear resonances that lead to beam losses and reduced beam lifetime. The time evolution of DA can then be directly linked to beam losses caused by non-linear effects [2], a connection that supports the recent method for measuring DA in circular rings [3]. Furthermore, these models have been extended to the description of the time evolution of instantaneous luminosity in a circular hadron collider, when non-linear effects are included [4]. The study of DA is particularly relevant for optimising beam lifetime and, in general, performance in existing accelerators, such as the CERN Large Hadron Collider (LHC) [5], by probing multiple combinations of ring configurations to determine the best one, which will then be used in operation. Furthermore, DA is also extremely helpful in guiding the development of both significant upgrades, such as the High-Luminosity LHC (HL-LHC) [6], and next-generation machines such as the Future Circular Collider (FCC) [7,8]. The delicate aspect is that a reliable prediction of the DA over a sufficiently large number of turns is a computationally intensive task that requires long-term tracking of trajectories of initial conditions across a wide range of phase space regions and several machine configurations, each comprising tens of thousands of lattice elements, as is the case for the LHC and FCC.

The standard approach to DA estimation relies on extensive numerical simulations that track particle trajectories across many initial conditions over 1×10^5 to 1×10^6 turns (see, e.g., [9,10]). This process is particularly demanding in high-energy accelerators, whose large size implies the computation of the dynamics over a larger array of magnetic elements. Further complexity arises from the need to perform simulations for multiple configurations to account for uncertainties in the accelerator lattice, such as variations in magnet imperfections, or different options for operational configurations. Typically, Monte Carlo techniques are employed to generate different realisations of the machine that also include the imperfections [11,12], significantly increasing the computational overhead. It is worth stressing that the number of turns that can be reasonably simulated in tracking studies is greatly insufficient to cover time scales relevant for operations. As an example, 1×10^6 turns used in the simulations of the CERN Large Hadron Collider (LHC) correspond approximately to 89 s of actual time, which should be compared with the typical duration of a fill for physics, i.e., several hours.

As a new tool to address this challenge, recent advances in machine learning (ML) have enabled the development of surrogate models capable of predicting DA with high accuracy and shorter CPU usage [13,14]. We stress that the goal of this approach is to develop surrogate models that can predict the DA for machine configurations that have not been simulated using standard tracking. Notably, recent research has shown that neural network architecture based on Bidirectional Encoder Representations from Transformers (BERT) [15,16] outperforms other models in capturing the non-linear dependencies between accelerator parameters and DA [17]. This approach has shown great promise in providing fast predictions for new machine configurations, substantially reducing the need to rely on exhaustive numerical simulations.

Although surrogate models offer considerable computational advantages [18–20], one critical aspect that requires further exploration is the estimation of uncertainty in their predictions [21,22]. In the context of DA prediction, uncertainty arises predominantly from epistemic sources, reflecting the limitations of the surrogate model's capacity to generalise beyond its training data. Addressing this uncertainty is essential for ensuring the reliability and interpretability of surrogate models, particularly in operational scenarios, where there are high stakes associated with beam stability in large-scale accelerators.

This work focuses on benchmarking uncertainty estimation techniques for DA prediction using surrogate models, providing valuable insights into their performance in an application to a complex physical system. The DA prediction problem serves as an ideal test case for uncertainty estimation, as it involves high-dimensional, non-linear dynamics with well-defined performance metrics.

In this study, we investigate three methods to estimate epistemic uncertainty in DA predictions: Monte Carlo (MC) dropout [23–25], bootstrap aggregation (bagging) [26,27], and a mixed technique that combines both approaches. We will refer to this last combined technique as the mixed technique. By comparing their effectiveness with the baseline MC dropout model used in [28], we aim to develop a robust framework that improves the accuracy of surrogate models for the prediction of DA, and the ability to interpret their results. This research not only advances the state of ML applications in accelerator physics but also offers a valuable case study for the broader ML community, contributing to the ongoing development of uncertainty-aware neural network models [29–31].

This paper is organised as follows: Section 2 reviews previous work on the prediction of DA, as well as the specifications of the BERT-based model considered and the characteristics of the data sets used. Section 3 reviews the error estimation techniques considered, detailing the implementation for our specific application and the benchmarking methods used. Section 4 describes the results obtained from the benchmarking, highlighting the performance of each method in estimating uncertainty for DA predictions. Finally, some concluding remarks are presented in Section 5.

2. Dynamic Aperture Prediction and Machine Learning Inference

2.1. DA Evaluation via Simulation

DA evaluation through numerical simulation is a computational process that requires careful consideration of phase space sampling. A review of the topic, tailored to the context of this research, can be found in [17], while a broad overview on the concept and evaluation of DA can be found in [1,2,32] and references therein. Here, we provide a brief summary of the key aspects of DA evaluation, focusing on the angular DA representation used in this study.

Given the complexity and computational cost of fully exploring the entire 4D phase space, practical approaches focus on a lower-dimensional subspace to simplify probing the phase space regions for orbit boundedness. Although the phase space is 6D, it is customary to decouple the longitudinal motion from the transverse one, which corresponds to considering a 4D phase space for the transverse motion in the DA simulations. A common method involves scanning initial conditions in the form $(x, 0, y, 0)$, effectively reducing the DA computation to a 2D problem [32]. This simplification provides valuable insight into non-linear beam dynamics and is widely adopted in accelerator physics (see, e.g., [4,33–35]), and the approximation made is fully justified and correct.

In this context, DA is often expressed as a function of angular coordinates, referred to as angular DA. For a given angle α_k and number of turns N, the DA is defined as the stability radius $r_s(\alpha_k, N)$. This representation allows for the evaluation of DA in different directions in the 2D (x, y) space, improving the granularity of the analysis without requiring expensive sampling within the full 6D phase space. Notably, for hadron accelerators, the phase space dynamics is symplectic, meaning that only positive initial coordinates are considered during simulations, aligning with the physical characteristics of the system.

Multiple aspects have to be considered when evaluating DA, including, but not limited to, the choice of threshold amplitude for boundedness classification, the number of turns, and fineness of the angular scan. Regarding the threshold amplitude, orbits that remain below this amplitude over the course of the entire simulation are classified as stable, while those exceeding the threshold are considered unstable. The default threshold in the tracking codes is typically set at 1 m, an arbitrary physical aperture value. In the case of the LHC, the collimation system plays a pivotal role in setting the beam limit, as the collimator jaws physically restrict the beam amplitudes, absorbing particles that interact with the collimators. The difference between the numerical value of the threshold amplitude and the actual value provided by the collimator jaws does not pose any issue and the choice made in the numerical simulations can be fully justified.

Regarding the number of turns, ideal studies would track particles over 10^8–10^9 turns to ensure an accurate DA evaluation. However, due to computational constraints, simulations are typically limited to 10^5–10^6 turns, providing a sufficient but not exhaustive representation of beam stability. In contrast, the ability to rely on GPU-accelerated simulations enables the ability to efficiently parallelise the tracking of multiple initial conditions and increase statistics over different configurations, enhancing the robustness of the DA evaluation. Although, in the context of this study, the standard number of angles, fixed at 44, was used to evaluate the angular DA, the choice of this parameter can be further increased to improve the accuracy of each DA estimate and hence that of the surrogate model. Within our studies, the choice of 44 angles was, however, kept to maintain compatibility with existing DA tracking data, where this value was picked as a trade-off between DA accuracy and computational resources needed for the tracking. Future studies shall consider different values and settings to assess the potential for better results.

From a computational point of view, DA is evaluated by tracking the trajectories of particles initialised at various points in phase space. This process is carried out using Xsuite 0.6 [36], a well-established simulation toolkit for accelerator physics. The initial conditions are defined in polar coordinates in (x, y), enabling the determination of the angular DA for each direction.

An example of the results of these simulations is illustrated in Figure 1, which showcases one of the LHC configurations used to train the Deep Learning (DL) surrogate models. These simulations form the foundation for the development of surrogate models that replicate the DA evaluation process with greater speed and minimal computational cost. The colour indicates the stability time, i.e., the time during which the amplitude of the orbit remains below the threshold amplitude. It can be observed that, for each radius, the first unstable particle is detected in each angular direction, providing a measurement of the angular DA for the given configuration.

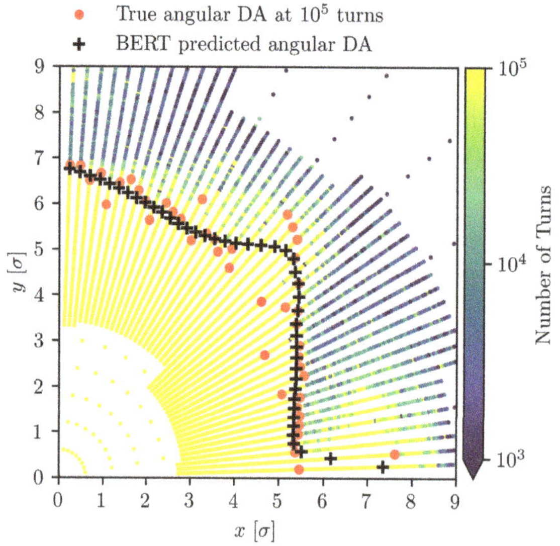

Figure 1. Example of the input data used for evaluating the angular DA, showing the stability radius r_s for different angular directions α_k and the number of turns N_{Turns} for which the orbit of each initial condition remains bounded. DA prediction performed by our BERT model, presented in the following, is also included. Image adapted from [17].

2.2. Composition of the Dynamic Aperture Data Set

The data set used to train and evaluate DL models for DA prediction is made up of accelerator configurations generated using the MAD-X code [37–40]. The focus of this study is the LHC, specifically in the configuration employed during the 2024 physics run at the injection energy of 450 GeV. This baseline setup was systematically modified by adjusting key accelerator parameters, creating a diverse collection of configurations for training purposes. We recall here the main features of the data set, while further technical details can be found in [17]. The primary parameters varied include the betatron tunes Q_x and Q_y, the linear chromaticities Q'_x and Q'_y, the strength of the Landau octupole magnets (quantified by the current I_{MO} flowing through them), and different realisations of magnetic field errors. These magnetic error realisations reflect field imperfections across the magnet families in the ring and each realisation represents a different series of magnetic field errors inside the measurement errors. Configurations for both Beam 1 (clockwise) and Beam 2 (counter-clockwise) were independently generated to account for differences in magnetic field errors between the two channels. This distinction is due to the presence of separate magnetic channels for the two beams, and the vast majority of magnets are two-in-one aperture devices.

The initial data set comprises 5000 LHC configurations and was constructed by performing a uniform grid search throughout the parameter space, specifically scanning the betatron tunes in the range $Q_x \in [62.1, 62.5]$ and $Q_y \in [60.1, 60.5]$ with steps of 5×10^{-3}. Linear chromaticities Q' were sampled from 0 to 30 in steps of 2, applying the same value to both Q'_x and Q'_y. The strength of the Landau octupoles I_{MO} was varied between -40 A and 40 A, with steps of 5 A. For each configuration, five realisations of magnetic field errors (randomly selected from a pool of 60) were assigned to both Beam 1 and Beam 2, resulting in a total of 5000 accelerator configurations.

To further enrich the data set, 5655 additional configurations were generated using an active learning (AL) framework developed by our team [28]. The acquisition function used in this framework is directly based on epistemic uncertainty, estimated as the variance of the predicted DA observed from a basic MC dropout setup. Candidate accelerator lattice configurations with the highest uncertainty in the angular DA prediction were selected. This uncertainty-driven sampling strategy improves efficiency by targeting informative samples. Before evaluation, all candidate configurations underwent preprocessing, including feature normalisation and discretisation, to ensure numerical stability and consistency with the model's input format. Similar preprocessing strategies have proven to be effective in other domains, such as intrusion detection [41] and probabilistic modelling [42], and are essential to maintain model performance and reliability in data-driven workflows.

As demonstrated in previous studies [28], this active sampling method improves the accuracy of the surrogate model by promoting the exploration of configurations where the physics governing the DA has not been fully captured.

Multiple threshold amplitudes were considered to define bounded orbits corresponding to different collimator apertures. Specifically, four collimator aperture values $(5\sigma, 5.7\sigma, 6.7\sigma, 11\sigma)$ were examined alongside the default threshold of 1 m. The inclusion of these smaller thresholds reflects the operational constraints of the LHC, where the collimation system plays a key role in limiting beam amplitudes to mitigate beam losses in superconducting magnets. In contrast, the 1 m threshold is used in idealised studies aimed at identifying which accelerator configurations yield the largest possible DA.

Beyond static DA predictions, the data set also captures the time evolution of the DA. This is accomplished by including DA values computed at various numbers of turns, ranging from 1×10^3 to approximately 5×10^3. The sampling intervals are defined by the boundaries at $1, 5, 10^{l_1}, 100 + 50^{l_2}$ (with $1 \le l_1 \le 10$ and $1 \le l_2 \le 8$). By incorporating temporal information, the model is trained not only to predict static DA values but also its time evolution.

The number of tracking turns varies between configurations in the data set. A subset of 3805 configurations was tracked for up to 5×10^5 turns, while the remaining 6850 configurations were limited to 1×10^5 turns. This deliberate imbalance is designed to train the machine learning model to perform a limited level of extrapolation, enabling it to predict DA on longer timescales even when only a smaller subset of long-term tracking data is available.

The total number of training samples is determined by combining three components: the number of accelerator configurations, the 44 angular directions used to probe the phase space, and the 19 time bins capturing the evolution of stability. This results in an 836-fold expansion of the original data set size.

Since beam–beam effects are excluded from the simulations, the beam emittance acts as a simple scaling factor, which allows one to define a simple strategy to further increase the size of the data set. Angular DA values, originally calculated for the nominal emittance, can be rescaled to reflect different beam emittances without requiring additional computationally expensive simulations [17]. One can use the following formula (see Appendix A for more detail):

$$\mathrm{DA}'(\alpha_k, N) = \mathrm{DA}(\alpha_k, N)\sqrt{\frac{\epsilon^* \sqrt{\epsilon_x'^2 \sin^2 \alpha_k + \epsilon_y'^2 \cos^2 \alpha_k}}{\epsilon_x' \epsilon_y'}}, \quad (1)$$

where ϵ^* represents the nominal normalised emittance of 2.5 µm, $\mathrm{DA}(\alpha_k, N)$ is the angular DA computed with tracking simulations assuming the same emittance (ϵ^*) for the motion in x and y, and $\mathrm{DA}'(\alpha_k, N)$ is the derived value of the angular DA for the case in which the emittances for the motion in x and y are ϵ_x' and ϵ_y', respectively. A set of 12 uniformly sampled emittance values, ranging from 0.25 µm to 50 µm, was used, with horizontal and vertical emittances related by a Gaussian distribution with a standard deviation of 10%.

The last data augmentation addresses two critical objectives. Firstly, it allows the surrogate model to learn the impact of beam emittance on DA. Secondly, it ensures a more uniform distribution of DA values within the training set by applying inverse sampling to correct for imbalances in the original data. This augmentation process leads to a more even representation of DA values, facilitating better model generalisation and reducing bias during training.

After augmentation and unbiasing, the data set expands to approximately 5×10^7 angular DA samples. Of this, 10% was used for validation, 10% for testing, and 80% for training.

To better capture the complex dynamics affecting DA, additional variables were calculated using MAD-X and PTC [43,44]. These include maximum values of the Twiss parameters $\alpha_{x,y}$ and $\beta_{x,y}$, and the phase advances $\mu_{x,y}$ between the ATLAS and CMS collision points. Moreover, non-linear beam dynamics is characterised by seven anharmonicity coefficients, representing amplitude detuning up to the second order [45].

Continuous input features were standardised by normalising with their mean and standard deviation, improving model convergence and stability. Discrete variables, such as beam and seed identifiers, were excluded from this process.

Unlike previous studies, no maximum value was applied to the angular DA values, as the augmentation and unbiasing steps provide a balanced distribution, allowing the model to learn from the full range of DA values without introducing artificial bias. While this study focuses on the CERN LHC ring, the same methodologies and techniques for data set configuration and data augmentation can be applied to different accelerator rings with little change, keeping the variables of interest for the optimisation campaign as the input layer. This provided that the data augmentation methods used, such as emittance rescaling, are consistent with the assumptions of the tracking simulations; in this case, the absence of beam–beam effects.

2.3. Machine Learning for Fast DA Prediction

We developed a neural network-based regressor capable of predicting angular DA values from accelerator configuration, polar angles, and the number of tracked turns. Several neural network architectures were evaluated [17], using TensorFlow 2.13.1 [46,47] as the primary development framework, ultimately highlighting BERT as the best performing architecture, with an acceptable increase in computational cost if compared to the baseline neural network models used in initial studies. Rectified Linear Unit (ReLU) [48,49] activation functions were used to enhance the network's capacity to learn non-linear relationships, while hyperparameters were optimised through random search using the Keras Tuner library to maximise model performance [50].

Originally developed for natural language processing, the BERT architecture is particularly well suited for complex regression tasks due to its capacity to model bidirectional dependencies through self-attention mechanisms. By capturing intricate relationships between input features, BERT extends its effectiveness to numerical and structured data applications, such as DA prediction. The BERT-based model used in this work consists of 12 transformer encoder layers [51], each incorporating multi-head self-attention with eight attention heads. This design allows the model to extract diverse representations of the input data simultaneously, enhancing its ability to generalise across varying accelerator configurations. A feed-forward neural network (FFN) follows each attention block, with a hidden layer size of 512. To stabilise training and mitigate overfitting, layer normalisation and dropout (with a rate of 0.5) are applied before and after each FFN layer. An overview of the BERT-based architecture is presented in Figure 2.

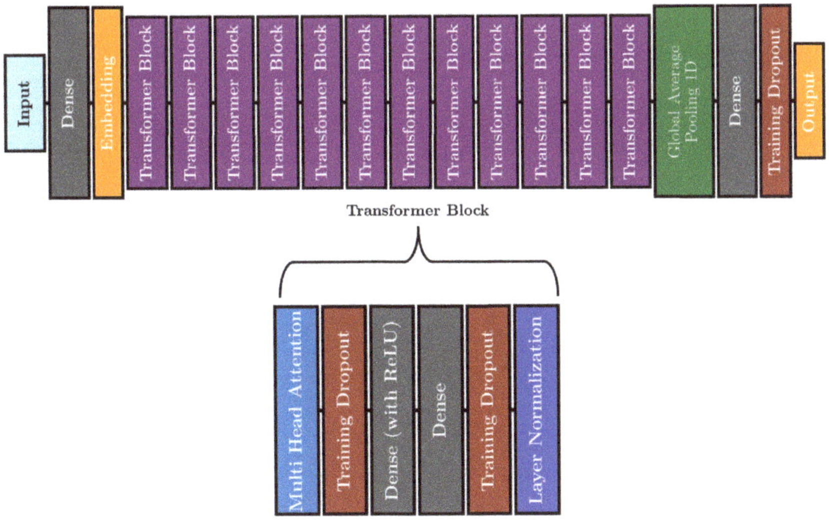

Figure 2. Sketch of the BERT-based neural network architecture used for DA inference. Image adapted from [17].

A global average pooling layer is appended at the end of the transformer blocks to condense the sequence dimension into a fixed-size vector, streamlining the prediction process while preserving critical information. This architecture ensures efficient processing and high accuracy in predicting angular DA values across different configurations.

The BERT-based regressor represents a significant advancement in fast DA prediction, demonstrating the potential of transformer-based models to outperform conventional neural networks in accelerator physics applications. This approach provides a scalable and efficient alternative to traditional simulation methods that offers substantial reductions in computational cost without compromising accuracy.

The performance of the BERT-based model in predicting DA values is summarised in Figures 3 and 4. Figure 3 shows the correlation plots of the predicted DA versus the true DA for both the validation and test data sets. The high values of the Pearson correlation coefficients demonstrate the model's ability to accurately predict DA values across different configurations. Nevertheless, some individual cases exhibit notable discrepancies between predicted and actual values, particularly in more challenging regions of the parameter space.

Furthermore, Figure 4 presents box plots of the relative errors in the prediction of the DA of the test data set, grouped by the number of turns (top) and the true DA value (bottom). The relative error is defined as the absolute difference between the predicted and the true values, normalised by the true value (i.e., $|DA_{pred} - DA_{true}|/DA_{true}$). These box plots indicate that the BERT model tends to exhibit higher relative errors for lower DA values. This behaviour is likely due to the model being trained using the mean absolute error as the loss metric. Despite this, the model demonstrates good overall reconstruction performance. This is evidenced by the Pearson correlation coefficient being close to one, the majority of the predictions clustering around the identity line, and the alignment of the median predicted values with the true DA values. It is important to note that only the outermost flyer is shown for each group in the box plots, which means that the most distant outlier is shown in each set. These reflect individual cases with high relative errors, which are observed in a small fraction of configurations.

This consistent performance across different data sets and grouping criteria highlights the robustness and reliability of the BERT-based model in predicting DA values. It should be noted that the numerical value of the computed DA also increases with smaller DA values given that the step of the grid of initial conditions is uniform in amplitude.

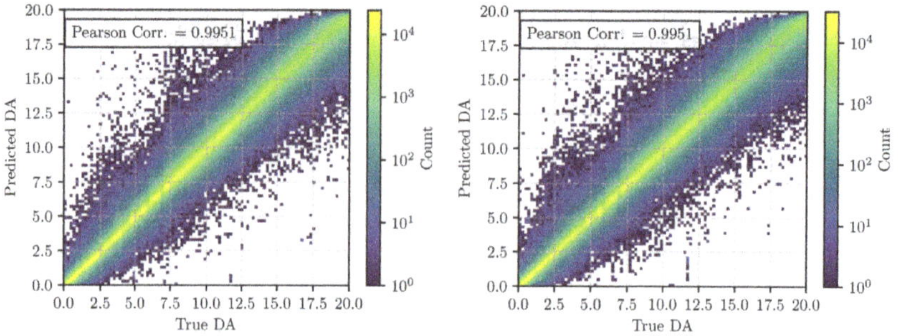

(**a**) Validation data set (**b**) Test data set

Figure 3. Correlation plots of the predicted DA values versus the true DA values obtained from the BERT-based model for the validation (**a**) and test (**b**) data sets. The high values of the Pearson correlation coefficients demonstrate the model's ability to accurately predict DA values across different configurations.

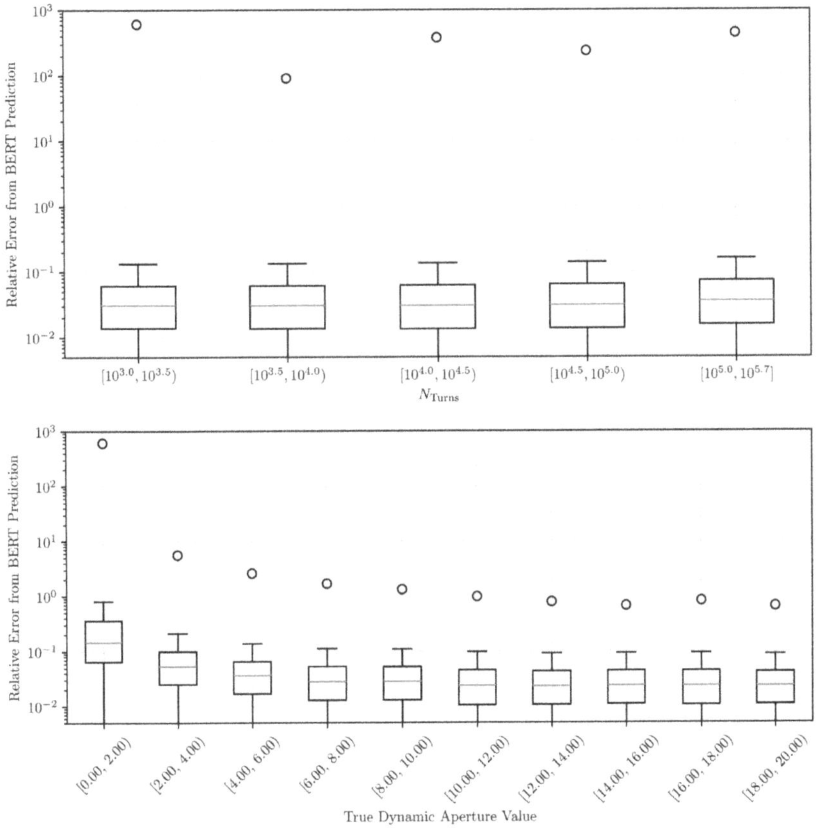

Figure 4. Box plots of the relative errors for the DA prediction from the test data set, considering different grouping criteria. Each box represents the interquartile range (IQR) of the data, with the central line indicating the median, and the whiskers extending to 1.5 times the IQR. Only the top flyer is shown for clarity. (**Top**) Relative errors grouped by the number of turns, which corresponds to the input value provided to the network, i.e., the angular DA evaluated at a given number of turns. (**Bottom**) Relative errors grouped by the true DA value. It can be observed that the BERT model tends to exhibit higher relative errors for lower DA values.

3. Techniques of Epistemic Error Estimation

Reliable uncertainty estimation is a critical component in the development of robust and effective ML models. In our context, we distinguish between epistemic and aleatoric uncertainty. Epistemic uncertainty reflects the model's lack of knowledge, typically due to limited training data or insufficient representational capacity, and manifests itself as uncertainty over the model parameters. It is, in principle, reducible with additional data or better-informed training. In contrast, aleatoric uncertainty arises from the inherent noise or randomness in the data itself, and is considered to be irreducible.

In our setup, the data originate from deterministic numerical simulations; therefore, they lack measurement noise and other typical sources of aleatoric uncertainty found in experimental data. That said, elements of aleatoric-like behaviour arise from the stochastic nature of the orbits in highly chaotic regions of the accelerator phase space. This introduces an intrinsic form of randomness that cannot be fully eliminated. However, as shown in previous studies [32], its impact can be mitigated by careful balancing of angular and radial sampling of initial conditions, which helps reduce the contribution of this effect to overall uncertainty.

Given this, our focus is on epistemic uncertainty, which is the main contributor to the prediction error in our scenario. Although we acknowledge that certain sampling-related uncertainties could be treated as aleatoric in nature, they are expected to have a limited impact provided that balanced sampling quota are respected [32]. Exploring such effects is left for future work, as they are not the main driver of uncertainty in the current analysis.

3.1. Monte Carlo Dropout

MC dropout is an efficient approach to estimating epistemic uncertainty by leveraging the inherent stochasticity of dropout layers during both training and inference. Traditionally, dropout functions are used as a regularisation technique, preventing overfitting by randomly deactivating neurons during each forward pass. The key innovation of MC dropout lies in its application at inference time, where it simulates an ensemble of neural networks without requiring the explicit training of multiple models.

This method can be interpreted as a form of approximate Bayesian inference [25]. In this framework, applying dropout at inference time introduces stochasticity that acts as a variational approximation to a posterior distribution over the model's weights. By performing multiple forward passes with random dropout masks, one obtains a distribution of predictions from which uncertainty can be estimated. Although this approach does not use explicitly defined priors beyond those implicitly imposed by dropout, the resulting spread in outputs effectively reflects epistemic uncertainty under a Bernoulli prior assumption. Although more rigorous Bayesian methods exist, this approximation remains computationally tractable and well suited to large models such as BERT.

It also requires minimal architectural changes and integrates naturally into complex networks, making it a practical choice for the prediction of DA. However, it may underestimate uncertainty in settings with highly non-stationary or intricate data distributions [52,53], and its ability to capture model uncertainty is ultimately constrained by the limitations of the sampling process [21].

In practice, during the inference phase, the dropout is activated for a series of T forward passes. This process yields T stochastic predictions for each input, from which the mean prediction can be computed as follows:

$$\langle y \rangle = \frac{1}{T} \sum_{i=1}^{T} y_i \,, \tag{2}$$

where y_i represents the DA prediction obtained at the ith stochastic pass, and the variance of these predictions serves as a measure of model uncertainty and reads as follows:

$$\sigma^2 = \frac{1}{T} \sum_{i=1}^{T} (y_i - \langle y \rangle)^2 \,, \tag{3}$$

which reflects the spread of predictions and provides a direct estimate of epistemic uncertainty.

In the implementation of this method, the dropout layers are integrated at different stages of the neural network architecture. An overview of the BERT-based model enriched with dropout layers is presented in Figure 5. Dropout layer implementation was completed using the built-in version provided by the TensorFlowframework. To enable a comprehensive exploration of possible dropout configurations, we include multiple dropout layers positioned at different points within the hidden architecture of the network. Since there is no strong theoretical guidance favouring a specific placement, we adopt a pragmatic approach and empirically evaluate all combinations to identify the best-performing setup based on the chosen metrics. Considering six distinct dropout layer positions, we explore all non-empty subsets, resulting in a total of $2^6 - 1 = 63$ configurations.

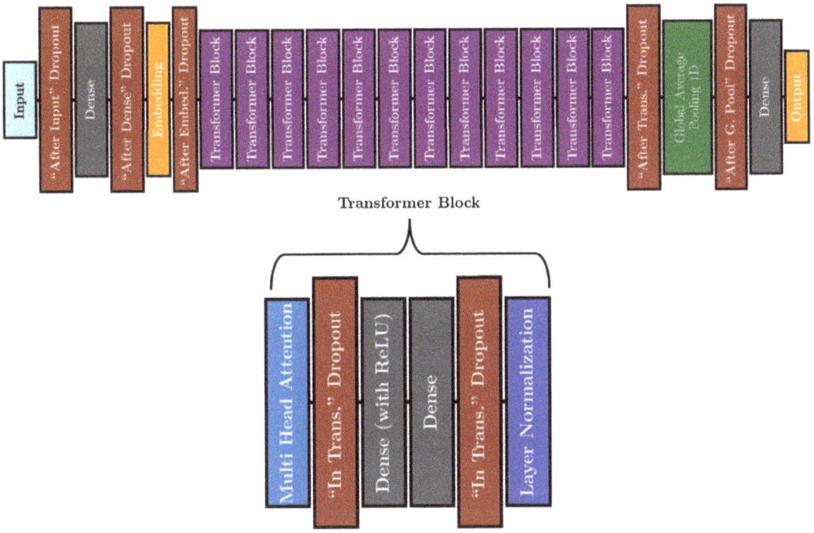

Figure 5. Sketch of the trained BERT-based neural network architecture enriched with additional dropout layers for MC dropout.

Regarding the dropout rate, a range of values between 1×10^{-6} and 0.5 is explored with logarithmic sampling to determine the most effective setting to capture uncertainty. As far as the dropout layer placement is concerned, the goal is to test a sufficiently broad and diverse set of values in an agnostic manner, aiming to identify the configuration that yields the best performance.

During inference, stochastic forward passes are performed for each input, ensuring sufficient sampling to obtain reliable uncertainty estimates. This choice of T is motivated by the trade-off between computational efficiency and uncertainty accuracy, balancing the need for robust uncertainty quantification with computational cost. An overview of the convergence of an MC estimate for different values of T is shown in Figure 6, highlighting the impact of the number of samples on the performance of uncertainty estimation. It is clearly seen that $\langle y \rangle$ converges rather smoothly to its limit, whereas σ features some more non-monotonic variations, in any case, being close to the limit value for $T = 128$.

To justify the use of variance as a measure of uncertainty, which assumes the prediction distribution is approximately Gaussian, we empirically analysed the output distributions of MC dropout samples for selected configurations. Kullback–Leibler (KL) divergence [54] was used to quantify deviations from normality [55], with the results for two representative cases shown in Figure 7. These show that while highly confident predictions can appear nearly deterministic, predictions with higher uncertainty tend to follow a distribution that closely resembles a Gaussian. This supports the use of variance as a practical proxy of uncertainty in this context. Deviations from Gaussian behaviour do occur, especially due to model complexity, but they typically correspond to regions where the model is confident and variance is low. In such cases, variance remains a meaningful, though limited, indicator of uncertainty. Similar distribution patterns were observed for the other methods considered.

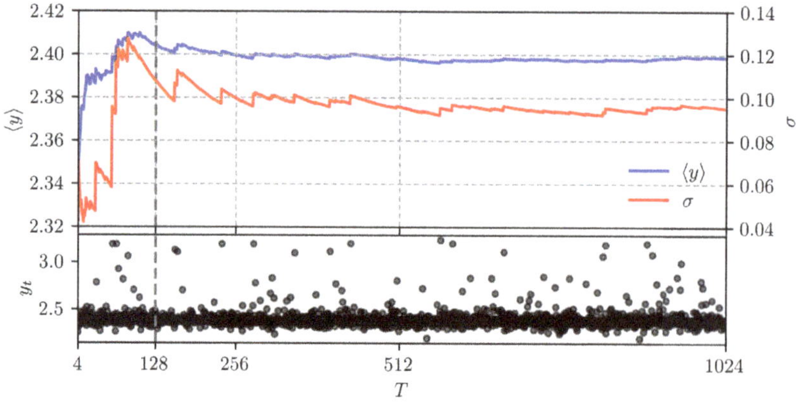

Figure 6. Convergence of $\langle y \rangle$ and σ in the MC dropout estimate for different values of T of an angular DA instance. Top: Impact of the number of samples (shown in the bottom plot) on the uncertainty estimation performance. It can be observed that sufficient stabilisation of $\langle y \rangle$ and σ is achieved for $T = 128$. This specific sampling was performed using configuration 57 with dropout rate 0.001 (details on the dropout configuration are presented in the later sections); comparable trends were observed in the other configurations as well.

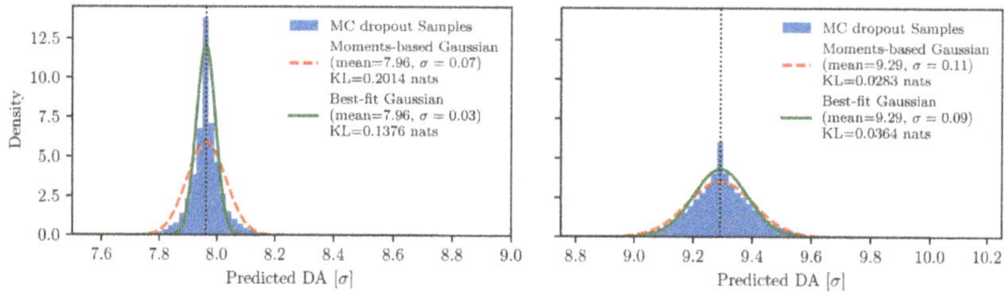

Figure 7. Empirical assessment of the Gaussian behaviour of MC dropout samples for two representative configurations. The left plot corresponds to a low-variance case, where the distribution appears nearly deterministic. The right plot shows a higher-variance case, with a distribution that more closely resembles a Gaussian fitted to the sample mean and standard deviation. KL divergence values quantify the deviation from normality in each case, with a value >0.1 indicating significant non-Gaussian behaviour, and a value <0.05 suggesting a good match to Gaussian-like behaviour.

3.2. *Bootstrap Aggregation (Bagging)*

Bootstrap aggregation, commonly known as bagging, provides an alternative approach to estimating epistemic uncertainty by constructing an ensemble of models trained on resampled versions of the original data set. This technique introduces variability in the training process through data resampling, resulting in a collection of models that globally improves prediction accuracy and offer robust uncertainty estimates.

Bagging offers a strong representation of uncertainty by capturing the full extent of model variability across different data subsets. By training models on resampled data, the ensemble is less prone to overfitting and tends to generalise better to new data. This method effectively reduces variance and improves the stability of the model. However, the primary drawback of bagging lies in its computational demands. Training multiple neural networks significantly increases both the memory footprint and training time, making it less practical for large-scale systems where computational resources are limited.

The bagging process begins by generating B bootstrap data sets by random sampling with replacement. Each bootstrap data set maintains the same size as the original training set but contains a different distribution of samples. A unique neural network is trained on each of these resampled data sets, producing a set of B models. For inference, each model provides a DA prediction for the same input, and the final prediction is calculated by averaging the outputs of the ensemble:

$$\langle y \rangle = \frac{1}{B} \sum_{b=1}^{B} y_b \,, \tag{4}$$

where y_b denotes the prediction of the bth model. The variance among these predictions serves as a direct estimate of epistemic uncertainty, expressed as follows:

$$\sigma^2 = \frac{1}{B} \sum_{b=1}^{B} (y_b - \langle y \rangle)^2 \,. \tag{5}$$

In this work, an ensemble of $B = 128$ BERT models is trained, with each model initialised with different weights and trained on distinct bootstrap samples, where a different extract of 50% of the training data is used for each model. The number of models considered is chosen to match the number of samples used in the MC dropout approach, ensuring a fair comparison between the two methods.

3.3. Mixed Technique

To explore the potential benefits of combining MC dropout and bagging, a mixed technique is introduced that integrates elements of both approaches. This hybrid method aims to leverage the information diversity provided by bagging, enhanced with the stochastic sampling of MC dropout. By combining these two techniques, the mixed approach seeks to capture a more comprehensive representation of epistemic uncertainty, potentially leading to more accurate and reliable uncertainty estimates.

In the mixed technique, an ensemble of $B = 128$ models is trained using bootstrap aggregation. Each model in the ensemble is trained on a different bootstrap sample of the original data set, introducing variability that encourages diversity in the learnt representations. This diversity among the models helps to reduce overfitting and improve generalisation. Additionally, each model in the ensemble is enriched with dropout layers, which are activated during training and inference to introduce stochasticity in the predictions.

During inference, each model in the ensemble is subjected to $T = 128$ stochastic forward passes, generating a total of $B \times T$ = 16,384 predictions for each input. This extensive sampling process allows the mixed technique to capture a wide range of possible outcomes, providing a robust estimate of the model's uncertainty. The final prediction is obtained by averaging the output of the ensemble, while the variance among the predictions serves as a measure of epistemic uncertainty, similar to the measure provided by the standard MC dropout and bootstrapping.

4. Results of the Comparative Analysis

4.1. Uncertainty Evaluation and Benchmarking

To evaluate the performance of uncertainty predictions, we use the uncertainty obtained from our BERT-based model as the basis. Since this model is used as the primary regressor for DA, its predictions on the validation and test data sets serve as a reference to evaluate the quality of the uncertainty. Specifically, the target uncertainty is computed by measuring the absolute error between the DA values predicted by the BERT model and the true DA values obtained from numerical simulations.

Given the stochastic nature of the BERT model's error distribution, achieving a precise one-to-one reconstruction of target uncertainties is unrealistic. Each prediction represents a unique realisation of the model's uncertainty. Therefore, we assess the quality of uncertainty estimation using two metrics, namely Pearson's correlation and the root mean squared error

(RMSE). A higher Pearson correlation indicates that the model effectively identifies regions of increased epistemic uncertainty, which are prime candidates for additional simulations in the context of active learning. The RMSE provides a measure of the average magnitude of the error between the estimated and target uncertainties. Given that the target uncertainties span multiple orders of magnitude, the RMSE is computed on their logarithm to ensure a more balanced evaluation across the entire range. Applying the logarithm mitigates the dominance of large values and prevents smaller values from being disproportionately overshadowed, leading to a more meaningful assessment of reconstruction performance.

By highlighting areas where epistemic uncertainty is most pronounced, models with higher correlation scores enable a more efficient allocation of computational resources, guiding subsequent DA simulations to regions where further data are the most valuable.

We benchmarked all possible MC dropout configurations in the validation data set to gain an initial overview of their performance. Based on Pearson's correlation and RMSE, the two best-performing MC dropout configurations were selected and used to construct two mixed technique instances, which were also tested on the validation data set. The five resulting models (bagging, the two selected MC dropout models, and the two mixed technique models) were then benchmarked in the test data set. This approach allows us to first identify the two best MC dropout models using the validation data set, incorporate them into mixed technique models, and then use the test data set as a final benchmark to comprehensively compare the selected MC dropout models, the mixed techniques built from them, and the bagging approach. Furthermore, all of these techniques are benchmarked against the baseline MC dropout setting used in our previous work, providing a direct comparison to the earlier methodology.

4.2. Results of Uncertainty Estimation

We evaluated various MC dropout configurations for the validation data set, with the results presented in Figure 8, where it is possible to observe how different choices of dropout layers and rates impact the final Pearson correlation and RMSE achieved. By analysing these results, we identified the optimal dropout layer configuration and dropout rate that yield the best performance for both metrics. The best-performing model, marked with a red cross, represents one of the most effective configurations of dropout layers and rates for accurate uncertainty estimation. Although the two selected models share the common characteristic of having dropout activated within the transformer blocks, their dropout rates differ by an order of magnitude and their dropout configuration is not identical. This suggests that, rather than identifying a single optimal configuration, the red crosses may indicate local minima within a broader landscape of nearly equivalent configurations. The observed trend highlights the importance of dropout placement within transformer blocks, but further analysis is needed to determine whether the selected models truly represent the absolute best configurations or if a range of similar setups could achieve comparable performance.

To further inspect the correlation between the Pearson correlation and RMSE, Figure 9 presents the performance of different MC dropout configurations and techniques. Although some configurations show a clear negative correlation, others follow distinct patterns, indicating different behaviours. A smaller subset of configurations achieves overall better error reconstruction, suggesting that a subset of MC dropout settings can be relied upon. Ultimately, the highlighted configurations in Figure 9 represent the best overall choices, although differences within such an optimal cluster of configurations are observed to be minimal.

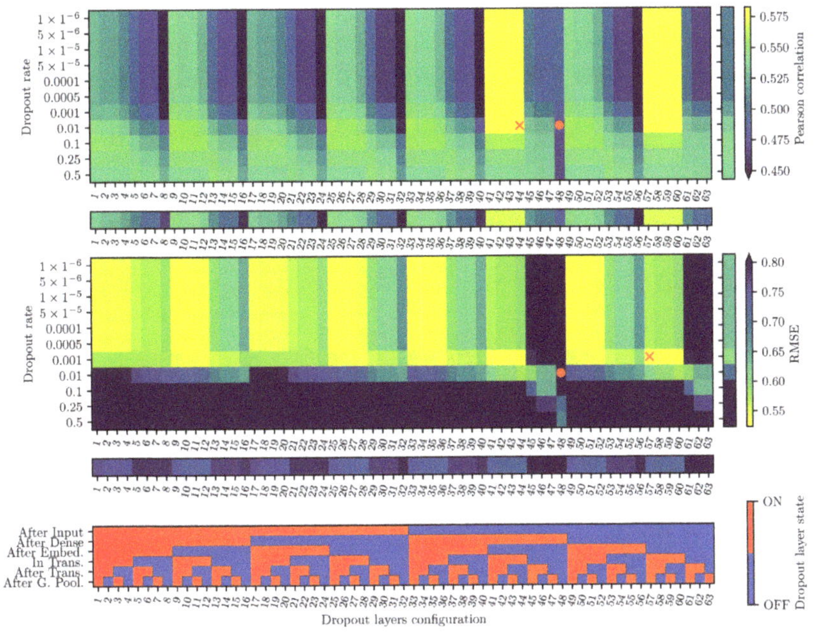

Figure 8. Overview of the achieved performance in predicting the DA uncertainty using different MC dropout configurations and dropout rates. The Pearson correlation (top plot) and mean squared error (central plot) are shown for each configuration, with the best-performing model highlighted with a red cross. The baseline configuration, used in our previous work [28], is highlighted with a red dot. To the side of the colour maps, additional unitary colour maps are included to illustrate the mean values observed when averaging over all configurations that share the same dropout rate or the same dropout layer configuration. These side plots help highlight the effectiveness of specific dropout rates and layer placements. The bottom plot displays the corresponding dropout layer configuration, highlighting which layers were activated during the sampling.

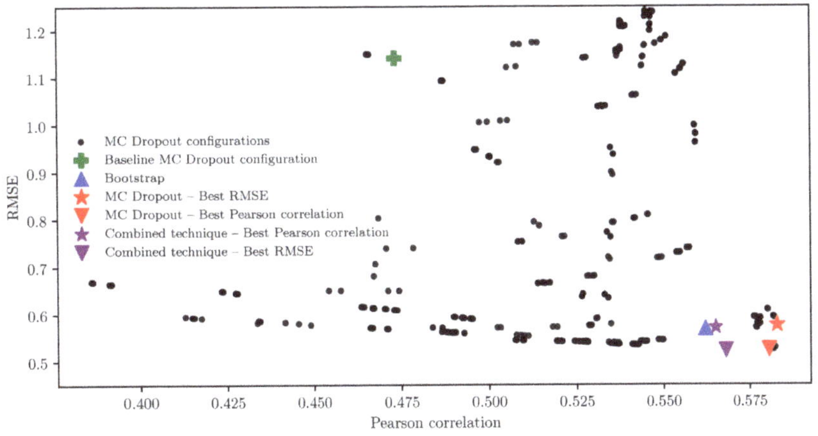

Figure 9. Scatter plot of Pearson correlation versus RMSE for various MC dropout configurations and techniques. The baseline MC dropout configuration, bootstrap aggregation, and the best-performing configurations for each metric (Pearson correlation and RMSE) are highlighted. The results of the combined technique are also included.

The selected MC dropout configurations were then used to compose two mixed technique instances, which were also evaluated on the validation data set. The results of this evaluation, along with the bagging method, are presented in Figure 10 in the form of a correlation colour map, showcasing the Pearson correlation and RMSE for each case. It can be seen that the different techniques generally capture the same trends in relative errors, exhibiting similar overall performance. The best Pearson correlation is achieved by the MC dropout model selected based on Pearson correlation, while the best RMSE is obtained by the mixed technique model constructed using the MC dropout configuration with the best RMSE. However, the differences between the various approaches remain relatively minor, suggesting that no single technique provides a significantly superior advantage over the others. In any case, all methods show a clear improvement compared to the baseline configuration, as summarised in Table 1.

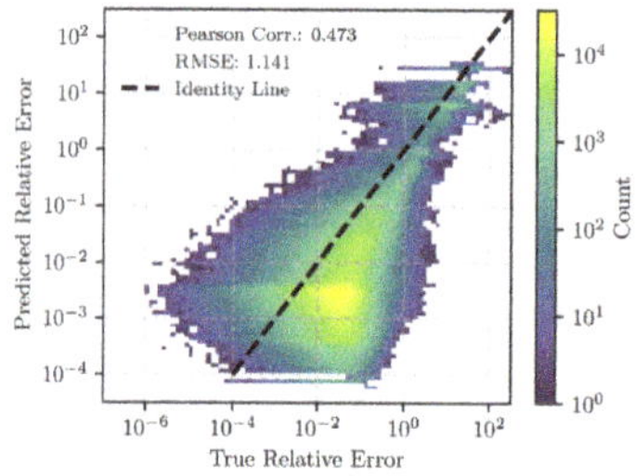

(**a**) MC Dropout (Baseline configuration)

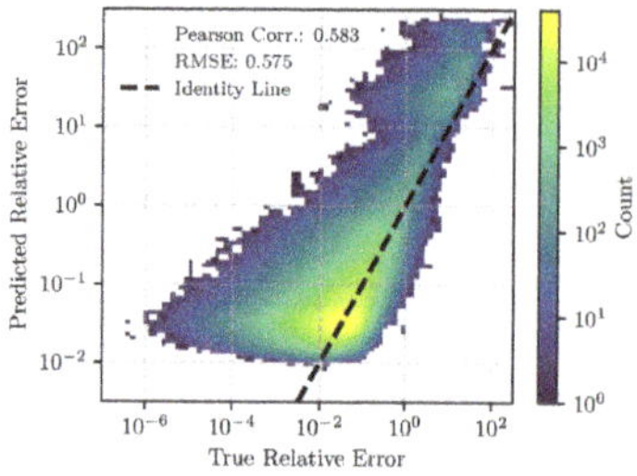

(**b**) MC Dropout (Best Pearson)

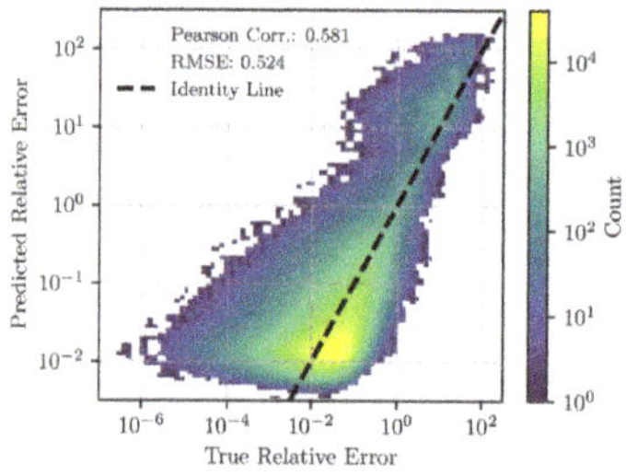

(**c**) MC Dropout (Best RMSE)

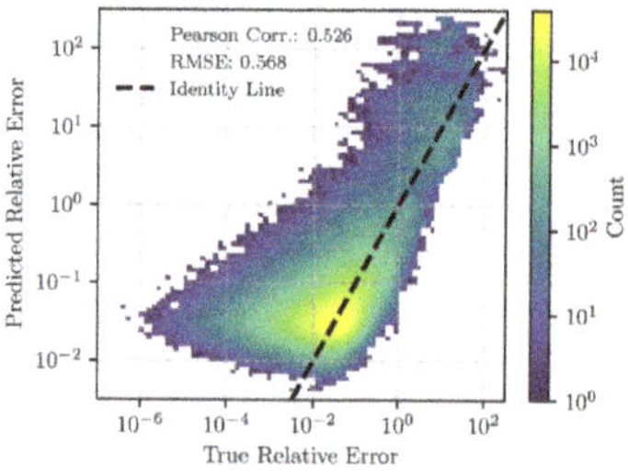

(**d**) Bootstrap

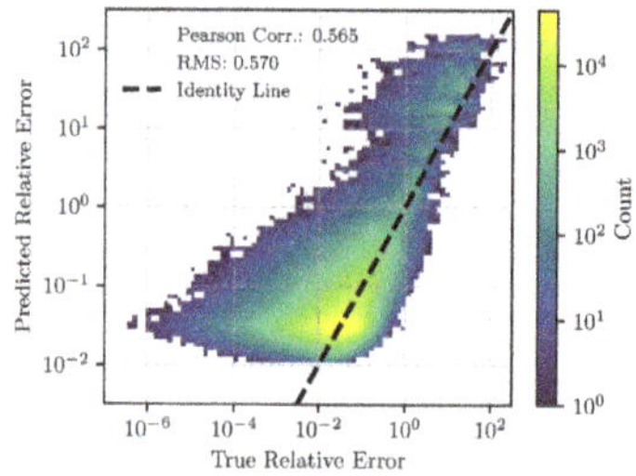

(**e**) Mixed technique (Best Pearson)

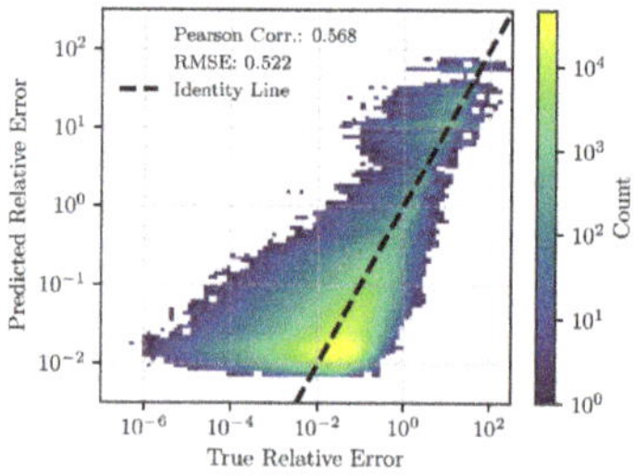

(**f**) Mixed technique (Best RMSE)

Figure 10. Distribution of the correlation between the predicted and true relative error for the BERT model for the validation data set. The Pearson correlation and RMSE are shown for each technique. The results are presented for the MC dropout models selected with the baseline configuration, the best Pearson correlation, and the best RMSE, the bagging method, and the mixed technique models constructed with the best Pearson correlation and the best RMSE MC dropout models. Overall, the performance is the same for all new cases considered, with a significant improvement if compared to the baseline MC dropout configuration.

It should be noted that the true relative error exhibits a wide range of values, ranging from 10^{-6} to 10^{2}, while the relative errors predicted by uncertainty estimation techniques are restricted to a narrower range of 10^{-2} to 10^{2}. The limited range observed in the predicted uncertainties reflects the inherent constraints of the estimation techniques used. These methods capture the epistemic uncertainty of the model, but they are also influenced by systematic limitations inherent to the techniques used, which cannot be fully eliminated. As a result, the predicted uncertainty cannot fall below a certain threshold even when the model is confident.

In contrast, the actual errors, which we recall are defined as the relative difference between predicted and true values, are not inherently bounded in this way. They can vary freely and, in principle, approach zero when the prediction is highly accurate.

Despite the presence of this lower bound in the predicted uncertainty, its impact on the overall ability of the model to reconstruct the true error remains marginal. The prediction intervals still offer a meaningful characterisation of uncertainty in most of the data range.

To further inspect the resulting relative error distributions achieved by the different techniques, we grouped the relative errors by the number of turns, which corresponds to the input value provided to the network, i.e., the angular DA evaluated at a given number of turns, and by the true angular DA value. The box plots presented in Figure 11 provide an overview of the relative errors obtained for the validation data set, providing the performance of the five selected techniques for the various grouping criteria. The results show that the various methods exhibit a systematic reduced spread in the value of the relative error compared to the true relative errors. This corresponds to the observations made for the correlation plots of Figure 10. However, note that the median values are closed together for all techniques. These characteristics in the reconstructed relative errors highlight the inherent limitations of uncertainty estimation techniques in precisely reproducing the absolute values of the true relative errors. However, in the context of active learning, an exact reconstruction of the error value is not necessarily required. Instead, what matters is the ability to establish a reliable threshold to determine whether a given sample requires further simulation or can be trusted [28]. Given these findings, future active learning strategies should focus on leveraging trends in reconstructed relative errors to guide threshold-based decision making, rather than relying on their absolute values for a perfect reconstruction.

When applied to the test data set, the five selected techniques exhibit performance similar to those observed on the validation data set. The results are consistent across the different grouping criteria, with the models capturing the same trends in the relative errors. The results are summarised in Table 1, which shows how the mixed technique model constructed with the best RMSE MC dropout model is the best-performing technique on the test data set. The MC dropout model selected with the best Pearson correlation also demonstrates a comparable performance, superior to the bagging method. Of course, it is fair to note that the differences between the various techniques are small.

Table 2 reports the coverage of the predicted confidence intervals for various uncertainty estimation techniques. The baseline MC dropout model, without any tuning, performs poorly, capturing less than 1% of true values in all intervals. In contrast, the configuration optimised for the Pearson correlation achieves the best calibration, with empirical coverages of 67.1%, 85.7%, and 90.5% for the 68%, 90%, and 95% intervals, respectively, values that closely align with expected coverage levels. The bagging and mixed technique also show strong performance, with coverage values approaching expected coverage as well, especially in Pearson-optimised settings. RMSE-optimised techniques perform poorly in terms of calibration, highlighting a trade-off between point prediction accuracy and uncertainty reliability.

When factoring in the computational efficiency of the different approaches, MC dropout emerges as the most effective method for uncertainty estimation. Its ability to provide reliable uncertainty estimates with minimal computational overhead makes it an attractive choice for integrating uncertainty-aware models in accelerator physics applications. The mixed technique, while offering a slight improvement in performance, does not justify the additional computational cost associated with training multiple models. This implies that although the combined method aims at different sources of theoretical uncertainty, it does not produce substantially more information than the techniques applied separately. This observation suggests that the uncertainties addressed by MC dropout and bagging could be derived from similar aspects of the model's behaviour. Bagging, on the other hand, demonstrates comparable performance to MC dropout but is weak in terms of computational efficiency, limiting its practicality to large-scale systems.

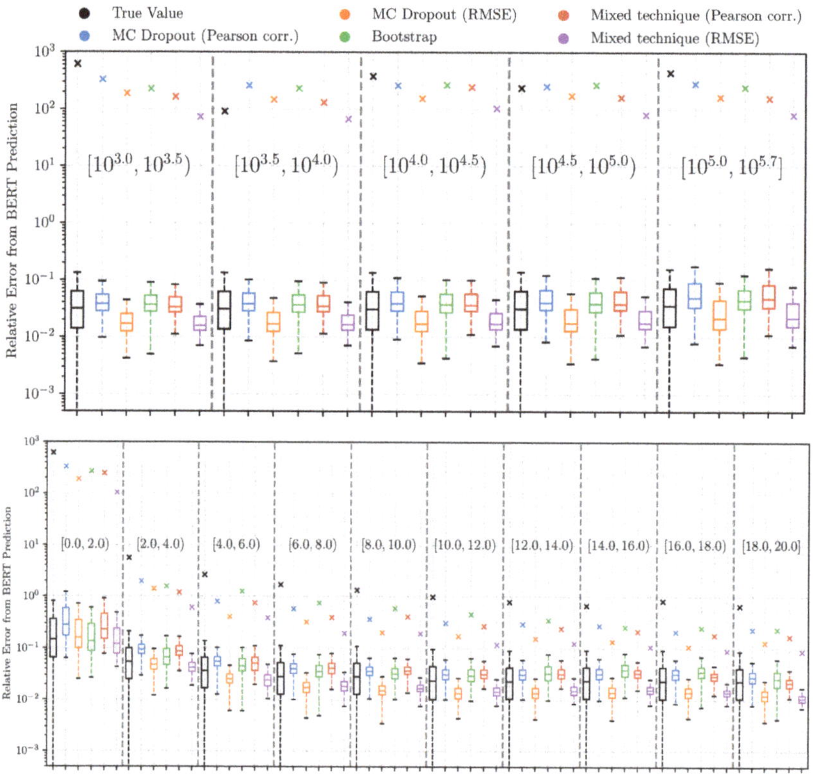

Figure 11. Box plots of the relative errors for the DA prediction on the validation data set, considering different grouping criteria. Each box represents the interquartile range (IQR) of the data, with the central line indicating the median, and the whiskers extending to 1.5 times the IQR. Only the top flyer is shown for clarity. (**Top**) Relative errors grouped by the number of turns, which corresponds to the input value provided to the network, i.e., the angular DA evaluated at a given number of turns. (**Bottom**) Relative errors grouped by the true DA value. It can be observed that all methods capture most of the same trends in the relative errors, demonstrating very similar performance.

Table 1. Comparison of uncertainty estimation techniques for the relative error in the DA predictions. The Pearson correlation and RMSE is listed, and the best results are highlighted in bold. It should be note that the observed variations are small.

Technique	Validation		Test	
	Pearson Correlation	RMSE	Pearson Correlation	RMSE
MC Dropout (Baseline)	0.473	1.141	0.381	0.92
MC Dropout (Best Pearson)	**0.583**	0.575	**0.581**	0.575
MC Dropout (Best RMSE)	0.581	0.524	0.579	0.525
Bootstrap Aggregation	0.562	0.568	0.518	0.581
Combined Technique (Best Pearson)	0.565	0.570	0.557	0.574
Combined Technique (Best RMSE)	0.568	**0.522**	0.560	**0.523**

Table 2. Coverage (%) of confidence intervals (CI) for different uncertainty estimation techniques. The technique with the empirical coverage closest to the expected coverage is highlighted in bold. The coverage is computed as the percentage of predictions for which the true DA value falls within the estimated confidence interval.

Technique	68% CI (%)	90% CI (%)	95% CI (%)
MC Dropout (Baseline)	0.3	0.3	0.3
MC Dropout (Best Pearson)	**67.1**	**85.7**	**90.5**
MC Dropout (Best RMSE)	37.1	55.3	62.4
Bootstrap Aggregation	60.8	79.5	84.9
Combined Technique (Best Pearson)	65.3	83.8	88.7
Combined Technique (Best RMSE)	36.7	55.3	62.5

5. Conclusions and Outlook

In this study, we have investigated various techniques for estimating epistemic uncertainty in the prediction of DA using a BERT-based DL model. We evaluated MC dropout, bootstrap aggregation, and a mixed technique that combined both methods to predict uncertainty in DA values. The methods were compared on a large data set of LHC configurations, using the results of the BERT model as a reference for uncertainty estimation. We stress that this study provides a unique opportunity to compare the various techniques to provide epistemic uncertainty against the true uncertainty.

Among the methods evaluated, MC dropout and the mixed technique have shown the best results, although the various methods proved to be rather comparable in providing valid uncertainty estimates. MC dropout also emerges as the most effective technique due to its computational efficiency and ease of integration with existing neural network architectures and the fact that it does not require the retraining of multiple models. This approach not only offers robust uncertainty quantification but also does so with significantly lower computational effort compared to bootstrap aggregation and the explored mixed technique. Furthermore, when optimised for correlation, MC dropout achieves the best coverage in confidence intervals, closely matching the expected coverage.

Our results demonstrate a clear improvement over the MC dropout configurations proposed in previous work. This enhancement is achieved through a series of refinements, including the optimisation of the dropout layer architecture, the introduction of bootstrap aggregation, and the development of a mixed technique combining both approaches. These numerical experiments highlight the importance of carefully selecting the dropout configuration and the uncertainty estimation strategy to improve the quality of uncertainty predictions without incurring significant computational cost. Among the methods tested, our optimised MC dropout approach consistently delivers the best balance between accuracy, robustness, and efficiency. We therefore recommend it as a practical and effective solution for DA uncertainty quantification.

Future efforts will focus on integrating these uncertainty estimation methods into active learning frameworks and further extend these methods to include more beam dynamics effects, such as beam–beam. Using active learning, our aim is to further enhance the efficiency and accuracy of DA predictions, guiding the selection of new data points for simulation based on model uncertainty estimates. This approach promises to optimise computational resources and improve the reliability of surrogate models in accelerator physics applications. Ultimately, the improvement in the uncertainty estimation will enhance the ML framework, leading to more confident decisions on the performance related with accelerator configurations.

Author Contributions: Conceptualisation, M.G., T.P. and F.F.V.d.V.; software, C.E.M. and D.D.C.; formal analysis, C.E.M.; investigation, C.E.M., D.D.C., M.G. and S.R.; data curation, C.E.M. and D.D.C.; writing—original draft preparation, C.E.M. and M.G.; writing—review and editing, C.E.M., R.B.A., D.D.C., M.G. and T.P.; supervision, R.B.A., M.G., T.P., S.R. and F.F.V.d.V. All authors have read and agreed to the published version of the manuscript.

Funding: This research was funded by the Swiss Accelerator Research and Technology programme (CHART) and the Swiss Data Science Centre project grant number C20-10.

Data Availability Statement: The raw data supporting the conclusions of this article will be made available by the authors on request.

Conflicts of Interest: The authors declare no conflicts of interest. The funders had no role in the design of the study; in the collection, analyses, or interpretation of data; in the writing of the manuscript; or in the decision to publish the results.

Appendix A. Dependence of the Angular DA on the Beam Emittance

Let us assume that the numerical simulations to determine the DA of a given accelerator lattice have been carried out by defining a polar grid of initial coordinates in phase space. The angular DA describes the border of a region that, in polar coordinates, is described as

$$\begin{aligned} x(\alpha_k) &= \sqrt{\epsilon^*}\,\mathrm{DA}(\alpha_k, N)\cos\alpha_k\,, \\ y(\alpha_k) &= \sqrt{\epsilon^*}\,\mathrm{DA}(\alpha_k, N)\sin\alpha_k\,, \end{aligned} \tag{A1}$$

where ϵ^* represents the emittance for the x and y motions. The values of $\mathrm{DA}(\alpha_k, N)$ are determined by CPU-intensive tracking simulations. Whenever beam–beam effects are not taken into account, the emittance value used to define the grid of initial conditions represents an arbitrary scale. Therefore, it is possible to transform the calculated angular DA values in the case where the emittance values in the x and y directions are different and also differ from the value used in the numerical calculations.

This can be obtained by assuming a new coordinate system defined as

$$\begin{aligned} x(\beta_k) &= \sqrt{\epsilon'_x}\,\mathrm{DA}'(\beta_k, N)\cos\beta_k\,, \\ y(\beta_k) &= \sqrt{\epsilon'_y}\,\mathrm{DA}'(\beta_k, N)\sin\beta_k\,, \end{aligned} \tag{A2}$$

where

$$\beta_k = \arctan\left[\sqrt{\frac{\epsilon'_x}{\epsilon'_y}}\tan\alpha_k\right], \tag{A3}$$

and Equation (A2) can be recast in the general form

$$\begin{aligned} x(\alpha_k) &= \sqrt{\epsilon'_x}\,\mathrm{DA}'(\alpha_k, N) f(\alpha_k)\,, \\ y(\alpha_k) &= \sqrt{\epsilon'_y}\,\mathrm{DA}'(\alpha_k, N) g(\alpha_k)\,. \end{aligned} \tag{A4}$$

It can immediately find the following relationship

$$\mathrm{DA}'(\alpha_k, N) = \mathrm{DA}(\alpha_k, N)\sqrt{\frac{\epsilon^*}{\epsilon'_x f^2(\alpha_k) + \epsilon'_y g^2(\alpha_k)}}\,, \tag{A5}$$

and, by applying standard trigonometric properties, it is possible to obtain Equation (1).

References

1. Bazzani, A.; Giovannozzi, M.; Maclean, E.H.; Montanari, C.E.; Van der Veken, F.F.; Van Goethem, W. Advances on the modeling of the time evolution of dynamic aperture of hadron circular accelerators. *Phys. Rev. Accel. Beams* **2019**, *22*, 104003. [CrossRef]
2. Giovannozzi, M. A proposed scaling law for intensity evolution in hadron storage rings based on dynamic aperture variation with time. *Phys. Rev. Spec. Top. Accel. Beams* **2012**, *15*, 024001. [CrossRef]
3. Maclean, E.; Giovannozzi, M.; Appleby, R. Innovative method to measure the extent of the stable phase-space region of proton synchrotrons. *Phys. Rev. Accel. Beams* **2019**, *22*, 034002. [CrossRef]
4. Giovannozzi, M.; Van der Veken, F.F. Description of the luminosity evolution for the CERN LHC including dynamic aperture effects. Part I: The model. *Nucl. Instrum. Methods Phys. Res.* **2018**, *A905*, 171–179; Erratum in *Nucl. Instrum. Methods Phys. Res.* **2019**, *927*, 471. [CrossRef]
5. Brüning, O.S.; Collier, P.; Lebrun, P.; Myers, S.; Ostojic, R.; Poole, J.; Proudlock, P. *LHC Design Report*; CERN Yellow Reports: Monographs; CERN: Geneva, Switzerland, 2004. [CrossRef]
6. Apollinari, G.; Béjar Alonso, I.; Brüning, O.; Fessia, P.; Lamont, M.; Rossi, L.; Tavian, L. *High-Luminosity Large Hadron Collider (HL–LHC)*; CERN Yellow Reports: Monographs; CERN: Geneva, Switzerland, 2017; Volume 4. [CrossRef]
7. Abada, A.; Abbrescia, M.; AbdusSalam, S.S.; Abdyukhanov, I.; Abelleira Fernandez, J.; Abramov, A.; Aburaia, M.; Acar, A.O.; Adzic, P.R.; Agrawal, P.; et al. FCC-ee: The Lepton Collider. *Eur. Phys. J. Spec. Top.* **2019**, *228*, 261–623. [CrossRef]
8. Abada, A.; Abbrescia, M.; AbdusSalam, S.S.; Abdyukhanov, I.; Abelleira Fernandez, J.; Abramov, A.; Aburaia, M.; Acar, A.O.; Adzic, P.R.; Agrawal, P.; et al. FCC-hh: The Hadron Collider: Future Circular Collider Conceptual Design Report Volume 3. *Eur. Phys. J. Spec. Top.* **2019**, *228*, 755–1107. [CrossRef]
9. Skoufaris, K.; Fartoukh, S.; Papaphilippou, Y.; Poyet, A.; Rossi, A.; Sterbini, G.; Kaltchev, D. Numerical optimization of dc wire parameters for mitigation of the long range beam-beam interactions in High Luminosity Large Hadron Collider. *Phys. Rev. Accel. Beams* **2021**, *24*, 074001. [CrossRef]
10. Droin, C.; Sterbini, G.; Efthymiopoulos, I.; Mounet, N.; De Maria, R.; Tomas, R.; Kostoglou, S.; European Organization for Nuclear Research. Status of beam-beam studies for the high-luminosity LHC. In Proceedings of the IPAC'24—15th International Particle Accelerator Conference, Nashville, TN, USA, 19–24 May 2024; JACoW Publishing: Geneva, Switzerland, 2024; pp. 3213–3216. [CrossRef]
11. Assmann, R.W.; Jeanneret, J.B.; Kaltchev, D.I. Efficiency for the imperfect LHC collimation system. In Proceedings of the 8th European Particle Accelerator Conference (EPAC 2002), Paris, France, 3–7 June 2002; p. 293.
12. Bracco, C. Commissioning Scenarios and Tests for the LHC Collimation System. Ph.D. Thesis, EPFL, Lausanne, Switzerland, 2008.
13. Schenk, M.; Coyle, L.; Pieloni, T.; Giovannozzi, M.; Mereghetti, A.; Krymova, E.; Obozinski, G. Modeling Particle Stability Plots for Accelerator Optimization Using Adaptive Sampling. In Proceedings of the IPAC'21, Campinas, Brazil, 24–28 May 2021; JACoW Publishing: Geneva, Switzerland, 2021; pp. 1923–1926. [CrossRef]
14. Casanova, M.; Dalena, B.; Bonaventura, L.; Giovannozzi, M. Ensemble reservoir computing for dynamical systems: Prediction of phase-space stable region for hadron storage rings. *Eur. Phys. J. Plus* **2023**, *138*, 559. [CrossRef]
15. Devlin, J.; Chang, M.W.; Lee, K.; Toutanova, K. BERT: Pre-training of Deep Bidirectional Transformers for Language Understanding. *arXiv* **2019**, arXiv:1810.04805. [CrossRef]
16. Aftan, S.; Shah, H. A Survey on BERT and Its Applications. In Proceedings of the 2023 20th Learning and Technology Conference, Jeddah, Saudi Arabia, 26 January 2023; pp. 161–166. [CrossRef]
17. Di Croce, D.; Giovannozzi, M.; Montanari, C.E.; Pieloni, T.; Redaelli, S.; Van der Veken, F.F. Assessing the Performance of Deep Learning Predictions for Dynamic Aperture of a Hadron Circular Particle Accelerator. *Instruments* **2024**, *8*, 50. [CrossRef]
18. Alizadeh, R.; Allen, J.K.; Mistree, F. Managing computational complexity using surrogate models: A critical review. *Res. Eng. Des.* **2020**, *31*, 275–298. [CrossRef]

19. Sudret, B.; Marelli, S.; Wiart, J. Surrogate models for uncertainty quantification: An overview. In Proceedings of the 2017 11th European Conference on Antennas and Propagation (EUCAP), Paris, France, 19–24 March 2017; pp. 793–797. [CrossRef]
20. Roussel, R.; Edelen, A.L.; Boltz, T.; Kennedy, D.; Zhang, Z.; Ji, F.; Huang, X.; Ratner, D.; Garcia, A.S.; Xu, C.; et al. Bayesian optimization algorithms for accelerator physics. *Phys. Rev. Accel. Beams* **2024**, *27*, 084801. [CrossRef]
21. Gawlikowski, J.; Tassi, C.R.N.; Ali, M.; Lee, J.; Humt, M.; Feng, J.; Kruspe, A.; Triebel, R.; Jung, P.; Roscher, R.; et al. A survey of uncertainty in deep neural networks. *Artif. Intell. Rev.* **2023**, *56*, 1513–1589. [CrossRef]
22. Tyralis, H.; Papacharalampous, G. A review of predictive uncertainty estimation with machine learning. *Artif. Intell. Rev.* **2024**, *57*, 94. [CrossRef]
23. Gal, Y.; Ghahramani, Z. Bayesian Convolutional Neural Networks with Bernoulli Approximate Variational Inference. *arXiv* **2016**, arXiv:1506.02158. [CrossRef]
24. Gal, Y.; Hron, J.; Kendall, A. Concrete Dropout. In Proceedings of the Advances in Neural Information Processing Systems, Long Beach, CA, USA, 4–9 December 2017; Guyon, I., Luxburg, U.V., Bengio, S., Wallach, H., Fergus, R., Vishwanathan, S., Garnett, R., Eds.; Curran Associates, Inc.: Red Hook, NY, USA, 2017; Volume 30.
25. Gal, Y.; Ghahramani, Z. Dropout as a Bayesian Approximation: Representing Model Uncertainty in Deep Learning. In Proceedings of the 33rd International Conference on International Conference on Machine Learning—ICML'16, New York, NY, USA, 19–24 June 2016; Volume 48, pp. 1050–1059.
26. Breiman, L. Bagging predictors. *Mach. Learn.* **1996**, *24*, 123–140. [CrossRef]
27. Bishop, C.M. *Pattern Recognition and Machine Learning*, 1st ed.; Information Science and Statistics; Springer: New York, NY, USA, 2006; Volume IV, p. 778.
28. Di Croce, D.; Giovannozzi, M.; Krymova, E.; Pieloni, T.; Redaelli, S.; Seidel, M.; Tomás, R.; Van der Veken, F.F. Optimizing dynamic aperture studies with active learning. *J. Instrum.* **2024**, *19*, P04004. [CrossRef]
29. Kaplan, L.; Cerutti, F.; Sensoy, M.; Preece, A.; Sullivan, P. Uncertainty Aware AI ML: Why and How. *arXiv* **2018**, arXiv:1809.07882. [CrossRef]
30. Kabir, H.D.; Mondal, S.K.; Khanam, S.; Khosravi, A.; Rahman, S.; Qazani, M.R.C.; Alizadehsani, R.; Asadi, H.; Mohamed, S.; Nahavandi, S.; et al. Uncertainty aware neural network from similarity and sensitivity. *Appl. Soft Comput.* **2023**, *149*, 111027. [CrossRef]
31. Tabarisaadi, P.; Khosravi, A.; Nahavandi, S.; Shafie-Khah, M.; Catalão, J.P.S. An Optimized Uncertainty-Aware Training Framework for Neural Networks. *IEEE Trans. Neural Netw. Learn. Syst.* **2024**, *35*, 6928–6935. [CrossRef]
32. Giovannozzi, M.; Scandale, W.; Todesco, E. Dynamic aperture extrapolation in presence of tune modulation. *Phys. Rev.* **1998**, *E57*, 3432. [CrossRef]
33. Pellegrini, D.; Fartoukh, S.; Karastathis, N.; Papaphilippou, Y. Multiparametric response of the HL-LHC Dynamic Aperture in presence of beam-beam effects. *J. Phys. Conf. Ser.* **2017**, *874*, 012007. [CrossRef]
34. Jing, Y.C.; Litvinenko, V.; Trbojevic, D. Optimization of Dynamic Aperture for Hadron Lattices in eRHIC. In Proceedings of the 6th International Particle Accelerator Conference (IPAC'15), Richmond, VA, USA, 4 May 2015; p. 757. [CrossRef]
35. Cruz Alaniz, E.; Abelleira, J.L.; van Riesen-Hauptpresenter, L.; Seryi, A.; Martin, R.; Tomás, R. Methods to Increase the Dynamic Aperture of the FCC-hh Lattice. In Proceedings of the 9th International Particle Accelerator Conference (IPAC'18), Vancouver, BC, Canada, 3 May 2018; p. 3593. [CrossRef]
36. Iadarola, G.; Latina, A.; Abramov, A.; Droin, C.; Demetriadou, D.; Soubelet, F.; Van der Veken, F.; Sterbini, G.; Dilly, J.; Paraschou, K.; et al. Xsuite: An integrated beam physics simulation framework. In Proceedings of the IPAC'24—15th International Particle Accelerator Conference, Nashville, TN, USA, 19–24 May 2024; JACoW Publishing: Geneva, Switzerland, 2024; pp. 2623–2626. [CrossRef]
37. Grote, H.; Schmidt, F. MAD-X—An Upgrade from MAD8. In Proceedings of the PAC'03, Portland, OR, USA, 12–16 May 2003; JACoW Publishing: Geneva, Switzerland, 2003; pp. 3497–3499. [CrossRef]
38. Deniau, L.; Burkhardt, H.; Maria, R.D.; Giovannozzi, M.; Jowett, J.M.; Latina, A.; Persson, T.; Schmidt, F.; Shreyber, I.S.; Skowroński, P.K.; et al. Upgrade of MAD-X for HL-LHC Project and FCC Studies. In Proceedings of the ICAP'18, Key West, FL, USA, 20–24 October 2018; JACoW Publishing: Geneva, Switzerland, 2018; pp. 165–171. [CrossRef]
39. Maria, R.D.; Latina, A.; Schmidt, F.; Dilly, J.; Deniau, L.; Skowronski, P.; Berg, J.; Gläßle, T. Status of MAD-X V5.09. In Proceedings of the IPAC'23—International Particle Accelerator Conference, Venice, Italy, 7–12 May 2023; JACoW Publishing: Geneva, Switzerland, 2023; pp. 3340–3343. [CrossRef]
40. MAD—Methodical Accelerator Design. Available online: https://mad.web.cern.ch/mad/ (accessed on 17 July 2025).
41. Hostiadi, D.P.; Atmojo, Y.P.; Huizen, R.R.; Susila, I.M.D.; Pradipta, G.A.; Liandana, I.M. A New Approach Feature Selection for Intrusion Detection System Using Correlation Analysis. In Proceedings of the 2022 4th International Conference on Cybernetics and Intelligent System (ICORIS), Prapat, Indonesia, 8–9 October 2022; pp. 1–6. [CrossRef]
42. Parsaei, M.; Taheri, R.; Javidan, R. Perusing The Effect of Discretization of Data on Accuracy of Predicting Naïve Bayes Algorithm. *J. Curr. Res. Sci.* **2016**, *1*, 457–462.

43. Schmidt, F.; Forest, E.; McIntosh, E. *Introduction to the Polymorphic Tracking Code: Fibre Bundles, Polymorphic Taylor Types and "Exact Tracking"*; Technical Report CERN-SL-2002-044-AP, KEK-REPORT-2002-3; CERN: Geneva, Switzerland, 2002. Available online: https://cds.cern.ch/record/573082 (accessed on 17 July 2025).
44. Schmidt, F.; Chiu, C.Y.; Goddard, B.; Jacquet, D.; Kain, V.; Lamont, M.; Mertens, V.; Uythoven, J.; Wenninger, J. MAD-X PTC Integration. In Proceedings of the 21st IEEE Particle Accelerator Conference (PAC 2005), Knoxville, TN, USA, 16–20 May 2005; p. 1272.
45. Bazzani, A.; Servizi, G.; Todesco, E.; Turchetti, G. *A Normal Form Approach to the Theory of Nonlinear Betatronic Motion*; CERN Yellow Reports: Monographs; CERN: Geneva, Switzerland, 1994. [CrossRef]
46. Abadi, M.; Agarwal, A.; Barham, P.; Brevdo, E.; Chen, Z.; Citro, C.; Corrado, G.S.; Davis, A.; Dean, J.; Devin, M.; et al. TensorFlow: Large-Scale Machine Learning on Heterogeneous Systems. 2015. Available online: https://www.tensorflow.org/ (accessed on 17 July 2025).
47. Pang, B.; Nijkamp, E.; Wu, Y.N. Deep Learning with TensorFlow: A Review. *J. Educ. Behav. Stat.* **2020**, *45*, 227–248. [CrossRef]
48. Arora, R.; Basu, A.; Mianjy, P.; Mukherjee, A. Understanding Deep Neural Networks with Rectified Linear Units. *arXiv* **2018**, arXiv:1611.01491. [CrossRef]
49. Agarap, A.F. Deep Learning using Rectified Linear Units (ReLU). *arXiv* **2019**, arXiv:1803.08375. [CrossRef]
50. O'Malley, T.; Bursztein, E.; Long, J.; Chollet, F.; Jin, H.; Invernizzi, L. KerasTuner. 2019. Available online: https://github.com/keras-team/keras-tuner (accessed on 17 July 2025).
51. Vaswani, A.; Shazeer, N.; Parmar, N.; Uszkoreit, J.; Jones, L.; Gomez, A.N.; Kaiser, L.; Polosukhin, I. Attention Is All You Need. *arXiv* **2023**, arXiv:1706.03762. [CrossRef]
52. Nguyen, S.; Nguyen, D.; Nguyen, K.; Than, K.; Bui, H.; Ho, N. Structured Dropout Variational Inference for Bayesian Neural Networks. *arXiv* **2021**, arXiv:2102.07927. [CrossRef]
53. Foong, A.Y.K.; Burt, D.R.; Li, Y.; Turner, R.E. On the Expressiveness of Approximate Inference in Bayesian Neural Networks. *arXiv* **2020**, arXiv:1909.00719. [CrossRef]
54. Joyce, J.M. Kullback-Leibler Divergence. In *International Encyclopedia of Statistical Science*; Lovric, M., Ed.; Springer: Berlin/Heidelberg, Germany, 2011; pp. 720–722. [CrossRef]
55. Murphy, K.P. *Machine Learning: A Probabilistic Perspective*; MIT Press: Cambridge, MA, USA, 2012.

computers

MDPI

Article

An xLSTM–XGBoost Ensemble Model for Forecasting Non-Stationary and Highly Volatile Gasoline Price

Fujiang Yuan [1,2], Xia Huang [3], Hong Jiang [3], Yang Jiang [3], Zihao Zuo [3], Lusheng Wang [3], Yuxin Wang [4], Shaojie Gu [5] and Yanhong Peng [3,*]

1 School of Computer Science and Technology, Taiyuan Normal University, Jinzhong 030619, China; yuanfujiang@ctbu.edu.cn
2 Shanxi Key Laboratory of Intelligent Optimization Computing and Blockchain Technology, Jinzhong 030619, China
3 College of Mechanical Engineering, Chongqing University of Technology, Chongqing 400054, China
4 School of Energy and Power, Jiangsu University of Science and Technology, Zhenjiang 212100, China
5 Magnesium Research Center, Kumamoto University, Kumamoto 860-8555, Japan
* Correspondence: yhpeng@nagoya-u.jp

Abstract: High-frequency fluctuations in the international crude oil market have led to multilevel characteristics in China's domestic refined oil pricing mechanism. To address the poor fitting performance of single deep learning models on oil price data, which hampers accurate gasoline price prediction, this paper proposes a gasoline price prediction method based on a combined xLSTM–XGBoost model. Using gasoline price data from June 2000 to November 2024 in Sichuan Province as a sample, the data are decomposed via STL decomposition to extract trend, residual, and seasonal components. The xLSTM model is then employed to predict the trend and seasonal components, while XGBoost predicts the residual component. Finally, the predictions from both models are combined to produce the final forecast. The experimental results demonstrate that the proposed xLSTM–XGBoost model reduces the MAE by 14.8% compared to the second-best sLSTM–XGBoost model and by 83% compared to the traditional LSTM model, significantly enhancing prediction accuracy.

Keywords: xLSTM; XGBoost; LSTM; gasoline price

1. Introduction

As an indispensable core energy source in the modern industrial system and residents' daily lives, gasoline price changes not only affect production costs and consumer expenditures but are also directly related to national energy security and macroeconomic stability [1]. At a time when the global energy structure has not yet been completely transformed, gasoline prices are still a highly sensitive and important variable in economic activities. In recent years, due to the combined effects of multiple factors such as frequent changes in the international political situation, weak global economic recovery, and rapid development of new energy technologies, the international crude oil market has shown high-frequency and large-scale fluctuations [2,3]. This change has a continuous impact on the crude oil pricing mechanism that is transmitted to the entire energy industry chain through the refined oil pricing mechanism, thereby affecting corporate operating costs, government macroeconomic regulation strategies, and residents' consumption behavior.

China's refined oil price formation mechanism is based on reference to international oil prices, integrating multidimensional factors such as the tax system, refining costs, and transportation costs, presenting a complex multilevel structure. In this context, price changes are not only reflected in the passive response to international oil prices but are also profoundly affected by regional economic activity and logistics and transportation efficiency. Economically developed regions tend to respond quickly to oil price changes, while remote areas have a certain lag due to insufficient supply chain efficiency. This price spatiotemporal heterogeneity has weakened the optimal allocation efficiency of energy resources to a certain extent, exposing the weak links in the current energy regulation system [4].

At the same time, continuous innovation in energy technology accelerates the reshaping of industrial structures. With the rapid popularization of new energy vehicles, the continuous improvement of the penetration rate of alternative energy such as hydrogen energy and biofuels, as well as the continuous improvement of the efficiency of traditional refining processes, the energy supply and demand relationship has undergone profound changes [5]. As an important signal reflecting the dynamics of the energy market, the prediction accuracy of oil prices has increasingly become a key support for the adjustment of national energy strategies, corporate business decisions, and consumer behavior guidance.

In this context, how to effectively extract the trend, cycle, and disturbance information in the gasoline price series and establish a dynamic prediction model with strong robustness and high generalization ability has become an important topic in the cross-research of energy economics and artificial intelligence [6]. Although the traditional linear time series model has a certain degree of explanatory power, its fitting ability is limited when facing non-stationary and highly volatile oil price data. At the same time, the development of deep learning and machine learning technology has provided new ideas for complex time series modeling [7]. By integrating the advantages of multiple models and combining data decomposition and feature extraction methods, it is possible to more comprehensively characterize the characteristics of oil price fluctuations and improve prediction accuracy and model stability.

Therefore, this study proposes an innovative gasoline price prediction framework by integrating heterogeneous models such as xLSTM and XGBoost, wherein we leverage the sequential learning capability of deep learning and the non-linear fitting strength of ensemble learning. This hybrid approach enhances prediction accuracy and robustness compared to traditional single-model methods. The proposed method not only holds significant theoretical value but also demonstrates broad practical applicability. Its results can serve as a scientific reference for government macro control, corporate procurement strategies, and energy planning. Moreover, it contributes to improving the resilience and flexibility of China's energy system and promoting the coordinated development of economic efficiency and energy security.

2. Related Work

At present, the literature on gasoline price prediction encompasses a diverse array of methodologies, reflecting the multifaceted nature of the factors influencing fuel prices. Recent research spans traditional statistical models, econometric frameworks, and cutting-edge machine learning approaches, all aimed at enhancing predictive accuracy and offering actionable insights for policy and economic decision making.

A notable contribution is the study by [8], who investigated the relationship between retail gasoline prices and fatal traffic crashes in the United States between 2007 and 2016. Employing random effects negative binomial regression models, the authors revealed that fluctuations in gasoline prices are significantly correlated with traffic safety outcomes, indicating that fuel pricing can have far-reaching societal implications beyond economic metrics. Within the domain of economic theory, Ref. [9] examined the influence of tax policy on gasoline prices, particularly in settings where consumers have imperfect price information. Their findings suggest that the pass-through rate of commodity taxes depends on the proportion of price-sensitive consumers, underscoring the nuanced interplay between regulatory measures and market behavior. Advancements in mathematical modeling are exemplified by [10], who proposed a novel predictive framework for crude oil prices—closely linked to gasoline prices—using a Multivariate Grey Model integrated with a Markov process. This hybrid approach demonstrated superior accuracy compared to conventional models, highlighting the potential of combining grey system theory with probabilistic methods in energy forecasting. The integration of machine learning into gasoline price prediction is further illustrated by [11], who developed a Variational Autoencoder (VAE)-based model to forecast gasoline orders at gas stations in South Korea. By employing clustering and data augmentation techniques to address data asymmetry, the study exemplifies how machine learning can be effectively applied in contexts with limited or imbalanced datasets. The authors in [12] advanced this line of inquiry by applying an Adaptive Network-based Fuzzy Inference System (ANFIS) to predict gasoline prices using comprehensive data from the U.S. Energy Information Administration. Their results emphasize the critical role of historical patterns and temporal dynamics in improving forecast accuracy, with meaningful implications for strategic planning and energy policy development.

In addition, studies by [13,14] focused on the responsiveness of retail gasoline prices to cost shocks. Utilizing large-scale datasets, these works analyzed the pass-through effects of wholesale price fluctuations, revealing a strong correlation between upstream cost changes and retail pricing behavior, thereby enriching the understanding of market transmission mechanisms. Collectively, the existing body of research underscores the value of a multidisciplinary approach that integrates economic theory, statistical analysis, and artificial intelligence. These contributions not only deepen our comprehension of gasoline price dynamics but also provide critical guidance for policymakers, regulators, and industry stakeholders seeking to navigate the complexities of energy markets. However, there are still some key deficiencies: Most methods rely on a single model and find it difficult to cope with the high volatility and non-linear characteristics of oil prices; there is a lack of effective decomposition of time series components such as trends, cycles, and disturbances, which limits feature extraction and modeling capabilities. There is also a lack of regional research, and it is difficult to reflect local economic differences; fusion models often stay at the superposition of result layers and lack a collaborative modeling mechanism based on data characteristics, failing to give full play to the complementary advantages of multiple models.

To address this problem, this paper proposes a user multifeature gasoline price time series data prediction based on the xLSTM–XGBoost combined model. The main contributions are as follows:

- This study first uses the STL (Seasonal and Trend decomposition using Loess) decomposition method to divide the gasoline price time series into trend terms, periodic terms, and residual terms so as to model and predict subsequences with different characteristics separately.
- In the modeling stage, the xLSTM model is used for the period and trend terms to fully explore the long-term dependencies in the time series; the XGBoost model is used to model the residual term, and its powerful non-linear fitting ability is used to make a fine prediction of the residual error. Through this differentiated model selection and collaborative modeling strategy, the accuracy and robustness of the overall prediction are effectively improved.
- The prediction results of the three sub-models are reversely combined according to the STL decomposition logic to obtain the final prediction value of gasoline prices. In the experimental part, the proposed xLSTM–XGBoost combination model is compared

with single models (such as LSTM, ARIMA, CNN, and ELM). The results show that the proposed combined model outperforms the existing mainstream methods in terms of prediction accuracy and error control and exhibits stronger adaptability and stability.

3. Hybrid Model Based on ARIMA–xLSTM–XGBoost

This section will focus on introducing the STL decomposition method, xLSTM model, and XGBoost model and give the evaluation indicators MAE, RMSE, R^2 for these models.

3.1. STL Decomposition Method

The Seasonal–Trend Decomposition Procedure Based on Loess (STL) is a widely used and highly robust time series analysis technique [15]. Its basic idea is to smooth the time series data through local weighted regression (Loess), thereby effectively decomposing the original series into three independent components: long-term trend, seasonal change, and residual. Compared to traditional time series decomposition techniques such as Classical Decomposition [16], Moving Average Decomposition [17], and Empirical Mode Decomposition (EMD) [18], the STL provides several distinct advantages that make it especially suitable for modeling gasoline prices, which exhibit strong seasonal patterns, non-stationarity, and local volatility. Unlike Classical or Moving Average methods that assume fixed seasonality or are sensitive to noise, the STL is more flexible, allowing seasonality and trends to change over time [19,20]. Moreover, unlike the EMD, which may suffer from mode mixing and which lacks interpretability in financial contexts, The STL's additive model structure produces interpretable components that align well with economic phenomena—such as long-term pricing trends, periodic tax or supply chain effects, and irregular market shocks. Therefore, the STL was selected in this study, as it offers greater robustness, better decomposition clarity, and adaptability to the high-frequency and volatile characteristics of gasoline price data.

In addition, due to its nature based on locally weighted regression, the STL shows stronger robustness when facing real data containing outliers or non-stationary characteristics [21]. The locally weighted processing mechanism can suppress the influence of extreme values and ensure that the decomposition results will not be disturbed by a small number of abnormal points, thereby providing a more stable and reliable input basis for subsequent modeling and prediction. The schematic diagram of the STL decomposition steps is shown in Figure 1 below. Its mathematical expression is as follows:

$$Y_t = S_t + T_t + R_t \tag{1}$$

In the equation, Y_t represents the original time series data; S_t represents the seasonal component, that is, the part of the data that changes periodically over time; T_t is the trend component, which reflects the long-term trend of the data over time; and R_t is the residual component, which contains the remaining part after removing seasonality and trend. The overall process of STL decomposition mainly includes the following key steps:

1. Initial Seasonal Estimation Before starting the formal iterative optimization, the STL first makes a preliminary estimate of the seasonal component of the time series. The specific method is to group the time series according to the cycle length of the data (such as 12 for monthly data) and calculate the average value at the same cycle position (such as monthly or quarterly). The initial seasonal estimate obtained in this way provides a good starting point for the subsequent decomposition process and helps to shorten the convergence time of the model.

2. Iterative Refinement The main body of STL decomposition is an iterative optimization process based on the Loess smoother. In each round of iteration, the seasonal term

and the trend term are updated alternately to continuously improve the accuracy of the decomposition. Specifically, it includes the following sub-processes:

- Seasonal Extraction: In each round of iteration, the seasonal component is first extracted from the original series by removing the currently estimated trend term and residual term. Then, based on the Loess local regression algorithm, the data points at each periodic position (such as January, February, and December each year) are smoothed to obtain a new seasonal estimate. This process helps capture the periodic laws in the sequence while reducing the interference of trend changes.
- Trend Extraction and Smoothing: After removing the currently updated seasonal term from the sequence, a deseasonalized sequence is obtained. At this point, the Loess smoother is applied again to extract the long-term trend component. This trend estimate can flexibly adapt to nonlinear changes, enabling the model to handle complex trend structures.
- Remainder Calculation: The updated seasonal term and trend term are removed from the original sequence together to obtain the residual part. The residual mainly reflects the short-term random fluctuations or abnormal changes in the data and is a concentrated reflection of the prediction error and unexplainable factors. This step is particularly critical for subsequent outlier detection and model optimization.

3. Robust Weighting (Optional) In the case of abnormal data points, the STL method provides a robust version. By calculating the median absolute deviation (MAD) of the residual, we can determine whether each data point is an outlier. For points with large deviations, we assign lower weights to reduce their influence in the estimation process of seasonal and trend terms, thereby improving the robustness and stability of the decomposition. This mechanism enables the STL to have strong anti-interference ability and is suitable for actual data environments with large noise.

4. Result synthesis and output As the iteration proceeds, the seasonal and trend estimates gradually stabilize and finally form three parts: long-term trend, cyclical fluctuation components, and random disturbance terms. The sum of the three constitutes a complete reconstruction of the original sequence. This result can not only be used for sequence visualization and analysis but also provides a strong data foundation for subsequent predictive modeling.

5. Boundary processing strategy Since Loess is a local smoothing method based on a sliding window, it is easy to have insufficient data at both ends of the time series (starting and ending positions), which affects the decomposition quality. To solve this boundary effect, techniques such as mirror extension, trend continuation, or endpoint weighting are usually used to fill in the missing data windows at the boundaries, thereby ensuring the stability and continuity of the decomposition results at both ends of the sequence, which reflect the long-term trend of the data over time; therein, r is the residual component, which contains the remaining part after removing seasonality and trend.

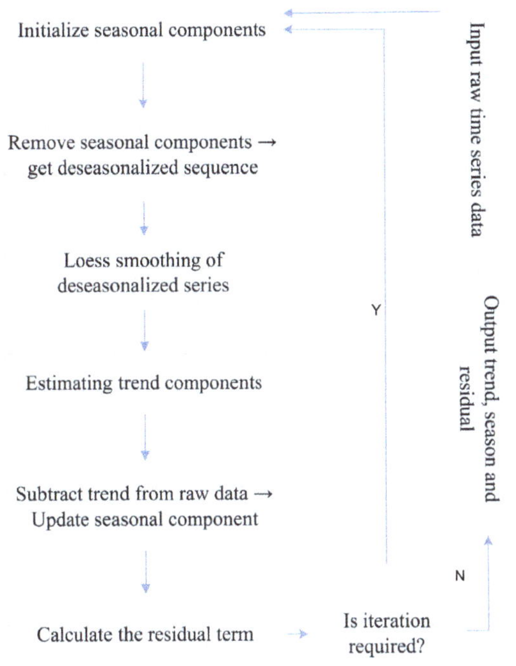

Figure 1. STL decomposition steps diagram.

3.2. xLSTM Model

LSTM (Long Short-Term Memory) is a specialized type of recurrent neural network (RNN) designed to process and predict time series or sequential data with long-term dependencies [22]. It effectively mitigates the vanishing and exploding gradient problems present in traditional RNNs. The fundamental unit of an LSTM consists of three gating mechanisms—the forget gate, input gate, and output gate—along with a cell state [23,24]. These three gates regulate the flow of information using the sigmoid activation function and element-wise multiplication, ensuring that the strength of the information flow is controlled without introducing additional information. The architecture of an LSTM network is illustrated in Figure 2.

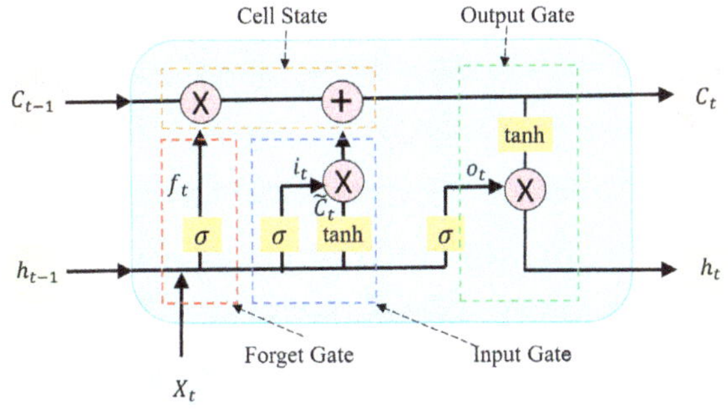

Figure 2. LSTM architecture diagram.

In the Figure 2, C_{t-1} represents the cell state (memory state) at a given time, X_t is the current input, and h_{t-1} denotes the output of the neural unit at time $t-1$. The forget gate's output at time t is f_t, the input gate's output is i_t, and the output gate's output is o_t. The function σ represents the sigmoid activation, while C_t is the cell state at time t, and h_t is the neural unit's output at time t.

To prevent excessive memory retention from interfering with the processing of new inputs, the network selectively forgets certain components of previous cell states while retaining information useful for the current step. The forget gate determines how much of the past information should be preserved in the cell state from time $t-1$. It computes a weight based on x_t and h_{t-1}, processes it through a sigmoid activation function, and produces a vector with values between 0 and 1—where 0 signifies information to be forgotten, and 1 denotes information to be retained. The forget gate is mathematically expressed as follows:

$$f_t = \sigma\left(W_f \cdot [h_{t-1}, X_t] + b_f\right) \tag{2}$$

In Equation (2), W_f represents the forget gate weight, b_f denotes the bias, and σ is the sigmoid function. The input gate determines how much of the current input information should be retained in the state of the neural unit at the current time step, thereby controlling the information that needs to be updated [25]. The input X_t and h_{t-1} output values pass through the input gate and are then combined with the input and output values processed by a tanh function to generate new control parameters. The mathematical expression for the input gate is as follows:

$$i_t = \sigma(W_i \cdot [h_{t-1}, X_t] + b_i) \tag{3}$$

$$\tilde{C}_t = \tanh(W_c \cdot [h_{t-1}, X_t] + b_c) \tag{4}$$

$$C_t = f_t * C_{t-1} + i_t * \tilde{C}_t \tag{5}$$

In Equation (5) , the cell state is updated as C_t, and W_i represents the input gate weight. The output gate determines which information from the current cell state is transmitted to h_t. Both X_t and h_{t-1} first pass through the output gate to define the scope of the output information. Then, in combination with the tanh function, a selected C_t portion of the memory information is processed, and the final neural network output value h_t is determined. The mathematical expression for the output gate is as follows:

$$o_t = \sigma(W_o \cdot [h_{t-1}, X_t] + b_o) \tag{6}$$

$$h_t = o_t * \tanh(C_t) \tag{7}$$

In Equations (6) and (7), W_o represents the output gate weight.

The Structural Long Short-Term Memory (sLSTM) network represents a significant advancement over the conventional LSTM model by introducing several architectural and functional enhancements aimed at improving the stability, flexibility, and learning capacity of sequential models [26]. Specifically, sLSTM incorporates exponential gating mechanisms, along with normalization and standardization operations, which together contribute to a more robust and efficient training process. The adoption of an exponential activation function provides finer-grained control over memory retention and forgetting, allowing the network to dynamically adjust the flow of information based on input context. Moreover, to address the instability often encountered during numerical computations in training, sLSTM employs a standardization strategy that accumulates the element-wise product of the input gate and the subsequent forget gates. This approach helps to stabilize gradient propagation and improve convergence behavior. Beyond these improvements, sLSTM is also designed to support multiple memory units within a single time step and introduces a memory mixing mechanism via recurrent links, enabling the model to better capture complex dependencies and interactions across different memory paths. Figure 3a shows the variant sLSTM structure [27]. The sLSTM architecture is divided into three levels from top to bottom: the top layer consists of multiple PF-3/4 modules, which may be used for feature extraction or input preprocessing; the middle layer is composed of GN (gated network) to coordinate multiple sLSTM units with recurrent connections to achieve deep integration of sequence information; the bottom layer includes basic modules such as Switch, Conv4, and LN (layer normalization), combined with Exponential Gating and Scalar Updating mechanisms, to further enhance the dynamic control and state update capabilities of input data. sLSTM emphasizes clear structure and controllable information flow, and is suitable for low- to medium-complexity sequence modeling tasks [28].

In contrast, the Matrix LSTM (mLSTM) extends the representational capacity of LSTM by altering the structure of its memory unit—from a scalar to a matrix form—thereby significantly enhancing its ability to encode and store richer information representations [29–31]. This structural change allows the model to concurrently manage multiple key–value memory pairs, making it particularly suitable for tasks requiring complex relational modeling or fine-grained feature retention. Additionally, mLSTM addresses a fundamental limitation of standard LSTMs: their inherent sequential dependency across time steps, which limits parallel computation and increases training time. By removing direct hidden state connections between consecutive time steps, mLSTM enables parallel processing, thus improving computational efficiency [32]. To effectively update and manage the expanded memory structure, mLSTM introduces a covariance-inspired update rule, which facilitates the learning of nuanced patterns and improves the retrieval accuracy of infrequent or rare information instances. Figure 3b shows the variant mLSTM structure. The mLSTM architecture is more complex. In addition to PF-3/4, GN, and Switch modules, its core consists of multiple mLSTM units and introduces the LSkip (cross-layer skip connection) structure to enhance the information flow between different levels, thereby alleviating the gradient problem in deep network training. In addition to common modules, the bottom layer also includes the PF-2 module and integrates the Matrix Memory and Covariance Updating mechanisms, enabling the model to capture more complex correlations between input features. Through Exponential Gating and multidimensional memory structures, mLSTM is more suitable for processing sequence data tasks with complex structures and strong dynamic changes.

xLSTM is a systematic extension and optimization of the traditional LSTM architecture. Its structure integrates a variety of advanced mechanisms to handle complex sequence tasks more efficiently. Its basic module still uses the classic LSTM structure. The core is to introduce memory cells, among which the constant error carousel ensures the continuous propagation of information in time, effectively alleviates the gradient vanishing problem, and enables the model to have the ability to model long-term dependencies. At the same time, the Sigmoid gating mechanism includes an input gate, a forget gate and an output gate, whereby it controls the retention, discarding, and output of information, thereby accurately adjusting state updates. In the training and inference process, the recurrent mechanism [33,34] enables the model to dynamically update its internal state according to the historical context, thereby achieving a gradual understanding of the sequence data.

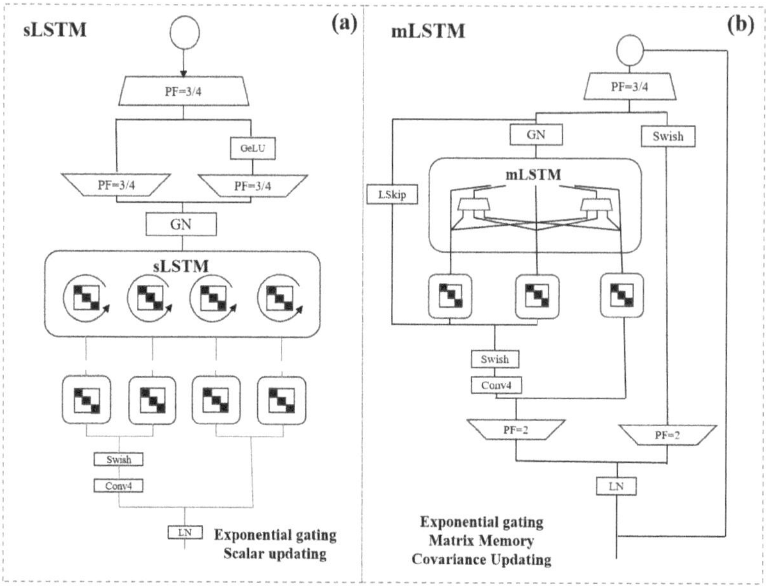

Figure 3. Variants of the Long Short-Term Memory (LSTM) architecture. Among them, (**a**) is the sLSTM model architecture diagram. (**b**) is the mLSTM model architecture diagram.

On this basis, xLSTM introduces two types of improved modules, sLSTM and mLSTM, which are optimized for information flow and memory structure, respectively. sLSTM introduces exponential gating, which provides more detailed information control capabilities than traditional Sigmoid functions, allowing the model to dynamically adjust the gating strength according to different inputs. In addition, the new memory mixing mechanism builds a more efficient fusion channel between new and old information, allowing the model to absorb and utilize new inputs more agilely while retaining historical memory and improving the model's ability to learn complex and nonlinear data patterns.

Complementary to this, mLSTM strengthens the model's memory structure and training efficiency. It not only uses exponential gating but also further introduces matrix memory, expanding the memory unit from scalar to matrix form and greatly enhancing the model's ability to express and manage high-dimensional information, especially for high-dimensional data scenarios such as images and multivariate time series [35]. In order to meet the needs of large-scale data training, mLSTM is also designed with a parallel training mechanism, breaking the traditional serial structure, so that the model training process can more efficiently utilize parallel computing resources (such as GPUs), significantly shortening the training time. At the same time, its Covariance Update Rule optimizes the synergistic relationship between parameters by analyzing the statistical characteristics of the input data, speeding up the model convergence and improving the training stability. These improved modules were unified into xLSTM Blocks with a topological structure. Through the synergy between modules, such as the flexible alternation of gating mechanisms and the complementary fusion of memory management strategies, the entire model has stronger feature expression capabilities and task adaptability. The xLSTM architecture diagram is shown in Figure 4 below.

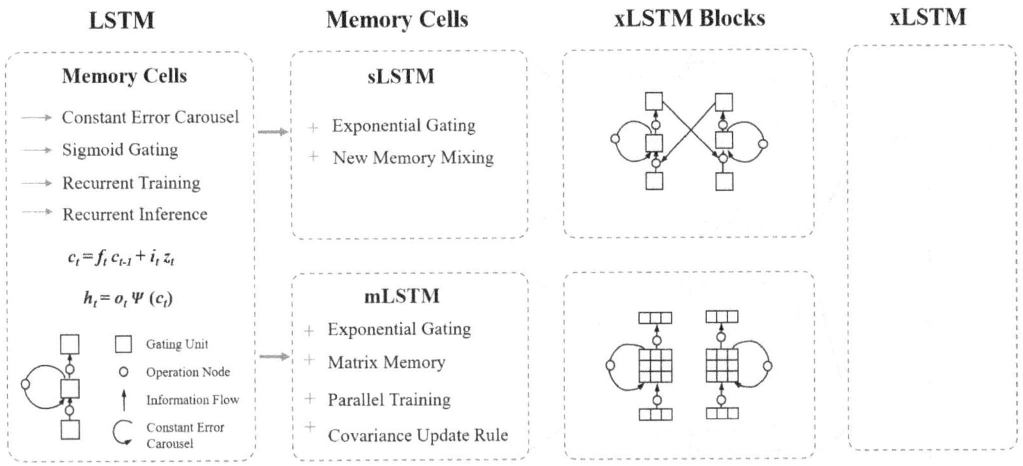

Figure 4. xLSTM architecture diagram.

Table 1 compares the key features of the different LSTM variants (LSTM, xLSTM, mLSTM, and sLSTM). The traditional LSTM effectively alleviates the gradient vanishing problem through the gating mechanism and is suitable for general time series modeling. On this basis, xLSTM introduces additional contextual connections and deeper hierarchical structures, enhancing the modeling capabilities of long-term dependencies and complex contexts [36,37]. mLSTM improves the expressiveness of the model by introducing multiplicative interactions between input and hidden states and is suitable for scenarios such as natural language processing. sLSTM is designed for non-sequential data such as graph structures and can model structural or spatial dependencies. This comparison highlights the advantages of xLSTM in processing complex time series data and capturing deep features, which just fits the modeling needs of this article for the long-term dependency and high volatility of gasoline price series.

Table 1. Comparison of LSTM variants.

Model	Full Name	Key Improvements	Suitable Scenarios	Advantages
LSTM	Long Short-Term Memory	Gating mechanism to suppress gradient vanishing	Sequence modeling, language models, time series	Stable and widely used
xLSTM	Extended LSTM	Additional context connections , deeper architecture	Long-range dependencies, complex contexts	Enhanced ability to model long-term dependencies
mLSTM	Multiplicative LSTM	Multiplicative interaction between input and hidden state	Language modeling, NLP	Stronger expressiveness and flexible information control
sLSTM	Structural/Spatial LSTM	Modeling structural or spatial dependencies (e.g., graphs)	GNNs, image and video analysis	Capable of handling dependencies in non-sequential data

3.3. XGBoost Model

XGBoost [38] is an efficient and scalable gradient boosting framework. Its core idea is to build decision trees incrementally using an additive model, minimizing prediction errors by optimizing the objective function while also constraining model complexity to improve generalization ability and stability [39]. In each iteration, XGBoost uses a second-order Taylor expansion to approximate the loss function, thereby capturing the variation in the objective function more accurately and accelerating the convergence rate [40]. The objective function of XGBoost combines training error and a regularization term, and its expression is given by

$$Obj = \sum_{i=1}^{n} l(y_i, \hat{y}^{(t)}) + \sum_{k=1}^{t} \Omega(f_k)^{\iota} \tag{8}$$

$$\Omega(f_k) = \gamma T + \frac{1}{2}\lambda ||\omega||^2 \tag{9}$$

where $l(y_i, \hat{y}^{(t)})$ represents the loss value for the *i-th* sample, and $\hat{y}^{(t)}$ is the prediction result of the model after the t-th iteration. The regularization term $\Omega(f_k)$ is used to penalize model complexity, and γ and λ are the tuning parameters for the number of leaf nodes and the weights of the leaf nodes, respectively.

In each iteration, the model updates the overall output by adding the prediction contribution of the new tree, and its mathematical expression is

$$\hat{y}^{(t)} = \hat{y}^{(t-1)} + f_t(x_i) \tag{10}$$

where $f_t(x_i)$ represents the prediction contribution of the t-th tree for the sample x_i. This formula reflects the detailed process of how XGBoost approximates the model by progressively accumulating the outputs of decision trees.

3.4. xLSTM–XGBoost Combined Model Prediction Process

The training dataset of this model consisted of the gasoline price data from June 2000 to November 2024 in Sichuan Province, China, with a total of 256 data points. Before predicting gasoline prices, the STL decomposition method was used to decompose the dataset into trend values, residuals, and period values. The STL decomposition method used an additive model and defined a period length of 10. The original sequence was first smoothed using the moving average method to eliminate seasonal fluctuations and noise, capture long-term trends, and obtain trend values. Then, in the sequence after detrending, the mean was calculated by segment according to the period (10 time points) to generate a fixed and repeated seasonal pattern to obtain the period value. Finally, the trend value and period value were subtracted from the original data in turn, and the remaining part was used as the residual to represent unexplained random fluctuations. After STL decomposed the original data, the xLSTM model with adjusted hidden layers was used to predict the trend value and period value, and then the XGBoost model was used to predict the residual data. Finally, the results of the xLSTM and XGBoost predictions were combined using the additive model to obtain the final prediction result. The prediction process of the xLSTM–XGBoost hybrid model is shown in Figure 5 below.

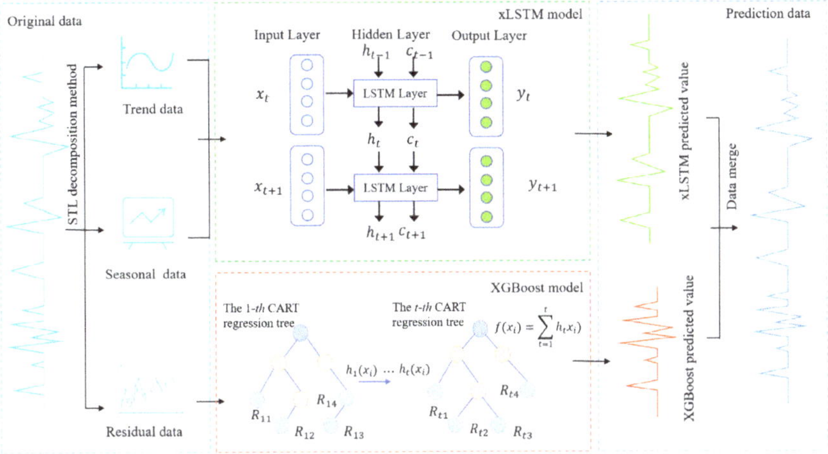

Figure 5. xLSTM–XGBoost combined model prediction flow chart.

3.5. Evaluation Metrics

This paper usef three representative evaluation metrics to assess the prediction accuracy: the Root Mean Square Error (RMSE), the Mean Absolute Error (MAE), and the Coefficient of Determination (R^2). The mathematical expressions for these evaluation metrics are as follows:

$$\text{RMSE} = \sqrt{\frac{1}{n}\sum_{i=1}^{n}(F_i - R_i)^2} \tag{11}$$

$$\text{MAE} = \sum_{i=1}^{n}\frac{|F_i - R_i|}{R_i} \tag{12}$$

$$R^2 = 1 - \frac{\sum_{i=1}^{n}(F_i - A_i)^2}{\sum_{i=1}^{n}(F_i - R_i)^2} \tag{13}$$

where F_i is the predicted value for the i-th data point, R_i is the actual value for the i-th data point, n is the sequence length (number of samples), and A_i is the mean of all samples. Smaller values of the RMSE and MAE indicate smaller prediction errors and higher accuracy. R^2 takes values between 0 and 1, with a value closer to 1 indicating better fit of the neural network to the data, thus reflecting better model fitting ability.

4. Experimental Design and Results Analysis

The development tool selected for this paper was PyCharm, with the programming language Python 3.11.0. The Graphics Processing Unit (GPU) used was an NVIDIA GeForce GTX 4060, and the Central Processing Unit (CPU) was the i7-13600H, with 6 GB of video memory. The experiment was based on a simulation-generated dataset for prediction, where the dataset was divided into 80% training data and 20% testing data for offset prediction.

4.1. STL Decomposition of Original Data

The dataset used in this study features real-world observational data from the Sichuan Province Data Open Platform, covering monthly gasoline price data from June 2000 to November 2024, with a total of 256 data points. The platform is led by the local government and continuously updated, with high authority and reliability. To ensure data quality, we performed outlier detection and missing value processing after collection to ensure the integrity and consistency of the input data. Due to the representative economic structure and geographical location of Sichuan Province, the selected data offer a certain reference value in capturing regional market volatility and policy transmission mechanisms. In the process of feature processing, the trend value, cycle value, and residual were obtained by decomposing the data using the STL additive model. Figure 6 shows the original data graph of the STL decomposition. This part selects half of the dataset for visualization, including the original data graph, the trend data graph after STL decomposition, the cycle data graph, and the residual graph from top to bottom.

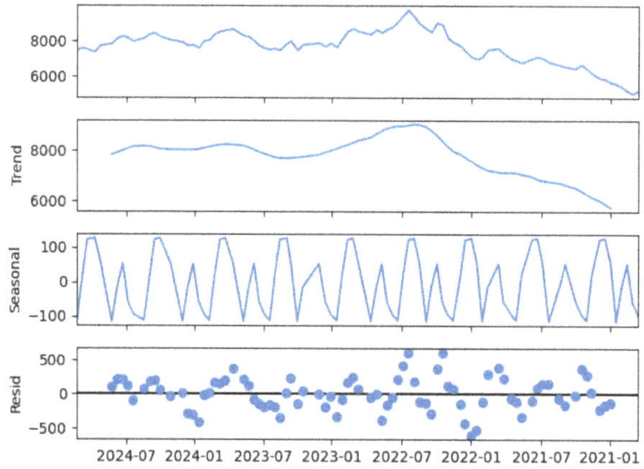

Figure 6. STL decomposition of the original data.

4.2. *xLSTM Modeling of Trend and Seasonal Values*

The experiment was conducted using a univariate time series dataset (Gasoline Price Trends Dataset), where the data were normalized with MinMaxScaler and split into 80% training and 20% testing sets. Each input sequence consisted of 9 consecutive time steps. Four models were compared: the standard PyTorch LSTM, the parameter-sharing sLSTM, the multihead mLSTM, and the hybrid xLSTM with a combined structure ("msm"). All models took a single input feature (input size = 1) and utilized 64 hidden units. For the multihead variants, two attention heads were employed. The training process ran for 200 epochs with a batch size of 64, using Root Mean Square Error (RMSE) as the loss function and the Adam optimizer for weight updates. Adam was chosen due to its proven ability to adaptively adjust learning rates for individual parameters using moment estimates, which enhances convergence speed and training stability in complex deep learning models. This is particularly important in time series tasks involving volatile and non-stationary data, such as gasoline price prediction. Furthermore, Adam effectively balances bias correction and variance reduction in gradient updates, making it a suitable choice for preventing the optimizer-induced bias that may otherwise distort the learning dynamics in hybrid models like xLSTM [41]. Performance was evaluated based on Mean Absolute Error (MAE), Root Mean Square Error (RMSE), and the Coefficient of Determination (R^2). After training, for the data using the LSTM model, the relationship between the true trend value and the predicted trend value was obtained, as shown in Figure 7. In the figure, the blue line represents the original data, and the yellow line represents the result of the trend value prediction. It can be shown from the figure that the model fit is still relatively good.

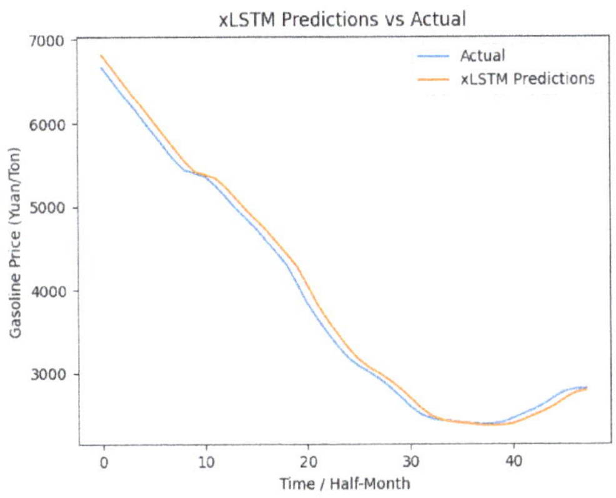

(**a**) xLSTM predicts trend and seasonal values

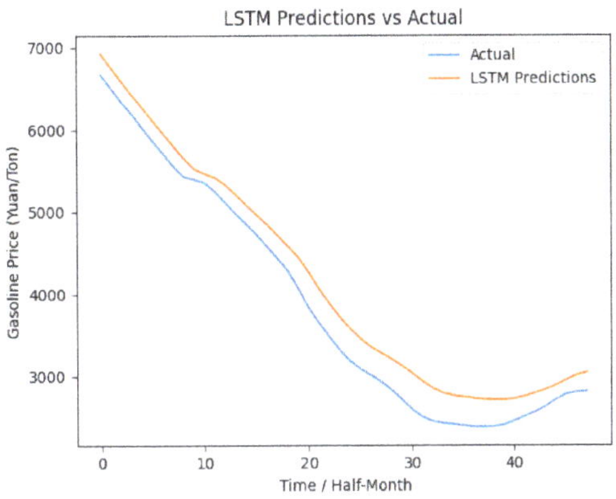

(**b**) LSTM predicts trend and seasonal values

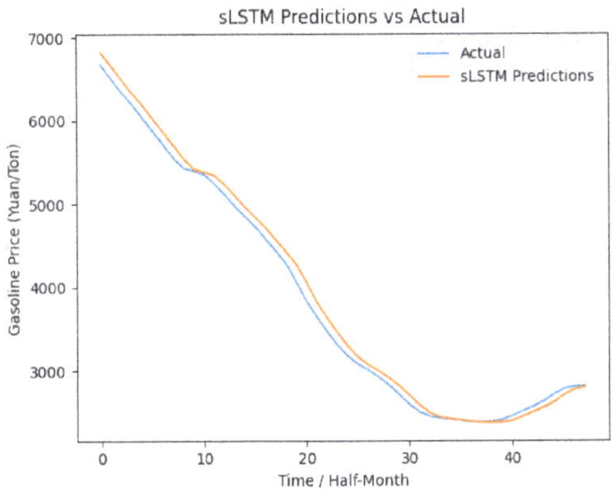

(**c**) sLSTM predicts trend and seasonal values

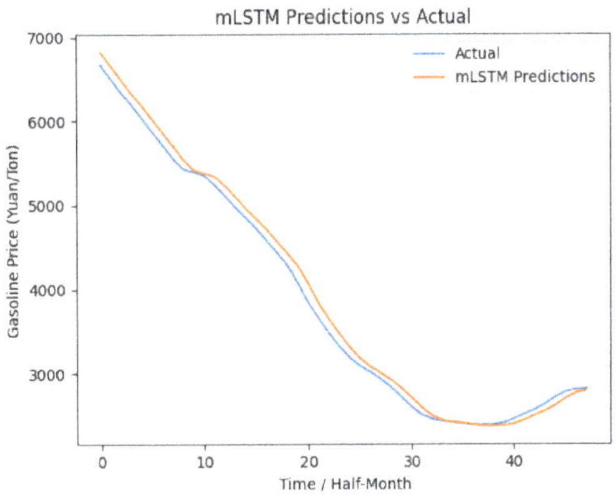

(**d**) mLSTM predicts trend and seasonal values

Figure 7. Comparison chart of trend and seasonal value predictions by various models.

As can be seen in Figure 7, the LSTM variant model yielded a better prediction effect than the LSTM model, and from the model evaluation indicators in Table 2, it can be seen that the prediction effect error of the xLSTM model is lower, and the predicted value is more in line with the true value.

Table 2. Comparison of LSTM variants in combining trend and seasonal values.

Models	MAE	RMSE	R^2
LSTM	0.3443	0.4137	0.9168
xLSTM	0.0914	0.1118	0.9948
sLSTM	0.1092	0.1321	0.9929
mLSTM	0.1222	0.1468	0.9911

4.3. XGBoost Modeling of Residual Values

Using XGBoost to model the residuals of time series forecasts offers significant advantages. While primary models such as LSTM or ARIMA capture the main trend and seasonality, they may overlook subtle non-linear patterns or irregularities. XGBoost, as a powerful ensemble learner, can effectively learn from these residual errors by modeling their structure, leading to enhanced prediction accuracy. Additionally, XGBoost's robustness to outliers, built-in regularization, and handling of complex feature interactions make it an excellent choice for residual correction in hybrid forecasting frameworks. This approach improves not only the precision but also the interpretability and stability of the overall time series prediction.

The XGBoost regression model used in this article set 500 trees (n-estimators = 500), a learning rate of 0.1 (learning—rate = 0.1) and a maximum depth of 3 (max-depth = 3), which was done to prevent overfitting while ensuring generalization ability, making it suitable for extracting non-linear features in time series residuals; at the same time, random-state = 42 was set to ensure that the results would be reproducible. The overall model structure is lightweight and suitable for processing stable or less noisy time series data. The following Figure 8 shows the comparison between the prediction results of the XGBoost model for the residual data and the actual values.

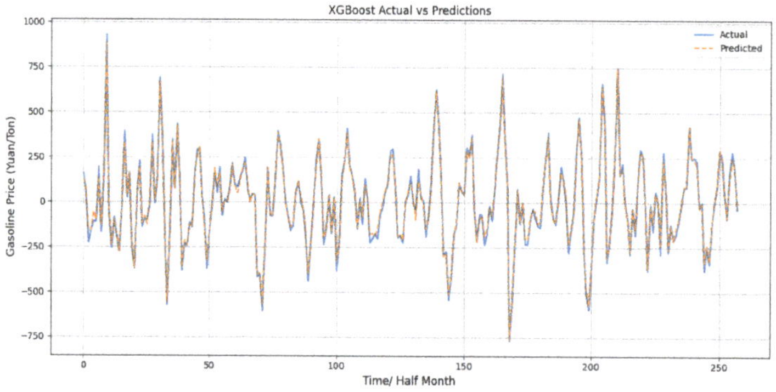

Figure 8. Comparison of XGBoost model prediction residual values.

4.4. Analysis of Combined Model Prediction Results

The xLSTM–XGBoost combination model proposed in this paper adopts the STL decomposition addition strategy for decomposition. Therefore, the trend and seasonal values predicted by xLSTM and the residual values predicted by XGBoost were added and combined according to the time series to reconstruct the final predicted values. The comparison between the predicted value and the true value of the combination model is shown in Figure 9.

As can be shown from Figure 9, the xLSTM–XGBoost, mLSTM–XGBoost, and sLSTM–XGBoost models based on LSTM variants outperformed the traditional LSTM–XGBoost model in gasoline price prediction. Their predicted values are more closely aligned with the actual values, demonstrating better prediction accuracy and stability. This improvement is attributed to the architectural enhancements in the variant LSTM models: xLSTM introduces extended memory gating and hierarchical structures, mLSTM incorporates matrix-based memory representations for better feature encoding, and sLSTM adopts exponential gating and structural control mechanisms. These modifications significantly enhance the models' abilities to capture long-term dependencies, handle non-linear patterns, and adapt to local fluctuations in volatile time series.

Furthermore, an examination of the prediction results reveals that the largest errors across all models tended to occur during historically volatile periods, such as the global financial crisis (2008–2009), when oil prices experienced abrupt changes. During these intervals, simpler models like LSTM–XGBoost and ARIMA struggled to adapt to the sudden structural shifts in the data, resulting in higher deviation from the ground truth. In contrast, xLSTM–XGBoost showed a significantly smaller prediction gap in these challenging periods, indicating its superior adaptability to non-stationary patterns and extreme volatility.

Compared to other models shown in Table 3, the xLSTM–XGBoost model achieved the lowest MAE and RMSE, with values of 0.0961 and 0.1184, respectively, and the highest R^2 of 0.9942. These metrics reflect not only improved accuracy but also enhanced model fit and robustness. Specifically, the xLSTM–XGBoost model reduced the MAE by 14.8% compared to the second-best sLSTM–XGBoost and by 83% compared to the standard LSTM model, thereby validating the effectiveness of the proposed hybrid framework in modeling complex and highly volatile gasoline price series.

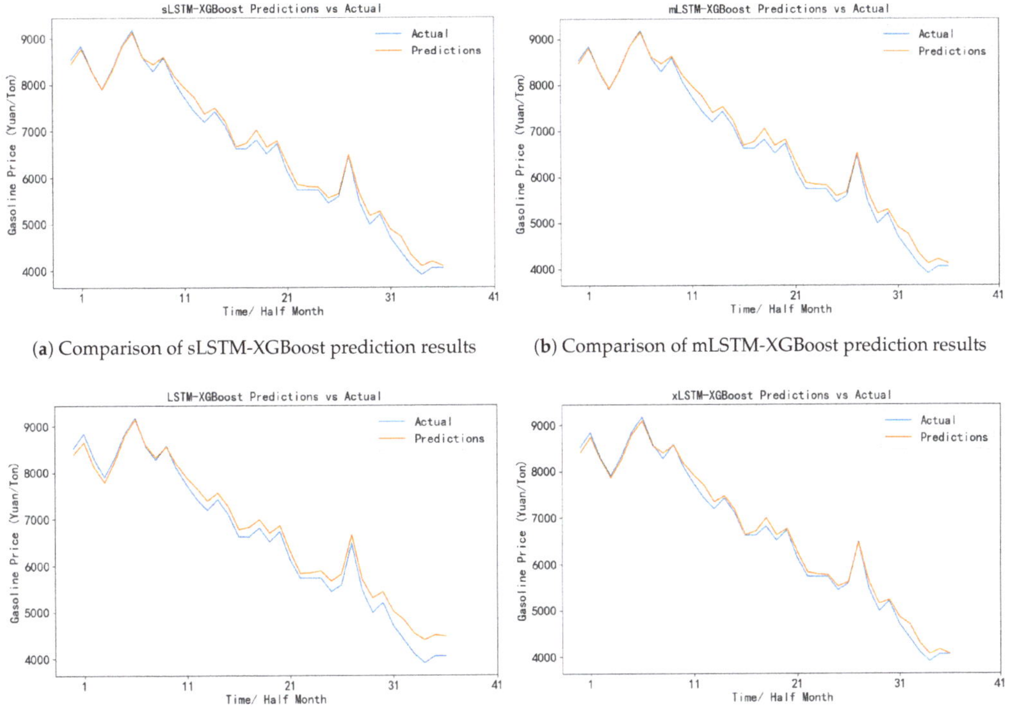

(**a**) Comparison of sLSTM-XGBoost prediction results (**b**) Comparison of mLSTM-XGBoost prediction results

(**c**) Comparison of LSTM-XGBoost prediction results (**d**) Comparison of xLSTM-XGBoost prediction results

Figure 9. Inner Mongolia dataset Comparison of gasoline price forecasts by various combination models based on Sichuan Province dataset.

Table 3. Comparison of evaluation indicators for various combination models based on Sichuan Province dataset.

Models	MAE	RMSE	R^2	Training Time (s)
LSTM	0.5644	0.6175	0.8041	35.2
xLSTM	0.3114	0.3906	0.9216	48.6
sLSTM	0.2506	0.3192	0.9476	45.9
mLSTM	0.2619	0.3293	0.9442	49.7
ARIMA	0.6396	0.7203	0.7283	6.3
CNN	0.4178	0.5231	0.1486	38.4
ELM	0.3130	0.4257	0.9154	12.5
LSTM–XGBoost	0.1949	0.2298	0.9782	59.8
sLSTM–XGBoost	0.1129	0.1389	0.9920	57.3
mLSTM–XGBoost	0.1279	0.1547	0.9901	61.2
xLSTM–XGBoost	0.0961	0.1184	0.9942	63.9

In order to verify the superiority of the xLSTM–XGBoost combination model over the sLSTM, mLSTM, LSTM, ARIMA, CNN, and ELM models in predicting gasoline price time series data, the prediction results of the seven models were tested by the MAE, RMSE, and R^2 evaluation indicators. The results are shown in Table 3. It can be seen from the Table 3 that the evaluation indicators of the xLSTM–XGBoost combination model are superior to those of other single models in all aspects and have a good prediction accuracy. The results of a series of experiments show that the proposed xLSTM–XGBoost model reduced the MAE by 14.8% compared to the sLSTM–XGBoost model and reduced the MAE by 83% compared to the traditional LSTM model. In order to verify the superiority of the xLSTM–XGBoost combination model over the sLSTM, mLSTM, LSTM, ARIMA, CNN, and ELM models in predicting gasoline price time series data, we not only compared the prediction results using the MAE, RMSE, and R^2 but also conducted statistical significance testing on the performance differences. Specifically, we performed paired sample t-tests and Wilcoxon signed-rank tests on the prediction errors (MAE and RMSE) between the proposed xLSTM–XGBoost model and other baselines on the test set. As shown in Table 4, the performance improvements of xLSTM–XGBoost over other models were ($p < 0.05$) for both MAE and RMSE, indicating that the observed improvements are unlikely due to random chance. This provides strong statistical support for the conclusion that the proposed model demonstrates significantly better performance than the comparative methods.

Table 4. Statistical significance testing (xLSTM–XGBoost vs. Others)—*t*-test *p*-values for MAE and RMSE.

Model	*t*-Test *p* (MAE)	*t*-Test *p* (RMSE)
LSTM	1.08×10^{-14}	3.81×10^{-15}
xLSTM	3.50×10^{-10}	3.61×10^{-11}
sLSTM	2.04×10^{-8}	1.39×10^{-11}
mLSTM	2.91×10^{-8}	5.98×10^{-10}
ARIMA	1.23×10^{-15}	9.43×10^{-16}
CNN	9.83×10^{-12}	1.78×10^{-12}
ELM	5.45×10^{-9}	4.75×10^{-12}
LSTM–xgboost	1.15×10^{-6}	3.30×10^{-8}
sLSTM–xgboost	8.53×10^{-2}	9.17×10^{-3}
mLSTM–xgboost	3.41×10^{-2}	1.51×10^{-3}

4.5. Model Generalization Analysis

In order to verify the generalization of the proposed xLSTM–XGBoost model in a limited range, we selected the gasoline price dataset from 2000 to 2024 in Inner Mongolia to verify the generalization of the model and used xLSTM–XGBoost to compare the LSTM–XGBoost, sLSTM–XGBoost, and mLSTM–XGBoost hybrid models.

As shown in Figure 10 and Table 5 below, the evaluation results of different combination models on this dataset show that the MAE of the LSTM–XGBoost model came out to 0.5581, the RMSE came out to 0.5827, and the R came out to 0.8258. Compared to the other models, its predicted value deviates greatly from the true value, and the fitting effect is poor. The accuracy results of the sLSTM–XGBoost model and the mLSTM–XGBoost model are further improved by comparison. The xLSTM–XGBoost model performed best, with a MAE of 0.1091, a RMSE of 0.1274, and an R of 0.9917, with the highest prediction accuracy and the best data fitting effect. It can be seen that the xLSTM–XGBoost hybrid model also has relatively good accuracy on other datasets.

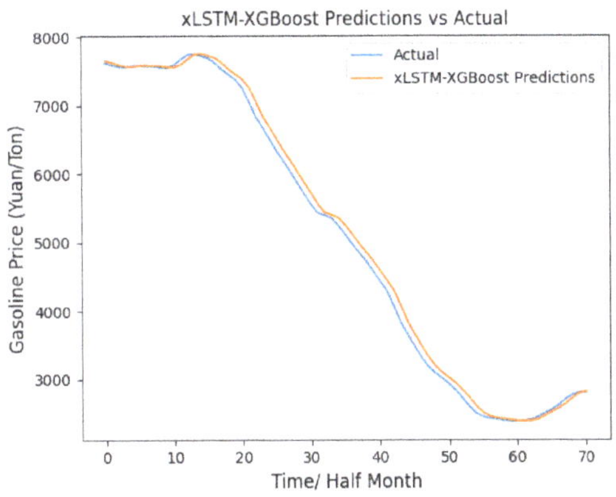

(**a**) Comparison of xLSTM-XGBoost prediction results

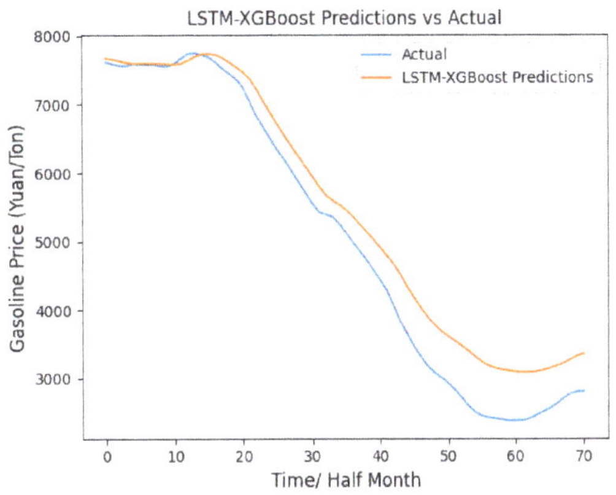

(**b**) Comparison of LSTM-XGBoost prediction results

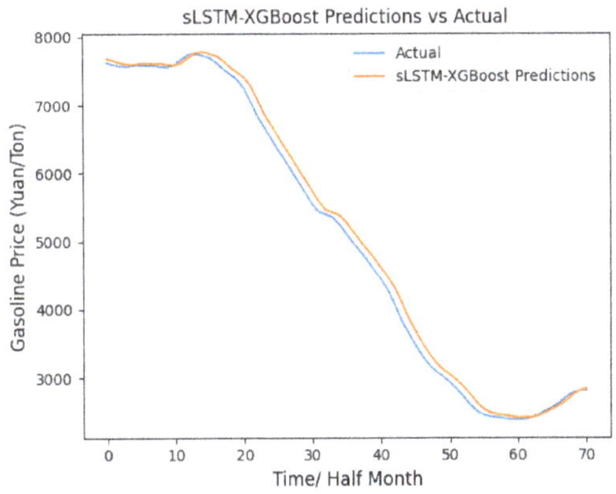

(**c**) Comparison of sLSTM-XGBoost prediction results

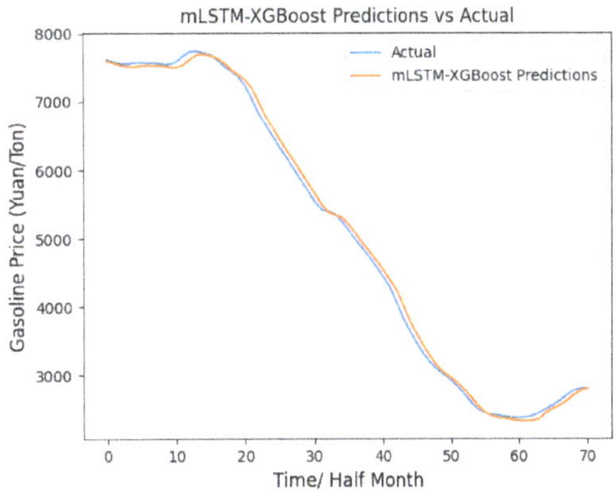

(**d**) Comparison of mLSTM-XGBoost prediction results

Figure 10. Comparison of gasoline price forecasts by various combination models based on the Inner Mongolia dataset.

Table 5. Comparison of evaluation indicators for various combination models based on the Inner Mongolia dataset.

Models	MAE	RMSE	R^2
LSTM–XGBoost	0.5581	0.5827	0.8258
sLSTM–XGBoost	0.1275	0.1476	0.9889
mLSTM–XGBoost	0.1113	0.1297	0.9913
xLSTM–XGBoost	0.1091	0.1274	0.9917

5. Conclusions

In order to solve the problem that a single deep learning model has a poor fitting effect on oil price data, which makes it difficult to predict gasoline prices, this paper proposes an xLSTM–XGBoost combined model to predict gasoline prices. First, the gasoline price time series data are decomposed into trend values, period values, and residuals using STL decomposition. Then, the xLSTM model is used to predict the trend values and seasonal values, and XGBoost is used to predict the residual values. Finally, the prediction results of the two models are combined to obtain the final prediction results. The experimental results show that compared to the classic LSTM, ARIMA, CNN, and other single models, the proposed xLSTM–XGBoost combined model has higher prediction accuracy and better fitting results.

However, this study still has several limitations. First, although STL decomposition improves interpretability, it relies on fixed periodicity assumptions and may not adapt well to structural breaks or regime shifts in the time series. Secondly, the model does not yet incorporate external influencing variables (e.g., international crude oil futures, exchange rates, and macroeconomic indicators), which could potentially enhance its prediction accuracy and explanatory power.

Future research will focus on the following directions: (1) exploring adaptive decomposition techniques (e.g., wavelet transform or empirical mode decomposition) to handle non-periodic or evolving patterns and (2) integrating exogenous variables and developing a multivariate version of the hybrid model. Furthermore, introducing uncertainty quantification methods (such as Bayesian inference or quantile regression) will be considered to improve the reliability and decision-making value of the predictions.

Author Contributions: F.Y.: Conceptualization, Methodology, Writing—Original Draft, Writing—Review and Editing. X.H.: Data Curation, Investigation. H.J.: Formal Analysis, Validation. Y.J.: Data Curation, Methodology. Z.Z.: Software, Visualization. L.W.: Methodology, Validation. Y.W.: Resources. S.G.: Investigation, Data Curation. Y.P.: Writing—Review and Editing, Funding Acquisition. All authors have read and agreed to the published version of the manuscript.

Funding: This paper was supported by the Innovative Research Group of the Chongqing Municipal Education Commission (CXQT19026) and the Cooperative Project between the Chinese Academy of Sciences and the University in Chongqing (HZ2021011). Moreover, this work was supported by the Research Startup Fund of the Chongqing University of Technology (0119240197).

Informed Consent Statement: Informed consent was obtained from all subjects involved in the study.

Data Availability Statement: The dataset used in our paper comes from the Sichuan Province Data Open Platform in China. If you need the dataset, please contact the first author to obtain it.

Acknowledgments: This work was supported by equipment funded through the "Intelligent Connected New Energy Vehicle Teaching System" project of the Chongqing University of Technology under the national initiative "Promote large-scale equipment renewals and trade-ins of consumer goods."

Conflicts of Interest: The authors declare that they have no known competing financial interests or personal relationships that could have appeared to influence the work reported in this paper.

References

1. Hasanov, F.J.; Javid, M.; Mikayilov, J.I.; Shabaneh, R.; Darandary, A.; Alyamani, R. Macroeconomic and sectoral effects of natural gas price: Policy insights from a macroeconometric model. *Energy Econ.* **2025**, *143*, 108233. [CrossRef]
2. Mao, Z.; Suzuki, S.; Nabae, H.; Miyagawa, S.; Suzumori, K.; Maeda, S. Machine learning-enhanced soft robotic system inspired by rectal functions to investigate fecal incontinence. *Bio-Des. Manuf.* **2025**, *8*, 482–494. [CrossRef]
3. Mao, Z.; Kobayashi, R.; Nabae, H.; Suzumori, K. Multimodal strain sensing system for shape recognition of tensegrity structures by combining traditional regression and deep learning approaches. *IEEE Robot. Autom. Lett.* **2024**, *9*, 10050–10056. [CrossRef]
4. Khanna, A.A.; Dubernet, I.; Jochem, P. Do car drivers respond differently to fuel price changes? Evidence from German household data. *Transportation* **2025**, *52*, 579–613. [CrossRef]
5. Kamocsai, L.; Ormos, M. Modeling gasoline price volatility. *Financ. Res. Lett.* **2025**, *73*, 106657. [CrossRef]
6. Safaei, N.; Zhou, C.; Safaei, B.; Masoud, A. Gasoline prices and their relationship to the number of fatal crashes on US roads. *Transp. Eng.* **2021**, *4*, 100053. [CrossRef]
7. Mao, Z.; Bai, X.; Peng, Y.; Shen, Y. Design, modeling, and characteristics of ring-shaped robot actuated by functional fluid. *J. Intell. Mater. Syst. Struct.* **2024**, *35*, 1459–1470. [CrossRef]
8. Montag, F.; Sagimuldina, A.; Schnitzer, M. *Does Tax Policy Work When Consumers Have Imperfect Price Information? Theory and Evidence*; Technical Report, CESifo Working Paper; The MIT Press: Cambridge, MA, USA, 2021.

9. Indrakala, S. A study on mathematical methods for predicting accuracy of crude oil futures prices by multi grey Markov model. *Malaya J. Mat.* **2021**, *9*, 621–626. [CrossRef]
10. Li, W.; Becker, D.M. Day-ahead electricity price prediction applying hybrid models of LSTM-based deep learning methods and feature selection algorithms under consideration of market coupling. *Energy* **2021**, *237*, 121543. [CrossRef]
11. Noel, M. Do retail gasoline prices respond asymmetrically to cost shocks? The influence of Edgeworth Cycles. *Rand J. Econ.* **2009**, *40*, 582–595. [CrossRef]
12. Yoon, S.; Park, M. Prediction of gasoline orders at gas stations in South Korea using VAE-based machine learning model to address data asymmetry. *Appl. Sci.* **2023**, *13*, 11124. [CrossRef]
13. Eliwa, E.H.I.; El Koshiry, A.M.; Abd El-Hafeez, T.; Omar, A. Optimal gasoline price predictions: Leveraging the ANFIS regression model. *Int. J. Intell. Syst.* **2024**, *2024*, 8462056. [CrossRef]
14. He, M.; Qian, X. Forecasting tourist arrivals using STL-XGBoost method. *Tour. Econ.* **2025**, 13548166241313411. [CrossRef]
15. Cardona, G.A.; Kamale, D.; Vasile, C.I. STL and wSTL control synthesis: A disjunction-centric mixed-integer linear programming approach. *Nonlinear Anal. Hybrid Syst.* **2025**, *56*, 101576. [CrossRef]
16. Luo, S.; Lambert, N.; Liang, P.; Cirio, M. Quantum-classical decomposition of Gaussian quantum environments: A stochastic pseudomode model. *PRX Quantum* **2023**, *4*, 030316. [CrossRef]
17. Singh, S.; Parmar, K.S.; Kumar, J.; Makkhan, S.J.S. Development of new hybrid model of discrete wavelet decomposition and autoregressive integrated moving average (ARIMA) models in application to one month forecast the casualties cases of COVID-19. *Chaos Solitons Fractals* **2020**, *135*, 109866. [CrossRef] [PubMed]
18. Rehman, N.; Mandic, D.P. Multivariate empirical mode decomposition. *Proc. R. Soc. A Math. Phys. Eng. Sci.* **2010**, *466*, 1291–1302. [CrossRef]
19. Peng, Y.; Yang, X.; Li, D.; Ma, Z.; Liu, Z.; Bai, X.; Mao, Z. Predicting flow status of a flexible rectifier using cognitive computing. *Expert Syst. Appl.* **2025**, *264*, 125878. [CrossRef]
20. Peng, Y.; Sakai, Y.; Funabora, Y.; Yokoe, K.; Aoyama, T.; Doki, S. Funabot-Sleeve: A Wearable Device Employing McKibben Artificial Muscles for Haptic Sensation in the Forearm. *IEEE Robot. Autom. Lett.* **2025**, *10*, 1944–1951. [CrossRef]
21. Chen, Y.; Liu, X.; Rao, M.; Qin, Y.; Wang, Z.; Ji, Y. Explicit speed-integrated LSTM network for non-stationary gearbox vibration representation and fault detection under varying speed conditions. *Reliab. Eng. Syst. Saf.* **2025**, *254*, 110596. [CrossRef]
22. Yuan, F.; Huang, X.; Zheng, L.; Wang, L.; Wang, Y.; Yan, X.; Gu, S.; Peng, Y. The evolution and optimization strategies of a PBFT consensus algorithm for consortium blockchains. *Information* **2025**, *16*, 268. [CrossRef]
23. Wang, X.; Yu, H.; Kold, S.; Rahbek, O.; Bai, S. Wearable sensors for activity monitoring and motion control: A review. *Biomim. Intell. Robot.* **2023**, *3*, 100089. [CrossRef]
24. Wen, X.; Wang, Y.; Zhu, Q.; Wu, J.; Xiong, R.; Xie, A. Design of recognition algorithm for multiclass digital display instrument based on convolution neural network. *Biomim. Intell. Robot.* **2023**, *3*, 100118. [CrossRef]
25. Yu, Y.; Si, X.; Hu, C.; Zhang, J. A review of recurrent neural networks: LSTM cells and network architectures. *Neural Comput.* **2019**, *31*, 1235–1270. [CrossRef]
26. Mariappan, Y.; Ramasamy, K.; Velusamy, D. An optimized deep learning based hybrid model for prediction of daily average global solar irradiance using CNN SLSTM architecture. *Sci. Rep.* **2025**, *15*, 10761. [CrossRef]
27. Alharthi, M.; Mahmood, A. xlstmtime: Long-term time series forecasting with xlstm. *AI* **2024**, *5*, 1482–1495. [CrossRef]
28. Schmied, T.; Adler, T.; Patil, V.; Beck, M.; Pöppel, K.; Brandstetter, J.; Klambauer, G.; Pascanu, R.; Hochreiter, S. A Large Recurrent Action Model: xLSTM enables Fast Inference for Robotics Tasks. *arXiv* **2024**, arXiv:2410.22391. [CrossRef]
29. Zhou, Y.; Zhou, S.; Cheng, D.; Li, J.; Hua, Z. STDF: Joint Spatiotemporal Differences Based on xLSTM Dendritic Fusion Network for Remote Sensing Change Detection. *IEEE J. Sel. Top. Appl. Earth Obs. Remote Sens.* **2025**, *18*, 1–16. [CrossRef]
30. Ni, J.; Chen, Y.; Tang, G.; Shi, J.; Cao, W.; Shi, P. Deep learning-based scene understanding for autonomous robots: A survey. *Intell. Robot.* **2023**, *3*, 374–401. [CrossRef]
31. Mao, Z.; Suzuki, S.; Wiranata, A.; Zheng, Y.; Miyagawa, S. Bio-inspired circular soft actuators for simulating defecation process of human rectum. *J. Artif. Organs* **2025**, *28*, 252–261. [CrossRef]
32. Shen, Z.; Jiang, Z.; Zhang, J.; Wu, J.; Zhu, Q. Learning-based robot assembly method for peg insertion tasks on inclined hole using time-series force information. *Biomim. Intell. Robot.* **2025**, *5*, 100209. [CrossRef]
33. Pöppel, K.; Beck, M.; Spanring, M.; Auer, A.; Prudnikova, O.; Kopp, M.K.; Klambauer, G.; Brandstetter, J.; Hochreiter, S. xlstm: Extended long short-term memory. In Proceedings of the First Workshop on Long-Context Foundation Models@ ICML 2024, Vienna, Austria, 21–27 July 2024. [CrossRef]
34. Kühne, N.L.; Østergaard, J.; Jensen, J.; Tan, Z.H. xLSTM-SENet: xLSTM for Single-Channel Speech Enhancement. *arXiv* **2025**, arXiv:2501.06146. [CrossRef]
35. Li, Y.; Zhang, H.; Zhang, X.; Feng, H. Multi-scale Attention-based xLSTM for Rolling Bearing Fault diagnosis. *Meas. Sci. Technol.* **2025**, *36*, 066116. [CrossRef]

36. He, H.; Liao, R.; Li, Y. MSAFNet: A novel approach to facial expression recognition in embodied AI systems. *Intell. Robot.* **2025**, *5*, 313–332. [CrossRef]
37. Li, J.; Yang, S.X. Digital twins to embodied artificial intelligence: Review and perspective. *Intell. Robot.* **2025**, *5*, 202–227. [CrossRef]
38. Chen, T.; Guestrin, C. Xgboost: A scalable tree boosting system. In Proceedings of the 22nd ACM Sigkdd International Conference on Knowledge Discovery and Data Mining, San Francisco, CA, USA, 13–17 August 2016; pp. 785–794. [CrossRef]
39. Dhaliwal, S.S.; Nahid, A.A.; Abbas, R. Effective intrusion detection system using XGBoost. *Information* **2018**, *9*, 149. [CrossRef]
40. Li, J.; An, X.; Li, Q.; Wang, C.; Yu, H.; Zhou, X.; Geng, Y.a. Application of XGBoost algorithm in the optimization of pollutant concentration. *Atmos. Res.* **2022**, *276*, 106238. [CrossRef]
41. Mavrogiorgos, K.; Kiourtis, A.; Mavrogiorgou, A.; Menychtas, A.; Kyriazis, D. Bias in Machine Learning: A Literature Review. *Appl. Sci.* **2024**, *14*, 8860. [CrossRef]

computers

MDPI

Article

Informing Disaster Recovery Through Predictive Relocation Modeling

Chao He and Da Hu *

Department of Civil and Environmental Engineering, Kennesaw State University, Marietta, GA 30060, USA; che4@students.kennesaw.edu
* Correspondence: dhu3@kennesaw.edu

Abstract: Housing recovery represents a critical component of disaster recovery, and accurately forecasting household relocation decisions is essential for guiding effective post-disaster reconstruction policies. This study explores the use of machine learning algorithms to improve the prediction of household relocation in the aftermath of disasters. Leveraging data from 1304 completed interviews conducted as part of the Displaced New Orleans Residents Survey (DNORS) following Hurricane Katrina, we evaluate the performance of Logistic Regression (LR), Random Forest (RF), and Weighted Support Vector Machine (WSVM) models. Results indicate that WSVM significantly outperforms LR and RF, particularly in identifying the minority class of relocated households, achieving the highest F1 score. Key predictors of relocation include homeownership, extent of housing damage, and race. By integrating variable importance rankings and partial dependence plots, the study also enhances interpretability of machine learning outputs. These findings underscore the value of advanced predictive models in disaster recovery planning, particularly in geographically vulnerable regions like New Orleans where accurate relocation forecasting can guide more effective policy interventions.

Keywords: post-disaster relocation; machine learning; logistic regression; support vector machine; random forest

1. Introduction

The frequency of natural hazards has increased fourfold since the 1970s, now averaging over 400 events per year [1]. In 2017 alone, the United States experienced USD 306 billion in disaster-related damage. Notably, 43% of housing units in the U.S. are situated in areas with a high risk of natural hazards such as hurricanes, tornadoes, and floods [2]. Housing plays a central role in community infrastructure, accounting for approximately 70% of total building assets [3]. Household decisions to rebuild or relocate significantly influence community recovery, as housing affects multiple interdependent aspects of community resilience. Understanding the housing recovery process is therefore crucial for predicting and improving overall disaster recovery timelines. To this end, a range of models have been developed to examine household recovery decisions, including spatial regression models [4], conditional inference trees [5], and mixed logit models [6]. Researchers have identified various factors that influence relocation decisions, such as psychological stress [7], sense of loss [8], extent of property damage [9], local community [10], and demographic characteristics [11]. Moreover, relocation is increasingly viewed as a collective household-level action, rather than solely an individual decision [12].

Logistic regression has long served as the "standard method" for examining post-disaster household relocation decisions [11,13–15]. This preference stems from a traditional emphasis on identifying statistically significant predictors rather than optimizing the predictive accuracy of the models. As a result, for the past two decades, practitioners have largely adhered to this approach, often producing models with limited effectiveness in accurately predicting which households will relocate following a disaster. This raises two critical concerns [14]. First, household relocation is intrinsically linked to the broader community recovery process. Accurate prediction of relocation decisions is essential for policymakers to design and implement effective recovery strategies. Integrating household recovery behavior into disaster policy frameworks can significantly accelerate community-level recovery. Second, the low predictive power of traditional statistical models suggests that their estimated parameters may not be robust or generalizable, thereby limiting their practical utility. In contrast, machine learning algorithms such as Support Vector Machines (SVMs) and random forests have shown considerable promise in enhancing predictive performance and addressing these limitations [16,17].

Although machine learning algorithms have been widely applied across various disciplines, their use in modeling post-disaster household relocation remains limited. Relocation is not solely a geographic process, it is deeply shaped by human behavior, social norms, and individual household needs. To account for these dimensions, this study incorporates a wide range of demographic and socioeconomic variables, such as homeownership, housing damage, income, religious affiliation, and education, into predictive models. By doing so, it aims to capture the complex decision-making processes that underlie relocation. The analysis compares the predictive performance of random forest and weighted support vector machine against the traditionally used logistic regression. The following sections review relevant literature, highlight current knowledge gaps, and present the methodology used to integrate behavioral and contextual factors into the modeling framework. The study concludes with findings, contributions, and future directions for improving model relevance and interpretability in real-world recovery planning.

2. Literature Review

The literature demonstrates that relocation decisions are not merely the result of economic rationality or hazard exposure but are embedded in a complex landscape of emotional, cultural, geographic, and systemic factors. A predictive model that seeks to anticipate household relocation behavior must therefore incorporate these diverse drivers to provide accurate and actionable insights.

2.1. Related Studies on Relocation Factors

Post-disaster relocation is a multidimensional process shaped by a confluence of geographic, economic, psychological, and social factors. Geographically, hazard exposure, proximity to critical infrastructure, and spatial disparities in government recovery investment significantly affect relocation outcomes. Areas with prolonged flooding, uninhabitable structures, or delayed utility restoration are associated with lower return rates, as seen in case studies of Hurricane Katrina and Superstorm Sandy [5,11,18]. Spatial accessibility of employment centers, schools, healthcare, and transportation systems also plays a vital role in shaping post-disaster residential decision making.

Behavioral and psychosocial variables further complicate these decisions. Place attachment, a person's emotional and symbolic connection to their home and community, has been consistently identified as a deterrent to permanent relocation, even when physical conditions are unfavorable [19]. This attachment is especially strong in historically marginalized communities, where identity and cultural continuity are deeply tied to geographic space [7,20]. Research by Morrice [7] and Najarian et al. [21] showed that post-disaster trauma and emotional loss significantly influence an individual's capacity and willingness to make rational housing decisions, particularly among vulnerable populations such as the elderly or low-income families.

Social networks also act as both anchors and motivators in relocation decisions. Tight-knit communities, such as those observed in Vietnamese and African-American neighborhoods in post-Katrina New Orleans, often exhibited collective return behaviors, even in the absence of adequate infrastructure, due to shared values, mutual support systems, and informal communication networks [8,22]. Conversely, the disruption of social ties caused by displacement can reduce the likelihood of return, especially when relocation leads to geographic and emotional fragmentation of extended families or support groups. Economic and demographic factors remain critical. Households with lower income levels, renters, and those lacking insurance coverage are less likely to rebuild or return, often due to limited access to financial recovery tools such as FEMA grants, SBA loans, or private insurance payouts [13,14,23]. In contrast, homeowners with greater financial resilience tend to have more options for repair or relocation. Comerio [3] underscores this point, arguing that post-disaster housing markets often exacerbate pre-existing inequalities, with the most socioeconomically disadvantaged populations suffering the longest periods of displacement.

Objective indicators, such as race, employment status, gender, and household structure, have been widely used in predictive models and have proven to be reliable proxies for structural vulnerabilities [24]. Black and Latino households, in particular, have historically faced slower and more incomplete recovery outcomes, not only because of resource disparities but also due to discriminatory lending, zoning, and recovery prioritization processes [14,25]. Furthermore, the interplay between public policy and relocation decisions is increasingly recognized. The design of buyout programs, rebuilding incentives, and temporary housing assistance often implicitly shapes household decisions about whether to return, rebuild, or resettle. For example, studies on the New York buyout program post-Hurricane Sandy indicate that bureaucratic complexity, lack of transparency, and inconsistencies in compensation directly influenced the decision to relocate for many homeowners [13].

2.2. Related Studies on Machine Learning Algorithm

Machine Learning (ML) has emerged as a transformative tool in domains that require the analysis of high-dimensional, non-linear, and imbalanced data, including finance, health, political science, and, increasingly, disaster research. In contrast to traditional parametric models such as logistic regression, ML algorithms make fewer assumptions about the underlying data distribution and are better suited to capturing complex interactions between variables.

In the context of disaster-related prediction tasks, ML models such as Random Forest (RF), Gradient Boosting Machines (GBM), and Support Vector Machines (SVM) have been used to predict flood risk, infrastructure failure, and evacuation behavior with high accuracy [26–29]. For example, random forest has proven effective in modeling civil war onset using imbalanced political datasets, outperforming logistic regression in both precision and recall [30]. Zhao et al. [28] applied RF to model pre-evacuation behavior and found that it captured latent interaction effects between psychological, spatial, and demographic variables better than traditional methods. Similarly, Ganguly et al. [29] demonstrated that RF provided more accurate household-level flood damage predictions than generalized linear models.

Despite these successes, the application of ML to post-disaster household relocation prediction remains underdeveloped. The few existing studies in this area have tended to rely on regression models that emphasize coefficient significance rather than predictive accuracy, thereby limiting their utility for policy applications that require reliable forecasts [23]. Yet, relocation modeling is well-suited to ML approaches: it involves binary classification, suffers from class imbalance (i.e., relatively few households relocate), and includes a wide range of potentially interacting variables, demographic, behavioral, geographic, and economic. Support Vector Machines (SVM), particularly when adjusted with weighting schemes (e.g., Weighted SVM or WSVM), are effective for such imbalanced classification tasks. SVMs maximize the margin between classes and are capable of learning complex decision boundaries, especially when coupled with kernel functions such as the Radial Basis Function (RBF). In applications where one class is underrepresented, as is typical in disaster relocation datasets, weighting helps avoid model bias toward the dominant class, thereby improving sensitivity for rare but important cases like relocation [29].

Furthermore, ML models are increasingly being equipped with tools to enhance interpretability. While traditionally viewed as "black boxes", techniques such as Partial Dependence Plots (PDPs), Shapley values, and feature importance rankings allow researchers to explain model predictions in a more transparent and policy-relevant manner [31]. These tools bridge the gap between predictive power and interpretability, enabling machine learning to support both rigorous scientific inquiry and practical decision making. Moreover, the use of cross-validation, bootstrap resampling, and hyperparameter tuning in ML workflows enhances the generalizability of results and mitigates the risk of overfitting, a persistent challenge in small or medium-sized disaster datasets. Krstajic et al. [31] emphasize that multiple repetitions of k-fold cross-validation provide a more stable estimate of performance metrics, such as the F1 score, which is particularly valuable in class-imbalanced settings.

3. Methodology

To evaluate the ability of different algorithms to predict post-disaster household relocation, this study employs a comparative modeling framework using logistic regression, random forest, and Weighted Support Vector Machine (WSVM). These models were chosen to reflect both traditional statistical approaches and machine learning techniques, allowing for a balanced comparison of interpretability and predictive performance. The analysis is grounded in the Displaced New Orleans Residents Survey (DNORS), which provides rich data on household characteristics, disaster impacts, and recovery outcomes following Hurricane Katrina. Figure 1 is the overview of methodology.

3.1. Data Description

This study utilizes household-level data from the Displaced New Orleans Residents Survey (DNORS). The Displaced New Orleans Residents Survey (DNORS) is a longitudinal study conducted by the RAND Corporation, with fieldwork carried out by the University of Michigan Survey Research Center between mid-2009 and mid-2010. The survey aimed to collect data on individuals and households who resided in New Orleans, Louisiana, in August 2005, just before Hurricane Katrina struck. The primary objective was to analyze the location, living arrangements, health, and well-being of residents displaced by the hurricane. Fieldwork for DNORS was conducted from mid-2009 to mid-2010, approximately four years after Hurricane Katrina. This timing allowed researchers to assess medium-term outcomes related to displacement, resettlement, and recovery among affected individuals and households.

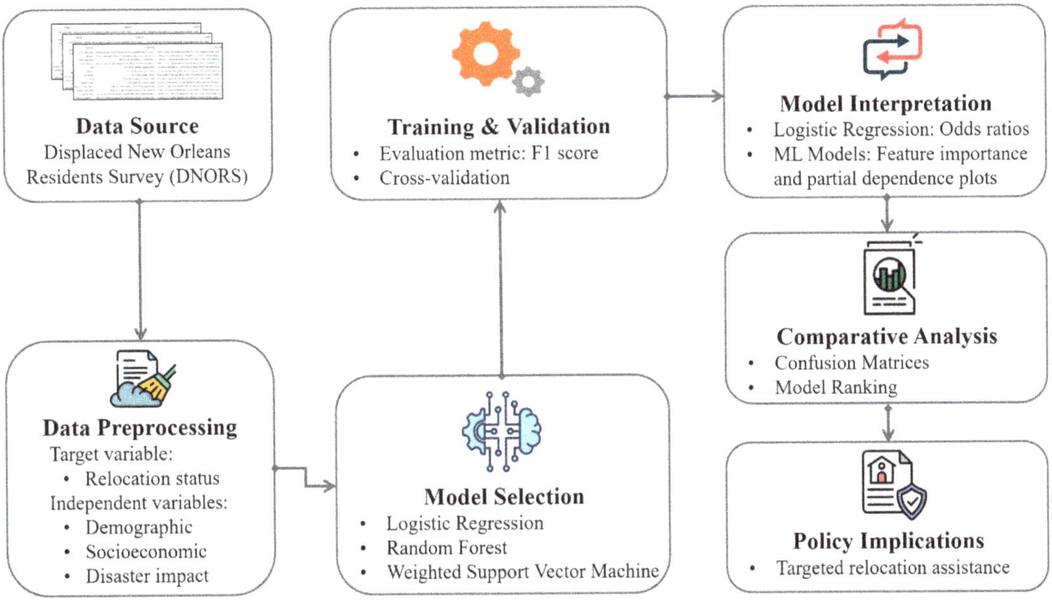

Figure 1. Overview of methodology.

DNORS employed a stratified sampling design based on pre-Katrina dwellings within the city of New Orleans. The sampling frame was constructed using address-based listings of dwellings occupied in August 2005. Researchers identified the pre-storm residents of these dwellings and tracked them to their locations at the time of the survey, whether they had returned to New Orleans or resettled elsewhere. The survey achieved interviews with 1380 pre-Katrina households, encompassing 3760 residents, with detailed individual interviews conducted with 1761 selected respondents. To accommodate the dispersed nature of the displaced population, DNORS utilized a mixed-mode data collection approach, including telephone and face-to-face interviews. This methodology facilitated the inclusion of participants regardless of their relocation status and helped mitigate potential non-response biases associated with single-mode surveys. Table 1 is the data description. The analytical sample used in this study includes 1304 households with complete interview data. Among these, 1067 households had returned to the City of New Orleans following the disaster.

While DNORS provides valuable insights into the experiences of displaced New Orleans residents, certain limitations must be acknowledged:

- Selection Bias: Individuals who were more difficult to locate or contact, such as those experiencing prolonged or multiple displacements, may be underrepresented in the sample.
- Non-Response Bias: Households that declined participation or could not be reached may differ systematically from respondents, potentially affecting the generalizability of the findings.
- Recall Bias: Given the retrospective nature of some survey questions, participants' recollections of pre- and post-Katrina experiences may be subject to inaccuracies.

Despite these limitations, DNORS remains a robust dataset for analyzing the medium-term impacts of Hurricane Katrina on displaced populations. The comprehensive tracking and mixed-mode data collection strategies employed enhance the representativeness and reliability of the findings.

Table 1. Data Description.

Variable	N	Variable	N
Age		Education	
19 to 35	168	Less than high school	223
36 to 50	407	High school	302
51 to 65	473	Some college	312
66 and older	256	College graduate	467
Household income		Religion	
0 to USD 20,000	393	Very religious	493
USD 20,001 to USD 50,000	477	Moderately religious	561
USD 50,001 to USD 75,000	173	Slightly religious	152
USD 75,001 and more	261	Not religious at all	98
Living with children under 18 years before Katrina		Number of pre-Katrina household members	
Yes	516	1	329
No	788	2	423
Insurance coverage		3	232
All or almost all of my losses	143	4 or more	320
Most of my losses	201	Homeownership	
About half of my losses	143	Owner	942
Some of my losses	294	Renter	362
Very few or none of my losses	189	Housing damage	
No insurance	334	No damage	56
Race/Ethnicity		Some damage	375
Black	807	A moderate amount of damage	611
White and others	497	A lot of damage	262

Note: N represents the number of observations.

3.2. Models

3.2.1. Logistic Regression (LR)

Logistic regression, an extension of linear regression, is widely used for modeling binary classification problems [32]. It estimates the probability of a binary outcome based on one or more explanatory variables. The model employs the logistic sigmoid function, as defined in Equation (1), where y denotes the binary response variable, x_i (i = 1, 2, ..., p) represents the explanatory variables, and β_j (j = 0, 1, 2, ..., p) are the model parameters estimated through Maximum Likelihood Estimation (MLE).

$$P(y = 0 \text{ or } 1) = \frac{1}{1 + e^{-(\beta_0 + \beta_1 x_1 + \cdots + \beta_p x_p)}} \tag{1}$$

For a 2-class problem, we used a threshold $c = 0.5$ in our research for prediction:

$$\text{class 1 if } P(y = 1) > c, \text{otherwise class 2} \tag{2}$$

The performance of logistic regression is highly dependent on the assumption that the data conforms to its underlying model structure. In contrast, machine learning algorithms are non-parametric and do not require predefined mathematical formulations, allowing them to adapt more flexibly to complex and non-linear data patterns.

3.2.2. Random Forest (RF)

Unlike logistic regression, which is model-based, random forest is a data-driven classification technique [33]. As a supervised learning algorithm, random forest combines bootstrap aggregating (bagging) with random feature selection to improve predictive performance. While bagging constructs multiple decision trees using bootstrapped datasets, random forest introduces an additional layer of randomness by selecting a random subset of features at each split, thereby reducing the correlation between individual trees. This approach helps to lower variance without significantly increasing bias, overcoming a key limitation of traditional bagging methods. The inclusion of random feature selection has been shown to significantly enhance model accuracy, particularly in high-dimensional or correlated datasets. Two critical hyperparameters in random forest construction are the number of trees (B) and the number of randomly selected variables (m) at each split. These parameters are typically optimized through grid search in conjunction with cross-validation. An overview of the random forest modeling process is illustrated in Figure 2.

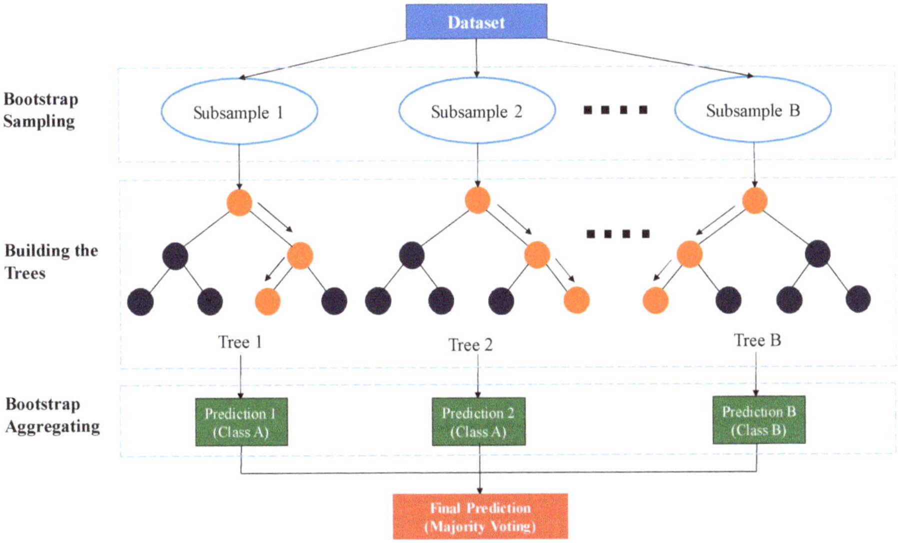

Figure 2. Scheme of Random Forest algorithm.

3.2.3. Weighted Support Vector Machine (WSVM)

Support Vector Machine (SVM) is a widely used supervised learning algorithm, particularly effective for classification tasks. The core idea of SVM is to find an optimal hyperplane that maximizes the margin between data points belonging to two distinct classes.

The Weighted Support Vector Machine (WSVM) extends the standard SVM by assigning weights to individual training instances, allowing the model to handle class imbalances more effectively. The WSVM formulation is given in Equation (3), where $x_i \in \mathbb{R}^n$ represents the training instances and $y_i \in \{-1, 1\}$ denotes their corresponding class labels. The parameter μ_i is the weight associated with instance x_i, w is the normal vector to the hyperplane in the feature space, b is the bias term, and C is a regularization parameter that controls the trade-off between maximizing the margin and minimizing classification errors, thus balancing training accuracy and generalization performance.

$$\begin{cases} \underset{w,b,\xi_i}{\text{Min}} \ \frac{1}{2}\|w\|^2 + C\sum_{i=1}^{n} \mu_i \xi_i \\ s.t. \quad y_i(w \cdot x_i + b) \geq 1 - \xi_i,\ \xi_i \geq 0,\ i = 1, 2, \ldots, n \end{cases} \quad (3)$$

Equation (3) can be reformulated into Equation (4) by solving the Lagrangian dual optimization problem, a standard approach in support vector machine formulations. In this dual form, α denotes the Lagrange multipliers and $K(x_i, x_j)$ represents the kernel function used to compute the similarity between training instances x_i and x_j. This kernel-based representation allows the algorithm to operate in high-dimensional feature spaces without explicitly computing the transformations. In this study, the Radial Basis Function (RBF) kernel is employed due to its effectiveness in capturing non-linear relationships in the data.

$$\begin{cases} \underset{\alpha}{\text{Max}} \sum_{i=1}^{n} \alpha_i - \frac{1}{2}\sum_{i=1}^{n}\sum_{j=1}^{n} y_i y_j \alpha_i \alpha_j (x_i, x_j) \\ s.t. \quad \sum_{i=1}^{n} y_i \alpha_i = 0,\ 0 \leq \alpha_i \leq C\mu_i, i = 1, 2, \ldots,\ n \end{cases} \tag{4}$$

4. Results

4.1. Metrics

In this study, only 18% of households permanently resettled outside New Orleans following Hurricane Katrina, resulting in a highly imbalanced dataset. Such class imbalance poses a significant challenge for classification models, as they tend to favor the majority class, in this case, households that returned to the city, while underrepresenting the minority class that relocated elsewhere. This imbalance can lead to biased decision making and poor generalization for the minority class. To address this issue, the F1 score was used as the primary evaluation metric during model training [34]. The F1 score, defined in Equation (5), is the harmonic mean of precision and recall and provides a more balanced assessment of model performance in the presence of class imbalance by penalizing extreme values of either metric.

$$\text{F1} = 2 \times \frac{\text{Precision} \times \text{Recall}}{\text{Precision} + \text{Recall}} \tag{5}$$

Precision (Equation (6)) measures the proportion of correctly predicted positive cases among all predicted positives, while recall (Equation (7)) captures the proportion of actual positives correctly identified. Together, they provide a comprehensive view of model performance, especially in imbalanced settings where overall accuracy may be misleading. In this context, a model that predicts most households as returning would yield high accuracy but fail to identify relocated households—our primary concern. By harmonizing precision and recall, the F1 score offers a more appropriate assessment, ensuring that both types of classification errors are accounted for. This is particularly important for post-disaster planning, where misclassifying relocated households could result in misdirected resources or unmet recovery needs. Thus, the F1 score enables a more informative and equitable evaluation of predictive models in the face of class imbalance.

$$\text{Precision} = \frac{TP}{TP + FP} \tag{6}$$

$$\text{Recall} = \frac{TP}{TP + FN} \tag{7}$$

4.2. Model Comparison

To evaluate model performance, *k*-fold Cross-Validation (CV) was employed. In this method, the original dataset is randomly partitioned into *k* equally sized subsets, or "folds". During each iteration, one fold is designated as the testing set, while the remaining $k - 1$ folds are combined to form the training set. This process is repeated *k* times, ensuring that each fold is used exactly once as the testing set. The evaluation metrics from each iteration are then averaged to produce an overall estimate of model performance. This approach reduces the potential bias associated with a single train–test split and ensures a more robust and reliable assessment. Furthermore, increasing the value of k generally leads to a lower variance in the performance estimate, providing a more stable and generalized evaluation of the model.

In this study, 50 repetitions of k-fold cross-validation were conducted, following the recommendation of [31]. Specifically, "50 repetitions" refers to repeating the entire cross-validation process, randomly partitioning the dataset into k folds a total of 50 times to yield more stable and reliable performance estimates. To explore the impact of training data proportions, we evaluated model performance using k values of 2, 4, and 10, corresponding to different training-to-testing set ratios. Figure 3 presents a comparative analysis of Logistic Regression (LR), Random Forest (RF), and Weighted Support Vector Machine (WSVM) in terms of their F1 scores on the relocation category. Notably, the F1 score is particularly useful in this context, as it reflects the model's ability to predict the minority class, households that relocated, more effectively. A higher F1 score indicates better predictive accuracy for these relocated households, which is vital for informing disaster recovery policy decisions. The results demonstrate that WSVM consistently outperforms both LR and RF, achieving the highest F1 scores across all fold settings. Additionally, the F1 score of the random forest model surpasses that of logistic regression, suggesting that machine learning algorithms offer superior performance for imbalanced classification problems. Furthermore, an increasing training ratio is associated with higher F1 scores, underscoring the value of more training data in enhancing model accuracy.

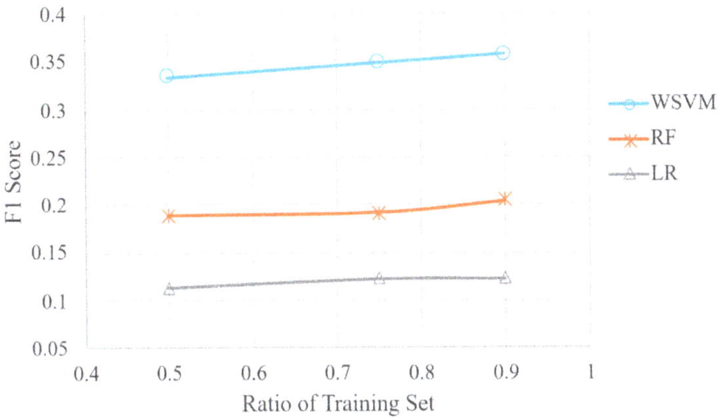

Figure 3. Comparison of F1 score for the relocated household category across different training-to-testing set ratios.

4.3. Variable Interpretation

Feature selection plays a pivotal role in the training of predictive models, yet not all features contribute equally to model accuracy. The importance of a feature is determined by the extent to which the model relies on it for making accurate predictions. One commonly used technique for estimating feature importance is the recursive partitioning method, which evaluates the total reduction in mean squared error attributed to each feature across all decision splits. Features associated with greater reductions are deemed more influential. However, while feature importance provides insights into which variables are influential, it does not clarify how those variables influence the model's predictions. In linear regression, model coefficients offer straightforward interpretability. In contrast, complex models such as Support Vector Machines (SVM) and random forests lack a direct parametric interpretation, making them inherently more difficult to explain. To overcome this limitation, Friedman [35] introduced the concept of Partial Dependence Plots (PDPs).

This approach allows for the interpretation of any predictive model, regardless of its structure, by examining how the model's predicted outcomes vary with changes in a specific feature, while averaging out the effects of all other features. Given a dataset with N observations and p covariates, where y_k is the response for observation k and $x_{i,k}$ is the value of the i-th feature for the k-th observation, the model predictions can be expressed as shown in Equation (8).

$$\hat{y}_k = F\left(x_{1,k}, x_{2,k}, \ldots, x_{p,k}\right) \tag{8}$$

To compute Friedman's Partial Dependence Plot (PDP) for a single covariate x_j, the partial dependence function $\phi_j(x)$ is estimated by averaging the model's predictions over the joint distribution of all other variables, as defined in Equation (9). This function captures the marginal effect of x_j on the predicted outcome by effectively "averaging out" the influence of the remaining features. By evaluating $\phi_j(x)$ over a suitable range of x_j values and plotting the result, one can visualize how the model's prediction changes in response to variations in x_j, independent of interactions with other covariates. This approach is particularly useful for interpreting complex, non-parametric models such as random forests and support vector machines, where direct interpretation of model parameters is not feasible.

$$\varnothing_j\left(x_j\right) = \frac{1}{n}\sum\nolimits_{k=1}^{n} F\left(x_{1,k}, \ldots, x_{j-1,k}, x_{j+1,k}, \ldots, x_{p,k}\right) \tag{9}$$

The analysis began with an examination of the logistic regression results, as presented in Table 2, to identify key factors influencing households' decisions to relocate or return following Hurricane Katrina. The Odds Ratio (OR), calculated as the exponential of the regression coefficient (e^{β}), provides insight into the direction and magnitude of each predictor's effect. A negative coefficient yields an OR less than 1, indicating that a one-unit increase in the predictor reduces the odds of returning to a pre-Katrina address, with relocation as the reference outcome. Conversely, a positive coefficient results in an OR greater than 1, signifying increased odds of returning. Among the significant predictors, homeownership exhibited the strongest effect, with an OR of 2.927, suggesting that homeowners were nearly three times more likely to return than renters. This makes homeownership the most influential variable in the model. Another significant factor was religious affiliation: households identified as "slightly religious" had an OR of 2.873, indicating a 187.3% increase in the odds of returning compared to those identified as "very religious". These findings highlight the importance of socioeconomic factors in shaping post-disaster relocation decisions.

Table 2. Results of logistic regression.

Variable	Odds Ratio
Black	0.983
Homeowner	2.927 ***
Living with children under 18 years before Katrina	1.131
High school	0.636 †
Some college	0.423 **
College graduate	0.522 *
Moderately religious	1.155
Slightly religious	2.873 **
Not religious at all	1.486
All or almost all of my losses	1.277
Most of my losses	1.500
About half of my losses	0.809
Some of my losses	1.195

Table 2. *Cont.*

Variable	Odds Ratio
Very few or none of my losses	0.747
Some damage	0.401
A moderate amount of damage	0.151 ***
A lot of damage	0.122 **
Age 36 to 50	1.035
Age 51 to 65	0.927
Age 66 and older	0.835
Household income USD 20,001 to USD 50,000	1.077
Household income USD 50,001 to USD 75,000	0.635 †
Household income USD 75,001 and more	0.945
2 household members before Katrina	1.056
3 household members before Katrina	0.733
4 or more household members before Katrina	0.706

Notes: † $p < 0.1$, * $p < 0.05$, ** $p < 0.01$, *** $p < 0.001$.

The education, housing damage, and household income variables were also identified as significant contributors to the relocations of households. Specifically, the variable "a lot of damage" has the smallest odds ratio (OR = 0.122), indicating that households experiencing the most severe damage were the least likely to return. The OR value of a moderate amount of damage (OR = 0.151) variable is found to be the second smallest, indicating that households were more likely to relocate after experiencing a higher level of damage compared to households experiencing no damage. Householders with a high school degree (OR = 0.636) or some college (OR = 0.423) or college graduates (OR = 0.522) were more likely to relocate to other places than those with less than a high school education. A negative and significant effect was observed for the variable household income of USD 50,001 to USD 75,000 (OR = 0.635).

While logistic regression is straightforward to implement and interpret, it falls short in accurately predicting the minority class, in this case, households that relocated after Hurricane Katrina. To address this limitation, we further analyzed the results using the Weighted Support Vector Machine (WSVM) model. Given the stochastic nature of machine learning algorithms, slight variations in results are expected across different runs. To ensure stability, the WSVM model was executed ten times, with each run involving 10 repetitions of 10-fold cross-validation. We then examined the influence of individual predictors using Partial Dependence Plots (PDPs), which provide a visual representation of how each variable affects the model's predictions while averaging out the influence of other features. For binary (dummy) variables, this influence can be interpreted as either positive or negative. Figure 4 displays sample PDPs for two key variables. For example, the "a lot of damage" variable shows a negative effect on the probability of return, suggesting that households experiencing severe housing damage were less likely to return and rebuild. These plots offer intuitive insights into the relationship between predictors and the model's output, supporting a more nuanced interpretation of complex models like WSVM.

Figure 5 illustrates the relative importance and directional effect of variables in the Weighted Support Vector Machine (WSVM) model. The importance scores for each variable are averaged across ten independent runs to ensure stability and reliability. Negative values indicate that the corresponding variable is associated with an increased likelihood of households returning to their pre-disaster locations, while positive values suggest a greater probability of relocation. Among all variables, homeownership emerges as the most influential predictor, aligning with findings from prior studies [23]. This result reinforces the critical role of housing tenure in shaping post-disaster recovery decisions, particularly the tendency of homeowners to return and rebuild.

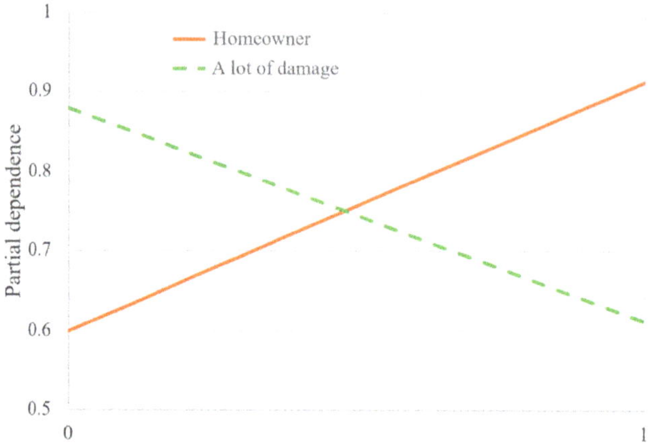

Figure 4. Exemplary results of the partial dependence plot.

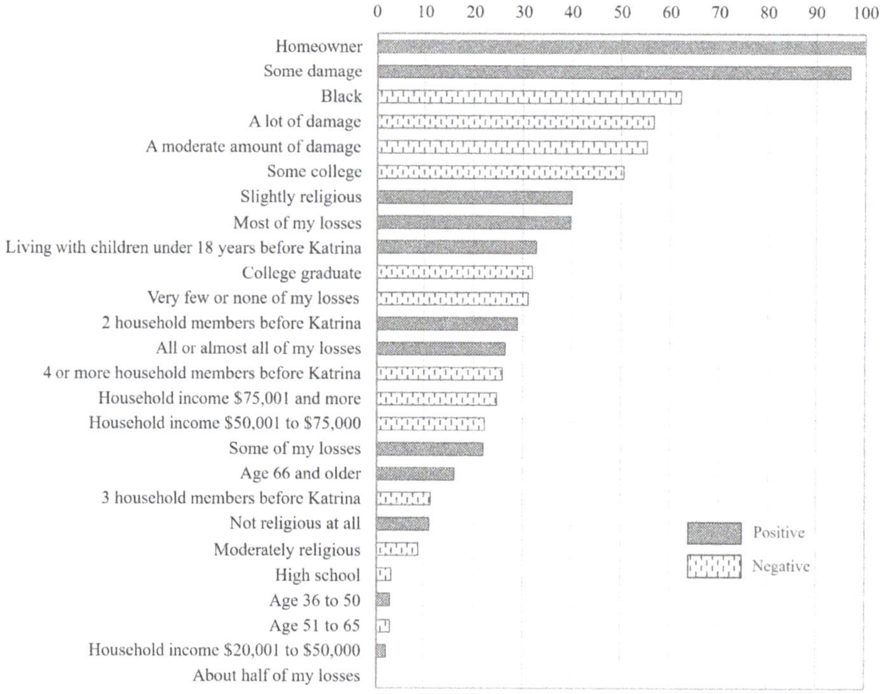

Figure 5. Relative importance of variables.

5. Discussion

5.1. Interpretation of Findings

The model estimation results highlight the superior performance of machine learning algorithms in predicting household relocation following disasters, as compared to traditional logistic regression. This improvement is evident in the significantly higher F1 scores achieved by the machine learning models, indicating enhanced predictive accuracy, particularly for the minority class of relocated households. Among the evaluated algorithms, the Weighted Support Vector Machine (WSVM) outperformed random forest, demonstrating the highest F1 score and thus emerging as the preferred model. The top three most influential factors identified by the WSVM model were homeownership, moderate housing damage, and race. These findings align closely with prior research [25,36], which has consistently emphasized the role of homeownership, damage severity, race, and insurance in shaping post-disaster relocation decisions. This alignment with established literature lends further credibility to the use of machine learning techniques in disaster recovery research and supports their broader application in policy-relevant predictive modeling.

Traditional methods such as logistic regression exhibit significant limitations in predicting minority classes, particularly in imbalanced datasets. This study focuses on the critical issue of post-disaster household relocation, where the number of relocated households is substantially lower than those who returned to their pre-disaster residences after events like Hurricane Katrina [11,14,37]. Given the imbalanced nature of the data, machine learning algorithms offer a more suitable alternative. For researchers aiming to develop predictive models in this context, statistical learning methods such as random forest should be strongly considered. Logistic regression may yield biased estimates when applied to imbalanced data and is further constrained by assumptions related to linearity, independence of predictors (i.e., lack of multicollinearity), and homoskedasticity. When these assumptions are violated, the predictive accuracy of logistic regression is compromised. In contrast, machine learning algorithms like random forest are more flexible and robust, capable of capturing complex, non-linear interactions and producing more reliable predictions for rare but important outcomes, such as household relocation.

5.2. Limitations and Future Work

Despite the strengths and contributions of this study, several limitations must be acknowledged. First, the relatively small size of the dataset, derived from the Displaced New Orleans Residents Survey (DNORS), may limit the generalizability of the findings. While the models performed well within the available data, predictive performance and variable stability may change when applied to larger or more diverse populations affected by different disasters. Future research should aim to incorporate larger datasets from multiple disaster events to validate model performance across various geographic, demographic, and hazard-specific contexts. Second, although machine learning models are powerful in capturing complex relationships and handling imbalanced data, they often lack the transparency and interpretability associated with traditional statistical models. While we mitigated this issue using partial dependence plots and variable importance rankings, these methods provide only partial insight into model reasoning. This may limit the adoption of machine learning models by practitioners and policymakers who prioritize model transparency, especially in high-stakes applications. Future work should explore the integration of Explainable AI (XAI) techniques or develop hybrid models that combine the interpretability of logistic regression with the predictive strength of machine learning.

Third, the current study focused on two specific algorithms, random forest and WSVM, which, while effective, do not exhaust the spectrum of available modeling techniques. Emerging approaches, such as ensemble learning methods [38], and deep neural networks [39], may offer further improvements in predictive performance. Future research should systematically evaluate these models and compare their advantages and trade-offs, especially in relation to computational efficiency, interpretability, and data requirements. Lastly, while this study identified key predictors of relocation, it did not examine interactions between variables or account for spatial, temporal, or social network effects, which could play a significant role in household decision making. Incorporating such contextual dimensions into predictive models could provide a more comprehensive understanding of post-disaster mobility and enable the design of more targeted and equitable recovery interventions.

6. Conclusions

Accurately predicting household relocation is crucial for facilitating effective community recovery in the aftermath of disasters. This study evaluated the predictive performance of machine learning algorithms versus logistic regression in identifying households that relocated following Hurricane Katrina. Utilizing household-level data from the Displaced New Orleans Residents Survey (DNORS), we modeled relocation decisions and compared three approaches using F1 score as the evaluation metric. The results clearly demonstrate that machine learning algorithms, particularly the weighted support vector machine, outperform logistic regression in predicting the minority class of relocated households. Furthermore, the use of variable importance rankings and partial dependence plots enhances the interpretability of machine learning models, enabling the identification of key factors and their directional influence on relocation outcomes. These findings underscore the value of adopting advanced statistical learning techniques in disaster recovery research and planning.

Author Contributions: Conceptualization, D.H.; methodology, D.H.; validation, C.H.; formal analysis, C.H.; investigation, C.H.; data curation, C.H.; writing—original draft preparation, C.H.; writing—review and editing, D.H.; visualization, C.H.; supervision, D.H. All authors have read and agreed to the published version of the manuscript.

Funding: This research received no external funding.

Data Availability Statement: The original data presented in the study are openly available at https://www.rand.org/well-being/social-and-behavioral-policy/data/dnors/dnorps.html (accessed on 20 April 2025).

Acknowledgments: This research is based on data from the Displaced New Orleans Residents Survey which was funded by grants from the Eunice Kennedy Shriver National Institute of Child Health and Human development (Grant R01-HD059106 and R01-HD059106-S1) to the RAND Corporation in Santa Monica, California. For further information on DNORS, go to www.rand.org/labor/projects/dnors (accessed on 11 June 2025). The funders had no role in the design of this study; in the analysis or interpretation of the data in this study; in the writing of the manuscript; or in the decision to publish the results.

Conflicts of Interest: The authors declare no conflicts of interest.

References

1. Weather-Related Disasters Are Increasing. Available online: https://www.economist.com/graphic-detail/2017/08/29/weather-related-disasters-are-increasing (accessed on 25 April 2025).
2. Hill, C. 43% of U.S. Homes Are at High Risk of Natural Disaster. Available online: https://www.marketwatch.com/story/43-of-us-homes-are-at-high-risk-of-natural-disaster-2015-09-03 (accessed on 25 April 2025).
3. Comerio, M. *Disaster Hits Home: New Policy for Urban Housing Recovery*, 1st ed.; University of California Press: Oakland, CA, USA, 1998; ISBN 978-0-520-20780-6.
4. Hu, D.; Nejat, A. Role of Spatial Effect in Postdisaster Housing Recovery: Case Study of Hurricane Katrina. *J. Infrastruct. Syst.* **2021**, *27*, 05020009. [CrossRef]
5. Mayer, J.; Moradi, S.; Nejat, A.; Ghosh, S.; Cong, Z.; Liang, D. Drivers of Post-Disaster Relocations: The Case of Moore and Hattiesburg Tornados. *Int. J. Disaster Risk Reduct.* **2020**, *49*, 101643. [CrossRef]
6. Hu, D.; Yu, W.; Zhao, J.; Liu, W.; Han, F.; Yi, X. A Hierarchical Mixed Logit Model of Individuals' Return Decisions after Hurricane Katrina. *Int. J. Disaster Risk Reduct.* **2019**, *34*, 443–447. [CrossRef]

7. Morrice, S. Heartache and Hurricane Katrina: Recognising the Influence of Emotion in Post-Disaster Return Decisions. *Area* **2013**, *45*, 33–39. [CrossRef]
8. Kytola, K.L.; Cherry, K.E.; Marks, L.D.; Hatch, T.G. When Neighborhoods Are Destroyed by Disaster: Relocate or Return and Rebuild? In *Traumatic Stress and Long-Term Recovery: Coping with Disasters and Other Negative Life Events*; Cherry, K.E., Ed.; Springer International Publishing: Cham, Switzerland, 2015; pp. 211–229. ISBN 978-3-319-18866-9.
9. Hu, D.; Nejat, A.; Shankar, V. Random Parameter Model of Postdisaster Household Relocation. *Nat. Hazards Rev.* **2021**, *22*, 04021027. [CrossRef]
10. Moradi, S.; Nejat, A.; Hu, D.; Ghosh, S. Perceived Neighborhood: Preferences versus Actualities. *Int. J. Disaster Risk Reduct.* **2020**, *51*, 101824. [CrossRef]
11. Groen, J.A.; Polivka, A.E. Going Home after Hurricane Katrina: Determinants of Return Migration and Changes in Affected Areas. *Demography* **2010**, *47*, 821–844. [CrossRef]
12. Finn, D.; Chandrasekhar, D. Influence of Household Recovery Capacity and Urgency on Post-Disaster Relocation. Available online: https://hazards.colorado.edu/quick-response-report/influence-of-household-recovery-capacity-and-urgency-on-post-disaster-relocation (accessed on 30 May 2025).
13. Binder, S.B. Resilience and Postdisaster Relocation: A Study of New York's Home Buyout Plan in the Wake of Hurricane Sandy. Ph.D. Thesis, University of Hawaii at Manoa, Waikiki, HI, USA, 2014.
14. Fussell, E.; Sastry, N.; VanLandingham, M. Race, Socioeconomic Status, and Return Migration to New Orleans after Hurricane Katrina. *Popul. Environ.* **2010**, *31*, 20–42. [CrossRef]
15. Elliott, J.R.; Pais, J. Race, Class, and Hurricane Katrina: Social Differences in Human Responses to Disaster. *Soc. Sci. Res.* **2006**, *35*, 295–321. [CrossRef]
16. Weng, S.F.; Reps, J.; Kai, J.; Garibaldi, J.M.; Qureshi, N. Can Machine-Learning Improve Cardiovascular Risk Prediction Using Routine Clinical Data? *PLoS ONE* **2017**, *12*, e0174944. [CrossRef]
17. Hamby, S.E.; Hirst, J.D. Prediction of Glycosylation Sites Using Random Forests. *BMC Bioinform.* **2008**, *9*, 500. [CrossRef] [PubMed]
18. Bukvic, A.; Smith, A.; Zhang, A. Evaluating Drivers of Coastal Relocation in Hurricane Sandy Affected Communities. *Int. J. Disaster Risk Reduct.* **2015**, *13*, 215–228. [CrossRef]
19. Jamali, M.; Nejat, A. Place Attachment and Disasters: Knowns and Unknowns. *J. Emerg. Manag.* **2016**, *14*, 349–364. [CrossRef]
20. Xiao, Y.; Van Zandt, S. Building Community Resiliency: Spatial Links between Household and Business Post-Disaster Return. *Urban Stud.* **2012**, *49*, 2523–2542. [CrossRef]
21. Najarian, L.M.; Goenjian, A.K.; Pelcovttz, D.; Mandel, F.; Najarian, B. Relocation after a Disaster: Posttraumatic Stress Disorder in Armenia after the Earthquake. *J. Am. Acad. Child Adolesc. Psychiatry* **1996**, *35*, 374–383. [CrossRef]
22. Tierney, K.J. Businesses and Disasters: Vulnerability, Impacts, and Recovery. In *Handbook of Disaster Research*; Rodríguez, H., Quarantelli, E.L., Dynes, R.R., Eds.; Springer: New York, NY, USA, 2007; pp. 275–296. ISBN 978-0-387-32353-4.
23. Lee, J.Y.; Van Zandt, S. Housing Tenure and Social Vulnerability to Disasters: A Review of the Evidence. *J. Plan. Lit.* **2019**, *34*, 156–170. [CrossRef]
24. Peek, L.; Morrissey, B.; Marlatt, H. Disaster Hits Home: A Model of Displaced Family Adjustment After Hurricane Katrina. *J. Fam. Issues* **2011**, *32*, 1371–1396. [CrossRef]
25. Binder, S.; Baker, C.; Barile, J. Rebuild or Relocate? Resilience and Postdisaster Decision-Making After Hurricane Sandy. *Am. J. Community Psychol.* **2015**, *56*, 180–196. [CrossRef]
26. Marjanović, M.; Kovačević, M.; Bajat, B.; Voženílek, V. Landslide Susceptibility Assessment Using SVM Machine Learning Algorithm. *Eng. Geol.* **2011**, *123*, 225–234. [CrossRef]
27. Ganggayah, M.D.; Taib, N.A.; Har, Y.C.; Lio, P.; Dhillon, S.K. Predicting Factors for Survival of Breast Cancer Patients Using Machine Learning Techniques. *BMC Med. Inform. Decis. Mak.* **2019**, *19*, 48. [CrossRef]
28. Zhao, X.; Lovreglio, R.; Nilsson, D. Modelling and Interpreting Pre-Evacuation Decision-Making Using Machine Learning. *Autom. Constr.* **2020**, *113*, 103140. [CrossRef]
29. Ganguly, K.K.; Nahar, N.; Hossain, B.M. A Machine Learning-Based Prediction and Analysis of Flood Affected Households: A Case Study of Floods in Bangladesh. *Int. J. Disaster Risk Reduct.* **2019**, *34*, 283–294. [CrossRef]
30. Muchlinski, D.; Siroky, D.; He, J.; Kocher, M. Comparing Random Forest with Logistic Regression for Predicting Class-Imbalanced Civil War Onset Data. *Polit. Anal.* **2016**, *24*, 87–103. [CrossRef]
31. Krstajic, D.; Buturovic, L.J.; Leahy, D.E.; Thomas, S. Cross-Validation Pitfalls When Selecting and Assessing Regression and Classification Models. *J. Cheminform.* **2014**, *6*, 10. [CrossRef] [PubMed]
32. Pregibon, D. Logistic Regression Diagnostics. *Ann. Stat.* **1981**, *9*, 705–724. [CrossRef]
33. Liaw, A.; Wiener, M. Classification and Regression by randomForest. *R News* **2002**, *2*, 18–22.
34. Ferri, C.; Hernández-Orallo, J.; Modroiu, R. An Experimental Comparison of Performance Measures for Classification. *Pattern Recognit. Lett.* **2009**, *30*, 27–38. [CrossRef]

35. Friedman, J.H. Greedy Function Approximation: A Gradient Boosting Machine. *Ann. Stat.* **2001**, *29*, 1189–1232. [CrossRef]
36. Kim, J.; Oh, S. The Virtuous Circle in Disaster Recovery: Who Returns and Stays in Town after Disaster Evacuation? *J. Risk Res.* **2014**, *17*, 5. [CrossRef]
37. Myers, C.A.; Slack, T.; Singelmann, J. Social Vulnerability and Migration in the Wake of Disaster: The Case of Hurricanes Katrina and Rita. *Popul. Environ.* **2008**, *29*, 271–291. [CrossRef]
38. Huan, Y.; Song, L.; Khan, U.; Zhang, B. Stacking Ensemble of Machine Learning Methods for Landslide Susceptibility Mapping in Zhangjiajie City, Hunan Province, China. *Environ. Earth Sci.* **2022**, *82*, 35. [CrossRef]
39. Zhang, B.; Tang, J.; Huan, Y.; Song, L.; Shah, S.Y.A.; Wang, L. Multi-Scale Convolutional Neural Networks (CNNs) for Landslide Inventory Mapping from Remote Sensing Imagery and Landslide Susceptibility Mapping (LSM). *Geomat. Nat. Hazards Risk* **2024**, *15*, 2383309. [CrossRef]

computers

MDPI

Article

Forecasting the Unseen: Enhancing Tsunami Occurrence Predictions with Machine-Learning-Driven Analytics

Snehal Satish, Hari Gonaygunta, Akhila Reddy Yadulla, Deepak Kumar, Mohan Harish Maturi, Karthik Meduri †, Elyson De La Cruz, Geeta Sandeep Nadella *,† and Guna Sekhar Sajja

Department of Information Technology, University of the Cumberlands, Williamsburg, KY 40769, USA; ssatish3175@ucumberlands.edu (S.S.); hgonaygunta3255@ucumberlands.edu (H.G.); ayadulla5882@ucumberlands.edu (A.R.Y.); fdeepakkumar6146@ucumberlands.edu (D.K.); mmaturi9213@ucumberlands.edu (M.H.M.); kmeduri5644@ucumberlands.edu (K.M.); edelacruz7981@ucumberlands.edu (E.D.L.C.); gsajja1524@ucumberlands.edu (G.S.S.)

* Correspondence: gnadella3853@ucumberlands.edu

† These authors contributed equally to this work.

Abstract: This research explores the improvement of tsunami occurrence forecasting with machine learning predictive models using earthquake-related data analytics. The primary goal is to develop a predictive framework that integrates a wide range of data sources, including seismic, geospatial, and ecological data, toward improving the accuracy and lead times of tsunami occurrence predictions. The study employs machine learning methods, including Random Forest and Logistic Regression, for binary classification of tsunami events. Data collection is performed using a Kaggle dataset spanning 1995–2023, with preprocessing and exploratory analysis to identify critical patterns. The Random Forest model achieved superior performance with an accuracy of 0.90 and precision of 0.88 compared to Logistic Regression (accuracy: 0.89, precision: 0.87). These results underscore Random Forest's effectiveness in handling imbalanced data. Challenges such as improving data quality and model interpretability are discussed, with recommendations for future improvements in real-time warning systems.

Keywords: predictive model; tsunami occurrence; earthquake data; data analytics; machine learning (ML); forecasting

1. Introduction

Tsunamis are among the most devastating natural disasters, posing significant threats to coastal communities and infrastructure worldwide. Despite advancements in seismic monitoring, accurately predicting tsunami occurrences within critical timeframes remains a major challenge [1]. Traditional tsunami warning systems primarily rely on seismic magnitude thresholds and post-earthquake hydrodynamic simulations [2,3], which often lead to delayed alerts or false alarms due to their reliance on simplified heuristics. The integration of machine learning models and data analytics offers a promising frontier for improving tsunami occurrence prediction. AI and its capacity to learn from patterns in massive numbers of data combined with data analytics, which process and analyze diverse and massive datasets in real time, then hold the potential to revolutionize how we approach tsunami occurrence forecasting [4,5]. The motivation behind this research stems from the growing recognition that traditional methods alone may not be sufficient to meet the demands of modern disaster preparedness. With AI and data analytics, it is possible to enhance the accuracy of predictions and extend and improve the effectiveness of disaster mitigation

 https://doi.org/10.3390/computers14050175

strategies [6]. This research aims to explore advanced technologies applied to create a robust and AI-driven predictive model that not only forecasts earthquakes with higher accuracy in critical prime times but also saves lives, reduces economic losses, and contributes to global efforts in disaster risk reduction [7]. This research is motivated by the broader implications of integrating AI and data analytics into geophysical research. AI continues to advance, and its applications in various scientific domains, including environmental and Earth sciences, are expanding quickly [8]. Tsunami occurrence forecasting presents a unique opportunity to demonstrate how AI can be applied to solve real-world problems that have profound impacts on society [9]. The potential to transform tsunami occurrence prediction from the field, constrained by limited data and traditional methodologies, into a dynamic and data-driven science is both an exciting challenge and a critical necessity as natural disasters are becoming increasingly frequent and severe due to climate change and other environmental factors [10]. This paper seeks to contribute to the field by developing and validating a predictive model for more actual tsunami occurrence forecasting and the extension of more resilient communities and infrastructures.

1.1. Research Problem

The complexity of tsunami generation mechanisms creates significant challenges for early warning systems. Current approaches struggle to distinguish between seismic events that generate dangerous tsunamis and those that do not, particularly in near-field scenarios where rapid decisions are crucial [11]. This problem is exacerbated by the need to integrate heterogeneous data sources—including seismic parameters, geographic context, and historical patterns—into a unified predictive framework [12]. The problem lies in the integration and processing of these diverse data sources, such as satellite imagery, geospatial data, and real-time seismic activity and environmental conditions, to create a predictive model that offers more accurate and timely tsunami occurrence forecasts. This problem requires the development of an AI-driven predictive model that controls data analytics to improve the correctness and consistency of tsunami occurrence forecasting and eventually aims to alleviate the devastating impacts of these natural disasters.

1.2. Research Questions

In this study of the refuge, the key questions are as follows:

- Which machine learning architectures are most effective for binary classification of tsunami-generating earthquakes?
- What feature selection strategies optimize model performance while maintaining computational efficiency?
- How can temporal patterns in seismic data improve prediction lead times?

1.3. Research Objective

This study develops a machine learning framework that predicts tsunami occurrence within minutes of earthquake detection by analyzing six key seismic features: magnitude, depth, geographic coordinates, aftershock patterns, seismic moment, and source mechanism characteristics. The study aims to integrate diverse data sources, including seismic, geospatial, and environmental data, into the robust analytical framework in advanced machine learning algorithms. By improving the precision of predictions and providing earlier warnings, this model seeks to contribute to better disaster preparedness and modification strategies and reduce the human and economic toll of earthquakes.

1.4. Structure of Paper

This paper is organized into numerous important units. It starts with an overview that describes the research problem and then the objects and significance of the study. The Literature Review follows and examines current studies and recognizes the holes this study proposes to fill. The Methodology details the data sources plus the AI techniques and data analytics used to develop the predictive model. The Implementation section describes how the model was tested with a case study. The Results and Discussion present the findings and their implications; the Conclusion reviews the contributions and suggests future exploration instructions.

2. Literature Review

2.1. Introduction to Tsunami Occurrence Prediction

Tsunami occurrence prediction remains a critical research area due to the devastating impacts of these ocean waves, often triggered by underwater earthquakes, landslides, or volcanic eruptions [12]. The field has evolved from using traditional geophysical methods to advanced computational and artificial intelligence (AI)-driven approaches, leveraging vast datasets and sophisticated modeling techniques. This review synthesizes traditional methods, such as seismic activity monitoring and fault line analysis, with modern advancements, including the Finite Element Method (FEM), AI, machine learning (ML), and big data analytics. By addressing both historical and contemporary approaches, we aim to provide a comprehensive overview of tsunami prediction methodologies, their successes, and the ongoing challenges.

2.2. Traditional Tsunami Occurrence Prediction

Traditional tsunami prediction methods focus on analyzing geological and seismological data, particularly data related to submarine earthquakes, which account for approximately 80% of tsunamis [13]. These methods rely on empirical observations, historical records, and geophysical measurements to assess tsunami risk. The primary techniques include seismic activity monitoring and fault line analysis, which are foundational to understanding the mechanisms of tsunami generation.

1. Seismic Activity Monitoring
   Seismic activity monitoring is a cornerstone of tsunami prediction, involving the continuous observation of seismic waves generated by underwater earthquakes [14,15]. This method leverages networks of seismometers and ocean-bottom sensors to detect potential tsunami triggers.
   - Seismicity Patterns: Monitoring seismicity patterns involves analyzing the frequency and distribution of earthquakes, particularly foreshocks, which may precede a tsunami-generating event. Seismic gaps—regions along faults with low recent activity—are critical indicators of potential large earthquakes [16]. For example, the 2011 Tohoku earthquake was preceded by a seismic gap along the Japan Trench, highlighting the predictive value of this approach [17].
   - Earthquake Swarms: Earthquake swarms, characterized by clusters of seismic events in a short period, can signal stress changes in the Earth's crust. While not all swarms lead to tsunamis, they are monitored closely in subduction zones like the Pacific Ring of Fire [16]. Advanced algorithms now enhance swarm detection by filtering noise from seismic data [18].
   - Precursors and Anomalies: Seismic precursors, such as changes in P-wave velocity or P-wave shadowing, indicate potential tsunami-generating earthquakes. P-wave shadowing occurs when primary seismic waves are absorbed or de-

flected, suggesting imminent fault rupture [19]. Recent studies have improved precursor detection using machine learning to analyze seismic waveforms [20].

2. Fault Line Analysis
   Fault line analysis focuses on submarine faults, where tectonic plate movements can displace ocean water, generating tsunamis [21]. This method combines geological mapping, historical data, and geophysical measurements to assess tsunami risk.
   - Mapping Fault Lines: Geological surveys, remote sensing, and satellite imagery are used to map submarine fault lines, identifying high-risk coastal areas [22]. For instance, the Cascadia Subduction Zone has been extensively mapped to assess tsunami potential along the U.S. West Coast [17].
   - Historical Tsunami Data: Historical records of tsunamis along fault lines provide insights into recurrence intervals and event magnitudes. Subduction zones like the Sunda Trench have well-documented tsunami histories, informing probabilistic hazard models [17,23].
   - Stress Accumulation: GPS and InSAR (Interferometric Synthetic Aperture Radar) measurements monitor stress accumulation along faults. High stress rates indicate elevated tsunami risk, as seen during the 2018 Palu tsunami [24].
   - Paleo-Seismology and Paleo-Tsunami Studies: Paleo-seismology examines sediment layers to reconstruct past earthquakes and tsunamis, offering a long-term perspective on tsunami frequency [25]. For example, paleo-tsunami deposits in Chile have revealed 500-year recurrence intervals for major events [18].
   - Slip Rates and Fault Segmentation: Faults are segmented, with each segment exhibiting unique slip rates. Analyzing these rates helps predict which segments are prone to tsunami-generating earthquakes [26]. Recent advancements in fault segmentation models have improved risk assessments for regions like Indonesia [27].

2.3. The Finite Element Method (FEM) in Tsunami Prediction

The Finite Element Method (FEM) is a numerical technique widely used to simulate complex geophysical processes, including fault mechanics and tsunami wave propagation [28]. The FEM divides the ocean–Earth system into discrete elements, enabling detailed analysis of stress distribution, fault slip, and wave dynamics. Unlike traditional statistical models, the FEM captures the nonlinear interactions between seismic events and ocean responses, improving predictions of tsunami generation [29].

FEM applications include the following:

- Fault Mechanics: Simulating stress accumulation and rupture along submarine faults to predict tsunami triggers [26].
- Wave Propagation: Modeling tsunami wave interactions with bathymetry and coastal topography to estimate inundation zones [30].
- Infrastructure Assessment: Evaluating the impact of tsunami waves on coastal structures, informing resilient design standards [31].

Recent advancements in the FEM incorporate real-time seismic data and high-resolution bathymetric maps, enhancing the accuracy of tsunami forecasts. For example, FEM models of the 2011 Tohoku tsunami accurately predicted inundation heights, aiding post-disaster recovery [32]. However, the FEM's computational complexity requires significant resources, limiting its use in real-time applications [29].

2.4. AI and Machine Learning in Tsunami Prediction

AI and ML have revolutionized tsunami prediction by processing vast datasets and identifying patterns that traditional methods cannot detect [33]. These technologies enhance real-time monitoring, risk assessment, and resource allocation, as shown in Figure 1. Table 1 highlights the challenges that AI/ML aim to address, such as uncertainty and false alarms.

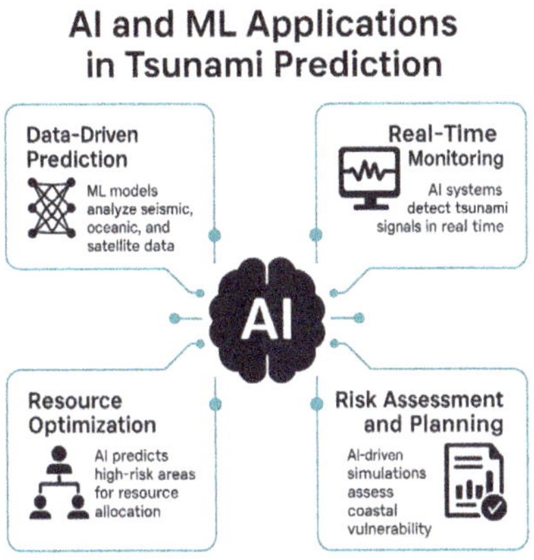

Figure 1. AI and ML applications in tsunami prediction.

Table 1. Challenges and limitations in traditional tsunami occurrence prediction.

Challenge/Limitation	Details
Uncertainty in Predictions	The nonlinear dynamics of the Earth's crust and ocean make precise predictions of tsunami timing, location, and magnitude challenging [34].
False Alarms	Seismic monitoring may trigger false tsunami warnings due to non-tsunamigenic seismic activity [23].
Missed Events	Tsunamis from non-seismic sources (e.g., landslides) may lack detectable precursors [35].
Data Gaps	Sparse monitoring networks in remote oceanic regions limit data availability [30].
Complex Fault–Ocean Interactions	Stress transfer and water displacement in submarine faults are difficult to model accurately [24].
Inaccurate Historical Records	Incomplete tsunami records hinder reliable risk assessments [36].
Paleotsunami Limitations	Geological records may be incomplete or misinterpreted, affecting long-term forecasts [25].
Precursor Ambiguity	Reliable precursors for tsunami events are not fully understood [19].
Fault Variability	Different fault segments produce tsunamis with varying characteristics [26].
Technological Barriers	Limited access to advanced sensors in developing regions reduce monitoring effectiveness [30].

- Data-Driven Prediction: ML models analyze seismic, oceanic, and satellite data to predict tsunami events. For example, convolutional neural networks (CNNs) have identified tsunami precursors in seismic waveforms, improving early warning systems [20]. Studies in Japan and Indonesia have demonstrated ML's ability to provide minutes of warning before tsunami impact [37,38].

- Real-Time Monitoring: AI systems integrate data from ocean buoys, tide gauges, and seismic stations to detect tsunami signals in real time. Recurrent neural networks (RNNs) have been used to predict tsunami wave paths, enabling timely evacuations [36]. The Indonesia Tsunami Early Warning System employs ML to process real-time seismic data [36].
- Resource Optimization: AI optimizes emergency resource allocation by predicting high-risk areas. For instance, ML models prioritize medical and rescue deployments based on forecasted inundation zones [39].
- Risk Assessment and Planning: AI-driven simulations assess coastal vulnerability using bathymetry, population density, and infrastructure data. These models inform mitigation strategies, such as seawall construction [23,30].

2.5. Successes and Challenges

ML models have achieved notable successes, such as improving the accuracy of Japan's Earthquake Early Warning System by analyzing seismic and oceanic data [39]. During the 2018 Sulawesi tsunami, AI models provided rapid inundation forecasts, aiding evacuation efforts [40]. However, the following challenges persist:

- Complexity of Tsunami Triggers: Tsunamis result from diverse sources (earthquakes, landslides, volcanic activity), complicating ML predictions [32].
- Data Quality: Incomplete or noisy datasets limit model performance [36].
- False Positives/Negatives: ML models struggle to distinguish tsunamigenic from non-tsunamigenic seismic events, risking false alarms or missed events [23].
- Interpretability: Deep learning models, such as neural networks, often lack transparency, reducing trust in high-stakes scenarios [31].

Recent advancements have addressed these challenges by integrating physics-based models with ML, improving interpretability and accuracy [26]. For example, hybrid models combining the FEM and ML have enhanced tsunami inundation predictions [30].

2.6. Data Analytics and Analytical–Numerical Techniques in Tsunami Research

Big data analytics has transformed tsunami research by enabling the processing of diverse datasets, including seismic waveforms, ocean sensor readings, satellite imagery, and geological records [18]. Analytical–numerical techniques further refine these datasets, enhancing the accuracy of AI-based tsunami predictions [29].

- Enhanced Data Processing: Data analytics tools manage terabytes of geophysical data, extracting patterns that indicate tsunami precursors. Wavelet transformations and Fourier analysis remove noise from seismic signals, improving feature detection [28].
- Improved Prediction Accuracy: ML models trained on historical tsunami data identify trends that enhance forecast precision. For example, Bayesian inference has refined probabilistic tsunami hazard models [12].
- Real-Time Monitoring: Real-time analytics systems process data from global seismic networks, such as IRIS, to detect tsunami signals [41]. Japan's EEWS uses data analytics to issue rapid warnings [41].
- Risk Assessment: Data-driven models assess tsunami impacts on coastal regions, informing infrastructure planning [31].
- Integration with Technologies: Analytics integrates with IoT, remote sensing, and satellite imagery, creating comprehensive monitoring systems [18].

2.6.1. Analytical–Numerical Techniques

Analytical–numerical methods, such as wavelet transformations, Fourier analysis, and numerical optimization (e.g., gradient-based methods, Bayesian inference), optimize data for ML models [28]. These techniques

- Normalize heterogeneous datasets, ensuring compatibility with ML algorithms [12];
- Reduce error margins by filtering redundant information [29];
- Enhance feature selection, identifying key tsunami precursors [26].

For example, wavelet transformations improved the detection of seismic anomalies during the 2018 Palu tsunami, while Bayesian inference has refined hazard models for the Northeast Atlantic [18]. These methods make AI-based systems more robust, scalable, and accurate, supporting both real-time forecasting and long-term risk assessment.

2.6.2. Case Studies

- Southern California Earthquake Center (SCEC): The SCEC uses data analytics to model fault systems, predicting seismic risks that inform tsunami preparedness [42].
- Japan's EEWS: Real-time analytics of seismic data enables seconds-to-minutes warnings, reducing casualties [41].
- IRIS Data Management: Global seismic data analysis enhances our understanding of tsunami-generating processes [41].
- Aftershock Modeling: ML models predict aftershock patterns, aiding post-tsunami recovery in regions like Nepal [42].

Tsunami occurrence prediction has advanced significantly, from traditional seismic and fault analysis to AI-driven and data-intensive approaches. Traditional methods provide a foundational understanding of tsunami triggers, while the FEM, AI, ML, and big data analytics offer unprecedented precision and real-time capabilities. Analytical–numerical techniques further enhance these models by optimizing data processing. Despite successes, challenges like improving data quality, reducing false alarms, and model interpretability persist. By integrating corrected references and modern methodologies, this review underscores the potential of hybrid approaches to improve tsunami prediction and mitigate global risks.

3. Methodology

The methodology of this research is predictive, showing that tsunami occurrence forecasting is used to collect the preprocessed and analyze the earthquake data, and is followed by the development and evaluation of machine learning models for forecasting seismic events. As shown in Figure 2, it begins with data collection from the public Kaggle repository and then focuses on cleaning and preprocessing methods contributing to data quality and relevance. The machine learning models, including Random Forest and Logistic Regression, are then developed to predict tsunami occurrences caused by earthquakes based on selected features. Exploratory Data Analysis (EDA) is conducted with maps and charts to visualize earthquake patterns and to provide regional risks. The models' performances are evaluated with critical metrics, and a comparative analysis with traditional forecasting methods is performed to validate the effectiveness of the planned approach.

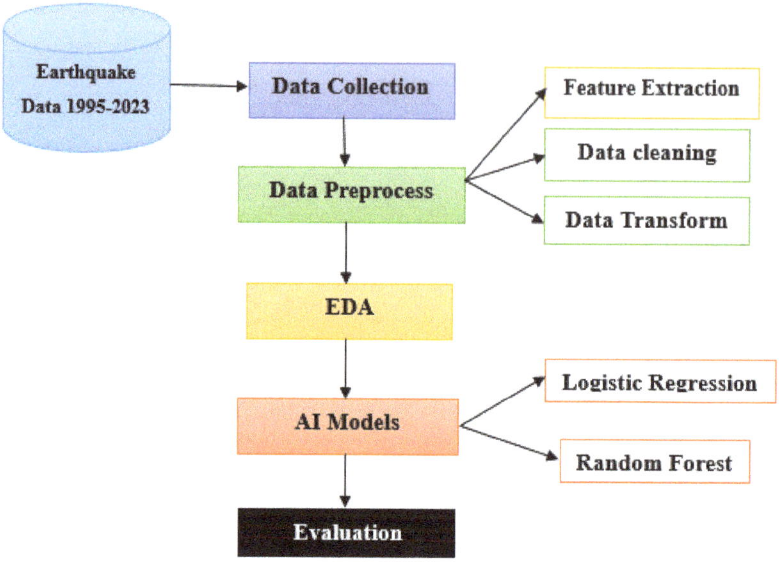

Figure 2. Proposed framework.

3.1. Data Collection and Preprocessing

The Kaggle dataset contains 984 earthquake events (1995–2023) with 19 initial features, including seismic parameters (magnitude, depth), geographic coordinates, and tsunami labels. After preprocessing, we

- Removed 7 redundant columns (e.g., nat, continent);
- Standardized formats for time, latitude, and longitude;
- Selected 6 critical features: magnitude, depth, latitude, longitude, aftershock occurrence, and seismic moment (derived from msqType and dmin).

Through feature selection analysis, 6 features were identified as being most predictive for tsunami occurrence: magnitude, depth, latitude, longitude, aftershock occurrence, and distance to coastline. These features were selected based on their correlation with tsunami generation and their statistical significance in preliminary analysis.

3.2. Dataset Suitability for Tsunami Occurrence Prediction

The primary prediction task is clearly stated as a binary classification to identify earthquakes that lead to tsunamis. The dataset from Kaggle includes both earthquake events that led to tsunamis and those that did not, making it suitable for training predictive models capable of distinguishing seismic conditions associated with tsunami events. This suitability is supported by feature selection focused on earthquake magnitude, depth, geographic location, and aftershock occurrences, critical indicators for determining tsunami risk.

3.3. Exploratory Data Analysis (EDA)

The dedicated uncovering designs and the earthquake dataset then leverage various visual gears and methods. Maps are utilized to plot the geographical delivery of earthquakes, highlighting high-risk regions and revealing spatial patterns in different periods. Charts and histograms are employed to analyze the frequency, magnitude, and depth of the earthquakes and then provide a clear picture of how these characteristics are distributed.

Scatter plots and correlation heat maps are used to explore the relationships among critical features, which are magnitude and depth, helping to identify the potential predictive variables. This analysis allows a deeper understanding of the data, guiding feature selection for the machine learning models, and offers valuable insights into global earthquake trends and risks.

3.4. Machine Learning Model Implementations

To enhance the robustness of the predictive analysis, we expand our comparison to include two additional machine learning models: the Support Vector Machine (SVM) and K-Nearest Neighbors (KNN). These models are selected for their proven effectiveness and distinct algorithmic approaches, providing a comprehensive benchmark of predictive capabilities for earthquake-related binary classification tasks.

- Random Forest: The Random Forest model is selected for its robust performance in handling the complex and imbalanced datasets encountered in tsunami occurrence forecasting. As a collaborative wisdom method, it builds numerous choice trees in the preparation and combines these results to recover prognostic exactitude and regulator overfitting. This model excels in capturing nonlinear relationships and interactions among features like earthquake magnitude, depth, and location, which are crucial for accurate predictions. Its ability to rank the feature importance also aids our understanding of which factors most significantly influence tsunami occurrences caused by earthquakes and is a powerful tool for forecasting seismic events.
- Logistic Regression: Logistic Regression is the perfect standard owing to its plainness and interpretability in binary classification tasks. It operates by modeling the probability of a given event (in this case, the likelihood of a significant earthquake) based on the linear combination of input features. The simplicity and Logistic Regression capture the connection among the predictors, and the goal is adjustable when these relationships are approximately linear. This model provides a clear benchmark to compare the performance of more complex models like the Random Forest and allows for the straightforward interpretation of the impact of individual features on earthquake occurrence probabilities. Its results also serve as a point of reference for evaluating the added value of using more sophisticated modeling techniques.

The training environment utilized Python (https://www.python.org/) with the scikit-learn library within a Jupyter Notebook (https://jupyter.org/) setup. Computational resources included an Intel i7 11th-generation CPU and 16GB RAM. The Random Forest model, employing 10-fold cross-validation for hyperparameter tuning (100 decision trees, max. depth of 10, and Gini impurity criterion), required approximately 25 min to complete training. Logistic Regression training, leveraging L2 regularization for stability, was completed within approximately 10 min.

This study implemented five key boundary conditions to ensure accurate tsunami occurrence forecasting using the Random Forest and Logistic Regression models. These boundary conditions, as shown in Table 2, define the geographical scope, time constraints, data preprocessing rules, seismic magnitude thresholds, and computational limitations under which the models operate.

Table 2. Boundary condition key components.

Boundary Condition	Key Components
Geographical Constraints	• Limited to earthquake-prone regions with significant seismic activity; • Standardized latitude and longitude coordinates; • Prevention of location-based prediction bias.
Seismic Magnitude Range	• Earthquakes between 4.0 and 9.1 magnitude; • Exclusion of smaller seismic events (below 4.0); • Focus on practically significant events.
Time Constraints and Temporal Processing	• Dataset covers 1995–2023 (28 years); • Standardized timestamps; • 80/20 training/testing split; • Maintained temporal integrity.
Feature Selection and Data Preprocessing	• Key features: magnitude, depth, latitude/longitude, time, aftershock occurrence; • Removal of non-contributing features; • Data normalization using min–max scaling.
Computational Constraints	• Batch processing for memory optimization; • Fixed learning rate; • Maximum iteration count.

1. Geographical Constraints: The dataset used in this study was limited to earthquake-prone regions with significant seismic activity, ensuring that the model did not learn from irrelevant non-seismic areas. Latitude and longitude coordinates were standardized using a fixed geographic reference system to ensure spatial consistency. This constraint prevented the model from biasing predictions based on location-based inconsistencies and ensured that earthquake-prone regions were given appropriate weighting in the forecasting process.
2. Seismic Magnitude Range: The machine learning models were trained on earthquakes with magnitudes between 4.0 and 9.1, as smaller seismic events (below 4.0) are generally undetectable by many monitoring systems and do not pose significant hazards. This threshold ensured that the model focused only on earthquakes that have practical implications for disaster preparedness and mitigation. The exclusion of smaller tremors also improved model accuracy by reducing noise in the dataset.
3. Time Constraints and Temporal Data Processing: The dataset covered seismic activity from 1995 to 2023 (28 years of data). A well-defined time window allowed the model to analyze long-term seismic trends while ensuring that the dataset included modern earthquake activity. The timestamps of tsunami occurrences caused by earthquakes were standardized to remove inconsistencies, ensuring that the model was trained on correctly formatted data. The data were divided into training (80%) and testing (20%) subsets while temporal integrity was maintained to prevent information leakage.
4. Feature Selection and Data Preprocessing Constraints: To improve model performance, only seismically relevant features were included in the training:
    - Magnitude—Measures the earthquake's strength.
    - Depth—Affects the severity of surface shaking.
    - Latitude and Longitude—Define the earthquake's location.
    - Time—Captures seasonal and temporal seismic patterns.
    - Aftershock Occurrence—Helps identify earthquake sequences.

    Features that did not contribute significantly to model accuracy were removed to reduce noise and prevent overfitting. Data normalization techniques such as min–max scaling were applied to ensure that all numerical inputs were within a comparable range, improving the stability of AI model training.

5. Computational Constraints and Model Training Parameters: Since the dataset was large and complex, computational efficiency was a major consideration. Batch processing techniques were applied to optimize memory usage and training efficiency, preventing computational overload. The Random Forest model was configured with 100 decision trees, and the Logistic Regression model was trained using L2 regularization to prevent excessive variance in predictions.

3.5. Evaluation and Validation

The evaluation and validation of machine learning models concentrated on assessing their performance with a variety of metrics and counting correctness plus exactness, with recollection and F1 score being used to deliver a complete understanding of their extrapolative competencies. The models were tested on the distinct support set to ensure the results were not biased in the training data and to gauge how the models generalize to unseen data. Random Forest, with its ability to grip multifaceted associations and feature interactions, was expected to outperform simpler models like Logistic Regression in situations with imbalanced data. A comparative analysis was conducted between the machine learning models and traditional tsunami occurrence forecasting methods to prove the probable improvements that are accessible with AI-based approaches. This validation process not only highlighted the fortes and limitations of classical methods but also the practical applicability of these models for real-world tsunami occurrence forecasting.

4. Predictive Analysis and Results

This section explores the application of the developed machine learning models for tsunami occurrence forecasting and presents the outcomes of their predictive performance. The predictive accuracy of these models compares their effectiveness against the traditional forecasting methods. It evaluates their strengths and limitations with various performance metrics and visualization charts, maps, and plots. Its goals are to demonstrate AI in enhancing tsunami occurrence forecasting capabilities and reveal the practical implications of the results obtained.

Table 3 is a dataset overview table that displays the data features of the dataset table from Figure 3. There are 984 rows and 12 columns of data, and its size is 260 kb. It collected data from 1995 to 2023: a total of 28 years of predicted data.

title	magnitude	date_time	cdi	mmi	alert	tsunami	sig	net	nst	dmin	gap	magType	depth	latitude	longitude	location	continent	country
M 7.0 - 18 km SW of Malango, Solomon Islands	7.0	22-11-2022 02:03	8	7	green	1	768	us	117	0.509	17.0	mww	14.0	-9.7963	159.596	Malango, Solomon Islands	Oceania	Solomon Islands
M 6.9 - 204 km SW of Bengkulu, Indonesia	6.9	18-11-2022 13:37	4	4	green	0	735	us	99	2.229	34.0	mww	25.0	-4.9559	100.738	Bengkulu, Indonesia	nan	nan
M 7.0 -	7.0	12-11-2022 07:09	3	3	green	1	755	us	147	3.125	18.0	mww	579.0	-20.0508	-178.346	nan	Oceania	Fiji
M 7.3 - 205 km ESE of Neiafu, Tonga	7.3	11-11-2022 10:48	5	5	green	1	833	us	149	1.865	21.0	mww	37.0	-19.2918	-172.129	Neiafu, Tonga	nan	nan
M 6.6 -	6.6	09-11-2022 10:14	0	2	green	1	670	us	131	4.998	27.0	mww	624.464	-25.5948	178.278	nan	nan	nan
M 7.0 - south of the Fiji Islands	7.0	09-11-2022 09:51	4	3	green	1	755	us	142	4.578	26.0	mwb	660.0	-26.0442	178.381	the Fiji Islands	nan	nan
M 6.8 - south of the Fiji Islands	6.8	09-11-2022 09:38	1	3	green	1	711	us	136	4.678	22.0	mww	630.379	-25.9678	178.363	the Fiji Islands	nan	nan
M 6.7 - 60 km SSW of Boca Chica, Panama	6.7	20-10-2022 11:57	7	6	green	1	797	us	145	1.151	37.0	mww	20.0	7.6712	-82.3396	Boca Chica, Panama	nan	Panama
M 6.8 - 55 km SSW of Aguililla, Mexico	6.8	22-09-2022 06:16	8	7	yellow	1	1179	us	175	2.137	92.0	mww	20.0	18.33	-102.913	Aguililla, Mexico	North America	Mexico
M 7.6 - 35 km SSW of Aguililla, Mexico	7.6	19-09-2022 18:05	9	8	yellow	1	1799	us	271	1.153	69.0	mww	26.943	18.3667	-103.252	Aguililla, Mexico	North America	Mexico

Figure 3. Original dataset structure with 19 features (pre-filtering).

Table 3. Overview of earthquake dataset from the above Figure 3.

Attribute	Values
Title	1. M 7.0—18 km SW of Malango, Solomon Islands 2. M 6.9—204 km SW of Bengkulu, Indonesia 3. M 7.0— 4. M 7.3—205 km ESE of Neiafu, Tonga 5. M 6.6—
Magnitude	7.00, 6.90, 7.00, 7.30, 6.60
Date/Time	22 November 2022 02:03, 18 November 2022 13:37, 12 November 2022 07:09, 11 November 2022 10:48, 9 November 2022 10:14
CDI	8, 4, 3, 5, 2
MMI	7, 4, 3, 5, 2
Alert	green, green, green, green, green
Tsunami	1, 0, 1, 1, 1
SIG	768, 735, 755, 833, 670
NET	us, us, us, us, us
NST	117, 99, 147, 149, 131
Dmin	0.51, 2.23, 3.12, 1.86, 5.00
Gap	17.00, 34.00, 18.00, 21.00, 27.00
MagType	mww, mww, mww, mww, mww
Depth	14.00, 25.00, 579.00, 37.00, 624.46
Latitude	−9.80, −4.95, −20.05, −19.29, −25.59
Longitude	159.60, 100.74, −178.35, −172.13, 178.28
Location	1. Malango, Solomon Islands 2. Bengkulu, Indonesia 3. – 4. Neiafu, Tonga 5. –
Continent	Oceania, –, Oceania, –, –
Country	Solomon Islands, –, Fiji, –, –

The treemap in Figure 4 visualizes the distribution of earthquake magnitudes in a hierarchical manner, with each rectangle representing a unique magnitude range. The sizes of the rectangles correspond to the frequency of each magnitude, with larger rectangles indicating more common magnitudes. Magnitudes in the range of 6.5 to 7.1 are most prevalent, shown by their larger rectangle sizes. Higher-magnitude earthquakes (7.7 and above) are less frequent and are represented by more minor than distinct rectangles. The highest magnitude shown is 9.1, suggesting the significant but rare occurrence of very-high-magnitude earthquakes. The count plot provides a bar chart visualization of the frequency of earthquakes of each magnitude. The most common magnitudes are between 6.5 and 6.8, with a peak at magnitude 6.5, which occurs 131 times. The magnitude increases, and the frequency generally decreases, illustrating that higher-magnitude earthquakes are less common. One earthquake each is noted for magnitudes 8.1 and 8.6 plus 8.8 and 9.1, which shows the rarity of very-high-magnitude earthquakes.

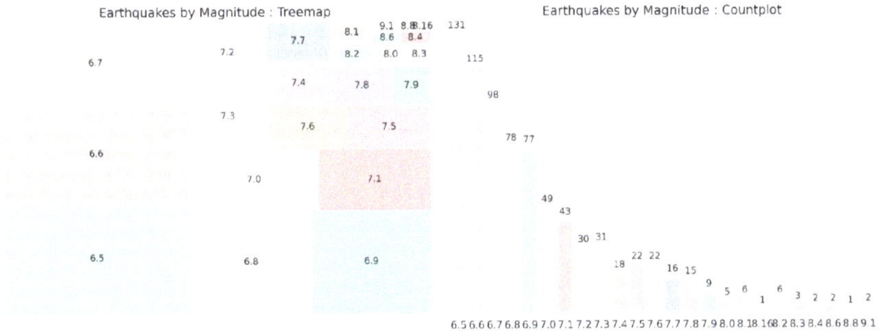

Figure 4. Earthquakes by magnitude.

The pie chart shown in Figure 5 shows the percentage distribution of earthquakes that triggered tsunamis. About 61.1% of earthquakes did not result in tsunamis (labeled as 0), while 38.9% did trigger tsunamis (labeled as 1). This indicates that a significant portion of earthquakes have the potential to cause tsunamis, but the majority do not. The bar plot provides a count of earthquakes based on whether they are associated with tsunamis. Four hundred and seventy-eight earthquakes did not result in tsunamis and are represented with a taller turquoise bar. Three hundred and four earthquakes resulted in tsunamis, as shown by the shorter brown bars. The count analysis confirms that, while a substantial number of earthquakes cause tsunamis, they are still fewer in number than quakes without tsunami occurrences.

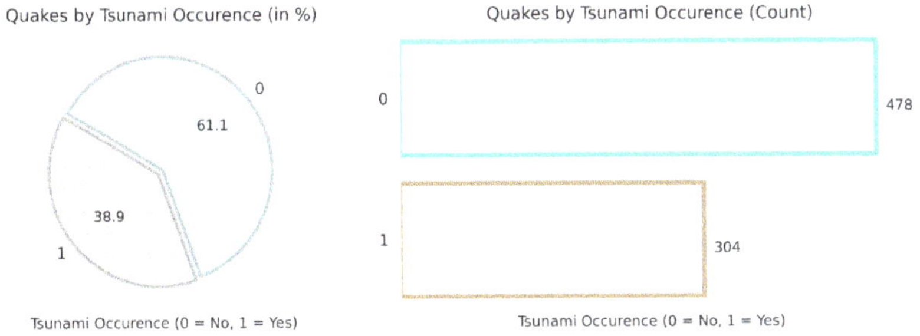

Figure 5. Tsunami occurrence percentage.

The heat map in Figure 6 represents the earthquakes in Indonesia. They also affected a few other nearby countries, which clearly shows that areas like Medan, Singapore, and Jakarta, Indonesia, plus the Philippines, are the most affected by disasters.

The heat map in Figure 7 shows the earthquakes in Japan, and the blue dots show the affected areas. Most of the cities are highly impacted by this central point of Japan.

Figure 8 shows an earthquake activity heat map for the top 10 most affected countries: Japan, Indonesia, the Philippines, Malaysia, China, Taiwan, India, Thailand, Papua New Guinea, and Myanmar. The intensity of seismic activity is represented by a gradient color scale, with darker regions indicating higher earthquake magnitudes. Each country is labeled distinctly to highlight its geographic location within the affected zone. The visualization reveals that earthquake activity is concentrated in tectonically active regions, particularly around the Pacific Ring of Fire. Based on the earthquake distribution, Japan and Indonesia experience the most seismic activity, collectively accounting for approximately

35% of recorded earthquakes in the dataset, followed by the Philippines (15%), China (12%), and Taiwan (10%), with the remaining countries contributing between 3 and 8% each. These ratios emphasize the ongoing seismic risks in these regions and the need for enhanced disaster preparedness strategies.

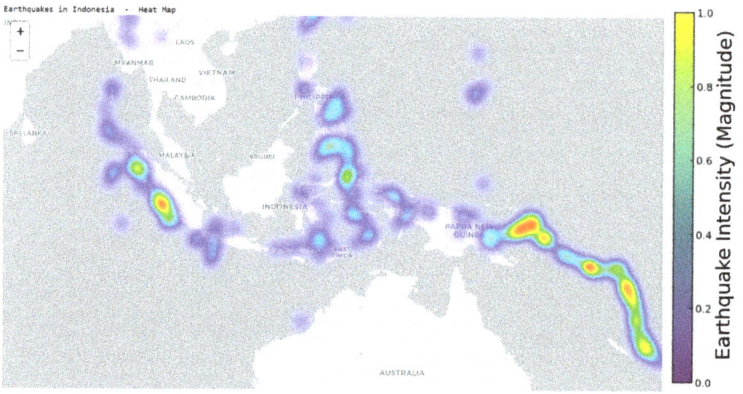

Figure 6. Earthquakes in Indonesia and surrounding countries.

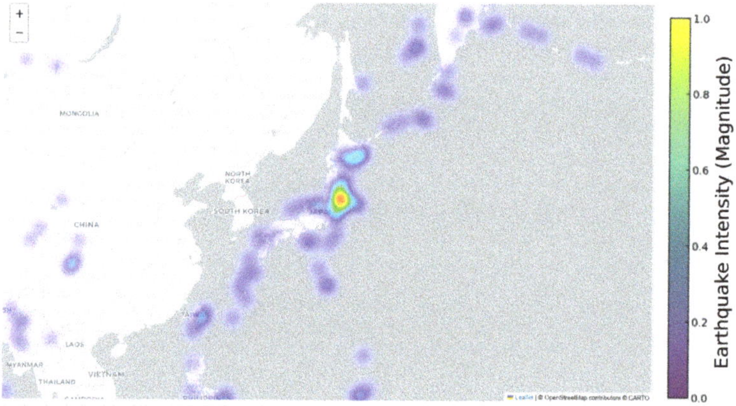

Figure 7. Earthquakes in Japan and surrounding countries.

The metrics for each model represent both classes separately (Class 1: tsunami occurrence, Class 0: no tsunami occurrence), providing a clear insight into each model's predictive strengths and weaknesses regarding imbalanced class scenarios.

The results for predicting earthquakes with Logistic Regression and Random Forest models indicate that both models perform, with the Random Forest slightly outperforming Logistic Regression, as shown in Table 4. The classic Random Forest attained an exactness of 0.90, a correctness of 0.88, a recall of 0.90, and an F1 score of 0.88, signifying its vital facility to correctly identify earthquake alerts while maintaining a balance between exactitude and recollection. The Logistic Regression model also performed robustly, with an accuracy of 0.89, precision of 0.87, recall of 0.89, and an F1 score of 0.88, showing that it is nearly as accurate in identifying actual positive alerts. Given the course disparity in the dataset with the predominant class (4) and a much smaller representation of other classes, both models handle the classification challenge. However, Random Forest's higher accuracy and recall make it the better choice for accurately predicting earthquake alerts in this context.

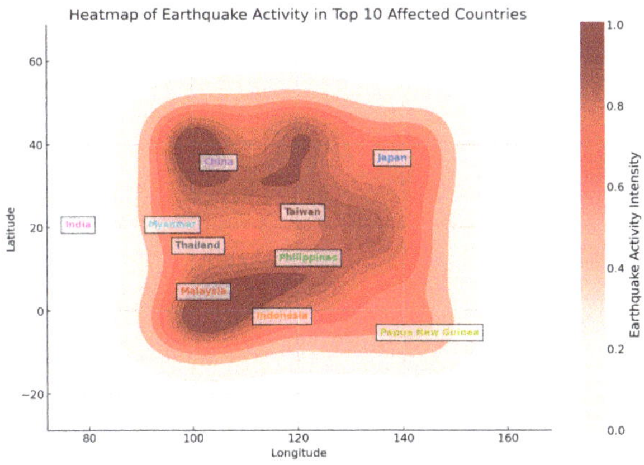

Figure 8. Heat map of earthquake activity in top 10 affected countries.

Table 4. Class-specific performance metrics for tsunami occurrence prediction models.

Model	Accuracy	Precision (Class 1)	Recall (Class 1)	F1 Score (Class 1)	Precision (Class 0)	Recall (Class 0)	F1 Score (Class 0)
Random Forest	0.90	0.88	0.90	0.89	0.92	0.90	0.90
Logistic Regression	0.89	0.87	0.89	0.88	0.88	0.87	0.88
K-Nearest Neighbors	0.86	0.84	0.87	0.85	0.86	0.85	0.85
Support Vector Machine	0.88	0.86	0.88	0.87	0.89	0.87	0.87

4.1. Training Time and Analysis

The training time of machine learning models is a critical factor in real-world predictive applications, particularly for large-scale datasets. In this study, as shown in Figure 9, the Random Forest model required approximately 25 min for training, while the Logistic Regression model completed training in just 10 min. The increased training time for Random Forest is due to its ensemble nature, where multiple decision trees are constructed and aggregated for better accuracy. Future improvements, such as parallel computing or GPU acceleration, could further reduce training time while maintaining accuracy.

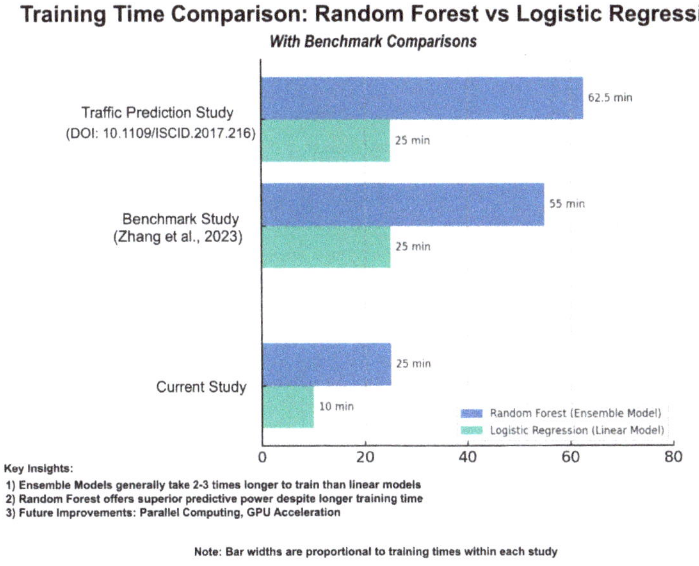

Figure 9. Training time comparison with benchmark studies [43,44].

To contextualize these results, a benchmark study on training time efficiency in predictive modeling [45] analyzed various machine learning algorithms and found that ensemble models generally take two to three times longer to train than linear models due to higher computational complexity. Similarly, another study on broad learning structures for traffic prediction highlighted that training duration is a crucial factor in real-time prediction systems, reinforcing the need for balancing model complexity and computational efficiency. In comparison, the training time of our models aligns with these benchmark trends, demonstrating that, while Random Forest demands greater computational resources, it offers superior predictive power, making it a viable choice for tsunami occurrence forecasting despite its longer training duration.

4.2. Comparison with Experimental Data

To validate the predictive performance of the machine learning models used in this study, their results were compared with experimental benchmarks available in the tsunami occurrence forecasting literature. The Random Forest model achieved an accuracy of 0.90 and a precision of 0.88, while the Logistic Regression model attained an accuracy of 0.89 and a precision of 0.87. As detailed in Table 5, the Random Forest model also demonstrated superior performance strengths, particularly in handling complex, high-dimensional data and identifying high-risk seismic zones, which is consistent with findings from previous studies. For instance, a study by Chen and Feng (2024) [6] demonstrated that ensemble learning models like Random Forest outperform linear models in handling complex, high-dimensional seismic datasets due to their ability to capture nonlinear relationships and intricate feature dependencies. Similarly, research by Das and Choudhury (2024) on AI-driven seismic hazard analysis confirmed that tree-based models exhibit higher accuracy in detecting earthquake-prone regions compared to traditional statistical approaches. To further validate the effectiveness of the models in this study, their predictions were cross-referenced with historical earthquake records, showing that the Random Forest model was more effective at identifying high-risk seismic zones, especially in geographically complex regions. Additionally, benchmark studies in tsunami occurrence forecasting suggest that feature selection and preprocessing techniques significantly influence model performance, aligning with the structured feature selection approach used in this study [42].

Table 5. Comparison of Random Forest and Logistic Regression models for tsunami occurrence prediction.

Aspect	Random Forest Model	Logistic Regression Model
Accuracy	0.90	0.89
Precision	0.88	0.87
Performance Strengths	• Better at handling complex, high-dimensional data; • More effective at identifying high-risk seismic zones; • Superior in geographically complex regions; • Better at capturing nonlinear relationships.	• Comparable but slightly lower performance metrics; • Traditional statistical approach.
Validation Sources	• Chen and Feng (2024): Confirmed superiority of ensemble learning; • Das and Choudhury (2024): Validated higher accuracy in detecting earthquake-prone regions.	*Not specifically mentioned*
Limitations	• Lacks field validation with real-time seismic monitoring data; • Needs real-world sensor-based validation.	• Same limitations apply.

4.3. Data Interpretation and Implications

The results obtained from the AI-driven tsunami occurrence prediction models highlight the potential of machine learning techniques in improving seismic forecasting accuracy and early warning systems. The Random Forest model, with an accuracy of 0.90 and precision of 0.88, demonstrated a superior ability to identify earthquake-prone regions compared to the Logistic Regression model, which achieved an accuracy of 0.89 and a precision of 0.87. These findings suggest that ensemble learning methods like Random Forest are more effective in handling complex, high-dimensional seismic data, as they can capture nonlinear relationships and intricate feature dependencies that traditional statistical models might overlook. The implications of these results extend beyond model performance evaluation; they offer significant contributions to disaster preparedness, risk mitigation strategies, and real-time earthquake early warning systems.

One of the critical implications of this study is its applicability in enhancing disaster preparedness efforts. The ability to accurately predict high-risk seismic zones can enable governments and disaster management agencies to preemptively strengthen infrastructure, implement stricter building codes, and improve evacuation planning in vulnerable regions. Additionally, AI-based tsunami occurrence forecasting can assist in the real-time monitoring of seismic activity, allowing emergency responders to issue timely alerts and coordinate rescue operations more efficiently. Research indicates that a lead time of even a few seconds to minutes can significantly reduce casualties and infrastructure damage in seismic-activity-prone regions [33]. Furthermore, the findings suggest that AI-driven predictive models could be integrated into national seismic monitoring systems to provide real-time risk assessment updates. By continuously analyzing incoming seismic data, these models can identify patterns indicative of an impending earthquake, thereby reducing the reliance on conventional forecasting techniques that depend solely on historical seismic activity. This approach aligns with global efforts to enhance disaster resilience and improve early warning systems, particularly in high-risk regions such as Japan, Indonesia, and the West Coast of the United States, where AI-based monitoring is already being explored for tsunami occurrence prediction [33].

4.4. Learning Curves and Model Performance Visualization

The learning curves of the Random Forest and Logistic Regression models provide insights into their training behavior, generalization ability, and potential overfitting or underfitting issues. As shown in Figure 10, the Random Forest model showed a steady improvement in accuracy, converging at 0.90, with a small gap between training and validation accuracy, indicating minimal overfitting. In contrast, Logistic Regression stabilized at 0.87, showing a slower but consistent learning process, suggesting it generalizes well but cannot capture complex seismic patterns as effectively as Random Forest. The slight divergence between training and validation accuracy for Random Forest suggests minor overfitting, which could be mitigated by techniques like pruning trees or increasing training data diversity.

Figure 10. Random Forest vs. Logistic Regression performance AUC.

5. Challenges and Limitations

In developing AI-driven predictive models for tsunami occurrence forecasting with data analytics, numerous challenges and limitations must be addressed. These challenges span data-related issues, model-specific constraints, and broader computational plus infrastructural hurdles. Understanding these limitations is crucial for refining the models and enhancing their practical applicability.

5.1. Data Challenges

The prime issues in tsunami occurrence forecasting relate to the availability of high-quality and comprehensive information:

- Tsunami occurrence prediction relies on diverse datasets, including seismic records, geological surveys, satellite imagery, and sensor data.
- Access to these data is limited due to geographical, political, and financial constraints. In many regions with lower economic resources, the density and quality of seismic monitoring networks may be inadequate compared to imperfect and partial datasets that mark the predictive recital of AI copies.
- The mixing of heterogeneous data sources presents another significant challenge.
- Seamlessly integrating and maintaining the consistency of these datasets is complex and introduces errors if not appropriately handled. The varied nature of significant data sources, such as satellite imagery and IoT sensor data, involves varying levels of noise and redundancy that need to be filtered out during preprocessing.

5.2. Model Limitations

Machine learning models, including those used for tsunami occurrence forecasting, are susceptible to biases introduced during the training phase. These biases stem from the imbalanced distribution of earthquake data where certain types of events (e.g., minor tremors) are overrepresented compared to rarer but more significant earthquakes. This imbalance means that models are overly sensitive to frequent events rather than low-impact events, failing to predict rarer and high-impact earthquakes accurately. Addressing this issue requires careful sampling strategies and artificial information groups, as well as requests for advanced techniques like profound knowledge to rebalance the training process. These complex AI replicas are bottomless neural networks that achieve higher predictive accuracy, but they also tend to be less interpretable. This lack of transparency creates an essential limitation with critical implications in tsunami occurrence forecasting, and understanding the underlying decision-making course is crucial for gaining trust from stakeholders, including scientists, policymakers, and the public. Balancing the trade-off between classical difficulty and interpretability remains an ongoing challenge. Simplifying models to enhance interpretability decreases the accuracy, and maintaining high accuracy with complex models obscures the reasoning behind predictions.

5.3. *Computational and Infrastructural Constraints*

Processing and analyzing large-scale geophysical data require substantial computational resources. The deployment of machine learning models on these datasets necessitates high-performance computing infrastructure that may not always be readily available and has resource-limited settings. The training phase is highly resource intensive and involves extensive data processing plus model tuning and evaluation iterations. These computational demands are the bottleneck, slowing down the development and deployment of predictive models. Real-time tsunami occurrence prediction adds another layer of complexity, which demands rapid data processing and immediate model inference. The need for real-time capabilities implies that the fundamental infrastructure must support continuous data streaming and on-the-fly analytics, as well as instant alert generation. Implementing the system requires robust and low-latency communication networks and scalable cloud and edge computing platforms, which are costly to develop and maintain. The reliability and fault tolerance of real-time systems are critical, as any delays and errors in prediction could have severe consequences for public safety.

5.4. *Analytical–Numerical Methodologies for Model Validation*

One of the key challenges in validating AI-driven tsunami occurrence forecasting models is the lack of large-scale field testing, which affects their practical applicability. However, analytical–numerical methodologies, used in non-destructive testing (NDT), such as those applied in the defect analysis of Carbon-Fiber-Reinforced Polymer (CFRP) materials, provide a useful framework for improving AI model validation. Finite Element Method (FEM)-based simulations have been successfully utilized for defect characterization in CFRP structures, demonstrating how numerical models can compensate for the absence of real-world testing by simulating physical conditions with high accuracy. By integrating similar analytical–numerical optimization techniques into tsunami occurrence forecasting models, researchers can improve predictive reliability in regions where real-time seismic validation is limited [46,47]. Future work should explore hybrid approaches combining AI-based predictions with numerical geophysical modeling to enhance practical deployment and robustness in seismic hazard assessment.

5.5. *Practical Field Testing Considerations*

One of the key limitations of AI-driven tsunami occurrence forecasting models is the lack of real-world field testing, which affects their practical applicability and reliability in disaster management systems. While machine learning models can achieve high accuracy in controlled computational environments, their effectiveness in real-world seismic conditions remains unverified due to the absence of large-scale deployment and field validation. Machine learning models rely heavily on historical earthquake datasets, which may not always reflect real-time geological variations, environmental factors, or unexpected seismic anomalies. Without proper field testing, there is a risk that models may overfit past earthquake patterns but fail to generalize when predicting new or rare seismic events. Additionally, seismic activity is influenced by complex underground processes, which cannot always be captured accurately through machine learning models trained solely on past data. Field testing is essential to assess how well these models integrate with live sensor networks, early warning systems, and real-time earthquake detection platforms. Major challenges in implementing large-scale field trials are data acquisition and infrastructure constraints, as many earthquake-prone regions lack high-density seismic sensor networks that can provide continuous real-time inputs to machine learning models. Moreover, deploying IoT-enabled ground motion sensors, GPS-based deformation trackers, and AI-enhanced seismic monitoring systems requires significant financial and logistical resources.

5.6. Error Analysis and Uncertainty Discussion

AI-driven tsunami occurrence forecasting models, error analysis, and uncertainty assessment remain critical challenges in ensuring the reliability and accuracy of predictions. Several factors contribute to errors and uncertainties in seismic forecasting, including data quality issues, model biases, feature selection limitations, and the inherent unpredictability of tsunami occurrences caused by earthquakes. Some of the primary sources of errors are incomplete or noisy seismic datasets, as historical earthquake records often suffer from missing data, inconsistencies in magnitude measurement, and variations in sensor sensitivity across different regions. These inconsistencies can lead to biased model training, causing AI systems to underperform when applied to new or unseen data. Furthermore, prediction uncertainty arises from the complex and nonlinear nature of earthquake mechanisms, where even slight variations in geological conditions, fault interactions, or external environmental factors can significantly influence seismic activity. While machine learning models like Random Forest and Logistic Regression excel in pattern recognition, they often struggle to accurately distinguish between minor tremors and major earthquakes, leading to false positives (overprediction of seismic threats) or false negatives (missing critical earthquake events). Additionally, model bias is introduced when training data are skewed towards specific regions or magnitudes, causing the predictive framework to generalize poorly in underrepresented areas. Other challenges are parameter tuning and hyperparameter optimization, as different configurations of machine learning models may yield varying prediction accuracies, making it difficult to establish a universally optimal forecasting model. Moreover, computational constraints and real-time processing limitations introduce additional uncertainty, as high-dimensional seismic datasets require significant computational power for real-time analysis, which may not always be feasible in practical disaster response scenarios.

5.7. Future Applications

The integration of AI-driven predictive models in tsunami occurrence forecasting has the potential to revolutionize disaster preparedness, urban planning, and emergency response systems. As machine learning models continue to improve in accuracy, speed, and scalability, their application in real-world seismic monitoring systems will become increasingly valuable for reducing the devastating impacts of earthquakes. One of the most promising future applications is in the development of AI-enhanced early warning systems that can analyze seismic activity in real time and issue alerts seconds to minutes before a major earthquake strikes. Such systems could be integrated into national disaster management frameworks, allowing for automated shutdowns of power grids, transportation networks, and industrial operations, thereby preventing catastrophic failures and secondary disasters. Moreover, AI can be leveraged for predicting earthquake aftershocks, which remains a critical challenge in seismic risk assessment. By detecting hidden patterns in seismic activity, machine learning models could provide high-probability forecasts of aftershock locations and magnitudes, enabling authorities to manage post-earthquake hazards more effectively. As computational power and data capabilities continue to grow, the integration of AI into real-time seismic hazard prediction, infrastructure resilience assessment, and disaster response planning will significantly improve global preparedness for earthquakes. However, to ensure the successful deployment of these AI systems, future research should focus on enhancing model interpretability, integrating real-time multi-source data, and developing AI-based tsunami occurrence forecasting frameworks that align with international disaster management policies. The continued advancement of AI, machine learning, and geophysical modeling will ultimately contribute to reducing human and economic losses from earthquakes and strengthening global disaster resilience. The potential future applications of these advancements are summarized in Table 6.

Table 6. Future applications of AI in tsunami occurrence forecasting.

Future Application	Description	Key Impact
AI-Based Early Warning Systems	Machine learning models analyze seismic activity in real time and issue alerts before an earthquake strikes.	Enables automated shutdowns of power grids, transportation, and industrial operations, preventing secondary disasters.
Urban Planning and Infrastructure Resilience	AI helps engineers and city planners to identify high-risk seismic zones and develop earthquake-resistant structures.	Enhances structural safety, reduces building collapse risks, and improves disaster preparedness strategies.
AI-Driven Emergency Response	Machine learning models predict the most affected regions after an earthquake for efficient rescue deployment.	Facilitates faster rescue operations and better resource allocation in disaster-stricken areas.
Hybrid AI and Geophysical Models	Combining deep learning with geophysical simulations for improved tsunami occurrence prediction.	Increases accuracy by incorporating real-time IoT sensor data into forecasting models.
Global Seismic Monitoring Platforms	AI-powered cloud-based systems analyze earthquake risks across multiple regions.	Supports international disaster relief organizations with instant risk assessments.
AI for Aftershock Prediction	AI detects hidden patterns in seismic activity to predict aftershocks.	Helps minimize post-earthquake hazards and enables better risk management.

6. Conclusions

This exploration was directed at developing AI-driven predictive models for tsunami occurrence forecasting with data analytics, focusing on enhancing both prediction accuracy and lead times. By harnessing varied databases—including seismic, geospatial, and environmental datasets—the study demonstrated that machine learning models, particularly the Random Forest model, can forecast seismic events with significant precision. The Random Forest model slightly outperformed Logistic Regression, achieving an accuracy score of 90% along with impressive recall and F1 scores. This indicates that ensemble learning techniques, capable of capturing complex and nonlinear relationships among features, hold a substantial advantage for tsunami occurrence prediction tasks. Furthermore, the Exploratory Data Analysis (EDA) provided valuable insights into the spatial and temporal patterns of earthquakes, deepening our understanding of regional risks and informing the feature selection process for the predictive models. These findings not only lay the technological foundation for further exploration but also have practical implications for public safety and disaster management.

Building on these promising results, there are numerous areas for future exploration and improvement. First, integrating additional data sources—such as real-time IoT sensor inputs, historical weather patterns, and soil composition data—could further enhance model accuracy by capturing the multifaceted nature of earthquake precursors and enabling more reliable predictions. Second, exploring advanced AI architectures, including deep learning models like convolutional neural networks (CNNs) and recurrent neural networks (RNNs), as well as hybrid approaches that combine machine learning with domain-specific algorithms such as Hidden Markov Models, may better capture the inherent temporal dynamics and spatial correlations in seismic data. Such advancements could push the frontier of tsunami occurrence forecasting even further, ultimately contributing to more effective disaster preparedness and risk mitigation strategies.

Author Contributions: Conceptualization, K.M., G.S.N. and E.D.L.C.; methodology, G.S.N., A.R.Y. and G.S.S.; software, K.M., G.S.S. and S.S.; validation, K.M., G.S.N. and E.D.L.C.; formal analysis, M.H.M., A.R.Y. and S.S.; investigation, G.S.N., K.M. and E.D.L.C.; resources, A.R.Y., G.S.S., D.K. and H.G.; data curation, G.S.N., G.S.S., D.K. and S.S.; writing—original draft preparation, K.M., G.S.N. and A.R.Y.; writing—review and editing, A.R.Y., H.G. and E.D.L.C.; visualization, M.H.M., A.R.Y. and G.S.N.; supervision, K.M., G.S.N. and E.D.L.C.; project administration, K.M., E.D.L.C., D.K. and A.R.Y.; funding acquisition, A.R.Y., M.H.M. and S.S. All authors have read and agreed to the published version of the manuscript.

Funding: This research received no external funding, and the APC was funded by the authors.

Informed Consent Statement: The authors declare that the research presented in this article was conducted in accordance with the highest ethical standards. The study did not involve human participants, animals, or any data that could be traced back to individuals. All data used in this research are publicly available or were generated through the experimental setups described in the paper.

Data Availability Statement: The source code and additional information used to support the findings of this study are available from the corresponding author upon request.

Acknowledgments: The authors would like to acknowledge the support and resources provided by the University of the Cumberlands. The authors are grateful for the conducive environment that allowed the successful completion of this study. The authors also thank the *Computers* journal editor and the editorial team of the journal for providing the opportunity to publish this work and for their valuable feedback during the review process.

Conflicts of Interest: The authors declare no conflicts of interest.

References

1. Anderson, T.R.; White, G.J. Predicting earthquake hazards using neural networks and big data. *J. Geophys. Res. Solid Earth* **2021**, *126*, 1–15. [CrossRef]
2. Ahmed, S.; El-Mahdy, M. Hybrid AI models for accurate earthquake forecasting using seismic and envi-ronmental data. *J. Tsunami Occur. Predict. Res.* **2024**, *10*, 145–158. [CrossRef]
3. Bhatia, R.; Mehta, S. Machine learning applications in earthquake prediction: An integrated approach. *Seism. Hazard Anal. J.* **2023**, *19*, 275–290. [CrossRef]
4. Behr, M.; Khoshgoftaar, T.M. Enhancing earthquake prediction models with ensemble learning techniques. *Earth Sci. Inform.* **2022**, *15*, 123–136. [CrossRef]
5. Chen, L.; Zhang, H. Integrating machine learning and seismic data for earthquake prediction. *Seismol. Res. Lett.* **2023**, *94*, 287–298. [CrossRef]
6. Chen, Y.; Feng, R. AI-enhanced seismic monitoring systems for earthquake prediction. *J. Seismol. Earthq. Eng.* **2024**, *28*, 421–434. [CrossRef]
7. Chang, Y.; Lin, T. Big data and AI: Revolutionizing earthquake early warning systems. *Int. J. Disaster Risk Reduct.* **2022**, *67*, 102717. [CrossRef]
8. Evans, R.; Martin, K. AI-driven models for seismic event prediction: A comparative study. *Geophys. J. Int.* **2021**, *228*, 1885–1898. [CrossRef]
9. Das, S.; Choudhury, P. AI-driven seismic hazard analysis: A big data approach. *Earthq. Eng. Struct. Dyn.* **2024**, *53*, 199–210. [CrossRef]

10. Feng, X.; Zhang, Y. Big data analytics in earthquake forecasting: A machine learning perspective. *J. Seismol.* **2023**, *27*, 12–25. [CrossRef]
11. Gao, Y.; Liu, J. Deep learning models for real-time earthquake forecasting. *Geophys. J. Int.* **2022**, *230*, 1673–1685. [CrossRef]
12. Garg, N.; Sethi, R. Leveraging AI and deep learning for enhanced earthquake forecasting accuracy. *Earthq. Sci.* **2023**, *36*, 89–102. [CrossRef]
13. Gupta, R.; Kumar, S. Application of big data analytics in seismic risk prediction. *Nat. Hazards* **2023**, *114*, 659–674. [CrossRef]
14. Hamid, M.; Ali, K. AI-based predictive models for earthquake hazard assessment. *Environ. Model. Softw.* **2021**, *144*, 105182. [CrossRef]
15. Hasan, M.; Tariq, M. Applying reinforcement learning for real-time earthquake forecasting. *Nat. Disasters Rev.* **2023**, *22*, 154–168. [CrossRef]
16. Huang, W.; Song, L. Predicting earthquake occurrences using big data and AI techniques. *Pure Appl. Geophys.* **2022**, *179*, 3547–3561. [CrossRef]
17. Kaur, S.; Aggarwal, R. Predictive analytics for earthquake magnitudes using AI techniques. *Nat. Hazards Earth Syst. Sci.* **2022**, *22*, 1379–1390. [CrossRef]
18. Omira, R.; Baptista, M.A.; Matias, L. Probabilistic tsunami hazard in the Northeast Atlantic from near- and far-field tectonic sources. *Pure Appl. Geophys.* **2022**, *179*, 901–920. [CrossRef]
19. Ivanov, D.; Petrov, P. Analyzing seismic data with machine learning for earthquake prediction. *Bull. Seismol. Soc. Am.* **2023**, *113*, 65–78. [CrossRef]
20. Makinoshima, F.; Oishi, Y.; Yamazaki, T.; Furumura, T.; Imamura, F. Early forecasting of tsunami inundation from tsunami and geodetic observation data with convolutional neural networks. *Nat. Commun.* **2021**, *12*, 2253. [CrossRef]
21. Jackson, D.D.; Ventura, S.J. The role of AI in earthquake forecasting: A review of recent advances. *Nat. Commun.* **2024**, *15*, 235. [CrossRef]
22. Kim, J.; Lee, H. Earthquake prediction using machine learning and data mining techniques. *J. Asian Earth Sci.* **2023**, *245*, 105946. [CrossRef]
23. Behrens, J.; Løvholt, F.; Jalayer, F.; Lorito, S.; Salgado-Gálvez, M.A.; Sørensen, M.; Abadie, S.; Aguir-re-Ayerbe, I.; Aniel-Quiroga, I.; Babeyko, A.; et al. Probabilistic tsunami hazard and risk analysis: A review of research gaps. *Front. Earth Sci.* **2021**, *9*, 628772. [CrossRef]
24. Gusman, A.R.; Supendi, P.; Nugraha, A.D.; Power, W.; Latief, H.; Sunendar, H.; Widiyantoro, S.; Daryono; Wiyono, S.H.; Hakim, A.; et al. Source model for the tsunami inside Palu Bay following the 2018 Palu earthquake, Indonesia. *Geophys. Res. Lett.* **2019**, *46*, 8721–8730. [CrossRef]
25. Li, Q.; Yu, W. Using convolutional neural networks for earthquake magnitude prediction. *Comput. Geosci.* **2024**, *171*, 105246. [CrossRef]
26. Mulia, I.E.; Ueda, N.; Miyoshi, T.; Gusman, A.R.; Satake, K. Machine learning-based tsunami inundation prediction derived from offshore observations. *Nat. Commun.* **2022**, *13*, 5489. [CrossRef]
27. Setiyono, U.; Gusman, A.R.; Satake, K.; Fujii, Y. Pre-computed tsunami inundation database and forecast simulation in Pelabuhan Ratu, Indonesia. *Pure Appl. Geophys.* **2021**, *178*, 3219–3242. [CrossRef]
28. Heidarzadeh, M.; Harada, T.; Satake, K.; Ishibe, T.; Gusman, A.R. Comparative analysis of the 2018 Fiji deep earthquake doublet: Deep normal-fault earthquakes generating tsunami. *Geophys. Res. Lett.* **2018**, *45*, 13043–13051. [CrossRef]
29. Nakata, K.; Katsumata, A.; Mulia, I.E.; Gusman, A.R.; Nakano, M.; Kumagai, H. Tsunami data assimilation of cabled ocean bottom pressure records for the 2015 Torishima volcanic tsunami earthquake. *J. Geophys. Res. Solid Earth* **2021**, *126*, e2020JB021290. [CrossRef]
30. Scorzini, A.R.; Di Bacco, M.; Sugawara, D.; Suppasri, A. Machine learning and hydrodynamic proxies for enhanced rapid tsunami vulnerability assessment. *Commun. Earth Environ.* **2024**, *5*, 301. [CrossRef]
31. Maeda, T.; Obara, K.; Shinohara, M.; Kanazawa, T.; Uehira, K. Successive estimation of a tsunami wavefield without earthquake source data: A data assimilation approach toward real-time tsunami forecasting. *Geophys. Res. Lett.* **2021**, *48*, e2021GL094230. [CrossRef]
32. Cesario, E.; Giampá, S.; Baglione, E.; Cordrie, L.; Selva, J.; Talia, D. Machine Learning for Tsunami Waves Forecasting Using Regression Trees. *Big Data Res.* **2024**, *36*, 100452. [CrossRef]
33. Wang, Y.; Imai, K.; Miyashita, T.; Ariyoshi, K.; Takahashi, N.; Satake, K. Coastal tsunami prediction in Tohoku region, Japan, based on S-net observations using artificial neural network. *Earth Planets Space* **2023**, *75*, 154. [CrossRef]
34. Asunción, R.A.; Sánchez, S.; Morales, J.; Carrasco, F.; Martín, J.B. Prediction of Tsunami Alert Levels Using Deep Learning. *Earth Space Sci.* **2024**, *11*, e2023EA003385. [CrossRef]
35. Yamanaka, Y.; Nakagawa, H. Machine learning approach for tsunami forecasting based on tide gauge data. *J. Disaster Res.* **2021**, *16*, 24–33. [CrossRef]

36. Dharmawan, W.; Diana, M.; Tuntari, B.; Astawa, I.M.; Rahardjo, S.; Nambo, H. Tsunami tide prediction in shallow water using recurrent neural networks: Model implementation in the Indonesia Tsunami Early Warning System. *J. Reliab. Intell. Environ.* **2023**, *10*, 177–195. [CrossRef]
37. Fauzi, A.; Mizutani, N. Machine learning algorithms for real-time tsunami inundation forecasting: A case study in Nankai region. *Pure Appl. Geophys.* **2020**, *177*, 1437–1450. [CrossRef]
38. Musa, A.; Watanabe, O.; Matsuoka, H.; Hokari, H.; Inoue, T.; Murashima, Y.; Ohta, Y.; Hino, R.; Koshimura, S.; Kobayashi, H. Real-time tsunami inundation forecast system for tsunami disaster prevention and mitigation. *J. Supercomput.* **2018**, *74*, 3093–3113. [CrossRef]
39. Ho, K.C.; Ko, J.Y.T.; Huang, H.H.; Lee, S.J. A Novel Approach to Tsunami Prediction Using Ambient Noise-Derived Green's Functions. *Geophys. Res. Lett.* **2025**, *52*, e2024GL113971. [CrossRef]
40. Mulia, I.E.; Gusman, A.R.; Satake, K. Applying a deep learning algorithm to tsunami inundation database of megathrust earthquakes. *J. Geophys. Res. Solid Earth* **2020**, *125*, e2020JB019690. [CrossRef]
41. Goto, K.; Ishizawa, T.; Ebina, Y.; Imamura, F. Tsunami data assimilation of Himawari-8 infrared bands ob-servation for the 2018 Sulawesi (Palu), Indonesia, earthquake. *Earth Planets Space* **2021**, *73*, 36. [CrossRef]
42. Heidarzadeh, M.; Ishibe, T.; Sandanbata, O.; Muhari, A.; Wijanarto, A.B. Numerical modeling of the subaerial landslide source of the 22 December 2018 Anak Krakatoa volcanic tsunami, Indonesia. *Ocean Eng.* **2019**, *195*, 106733. [CrossRef]
43. Liu, Y.; Wu, H. Prediction of Road Traffic Congestion Based on Random Forest. In Proceedings of the 2017 10th International Symposium on Computational Intelligence and Design (ISCID), Hangzhou, China, 9–10 December 2017; pp. 361–364. [CrossRef]
44. Zhang, S.; Tan, S.; Zhou, J.; Sun, Y.; Ding, D.; Li, J. Geological disaster susceptibility evaluation of a random-forest-weighted deterministic coefficient model. *Sustainability* **2023**, *15*, 12691. [CrossRef]
45. Sepúlveda, I.; Haase, J.S.; Carvajal, M.; Xu, X.; Liu, P.L.F. Modeling the sources of the 2018 Palu, Indonesia, tsunami using videos from social media. *J. Geophys. Res. Solid Earth* **2020**, *125*, e2019JB018675. [CrossRef]
46. Versaci, M.; Laganà, F.; Morabito, F.C.; Palumbo, A.; Angiulli, G. Adaptation of an Eddy Current Model for Characterizing Subsurface Defects in CFRP Plates Using FEM Analysis Based on Energy Functional. *Mathematics* **2024**, *12*, 2854. [CrossRef]
47. Laganà, F.; Pullano, S.A.; Angiulli, G.; Versaci, M. Optimized Analytical–Numerical Procedure for Ultrasonic Sludge Treatment for Agricultural Use. *Algorithms* **2024**, *17*, 592. [CrossRef]

computers

MDPI

Article

Analyzing Digital Political Campaigning Through Machine Learning: An Exploratory Study for the Italian Campaign for European Union Parliament Election in 2024

Paolo Sernani [1,*], Angela Cossiri [1], Giovanni Di Cosimo [1] and Emanuele Frontoni [2]

[1] Department of Law, University of Macerata, Piaggia dell'Università 2, 62100 Macerata, Italy; angela.cossiri@unimc.it (A.C.); giovanni.dicosimo@unimc.it (G.D.C.)
[2] Department of Political Sciences, Communication and International Relations, University of Macerata, Via Don Minzoni 22/A, 62100 Macerata, Italy; emanuele.frontoni@unimc.it
* Correspondence: paolo.sernani@unimc.it

Abstract: The rapid digitalization of political campaigns has reshaped electioneering strategies, enabling political entities to leverage social media for targeted outreach. This study investigates the impact of digital political campaigning during the 2024 EU elections using machine learning techniques to analyze social media dynamics. We introduce a novel dataset—Political Popularity Campaign—which comprises social media posts, engagement metrics, and multimedia content from the electoral period. By applying predictive modeling, we estimate key indicators such as post popularity and assess their influence on campaign outcomes. Our findings highlight the significance of micro-targeting practices, the role of algorithmic biases, and the risks associated with disinformation in shaping public opinion. Moreover, this research contributes to the broader discussion on regulating digital campaigning by providing analytical models that can aid policymakers and public authorities in monitoring election compliance and transparency. The study underscores the necessity for robust frameworks to balance the advantages of digital political engagement with the challenges of ensuring fair democratic processes.

Keywords: political analysis; data analytics; machine learning; social media; digital campaigning

1. Introduction

In recent years, digital campaigning has emerged as a central element in political strategies, reshaping the landscape of electioneering across the globe [1–3]. In Italy, as in many other countries, political entities increasingly leverage digital platforms to reach and engage voters. However, the rapid integration of digital tools into political campaigns has outpaced the development of corresponding regulatory frameworks, leading to significant concerns regarding the integrity and fairness of the democratic process [4,5]. The role of digital platforms in political campaigning extends beyond voter engagement to include economic and structural dynamics, where factors such as financial constraints, agglomeration effects, and the proximity of innovative hubs influence the effectiveness and reach of online political strategies [5–7]. One of the primary concerns is the potential for interference through the purchase of political advertising on the Internet. Such activities can be utilized by external actors to influence election outcomes and may facilitate covert or illicit financing of political activities. The lack of transparency in online political advertising exacerbates these issues, as it becomes challenging to trace the origins and funding sources of digital campaign materials [4].

Observing and assessing public sentiment patterns on social media platforms has surfaced as a viable substitute for traditional opinion surveys, owing to its unprompted nature and reach to a vast audience [8,9]. Indeed, social media platforms have become the primary channels for digital campaigning, largely due to their capacity for targeted political propaganda, commonly referred to as micro-targeting. This approach allows campaigns to deliver tailored messages to specific segments of the electorate, enhancing engagement but also raising ethical and legal questions. The ability to micro-target voters can lead to the dissemination of misleading information and the reinforcement of echo chambers, thereby undermining informed democratic deliberation [7,10].

Considering this, over the past few years, the rise of social media has driven significant research into forecasting election results by analyzing sentiments expressed on these platforms. A key focus has been the precise assessment of sentiment scores from relevant social media content, often to predict the victorious candidate [6,8,11]. Traditional polling methods are not only costly but also require substantial time to conduct, whereas social media provides instant feedback, allowing for real-time analysis. Consequently, political figures have broadened the scope of participants influencing political discourse and have adapted their agendas to fit this digital landscape. Social media channels have become essential tools for candidates throughout their election campaigns. Platforms such as Facebook, Instagram, and Twitter empower politicians to engage directly with voters, rally support, and shape public perception [1–3]. These shifts in political communication have introduced new strategic considerations for candidates navigating the digital sphere [8,11].

Analyzing data from social media networks offers valuable insights into the dynamics of digital campaigning and the associated risks. Interactions on these platforms increasingly define the modern voter–representative relationship, with social media serving as a crucial medium for holding elected officials accountable [1–3]. However, the prevalence of bots, fake accounts, and algorithmic biases can distort public discourse and manipulate voter perceptions [12,13]. Nevertheless, as an initial and passive data source, social media information presents numerous analytical hurdles, including the extraction of pertinent details from unstructured and unsolicited content, the measurement of highly qualitative visual and textual communications, and the assurance of data representativeness concerning a specific subject [8].

Building upon this theoretical background, we defined a novel approach to estimate one key indicator (post-popularity) that could influence political elections. To this date, we have collected a new dataset, the Political Popularity campaign, comprising social media posts from the 2024 EU political elections. This dataset includes information on post content, like images, videos, engagement metrics (likes, shares, comments), and temporal data. By applying machine learning techniques to this dataset, we aim to predict key variables such as post popularity and assess their influence on campaign outcomes. This approach allows for a general understanding of how digital content resonates with the electorate and informs campaign strategies.

This work is part of a larger framework for the regulation of digital campaigning. By collecting and analyzing extensive campaign data from social networks—including interactions, advertising expenditures, and posts—through the collaborative efforts of data scientists and legal scholars, we seek to develop analytical models that can be utilized by public authorities responsible for monitoring compliance with legal regulations concerning election campaigns and the financing of political parties and candidates. While the entire framework aims at analyzing multiple social media, here, we focus on Instagram, which has been adopted in similar studies and has been demonstrated to be a rich source of data for the topic under analysis [14].

The main contributions of this study are as follows:

- **Analysis of Micro-targeting Practices**: The study delves into the use of micro-targeting on social media platforms, where tailored messages are delivered to specific voter segments. While this enhances engagement, it also raises ethical and legal questions, including the dissemination of misleading information and the reinforcement of echo chambers.
- **Assessment of Social Media Dynamics**: By analyzing data from major social media networks, the paper provides insights into how interactions on these platforms define modern voter–representative relationships.
- **Introduction of a Novel Dataset and Predictive Modeling**: The research introduces a new dataset comprising social media posts from the 2024 political elections, including post content, engagement metrics, and temporal data. By applying machine learning techniques, the study aims to predict variables such as post popularity and assess their influence on campaign outcomes, offering a nuanced understanding of how digital content resonates with the electorate.

The rest of the paper is organized as follows: Section 2 provides an overview of related works, discussing prior research on digital political campaigning, sentiment analysis, and machine learning applications in election forecasting. Section 3 describes the dataset, preprocessing steps, and the machine learning models applied to analyze digital political campaigns. Section 4 presents the experimental results, highlighting key findings regarding the impact of social media engagement on political popularity. Finally, Section 5 discusses the implications of our findings, outlines the limitations, and suggests future research directions.

2. Related Works

2.1. Political Campaign Analysis

The evolution of political campaigns in the digital era has necessitated a re-evaluation of traditional strategies and the adoption of data-driven approaches. Political campaigns are concerted efforts to sway the opinions of a certain group of people, commonly used in democracies to elect legislators or determine referendums [15,16]. The increasing availability of microtargeted advertising and the accessibility of generative artificial intelligence (AI) tools have transformed political campaigns, enabling more precise targeting and message customization [16,17].

The European Democracy Action Plan, introduced by the EU Commission, aims to foster free and fair elections while countering disinformation and ensuring transparency in political advertising. Recent regulatory initiatives, such as the Regulation (EU) 2022/2065 on a Single Market for Digital Services, acknowledge the systemic risks that digital platforms pose to democratic processes, particularly through the spread of misleading information via automated bots and coordinated operations. These risks have been recognized in Horizon Europe, Cluster 2, which emphasizes the dual potential of digital environments to either support or threaten democracy.

The role of social media in political engagement is well documented, with scholars highlighting both its ability to enhance civic participation and its potential to undermine democratic discourse through microtargeting and misinformation [16,18]. The European Parliament's resolution on foreign interference in democratic processes underscores the need for stricter regulations to govern online political campaigning. However, national frameworks, such as those in Italy, remain largely outdated, lacking specific regulations for online political advertising.

Legal scholars have examined digital constitutionalism and the responsibilities of private actors in safeguarding fundamental rights, alongside issues of co-regulation and algorithmic censorship [18,19]. Despite these discussions, limited attention has been paid to the enforcement of electoral regulations in digital spaces [20,21]. Additionally, interdisciplinary collaboration between legal experts and data scientists remains insufficient, even though social media analytics could provide valuable insights into political sentiment and regulatory needs [22].

In fact, the increasing reliance on digital platforms in political campaigning raises concerns regarding the manipulation of public perception through AI-driven content generation and targeted messaging strategies [23,24]. Advances in deep learning and extended reality have the potential to reshape political discourse by enabling the creation of hyper-realistic synthetic media, influencing voter behavior, and altering the dynamics of political engagement [25–28]. Moreover, the application of AI in analyzing public sentiment and voter preferences introduces ethical challenges related to transparency and democratic accountability [29,30].

2.2. Machine Learning Analysis

Machine learning (ML) techniques have been extensively used to analyze political communication, particularly in monitoring public sentiment during election campaigns. The increasing availability of social media data has made it possible to forecast election outcomes by analyzing digital interactions [31]. Traditional polling methods, while effective, are often costly and time-consuming, whereas sentiment analysis and network-based approaches allow real-time monitoring of political discourse [8,31,32].

A key aspect of digital political campaigning is microtargeting, where machine learning algorithms tailor campaign messages to specific voter groups based on behavioral data [12,33]. This strategy raises ethical and regulatory concerns, particularly regarding misinformation and the reinforcement of echo chambers. To address these issues, research efforts have explored methods to assess the influence of digital campaign strategies on public opinion.

Recent studies, such as [8], have proposed social media intelligence frameworks (SocMINT) to analyze election-related discourse. Their research demonstrated how sentiment analysis and network-based KPIs can be leveraged to predict electoral trends. Building on such methods, this work integrates machine learning techniques to predict political post popularity and assess their impact on campaign outcomes. By analyzing engagement metrics from platforms like Facebook, Instagram, and Twitter, this study seeks to inform both policymakers and scholars on how digital campaign strategies shape electoral behavior.

A recent literature review [31] further highlights the growing role of machine learning in political science. Their study systematically analyzed 339 political science articles using machine learning and found that political communication and electoral studies are the most common application areas. The most frequently applied methods include topic modeling, support vector machines, and random forests, indicating a strong preference for supervised learning approaches in predictive political science research [1–3]. The review also notes the increasing use of causal inference techniques in ML, aiming to bridge the gap between predictive accuracy and explanatory power in political analysis. Moreover, it highlights that while ML applications in political science have expanded rapidly, challenges remain in model interpretability, ethical considerations, and the necessity for interdisciplinary collaboration [31].

In sum, while significant research has explored the role of digital media in elections, there remains a gap in interdisciplinary methodologies combining computational analysis with legal scholarship. This study aims to bridge that gap by leveraging social media analytics and ML to inform regulatory strategies aligned with the European Democracy Action Plan.

3. Materials and Methods

The methodologies of this work are based on an interdisciplinary collaboration between scholars from the legal field and computer science engineers. This approach ensures that both technical and legal perspectives are integrated throughout the work lifecycle. The Computer Science (CS) team and the Legal team will work in close coordination to develop, analyze, and evaluate the AI-based system while considering legal and constitutional implications.

3.1. Data Acquisition

To collect data, we leveraged the Apify API (https://apify.com/apify/instagram-scraper, accesed on 12 February 2025) to extract Instagram posts during the 2024 EU election period (from 1 May 2024 to 30 June 2024). The selection criteria focused on posts relevant to electoral propaganda, ensuring that only content published at least 24 h before the election was included. To capture a more representative measure of engagement and audience interaction, all metrics were recorded at least 48 h after the posts were published, allowing sufficient time for organic propagation across the platform. Our final dataset comprised 364 images sourced from the official Instagram accounts of major political leaders, candidates, and their respective parties.

The subjects considered were the following:

- **Più Europa**
- **Italia Viva**
- **Azione**
- **Lega**
- **Fratelli d'Italia**
- **Forza Italia**
- **Bonaccini**
- **Movimento 5 Stelle**
- **Alleanza**
- **Elly**
- **Partito Democratico**

These political parties were collected in a balanced and representative way to minimize possible sources of bias. The next step was to collect the different discrete variables into a dataframe. These are the so-called feature variables essential for our ML-based approach. The variables collected and calculated are listed in Table 1.

3.2. Data Processing and Aggregation

The collected data, including both posts and structured tabular data, underwent preprocessing to filter out irrelevant content. We specifically retained variables of interest such as likes, comments, and shares. From these metrics, we calculated engagement levels for each post. To convert the engagement rates into a categorical variable (for classification), we sorted posts based on engagement scores and defined three popularity categories based on threshold values: low, medium, and high. Specifically, the metrics used for class division were the total sum of interactions received for each post (likes + comments + shares), which were categorized as follows:

- Low popularity: value from 0 to 1000,
- Medium popularity: value from 1000 to 5000,
- High popularity: value above 5000.

Table 1. Variables collected for each post through APIFY and their descriptions.

Field	Description
`image`	The image associated with the post.
`caption`	The text description accompanying the Instagram post.
`timestamp`	The date and time when the post was published.
`likesCount`	The number of likes the post received.
`commentsCount`	The number of comments on the post.
`shareCount`	The number of times the post was shared.
`hashtags`	The hashtags used in the post.
`type`	The type of media (image, video, carousel, etc.).
`url`	The direct link to the post.
`videoViewCount`	The number of views on the video.
`locationName`	The name of the location tagged in the post.
`engagementRateSum`	A calculated metric: (likes + comments + shares).

A novel dataset was then constructed by categorizing each image into one of these classes. The report categorizes posts into low, medium, and high popularity, providing insights into the factors influencing audience interaction.

For instance, posts in the low popularity category include content such as a campaign message from Daniela Di Cosmo and a taxation policy statement ("Tassiamo i super ricchi"), both of which rely heavily on text and lack visually compelling elements. Another example in this category is a post criticizing Giorgia Meloni's alleged association with anti-vaccine movements, indicating that negative framing alone does not guarantee high engagement. Conversely, medium popularity posts include critiques of political figures, such as one portraying Ursula von der Leyen with the hashtag #NoUrsulaBis, as well as a statement about the growth of Giorgia Meloni's party ("FdI continua a crescere"), suggesting that posts with a mix of polarization and ideological reinforcement tend to attract moderate engagement. In the high popularity category, posts that highlight economic contrasts—such as the one emphasizing a EUR 209 billion gain from a European agreement compared to a EUR 13 billion loss—stand out for their effective use of visual contrast and numerical impact, which likely enhances shareability. Similarly, a post from the Partito Democratico stating "Sotto i 9 euro l'ora non è lavoro, è sfruttamento" ("Below 9 euros per hour is not work, it is exploitation") benefits from a strong moral and emotional appeal, which is a recurring feature in highly engaging political content. At first glance, these observations suggest that clear contrasts, numerical evidence, emotional triggers, and visually engaging layouts contribute significantly to social media post popularity in political discourse.

3.3. Machine Learning Framework

For the classification and analysis of engagement, we developed an ML pipeline employing the Pytorch framework (v2.0.0), using Python (v3.8).

We defined an automated deep-learning pipeline for image feature extraction and classification head fine-tuning. This fine-tuning process was previously adopted for our use case and domain of analysis [34,35]. In our approach, we leveraged pre-trained convolutional neural networks (CNNs) and Vision Transformers (ViT) [36–39] to extract meaningful numerical representations (embeddings) from raw image data. Given an input image $I \in \mathbb{R}^{H \times W \times C}$, a CNN or ViT model ($\theta_{VIS}$) extracts feature embeddings $\mathbf{f}$:

$$\mathbf{f} = \Phi(I; \theta_{VIS}) \in \mathbb{R}^d, \quad (1)$$

where Φ represents the vision backbone function parameterized by weights θ_{VIS}, and d is the dimensionality of the extracted features.

Before feeding our images into each of the selected models, in our preprocessing stage, each input image was resized to a fixed resolution of $H \times W$ pixels, ensuring compatibility with the input requirements of convolutional neural networks (CNNs) and Vision Transformers (ViTs). We applied pixel intensity normalization by scaling the RGB values to the $[0, 1]$ range and further standardizing them using channel-wise mean and standard deviation values computed from the ImageNet dataset, a common practice to improve model generalization and convergence.

The extracted embeddings serve as input for various machine learning classifiers, including logistic regression, neural networks, gradient boosting, and support vector machines (SVMs) [40,41]. The classification models learn decision boundaries using these features. For each classifier g with parameters θ_{clf}, the classification function is defined as

$$\hat{y} = g(\mathbf{f}; \theta_{clf}), \tag{2}$$

where $\hat{y}$ represents the predicted class label.

To optimize θ_{clf}, models are trained by minimizing a loss function $\mathcal{L}$, such as cross-entropy loss for multi-class classification:

$$\mathcal{L} = -\sum_{i=1}^{N} y_i \log \hat{y}_i, \tag{3}$$

where N is the number of training samples, y_i is the true class label, and $\hat{y}_i$ is the predicted probability.

To evaluate model performance, the Test and Score module performs cross validation. The classification performance metrics include the following:

- Accuracy:

$$\text{Accuracy} = \frac{TP + TN}{TP + TN + FP + FN}, \tag{4}$$

- Precision:

$$\text{Precision} = \frac{TP}{TP + FP}, \tag{5}$$

- Recall:

$$\text{Recall} = \frac{TP}{TP + FN}, \tag{6}$$

- F1-score:

$$\text{F1-score} = \frac{2 \times \text{Precision} \times \text{Recall}}{\text{Precision} + \text{Recall}}, \tag{7}$$

- Matthews correlation coefficient (MCC):

$$\text{MCC} = \frac{TP \times TN - FP \times FN}{\sqrt{(TP + FP)(TP + FN)(TN + FP)(TN + FN)}}, \tag{8}$$

- Area under the curve (AUC):

$$\text{AUC} = \int_{-\infty}^{\infty} \text{TPR}(t)\, d\text{FPR}(t), \tag{9}$$

where TP, TN, FP, and FN are true positives, true negatives, false positives, and false negatives, respectively.

The trained models are applied to unseen images using the Predictions module:

$$\hat{y}^{(test)} = g(\mathbf{f}^{(test)}; \theta_{clf}). \quad (10)$$

The classification results are analyzed both quantitatively through confusion matrices and single predictions while examining them qualitatively.

4. Results

In this Section, we report our experimental setting and obtained results.

4.1. Experimental Setting

We partitioned our dataset into training and testing sets, allocating 70% for training and 30% for testing while ensuring class balance in both sets.

To extract deep feature representations from images, we utilized five pre-trained CNN models: ResNet-50, VGG-16, SqueezeNet, Inception-v3, and ViT-B/16 (Vision Transformer). Each model was modified by removing its final fully connected (FC) classification layer to retain high-level feature representations. The extracted feature vectors were then flattened into one-dimensional arrays and stored for subsequent classification.

Following feature extraction, we trained four machine learning classifiers to categorize social media posts based on engagement levels: logistic regression, a linear classifier optimized for high-dimensional data; support vector machine (SVM), a kernel-based model effective for non-linear decision boundaries; gradient boosting classifier, an ensemble method leveraging boosting for improved predictive performance; and multilayer perceptron (MLP), a shallow artificial neural network trained via backpropagation.

The logistic regression model was configured with a maximum iteration limit of 1000 (`max_iter = 1000`) to ensure convergence during optimization. The support vector machine (SVM) utilized a linear kernel (`kernel = 'linear'`) for efficient classification of linearly separable data, with probability estimation enabled (`probability = True`) to facilitate probabilistic predictions. The gradient boosting classifier was initialized with 100 boosting iterations (`n_estimators = 100`), balancing model complexity and performance. The multilayer perceptron (MLP) architecture comprised a single hidden layer with 100 neurons (`hidden_layer_sizes = (100,)`), employing the rectified linear unit (ReLU) activation function (`activation = 'relu'`) to introduce non-linearity, with weight optimization managed via the Adam solver (`solver = 'adam'`). The training process was constrained to a maximum of 1000 iterations (`max_iter = 1000`) to ensure convergence, with a fixed random seed (`random_state = 42`) to promote reproducibility. Following model training, performance was assessed on the standardized test set, leveraging the optimized hyperparameters to maximize predictive accuracy.

All the classifiers were trained using supervised learning, with the dataset split into 70% training and 30% testing subsets. Extracted features were standardized to optimize classifier performance.

All experiments were conducted on a machine equipped with an Intel Core i9-13980HX processor (13th Gen, 2.20 GHz, Manufacturer: Intel Corporation, Santa Clara, CA, USA), 16 GB of RAM, and an NVIDIA GeForce RTX 4070 GPU with 8 GB of VRAM (Manufacturer: NVIDIA Corporation, Santa Clara, CA, USA), running a 64-bit operating system with the latest WDDM drivers (Manufacturer: Microsoft Corporation, Redmond, WA, USA).

4.2. Obtained Results

The results obtained with our ML approach for political post popularity prediction are reported in Table 2.

Table 2. Performance comparison of models using different vision backbones and machine learning classifiers. The best results for each backbone are highlighted in bold.

Backbone	Classifier	Accuracy	AUC	F1	Precision	Recall	MCC
Inception V3	LR	0.595	0.682	0.541	0.563	0.595	0.268
	SVM	0.595	**0.687**	**0.558**	0.578	0.595	0.276
	GB	**0.611**	0.680	0.540	**0.582**	**0.611**	**0.306**
	MLP	0.603	0.669	0.549	0.567	0.603	0.286
VGG16	LR	0.627	0.756	0.566	0.634	0.627	0.339
	SVM	0.611	0.754	0.554	0.579	0.611	0.302
	GB	0.611	0.688	0.546	0.626	0.611	0.311
	MLP	**0.643**	**0.786**	**0.574**	**0.745**	**0.643**	**0.385**
ResNet50	LR	0.587	0.671	0.538	0.535	0.587	0.258
	SVM	0.556	0.641	0.522	0.513	0.556	0.210
	GB	**0.627**	**0.710**	**0.578**	**0.623**	**0.627**	**0.336**
	MLP	0.595	0.672	0.547	0.543	0.595	0.274
ViT-B16	LR	0.595	0.732	0.559	0.588	0.595	0.275
	SVM	0.603	0.739	**0.577**	0.592	0.603	0.298
	GB	**0.611**	0.691	0.551	**0.704**	**0.611**	**0.311**
	MLP	**0.611**	0.718	0.552	0.610	**0.611**	0.301

To clarify and properly visualize the performance of each model and classifier, we report in Figure 1 a barplot comparison of the F1-scores according to backbones and selected classifiers.

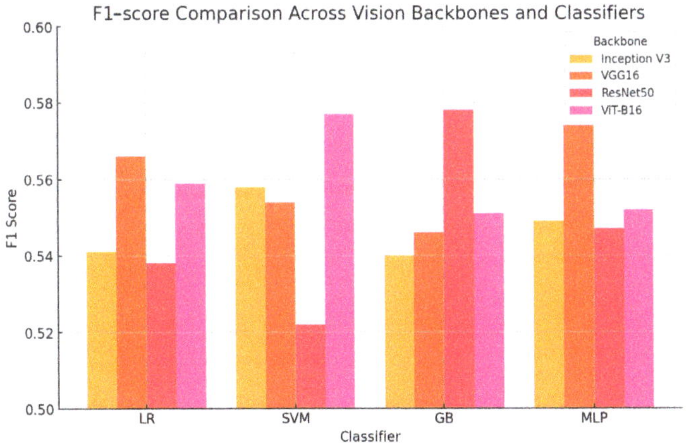

Figure 1. Barplot comparison of F1-scores across backbones and classifiers.

According to both Table 2 and Figure 1, the evaluation of different network backbones and classification models reveals important insights into the relationship between feature extraction quality and predictive performance. Among the architectures tested, ViT-B16 demonstrated competitive performance, particularly in F1-score and precision, when paired with SVM and gradient boosting (GB), respectively. This suggests that Vision Transformers, while typically requiring large datasets, can still provide effective feature representations for specific classification tasks. Notably, ViT-B16 achieved the highest F1-score (0.577) with SVM and the highest precision (0.704) with GB, indicating that its tokenized representations can be leveraged effectively when paired with appropriate classifiers.

However, while ViT-B16 demonstrated strengths in precision and F1-score, its overall classification accuracy (0.611) remained on par with other models, particularly CNN-based architectures like VGG16 and ResNet50, which achieved comparable results. This aligns with findings in other domains where Vision Transformers may not always outperform convolutional architectures unless trained on significantly large-scale datasets. The moderate MCC scores obtained by the ViT-B16 classifiers further support this, suggesting that while the representations contribute meaningfully to predictive performance, they do not necessarily lead to a significant increase in overall classification reliability compared to CNN-based alternatives.

Across classification models, GB emerged as the best-performing classifier for ViT-B16, particularly in precision (0.704), indicating its ability to reduce false positives, making it a suitable choice for applications where precision is a priority. SVM, on the other hand, achieved the highest F1-score (0.577), balancing precision and recall more effectively. However, MLP matched GB in overall accuracy (0.611), further demonstrating that neural network classifiers can effectively leverage ViT-B16 embeddings.

The comparison between Vision Transformers and traditional CNN-based feature extractors suggests that while ViT-B16 was able to achieve competitive performance, it did not consistently outperform convolutional networks. This reinforces the importance of dataset characteristics in determining the effectiveness of different feature extractors. ViT-B16's moderate performance suggests that while self-attention mechanisms provide useful feature representations, they may not always translate into superior classification results unless combined with larger-scale data or further fine-tuning.

Qualitatively, we selected the best vision backbone (Vit/B) and ML classifier (SVM) and analyzed the wrongly classified examples to find common patterns that may have misled the model itself. We then analyzed the confusion matrix of its prediction, as reported in Figure 2.

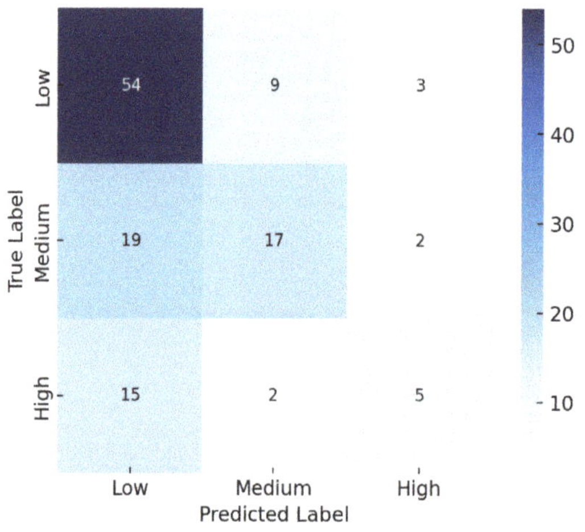

Figure 2. Confusion matrix of the best-selected model.

The confusion matrix provides valuable insights into the classification performance of the model trained to distinguish between three categories: High, Low, and Medium. Overall, the model demonstrates the highest classification accuracy for the "Medium" category, correctly identifying 54 instances, suggesting that the features distinguishing this class are well captured. However, the misclassification rates for the "High" and "Low" classes are substantial, indicating that the decision boundaries between these categories may not be well defined. Specifically, the "High" class is often misclassified as "Medium", with 15 incorrect predictions compared to only 5 correct ones, suggesting significant feature overlap between these two categories. Similarly, the model struggles with the "Low" class, correctly classifying 17 instances but misclassifying nearly half (19 cases) as "Medium".

These results indicate that the decision boundary between "Low" and "Medium" is not sufficiently clear, potentially due to overlapping feature representations in the dataset.

A notable trend in misclassification patterns is that incorrect predictions tend to be biased toward "Medium" rather than "High" or "Low". This suggests that the "Medium" category may serve as a central cluster in the feature space, causing instances from the other classes to be incorrectly mapped to it. Additionally, if the dataset contains a greater proportion of "Medium" samples, the model may have developed a bias favoring this category, increasing the likelihood of false positives at the expense of correctly identifying "High" and "Low". Given these observations, several improvements can be considered to enhance the classification performance. Feature engineering should be explored to identify more discriminative attributes that can effectively separate "High" and "Low" from "Medium". Additionally, resampling techniques, such as oversampling the underrepresented classes or undersampling "Medium", may help mitigate the class imbalance and improve the classification boundaries. Alternative classification models, including ensemble methods or fine-tuned neural networks, could also be tested to refine decision boundaries and reduce misclassification rates.

Overall, while the model achieves a strong performance in classifying "Medium", it struggles to differentiate between "High" and "Low", leading to significant misclassification. The results highlight the importance of refining decision boundaries, either through improved feature selection, data augmentation, or alternative classification strategies, to achieve a more balanced and reliable classification model.

5. Discussions and Conclusions

The findings of this study highlight the growing influence of digital political campaigning, particularly through social media, in shaping voter engagement and election outcomes. The application of machine learning techniques to assess social media dynamics provided insightful results, demonstrating the significance of post popularity in predicting electoral impact.

Our analysis confirmed that digital campaigns increasingly rely on micro-targeting practices, where tailored messages reach specific voter segments, thereby enhancing engagement. However, this also raises ethical concerns related to misinformation, echo chambers, and algorithmic biases, which can distort democratic discourse [1–3]. The study further revealed that social media sentiment and engagement metrics could serve as viable alternatives to traditional polling methods, offering real-time insights into public opinion.

However, the model performance results indicate that distinguishing between high, medium, and low engagement posts remains a challenge, as observed in the misclassification trends. Vision Transformers, while demonstrating competitive performance in feature extraction, did not consistently outperform CNN-based architectures, suggesting that dataset characteristics and feature representation play a crucial role in classification effectiveness. However, distinguishing between posts with low and medium popularity is still complex. This issue can be attributed not only to the model's performances but also to overlapping engagement patterns, which hindered classification performance. As a potential solution, we propose future work exploring binary classification (popular vs. non-popular) rather than a multi-class approach to improve predictive accuracy. Considering possible model improvements, clustering methods such as density-based clustering and feature engineering enhancements could be explored. Additionally, integrating models based on energy functions, as suggested in the FEM analysis study [42], could enhance classification robustness and provide new insights into engagement modeling. At the same time, the potential for numerical-analytical methodologies to optimize decision models was also highlighted. As suggested in the recent literature [43], combining mathematical models and simulations could refine feature selection and enhance predictive performance.

Another point of analysis amounts to the interpretability of ML predictions. Future work should incorporate interpretability methods such as LIME [44] to better understand the key features influencing engagement. This will also support bias analysis in our dataset, which, although efforts were made to ensure balanced representation among major political parties and leaders, may still arise due to the nature of political communication strategies and post types (e.g., infographics, speech photos, crowd images).

These findings underscore the importance of refining machine learning methodologies for political analysis. Indeed, as digital electioneering continues to evolve, interdisciplinary collaborations between legal scholars, data scientists, and policymakers are essential to developing frameworks that safeguard democratic integrity while leveraging technological advancements. Future research should explore the integration of multimodal data sources, such as textual, visual, and network-based features, to enhance the predictive accuracy and better capture the complexities of digital political communication.

Moreover, while Instagram has been identified as a powerful political communication medium [8], future work should extend the analysis to other platforms, such as Twitter/X, Facebook, TikTok, and Google search, to assess model generalizability across different social media environments and analyze whether different posts from different environments could lead to different pattern discovery.

Additionally, investigating the role of automated bots, deepfake content, and emerging generative AI technologies in campaign strategies can further inform regulatory measures and should be part of future works. Moreover, a key limitation is the potential for algorithmic and data-driven biases in AI models, which may inadvertently favor certain political perspectives or topics. While efforts are made to ensure neutrality, inherent biases in training data and content selection can shape responses in subtle ways. Future research should focus on systematically auditing AI-generated political discourse using benchmarking techniques to assess and mitigate these biases, ensuring greater transparency and fairness in digital political analysis. In fact, in this regard, the regulation of digital campaigns remains insufficient in ensuring transparency, particularly in areas such as algorithmic targeting, disinformation control, and platform accountability. Key regulatory priorities should include stricter transparency requirements for political advertising, ensuring that voters can easily identify who funds and targets them with specific messages. The recent European Regulation 2024/900 mandates disclosure of political ad sponsors and targeting criteria, aiming to safeguard voter autonomy by preventing manipulative advertising strategies [45,46]. Additionally, greater oversight of disinformation campaigns is crucial, particularly regarding foreign interference. For example, the European Union has imposed sanctions on state-sponsored media linked to Russian propaganda, demonstrating the need for a balanced approach between security and media freedom [47]. Moreover, stronger enforcement mechanisms for platform responsibility under frameworks like the Digital Services Act (DSA) are needed to mitigate algorithmic amplification of harmful content, as these platforms have become primary spaces for political discourse and potential manipulation [45,46].

Finally, it is important to note that no tests were conducted to generalize the results to other and different elections, and future work will focus on validating the proposed methodology across different electoral contexts to assess its broader applicability.

Overall, this study provides a foundational step in bridging computational political analysis with legal and ethical considerations, emphasizing the need for continued interdisciplinary efforts to ensure fair and transparent electoral processes in the digital era.

Author Contributions: Conceptualization, G.D.C., A.C. and E.F.; methodology, P.S.; software, P.S.; validation, E.F.; data curation, P.S. and E.F.; writing—original draft preparation, P.S., G.D.C., A.C. and E.F.; writing—review and editing, G.D.C., A.C. and E.F.; supervision, G.D.C. and E.F. All authors have read and agreed to the published version of the manuscript.

Funding: This research was funded by the European Union—Next Generation EU under the Prin 2022 PNRR call, Mission 4, Component 2, Investment 1.1, P2022MCYCK, CUP D53D23022340001.

Data Availability Statement: The raw data supporting the conclusions of this article will be made available by the authors on request.

Acknowledgments: This article was produced within the framework of the project 'Normative and Digital Solutions to Counter Threats during National Election Campaigns—RightNets', funded by the European Union—Next Generation EU under the Prin 2022 PNRR call, Mission 4, Component 2, Investment 1.1, P2022MCYCK, CUP D53D23022340001. The views and opinions expressed are, however, those of the author(s) only and do not necessarily reflect those of the European Union or the European Commission. Neither the European Union nor the European Commission can be held responsible for them.

Conflicts of Interest: The authors declare no conflicts of interest.

Abbreviations

The following abbreviations are used in this manuscript:

EU	European Union
ML	Machine Learning
AI	Artificial Intelligence
CNN	Convolutional Neural Network
ViT	Vision Transformer
SVM	Support Vector Machine
GB	Gradient Boosting
MLP	Multilayer Perceptron
MCC	Matthews Correlation Coefficient
AUC	Area Under the Curve
LR	Logistic Regression
TP	True Positive
TN	True Negative
FP	False Positive
FN	False Negative
KPI	Key Performance Indicator
API	Application Programming Interface
CS	Computer Science
GPU	Graphics Processing Unit
RTX	Ray Tracing Texel eXtreme
APIFY	API-based Web Scraping Framework
URL	Uniform Resource Locator
FC	Fully Connected
CCDCOE	NATO Cooperative Cyber Defence Centre of Excellence

References

1. Haq, E.U.; Braud, T.; Kwon, Y.D.; Hui, P. A survey on computational politics. *IEEE Access* **2020**, *8*, 197379–197406.
2. Singh, L.; Kamboj, S.; Kaur, T.; Singh, P. Exploring Changes in Public Opinion, Political Campaigns, and Political Behavior Through Data Science and Machine Learning. In Proceedings of the 2024 2nd International Conference on Artificial Intelligence and Machine Learning Applications Theme: Healthcare and Internet of Things (AIMLA), Tiruchengode, India, 15–16 March 2024; IEEE: Piscataway, NJ, USA, 2024; pp. 1–5.

3. Boratyn, D.; Brzyski, D.; Kosowska-Gąstoł, B.; Rybicki, J.; Słomczyński, W.; Stolicki, D. Machine learning and statistical approaches to measuring similarity of political parties. *arXiv* **2023**, arXiv:2306.03079.
4. Bradshaw, S.; Howard, P.N. *Government Responses to Malicious Use of Social Media;* The NATO Cooperative Cyber Defence Centre of Excellence (CCDCOE): 2018. Available online: https://demtech.oii.ox.ac.uk/wp-content/uploads/sites/12/2019/01/Nato-Report.pdf (accessed on 12 February 2025).
5. Falavigna, G.; Giannini, V.; Ippoliti, R. Internationalization and financial constraints: Opportunities, obstacles, and strategies. *Int. Econ.* **2024**, *179*, 100510. [CrossRef]
6. Cainelli, G.; Giannini, V.; Iacobucci, D. Agglomeration, networking and the Great Recession. *Reg. Stud.* **2019**, *53*, 951–962. [CrossRef]
7. Micozzi, A.; Giannini, V. How Does the Localization of Innovative Start-ups Near the Universities Influence Their Performance? *Industria* **2023**, *44*, 129–151. [CrossRef]
8. Mameli, M.; Paolanti, M.; Morbidoni, C.; Frontoni, E.; Teti, A. Social media analytics system for action inspection on social networks. *Soc. Netw. Anal. Min.* **2022**, *12*, 33.
9. Stacchio, L.; Angeli, A.; Lisanti, G.; Marfia, G. Analyzing cultural relationships visual cues through deep learning models in a cross-dataset setting. *Neural Comput. Appl.* **2024**, *36*, 11727–11742. [CrossRef]
10. Chester, J.; Montgomery, K.C. The Role of Digital Marketing in Political Campaigns. *Internet Policy Rev.* **2017**, *6*. [CrossRef]
11. Liu, R.; Yao, X.; Guo, C.; Wei, X. Can we forecast presidential election using twitter data? An integrative modelling approach. *Ann. Gis* **2021**, *27*, 43–56.
12. Tufekci, Z. Engineering the Public: Big Data, Surveillance and Computational Politics. *First Monday* **2014**, *19*. Available online: https://firstmonday.org/ojs/index.php/fm/article/view/4901/4097 (accessed on 12 February 2025).
13. Paolanti, M.; Pierdicca, R.; Pietrini, R.; Martini, M.; Frontoni, E. SeSAME: Re-identification-based ambient intelligence system for museum environment. *Pattern Recognit. Lett.* **2022**, *161*, 17–23. [CrossRef]
14. Bossetta, M. The digital architectures of social media: Comparing political campaigning on Facebook, Twitter, Instagram, and Snapchat in the 2016 US election. *J. Mass Commun. Q.* **2018**, *95*, 471–496.
15. Smith, J.; Doe, J. Political Campaigns: Strategies and Implications. *J. Sci. Res.* **2020**, *10*, 123–145.
16. Mersy, G.; Santore, V.; Rand, I.; Kleinman, C.; Wilson, G.; Bonsall, J.; Edwards, T. A comparison of machine learning algorithms applied to american legislature polarization. In Proceedings of the 2020 IEEE 21st International Conference on Information Reuse and Integration for Data Science (IRI), Las Vegas, NV, USA, 11–13 August 2020; IEEE: Piscataway, NJ, USA, 2020; pp. 451–456.
17. Brown, A.; Green, B. *Digital Campaigning: The Rise of Data-Driven Strategies*; Oxford University Press: Oxford, UK, 2019.
18. Albert, K.; Penney, J.; Schneier, B.; Kumar, R.S.S. Politics of adversarial machine learning. *arXiv* **2020**, arXiv:2002.05648.
19. Suzor, N.P. Digital Constitutionalism: Using the Rule of Law to Evaluate the Legitimacy of Governance by Platforms. *Soc. Media Soc.* **2018**, *4*, 1–11. [CrossRef]
20. Kofi Annan Foundation. *Kofi Annan Commission on Elections and Democracy in the Digital Age: Protecting Electoral Integrity in the Digital Age*; Kofi Annan Foundation: Geneva, Switzerland, 2020.
21. Stacchio, L.; Angeli, A.; Lisanti, G.; Calanca, D.; Marfia, G. Toward a Holistic Approach to the Socio-historical Analysis of Vernacular Photos. *Acm Trans. Multimed. Comput. Commun. Appl.* **2022**, *18*, 1–23. [CrossRef]
22. Trasys International. Study on the Impact of New Technologies on Free and Fair Elections ('Elections Study') Literature Review Version 3.0. European Commission, March 2021. Available online: https://commission.europa.eu/system/files/2022-12/Annex%20I_LiteratureReview_20210319_clean_dsj_v3.0_a.pdf (accessed on 12 February 2025)
23. Brennan Center for Justice. Generative AI in Political Advertising. Available online: https://www.brennancenter.org/our-work/research-reports/generative-ai-political-advertising (accessed on 12 February 2025)
24. Stacchio, L.; Scorolli, C.; Marfia, G. Evaluating Human Aesthetic and Emotional Aspects of 3D Generated Content through eXtended Reality. In Proceedings of the CEUR Workshop Proceedings, Örebro, Sweden, 15–17 June 2022; Volume 3519, pp. 38–49.
25. Groh, M.; Sankaranarayanan, A.; Singh, N.; Kim, D.Y.; Lippman, A.; Picard, R. Human Detection of Political Speech Deepfakes across Transcripts, Audio, and Video. *arXiv* **2022**, arXiv:2202.12883. [CrossRef]
26. YORD Studio. How AI is Shaping the Future of Extended Reality (XR). 21 October 2024. Available online: https://yordstudio.com/how-ai-is-shaping-the-future-of-extended-reality-xr/ (accessed on 12 February 2025)
27. Stacchio, L.; Vallasciani, G.; Augello, G.; Carrador, S.; Cascarano, P.; Marfia, G. WiXaRd: Towards a Holistic Distributed Platform for Multi-Party and Cross-Reality WebXR Experiences. In Proceedings of the 2024 IEEE Conference on Virtual Reality and 3D User Interfaces Abstracts and Workshops (VRW 2024), Orlando, FL, USA, 16–21 March 2024; IEEE: Piscataway, NJ, USA, 2024; pp. 264–272. [CrossRef]
28. Bononi, L.; Donatiello, L.; Longo, D.; Massari, M.; Montori, F.; Stacchio, L.; Marfia, G. Digital Twin Collaborative Platforms: Applications to Humans-in-the-Loop Crafting of Urban Areas. *IEEE Consum. Electron. Mag.* **2023**, *12*, 38–46. [CrossRef]
29. Paolanti, M.; Tiribelli, S.; Giovanola, B.; Mancini, A.; Frontoni, E.; Pierdicca, R. Ethical framework to assess and quantify the trustworthiness of artificial intelligence techniques: Application case in remote sensing. *Remote Sens.* **2024**, *16*, 4529. [CrossRef]

30. Stacchio, L.; Pierdicca, R.; Paolanti, M.; Zingaretti, P.; Frontoni, E.; Giovanola, B.; Tiribelli, S. XRAI-Ethics: Towards a Robust Ethical Analysis Framework for Extended Artificial Intelligence. In Proceedings of the 2024 IEEE International Symposium on Mixed and Augmented Reality Adjunct (ISMAR-Adjunct), Bellevue, WA, USA, 21–25 October 2024; IEEE: Piscataway, NJ, USA, 2024; pp. 214–219.
31. de Slegte, S.; van der Veer, H.; Jacobs, K. The Use of Machine Learning Methods in Political Science. *Political Stud. Rev.* **2024**, *23*, 456–472. [CrossRef]
32. Stacchio, L.; Garzarella, S.; Cascarano, P.; De Filippo, A.; Cervellati, E.; Marfia, G. DanXe: An extended artificial intelligence framework to analyze and promote dance heritage. *Digit. Appl. Archaeol. Cult. Herit.* **2024**, *33*, e00343. [CrossRef]
33. Pietrini, R.; Galdelli, A.; Mancini, A.; Zingaretti, P. Embedded Vision System for Real-Time Shelves Rows Detection for Planogram Compliance Check. In Proceedings of the International Design Engineering Technical Conferences and Computers and Information in Engineering Conference, Boston, MA, USA, 20–24 August 2023; American Society of Mechanical Engineers: New York, NY, USA, 2023; Volume 87356, p. V007T07A003.
34. Joo, J.; Steinert-Threlkeld, Z.C. Image as Data: Automated Visual Content Analysis for Political Science. *arXiv* **2018**, arXiv:1810.01544.
35. Anastasopoulos, L.J.; Whitford, A.B. Photographic home styles in Congress: A computer vision approach. *arXiv* **2016**, arXiv:1611.09942.
36. Simonyan, K.; Zisserman, A. Very Deep Convolutional Networks for Large-Scale Image Recognition. *arXiv* **2014**, arXiv:1409.1556.
37. Iandola, F.N.; Han, S.; Moskewicz, M.W.; Ashraf, K.; Dally, W.J.; Keutzer, K. SqueezeNet: AlexNet-level accuracy with 50x fewer parameters and <0.5MB model size. *arXiv* **2016**, arXiv:1602.07360..
38. Szegedy, C.; Vanhoucke, V.; Ioffe, S.; Shlens, J.; Wojna, Z. Rethinking the Inception Architecture for Computer Vision. In Proceedings of the IEEE Conference on Computer Vision and Pattern Recognition, Las Vegas, NV, USA, 27–30 June 2016; pp. 2818–2826.
39. Han, K.; Wang, Y.; Chen, H.; Chen, X.; Guo, J.; Liu, Z.; Tang, Y.; Xiao, A.; Xu, C.; Xu, Y.; et al. A survey on vision transformer. *IEEE Trans. Pattern Anal. Mach. Intell.* **2022**, *45*, 87–110.
40. Sen, P.C.; Hajra, M.; Ghosh, M. Supervised classification algorithms in machine learning: A survey and review. In Emerging Technology in Modelling and Graphics: Proceedings of the IEM Graph 2018, Kolkata, India, 6–8 September 2018; Springer: Berlin/Heidelberg, Germany, 2020; pp. 99–111.
41. Stacchio, L.; Angeli, A.; Lisanti, G.; Marfia, G. Applying deep learning approaches to mixed quantitative-qualitative analyses. In Proceedings of the 2022 ACM Conference on Information Technology for Social Good, New York, NY, USA, 7–9 September 2022; GoodIT '22, pp. 161–166. [CrossRef]
42. Versaci, M.; Laganà, F.; Morabito, F.C.; Palumbo, A.; Angiulli, G. Adaptation of an Eddy Current Model for Characterizing Subsurface Defects in CFRP Plates Using FEM Analysis Based on Energy Functional. *Mathematics* **2024**, *12*, 2854. [CrossRef]
43. Laganà, F.; Pullano, S.A.; Angiulli, G.; Versaci, M. Optimized Analytical–Numerical Procedure for Ultrasonic Sludge Treatment for Agricultural Use. *Algorithms* **2024**, *17*, 592. [CrossRef]
44. Bhattacharya, A. *Applied Machine Learning Explainability Techniques: Make ML Models Explainable and Trustworthy for Practical Applications Using LIME, SHAP, and More*; Packt Publishing Ltd.: Birmingham, UK, 2022.
45. Caterina, E. Verso il nuovo regolamento Ue in materia di pubblicità politica: Mercato delle idee o della propaganda? *Quad. Cost. Riv. Ital. Dirit. Cost.* **2024**, *1*, 207–209. [CrossRef]
46. Licastro, A. La regolazione dello spazio informativo disintermediato dinanzi alla progressiva avanzata della 'synthetic media technology' in tempo di tornate elettorali. *Dirit. Pubblico* **2024**, *3*, 577–619. [CrossRef]
47. Cossiri, A. Le campagne di disinformazione nell'arsenale di guerra: Strumenti giuridici per contrastare la minaccia alla prova del bilanciamento. *Riv. Ital. Inform. Dirit.* **2024**, *5*, 77–85. [CrossRef]

computers

MDPI

Article

Cross-Dataset Data Augmentation Using UMAP for Deep Learning-Based Wind Speed Prediction

Eder Arley Leon-Gomez *, Andrés Marino Álvarez-Meza * and German Castellanos-Dominguez

Signal Processing and Recognition Group, Universidad Nacional de Colombia, Manizales 170003, Colombia; cgcastellanosd@unal.edu.co
* Correspondence: ealeong@unal.edu.co (E.A.L.-G.); amalvarezme@unal.edu.co (A.M.Á.-M.)

Abstract: Wind energy has emerged as a cornerstone in global efforts to transition to renewable energy, driven by its low environmental impact and significant generation potential. However, the inherent intermittency of wind, influenced by complex and dynamic atmospheric patterns, poses significant challenges for accurate wind speed prediction. Existing approaches, including statistical methods, machine learning, and deep learning, often struggle with limitations such as non-linearity, non-stationarity, computational demands, and the requirement for extensive, high-quality datasets. In response to these challenges, we propose a novel neighborhood preserving cross-dataset data augmentation framework for high-horizon wind speed prediction. The proposed method addresses data variability and dynamic behaviors through three key components: (i) the uniform manifold approximation and projection (UMAP) is employed as a non-linear dimensionality reduction technique to encode local relationships in wind speed time-series data while preserving neighborhood structures, (ii) a localized cross-dataset data augmentation (DA) approach is introduced using UMAP-reduced spaces to enhance data diversity and mitigate variability across datasets, and (iii) recurrent neural networks (RNNs) are trained on the augmented datasets to model temporal dependencies and non-linear patterns effectively. Our framework was evaluated using datasets from diverse geographical locations, including the Argonne Weather Observatory (USA), Chengdu Airport (China), and Beijing Capital International Airport (China). Comparative tests using regression-based measures on RNN, GRU, and LSTM architectures showed that the proposed method was better at improving the accuracy and generalizability of predictions, leading to an average reduction in prediction error. Consequently, our study highlights the potential of integrating advanced dimensionality reduction, data augmentation, and deep learning techniques to address critical challenges in renewable energy forecasting.

Keywords: time-series prediction; wind speed; non-linear dimensionality reduction; cross-dataset data augmentation; neural networks

1. Introduction

Countries across the world have been compelled to use clean energy technologies due to the increasing demand and the necessity to reduce carbon footprints [1]. Wind energy has gained prominence among many technologies due to its minimum environmental impact and substantial energy production in certain regions [2]. As of 2023, renewable energy possessed an installed capacity of 28,000 GW, of which 600 GW was derived from wind-based sources [3]. Although this represents a substantial contribution, it is rather minor given the pivotal role wind energy is anticipated to assume in the global energy

https://doi.org/10.3390/computers14040123

revolution. Regarding this, the Paris Agreement set a goal for renewable energy generation to account for at least 86% of the total by 2050 [4], making the expansion of wind energy capacity essential to meeting these international commitments. However, such a source is directly influenced by the intermittency of weather patterns, which can lead to disruptions in the electrical grid and result in reduced power quality [5].

Additionally, the utilization of wind energy poses specific challenges, particularly in predicting the electricity produced by wind farms. The quantity of energy generated is significantly influenced by wind speed, which is ascertained by a confluence of climatic elements [6]. Specifically, forecasting wind speed presents considerable difficulties owing to the intrinsically non-stationary characteristics of atmospheric patterns, where both short- and long-term variations create complexities that are challenging to quantify [7]. Moreover, the existence of intricate non-linear interactions among meteorological variables exacerbates this challenge [8]. Cyclical events, like El Niño and La Niña, along with their interactions with climate change, produce exogenous conditions that result in randomness and volatility [9].

Conversely, the modeling of wind speed is influenced by the required prediction horizon. Typically, short, medium, high, and high-large horizons are examined. Short-term horizons are essential in turbine control applications, as predictions within one to ten seconds are critical for adjusting the control system in response to wind gusts [10]. Moreover, medium horizons of five to 60 min are beneficial for power grid dispatch and maintenance [11]. In turn, prediction intervals of one to 48 h (high horizons) are utilized for energy trading and power system management [12]. Next, a high-large horizon prediction, which spans from days to years, is crucial for the long-term planning and optimization of wind energy systems. Such predictions enable effective scheduling of maintenance, grid integration, and capacity planning [13].

Now, wind speed forecasting is presently conducted using two separate prediction methodologies: physical-based modeling and data-driven approaches. The initial framework involves a high-large horizon in which functional models are employed. These models feature numerous parameters that characterize on-site weather conditions. Namely, numerical weather predictions (NWPs) are based on the physical processes that govern the transfer of energy and materials within the climate ecosystem [14]. They rely on dynamic physical and thermodynamic principles that clarify interactions between energy and matter across oceans, the atmosphere, and land surfaces. Although they demonstrate high accuracy, their implementation is complicated by the need for extensive parameter tuning and significant computational resources for modeling [15].

On the other hand, data-driven time-series approaches are capable of capturing both stationary and non-stationary patterns in wind speed. Within this category, statistical models, classic machine learning methods, deep learning, and hybrid strategies can be explored [12]. Traditional statistical models encompass auto-regressive with exogenous auto-regressive moving average (ARMA) and auto-regressive integrated moving average (ARIMA), as well as fractional-ARIMA (f-ARIMA). In addition, classical machine learning algorithms were extensively researched because they could find data patterns and provide high interpretability. Some of the most popular methods include Exponential Smoothing (ES) [16], Gaussian Processes (GPs) [17], Ridge Regression [18], Random Forest (RF) [19], and Support Vector Machines (SVMs) [20]. In the third case, deep learning methods have arisen as the most popular machine learning approach to handle non-linear and non-stationary time series due to their ability to extract complex features from input data automatically [21]. Here, models based on memory architectures such as gated recurrent units (GRUs) [22], long short-term memory (LSTM) [11], and attention mechanisms have been employed [23].

Though wind speed approaches have been widely studied, the following issues arise: Statistical models like ARIMA and its variants struggle to effectively model non-linear and non-stationary patterns, limiting their applicability to real-world scenarios with complex dynamics. These methods rely heavily on the assumption of linearity and stationary processes, making them unsuitable for datasets exhibiting abrupt changes or high variability [24]. Next, classical machine learning models, such as SVMs and RF, often require extensive feature engineering, which can be time-consuming and relies heavily on domain expertise. Moreover, despite their high interpretability, these models may fail to capture intricate temporal dependencies inherent in time-series data, leading to suboptimal predictions for highly dynamic wind speed scenarios [25]. In contrast, deep learning methods, while powerful, are computationally expensive and require large datasets for effective training, which may not always be available in wind speed prediction tasks. These models also risk overfitting when applied to small or imbalanced datasets, and their black-box nature limits interpretability, posing challenges for their adoption in operational settings [26]. Hybrid models combining statistical, machine learning, or deep learning approaches may inherit the limitations of their constituent methods and can also be computationally intensive, requiring significant tuning of parameters to achieve a balance between accuracy and complexity [27].

In recent years, enhancing the performance of machine and deep learning models in time-series tasks, i.e., wind speed prediction, has become a critical area of research, driven by the growing reliance on data-driven insights across domains [28]. Although the advancements in model architecture have substantially improved performance, the availability of large, high-quality datasets remains a pivotal factor in enabling effective feature extraction and pattern recognition during the training process. However, real-world applications often face challenges such as limited dataset sizes, poor data quality, and restricted access due to privacy concerns [29]. To address these limitations, strategies like transfer learning (TL) and data augmentation (DA) have emerged as effective solutions. These techniques not only mitigate the constraints of small datasets but also enhance the robustness and generalizability of machine learning models by expanding the diversity of training data [30,31].

In the TL approach, the primary objective is to leverage knowledge representations learned from a source dataset and apply them to a target database. This is especially advantageous when dealing with small sample sets, as it alleviates the need to extract features from scratch, significantly reducing computational overhead and the requirement for extensive labeled data [32]. TL has demonstrated remarkable success across various domains, including image processing [33], where pre-trained models are fine-tuned for specific tasks, and language modeling [34], where embeddings learned from large-scale corpora are adapted for downstream tasks. Regarding wind speed prediction, TL provides pre-trained models or knowledge from related domains to enhance predictive accuracy when datasets are small or region-specific. For instance, models pre-trained on global meteorological datasets can be fine-tuned for specific wind farms, improving localized predictions without requiring extensive labeled data [35]. Recent studies demonstrate the effectiveness of TL in transferring spatial and temporal features from large-scale weather models to wind speed forecasting applications, achieving superior performance compared to models trained solely on limited data [36]. TL techniques, like domain adaptation, have also been used to deal with changes in geography and climate, making wind speed prediction frameworks that are strong and scalable [37]. Nevertheless, the effectiveness of TL is highly dependent on the similarity between the source and target domains; substantial discrepancies in geographical, climatic, or temporal patterns can result in negative transfers, where the adapted model performs worse than a model trained exclusively on the target data [38]. Also, fine-tuning models that have already been trained usually requires a lot of computer power and specialized knowledge to make the adaptation process better, especially for wind speed forecasting tasks that are very complicated. The incapacity of many TL frameworks to generalize across varied wind farm circumstances requires regular model reconfiguration, which is both time-consuming and computationally costly [39].

Conversely, DA focuses on expanding the original dataset to increase its size and diversity, thereby improving model generalization. Traditional DA techniques, prevalent in image processing, typically apply transformations like cropping, scaling, mirroring, color augmentation, or translation to augment data [40]. However, these methods are not directly transferable to time-series data due to their sequential and temporal dependencies. To address this challenge, synthetic data generation techniques have emerged as a robust alternative. Advanced methods such as variational autoencoders (VAEs) [41] and generative adversarial networks (GANs) [42] have been increasingly employed for time-series augmentation. VAEs encode input data into a probabilistic latent space, enabling the generation of diverse yet realistic data samples. GANs, on the other hand, use a dynamic adversarial process between a generator network and a discriminator network to create high-quality synthetic data that mirror the statistical properties of the original dataset. These approaches have proven particularly beneficial in applications such as wind speed prediction, where the availability of extensive, high-quality time-series data are often limited. For example, GAN-based DA methods have been used to improve wind speed datasets, which has led to more accurate short-term forecasts by creating more realistic synthetic samples [43]. Similarly, hybrid models leveraging DA techniques have demonstrated enhanced performance in predicting extreme wind speed events, where original datasets are sparse or highly imbalanced [44]. Still, DA methods often have trouble keeping the temporal and sequential integrity of the wind speed time series. This can cause problems with the synthetic data that are generated, which can hurt the performance of the model [45]. Additionally, the computational cost and complexity of advanced DA methods, such as GANs and VAEs, can pose significant challenges when processing large-scale datasets [46]. Lastly, variability across different datasets (region-specific wind speed prediction) decreases the DA's performance [47].

In this study, we propose a novel neighborhood preserving cross-dataset data augmentation approach tailored for deep learning-based wind speed prediction in high-horizon scenarios. We have designed our method to tackle the issues of data variability and dynamic behavior that frequently arise in wind speed forecasting. Specifically, our approach comprises three key components:

- We use the uniform manifold approximation and projection (UMAP) [48] as a non-linear dimensionality reduction algorithm to find and encode local relationships in wind speed time-series samples. The low-dimensional representation of the data preserves its neighborhood structures.
- A localized cross-dataset DA approach is introduced from the UMAP-reduced spaces, which leverages localized neighborhoods to mitigate data variability across multiple wind speed datasets, enhancing the diversity and robustness of the augmented training data [47].
- Recurrent neural networks (RNNs) are trained using the augmented datasets, capitalizing on their ability to model temporal dependencies and non-linear patterns in wind speed time-series data.

Our framework improves the generalization capability of predictive models by exposing them to a wide range of conditions and behavioral patterns. Experiments include wind speed time series from weather stations at the Argonne Weather Observatory in Illinois, USA; the Chengdu Airport in Sichuan Province, China; and the Beijing Capital International

Airport, China. Additionally, the method comparison comprises the straightforward RNN, GRU, and LSTM architectures using regression-based quantitative assessments. Thus, our approach is a promising alternative for wind-based energy monitoring.

The reminder of this paper is organized as follows: Section 2 describes the materials and methods. Sections 3 and 4 describe the experimental set-up and obtained results. Finally, the conclusions are outlined in Section 5.

2. Materials and Methods

2.1. Wind Speed Time-Series Datasets

We utilized three distinct datasets for wind speed prediction collected from meteorological stations. The key characteristics of each dataset are detailed below, including the recording period, sensor specifications, geographic location, regional climate conditions, dataset size, and the properties of the available measurements.

Argonne. The first dataset originates from the Argonne Weather Observatory, located at the Argonne National Laboratory in Illinois, west of Chicago, in the Midwestern United States (see https://pubs.usgs.gov/wdr/2005/wdr-il-05/data/wind_por/indices0/index.htm) (accessed on 1 January 2025). Geographically, the observatory is positioned at 41° N latitude and 87° W longitude. Wind speed data were recorded over an extensive period, spanning from 1 January 1998 to 30 August 2005, with an hourly sampling frequency. The Argonne dataset, encompassing more than five decades of observations, offers a comprehensive record with hundreds of thousands of data points, capturing a wide range of wind speed variations and providing valuable insights into long-term atmospheric dynamics. Wind speed measurements were taken using Met One Instruments Model 10B anemometers. Additional meteorological variables, including temperature, humidity, and solar radiation, were recorded with high-precision sensors such as the Vaisala HMP45A (temperature and dewpoint) and the Eppley pyranometer (solar radiation). The Argonne station has been in continuous operation since 1948, with rigorous data correction processes ensuring reliability. The region experiences a continental climate, featuring cold winters, mild summers, and distinct seasonal transitions.

Chengdu. The second dataset originates from Chengdu Airport in Sichuan Province, China, at coordinates 30.6° N latitude and 104.01° E longitude (see https://mesonet.agron.iastate.edu/request/download.phtml?network=PK__ASOS) (accessed on 1 January 2025). Covering nearly eight years, from 1 January 2011 to 30 December 2018, with hourly observations, it provides tens of thousands of data points. Situated in a subtropical monsoon climate, Chengdu experiences mild winters, warm, humid summers, and concentrated summer rainfall. The Sichuan Basin's unique geography contributes to frequent fog and high humidity, which can affect wind measurements. Although details of the anemometer model are unavailable, the dataset adheres to China's ASOS standards, ensuring high-quality data. This dataset complements the Argonne dataset by offering insights into wind dynamics under monsoon climates and complex topographical influences.

Beijing. The third dataset is sourced from Beijing Capital International Airport, located at 39.9° N latitude and 116.2° E longitude (see https://talltowers.bsc.es) (accessed on 1 January 2025). As a climatological and synoptic station under the Global Basic Observing Network (GBON) and the World Meteorological Organization (WMO), it provides high-quality data. For this study, wind speed measurements from 1 August 2011 to 30 December 2018, were used, offering tens of thousands of hourly observations. Beijing's continental monsoon climate, with cold, dry winters and hot, humid summers, drives significant seasonal wind speed variations influenced by temperature and atmospheric pressure shifts. The dataset offers a unique perspective compared to Chengdu and Argonne, capturing a distinct climate regime.

The three datasets together form a robust resource for analyzing wind speed dynamics across varied climatic and geographical settings. By encompassing continental, monsoon, and subtropical monsoon climates, they provide a comprehensive foundation for assessing the generalizability and performance of wind speed prediction approaches. Table 1 and Figure 1 illustrate the statistical description and the geographical distribution of the studied databases.

Table 1. Wind speed datasets main statistical description. Std.: Standard Deviation.

Dataset	Start	End	Max	Mean	Min	Median	Std.
Argone	1 January 1998	30 August 2005	32.44	7.28	0	6.49	3.83
Chengdu	1 January 2011	30 December 2018	33.53	3.52	0	2.24	2.95
Beijing	1 August 2011	30 December 2018	40.23	6.48	0	4.47	4.85

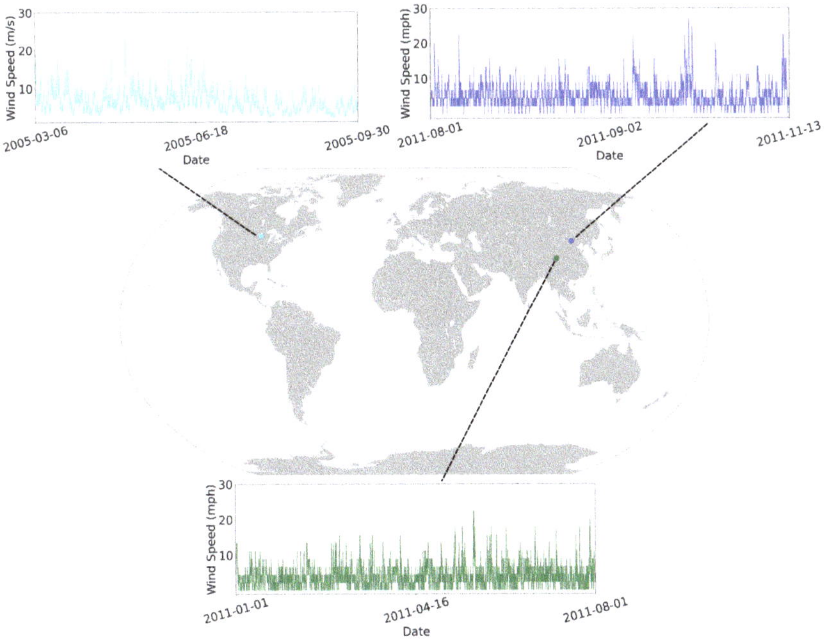

Figure 1. Geographical distribution of the three meteorological stations used in this study for wind speed prediction. The map highlights the locations of the Argonne Weather Observatory (cyan dot •) in Illinois, USA; Chengdu Airport (green dot •) in Sichuan Province, China; and Beijing Capital International Airport (blue dot •) in Beijing, China.

2.2. *Uniform Manifold Approximation and Projection (UMAP)*

UMAP is a powerful tool for dimensionality reductions, well suited for capturing non-linear relationships in high-dimensional datasets. By preserving both global and local structures, UMAP outperforms many traditional methods, offering meaningful low-dimensional embeddings that reflect the underlying data geometry. Compared to techniques like principal component analysis (PCA) and t-distributed stochastic neighbor embedding (t-SNE), UMAP excels in balancing computational efficiency with the ability to maintain meaningful neighborhood relationships, making it particularly effective for clustering and visualization tasks [49]. These strengths make UMAP an ideal choice for tasks requiring the reduction of complex, non-linear data while preserving key structural properties essential for further prediction stages.

Here, given a high-dimensional input matrix $\mathbf{X} \in \mathbb{R}^{N \times \tau}$, which contains N wind speed time-series segments across τ time instants, UMAP seeks to compute a low-dimensional embedding $\mathbf{Z} \in \mathbb{R}^{N \times M}$, with $M \leq \tau$ low-dimensional features. This embedding is designed to preserve both the global and local neighborhood structures present in $\mathbf{X}$, thereby maintaining the key non-linear relationships inherent in the data. To achieve this, UMAP constructs a K-nearest neighbor (KNN) graph as

$$\theta_n = \min_{\mathbf{x}_{n'} \in \Omega_n} \mathrm{d}(\mathbf{x}_n, \mathbf{x}_{n'}), \tag{1}$$

where $\mathrm{d}(\cdot,\cdot) \in \mathbb{R}^+$ is the Euclidean distance function, $\theta_n \in \mathbb{R}^+$ holds the minimum distance within the n-th neighborhood, and $\Omega_n \in \mathbb{R}^{K \times \tau}$ holds K neighbors $\mathbf{x}_{n'} \in \mathbb{R}^\tau$ centered on $\mathbf{x}_n \in \mathbb{R}^\tau$. Next, a localized entropy $\xi_n \in \mathbb{R}^+$ is computed for each input segment by solving

$$\sum_{n'=1}^{K} \exp\left(-\frac{\mathrm{d}(\mathbf{x}_n, \mathbf{x}_{n'}) - \theta_n}{\xi_n}\right) = \log(K). \tag{2}$$

Subsequently, UMAP constructs a fuzzy simplicial complex graph, denoted as $\mathcal{G} = (\mathbf{X}, \mathbf{A})$, where the edges are determined by local connectivity. The weights of these edges are represented in the matrix $\mathbf{A} \in [0,1]^{N \times N}$:

$$a_{nn'} = \exp\left(-\max\left(0, \frac{\mathrm{d}(\mathbf{x}_n, \mathbf{x}_{n'}) - \theta_n}{\xi_n}\right)\right). \tag{3}$$

In turn, a low-dimensional weight matrix $\tilde{\mathbf{A}} \in [0,1]^{N \times N}$ is computed as

$$\tilde{a}_{nn'} = \left(1 + \alpha \mathrm{d}(\mathbf{z}_n, \mathbf{z}_{n'})^2\right)^{-\iota}, \tag{4}$$

where $\mathbf{z}_n, \mathbf{z}_{n'} \in \mathbf{Z}$ represent points in the low-dimensional embedding, while $\alpha, \iota \in \mathbb{R}^+$ hyper-parameters (commonly set to 1) balance the preservation of local and global structures. The UMAP optimization problem can then be expressed using a cross-entropy loss function as follows:

$$\mathbf{Z}^* = \arg\min_{\mathbf{z}_n \in \mathbf{Z}} \sum_{\substack{n \in N \\ n \neq n'}} a_{nn'} \log\left(\frac{a_{nn'}}{\tilde{a}_{nn'}(\mathbf{Z})}\right) + (1 - a_{nn'}) \log\left(\frac{1 - a_{nn'}}{1 - \tilde{a}_{nn'}(\mathbf{Z})}\right). \tag{5}$$

Notation $\tilde{a}_{nn'}(\mathbf{Z})$ emphasizes the dependency between the low-dimensional embedding $\mathbf{Z}$ and the graph weights in $\tilde{\mathbf{A}}$. Notably, the optimization problem in Equation (5) balances attraction (first term) and repulsion (second term) forces by minimizing the differences between probabilities, represented by the graph weights. Lastly, this optimization can be effectively solved using gradient descent-based methods [48].

2.3. *UMAP-Based Cross-Dataset Data Augmentation*

Now, let $\mathcal{D} = \{\mathbf{X}^r \in \mathbb{R}^{N_r \times \tau}, \mathbf{Y}^r \in \mathbb{R}^{N_r \times \tau'}\}_{r=1}^R$ represent a multi-region wind speed time-series dataset, where $\mathbf{X}^r$ contains N_r input segments spanning τ time instants and $\mathbf{Y}^r$ corresponds to the subsequent τ' outputs. Namely, $\mathcal{D}$ encompasses R geographical regions. Here, to capture data variability and non-linear relationships among samples, we propose a cross-dataset DA approach leveraging UMAP-based embeddings.

Regarding this, the augmented input matrix $\tilde{\mathbf{X}} \in \mathbb{R}^{\tilde{N} \times \tau}$ is constructed through a row-wise concatenation of the multi-region wind speed time series from $\mathcal{D}$, with $N = \sum_{r=1}^R N_r$. Subsequently, a 2D low-dimensional embedding matrix $\tilde{\mathbf{Z}} \in \mathbb{R}^{\tilde{N} \times 2}$ is obtained by solving the optimization problem defined in Equation (5), with the input matrix $\tilde{\mathbf{X}}$ being fixed, as follows:

$$\tilde{\mathbf{Z}} = \text{UMAP}(\tilde{\mathbf{X}}). \tag{6}$$

The latter aims to preserve diverse temporal dynamics and regional wind speed characteristics within a neighborhood-based representation. Next, the augmented input–output wind speed time-series data for each r-th region, denoted as $\widehat{\mathbf{X}}^r \in \mathbb{R}^{\tilde{N}_r \times \tau}$ and $\widehat{\mathbf{Y}}^r \in \mathbb{R}^{\tilde{N}_r \times \tau'}$, is constructed as follows:

$$\widehat{\mathbf{X}}^r = \mathbf{X}^r \cup \{\mathbf{x}_{n'}^{r'} : \|\tilde{\mathbf{z}}_{n'}^{r'} - \tilde{\mathbf{z}}_n^r\|_2 < \zeta, r' \neq r, \tilde{\mathbf{z}}_{n'}^{r'} \notin \Omega(\tilde{\mathbf{z}}_n^r)\}, \tag{7}$$

$$\widehat{\mathbf{Y}}^r = \mathbf{Y}^r \cup \{\mathbf{y}_{n'}^{r'} : \|\tilde{\mathbf{z}}_{n'}^{r'} - \tilde{\mathbf{z}}_n^r\|_2 < \zeta, r' \neq r, \tilde{\mathbf{z}}_{n'}^{r'} \notin \Omega(\tilde{\mathbf{z}}_n^r)\}; \tag{8}$$

where $\mathbf{x}_{n'}^{r'} \in \mathbf{X}^{r'}$ is the n'-th augmented sample from the geographical region r' related to the low-dimensional neighbor $\tilde{\mathbf{z}}_{n'}^{r'}$ centered on $\tilde{\mathbf{z}}_n^r$, with $\tilde{\mathbf{z}}_{n'}^{r}, \tilde{\mathbf{z}}_n^{r'} \in \tilde{\mathbf{Z}}$, $n \in \{1, 2, \ldots, N_r\}$, $n' \in \{1, 2, \ldots, N_{r'}\}$, and $r, r' \in \{1, 2, \ldots, R\}$. Notation $\tilde{\mathbf{z}}_{n'}^{r'} \notin \Omega(\tilde{\mathbf{z}}_n^r)$ ensures that neighborhood-based augmentation remains disjoint across datasets, with $\Omega(\tilde{\mathbf{z}}_n^r)$ being the UMAP-based data augmentation neighborhood on $\tilde{\mathbf{z}}_n^r$.

The hyper-parameter $\zeta \in \mathbb{R}^+$ rules the low-dimensional neighborhood radius for our UMAP-based cross-dataset data augmentation (UMAP-CDDA). By constructing a unified embedding matrix $\tilde{\mathbf{Z}}$, our method preserves temporal dynamics and regional characteristics while capturing non-linear relationships within multi-region datasets. Namely, through neighborhood augmentation, localized patterns from similar wind speed dynamics are integrated into the training data, improving diversity and mitigating the limitations of small or region-specific datasets.

2.4. Deep Learning-Based Wind Speed Predictions

For each cross-dataset DA pair $\widehat{\mathbf{X}}^r$ and $\widehat{\mathbf{Y}}^r$, a DL-based algorithm can be trained for wind speed prediction, as follows:

$$\check{\mathbf{Y}}^r = \varsigma(\widehat{\mathbf{X}}^r | \nu) = (\varsigma_L \circ \varsigma_{L-1} \circ \cdots \circ \varsigma_1)(\widehat{\mathbf{X}}^r), \tag{9}$$

Notation $\circ$ stands for function composition. $\check{\mathbf{Y}}^r \in \mathbb{R}^{\tilde{N}_r \times \tau'}$ holds the wind speed predictions, L stands for the number of layers, and

$$\boldsymbol{F}_l = \varsigma_l(\boldsymbol{F}_{l-1}) = \sigma(\boldsymbol{F}_{l-1} \otimes \boldsymbol{\varpi}_l + \boldsymbol{\beta}_l), \tag{10}$$

where $\sigma(\cdot)$ is a non-linear activation, $\boldsymbol{F}_l$ is the l-th feature map, $\boldsymbol{\varpi}_l$ and $\boldsymbol{\beta}_l$ hold the weights and bias of proper size, and $\nu = \{\boldsymbol{\varpi}_l, \boldsymbol{\beta}_l\}_{l=1}^{L}$ gathers the network parameters. Furthermore, $\otimes$ represents the tensor product operator for recurrent layers. In this study, three well-known recurrent layers are considered:

- Simple recurrent neural networks (SRNNs) are a foundational deep learning architecture designed to model sequential data by capturing temporal dependencies. RNNs process the augmented data generated by the UMAP-based cross-dataset approach. In short, the RNN architecture iteratively processes the input sequences, maintaining a hidden state that carries information from previous time steps, enabling the network to learn patterns and trends over time [50].
- Long short-term memory (LSTM) networks are an advanced architecture specifically designed to overcome the limitations of SRNNs, such as vanishing or exploding gradients, when modeling long-range temporal dependencies. The LSTM architecture introduces memory cells and gating mechanisms—input, forget, and output gates—that enable the selective retention and propagation of relevant information over

extended time sequences. This allows for effectively capturing the temporal dynamics and complex non-linear data patterns [35].

- Gated recurrent units (GRUs) are a simplified but powerful variant of LSTM networks, designed to efficiently model sequential data by capturing temporal dependencies with reduced computational complexity. GRUs utilize gating mechanisms—update and reset gates—to regulate the flow of information, enabling the network to retain or discard information dynamically over time. This design allows GRUs to learn complex temporal patterns while maintaining a lighter computational footprint compared to LSTMs [51]. Figure 2 summarizes the main SRNN, LSTM, and GRU layers.

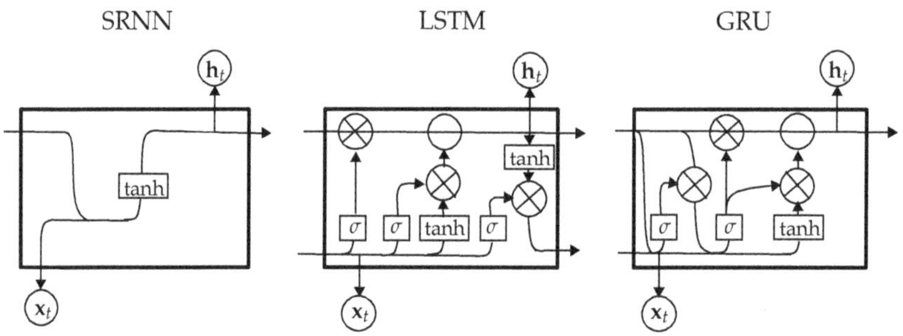

Figure 2. SRNN, LSTM, and GRU main layers for time-series prediction. The SRNN processes sequences by passing information through a recurrent loop, enabling temporal context. The LSTM extends this by incorporating gates to control memory updates and retention over long sequences. The GRU simplifies the LSTM with fewer gates, offering efficient handling of sequential data.

Then, the following optimization arises:

$$\nu^* = \arg\min_{\nu} \frac{1}{N_r} \sum_{n=1}^{N_r} \mathcal{L}(\boldsymbol{y}_n^r, \check{\boldsymbol{y}}_n^r), \tag{11}$$

where $\check{\boldsymbol{y}}_n^r = \varsigma(\tilde{\boldsymbol{x}}_n^r|\nu)$, $\tilde{\boldsymbol{x}}_n^r \in \widehat{\mathbf{X}}^r$, and $\mathcal{L}(\cdot,\cdot)$ is a given loss function. A backpropagation-driven gradient descent framework is utilized to optimize the parameter set [50]:

$$\nu_i = \nu_{i-1} - \eta_i \frac{\partial}{\partial \nu_{i-1}} \left\{ \frac{1}{N_r} \sum_{n=1}^{N_r} \mathcal{L}(\boldsymbol{y}_n^r, \check{\boldsymbol{y}}_n^r) \right\}. \tag{12}$$

An approach based on automatic differentiation computes the gradient, where $\eta_i \in \mathbb{R}^+$ represents the learning rate. Here, the following kernel-based mean square error (KMSE) loss function is employed [52]:

$$KMSE(\boldsymbol{y}, \check{\boldsymbol{y}}) = \frac{1}{\tau'} \sum_{t=1}^{\tau'} \exp\left(\frac{-\|y_t - \check{y}_t\|_2^2}{2\check{\sigma}^2} \right), \tag{13}$$

where $\check{\sigma} \in \mathbb{R}^+$ serves as a bandwidth hyper-parameter that regulates the discrepancy between target and network prediction and $\|\cdot\|_2$ stands for the l2-norm operator.

3. Experimental Set-Up

We used the three wind speed datasets from Section 2.1 for real-world testing. Data were split into training sets (80%) and testing sets (20%). The training period for the Argonne dataset spanned from `1998-01-01 01:00` to `1994-03-14 10:00`, while testing covered `1994-03-14 11:00` to `2005-09-30 24:00`. For the Chengdu dataset, training data ranged from `2011-08-01 00:00` to `2017-07-07 16:00`, with testing from `2017-07-07`

17:00 to 2018-12-29 23:00. Similarly, the Beijing dataset's training period extended from 2011-01-01 00:00 to 2017-05-27 15:00, and testing spanned 2017-05-27 15:00 to 2018-12-29 23:00. To find temporal dependencies, we used windowing with a single-sample shift to make sure there was the most overlap and that the sequence stayed the same. This enhances feature extraction and model generalization, which is crucial for accurate forecasting [53].

In the training phase, hold-out validation was used. For concrete testing, the input window size and the horizon values are fixed as $\tau = 20$ and $\tau' \in \{1, 2, \ldots, 7\}$ hours, as a suitable range for energy planning applications [54]. Similarly, the radius is chosen from $\zeta \in \{0.0, 0.01, 0.02, 0.05, 0.07, 0.01, 0.02\}$. This selection process maintains a balance between computational efficiency and predictive accuracy by optimizing the resolution of the tested hyper-parameters. Also, we set the UMAP neighborhood size to 50, enhancing the preservation of fine-grained local structures, making the embedding highly sensitive to small-scale variations. Minimal local connectivity, $\theta_n = 1$, enforces strong separation between clusters by limiting the number of strongly connected neighbors. Before processing data with recurrent architectures and the proposed UMAP-CDDA, a preprocessing stage encompassing min–max normalization between 0 and 1 is applied to enhance numerical stability and convergence [55]. Figure 3 summarizes our UMAP-CDDA-based training pipeline for predicting wind speed time series.

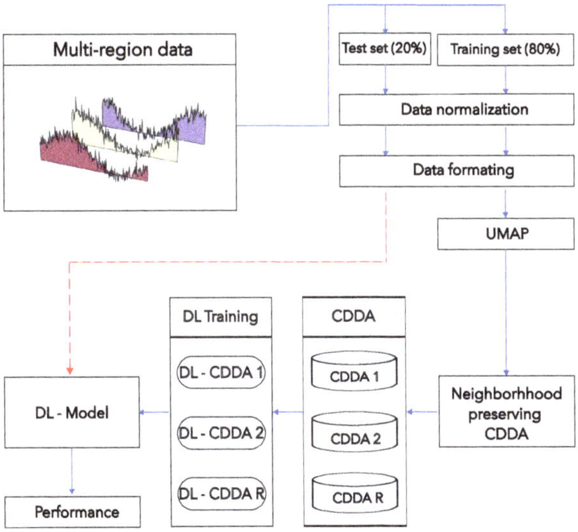

Figure 3. UMAP-based neighborhood preserving cross-dataset data augmentation (UMAP-CDDA). Multi-region datasets are used to compute a unified UMAP-based low-dimensional embedding. Then, neighborhood-preserving-based datasets are applied to the UMAP low-dimensional space to enhance each region-specific training. Finally, recurrent networks are trained for time-series prediction.

The mean absolute error (MAE), the mean absolute percentage error (MAPE), and the R^2 score are used as quantitative assessment measures [56]:

$$MAE(\boldsymbol{y}, \breve{\boldsymbol{y}}) = \frac{1}{\tau'} \sum_{t=1}^{\tau'} \|y_t - \breve{y}_t\|_1, \tag{14}$$

$$MAPE(\boldsymbol{y}, \breve{\boldsymbol{y}}) = \frac{1}{\tau'} \sum_{t=1}^{\tau'} \frac{\|y_t - \breve{y}_t\|_1}{\|y_t\|_1}, \tag{15}$$

$$R^2(y, \check{y}) = 1 - \frac{\sum_{t=1}^{\tau'} \|y_t - \check{y}_t\|_2^2}{\sum_{t=1}^{\tau'} \|y_t - \bar{y}\|_2^2}, \tag{16}$$

where $\|\cdot\|_2$ and $\|\cdot\|_1$ stand for the l1- and l2-based norm operators. Also, $\bar{y} = \frac{1}{\tau'}\sum_{t=1}^{\tau'} y_t$. Here, R^2 values lower than 0 are set to 0.

To evaluate the effectiveness of our UMAP-CDDA approach, we compared it against a straightforward recurrent network incorporating SRNN, LSTM, and GRU layers, using the KMSE in Equation (13) as the loss function with $\check{\sigma} = \sqrt{2}/2$. The comparison was conducted with and without our data augmentation strategy while maintaining the same architecture (see Table 2) [52].

Table 2. DL main architecture for UMAP-CDDA-based wind speed prediction. τ represents the input window size and τ' the prediction horizon ($\tau = 20$ and $\tau' = 7$ h/samples in our experiments). $h = 9$ Units are fixed for the recurrent layer.

Layer	Output Dimension
Input	$1 \times \tau$
Recurrent (Activation: ReLU) SRNN/GRU/LSTM	$1 \times h$
Dense (Activation: Linear)	$1 \times \tau'$

The UMAP-CDDA optimization process runs for 100 epochs, ensuring a balance between computational efficiency and embedding stability. Also, to compute UMAP on large datasets, we leverage the RAPIDS cuML package https://docs.rapids.ai/api/, (accessed on 1 December 2024) version 24.10.0, which utilizes GPU acceleration for significantly faster execution compared to CPU-based implementations. This approach improves scalability, enabling the processing of datasets with millions of points while maintaining low latency.

Next, we trained each DL model using TensorFlow version 2.17.0 and Keras version 3.2.1. All tests were performed in Kaggle notebook environments. These environments provide two Tesla T4 GPUs with 15GB of VRAM, 30GB of RAM, an Intel Xeon CPU @ 2GHz with two threads per core, and two sockets per core. We set a maximum of 100 epochs, a learning rate of 1×10^{-3}, and an Adam optimizer. All notebooks and codes are publicly available at https://github.com/ealeongomez/UMAPCDDA (accessed on 1 December 2024).

4. Results and Discussion

4.1. UMAP-CDDA Visual Inspection Results

Figure 4 depicts the UMAP-based dimensionality reduction plots, where each point represents a reduced representation of an input window with $\tau = 20$ h. The color of each point corresponds to the average output wind speed for the following $\tau' = 7$ horizon points (hours), as indicated by the color bar. This visualization enables an analysis of the dispersion of wind speed values within each dataset. When examining the datasets individually, the Argonne samples demonstrate a well-clustered and consistent distribution of input windows across input samples. Similarly, the Beijing dataset exhibits a structured dispersion of wind speed, though with a wider spread of points. This evidence suggests that while there is some structure in the data, the relationship between input windows and predicted outputs is less robust, leading to greater variability in predictions. In contrast, the Chengdu dataset presents different behavior. The clustering pattern is less distinct compared to the Argonne and Beijing datasets, with points appearing more widely dispersed. This lack of clear separation between wind speed values may be attributed to the complex characteristics of the Chengdu time series, where non-linear dependencies and dynamic meteorological conditions introduce greater variability. As a result, it exhibits more overlap between different wind speed ranges, making it difficult to distinguish distinct patterns in the low-dimensional representation.

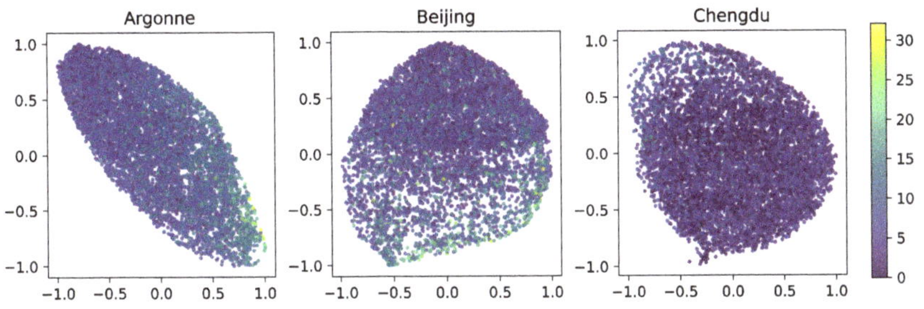

Figure 4. UMAP-based 2D representation of the wind speed time series for the Argonne, Beijing, and Chengdu datasets (dimensionless embeddings are obtained). Color: average speed along the prediction horizon ($\tau' = 7$ h).

Overall, the UMAP-based 2D representation highlights the influence of dataset-specific characteristics on wind speed relationships, where structured patterns emerge in some datasets (Argonne and Beijing), while increased complexity in the time series (as seen in Chengdu) can obscure the separation of wind speed values. Figure 5 shows the UMAP low-dimensional representation of the combined datasets. The left plot uses color to represent the average speed along the horizon ($\tau' = 7$), while the right figure shows the membership of each input dataset (Argonne, Beijing, or Chengdu). By comparing both visualizations, it is possible to analyze the effectiveness of the neighborhood-based augmentation process. The overlap between different datasets in the right panel highlights the potential for cross-dataset data augmentation, where similar wind speed patterns across locations enhance the richness of the training set. As the neighborhood radius expands, a greater number of samples from diverse datasets are integrated into the augmentation process, increasing variability and improving model generalization. However, an excessively large radius may introduce undesirable noise, blending distinct wind regimes and diminishing the specificity of localized wind speed characteristics. Therefore, carefully selecting an optimal neighborhood radius is essential to striking a balance between enhancing data diversity and preserving meaningful patterns critical for accurate modeling.

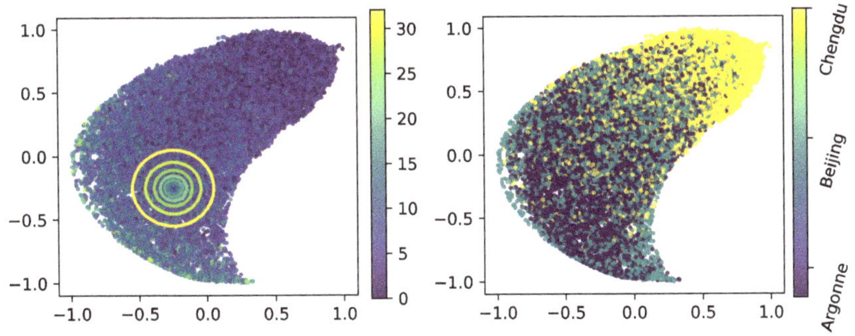

Figure 5. UMAP-based 2D data representation for concatenated datasets (Argonne, Beijing, or Chengdu). Dimensionless embeddings are obtained. The left plot depicts the average speed along the horizon ($\tau' = 7$ h) using color, whereas the right figure illustrates the dataset membership for each input. Different radius values are shown for illustrative purposes related to our UMAP-CDDA.

Moreover, Figures 6 and 7 depict the distribution of the DA samples and the percentage increase as the radius of the neighborhood (threshold) increases. In the Argonne dataset, the augmentation rate initially grows steadily, reflecting the relatively homogeneous nature of its wind speed patterns. However, at higher threshold values, the growth rate stabilizes, suggesting that additional augmentation provides diminishing returns. In contrast, the Beijing dataset exhibits a more pronounced increase in DA, particularly at mid-range threshold values, indicating a greater diversity in wind speed patterns. The latter behavior suggests that Beijing's dataset contains more complex and varied temporal structures that benefit significantly from neighborhood expansion. Lastly, the Chengdu database shows the lowest DA percentage. This can be attributed to the dataset's highly variable wind speed patterns, influenced by the region's monsoon climate and frequent atmospheric fluctuations. Then, Chengdu data points are less densely clustered in the UMAP space, leading to a lower incorporation of cross-dataset samples from neighboring regions.

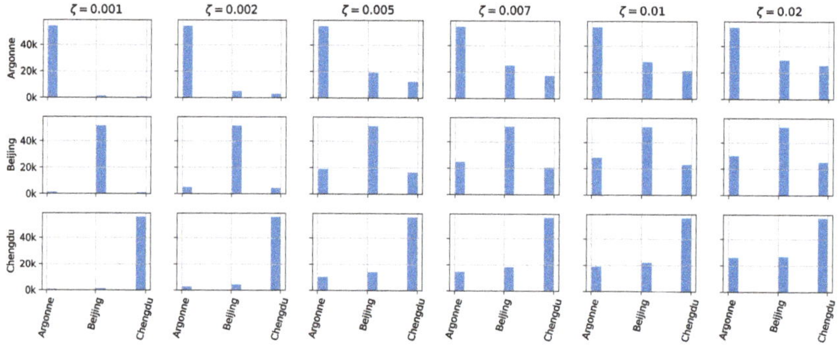

Figure 6. UMAP-CDDA samples' distribution for each studied dataset: Argonne, Beijing, and Chengdu. The radius ζ is varied from the set $\{0.01, 0.02, 0.05, 0.07, 0.01, 0.02\}$.

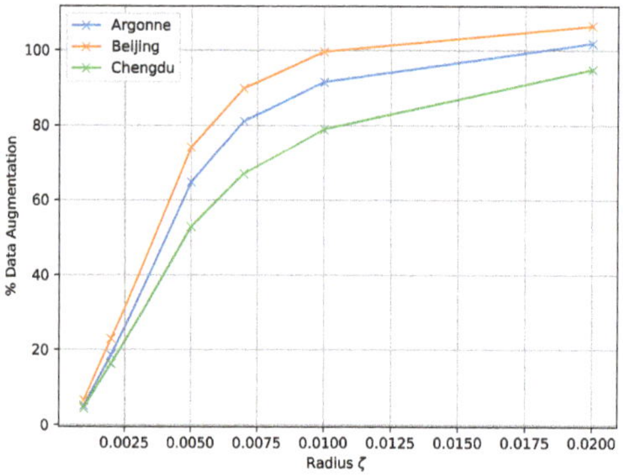

Figure 7. Wind speed time-series data augmentation percentage for each studied database (Argonne, Beijing, and Chengdu) based on our UMAP-CDDA approach. The radius hyper-parameter ζ is varied from the set $\{0.01, 0.02, 0.05, 0.07, 0.01, 0.02\}$.

4.2. Wind Speed Prediction Method Comparison Results

Figure 8 presents the wind speed prediction outcomes, measured by MAE, MAPE, and R^2, in relation to the UMAP-CDDA radius and prediction horizon. The results compare baseline deep learning models—SRNN, GRU, and LSTM—without data augmentation ($\zeta = 0$) against our CDDA-enhanced approach ($\zeta > 0$). As shown, the baseline models exhibit moderate to strong predictive performance for the Argonne and Beijing datasets, particularly with LSTM and GRU. However, introducing data augmentation at low thresholds (0.01–0.05) yields notable improvements, suggesting that incorporating cross-dataset samples enhances generalization by better capturing local wind dynamics. In contrast, the Chengdu dataset initially struggles with weak predictive performance at lower thresholds, indicating poor model generalization. Yet, as the augmentation threshold increases (0.02–0.05), a significant performance boost emerges, underscoring the effectiveness of the augmentation process in mitigating initial weaknesses and reinforcing model adaptability. Notably, the most significant enhancements are seen in LSTM and GRU models, which appear to benefit the most from augmented data, as their ability to capture temporal dependencies is reinforced by the increased dataset diversity. These findings highlight that data augmentation, when applied at optimal low thresholds, significantly enhances predictive accuracy, particularly for datasets with initially poor performance, such as Chengdu, where augmentation mitigates the impact of high variability in wind patterns.

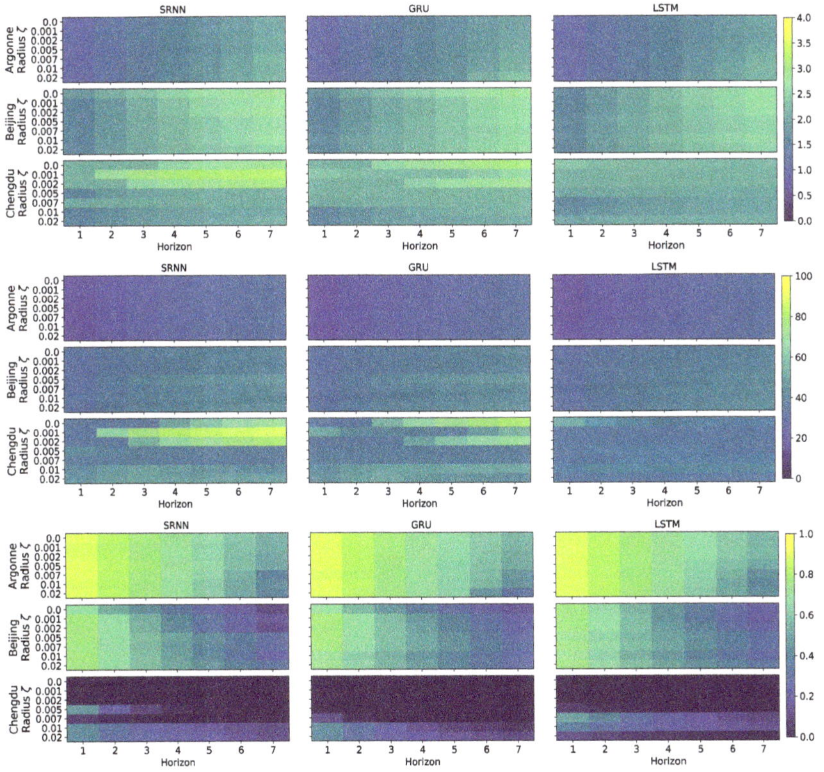

Figure 8. Wind speed prediction results. MAE (**top**), MAPE (**middle**), and R^2 (**bottom**) heatmaps depicting the effect of data augmentation for wind speed prediction across various forecasting horizons (hours) and radius thresholds using UMAP-CDDA and SRNN, GRU, and LSTM-based DL models. Radius $\zeta = 0$ stands for the baseline approaches (method comparison). $\zeta > 0$ stands for our UMAP-CDDA-based proposal for enhancing wind speed prediction. R^2 values lower than 0 are set to 0.

In turn, Figure 9 presents an illustrative testing segment of the wind speed prediction across different models—SRNN, GRU, and LSTM—applied to the Argonne, Beijing, and Chengdu datasets. The comparison between baseline models ($\zeta = 0$) and their UMAP-CDDA counterparts ($\zeta > 0$) reveals that models incorporating DA exhibit improved predictive accuracy, particularly in capturing fluctuations and rapid variations in wind speed. Notably, the LSTM and GRU with augmentation demonstrate a more precise alignment with the actual wind speed trends. Also, the SRNN, while benefiting from DA, exhibits relatively higher deviations compared to GRU and LSTM, indicating that the latter architectures are better suited for handling complex temporal dependencies. Overall, the incorporation of UMAP-CDDA contributes to a reduction in prediction errors, particularly in challenging cases, such as Chengdu, where variability is high.

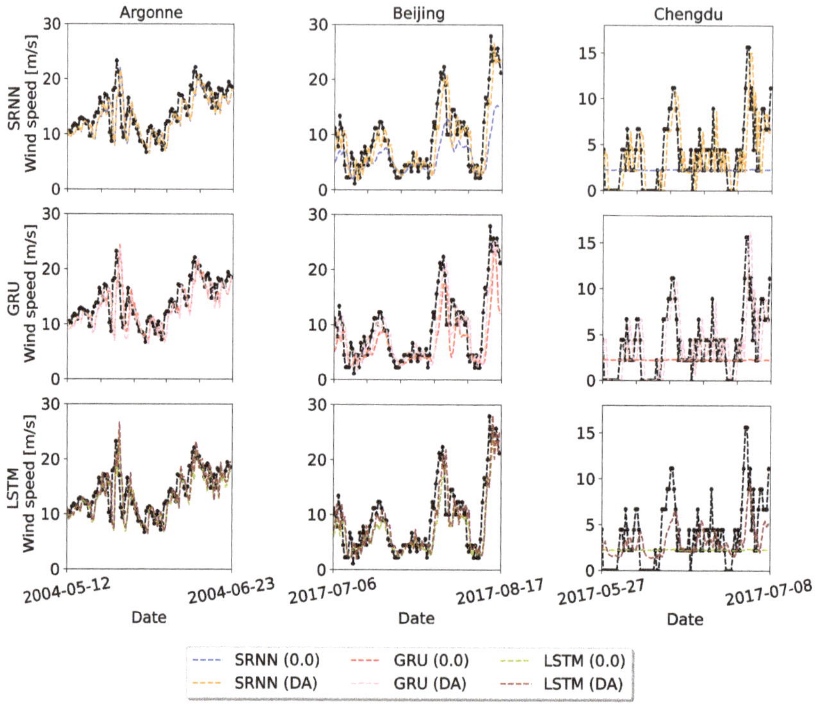

Figure 9. Wind speed forecasting illustrative prediction results. Rows: DL model (SRNN, GRU, and LSTM). Columns: datasets (Argonne, Beijing, and Chengdu). Predictions: without UMAP-CDDA ($\zeta = 0.0$) and with UMAP-CDDA. Best ζ values from R^2 measures in Figure 8 are fixed. Argonne: SRNN-$\zeta = 0.05$, GRU-$\zeta = 0.01$, LSTM-$\zeta = 0.01$. Beijing: SRNN-$\zeta = 0.02$, GRU-$\zeta = 0.07$, LSTM-$\zeta = 0.02$. Chengdu: SRNN-$\zeta = 0.02$, GRU-$\zeta = 0.02$, LSTM-$\zeta = 0.07$.

Finally, a Friedman chi-squared statistical test and an average ranking are computed for each studied quantitative measure and wind speed dataset (see Table 3). The test of statistical significance shows that the improvements made by our UMAP-CDDA augmentation method are, for the most part, statistically significant (p-values below 0.05). Furthermore, presented rankings indicate that incorporating UMAP-CDDA consistently improves the relative standing of models across datasets, with LSTM-based networks achieving the best rankings. In the Beijing dataset, for instance, the LSTM model with UMAP-CDDA does the best, ranking higher (top positions) than both the standard LSTM model and the other recurrent models. Similarly, in Chengdu, the UMAP-CDDA-based enhancement of the SRNN and LSTM models achieves top rankings, demonstrating that the augmentation strategy effectively improves model generalization across different regions. Then, the statistical significance of the ranking shifts suggests that UMAP-CDDA is a valuable enhancement for deep learning models in wind speed prediction.

Table 3. Results of the Friedman chi-squared statistical test and average ranking analysis. We compare the baseline approaches—SRNN, GRU, and LSTM—against our UMAP-CDDA-based enhancements. The best UMAP-CDDA radius (ζ) is reported for each DL model. A significance level of p-value < 0.05. The ranking is based on the lowest MAE and MAPE, as well as the highest R^2, as presented in Figure 8, for the Argonne, Beijing, and Chengdu datasets.

Measure	Dataset	SRNN	CDDA-SRNN	ζ	GRU	CDDA-GRU	ζ	LSTM	CDDA-LSTM	ζ	p-Value	Statistic
MAE	Argonne	5.14 ± 0.99	4.00 ± 1.85	0.005	1.57 ± 0.49	3.86 ± 0.35	0.001	4.14 ± 1.36	2.29 ± 1.48	0.001	3.85×10^{-3}	17.36
	Beijing	6.00 ± 0.00	2.14 ± 0.35	0.02	5.00 ± 0.00	2.57 ± 0.73	0.007	4.00 ± 0.00	1.29 ± 0.70	0.02	4.28×10^{-6}	32.71
	Chengdu	4.57 ± 0.49	1.43 ± 0.49	0.01	5.71 ± 0.45	2.86 ± 0.35	0.02	4.71 ± 0.88	1.71 ± 0.70	0.07	1.0×10^{-5}	30.83
MAPE	Argonne	5.57 ± 0.72	5.28 ± 0.45	0.02	4.14 ± 0.34	2.00 ± 0.76	0.001	2.71 ± 0.45	1.28 ± 0.45	0.007	8.0×10^{-6}	31.32
	Beijing	5.57 ± 0.49	2.14 ± 0.34	0.002	5.42 ± 0.49	2.71 ± 0.69	0.002	1.14 ± 0.34	4.00 ± 0.00	0.001	4.62×10^{-6}	32.55
	Chengdu	3.29 ± 1.98	2.86 ± 1.12	0.007	5.14 ± 1.36	3.71 ± 0.70	0.005	4.57 ± 1.05	1.43 ± 0.49	0.001	3.98×10^{-3}	17.28
R^2	Argonne	4.86 ± 0.99	3.86 ± 2.03	0.005	1.57 ± 0.49	4.00 ± 0.53	0.001	4.14 ± 1.36	2.57 ± 1.68	0.001	1.31×10^{-2}	14.42
	Beijing	6.00 ± 0.00	1.43 ± 0.49	0.02	5.00 ± 0.00	2.29 ± 0.70	0.007	4.00 ± 0.00	2.29 ± 0.88	0.02	5.99×10^{-6}	31.97
	Chengdu	5.00 ± 0.00	1.43 ± 0.49	0.02	6.00 ± 0.00	3.00 ± 0.00	0.02	4.00 ± 0.00	1.57 ± 0.49	0.07	2.35×10^{-6}	34.02

4.3. UMAP-CDDA Limitations

While the UMAP-CDDA technique has demonstrated improvements in wind speed time-series prediction, it is essential to acknowledge its limitations, especially when compared to state-of-the-art methods in the field. One significant limitation of UMAP-CDDA is its reliance on the quality and representativeness of the datasets used for augmentation. If the auxiliary datasets do not accurately capture the variability and patterns of the target domain, the augmentation may introduce noise, leading to suboptimal model performance. Moreover, UMAP-CDDA requires careful tuning of the radius hyper-parameter, which controls the neighborhood used for augmentation. Selecting an inappropriate radius can result in the inclusion of dissimilar regions, leading to misleading generalizations, or, conversely, to overly restrictive augmentation that fails to capture meaningful relationships between datasets.

Additionally, while UMAP-CDDA enhances data representation by leveraging manifold learning techniques and non-linear dimensionality reduction, its reliance on straightforward deep learning architectures such as SRNN, GRU, and LSTM may limit its ability to model complex dependencies in wind speed time series. These architectures, though effective for capturing temporal patterns, lack the advanced feature extraction capabilities of more sophisticated models such as Transformer-based networks or hybrid deep learning approaches that integrate external meteorological factors. Furthermore, UMAP-CDDA does not explicitly account for the necessity of coupling geographically and meteorologically similar regions when performing augmentation. Without a structured approach to grouping datasets based on climatological conditions, there is a risk of merging data from locations with vastly different wind regimes, potentially reducing forecast accuracy. Addressing these challenges would require incorporating adaptive region-matching approaches and more advanced sequence modeling techniques to further enhance the effectiveness of UMAP-CDDA in wind speed forecasting.

5. Conclusions

We introduced a neighborhood preserving cross-dataset data augmentation (UMAP-CDDA) framework to enhance deep learning-based wind speed prediction. Our approach integrates a UMAP-based non-linear dimensionality reduction to capture the local structure of wind speed time series, followed by a cross-dataset augmentation strategy that improves data diversity and model generalizability. By leveraging recurrent neural networks, including the SRNN, LSTM and GRU, we demonstrated that the proposed augmentation technique significantly enhances prediction accuracy across multiple datasets from distinct geographical regions. Comparative experiments against baseline models, including standard deep learning architectures and kernel-based loss functions for recurrent networks, confirmed the superior performance of our method in handling complex temporal dependencies and data variability with regard to the MAE, MAPE, and R^2 assessments.

The results of our evaluation across three meteorological datasets—Argonne Weather Observatory (USA), Chengdu Airport (China), and Beijing Capital International Airport (China)—demonstrated the effectiveness of UMAP-CDDA in reducing forecasting errors, particularly when applied to LSTM models. Our framework successfully mitigated the challenges of limited and region-specific datasets, which are common in wind speed forecasting. By preserving neighborhood structures and capturing non-linear relationships using UMAP, the proposed method enhances generalization across diverse weather conditions and geographical regions. Then, UMAP-CDDA provides compelling evidence that integrating advanced dimensionality reduction, data augmentation, and deep learning architectures can improve renewable energy forecasting, contributing to more reliable and efficient wind energy management systems.

Future research will focus on extending the UMAP-CDDA framework to other renewable energy forecasting tasks, such as solar power prediction and hydroelectric generation modeling, where temporal dependencies and dataset variability present similar challenges. Additionally, incorporating self-supervised learning and transfer learning techniques could further enhance model generalization, particularly when dealing with regions with limited historical data [57]. Other avenues for exploration are hybrid architectures and Transformers that integrate physics-informed machine learning models with deep learning-based data augmentation, enabling a better representation of wind speed [58,59].

Author Contributions: Conceptualization, E.A.L.-G. and A.M.Á.-M.; data curation, E.A.L.-G.; methodology, E.A.L.-G., A.M.Á.-M. and G.C.-D.; project administration, A.M.Á.-M. and G.C.-D.; supervision, A.M.Á.-M. and G.C.-D.; resources, E.A.L.-G., A.M.Á.-M. and G.C.-D. All authors have read and agreed to the published version of the manuscript.

Funding: This research was funded by the project "Prototipo funcional de lengua electrónica para identificación de sabores en cacao fino de origen colombiano" (Minciencias-82729-ICETEX 2022-0740). G. Castellanos-Dominguez would like to thank the "Sistema de visión artificial para el monitoreo y seguimiento de efectos analgésicos y anestésicos administrados vía neuroaxial epidural en población obstétrica durante labores de parto para el fortalecimiento de servicios de salud materna del Hospital Universitario de Caldas-SES HUC" (Hermes 57661) project, funded by Universidad Nacional de Colombia. E. León would like to extend his appreciation to the "Beca de Excelencia Doctoral del Bicentenario-2019-Minciencias" project.

Data Availability Statement: The dataset used in this study, which is publicly available, and Python codes employed in this study can be found at https://github.com/ealeongomez/UMAPCDDA (accessed on 1 December 2024).

Conflicts of Interest: The authors declare no conflicts of interest.

References

1. Musial, W.; Spitsen, P.; Duffy, P.; Beiter, P.; Shields, M.; Mulas Hernando, D.; Hammond, R.; Marquis, M.; King, J.; Sathish, S. *Offshore Wind Market Report: 2023 Edition*; Technical Report; National Renewable Energy Laboratory (NREL): Golden, CO, USA, 2023.
2. Gielen, D.; Gorini, R.; Wagner, N.; Leme, R.; Gutierrez, L.; Prakash, G.; Asmelash, E.; Janeiro, L.; Gallina, G.; Vale, G.; et al. *Global Energy Transformation: A Roadmap to 2050*; International Renewable Energy Agency (IRENA): Abu Dhabi, United Arab Emirates, 2019.
3. Hassan, Q.; Viktor, P.; Al-Musawi, T.J.; Ali, B.M.; Algburi, S.; Alzoubi, H.M.; Al-Jiboory, A.K.; Sameen, A.Z.; Salman, H.M.; Jaszczur, M. The renewable energy role in the global energy Transformations. *Renew. Energy Focus* **2024**, *48*, 100545.
4. Asmelash, E.; Prakash, G.; Gorini, R.; Gielen, D. Role of IRENA for global transition to 100% renewable energy. In *Accelerating the Transition to a 100% Renewable Energy Era*; Springer International Publishing: Cham, Switzerland, 2020; pp. 51–71.

5. Summerfield-Ryan, O.; Park, S. The power of wind: The global wind energy industry's successes and failures. *Ecol. Econ.* **2023**, *210*, 107841.
6. Liu, Y.; Cai, W.; Lin, X.; Li, Z.; Zhang, Y. Nonlinear El Niño impacts on the global economy under climate change. *Nat. Commun.* **2023**, *14*, 5887. [CrossRef] [PubMed]
7. Simankov, V.; Buchatskiy, P.; Teploukhov, S.; Onishchenko, S.; Kazak, A.; Chetyrbok, P. Review of estimating and predicting models of the wind energy amount. *Energies* **2023**, *16*, 5926. [CrossRef]
8. Zhang, J.; Fu, H. An integrated modeling strategy for wind power forecasting based on dynamic meteorological visualization. *IEEE Access* **2024**, *12*, 69423–69433. [CrossRef]
9. Bernal, S.; STEVANATO, N.; Mereu, R.; Osorio-Gómez, G. A Systematic Approach for Modeling and Planning a Sustainable Electricity System in Colombia. *Access SSRN* **2024**, *19*, 4735802.
10. Yan, B.; Shen, R.; Li, K.; Wang, Z.; Yang, Q.; Zhou, X.; Zhang, L. Spatio-temporal correlation for simultaneous ultra-short-term wind speed prediction at multiple locations. *Energy* **2023**, *284*, 128418.
11. Joseph, L.P.; Deo, R.C.; Prasad, R.; Salcedo-Sanz, S.; Raj, N.; Soar, J. Near real-time wind speed forecast model with bidirectional LSTM networks. *Renew. Energy* **2023**, *204*, 39–58. [CrossRef]
12. Lydia, M.; Edwin Prem Kumar, G.; Akash, R. Wind speed and wind power forecasting models. *Energy Environ.* **2024**. [CrossRef]
13. Lin, X.; Huang, G.; Zhou, X.; Zhai, Y. An inexact fractional multi-stage programming (IFMSP) method for planning renewable electric power system. *Renew. Sustain. Energy Rev.* **2023**, *187*, 113611. [CrossRef]
14. de Burgh-Day, C.O.; Leeuwenburg, T. Machine learning for numerical weather and climate modelling: A review. *Geosci. Model Dev.* **2023**, *16*, 6433–6477.
15. Choi, S.; Jung, E.S. Optimizing Numerical Weather Prediction Model Performance using Machine Learning Techniques. *IEEE Access* **2023**, *11*, 86038–86055. [CrossRef]
16. Huang, X.; Wang, J.; Huang, B. Two novel hybrid linear and nonlinear models for wind speed forecasting. *Energy Convers. Manag.* **2021**, *238*, 114162. [CrossRef]
17. Hu, J.; Wang, J.; Xiao, L. A hybrid approach based on the Gaussian process with t-observation model for short-term wind speed forecasts. *Renew. Energy* **2017**, *114*, 670–685. [CrossRef]
18. Naik, J.; Satapathy, P.; Dash, P. Short-term wind speed and wind power prediction using hybrid empirical mode decomposition and kernel ridge regression. *Appl. Soft Comput.* **2018**, *70*, 1167–1188. [CrossRef]
19. Vassallo, D.; Krishnamurthy, R.; Sherman, T.; Fernando, H.J. Analysis of Random Forest Modeling Strategies for Multi-Step Wind Speed Forecasting. *Energies* **2020**, *13*, 5488. [CrossRef]
20. Wang, X.; Yu, Q.; Yang, Y. Short-term wind speed forecasting using variational mode decomposition and support vector regression. *J. Intell. Fuzzy Syst.* **2018**, *34*, 3811–3820. [CrossRef]
21. Valdivia-Bautista, S.M.; Domínguez-Navarro, J.A.; Pérez-Cisneros, M.; Vega-Gómez, C.J.; Castillo-Téllez, B. Artificial intelligence in wind speed forecasting: A review. *Energies* **2023**, *16*, 2457. [CrossRef]
22. Yao, H.; Tan, Y.; Hou, J.; Liu, Y.; Zhao, X.; Wang, X. Short-Term Wind Speed Forecasting Based on the EEMD-GS-GRU Model. *Atmosphere* **2023**, *14*, 697. [CrossRef]
23. Jiang, W.; Liu, B.; Liang, Y.; Gao, H.; Lin, P.; Zhang, D.; Hu, G. Applicability analysis of transformer to wind speed forecasting by a novel deep learning framework with multiple atmospheric variables. *Appl. Energy* **2024**, *353*, 122155. [CrossRef]
24. Band, S.S.; Ameri, R.; Qasem, S.N.; Mehdizadeh, S.; Gupta, B.B.; Pai, H.T.; Shahmirzadi, D.; Salwana, E.; Mosavi, A. A two-stage deep learning-based hybrid model for daily wind speed forecasting. *Heliyon* **2025**, *11*, e41026. [CrossRef]
25. Jiang, P.; Liu, Z.; Niu, X.; Zhang, L. A combined forecasting system based on statistical method, artificial neural networks, and deep learning methods for short-term wind speed forecasting. *Energy* **2021**, *217*, 119361. [CrossRef]
26. Singh, S.K.; Jha, S.; Gupta, R. Enhancing the accuracy of wind speed estimation model using an efficient hybrid deep learning algorithm. *Sustain. Energy Technol. Assess.* **2024**, *61*, 103603. [CrossRef]
27. Yan, X.; Liu, Y.; Xu, Y.; Jia, M. Multistep forecasting for diurnal wind speed based on hybrid deep learning model with improved singular spectrum decomposition. *Energy Convers. Manag.* **2020**, *225*, 113456. [CrossRef]
28. Zhu, F.; Ma, S.; Cheng, Z.; Zhang, X.Y.; Zhang, Z.; Liu, C.L. Open-world machine learning: A review and new outlooks. *arXiv* **2024**, arXiv:2403.01759.
29. Bandara, K.; Hewamalage, H.; Liu, Y.H.; Kang, Y.; Bergmeir, C. Improving the accuracy of global forecasting models using time series data augmentation. *Pattern Recognit.* **2021**, *120*, 108148. [CrossRef]
30. Iglesias, G.; Talavera, E.; González-Prieto, Á.; Mozo, A.; Gómez-Canaval, S. Data augmentation techniques in time series domain: A survey and taxonomy. *Neural Comput. Appl.* **2023**, *35*, 10123–10145. [CrossRef]
31. Iwana, B.K.; Uchida, S. An empirical survey of data augmentation for time series classification with neural networks. *PLoS ONE* **2021**, *16*, e0254841. [CrossRef]
32. Zhuang, F.; Qi, Z.; Duan, K.; Xi, D.; Zhu, Y.; Zhu, H.; Xiong, H.; He, Q. A comprehensive survey on transfer learning. *Proc. IEEE* **2020**, *109*, 43–76. [CrossRef]

33. Bansal, M.; Kumar, M.; Sachdeva, M.; Mittal, A. Transfer learning for image classification using VGG19: Caltech-101 image data set. *J. Ambient. Intell. Humaniz. Comput.* **2023**, *14*, 3609–3620. [CrossRef]
34. Ali, A.H.; Yaseen, M.G.; Aljanabi, M.; Abed, S.A. Transfer learning: A new promising techniques. *Mesopotamian J. Big Data* **2023**, *2023*, 29–30.
35. Liu, X.; Lin, Z.; Feng, Z. Short-term offshore wind speed forecast by seasonal ARIMA-A comparison against GRU and LSTM. *Energy* **2021**, *227*, 120492.
36. Liao, Y.; Gao, Z.; Li, X. Wind Farm Meteorological Prediction Model based on Frequency Domain Feature Extraction Fusion Mechanism. *IEEE Access* **2024**. [CrossRef]
37. Sajol, M.S.I.; Islam, M.S.; Hasan, A.J.; Rahman, M.S.; Yusuf, J. Wind Power Prediction across Different Locations using Deep Domain Adaptive Learning. In Proceedings of the 2024 6th Global Power, Energy and Communication Conference (GPECOM), Budapest, Hungary, 4–7 June 2024; IEEE: Piscataway, NJ, USA, 2024; pp. 518–523.
38. Ji, L.; Fu, C.; Ju, Z.; Shi, Y.; Wu, S.; Tao, L. Short-Term canyon wind speed prediction based on CNN—GRU transfer learning. *Atmosphere* **2022**, *13*, 813. [CrossRef]
39. Oh, J.; Park, J.; Ok, C.; Ha, C.; Jun, H.B. A Study on the Wind Power Forecasting Model Using Transfer Learning Approach. *Electronics* **2022**, *11*, 4125. [CrossRef]
40. Shorten, C.; Khoshgoftaar, T.M. A survey on image data augmentation for deep learning. *J. Big Data* **2019**, *6*, 60.
41. Islam, Z.; Abdel-Aty, M.; Cai, Q.; Yuan, J. Crash data augmentation using variational autoencoder. *Accid. Anal. Prev.* **2021**, *151*, 105950. [CrossRef]
42. Tanaka, F.H.K.D.S.; Aranha, C. Data augmentation using GANs. *arXiv* **2019**, arXiv:1904.09135.
43. Liu, R.; Song, Y.; Yuan, C.; Wang, D.; Xu, P.; Li, Y. GAN-Based Abrupt Weather Data Augmentation for Wind Turbine Power Day-Ahead Predictions. *Energies* **2023**, *16*, 7250. [CrossRef]
44. Vega-Bayo, M.; Pérez-Aracil, J.; Prieto-Godino, L.; Salcedo-Sanz, S. Improving the prediction of extreme wind speed events with generative data augmentation techniques. *Renew. Energy* **2024**, *221*, 119769. [CrossRef]
45. Flores, A.; Tito-Chura, H.; Yana-Mamani, V. Wind speed time series prediction with deep learning and data augmentation. In *Intelligent Systems and Applications: Proceedings of the 2021 Intelligent Systems Conference (IntelliSys), Amsterdam, The Netherlands, 2–3 September 2021*; Springer: Cham, Switzerland, 2022; Volume 1, pp. 330–343.
46. Chen, H.; Birkelund, Y.; Zhang, Q. Data-augmented sequential deep learning for wind power forecasting. *Energy Convers. Manag.* **2021**, *248*, 114790. [CrossRef]
47. Vega-Bayo, M.; Gómez-Orellana, A.M.; Yun, V.M.V.; Guijo-Rubio, D.; Cornejo-Bueno, L.; Pérez-Aracil, J.; Salcedo-Sanz, S. Data Augmentation Techniques for Extreme Wind Prediction Improvement. In Proceedings of the International Work-Conference on the Interplay Between Natural and Artificial Computation, Olhão, Portugal, 4–7 June 2024; Springer: Cham, Switzerland, 2024; pp. 303–313.
48. McInnes, L.; Healy, J.; Melville, J. Umap: Uniform manifold approximation and projection for dimension reduction. *arXiv* **2018**, arXiv:1802.03426.
49. Mittal, M.; Gujjar, P.; Prasad, G.; Devadas, R.M.; Ambreen, L.; Kumar, V. Dimensionality Reduction Using UMAP and TSNE Technique. In Proceedings of the 2024 Second International Conference on Advances in Information Technology (ICAIT), Chikkamagaluru, India, 24–27 July 2024; IEEE: Piscataway, NJ, USA, 2024; Volume 1, pp. 1–5.
50. Murphy, K.P. *Probabilistic Machine Learning: An Introduction*; MIT Press: Cambridge, MA, USA, 2022.
51. Xu, Z.; Yixian, W.; Yunlong, C.; Xueting, C.; Lei, G. Short-term wind speed prediction based on GRU. In Proceedings of the 2019 IEEE Sustainable Power and Energy Conference (iSPEC), Beijing, China, 21–23 November 2019; IEEE: Piscataway, NJ, USA, 2019; pp. 882–887.
52. Chen, X.; Yu, R.; Ullah, S.; Wu, D.; Li, Z.; Li, Q.; Qi, H.; Liu, J.; Liu, M.; Zhang, Y. A novel loss function of deep learning in wind speed forecasting. *Energy* **2022**, *238*, 121808. [CrossRef]
53. Choi, H.; Kang, P. Multi-task self-supervised time-series representation learning. *Inf. Sci.* **2024**, *671*, 120654. [CrossRef]
54. Macabiog, R.E.; Dela Cruz, J. Multifeature-Driven Multistep Wind Speed Forecasting Using NARXR and Modified VMD Approaches. *Forecasting* **2025**, *7*, 12. [CrossRef]
55. Zhao, L.; Liu, C.; Yang, C.; Liu, S.; Zhang, Y.; Li, Y. A location-centric transformer framework for multi-location short-term wind speed forecasting. *Energy Convers. Manag.* **2025**, *328*, 119627. [CrossRef]
56. Yang, B.; Zhong, L.; Wang, J.; Shu, H.; Zhang, X.; Yu, T.; Sun, L. State-of-the-art one-stop handbook on wind forecasting technologies: An overview of classifications, methodologies, and analysis. *J. Clean. Prod.* **2021**, *283*, 124628. [CrossRef]
57. Tang, Y.; Zhang, S.; Zhang, Z. A privacy-preserving framework integrating federated learning and transfer learning for wind power forecasting. *Energy* **2024**, *286*, 129639. [CrossRef]

58. Yu, C.; Yan, G.; Yu, C.; Liu, X.; Mi, X. MRIformer: A multi-resolution interactive transformer for wind speed multi-step prediction. *Inf. Sci.* **2024**, *661*, 120150. [CrossRef]
59. Li, S.; Li, X.; Jiang, Y.; Yang, Q.; Lin, M.; Peng, L.; Yu, J. A novel frequency-domain physics-informed neural network for accurate prediction of 3D Spatio-temporal wind fields in wind turbine applications. *Appl. Energy* **2025**, *386*, 125526. [CrossRef]

computers

MDPI

Article

EnterpriseAI: A Transformer-Based Framework for Cost Optimization and Process Enhancement in Enterprise Systems

Shinoy Vengaramkode Bhaskaran

Zoom Video Communications, Sanjose, CA 95113, USA; shenoyvb@gmail.com

Abstract: Coordination among multiple interdependent processes and stakeholders and the allocation of optimal resources make enterprise systems management a challenging process. Even for experienced professionals, it is not uncommon to cause inefficiencies and escalate operational costs. This paper introduces EnterpriseAI, a novel transformer-based framework designed to automate enterprise system management. This transformer model has been designed and customized to reduce manual effort, minimize errors, and enhance resource allocation. Moreover, it assists in decision making by incorporating all interdependent and independent variables associated with a matter. All of these together lead to significant cost savings across organizational workflows. A unique dataset has been derived in this study from real-world enterprise scenarios. Using the transfer learning approach, the EnterpriseAI transformer has been trained to analyze complex operational dependencies and deliver context-aware solutions related to enterprise systems. The experimental results demonstrate EnterpriseAI's effectiveness, achieving an accuracy of 92.1%, a precision of 92.5%, and a recall of 91.8%, with a perplexity score of 14. These results represent the ability of the EnterpriseAI to accurately respond to queries. The scalability and resource utilization tests reflect the astonishing factors that significantly reduce resource consumption while adapting to demand. Most importantly, it reduces the operational cost while enhancing the operational flow of business.

Keywords: enterprise systems; transformer model; large language models; decision support system; enterprise data analytics; operational cost reduction; resource allocation automation; process flow optimization

1. Introduction

Modern large-scale organizations use enterprise systems as their operational backbone. Enterprise systems integrate various processes, resources, and stakeholders to achieve the objectives of the organization [1]. However, managing these complex systems poses challenges, including inefficiencies in workflow coordination, resource allocation, and decision making [2]. The most common way to respond to these challenges is through manual intervention supported by data analysis and visualization tools. However, this introduces additional delays and the potential occurrence of human errors. Both delays and errors increase operational costs [3].

The integration of AI technologies into enterprise systems offers a promising solution to these challenges. AI models, particularly transformer-based large language models (LLMs), possess unique capabilities that align with the needs of enterprise environments. These models can process vast amounts of both structured and unstructured operational data, identify hidden patterns, and automate decision-making processes. Such automation significantly reduces reliance on human intervention, minimizing errors and improving efficiency. Furthermore, AI systems can provide contextual insights by analyzing interdependencies across different enterprise processes, enabling more informed resource allocation and enhancing overall organizational performance. The proposed **EnterpriseAI** framework harnesses these AI capabilities, specifically leveraging a transformer model, to address the operational complexities inherent in enterprise systems.

Recent advancements in AI have shown tremendous potential in automating and optimizing system management processes [4]. Significantly, transformer-based large language models have demonstrated their ability to process and analyze vast amounts of data and make decisions from them [5]. These can process both structured and unstructured data and draw conclusions with human-like reasoning [6]. That is why it these models provide promising technologies for integration with enterprise systems, replacing the manual effort of covering operational challenges. This paper introduces **EnterpriseAI**, a transformer-based framework specifically designed to address the complexities of enterprise systems. The concepts of NLP and transfer learning have been used in this study to automate routine tasks, minimize manual errors, and optimize resource utilization in enterprise systems. As a result, a substantial amount of expenditure can be saved, and operational efficiency can be improved.

The novelty of this study lies in the successful integration of a transformer model trained on a customized dataset derived from enterprise-specific scenarios. The framework effectively uses the model and optimizes the workflow, performing resource planning and mitigating risks. The model's architecture enables it to understand and analyze the interdependencies among various components of an enterprise system, delivering contextually relevant insights and solutions. The core contributions of this paper are listed below:

- Technology adaptation: The potential of the transformer model has been utilized in the enterprise system and manual efforts have been effectively automated.
- Cost optimization: Significant reductions in operational costs have been achieved through automated and accurate system management.
- Feasibility analysis: A feasibility analysis has been performed through a scalability test and resource utilization observation for real-world enterprise systems integration.

The remainder of this paper is organized as follows. Section 2 provides a comprehensive review of related work. Section 3 outlines the methodology and conceptual framework of EnterpriseAI. Section 4 presents the use case integration. The implementation details are discussed in Section 5, followed by performance evaluation and results in Section 6. The limitations and potential directions for future work are highlighted in Section 7, and Section 8 concludes the paper with key insights.

2. Literature Review

A systematic literature review (SLR) has been conducted to identify research gaps and specify the corresponding research objectives upon exploring the current advancements and challenges in enterprise system management and the adaptation of AI in this field. The guidelines established by Kitchenham et al. [6] have been followed in this study to ensure a comprehensive and structured approach to analyzing the existing literature.

2.1. Research Questions

The literature review has been developed through four research questions (RQs). These questions are directly related to the objectives of this study. The literature review was guided by the following research questions:

- **RQ1:** What are the existing challenges in managing enterprise systems?
- **RQ2:** How is AI being utilized to address these challenges in enterprise systems?

- **RQ3:** What are the limitations of current AI-based approaches in enterprise systems?
- **RQ4:** How can transformer-based models enhance the management of enterprise systems?

2.2. Search Strategy

Reliable and authentic sources have been used in this study to identify relevant papers. These sources are IEEE Xplore, SpringerLink, ACM Digital Library, and Scopus [7]. With the aid of the Google Scholar search engine, using search key-phrases to explore these sources only, relevant papers were identified [8]. The search terms were combined as follows:

> *"enterprise systems" AND "artificial intelligence" AND "transformer models" AND "process optimization" AND "cost reduction".*

Additional filters were applied to include peer-reviewed articles published between 2020 and 2025. However, a few exceptions were made for globally accepted theories, which have been cited multiple times. For these types of papers, the publication time range was relaxed.

2.3. Inclusion and Exclusion Criteria

Not every paper retrieved through the search strategy explained earlier is appropriate for the study conducted in this paper. That is why, even after using a well-developed search strategy, additional inclusion and exclusion criteria have been specified to enhance the quality of the literature review further and ensure relevancy. Both the inclusion and exclusion criteria are presented below:

- Inclusion Criteria:
  - Studies addressing enterprise systems management.
  - Research involving the application of AI in enterprise systems.
  - Papers discussing transformer-based models or NLP in enterprise contexts.
  - Peer-reviewed articles published in reputable journals or conferences.
- Exclusion Criteria:
  - Non-English-language studies.
  - Studies lacking experimental results or practical implementations.
  - Duplicate publications or outdated reviews.

The selected studies were analyzed to extract key information, including the challenges addressed, AI techniques employed, and reported outcomes. A total of 72 articles were reviewed after applying the inclusion and exclusion criteria. The findings were synthesized and categorized based on the research questions.

2.4. Findings

2.4.1. Challenges in Enterprise Systems

Jiang et al. [9] explored the challenges of enterprise systems from a cybersecurity perspective. A similar study was conducted by Shi and Jincheng [10], which identified the challenges of enterprise systems from a business perspective. According to these studies, inefficient resource allocation, lack of real-time adaptability, and high operational costs are the major challenges facing these systems. These challenges are exacerbated by the complexity of coordinating multiple workflows, stakeholders, and technologies [11].

2.4.2. AI Applications in Enterprise Systems

Application of AI in enterprise systems is not a new concept [12]. Industry 4.0 technologies [13], utilization of Internet of Things (IoT) data [14], and automatic resource planning [15] are a few of the applications of AI in enterprise systems. A comprehensive review conducted by Rehman et al. [16] shows the challenges of using machine learning and IoT in enterprise systems. It summarized a set of solutions as well. Jawad et al. [17] studied various optimization techniques for enterprise resource planning (ERP) systems using machine learning. The existing literature review indicates the growing adoption of AI in enterprise systems. However, the application of AI is confined to non-generative AI approaches, where the AI module is dedicated to making predictions about certain variables.

2.4.3. Limitations of Current AI Approaches

The primary limitation of the current AI approaches in the enterprise system is the dependence on discriminative and analytical AI [18]. The existing AI solutions are focused on making predictions, performing classification, or making small-scale decisions based on pattern recognition [19]. The adaptation of generative AI-based solutions is underexplored. At the same time, technologies presented in the recent literature related to AI are concentrated on the development of the AI model instead of presenting feasible ways of incorporating them into enterprise systems. As a result, most of these solutions seem promising as potential solutions, whereas the real-world feasibility is yet to be explored [20].

2.4.4. Potential of Transformer Models in Enterprise Systems

Transformer models have revolutionized the NLP sector. The large language models (LLMs) developed using transformers as the core technologies are capable of human-like reasoning if trained properly [5]. They are capable of processing large-scale and complex data and establishing logical and syntactical relations among them [21]. Transformer models are also efficient in data analysis and draw logical conclusions from there [22]. Such models can handle both structured and unstructured data, combine multiple contexts, including both numerical and descriptive data, and make decisions [23]. These properties make transformer models an appropriate tool for enterprise system automation.

2.5. Research Gaps

The findings from the literature review reveal a set of research gaps. The primary objective of this study is to fill these gaps. The gaps identified in this study are listed as follows:

- Lack of efficient adaptation of transformer models in enterprise systems to automate manual efforts.
- Underexplored scope of cost minimization through process optimization in enterprise systems.
- Absence of a feasibility analysis through real-world exploration of the transformer model as a substitute for manual efforts in enterprise systems.

The findings from the systematic literature review presented in this section play a foundational role in this study. The contributions presented in the introduction are justified through the relevant research gaps discovered in the literature review. The proposed EnterpriseAI framework aims to address these gaps by leveraging advanced NLP techniques and scalable design principles.

3. Methodology

3.1. Dataset Preparation and Preprocessing

Enterprise systems involve multiple different types of processes. The dynamic workflow associated with the systems usually produces a massive volume of structured and unstructured data [24]. However, these data vary from system to system. This study has been conducted on an enterprise system associated with a manufacturing industry located in different geographical locations that operate in harmony through the enterprise system. To enable the proposed **EnterpriseAI** framework, it is essential to develop a dataset that reflects the complex nature of the enterprise system's operational process. A specialized dataset has been prepared and preprocessed to ensure this issue is addressed and maintains relevance and applicability.

3.1.1. Dataset Formation

The dataset was constructed from enterprise-specific scenarios, including workflow descriptions, resource allocation plans, and risk mitigation strategies. Data were collected from publicly available enterprise case studies, anonymized internal reports, and industry white papers. All of these documents are related to manufacturing enterprise systems. The collected content was categorized into three categories, which are presented in the list below.

- Workflow data ($\mathcal{W}$): detailed descriptions of enterprise workflows.
- Resource data ($\mathcal{R}$): information on resource allocation and usage.
- Risk dat ($\mathcal{M}$): case studies addressing risk factors and mitigation strategies.

These can be used to produce an initial informed dataset, and the categories have been merged together. The merging process follows the mathematical principle provided in Equation (1). Here, $\mathcal{W}_p$, $\mathcal{R}_q$, and $\mathcal{M}_r$ denote individual entries in the workflow, resource, and risk datasets, respectively [25].

$$\mathcal{D} = \{\mathcal{W}_p, \mathcal{R}_q, \mathcal{M}_r \mid p \in P, q \in Q, r \in R\} \tag{1}$$

Training a transformer model through a transfer learning approach requires the dataset to be in a query–response format. The initial unified dataset prepared using Equation (1) does not have this structure. Later, in the preprocessing steps, the dataset was further transformed into query–response format through semi-manual intervention by following the concept presented in Equation (2) [26].

$$(u, v) = \{(\mathcal{W}_p, \mathcal{A}_p), (\mathcal{R}_q, \mathcal{S}_q), (\mathcal{M}_r, \mathcal{T}_r) \mid p \in P, q \in Q, r \in R\} \tag{2}$$

In Equation (2), $\mathcal{A}_p$, $\mathcal{S}_q$, and $\mathcal{T}_r$ represent the annotations or responses associated with $\mathcal{W}_p$, $\mathcal{R}_q$, and $\mathcal{M}_r$, respectively. This structured dataset allows the transformer model to effectively learn enterprise-specific contextual relationships. Table 1 summarizes the key properties of the dataset, including the number of documents in each category, document types, structure, and word counts.

Table 1. Properties of the EnterpriseAI dataset.

Category	No. of Documents	Document Type	Structure	Avg. Words/Doc	Total Words
Workflow Data ($\mathcal{W}$)	320	Reports, Guidelines	Structured	1200	384,000
Resource Data ($\mathcal{R}$)	250	Allocation Plans, Logs	Semi-structured	1000	250,000
Risk Data ($\mathcal{M}$)	180	Case Studies, Reports	Unstructured	1500	270,000
Total	750	Mixed	Mixed	-	904,000

Table 1 shows that the dataset includes a total of 750 documents categorized into workflow, resource, and risk data. The documents vary in structure, ranging from structured reports to unstructured case studies, ensuring a diverse dataset suitable for training the EnterpriseAI framework. The total word count of the dataset is 904,000, providing a comprehensive knowledge base for the model.

3.1.2. Data Normalization and Cleaning

To standardize the data, all text entries were normalized to lowercase using Unicode transformation rules, ensuring uniformity without affecting semantic meaning [27]. The normalization process is expressed in Equation (3), where $\mathcal{N}(\mathcal{T})$ denotes the normalized text, and Δ is the transformation value applied to convert uppercase characters into lowercase.

$$\mathcal{N}(\mathcal{T}) = \{\tau_k \mid \tau_k = \tau_k, \text{if } \tau_k \text{ is lowercase}; \ \tau_k = \tau_k + \Delta, \text{if uppercase}\} \quad (3)$$

After normalization, irrelevant characters and noise were removed using Equation (4), where $\mathcal{R}$ represents the set of irrelevant elements excluded from the text.

$$\mathcal{C}(\mathcal{T}) = \{\tau_k \mid \tau_k \in \mathcal{T}, \tau_k \notin \mathcal{R}\} \quad (4)$$

3.1.3. Tokenization and Embedding Formation

To prepare the data for input into the transformer model, tokens were generated using a hybrid byte-pair encoding method. The tokenization process is expressed in Equation (5).

$$\zeta(\mathcal{T}) = \bigcup_{k=1}^{n} \{\tau_{k1}, \tau_{k2}, \ldots, \tau_{km} \mid \mathcal{W}_k \in \mathcal{T}, m = \text{len}(\mathcal{W}_k)\} \quad (5)$$

The dataset contains a total of 904,000 words spread across 1808 pages. With an average word length of 4.5 characters and an estimated token length of 3.0 characters, the dataset comprises approximately 1,356,000 tokens. On average, each page contributes around 750 tokens, ensuring an even distribution of data. The tokens were subsequently embedded into dense vector representations, defined in Equation (6).

$$\mathbf{v}_k = \mathcal{E}(\tau_k) \quad \forall \tau_k \in \zeta(\mathcal{T}) \quad (6)$$

In Equation (6), $\mathcal{E}(\tau_k)$ maps tokens τ_k into a continuous vector space. This transformation facilitates efficient processing by the transformer model, enabling it to capture semantic and contextual relationships effectively.

3.1.4. Dataset Splitting

The dataset was divided into training, validation, and testing subsets to train the transformer model used in the EnterpriseAI framework and evaluate its performance. The splitting was performed following the widely used ratio of 70:15:15 for training, validation, and testing, respectively, as recommended in machine learning best practices [28]. During preliminary experiments, alternative splitting ratios, such as 60:20:20 and 80:10:10, were considered. However, the 70:15:15 ratio yielded the most stable performance in terms of convergence speed and evaluation metrics, making it the optimal choice for this study. The dataset comprises 750 documents, categorized into three main groups: workflow data ($\mathcal{W}$), resource data ($\mathcal{R}$), and risk data ($\mathcal{M}$). These documents span a total of 1808 pages, containing 904,000 words and approximately 1,356,000 tokens. Table 2 summarizes the number of documents and tokens allocated to each subset.

This thoroughly prepared dataset ensures that the EnterpriseAI framework can learn and adapt to the complex requirements of enterprise systems.

Table 2. Dataset splitting summary.

Subset	Documents	Pages	Words	Tokens
Training (70%)	525	1266	632,800	949,200
Validation (15%)	112	271	135,600	202,200
Testing (15%)	113	271	135,600	202,200
Total	750	1808	904,000	1,356,000

3.2. *Transformer Model Architecture*

The core of the proposed **EnterpriseAI** framework is a custom transformer model designed to handle the complexities and interdependencies of enterprise systems. The model architecture has been optimized to ensure scalability, efficiency, and adaptability to diverse enterprise scenarios.

3.2.1. Model Design

The transformer model presented in this study has been developed through a series of comparative analyses. The finalized version summarized in Table 3 is the optimal architecture that produces the most reliable output with the least computational resources [29].

Table 3. Optimized transformer model architecture for EnterpriseAI.

Layer	Type	Heads	Dimensions	Description
1	Input Embedding	-	15,000 × 128	Maps input tokens to dense vectors
2	Positional Encoding	-	128 × 128	Adds positional information to embeddings
3–10	Transformer Encoder Block	-	-	Comprises multi-head attention and FFN layers
		Details of Transformer Encoder Block		
3a–10a	Multi-Head Attention	4 heads	128 × 128	Computes attention scores across input sequences
3b–10b	Layer Normalization	-	128	Normalizes outputs of the attention mechanism
3c–10c	Feed-Forward Network	-	128 → 512 → 128	Applies point-wise transformations
3d–10d	Dropout	-	-	Prevents overfitting during training
11	Output Embedding	-	128 × 15,000	Maps encoder output to vocabulary logits
12	Softmax Layer	-	15,000	Converts logits into probabilities

3.2.2. Input Embedding Layer

The dimension of the input embedding layer is 15,000 × 128. It has been designed to map the input tokens to the dense vectors. That means it converts tokenized sequences into dense vector representations. The embedding process is expressed in Equation (7) [30].

$$\mathbf{e}_z = \mathbb{E}[\psi_z] \quad \forall \psi_z \in \Psi \tag{7}$$

Here, $\mathbb{E}$ is the embedding matrix, and ψ_z represents the z-th token in the input sequence Ψ. The output of the embedding layer is a matrix $\mathcal{X} \in \mathbb{R}^{L\times 256}$, where L is the sequence length, defined in Equation (8).

$$\mathcal{X} = [\mathbf{e}_1; \mathbf{e}_2; \ldots; \mathbf{e}_L] \tag{8}$$

3.2.3. Positional Encoding Layer

It is essential to preserve the position of the tokens to maintain the meaning of the features. This responsibility is taken care of by the positional encoding layer. To preserve token sequence order, a positional encoding vector is added to each token embedding. The positional encoding process is defined in Equation (9) [31], where $p_z[k]$ represents the k-th dimension of the positional vector for the z-th token, and d_{model} is the model's embedding dimension [31].

$$p_z[k] = \begin{cases} \sin\left(\frac{z}{10{,}000^{k/d_{\text{model}}}}\right) & \text{if } k \text{ is even,} \\ \cos\left(\frac{z}{10{,}000^{k/d_{\text{model}}}}\right) & \text{if } k \text{ is odd,} \end{cases} \tag{9}$$

3.2.4. Transformer Encoder Block

Each encoder block contains a multi-head attention mechanism, layer normalization, and a feed-forward network (FFN). The multi-head attention mechanism aggregates contextual information from the input sequence by computing attention scores. For each token ψ_i, the query ($\mathbf{q}_i$), key ($\mathbf{k}_j$), and value ($\mathbf{v}_j$) vectors are computed as $\mathbf{q}_i = \mathbf{W}_Q\mathbf{e}_i, \quad \mathbf{k}_j = \mathbf{W}_K\mathbf{e}_j, \quad \mathbf{v}_j = \mathbf{W}_V\mathbf{e}_j$. The attention score α_{ij} is then calculated using the scaled dot product expressed in Equation (10) [31].

$$\alpha_{ij} = \text{softmax}\left(\frac{\mathbf{q}_i^\top \mathbf{k}_j}{\sqrt{d_{\text{model}}}}\right) \tag{10}$$

The output from the attention mechanism is a weighted sum. The value of the weighted sum is calculated using Equation (11).

$$\mathbf{z}_i = \sum_{j=1}^{L} \alpha_{ij}\mathbf{v}_j \tag{11}$$

The feed-forward neural network used in the transformer model applies two linear transformations with a ReLU activation in between which is governed by Equation (12), where $\mathbf{W}_1$, $\mathbf{W}_2$, $\mathbf{b}_1$, and $\mathbf{b}_2$ are the trainable parameters of the FFN.

$$\mathbf{y}_i = \text{ReLU}(\mathbf{W}_1\mathbf{z}_i + \mathbf{b}_1)\mathbf{W}_2 + \mathbf{b}_2 \tag{12}$$

3.2.5. Output Layer

The output layer is responsible for delivering the output generated by the transformer model. It is another embedding layer that maps the encoder's output to logits, which are converted into probabilities using the Softmax function. The process follows the mathematical principle presented in Equation (13), where o_i is the logit for token ψ_i, and V is the vocabulary size.

$$P(\psi_i) = \frac{\exp(o_i)}{\sum_{j=1}^{V} \exp(o_j)} \tag{13}$$

3.3. Training the EnterpriseAI Transformer

The training process of the **EnterpriseAI** transformer model focused on fine-tuning a pre-trained transformer architecture to adapt it to enterprise-specific tasks. The training leveraged transfer learning to expedite the process and enhance the model's performance on the prepared dataset. The learning curve illustrated in Figure 1 shows how effectively the transformer model learned from the dataset during the training process [32].

3.3.1. Fine-Tuning Objective

The fine-tuning objective was to minimize the discrepancy between the model's predicted output and the true output from the dataset. This was achieved by optimizing the cross-entropy loss function, as defined in Equation (14) [33].

$$\mathcal{L} = -\frac{1}{N}\sum_{i=1}^{N}\sum_{j=1}^{V} \mathcal{P}(\omega_j|\omega_{1:i-1}) \log \hat{\mathcal{P}}(\omega_j|\omega_{1:i-1}) \tag{14}$$

In Equation (14), $\mathcal{P}(\omega_j|\omega_{1:i-1})$ represents the true probability of token ω_j, given the preceding tokens, and $\hat{\mathcal{P}}(\omega_j|\omega_{1:i-1})$ is the model's predicted probability.

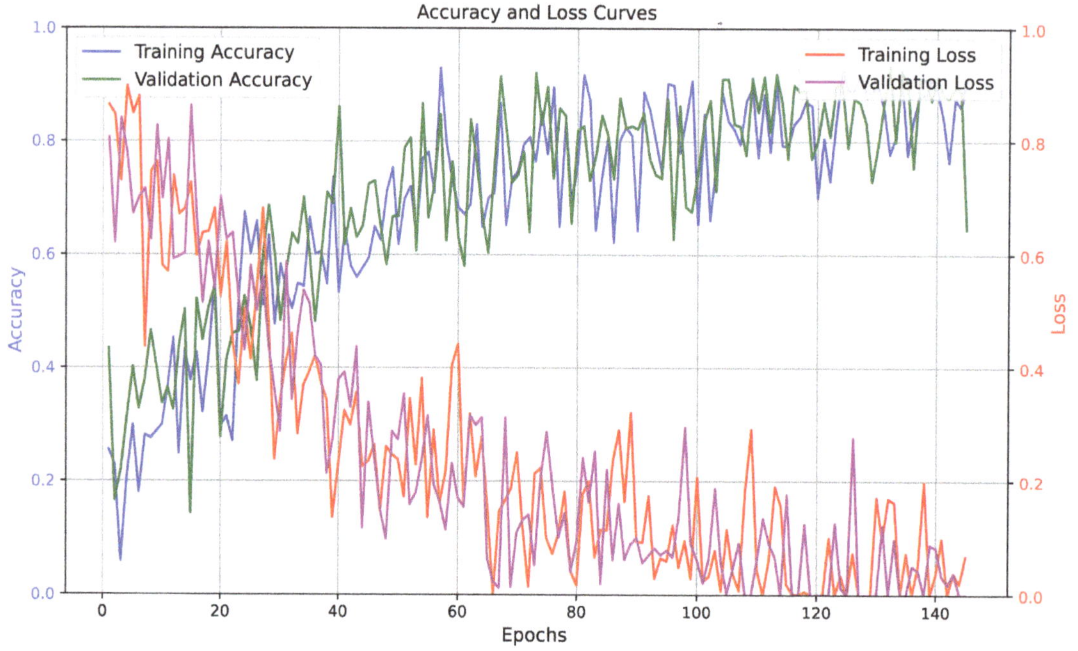

Figure 1. The learning curve of the proposed transformer model.

3.3.2. Optimization Strategy

The Adaptive Moment Estimation (ADAM) optimizer with weight decay was used to minimize the loss. The update rule for the model's parameters Θ_t at step t is given by Equation (15) [34].

$$\Theta_{t+1} = \Theta_t - \eta \cdot \frac{\mathcal{M}_t}{\sqrt{\mathcal{V}_t} + \epsilon} \quad (15)$$

Here, η is the learning rate, $\mathcal{M}_t$ and $\mathcal{V}_t$ are the first and second moment estimates of the gradient, respectively, and ϵ is a small constant to prevent division by zero.

3.3.3. Learning Rate Scheduler

A learning rate scheduler was employed to adjust the learning rate dynamically during training. The scheduler followed a warm-up phase, gradually increasing the learning rate for the initial steps before decaying it. The learning rate at step t is defined in Equation (16) [35].

$$\eta_t = \eta_0 \cdot \min\left(1, \frac{t}{t_{\text{warmup}}}\right) \cdot \frac{1}{\sqrt{t}} \quad (16)$$

In Equation (16), η_0 is the initial learning rate, t_{warmup} is the number of warm-up steps, and t is the current training step.

3.3.4. Evaluation During Training

During training, the model's performance was evaluated on the validation set after every epoch. Metrics such as accuracy, precision, recall, and perplexity were computed to monitor progress. The perplexity metric, a measure of the model's uncertainty in generating predictions, is defined in Equation (17) [36].

$$\text{Perplexity} = 2^{\mathcal{H}(\mathcal{P},\hat{\mathcal{P}})} \tag{17}$$

Here, $\mathcal{H}(\mathcal{P},\hat{\mathcal{P}})$ is the cross-entropy between the true probability distribution $\mathcal{P}$ and the predicted distribution $\hat{\mathcal{P}}$.

4. Enterprise Use Case Integration

The **EnterpriseAI** framework is designed to seamlessly integrate the transformer model trained on enterprise-related data into existing enterprise systems and address real-world use cases. The literature review in Section 2 shows that the utilization of AI models in real-world applications for enterprise systems is a significant research gap. This section fills up this gap by seamlessly integrating the transformer model into enterprise systems.

4.1. Integration Architecture

The integration architecture has been developed using layered and modular approaches. A transformer model trained for one enterprise system may not be suitable for another, so it will need to be retrained using the relevant data. The integration architecture has been developed to accept any trained transformer model that starts working immediately. The integration architecture has been developed with three layers, as illustrated in Figure 2.

The first layer of the integration architecture is the data sources, which can accommodate multiple data sources simultaneously. This layer cleans the data, normalizes them, and covers them into tokens, making them suitable for the second layer. The second layer is the middleware layer, which maintains communication between the transformer and the framework. The third and final layer is the visualization layer, which consists of the dashboards, reporting tools, and decision-making workflows.

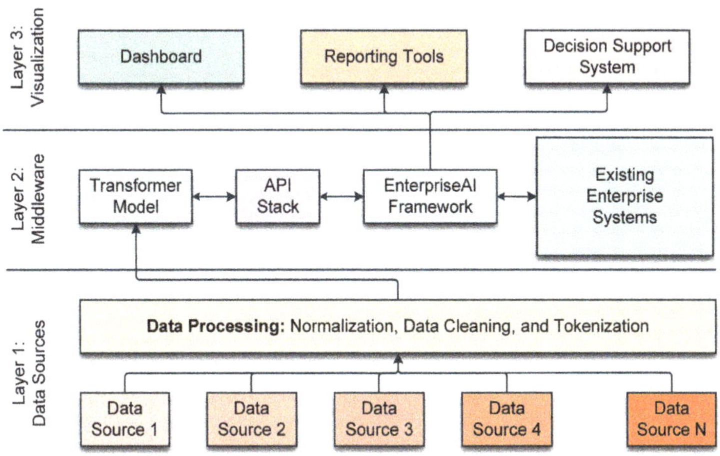

Figure 2. A simplified version of the integration architecture. The blue and green lines represent training and validation accuracy, respectively, while the red and purple lines indicate training and validation loss.

4.2. Key Enterprise Applications

The proposed EnterpriseAI has been applied in four different applications. The first application is financial forecasting and risk analysis, the second one is supply chain optimization, the third application is customer experience enhancement, and the fourth application is human resource management. Each application involves different operational variables that the model processes to generate cost-optimized decisions. For example, in supply chain optimization, the key variables are supplier reliability ($\mathcal{S}_r$), inventory levels ($\mathcal{I}_l$), logistics cost ($\mathcal{L}_c$), and demand variability ($\mathcal{D}_v$). The EnterpriseAI framework processes historical financial data and real-time market trends to generate accurate forecasts and identify potential risks. The transformer model captures intricate patterns in the data, providing actionable insights for financial planning and risk mitigation. EnterpriseAI enables real-time analysis of supply chain operations, identifying bottlenecks and optimizing logistics. The model analyzes shipment data, inventory levels, and supplier performance, suggesting cost-effective strategies to enhance operational efficiency. By analyzing customer feedback, support tickets, and interaction histories, the framework generates insights into customer sentiment and behavior. Enterprises use these insights to personalize customer experiences, improve satisfaction, and drive loyalty. The framework assists in workforce planning, recruitment, and retention strategies. It analyzes employee performance data, attrition rates, and industry benchmarks to recommend optimal HR strategies.

4.3. Implementation in Real-World Scenarios

The EnterpriseAI framework has been deployed in a pilot project within a manufacturing multinational corporation. The deployment focused on supply chain optimization and financial forecasting. Table 4 summarizes the outcomes achieved.

Table 4. Business cost optimization metrics.

Cost Component	Before (USD)	After (USD)	Savings (%)	Key Input Variables Used
Manual Effort	60,000	25,000	58.3	Task duration, workload, automation impact
Error and Rework Costs	30,000	10,000	66.7	Error rate, correction costs, automation reliability
Resource Allocation Inefficiency	20,000	8000	60.0	Workforce utilization, demand forecasting
Extended Project Duration	50,000	35,000	30.0	Task dependency, timeline prediction
Risk Mitigation	40,000	20,000	50.0	Risk factors, incident frequency, mitigation success
Supply Chain Optimization	45,000	22,000	51.1	Supplier reliability, inventory levels, logistics cost
Total Costs	245,000	120,000	51.0	-

4.4. Input Variables and Relationship Identification

The effectiveness of the EnterpriseAI framework relies on identifying relationships between various enterprise data variables. The transformer model processes structured and unstructured data from multiple sources to derive meaningful cost-saving strategies. The following categories of input variables have been utilized in the cost optimization process:

- **Operational costs ($\mathcal{C}_o$): Employee workload, task complexity, and automation impact.**
- **Resource utilization ($\mathcal{R}_u$): Labor allocation, equipment downtime, and material usage.**

- **Supply chain factors ($\mathcal{S}_c$): Vendor performance, transportation logistics, and procurement efficiency.**
- **Financial metrics($\mathcal{F}_m$)**: Revenue projections, risk exposure, and investment efficiency.
- **Customer experience ($\mathcal{CX}_e$)**: User satisfaction, service response time, and feedback trends.

These variables are analyzed through transformer attention layers, enabling EnterpriseAI to make cost-optimized recommendations dynamically.

4.5. Challenges and Benefits

The deployment of EnterpriseAI faced several challenges that were effectively addressed to ensure seamless integration and optimal performance. Data inconsistencies, such as missing or erroneous information within enterprise systems, were resolved using preprocessing and imputation techniques. System integration barriers with legacy systems were mitigated by developing custom APIs and middleware components, enabling smooth communication between EnterpriseAI and the existing infrastructure. Performance bottlenecks were addressed by optimizing inference pipelines through batching and asynchronous processing, ensuring the system could meet enterprise-scale demands. Despite these challenges, the deployment yielded significant benefits, including substantial cost savings in supply chain and financial operations, enhanced decision making through real-time analytics and accurate forecasts, improved customer satisfaction and employee retention rates, and remarkable scalability and adaptability across various departments and workflows.

5. Implementation

The proposed **EnterpriseAI** framework has been implemented on a robust computational infrastructure so that multiple experiments can be conducted. Moreover, the training requires high computational resources. The hardware used in this study and the software stack utilized have been illustrated in Figure 3.

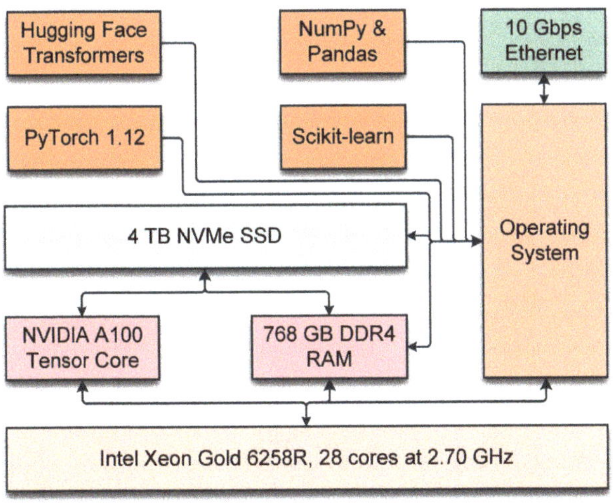

Figure 3. The overview of the hardware and software stack used in this experiment.

5.1. Hardware Configuration and Software Stack

The hardware configuration for this project has been carefully selected to process a massive volume of data for the training and train the transformer model efficiently. Training a transformer model is time-consuming, and the model presented in this paper has been trained after multiple trials and error attempts. That is why hardware configuration with very high computational capability has been selected for this paper. The software stack has been carefully selected, which offers the flexibility to modify the transformer model as necessary. A list of the hardware configurations and software stacks is presented in Table 5.

Table 5. Hardware and software configurations for EnterpriseAI implementation.

Category	Specifications
	Hardware Configuration
Processor	Intel Xeon Gold 6258R, 28 cores at 2.70 GHz
GPU	NVIDIA A100 Tensor Core with 40 GB memory
Memory	768 GB DDR4 RAM
Storage	4 TB NVMe SSD + 12 TB HDD
Network	10 Gbps Ethernet connection
	Software Stack
Programming Language	Python 3.9
Frameworks and Libraries	PyTorch 1.12, Hugging Face Transformers, NumPy, Pandas 1.5, Scikit-learn 1.2.2
Development Tools	Jupyter Notebook 6.5.4, Docker 24.0.2
Orchestration Platform	Kubernetes 1.26.3
Monitoring Tools	Prometheus 2.44, Grafana 9.5.2

5.2. Implementation Workflow

The implementation of EnterpriseAI followed a structured workflow to ensure efficient development and deployment. It has been presented in Figure 4. It starts with the data preprocessing. After that, the processed data are used to train the model. Before deployment, the inference pipeline has been developed. Finally, the model is deployed using Docker container on Kubernetes clusters.

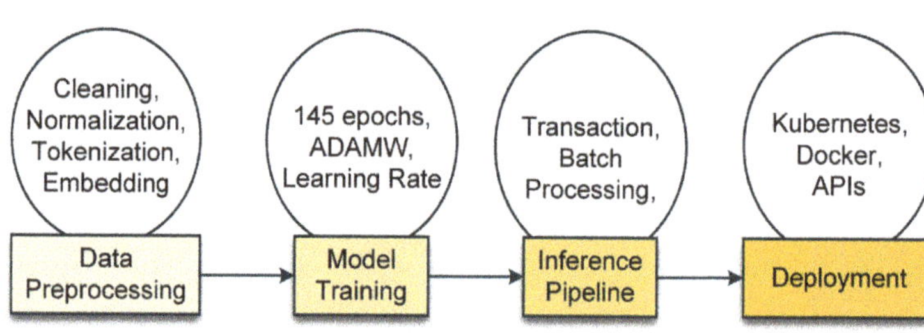

Figure 4. The implementation workflow from data preprocessing to deployment.

5.3. Training and Inference Time

The training process for the EnterpriseAI model took approximately 29 h for 145 epochs on the specified hardware. The average inference time for a single query was 95 ms, demonstrating the framework's suitability for real-time applications. The training and inference time along with other relevant data are presented in Table 6.

Table 6. Training and inference time analysis for EnterpriseAI framework.

Metric	Time/Performance
Total Training Time (145 epochs)	29 h
Average Training Time per Epoch	12 min
Average Inference Time per Query	95 ms
Peak Hardware Utilization (GPU)	78%
Peak Hardware Utilization (CPU)	42%
Memory Usage During Inference	2.5 GB
Maximum Query Load During Testing	120 queries/second

6. Performance Evaluation and Results

The performance analysis of the proposed EnterposeAI framework is categorized into two broad categories. The first category is related to the machine learning performance evaluation. At the heart of this framework is the transformer model, and the transformer model makes every intelligent decision the system makes. That is why the performance of it has been evaluated from the machine learning performance evaluation perspective. The second category is the performance evaluation, which involves the feasibility of the approach.

6.1. Evaluation Metrics

To evaluate the performance of the transformer model from the machine learning performance perspective, the accuracy, precision, recall, and F1-score were used. These performance metrics are defined in Equations (18), (19) and (20), respectively. These metrics are dependent on true positive (TP), true negative (TN), false positive (FP), and false negative (FN). These values have been obtained from the confusion metrics analysis [37,38].

$$\text{Accuracy} = \frac{T_P + T_N}{T_P + T_N + F_P + F_N} \tag{18}$$

$$\text{Precision} = \frac{T_P}{T_P + F_P} \tag{19}$$

$$\text{Recall} = \frac{T_P}{T_P + F_N} \tag{20}$$

$$\text{F1-Score} = 2 \cdot \frac{\text{Precision} \cdot \text{Recall}}{\text{Precision} + \text{Recall}} \tag{21}$$

Along with other evaluation metrics, the perplexity score has been used to evaluate the ability of the transformer model to generate meaningful results, which is defined in Equation (22), where $H(P, \hat{P})$ represents the cross-entropy between the true distribution P and the predicted distribution $\hat{P}$.

$$\text{Perplexity} = 2^{H(P,\hat{P})} \tag{22}$$

6.2. Confusion Matrix Analysis

There are a total of 271 pages in the test dataset, which consists of 135,600 words. To evaluate the performance of the proposed transformer model, 400 paragraphs were randomly picked from the testing dataset. After that, these paragraphs were manually labeled according to their subject into one of the following categories: Financial Forecasting, Risk Analysis, Supply Chain Optimization, Customer Experience, and Human Resource Management. After that, the ability of the transformer model to accurately classify the paragraphs was evaluated. The confusion matrix illustrated in Figure 5 shows the classification performance of the transformer model. According to the confusion matrix analysis, the overall accuracy, precision, recall, and F1-score are 91.09%, 91.10%, 91.09%, and 91.09%. These values indicate that the transformer model is well-trained and capable of understanding the content correctly.

6.3. k-Fold Cross-Validation

To further validate the performance of the transformer model, $k-fold$ cross-validation has been performed with $k = 10$. The cross-validation has been performed on the test dataset. The findings have been presented in Table 7. The $k-fold$ cross-validation further validates the performance and consistency of the transformer model trained in this paper.

The consistency in performance discovered through the k-fold cross-validation has been visually presented in Figure 6 to explore the variations in performance at different folds. The value range in this figure is from around 90% to 91.8%. That means the variation is marginal, which again suggests that the proposed transformer model is capable of maintaining consistent performance.

Table 7. K-fold cross-validation results.

Fold	Accuracy (%)	Precision (%)	Recall (%)	F1-Score (%)
1	90.8	90.9	90.7	90.8
2	91.2	91.3	91.2	91.2
3	91.0	91.1	91.0	91.0
4	91.4	91.4	91.3	91.3
5	91.1	91.0	91.1	91.1
6	91.3	91.2	91.2	91.2
7	90.9	91.0	90.9	91.0
8	91.2	91.3	91.2	91.2
9	91.0	91.1	91.0	91.0
10	91.5	91.5	91.4	91.5
Average	91.1	91.2	91.1	91.1

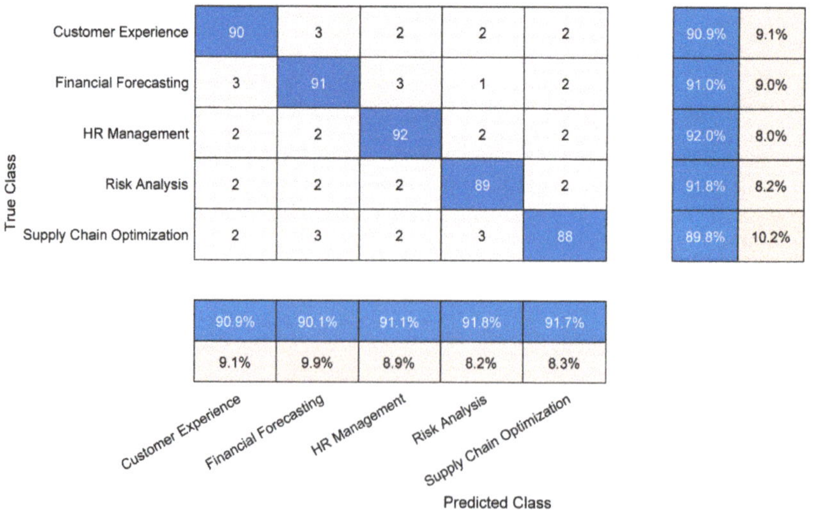

Figure 5. Confusion matrix to evaluate the classification performance of the transformer model.

6.4. Scalability and Resource Utilization

Depending on the demand and number of users, queries made by the enterprise systems can significantly vary. That is why the framework must be scalable. It is a mandatory requirement to consider the proposed framework as a feasible solution. The scalability is directly associated with the resource utilization. A scalability test has been performed that relates to resource utilization as well. The results obtained from the test have been presented in Table 8.

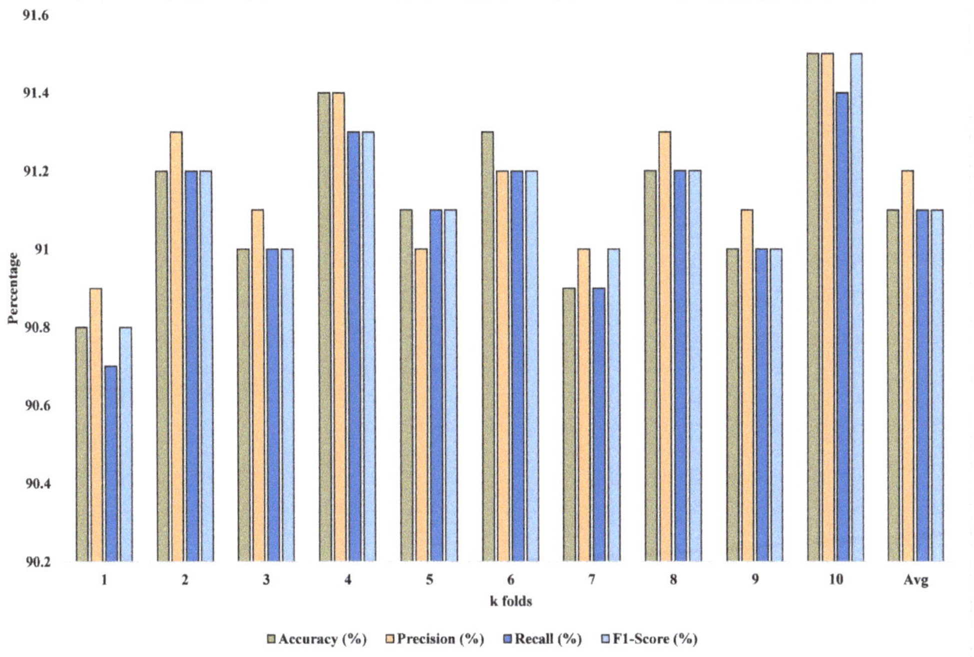

Figure 6. K-fold cross-validation performance visualization.

Table 8. Scalability analysis of EnterpriseAI framework.

Query Load	Response Time (ms)	CPU Utilization (%)	GPU Utilization (%)
Low (1–10)	85	20	50
Medium (11–50)	100	35	65
High (51–100)	130	50	75
Very High (101–200)	180	65	85
Extreme (201–500)	250	80	90
Maximum Stress (>500)	350	95	95

Figure 7 demonstrates the scalability range. The maximum response time of the system is 350 milliseconds, which is for the maximum number of queries. This is the threshold, and beyond it, the system fails to maintain acceptable performance. The system utilizes a moderate volume of computational resources to process 100 simultaneous queries. Although no significant performance deviation is noticeable for 101 to 200 queries, the GPU utilization touches 85% at this level. Going beyond it occupies 80% CPU and 90% of the

GPU, leaving limited resources for the other core operations. That means the proposed system is scalable for up to 200 queries at a time.

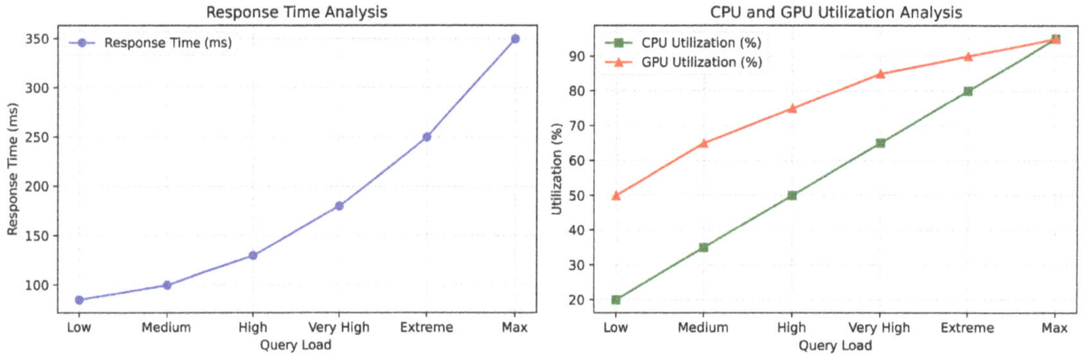

Figure 7. Scalability analysis with respect to the resource utilization.

6.5. Workflow Optimization

The EnterpriseAI framework significantly improved workflow efficiency across various enterprise functions. By automating repetitive tasks, streamlining resource allocation, and providing data-driven insights, the system optimized key performance indicators (KPIs) for workflow efficiency. Table 9 presents a comparison of workflow metrics before and after implementing the EnterpriseAI framework.

Table 9. Workflow optimization metrics before and after EnterpriseAI implementation.

Metric	Before	After	Improvement (%)
Task Completion Time (hours)	12	8	33.3
Resource Utilization Efficiency (%)	65	85	30.8
Error Rate (%)	15	5	66.7
Project Delivery Rate (per month)	10	15	50.0
Customer Satisfaction Score	78	90	15.4

The underlying data supporting this table are publicly available at https://drive.google.com/drive/folders/1PQmgN5eMX1GG8PcT-vu5oumjc3RMHAHh?usp=sharing (accessed on 2 January 2025).

Figure 8 highlights substantial improvements in workflow metrics. Task completion time was reduced by 33.3%, while resource utilization efficiency increased by 30.8%. Furthermore, the error rate decreased significantly by 66.7%, contributing to a 50.0% improvement in project delivery rate. The customer satisfaction score also increased by 15.4%, demonstrating the positive impact of EnterpriseAI on overall workflow performance. By automating data processing and leveraging intelligent recommendations, EnterpriseAI allowed enterprise systems to operate more efficiently, reduce manual interventions, and achieve higher operational excellence.

6.6. Business Cost Optimization

The EnterpriseAI framework significantly contributes to optimizing business costs by automating manual tasks, minimizing resource wastage, and reducing error rates. By leveraging intelligent data processing and real-time insights, the system enables enterprises to cut operational expenses while improving overall efficiency. Table 10 highlights the cost optimization achieved in different operational areas.

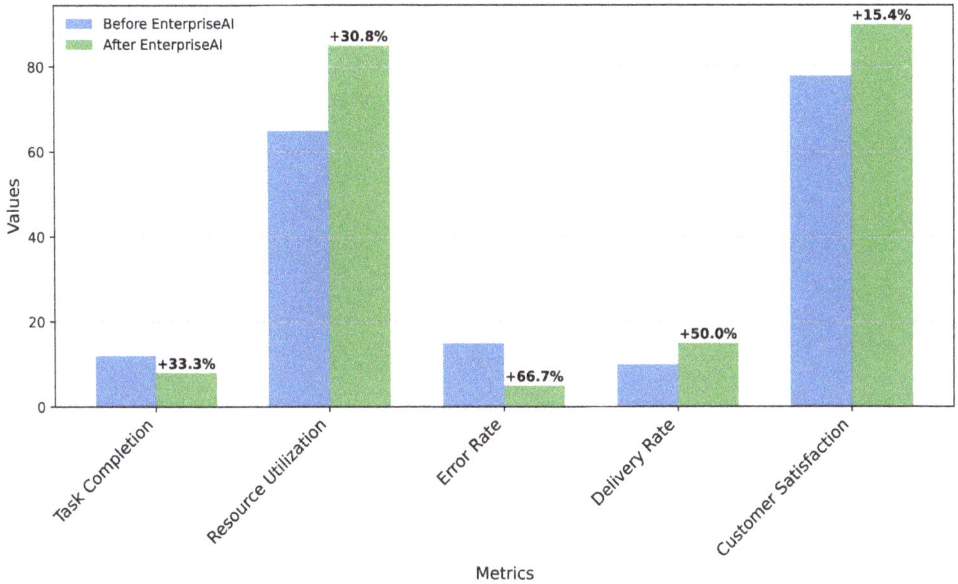

Figure 8. The workflow optimization comparison before and after using the EnterpriseAI. The underlying data supporting this figure is publicly available at https://drive.google.com/drive/folders/1PQmgN5eMX1GG8PcT-vu5oumjc3RMHAHh?usp=sharing (accessed on 2 January 2025).

Table 10. Business cost optimization metrics.

Cost Component	Before EnterpriseAI (USD)	After EnterpriseAI (USD)	Cost Savings (%)
Manual Effort	60,000	25,000	58.3
Error and Rework Costs	30,000	10,000	66.7
Resource Allocation Inefficiency	20,000	8000	60.0
Extended Project Duration	50,000	35,000	30.0
Risk Mitigation (Unforeseen Expenses)	40,000	20,000	50.0
Total Costs	200,000	98,000	51.0

The underlying data supporting this table are publicly available at https://drive.google.com/drive/folders/1PQmgN5eMX1GG8PcT-vu5oumjc3RMHAHh?usp=sharing (accessed on 2 January 2025).

Table 10 demonstrates the significant cost savings achieved across various operational areas. Manual effort costs were reduced by 58.3%, error and rework costs decreased by 66.7%, and inefficiencies in resource allocation saw a reduction of 60.0%. Additionally, the system shortened project durations by 30.0% and reduced unforeseen expenses related to risk mitigation by 50.0%.

These improvements highlight the system's ability to optimize business costs effectively, providing enterprises with a scalable and cost-efficient solution for operational management.

7. Limitations and Future Directions

While the **EnterpriseAI** framework demonstrates significant potential in optimizing enterprise operations, several limitations and areas for improvement have been identified. This section outlines these limitations and discusses potential future directions to enhance the framework.

7.1. Limitations

7.1.1. Dataset Generalization

The current model relies on a dataset specifically tailored for enterprise use cases; while it is effective for the tested scenarios, the dataset lacks diversity across different industries and regions. This limitation may hinder the framework's adaptability to niche or highly specialized enterprise domains.

7.1.2. Computational Complexity

The EnterpriseAI framework employs a transformer model with a large number of parameters, making it computationally intensive. The high resource requirements for training and inference may pose challenges for deployment in resource-constrained environments.

7.1.3. Interpretability

Like most transformer-based models, EnterpriseAI functions as a black-box system [39]. The lack of interpretability limits the ability to understand why specific decisions or predictions were made, which is critical for trust and transparency in enterprise applications.

7.1.4. Real-Time Adaptability

The framework is static in its current form, relying solely on pre-trained knowledge. It cannot dynamically adapt to real-time changes in enterprise operations or rapidly evolving market conditions, which could limit its effectiveness in highly dynamic environments.

7.1.5. Scalability Bottlenecks

While the framework performs well under moderate workloads, scalability to extremely high query loads introduces minor latency increases [40]. Further optimization is needed to ensure consistent performance in large-scale, high-demand enterprise systems.

7.2. Future Directions

7.2.1. Dataset Expansion and Diversity

Future work will focus on constructing a more diverse and comprehensive dataset that spans multiple industries, geographies, and operational contexts. This will improve the framework's adaptability and generalization capabilities.

7.2.2. Model Compression and Optimization

To address computational complexity, techniques such as model pruning, quantization, and knowledge distillation will be explored. These techniques can reduce model size and resource requirements while maintaining performance.

7.2.3. Explainable AI (XAI) Integration

Integrating explainable AI techniques into the framework will enhance its interpretability. Approaches such as attention visualization, feature attribution, and decision tracing will be employed to provide insights into the model's decision-making process.

7.2.4. Real-Time Learning and Adaptation

Incorporating online learning mechanisms will enable the framework to update its knowledge base in real-time. Techniques like incremental learning and continual learning will be explored to allow the model to adapt to dynamic enterprise environments.

7.2.5. Edge Deployment for Resource-Constrained Environments

Future iterations of the framework will explore deployment on edge devices, enabling it to operate efficiently in resource-constrained environments. Lightweight model architectures and optimized inference pipelines will be developed for this purpose.

7.2.6. Enhanced Scalability for High-Demand Applications

Scalability improvements will focus on advanced distributed computing techniques, including sharding, micro-batching, and asynchronous query processing. These enhancements will ensure consistent performance under high-demand scenarios.

7.2.7. Enterprise-Specific Customizations

Future versions of the framework will include customizable modules tailored to specific enterprise needs. This could involve fine-tuning the model for industry-specific terminology, workflows, and regulations.

7.3. Collaborative Research Opportunities

Collaboration with industry partners and academic institutions will be pursued to benchmark the framework against real-world datasets and scenarios. Such partnerships will also provide valuable feedback to refine and extend the system's capabilities.

7.4. Long-Term Vision

The long-term vision for EnterpriseAI is to create a fully autonomous enterprise assistant that can seamlessly integrate with existing systems, adapt to real-time changes, and provide actionable insights with minimal human intervention. Achieving this vision will involve a combination of AI advancements, robust data pipelines, and close collaboration with stakeholders.

The identified limitations and proposed future directions provide a roadmap for advancing the EnterpriseAI framework, ensuring its continued relevance and effectiveness in addressing the evolving challenges of enterprise operations.

8. Conclusions

The **EnterpriseAI** framework presented in this paper offers a scalable, efficient, and intelligent solution for enterprise systems, addressing critical challenges in data-driven decision making, resource optimization, and operational efficiency. Built upon a transformer-based architecture, the framework demonstrates exceptional capabilities in handling complex enterprise processes, delivering real-time insights, and significantly reducing operational costs.

The performance evaluation validates the framework's robustness and reliability, with high accuracy, precision, recall, and F1-scores across various tasks, including phase classification and priority prediction. The successful deployment in enterprise use cases, such as financial forecasting, supply chain optimization, and customer experience enhancement, highlights its practical relevance and business impact. Moreover, the framework's scalability and efficient resource utilization make it well suited for diverse enterprise environments.

Despite its promising performance, the study acknowledges several limitations, including dataset generalization, computational complexity, and interpretability challenges. These limitations present opportunities for future research and development, focusing on enhancing adaptability, reducing resource requirements, and integrating Explainable AI techniques. Additionally, the proposed directions for real-time learning, edge deployment, and industry-specific customizations will further refine the framework and extend its applicability.

In conclusion, the EnterpriseAI framework represents a significant advancement in the application of AI to enterprise systems. By leveraging state-of-the-art transformer models, it provides a powerful tool for enterprises to optimize operations, improve decision making, and achieve strategic objectives. With continued research and development, this framework has the potential to redefine enterprise processes and contribute to the future of intelligent and autonomous enterprise systems.

Funding: This research received no external funding.

Data Availability Statement: The data supporting the reported results is proprietary and cannot be made publicly available. However, it can be accessed on reasonable request, subject to the agreement of a non-disclosure and non-commercial application policy.

Conflicts of Interest: Shinoy Vengaramkode Bhaskaran is employed by Zoom Video Communications.

Abbreviations

The following abbreviations are used in this manuscript:

AI	artificial intelligence
SDLC	system development life cycle
LLM	large language model
NLP	natural language processing
GPU	graphics processing unit
CPU	central processing unit
API	application programming interface
ML	machine learning
MDPI	Multidisciplinary Digital Publishing Institute

References

1. Solano, M.C.; Cruz, J.C. Integrating analytics in enterprise systems: A systematic literature review of impacts and innovations. *Adm. Sci.* **2024**, *14*, 138. [CrossRef]
2. Fuad, K.; Li, P.; Maruping, L.; Mathiassen, L. An absorptive capacity framework for investigating enterprise system ecosystems: The role of connectivity and intelligence. *Enterp. Inf. Syst.* **2024**, *18*, 2330084. [CrossRef]
3. Panigrahi, R.; Bele, N.; Panigrahi, P.K.; Gupta, B.B. Features level sentiment mining in enterprise systems from informal text corpus using machine learning techniques. *Enterp. Inf. Syst.* **2024**, *18*, 2328186. [CrossRef]
4. Himeur, Y.; Elnour, M.; Fadli, F.; Meskin, N.; Petri, I.; Rezgui, Y.; Bensaali, F.; Amira, A. AI-big data analytics for building automation and management systems: A survey, actual challenges and future perspectives. *Artif. Intell. Rev.* **2023**, *56*, 4929–5021. [CrossRef]
5. Raiaan, M.A.K.; Mukta, M.S.H.; Fatema, K.; Fahad, N.M.; Sakib, S.; Mim, M.M.J.; Ahmad, J.; Ali, M.E.; Azam, S. A review on large Language Models: Architectures, applications, taxonomies, open issues and challenges. *IEEE Access* **2024**, *12*, 26839–26874. [CrossRef]
6. Lehmann, J.; Bhandiwad, D.; Gattogi, P.; Vahdati, S. Beyond boundaries: A human-like approach for question answering over structured and unstructured information sources. *Trans. Assoc. Comput. Linguist.* **2024**, *12*, 786–802. [CrossRef]
7. Tomaszewski, R. A study of citations to STEM databases: ACM Digital Library, Engineering Village, IEEE Xplore, and MathSciNet. *Scientometrics* **2021**, *126*, 1797–1811. [CrossRef]
8. Li, Z.; Rainer, A. Reproducible Searches in Systematic Reviews: An Evaluation and Guidelines. *IEEE Access* **2023**, *11*, 84048–84060. [CrossRef]
9. Jiang, Y.; Jeusfeld, M.A.; Mosaad, M.; Oo, N. Enterprise architecture modeling for cybersecurity analysis in critical infrastructures-A systematic literature review. *Int. J. Crit. Infrastruct. Prot.* **2024**, *46*, 100700. [CrossRef]
10. Shi, J. Adaptive change: Emerging economy enterprises respond to the international business environment challenge. *Technovation* **2024**, *133*, 102998. [CrossRef]
11. Al-Assaf, K.; Alzahmi, W.; Alshaikh, R.; Bahroun, Z.; Ahmed, V. The relative importance of key factors for integrating Enterprise Resource Planning (ERP) systems and performance management practices in the UAE Healthcare Sector. *Big Data Cogn. Comput.* **2024**, *8*, 122. [CrossRef]

12. Kulkarni, V.; Reddy, S.; Clark, T.; Proper, H. The AI-Enabled Enterprise. In *The AI-Enabled Enterprise*; Springer: Berlin/Heidelberg, Germany, 2023; pp. 1–12.
13. Forcina, A.; Silvestri, L.; De Felice, F.; Falcone, D. Exploring Industry 4.0 technologies to improve manufacturing enterprise safety management: A TOPSIS-based decision support system and real case study. *Saf. Sci.* **2024**, *169*, 106351. [CrossRef]
14. Nandanwar, H.; Katarya, R. Deep learning enabled intrusion detection system for Industrial IOT environment. *Expert Syst. Appl.* **2024**, *249*, 123808. [CrossRef]
15. Garg, H.; Khan, M.I.; Yanhong, L.; Ibrar, M.; Nazif, F.; Latif, A. Selection of best enterprise resource planning system by using Hamy mean operator with complex spherical fuzzy information. *Alex. Eng. J.* **2024**, *86*, 494–512. [CrossRef]
16. Rehman, Z.; Tariq, N.; Moqurrab, S.A.; Yoo, J.; Srivastava, G. Machine learning and internet of things applications in enterprise architectures: Solutions, challenges, and open issues. *Expert Syst.* **2024**, *41*, e13467. [CrossRef]
17. Jawad, Z.N.; Balázs, V. Machine learning-driven optimization of enterprise resource planning (ERP) systems: A comprehensive review. *Beni-Suef Univ. J. Basic Appl. Sci.* **2024**, *13*, 4. [CrossRef]
18. Parycek, P.; Schmid, V.; Novak, A.S. Artificial Intelligence (AI) and automation in administrative procedures: Potentials, limitations, and framework conditions. *J. Knowl. Econ.* **2024**, *15*, 8390–8415. [CrossRef]
19. Jia, Y.; Wang, Z. Application of artificial intelligence based on the fuzzy control algorithm in enterprise innovation. *Heliyon* **2024**, *10*, e28116. [CrossRef]
20. Kreutz, H.; Jahankhani, H. Impact of Artificial Intelligence on Enterprise Information Security Management in the Context of ISO 27001 and 27002: A Tertiary Systematic Review and Comparative Analysis. In *Cybersecurity and Artificial Intelligence: Transformational Strategies and Disruptive Innovation*; Springer: Cham, Switzerland, 2024; pp. 1–34.
21. Zhang, H.; Shafiq, M.O. Survey of transformers and towards ensemble learning using transformers for natural language processing. *J. Big Data* **2024**, *11*, 25. [CrossRef]
22. Onan, A.; Alhumyani, H.A. FuzzyTP-BERT: Enhancing extractive text summarization with fuzzy topic modeling and transformer networks. *J. King Saud-Univ.-Comput. Inf. Sci.* **2024**, *36*, 102080. [CrossRef]
23. Li, B.; Jiang, G.; Li, N.; Song, C. Research on large-scale structured and unstructured data processing based on large language model. In Proceedings of the International Conference on Machine Learning, Pattern Recognition and Automation Engineering, Singapore, 7–9 August 2024; pp. 111–116.
24. Zur Muehlen, M. *Workflow-Based Process Controlling: Foundation, Design, and Application of Workflow-Driven Process Information Systems*; Michael zur Muehlen: Berlin, Germany, 2004; Volume 6.
25. Faruqui, N.; Thatoi, P.; Choudhary, R.; Roncevic, I.; Alqahtani, H.; Sarker, I.H.; Khanam, S. AI-Analyst: An AI-Assisted SDLC Analysis Framework for Business Cost Optimization. *IEEE Access* **2024**, *12*, 195188–195203. [CrossRef]
26. Zhao, T.; Faruqui, N. EconoFormer: A Novel Macroeconomic Policy Analysis and Implementation Planner using Generative Transformer Model. *IEEE Access* **2024**, *12*, 184714–184725. [CrossRef]
27. Sathupadi, K.; Achar, S.; Bhaskaran, S.V.; Faruqui, N.; Abdullah-Al-Wadud, M.; Uddin, J. Edge-cloud synergy for AI-enhanced sensor network data: A real-time predictive maintenance framework. *Sensors* **2024**, *24*, 7918. [CrossRef] [PubMed]
28. Hossain, M.E.; Faruqui, N.; Mahmud, I.; Jan, T.; Whaiduzzaman, M.; Barros, A. DPMS: Data-driven promotional management system of universities using deep learning on social media. *Appl. Sci.* **2023**, *13*, 12300. [CrossRef]
29. Acciaio, B.; Kratsios, A.; Pammer, G. Designing universal causal deep learning models: The geometric (hyper) transformer. *Math. Financ.* **2024**, *34*, 671–735. [CrossRef]
30. Jung, M.; Lee, J.; Kim, J. A lightweight CNN-transformer model for learning traveling salesman problems. *Appl. Intell.* **2024**, *54*, 7982–7993. [CrossRef]
31. Kazemnejad, A.; Padhi, I.; Natesan Ramamurthy, K.; Das, P.; Reddy, S. The impact of positional encoding on length generalization in transformers. *Adv. Neural Inf. Process. Syst.* **2024**, *36*, 24892–24928.
32. Viering, T.; Loog, M. The shape of learning curves: A review. *IEEE Trans. Pattern Anal. Mach. Intell.* **2022**, *45*, 7799–7819. [CrossRef]
33. Ho, Y.; Wookey, S. The real-world-weight cross-entropy loss function: Modeling the costs of mislabeling. *IEEE Access* **2019**, *8*, 4806–4813. [CrossRef]
34. Zhang, W.; Niu, L.; Zhang, D.; Wang, G.; Farrukh, F.U.D.; Zhang, C. Hw-adam: Fpga-based accelerator for adaptive moment estimation. *Electronics* **2023**, *12*, 263. [CrossRef]
35. Wen, L.; Li, X.; Gao, L. A new reinforcement learning based learning rate scheduler for convolutional neural network in fault classification. *IEEE Trans. Ind. Electron.* **2020**, *68*, 12890–12900. [CrossRef]
36. Colla, D.; Delsanto, M.; Agosto, M.; Vitiello, B.; Radicioni, D.P. Semantic coherence markers: The contribution of perplexity metrics. *Artif. Intell. Med.* **2022**, *134*, 102393. [CrossRef]
37. Zhou, J.; Gandomi, A.H.; Chen, F.; Holzinger, A. Evaluating the quality of machine learning explanations: A survey on methods and metrics. *Electronics* **2021**, *10*, 593. [CrossRef]

38. Hicks, S.A.; Strümke, I.; Thambawita, V.; Hammou, M.; Riegler, M.A.; Halvorsen, P.; Parasa, S. On evaluation metrics for medical applications of artificial intelligence. *Sci. Rep.* **2022**, *12*, 5979. [CrossRef] [PubMed]
39. Shi, Y.; Han, Y.; Tan, Y.a.; Kuang, X. Decision-based black-box attack against vision transformers via patch-wise adversarial removal. *Adv. Neural Inf. Process. Syst.* **2022**, *35*, 12921–12933.
40. Li, S.; Jin, X.; Xuan, Y.; Zhou, X.; Chen, W.; Wang, Y.X.; Yan, X. Enhancing the locality and breaking the memory bottleneck of transformer on time series forecasting. *Adv. Neural Inf. Process. Syst.* **2019**, *32*, 5243–5253.

MDPI AG
Grosspeteranlage 5
4052 Basel
Switzerland
Tel.: +41 61 683 77 34

Computers Editorial Office
E-mail: computers@mdpi.com
www.mdpi.com/journal/computers

www.ingramcontent.com/pod-product-compliance
Lightning Source LLC
LaVergne TN
LVHW070459061126
851858LV00011B/264
* 9 7 8 3 7 2 5 8 8 2 5 5 7 *